Certified Management Accountant Review

Edited by Grant W. Newton   CMA, Ph.D., CPA
Professor of Accounting, Pepperdine University, Malibu

Contributing Authors

Andrew D. Bailey, Jr.   CMA, Ph.D., CPA
Professor of Accounting, University of Arizona

Roger N. Blakeney   Ph.D.
Associate Professor of Organizational Behavior and Management, University of Houston

Michael A. Diamond   Ph.D., CPA
Dean, School of Accounting, University of Southern California

James B. Edwards   CMA, Ph.D., CPA, CIA, CDP
Professor of Accounting, University of South Carolina

William D. Gunther   Ph.D.
Professor of Economics, The University of Alabama

John Kostolansky   Ph.D., CPA
Associate Professor of Accounting, Loyola University, Chicago

George C. Mead   Ph.D., CPA
Professor of Accounting, Michigan State University

Larry J. Merville   Ph.D.
Professor of Finance, University of Texas at Dallas

Cynthia J. Rooney   CMA, Ph.D., CPA
Associate Professor of Accounting, Xavier University

Arthur A. Thompson, Jr.   Ph.D.
Professor of Economics and Business Administration, The University of Alabama

Certified Management Accountant Review

Part 3
Management Reporting, Analysis, and Behavioral Issues

Fourth Edition

Malibu Publishing Company, Inc.
31312 Via Colinas, Suite 101
Westlake Village, CA 91362
(818) 889-1495   Fax (818) 889-5107

Certified Management Accountant Review, Part 3, Management Reporting, Analysis, and Behavioral Issues

Material from the Certified Management Accountant Examination, copyright© 1972-1993 by the Institute of Management Accountants, is used by permission.

International Standard Book Number: 0-918937-23-X

Library of Congress Number: 78-56493

Contents

Preface

These volumes provide a comprehensive review of the concepts covered on the Certified Management Accountant examination. They are designed for use either as a text in a CMA review course or as a guide for independent study. Parts of Volumes 2, 3, and 4 would also be helpful in preparing for the CPA examination.

These volumes contain a detailed discussion of concepts and previous CMA examination questions which should provide the candidate with all of the information needed to prepare for the CMA examination. The discussion commences at an elementary level and progresses to the level required by the examination. Someone with limited accounting training should, with proper study, be able to adequately prepare for the examination using these tests. Also, this format will serve as a good review for those whose formal training ended several years ago.

The content of the four volumes is as follows:

Part 1: Economics and Business Finance
Part 2: Financial Accounting and Reporting
Part 3: Management Reporting, Analysis, and Behavioral Issues
Part 4: Decision Analysis and Information Systems.

Each volume contains a discussion of the concepts for the part of the examination covered, illustrative questions and problems, and approaches to solutions; additional questions and problems covering the concepts discussed are found at the end of each chapter. The solutions to these questions and problems are also included.

The books are divided in a manner consistent with the examination. Each volume begins with a description of the subject matter of the examinations. To facilitate study and discussion, each volume is divided into chapters. This allows the candidate to study selected concepts, examine previous examination questions on these concepts, and then check his/her understanding by solving some of the problems at the end of each chapter. This categorization also provides for considerable flexibility for CMA review course directors in organizing review courses.

Acknowledgements

I owe a great deal to many for their help in developing this work. Most of all I am appreciative of the excellent cooperation and assistance received from the contributing authors. It would have been impossible for me to have selected a group of contributing authors who were more supportive and understanding.

I acknowledge with appreciation permission from the Institute of Certified Management Accountants of the Institute of Management Accountants to use problems from past CMA examinations, and from the American Institute of Certified Public Accountants to quote from its pronouncements and to use problem material from the CPA examination (Copyright© by the American Institute of Certified Public Accountants).

Finally, I thank Valda L. Newton for her considerable editorial assistance.

It should be emphasized that the final responsibility for the information in the text is that of the author alone.

G.W.N.

Malibu, California

Introduction
Grant W. Newton

The Institute of Management Accountants (IMA) has established the Certified Management Accountant program to recognize professional competence and educational attainment.

Basic objectives of the program are:

1. To establish management accounting as a recognized profession by identifying the role of the management accountant and the underlying body of knowledge, and by outlining a course of study by which such knowledge can be acquired;

2. To foster higher educational standards in the field of management accounting;

3. To assist employers, educators, and students by establishing an objective measure of an individual's knowledge and competence in the field of management accounting.

The CMA program requires candidates to pass a series of uniform examinations and meet specific educational and professional standards to qualify for and maintain the CMA certification. The IMA has established the Institute of Certified Management Accountants to administer the program, conduct the examinations, and grant certificates to those who qualify.

The examination is given semiannually in June and December in many locations throughout the United States and several other countries. Additional information about the requirements, application forms, examination sites, and a brochure describing the program may be obtained from the Institute of Certified Management Accountants.

Content of the Examination

The following outlines indicate the subject matter that will be covered in each part of the examination.

Part 1: Economics, Finance and Management

A. Microeconomics (10% - 15%) Factors affecting the individual firm including demand, supply, and elasticity and their interaction; comsumption of goods; production factors and their cost; market structures and pricing; various economic markets including the demand for resources, the labor market, and the capital market.

B. Macroeconomics and International Economics (10% - 15%) National income accounting, aggregate demand and supply, business cycles, fiscal and monetary policies, and other macroeconomic issues such as inflation, unemployment, and economic growth. International economics including trade policies, foreign exchange markets, and the role of U.S. business in the world economy.

---

1. *Certified Management Accountant* (New York: Institute of Management Accountants, 1993-1994 announcement). pp.4-7.

C. Institutional Environment of Business (10% - 15%) Legal environment of business including the legal forms of business and the structure of government regulation; the impact on business of external forces including employee protection, antitrust policies, social legislation, and non-governmental groups such as consumer and environmental organizations, and financial institutions.

D. Working Capital Management (10% - 15) Evaluating optimum levels of current assets and current liabilities and balancing profitability and risk; policies for the management of cash, marketable securities, accounts receivable, and inventories; short-term credit for financing current assets.

E. Long-term Finance and Capital Structure (10% - 15%) Factors influencing the optimum capital structure including types of risk and leverage; objectives and policies of long-term financing; cost of capital; types of long-term financing instruments; dividend policies.

F. Organizational and Management Theory (20% - 30%) Evolution of theory and practice; decision making in the organizational environment; planning concepts and practices; structure of organizations and their social and cultural environment; effective organization of jobs and groups. Roles and skills of managers; staffing and managing human resources; management theory and leadership styles; motivational theories and methods to influence behavior.

G. Communication (10% - 15%) Communication models; formal and informal organizational communication; deterrents to effective communication; managing communication and information content.

Part 2: Financial Accounting and Reporting

A. Financial Statements (30% - 40%) Objectives of external financial reporting; types, purposes, and timing of principal financial statements; external users of financial statements and their needs; conceptual framework of financial accounting; generally accepted accounting principles governing the recognition and valuation of assets, liabilities, owners' equity, revenue, and expense; limitations of financial statement information.

B. Reporting Requirements (30% - 40%) Public reporting standards regulating financial reporting; disclosure requirements in financial statements; the annual report; accounting for corporate income taxes; accounting standard setting organizations and the processes by which standards are set; the SEC and its reporting requirements.

C. Analysis of Accounts and Statements (15% - 20%) Interpretation and analysis of financial statements including activity ratio analysis and comparative analysis; analysis of accounts including aging accounts receivable and uncollectible accounts, inventory valuation and control, and analysis and valuation of fixed and intangible assets, depreciation, and depletion.

D. External Auditing (10% - 15%) External audit services; auditor and management responsibilities; professional standards of the external auditor; evidence and procedures used by external auditors; audit reports.

Part 3: Management Reporting, Analysis, and Behavioral Issues

A. Cost Measurement (20% - 30%) Cost concepts, flows and terminology; alternative cost objectives; cost measurement concepts; cost accumulation systems including job order costing, process costing, and activity-based costing; overhead cost allocation to cost objectives.

B. Planning (20% - 30%) Strategic plans; purposes of budgeting; budgeting concepts; annual profit plans and supporting schedules; financial budgeting including fixed assets, cash flow, and statement of financial position.

C. Control and Performance Evaluation (20% - 30%) Factors to be analyzed for control and performance evaluation including revenues, costs, profits, and investment in assets; techniques to control and evaluate operations including variance analysis based on flexible budgets and standard costs; techniques to evaluate and report performance including responsibility accounting for revenue, cost, contribution and profit centers.

D. Behavioral Issues (20% - 30%) Alignment of managerial and organizational goals; behavioral issues in developing and using budgets and standards; behavioral and communication issues in reporting and performance evaluation including segment reporting, transfer pricing, and allocation of common costs.

Part 4: Decision Analysis and Information Systems

A. Decision Theory and Operational Decision Analysis (20% - 30%) Logical steps to reach a decision; relevant data concept; cost/volume/profit analysis; marginal analysis; cost-based pricing; financial statement modeling; inventory models and systems. Income tax implications for operational decision analysis.

B. Investment Decision Analysis (20% - 30%) Cash flow estimates; time value of money; discounted cash flow concepts; net present value; internal rate of return; and non-discounting analysis techniques. Income tax implications for investment decision analysis.

C. Quantitative Methods for Decision Analysis (10% - 15%) Quantitative methods and techniques including regression analysis, learning curves, linear programming, sensitivity analysis, network analysis, probability concepts and expected values, decision trees, simulation, expert systems and artificial intelligence, and other appropriate aids to decision making.

D. Information Systems (20% - 30%) Nature of management and accounting information systems; systems development and design; techniques and terminology applicable to the development of computer-based accounting information systems; sys-terms controls and security measures in an accounting information system.

E. Internal Auditing (10% - 15%) Objectives and scope of internal auditing; fundamentals of internal organizational control; professional standards and procedures for administering operational and financial internal audits; internal audit reports; assessing the adequacy of internal controls, particularly in an accounting information system; auditing in an EDP environment.

Suggestions for Independent Study[2]

The CMA Examination tests the candidates' understanding of the fundamental principles underlying the specific areas covered on the examination. The examination recognizes that a management accountant is required to possess high levels of skill covered in Parts 4 and 5, while a reduced level of specialized knowledge is required in the subjects covered in Parts 1, 2, and 3. These levels of sophistication are considered in the administration of the examination. The candidate is also challenged to prepare lucid, professional statements with respect to specific situations faced on the examination. A successful candidate must have a comprehensive knowledge of the specific areas covered and the ability to organize and present such knowledge in writing. These volumes are designed to present a systematic review of concepts, a study of previous examinations and other sample questions and problems, and suggested answers and their organization.

The following suggestions will guide you in your study. These ideas are of a general nature as each candidate's study should be based upon his or her individual training and preparedness.

Establish Review Program

A review program substitutes a structured program for haphazard study. It is recommended that you establish a plan of how you are going to use your time in preparing for the examination. Allocate a certain amount of time each week to CMA examination preparation and put forth a great deal of effort to abide by your plan. It is also suggested that you set aside a specific number of weeks for each part of the examination and concentrate on those areas where you are weakest.

It is also important to set aside some time just before the examination to review the areas previously studied. To set up a time period for study, take the number of weeks that you will have available to study for the examination and divide this by the number of parts of the examination you are taking plus one. If a candidate plans to take all five parts and has 20 weeks before the examination and if some time will be devoted to the study in all but two weeks, the time for each part would be 3 weeks (18 ÷ 6), and the last three weeks would be devoted to a review of all 5 parts. Before you begin your study, set aside so many hours per week and make every effort to abide by the schedule.

2. The contributions of the CPA Review Faculty, the Accounting and Information Systems Department, The University of Alabama, to this section are gratefully acknowledged.

Approach to Study

After planning the review work, the next step is to discuss how the studying is to be done. The importance of advance study necessitates that it be carried out carefully. The first thing is to acquaint yourself with the subjects to be covered on the examination. Each volume is broken down by chapters consisting of a discussion of concepts, illustrations of how to solve selected problems, and a section of previous questions and problems to assist you in preparing for the examination. An effort was made to keep the reading material at a minimum and at the same time cover all areas of the examination.

Survey your personal strengths and weaknesses. In your review program, areas in which you are deficient will become apparent. Spend proportionately more time on these areas in order to maximize your examination performance. You may find it desirable to first study the part of the examination with which you are most familiar. This should give you confidence and encouragement. Do not, however, postpone the most difficult area to last. Why not attempt it second?

Initially the text material for any given subject should be read. Familiarize yourself with the basic concepts and principles that are common to each specialized subject. Study the illustrated problems, giving particular attention to the solution technique and to the items with which you are not familiar.

Problem Solving

Once you have studied the text material, work out the problems at the end of the Chapter. It is very important that the problems (at least some in each Chapter) actually be worked out on paper, because the mere reading of text material or the reading through of a problem with a mental decision that you know how to solve it constitutes only partial training. Do not, however, waste time solving similar problems in areas where you are very strong.

In preparing for the practical problems and cases, which are found in all parts of the examination, practice is required. This practice is necessary to develop (1) ability to analyze, (2) ability to plan, (3) technique, (4) correctness, and (5) speed. Sometimes the problems contain irrelevant information, and in such cases you must discriminate between the essential and nonessential. The ability to analyze is essential to the successful solution of practical accounting problems. To analyze means to classify the whole into its component parts. It is absolutely necessary to plan the answer before it is given. Time precludes you from experimenting as to how the answer should be made. To know in a general way, for instance, the nature of a statement of changes in financial position is insufficient, because the time allotted does not permit a trial-and-error search for the proper form of the statement. In planning solutions, accounting technique is of vital importance. Either before or after the problem is presented, the work required is indicated. Special care should be taken to meet this requirement. To prepare an acceptable solution in the allotted time, the student must get a sharp focus on the specific problem, discern the underlying principles involved, and form a mental picture of the best approach to its solution. Correctness and speed naturally improve as the previous essentials are developed. It is advisable to work some problems under simulated time constraints so the candidate can adjust to this pressure which is added during the taking of the examination. To help in this area, the suggested time for each problem at the end of the chapters is stated.

The actual solving of a problem will present many points which were missed in cursory reading. In addition, two other advantages occur; first, the ideas and concepts set forth in the problem are crystallized; and second, it provides a written record for direct comparison with a model solution. You may be unable to solve many of the problems completely. Do not let this discourage you, as the exact solution of these specific problems is not the primary purpose of your study. Rather, they serve to familiarize you with the type of problem often encountered, develop your analytical abilities, and hasten your completing an accepted approach to its solution. A good start gives encouragement; an uncertain approach is often demoralizing to the CMA candidate.

Do not look at the solution to a particular problem before attempting to solve it. Once your solution is prepared, compare it with the suggested solution. Determine the reason for the difference, if any, and be sure you understand the concepts involved.

Suggestions for Taking the Examination

If the candidate must take the exam in another city, it is advisable to make hotel reservations in advance. By making reservations, the candidate can be assured of being near the place where the examination is being given. The candidate should go to the area where the exam is being given a day early so she/he can recover from any travel fatigue and locate the testing center.

In taking the exam, candidates can improve their performance by doing the following:

1. Look at the requirements of the problem before reading the problem. Generally it is best to read the problem twice. The first time, scan the problem to determine what type it is and generally what is required. The second time, read it very carefully. Candidates may find it helpful to underline important data in the problem and make notations in the margins. Before attempting to write an answer, be sure the problem and its requirements are understood.

2. Budget your time according to the suggested time for the problem. Do not waste time on one problem when there are others to work. On the other hand, do try to solve all of the problems. A partial answer is better than none.

Not attempting to work a problem at all significantly reduces the chances to pass the examination. For example, if a 30 minute question is not answered, an average of 80 on the rest of the examination must be attained to end up with the passing average 70. If the suggested time for the question is 45 minutes, an average of 86 is required. Since most candidates who pass the examination do not have an average of 80, the failure to budget time so that all problems are attempted will almost ensure that this part of the examination will be failed.

Each part of the examination lasts four hours. The cover page of the examination lists the problems for the particular part by number and estimated time. Write down the time at

which each problem should be completed before you start the examination, and refer to this schedule to be sure you do not get behind. An example is as follows:

Friday, June 17; 1:00 p.m. to 5:00 p.m.

	Estimated Time	*Latest Completion Time*
Section A		
Number 1	60 minutes	*2:00*
Number 2	30 minutes	*2:30*
Number 3	30 minutes	*3:00*
Number 4	30 minutes	*3:30*
Number 5	30 minutes	*4:40*
Section B (answer only two of the three questions) Number		
6, 7, or 8	60 minutes each	*4:30 first option*
		5:00 second option

3. Check answers for clarity of thought and proper grammatical structures. The ease with which a grader can read the answer will have a positive influence on the grade given. Try to be as neat as possible.

4. Place your number and the examination part on the answer sheets as soon as they are distributed so you will not have to do this during the examination.

5. Candidates may use calculators during the examination. Select the calculator in advance and be sure you know how to operate it effectively. It is a good idea to take an extra calculator to the examination center, in case problems develop with the first one. Make sure batteries are fully charged.

6. The use of a calculator should not in any way reduce the amount of support you show for your answers. The exact steps which you took to solve the problem must be clearly shown. If you place the wrong amount in the calculator, but itemize your calculations, the grader will be able to see that the reason for the incorrect answer was a mechanical error, rather than a failure to understand a given concept.

Nature of Questions

The first problem on each examination will most likely be multiple choice. It is anticipated that each part will have at least 60 minutes of multiple choice questions. Over time, the time devoted to multiple choice questions will most likely increase.

Based on prior examinations, the rest of the exam will most likely consist of six 30-minute questions. With the ICMA now setting the percent of exam time devoted to each subject, there may be variation in this practice. In prior exams there have been some questions that required 20, 40, or 60 minutes. On some earlier examinations there have also been two or three 30-minute questions that related to the same set of facts.

While the ICMA is not bound by the policy of giving the candidate the option to answer two out of three questions during the last hour of the examination, most of the exams have followed this format. Again, to stay within the percentage guidelines, the ICMA may have to deviate from this practice. However, it is the policy of the ICMA to continue to offer options.

The most common type of question used is the situation problem. The question contains information about a problem, often related to a specific company. The candidate may first be asked to define or explain the meaning in general terms of the concept addressed in the question. The second part of the question usually deals with the application of the concepts to the facts in the question.

In addition, almost all questions that involve calculations also require some analysis or intrepetation of the calculated values. For example, if you are preparing for Part 1 of the exam, do not end your study by knowing how to calculate the weighted average cost of capital, but learn how to analyze the answer and know alternative approaches.

Content Specification Outlines

The CMA examination content specification outlines were approved by the ICMA Board of Regents in June 1990. These outlines represent the body of knowledge that will be covered on the CMA examination and expand upon content descriptions that appear in the CMA Program Announcement. The outlines may be changed in the future when new subject matter becomes part of the common body of knowledge for management accountants.

Candidates are responsible for being informed on the most recent developments in the areas covered in the outline. This includes understanding public pronouncements issued by accounting organizations as well as being up-to-date on recent developments reported in current accounting and business periodicals.

The content specification outlines serve several purposes. These include:

1. Establishing the foundation from which each CMA examination will be developed.

2. Providing consistent coverage on the CMA examination over time.

3. Communicating to interested parties more detail as to the content of each examination part.

4. Aiding candidates in their preparation for the examination.

5. Providing information to those who offer courses designed to assist candidates in preparing for the examination.

Important additional information about the content specification outlines and the CMA examination is listed below.

1. The percentage range given for each major topic within each examination part represents the relative weight range given to that topic in an examination part. A candidate will be required to answer questions that equal the minimum relative weight but do not exceed the maximum relative weight for a topic.

2. Each examination will sample from the subject areas contained within each major topic area to meet the relative weight specifications. No relative weights have been assigned to the subject areas within each major topic. No inference should be made from the order in which the subject areas are listed or from the number of subject areas as to the relative weight or importance of any of the subjects.

3. The topics for each of the four examination parts have been selected to minimize the overlapping of subject areas among the examination parts.

4. The major topics within an examination part and the subject areas within topics may be combined in individual questions.

5. The CMA examination will continue to have optional questions. However, from time to time, a part may have no optional questions.

6. Questions containing ethical issues can appear on any part of the examination. Ethical issues will appear on at least two parts at every examination offering. The ethical issues will be addressed within the context of specific subject areas. Over the four parts of an examination, the ethical issues content will not be less than the equivalent of one 30 minute question nor more than two 30 minute questions. For determining the relative weight distribution of an examination, the questions containing ethical issues will be counted in the major topic area in which the ethical issues are raised.

7. Federal income taxation issues will be divided into two categories and be contained in questions that relate to the two categories.

    a. Accounting for income taxes. The financial reporting requirements for income taxes including the proper treatment of deferred income taxes will be contained in questions in Part 2, Financial Accounting and Reporting.

    b. Tax implications for decisions. The tax code provisions that impact decisions will be contained in the decision analysis questions in Part 4, Decision Analysis and Information Systems. They also will be contained in questions that require decision analysis regarding debt versus equity issues in Part 1, Economics, Finance, and Management.

Part 3 - Management Reporting, Analysis, and Behavioral Issues

A. Cost measurement (20-30%)
  1. Cost concepts and flow
    a. Alternative cost objectives
    b. Cost terminology

  2. Cost measurement concepts
    a. Cost behavior
    b. Method of charging to cost objects
    c. Alternative measurement concepts
    d. Joint product and by-product costing
    e. Historical versus replacement cost
  3. Cost accumulation systems
    a. Operation costing
    b. Constnat flow manufacturing
    c. Activity-based costing
    d. Job order costing
    e. Process costing
  4. Alternative methods for accumulating and assigning overhead costs to products and services
    a. Considerations in measuring and assigning overhead

b. Plant-wide versus departmental overhead

c. Allocation of service department costs

B. Planning (20-30%)

  1. Hierarchy of planning

    a. Mission and strategic goals

    b. Strategic objectives and plans

    c. Tactical objectives and plans

    d. Operational objectives and plans

    e. Contingency plans

  2. Purposes of budgeting

    a. Plan operations and performance goals

    b. Implement plans and motivate people

    c. Frame of reference for performance evaluation

    d. Communicate and coordinate activities among organizational units

    e. Authorize action

  3. Budget concepts

    a. Relating planning to organizational structure

    b. The budget process

    c. Mechanics in budgeting

    d. Types of budget systems

  4. Annual profit plan and the supporting schedules

    a. Sales budget

    b. Production budget

    c. Direct materials budget

    d. Direct labor budget

    e. Overhead budget

    f. Cost of goods sold budget

    g. Selling and administrative budget

    h. Budget for acquisition of capital assets

    i. Cash budget and cash management plans

    j. Pro forma income statement

    k. Pro forma statement of financial position

    l. Pro forma statement of cash flows

C. Control and performance evaluation (20-30%)

  1. Factors to be analyzed for control and performance evaluation

    a. Regular operations

    b. Investment base and financing costs

c. Product quality

  2. Techniques to control and evaluate operations

    a. Comparison of actual results to the annual budget

    b. Use of flexible budgets to analyze performance

    c. Types of variation measures

    d. Use of standard cost systems

  3. Techniques to evaluate and report performance

    a. Type of responsibility segments

    b. Factors needed to exercise control

    c. Reporting in a responsibility setting

    d. Divisional performance measures

D. Behavioral issues (20-30%)

  1. Alignment of managerial and organizational goals

    a. Goal congruence with respect to purpose and use of budgets and standards

    b. Establishing authority and responsibility for activities

  2. Behavioral issues in developing budgets and standards

    a. Approaches to development of budgets and standards

    b. Advantages to participatory development

    c. Potential problems of participatory development

  3. Behavioral issues in reporting and performance evaluation

    a. Frequency and form of performance feedback

    b. Controllability of costs for accountability

    c. Arbitrary allocations of common costs

    d. Use of flexible budgets rather than static budgets

    e. Multiple measures of performance

    f. Specific issues related to segment reporting

The topics and subject areas above may include ethical considerations in management reporting, analysis, and behavioral issues of concern to management accountants.

  • Statement on Management Accounting No. 1C, "Standards of Ethical Conduct for Management Accountants"

    - Competence

    - Confidentiality

    - Integrity

    - Objectivity

  • Manipulation of analyses and results

  • Unethical behavior in developing budgets and standards

Chapter 1

Information, Communication, and Accounting

James R. Morton and
Grant W. Newton

Financial statements are the means by which information accumulated and processed in financial accounting is periodically communicated to those who use it. They are designed to serve the needs of a variety of users, particularly owners and creditors.[1]

In its broadest sense, accounting is concerned with providing financial information to users. The financial statements themselves are the means by which such information is transmitted to users. It is appropriate, therefore, before proceeding to a discussion of the individual financial statements in the conventional financial statement set, to examine some of the relevant communication and information concepts, as well as the underlying accounting principles and objectives pertinent to these financial statements.

Information and Communication Concepts

As it is used in the field of communication, the term **information** has been defined as "the property of a signal or message enabling it to convey something unpredictable by and meaningful to the recipient of the message."[2] **Communication** has been defined as "the process of transmitting ideas or thoughts from one person (or group) to another, or within a single person, for the purpose of creating understanding in the thinking of the person (or group) receiving the communication."[3]

On the basis of these definitions, three characteristics of information are apparent: (1) the message is conveyed to (understood by) the recipient; (2) the message resolves uncertainty (that is, it is not common knowledge to the recipient); and (3) the message is meaningful (relevant) to the recipient. Information is distinguished from **data** in terms of these three characteristics.

Data may be thought of as raw materials from which information is derived. However, in their raw state, data are merely facts—perhaps irrelevant, perhaps not understood, and/or perhaps already known to the recipient. The essence of information is its ability to reduce uncertainty on the part of the recipient of the message.

Conceptually, information measurement has been likened to the measurement of entropy in thermodynamics. Entropy is the tendency for the organization of any closed system to deteriorate and become more chaotic. The amount of entropy in such a system, then, is the difference between the amount of chaos in the system at the beginning and the amount at the end. The greater the difference, the greater is the system's propensity for variety. Similarly, information content of a message is measured by the difference between initial ignorance of the recipient and the recipient's ignorance after receipt of the message. A small difference, as one might expect, indicates a message containing little information. (The reader should note that information is related to uncertainty and is not necessarily related to the amount of data contained in a message.)

1. AICPA, *Professional Standards*. Volume 3, July 1, 1981 (Chicago: Commerce Clearing House), par. 1022.02 (Hereinafter referred to as *Professional Standards)*
2. William C. Himstreet and Wayne Murlin Baty, *Business Communications: Principles and Methods* (Belmont, California: Wadsworth Publishing Co., Inc., 1973), p. 5.
3. C. G. Browne, "Communication Means Understanding," in William G. Scott, *Organization Theory: A Behavioral Analysis for Management* (Homewood, Illinois: Richard D. Irwin, 1967), pp. 152-153.

Notwithstanding this difference between information and data, much of accounting literature is found to ignore such a distinction. The following footnote, for example, appears in the Accounting Principles Board's Statement No. 4:

> The term information is sometimes applied only to relevant data. This statement does not distinguish between the terms **information** and **data**.[4]

In this book we will defer to the bulk of accounting literature and treat the terms **information** and **data** as synonyms. However, the reader should be cautioned that information content, in the strict sense, can be attributed to financial statements only to the extent that the statements satisfy the requirements of relevance, understandability, and reduction of uncertainty.

Influences on Accounting Information

The ability of financial statements to satisfy the above requirements is affected by numerous factors influencing the nature of the information contained therein. In this section we will discuss these factors, and in the following section we will examine the qualitative attributes identified by the Accounting Principles Board (APB) as necessary to make financial statements useful.

Variety of Users and Information Needs

A significant factor influencing the nature of accounting information included in accounting reports is the fact that the audience for whom such reports are prepared is made up of a variety of potential users having diverse information needs. Broadly, these users can be divided into two categories: internal users and external users.

Internal Users   Internal users include all levels of management within the reporting entity's organizational framework (that is, top management, middle management, and first-line management). Within this broad grouping, user needs are largely concerned with planning and control decisions regarding **organizational** effectiveness and efficiency. However, even within this seemingly homogeneous internal user category, the information needs do differ according to the duties and responsibilities at each management level.

Reporting for internal management is not, strictly speaking, a "financial accounting" matter, but accounting reports, based at least in part on the entity's accounting records, are the means by which management planning and control information is transmitted to the various management levels. A distinctive feature of internal accounting reports is that they can be—and are—tailored to the needs of users within the reporting entity; this feature is not so readily accomplished in external reporting, as we shall see later.

4. *Professional Standards*, para. 1023.04.

All levels of management are involved to some extent in both planning and control activities. However, the relative importance and the nature of these activities differ among the different management levels. Generally, the planning function receives relatively greater attention at higher levels of management; the control function receives relatively greater attention at lower levels. Also, the nature of the planning and control activities is generally longer ranged and organizationally broader at higher management level than at lower levels.

At the top management level of the organization, information needs are primarily planning-oriented; this is consistent with the responsibility of top management for achievement of overall organizational objectives. Consequently, accounting reports intended for this level should emphasize information pertinent to long-range planning activities and to the resolution of special problems confronting the organization as a whole. Since the control responsibilities of top management are, by definition, broader in scope than those at lower management levels, and since top management is organizationally and temporally removed from the day-to-day operations of organization subunits, control-oriented reports intended for this level of management can be far less detailed and less frequent than reports intended for lower levels.

First-line managers are directly accountable for the day-to-day operating performance of their organizational unit and are in the best position to influence their unit's performance immediately. For this reason, control-oriented information at this level is very important. In addition, the planning efforts of first-line managers are, for the most part, short-ranged and center on efficient acquisition, allocation, and utilization of inputs to the operating unit. That is, first-line planning activities are primarily concerned with control considerations, and control-oriented information is again required. Since it is at the operating level that relatively minute adjustments are made to operations, reports intended for this level of management should contain greater performance detail than reports intended for higher management levels.

Middle management personnel are involved in both planning and control activities for the organizational subunits for which they are responsible. Planning efforts at the mid-management level are longer ranged than at the first-line management level, but because mid-management plans must conform to plans of top management, they are necessarily shorter ranged than those of top management. Further, since middle managers are typically responsible for several organizational subunits, and are somewhat removed from the day-to-day operations of those units, control-oriented reports should be less detailed than the reports intended for first-line management use. Also, in line with the philosophy of **management by exception** (a philosophy that calls for management to concentrate their efforts on significant departures from expected norms), these reports should emphasize areas of performance where corrective action is indicated.

External Users   External users of accounting reports are even less homogeneous in their needs than internal users. The external user category includes all interested parties who do not, by virtue of their relationship with the organization, have direct access to the firm's financial data bank. *APB Statement No. 4* lists 13 potential external user groups having either direct or indirect economic interests in business enterprises.[5] Among the users identified as having a direct interest are: owners, creditors, and suppliers; potential owners, creditors, and suppliers; taxing authorities; employees; and customers. Included among users having indirect interests are: financial analysts and advisors; stock exchanges; lawyers, regulatory or registration authorities; financial press and reporting agencies; trade associations; and labor unions.

Because the number of potential external users of financial statements is so great and their information needs so diverse, the tailoring of accounting reports for each potential external user group is not a feasible alternative. It should be pointed out here that the listing above is not meant to be—nor is it—an exhaustive listing of all possible users. However, pressures from these various groups have had, and continue to have, an important impact on the form and content of financial statements intended for external users. The form and content of these statements will be examined in subsequent sections of this chapter.

In addition to the diverse information needs of financial statement users, several other environmental factors exist that influence the nature of the data presented in financial statements. Some of these factors are exogenous to the accounting profession, while others are self-imposed.

Economic Activity

While all societies engage in the economic activities of production, consumption, exchange, income distribution, saving, and investment, the relative importance of each of these activities varies among societies at different levels of economic development and/or different economic structures. Savings and investment patterns in economically underdeveloped societies, for example, are significantly different from the complex process in the United States. And income distribution and resource allocation processes characteristic of capitalistic societies contrast markedly with such processes in socialistic societies.

Since accounting is concerned with the communication of economic events for the purpose of assisting in economic decision making, the configuration of the economic system in which the accounting reports are to be used is of considerable importance. The nature of accounting and accounting reports can be expected to evolve along lines consistent with the economic process they seek to describe and the economic decisions for which they are intended.

Social Concerns

The nature of accounting and reporting practices among different societies are affected by cultural considerations of a noneconomic nature, as well as by cross-cultural economic differences. For example, we have seen the focus of financial accounting in most Western economies evolve from a predominantly internal record-keeping focus, through a pre-

dominantly stewardship focus, to what can now best be described as an income determination focus. While this shift in accounting orientation is generally attributed to the widespread adoption of the corporate form of business organization, it is fair to say that public reporting practices would have proceeded at a far slower pace than they have, were it not for a concomitant increase in concern over the rights of outside investors.

In recent years, some of the social concern over the economic well-being of the United States' economy has been displaced by a growing concern over the mental and physical well-being of the nation's citizens. The once popular belief that "what is good for industry, is good for the country" is being questioned on all fronts. This shift in social concern has begun to manifest itself in publications calling for social responsibility accounting and in supplemental disclosures in corporate financial statements reporting the company's *social* (as contrasted with *economic*) contribution. To be sure, such disclosures are voluntary and have been rather rudimentary to date; but the influence of social concerns on the nature of information included in financial statements cannot be denied.

Information Technology

Economic activities and social concerns are positive factors influencing the nature of accounting information in that they describe the kinds of decisions for which the financial statements are to be used and the environment within which the decisions are to be made.

The state of development of information technology, however, might be viewed as a limiting factor with respect to information supplied in financial statements. The ability of the accounting profession to respond to users' information needs depends upon the availability of appropriate measurement and communication techniques. Thus, even though a significant concern may already exist regarding corporate social accountability, existing measurements of social costs and social benefits are far from well developed. Until such time as these measurements are developed (and can be understood by users), it is unlikely that social accountability disclosures will progress beyond their present status of voluntary and unaudited supplemental representations of corporate management.

Accounting Conventions

In addition to the exogenous environmental factors discussed above, certain accounting and reporting conventions have been adopted by the accounting profession, which influence the nature of information transmitted through financial statements to external parties. Although these conventions are self-imposed, they nevertheless represent the accountant's response to environmental factors and are considered necessary in order to make financial statements more useful to users.

Conservatism   Conservatism is perhaps the most widely publicized yet least understood of the self-imposed accounting

---

5. *Ibid.,* par. 1023.04-1023.06

conventions. Historically, during a period when debt was the primary source of business financing, conservatism in financial statements was viewed as a virtue; however, much of the contemporary commentary on conservatism in present-day financial statements is negative.

In its simplest sense, **conservatism** is defined as the practice in financial reporting of anticipating no gains and allowing for all losses. This definition, however, is an oversimplification of the true nature of conservatism in accounting. Ideally, the accountant strives to obtain and report financial measures that neither overstate nor understate the true situation. When an uncertainty exists regarding financial statement valuations and/or earnings, however, a conservative posture is adopted in order to minimize the ill-effects of measurement errors. It has long been the accountant's position that the ill-effects of overoptimism in financial statements are more damaging to users in general than are the ill-effects of pessimism.

Examples of conservatism in financial statements include: the practice of valuing inventories and marketable securities at the lower of cost or market, where losses in value are reflected in income currently but gains in value above cost are not reflected in income until the asset is sold at the higher price; accrual of contingent losses currently if there is a high probability that the loss will be incurred sometime in the future, while not accruing gains that are equally probable; and recognizing expected losses from disposals of segments of a business as soon as management commits itself to a formal plan to dispose of the segment, while generally not recognizing a gain until the segment is actually disposed of—that is, until the disposal is a *fait accompli*.

The double-edged nature of conservatism requires judicious application of the concept. Indiscriminate application of the conservatism doctrine that causes overly pessimistic financial statement representations currently will inevitably lead to overly optimistic representations in future periods. For example, excessive write-downs of inventory in the current period will understate income of the period of the write-down and will correspondingly overstate income in the period in which the inventory is sold.

Emphasis on Income   Emphasis on income is a self-imposed convention that has evolved as a result of, and in response to, the changing needs of financial statement users. As suggested earlier, the growth in importance of the corporate form of business organization was largely responsible for redirecting the focus of financial statement users from balance sheet valuations to reported income numbers.

The growth in incorporated businesses precipitated a growth in the number of equity investors; and equity investors, as residual owners of the corporate enterprise, tended to be more concerned with the ability of the enterprise to generate cash flow through operations than with reported net asset values. Consequently, even though the contention raises serious questions concerning the meaning of the traditional balance sheet as well as the relationship between the balance sheet and the income statement, the APB's position regarding the income emphasis in financial reporting is summed up as follows:

Although balance sheets formerly were presented without income statements, the income statement has in recent years come to be regarded as the most important of the financial statements. Accounting principles that are deemed to increase the usefulness of the income statement are therefore sometimes adopted by the profession as a whole regardless of their effect on the balance sheet.[6]

How it is possible, in light of the fundamental relationship that is supposed to exist between the financial statements, for an accounting principle to be appropriate to the income statement and inappropriate to the balance sheet is a conceptual question left unanswered by the APB.

Application of Accountant's Judgment   Application of accountant's judgment is a long-standing and fiercely defended convention in financial accounting calling for the accountant's independent determination of the correct or most appropriate accounting treatment in situations involving new, unusual, or vague circumstances. The convention is interpreted to mean that accountants, because of their background of knowledge and experience, are in the best position to make determinations concerning appropriate accounting and reporting procedures.

Critics of contemporary financial accounting practices cite the judgment convention as the source of several real or potential financial accounting and reporting problems. First, the judgment convention is merely an excuse for the inability of the public accounting profession to execute its assumed responsibility of prescribing accounting standards. Second, the latitude permitted by the judgment convention bestows upon the independent accountant, both individually and corporately, far too much authority over the contents of published financial statements. Finally, independent judgments regarding different situations with similar circumstances all too often result in different conclusions. Thus, one of the basic desirable attributes of financial statements—comparability—is compromised.

Despite these arguments, however, application of the accountant's judgment in prescribing accounting and reporting practices is essential. It is impossible to prescribe in advance principles covering every conceivable situation that may arise and may affect published financial statements. Also, while similar situations have undoubtedly been interpreted differently by different accountants, such occurrences are rare. The vast majority of apparent inconsistencies in accounting are not in fact inconsistencies at all, but rather reflect inherent differences in the situation itself that are not obvious to the untrained outside observer. To the extent that standards of financial reporting can be prescribed in advance, the Financial Accounting Standards Board (FASB), as an independent representative of financial statement preparers and users, as well as accountants, determines the content of published financial statements. In situations requiring judgmental discretion, who but the professional accountant is better qualified to exercise that judgment? And, whose interests would be served by transferring this responsibility elsewhere?

---

6. *Ibid.*, par. 1026.35.

Qualitative Objectives of Financial Statements

The overall objective of financial reporting was broadly stated earlier as the presentation of financial data that are intended to be useful to a variety of users. What constitute "useful" data is a question accountants have struggled with for some time, and the answer is not an easy one to come by. Nevertheless, the Accounting Principles Board outlined in *APB Statement No. 4* seven qualitative objectives of financial data that it felt would tend to enhance the usefulness of financial statements.

Relevance

Of these seven qualitative objectives, relevance, described as information that "bears on the economic decisions for which it is used,"[7] is identified as the primary objective. Relevance is considered the primary qualitative objective of financial data because data that do not bear on the decision for which they are used are not useful, regardless of the extent to which other objectives are satisfied. Furthermore, in light of the variety of financial statement users, relevance is defined in *APB Statement No. 4* in terms of the common needs of all users rather than the specific needs of individual users.

Exhibit 1-1 illustrates this generalized interpretation of relevance by a simple Venn diagram depicting information needs of four hypothetical financial statement user groups (A, B, C, D). Each user group has unique information needs, but there is some area of common need (represented by the darkened area) that is satisfied with a single set of general purpose financial statements. A problem associated with this generalized interpretation is also illustrated by the diagram, however. That is, while it is perhaps possible to satisfy the common needs of many user groups, a significant portion of individual users' needs may go unsatisfied.

Understandability

In order for data to be useful, they not only must bear on the decision for which they are to be used, but they must be understood by those who would use them. Data, even though relevant, are not useful if their meaning is not conveyed to the user. Because the level of sophistication of financial statement users varies both within and between user groups, presentation of data understandable to all parties is a problem inherent in general purpose financial statements.

Either the financial statements must be prepared under a "lowest common denominator" approach—that is, financial statements are prepared for the least sophisticated user; or they are prepared for users having some assumed level of technical competence regarding accounting and economic concepts and terminology.

A recent publication of the Financial Accounting Standards

7. *Ibid.*, par. 1024.16.

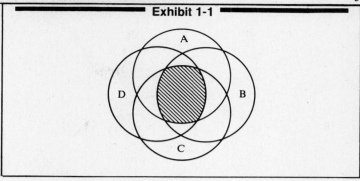

Exhibit 1-1

Board, issued in connection with the FASB's Conceptual Framework Project, adopts the latter approach.

> Financial reporting should provide information that is useful to present and potential investors and creditors and other users in making rational investment, credit, and similar decisions. The information should be comprehensible to those who have a reasonable understanding of business and economic activities and are willing to study the information with reasonable diligence.

Verifiability

There is general agreement that usefulness of financial information is enhanced if the information can be verified by independent determination. Thus it is that verifiability—the ability to corroborate financial information independently—is considered a desirable attribute of measurements in published financial statements.

It is important to recognize, however, that verifiability is not a dichotomous (verifiable/not verifiable) choice, but rather is a matter of degree. If the choice were between verifiable fact and an unsubstantiable assertion, the choice would be a simple matter. Such is not the case, however. A particular measure may be more or less verifiable than some other measure on a continuum of verifiability anchored only at the extremes by positive (verifiable) and negative (not verifiable) absolutes.

The question concerning verifiability is, therefore, whether the greater verifiability of certain measures causes those measures to be more useful than less verifiable measures. The question is not an easy one to answer because verifiability, like other attributes of financial information, is not independent of other considerations. Specifically, the inherent verifiability of historical cost numbers—rather than current (fair) values— is often suggested as justification for their use in financial statements. Fair value advocates, on the other hand, argue that historical cost numbers are generally not as relevant to users of financial statements as are some forms of fair value measures. The crux of their argument is illustrated in Exhibit 1-2.

8. Financial Accounting Standards Board, *Statement of Financial Accounting Concepts No. 1: Obectives of Financial Statements by Business Enterprises* (Stamford, Connecticut: FASB), p. 3.

Exhibit 1-2

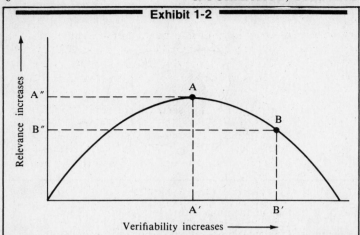

In general, the need for some corroborative evidence of financial measures is conceded. However, incremental gains in verifiability contribute to smaller and smaller gains in relevance until, at some point (A' in Exhibit 1-2) an additional increment in verifiability would detract from relevance. Thus, while historical cost (at say point B') is perhaps more verifiable than fair value (at say point A') a sacrifice of verifiability to the extent of A' − B' would yield an increase in relevance of A'' − B''.

Neutrality

Because of the diverse information needs of potential financial statement users; their varying levels of sophistication with respect to accounting and business and economic matters; and the impracticality of preparing separate financial statements for each potential user group; the single set of general purpose financial statements has long been seen as the most feasible approach to satisfying information needs. Specifically, *APB Statement No. 4* defines neutral financial accounting information as ". . . information that is directed toward the common needs of users and is independent of presumptions about the particular needs and desires of specific users of the information."[9] Thus, financial statements should not be designed to enhance the usefulness to a particular user segment to the detriment of other segments. Potential problems with this approach were discussed earlier in this section concerning the relevance of such financial statements.

The recent position of the FASB, which seems to narrow the intended audience for whom financial statements are prepared, is an indication that current thinking places greater importance on the information needs of informed creditor and investor user groups. The FASB apparently believes that by satisfying the needs of investor and creditor groups, other user groups' needs will be satisfied as well.

Timeliness

In its simplest form, timeliness of financial information means that the information should be provided early enough for that information to be used for the purpose intended. The

---

9. AICPA, *Professional Standards,* par. 1024.19.

timeliness objective of financial information, although obviously important in its own right, is an elaboration on one aspect of the primary objective, relevance.

Relevance and timeliness are inseparable by definition. Information that is provided too late for it to affect the decision for which it was intended is not relevant. However, timeliness may pose a conflict with the verifiability objective mentioned earlier. Perhaps the best example of this potential conflict concerns the presentation of financial forecasts. There is little doubt that forecast financial data are less verifiable than historical cost data. Nevertheless, the future expectations of an enterprise are unquestionably important inputs to investors, creditors, and others interest in the enterprise's long-term health.

Comparability

Comparability in financial reporting is a two-dimensional objective. First, comparability **within the reporting enterprise** is necessary in order that determinations of the enterprise's progress over time can be made. Thus, consistent accounting and reporting practices should be followed by the enterprise in successive accounting periods. When situations arise that call for departures from previously applied principles, disclosures should be made so that financial statement users can gauge the effect of the change on the current financial statements, as well as the implications of the change with respect to previously issued financial statements.

Second, comparability **between reporting enterprises** is required in order that comparisons between enterprises can be made. Specifically, differences in operating performance and financial position between enterprises should be attributable to real differences between the firms and/or their transactions; they should not merely be differences in accounting principles and procedures used by the firms. The major barrier to comparability between enterprises is the general acceptance of alternative accounting practices where such alternatives are not justified by true differences

Completeness

Completeness involves a delicate balance between reporting all information that is considered useful (that is, meets the other six qualitative objectives) and being overly redundant. Incomplete information may exclude disclosures that would be considered by some users as essential to their decision-making process, while excessive information may only be confusing and may conceal information that is essential to the decision-making process.

Nature of Financial Accounting Reports

The nature of accounting information is summed up in the kinds of reports included in the conventional financial statement set. In this section, we shall briefly introduce these financial reports (a more definitive discussion is presented in Part 2) and discuss some of the basic features and elements of these reports.

The Statement of Financial Position (Balance Sheet)

The statement of financial position, or balance sheet, consists of three basic elements—assets, liabilities, and owners' equity —that respectively purport to reflect the entity's stock of economic resources, its economic obligations, and the residual amount of its owners' equity in entity assets. The statement is static in the sense that it reflects the entity's resources, and the equities of owners and creditors at a particular point of time (that is, as of the close of business on the balance sheet date).

The relationship among the three basic elements is depicted by the basic accounting equation:

$$\text{Assets} = \text{Liabilities} + \text{Owners' equity.}$$

The left-hand member of the equation reflects the cost of the economic resources under the entity's control, and the right-hand members indicate the sources of resource financing (that is, by debt or by equity investment). Details of balance sheet reporting requirements are presented in Part 2.

The Income Statement

The income statement, like the balance sheet, consists of three basic elements—in this case, revenue, expenses, and net income. The relationship among the three elements is expressed as: Revenues − Expenses = Net income.

Revenues "are inflows or other enhancements of assets of an entity or settlements of its liabilities (or a combination of both) during a period from delivering or producing goods, rendering services, or other activities that constitute the entity's ongoing major or central operations."[10]

Expenses "are outflows or other using up of assets or incurrences of liabilities (or a combination of both) during a period from delivering or producing goods, rendering services, or carrying out other activities that constitute the entity's ongoing major or central operations."[11]

Revenues are recognized in the income statement when they are realized (generally at the point of sale); expenses are recognized in the income statement as they are directly associated with revenue realization (for example, cost of goods sold), or they are associated with a time period on a systematic and rational allocation basis (for example, depreciation). Thus, **net income,** the third basic element of the income statement, is merely the excess of revenues over expenses (or expenses over revenues in the case of a loss) for the period in which such revenues and expenses were recognized. Specific income statement presentations are discussed in detail in Part 2.

The Statement of Changes in Financial Position

There are two primary elements in the statement of changes

in financial position, or funds statement. They are: sources of funds and uses of funds. The term **funds**, as it is used in the statement of changes in financial position, generally means working capital or cash, whichever is the more informative for the reporting entity. However, whichever definition is used for the term, the statement itself must be prepared on a basis that reflects all significant financing and investing activities of the enterprise, whether or not cash or working capital is directly affected. The means by which such disclosures are accomplished is known as the "all financial resources approach" and is discussed in Part 2.

The objectives of the funds statement are:

1. to summarize the financing and investing activities of the entity, including the extent to which the enterprise has generated funds from operations during the period, and

2. to complete the disclosure of changes in financial position during the period.[12]

The relationship between the statement of changes in financial position and the two primary financial reports already discussed is described in *APB Opinion No. 19* as follows:

> The funds statement is related to both the income statement and the balance sheet and provides information that can be obtained only partially, or at best in piecemeal form, by interpreting them. . . . The funds statement cannot supplant either the income statement or the balance sheet but is intended to provide information that the other statements either do not provide or provide only indirectly about the flow of funds and changes in financial position during the period.[13]

A discussion of detailed reporting requirements relative to the statement of changes in financial position is presented in Part 2.

The FASB has placed more emphasis on cash flows than on the statement of changes in financial position. For example in describing the objectives of financial reporting, the FASB stated in *Statement of Financial Accounting Concept No. 1* (Highlights) that:

> Financial reporting should provide information to help present and potential investors and creditors and other users in assessing the amounts, timing, and uncertainty of prospective cash receipts from dividends or interest and the proceeds from the sale, redemption, or maturity of securities or loans. Since investors' and creditors' cash flows are related to enterprise cash flows, financial reporting should provide information to help investors, creditors, and others assess the amounts, timing, and uncertainty of prospective net cash inflows to the related enterprise.

Also, in the proposed concept dealing with recognition and measurement that is discussed below, cash flow is one of the principal financial statements.

Complete Set of Financial Statements

The FASB, in its exposure draft on the proposed statement of financial accounting concepts on Recognition and Measurement in Financial Statements of Business Enterprises, suggests that a complete set of financial statements for a period should show:

---

10. Financial Accounting Standards Board, *Statement of Financial Accounting Concepts No. 3: Elements of Financial Statements of Business Enterprises* (Stamford, Connecticut: FASB, 1980), par. 63.
11. *Ibid.,* par. 65.

12. *Professional Standards,* par. 2021.04.
13. *Ibid.,* par. 2021.05.

1. Financial position at the end of the period

2. Cash flows during the period

3. Earnings for the period

4. Comprehensive income for the period

5. Investments by and distributions to owners during the period.[14]

The FASB states that some of the information listed above might be combined into a single statement.

The FASB indicates that general purpose financial statements are directed toward the common interest of various potential users in the ability of a business enterprise to generate favorable cash flows. General purpose financial statements are feasible only because groups of users of financial information have generally similar needs. But "general purpose" does not mean "all purpose," and financial statements do not necessarily satisfy all users equally well. Financial statements are prepared after simplifying, condensing, and aggregating masses of data. Thus they convey information that would be obscured if greater detail about each transaction or event were provided. However, the FASB concludes that summary information—such as the amount of net assets, comprehensive income, earnings, or earnings per share—may be useful as a general indicator of investment or overall performance, but that it is important to avoid focusing too much attention on the bottom line.[15]

Financial statements are said to articulate because they reflect different aspects of the same transaction or other events affecting an entity. Important financial ratios, such as rates of return and turnover ratios, depend on interrelationships between financial statements. For example financial statements complement each other:

1. Statements of financial position include information that is often used in assessing an entity's liquidity and financial flexibility, but a statement of financial position provides only an incomplete picture of either liquidity or financial flexibility unless it is used in conjunction with at least a cash flow statement.

2. Statements of cash flows commonly show a great deal about an entity's current cash receipts and payments, but a cash flow statement provides an incomplete basis for assessing prospects for future cash flows because it cannot show interperiod relationships.

3. Statements of earnings and comprehensive income generally reflect a great deal about the profitability of an entity during a period, but that information can be interpreted most meaningfully or compared with that of the entity for other periods or that of other entities only if it is used in conjunction with a statement of financial position, for example, by computing rates of return on assets or equity.

4. Statements of investments by and distributions to owners provide information about significant sources of increases

and decreases in assets, liabilities, and equity, but that information is of little practical value unless used in conjunction with other financial statements, for example, by comparing distributions to owners with earnings and comprehensive income or by comparing investments by and distributions to owners with borrowings and repayments of debt.[16]

Statement of Financial Position   The FASB indicates that a

statement of financial position provides information about an entity's assets, liabilities, and equity and their relationships to each other at a moment in time. The statement delineates the entity's resource structure—major classes and amounts of assets—and its financing structure—major classes and amounts of liabilities and equity. A statement of financial position does not purport to show the value of a business enterprise but, together with other financial statements and other information, should provide information that is useful to those who desire to make their own estimates of the enterprise's value.[17]

Statement of Cash   A statement of cash flows reflects an entity's cash receipts classified by major sources and its cash payments classified by major uses during a period, including cash flow information about its operating, financing, and investing activities.[18]

Earnings   Earnings is a measure of entity performance during a period. It measures the extent to which asset inflows (revenues and gains) associated with substantially completed cash-to-cash cycles exceed asset outflows (expenses and losses) associated, directly or indirectly, with the same cycles.[19]

Comprehensive Income   Comprehensive income is a broad measure of the effects of transactions and other events on an entity, comprising all recognized changes in equity (net assets) of the entity during a period from transactions and other events and circumstances except those resulting from investments by owners and distributions to owners. Comprehensive income is based on the concept of financial capital maintenance.[20]

The FASB concludes in this proposed concepts statement that earnings and comprehensive income are not the same because certain gains and losses are included in comprehensive income but are excluded from earnings. Those items fall into two classes that are illustrated by certain present practices:

• Effects of certain accounting adjustments of earlier periods that are recognized in the current period, such as cumulative effects of a change in accounting principle.

• Certain other changes in net assets (principally certain holding gains and losses) that are recognized in the period but are excluded from earnings, such as some changes in market values of investments in marketable equity securities classified as noncurrent assets, some changes in market values of investments in industries having specialized accounting practices for marketable securities, and foreign currency translation adjustments.[21]

14. Financial Accounting Standards Board, *Proposed Statement of Financial Accounting Concepts: Recognition and Measurement in Financial Statements of Business Enterprises* (Stamford, Ct.: FASB, 1983), p. 4.
15. *Ibid.*, pp. 6-7.

16. *Ibid.*, pp. 7-8.
17. *Ibid.*, p. 8.
18. *Ibid.*, p. viii.
19. *Ibid.*
20. *Ibid.*
21. *Ibid.*, p. ix.

State of Investments by and Distributions to Owners A statement of investments by and distributions to owners reflects an entity's capital transactions during a period—the extent to which and in what ways the equity of the entity increased or decreased from transactions with owners *as owners*. Transactions with owners present no special recognition problems.[22]

So far we have dealt with financial statements that are issued primarily to outsiders. There are many statements and reports that are used internally. Most of this book will deal with these reports. However, the National Association of Accountants (NAA) has begun to issue statements dealing with management accounting that apply to both internal and external reporting. The balance of this chapter will deal with these statements, since they have served as the basis for one exam question and most likely will appear on future exams.

NAA Statements on Management Accounting

The principal reponsibility for development of Statements on Management Accounting within the NAA is assumed by the Management Accounting Practices (MAP) Committee's Subcommittee on MAP Statement Promulgation. The Subcommittee identifies the subjects to be explored and oversees the progress on each project from inception to completion. When the Subcommittee deems it appropriate, a project report is recommended to the MAP Committee for approval.

In order to utilize the expertise of NAA membership, early announcement of a project's existence is made in *Management Accounting*. After considering any comments received and upon completion of research, the Subcommittee prepares a draft statement for circulation to a panel of approximately 20 persons selected by the Subcommittee on the basis of background and expertise in the business and financial community, and to another panel of about 20 persons chosen from NAA membership-at-large on a stratified random sampling basis.

When comments from members of the panels have been received and evaluated, the Subcommittee considers modifications to its draft and recommends that the MAP Committee promulgate the revised version as a Statement on Management Accounting. The MAP Committee will then review the proposed Statement and, if approved, arrange for its distribution to members and the financial community. The objectives of the MAP Committee are:

• to express the official position of NAA on relevant accounting matters to other professional groups, government bodies, the financial community, and the general public.

• to provide guidelines to the membership of the Association and business management on management accounting concepts, policies, and practices.

Definition of Management Accounting

Statement on Management Accounting (SMA) No. 1A defined management accounting as the process of identification, measurement, accumulation, analysis, preparation, interpretation, and communication of financial information used by management to plan, evaluate, and control within an organization and to assure appropriate use of and accountability for its resources. Management accounting also comprises the preparation of financial reports for nonmanagement groups such as shareholders, creditors, regulatory agencies, and tax authorities.

SMA No. 1 concludes by stating that "many of the activities constituting the field of management accounting are interrelated and thus must be coordinated, ranked, and implemented by the management accountant in such a fashion as to meet the objectives of the organization as perceived by him or her. A major function of the management accountant is that of tailoring the application of the process to the organization so that the organization's objectives are achieved effectively."

SMA No. 1B states that management accounting is intended to include persons involved in such functions as controllership, treasury, financial analysis, planning and budgeting, cost accounting, internal audit, systems, and general accounting. Management accountants thus may have titles such as chief financial officer, vice president of finance, controller, treasurer, budget analyst, cost analyst, and accountant, among many others. High-level personnel outside the United States often have distinctly different titles; one that is often used is finance director.

Objectives of Management Accounting

As objectives of management accounting, SMA No. 1B indicates that management accountants provide information and participate in the management process. They select and provide, to all levels of management, information needed in:

1. planning, evaluating, and controlling operations

2. safeguarding the organization's assets

3. communicating with interested parties outside the organization, such as shareholders and regulatory bodies.

Regarding participation, the statement indicates that "Management accountants at appropriate levels are involved actively in the process of managing the entity. This process includes making strategic, tactical, and operating decisions and helping to coordinate the efforts of the entire organization. The management accountant participates, as part of management, in assuring that the organization operates as a unified whole in its long-run, intermediate, and short-run best interests."

Responsibilities of Management Accountants

SMA No. 1B identifies five major responsibilities that management accountants accept to fulfill the objectives of providing information and participating in the management process. These responsibilities are:

1. **Planning**—Quantifying and interpreting the effects on the organization of planned transactions and other economic events. The planning responsibility, which includes strategic, tactical, and operating aspects, requires that the accountant provide quantitative historical and prospective information

---

22. *Ibid.*

to facilitate planning. It includes participation in developing the planning system, setting obtainable goals, and choosing appropriate means of monitoring the progress toward the goals.

2. **Evaluating**—Judging implications of historical and expected events and helping to choose the optimum course of action. Evaluating includes translating data into trends and relationships. Management accountants must communicate effectively and promptly the conclusions derived from the analyses.

3. **Controlling**—Assuring the integrity of financial information concerning an organization's activities and resources; monitoring and measuring performance and inducing any corrective actions required to return the activity to its intended course. Management accountants provide information to executives operating in functional areas who can make use of it to achieve desirable performance.

4. **Assuring accountability of resources**—Implementing a system of reporting that is aligned with organizational responsibilities. This reporting system will contribute to the effective use of resources and measurement of management performance. The transmission of management's goals and objectives throughout the organization in the form of assigned responsibilities is a basis for identifying accountability. Management accountants must provide an accounting and reporting system that will accumulate and report appropriate revenues, expenses, assets, liabilities, and related quantitative information to managers. Managers then will have better control over these elements.

5. **External reporting**—Preparing financial reports based on generally accepted accounting principles, or other appropriate bases, for nonmanagement groups such as shareholders, creditors, regulatory agencies, and tax authorities. Management accountants should participate in the process of developing the accounting principles that underlie external reporting.

Activities

Management accountants discharge their responsibilities according to SMA No. 1B by organizing and implementing activities in the following categories:

1. **Reporting**—Reporting relates to both internal and external needs for information about past or future events and circumstances. Management accountants make available to managers timely reports that provide the information and perspective necessary for them to make decisions in a goal-congruent manner. The reports may concern financial, physical, and human resources and the markets and regulatory environments in which entities operate. In addition to reporting internally, management accountants make appropriate information available to shareholders, creditors, and governmental regulatory agencies and tax authorities.

2. **Interpretation**—Management accountants interpret all forms of internal and external information pertinent to the various segments of the organization and communicate the implications of the information being reviewed, including

its relevance and reliability. Management accountants thus must understand both the sources and uses of the information.

3. **Resource Management**—Management accountants must establish systems which facilitate planning and control of the organization's resources to ensure that their use is consistent with established policies. These systems also should meet the needs of management, investors, creditors, and other interested parties. Some of these needs are:

• Custody and management of working capital, including credit and collections and inventory management

• Creating and maintaining the most appropriate debt and equity capital structure

• Developing and implementing a system to control plant, property, and equipment

• Administering a pension or similar plan

• Tax planning and compliance

• Insurance management

• Creating and operating a system of internal accounting control that can detect misuses of assets, taking into account the cost/benefit aspects of the control system

4. **Information Systems Development**—Design and development of the overall management information system implies:

• Determining the output required by users

• Specifying the data inputs needed to obtain the required output

• Developing the requirements for a processing system that converts input to output

• Managing and securing the data bases

5. **Technological Implementation**—Modern equipment and techniques should be employed to facilitate the selection, accumulation, transmission, analysis, and safeguarding of information. Management accountants therefore should be familiar with current technology relative to information processing and the accounting techniques appropriate to controlling and using the information. Some examples are:

• Computer applications

    —basic accounting functions and data-base management

    —techniques in financial planning and decision making, such as models for optimizing asset utilization and resource allocation

• Network and communications systems

6. **Verification**—Management accountants assure the accuracy and reliability of information derived from the accounting system or related sources that is used throughout the organization. They also must be satisfied that actions taking place throughout the entity are consistent with policies of the organization. Both of these activities use the internal control system and are reviewed by internal audit.

7. **Administration**—Administration includes development and maintenance of an effective and efficient management accounting organization. This organization addresses and resolves issues relevant to the accounting and financial structure such as:

- Assignment of management accounting responsibilities

- Interface between accounting and other operations

- Delegation of authority and determinations relevant to centralization or decentralization

- Recruiting, training, and developing personnel in the various areas of responsibility

- Separation of duties

Other important administrative activities performed by management accountants include the development and maintenance of:

- Accounting policy and procedure manuals

- A cost-effective records management program

- Records adequate to meet the requirements of tax laws, other laws and regulatory agencies, and independent auditors

Processes

SMA No. 1B concludes with an identification of certain operation processes that are inherent throughout the range of activities described above. These processes include:

1. **Identification**—recognition and evaluation of business transactions and other economic events for appropriate accounting action.

2. **Measurement**—quantification, including estimates, of business transactions or other economic events that have occurred or forecasts of those that may occur.

3. **Accumulation**—disciplined and consistent approaches to recording and classifying appropriate business transactions and other economic events.

4. **Analysis**—determination of the reasons for the reported activity and its relationship with other economic events and circumstances.

5. **Preparation and Interpretation**—meaningful coordination of accounting and/or planning data to provide information, presented logically, and including, if appropriate, the conclusions drawn from those data.

6. **Communication**—reporting pertinent information to management and others for internal and external uses.

Standards of Ethical Conduct

SMA No. 1C contains the "Standards of Ethical Conduct for Management Accountants" developed by the ICMA and the NAA. Under the new exam format, ethics questions may appear on any part of the test and will be included in at least two parts. The candidate should be thoroughly familiar with the standards in SMA No. 1C, as they should be used in answering ethics problems. The standards are as follows:

Standards of Ethical Conduct for Management Accountants

Management accountants have an obligation to the organizations they serve, their profession, the public and themselves to maintain the highest standards of ethical conduct. In recognition of this obligation, the Institute of Certified Management Accountants and the National Association of Accountants have adopted the following standards of ethical conduct for management accountants. Adherence to these standards is integral in achieving the objectives of management accounting. Management accountants may not commit acts contrary to these standards nor shall they condone the commission of such acts by others within their organizations.

Competence

Management accountants have a responsibility to:

- Maintain an appropriate level of professional competence by ongoing development of their knowledge and skills.

- Perform their professional duties in accordance with relevant laws, regulations and technical standards.

- Prepare complete and clear reports and recommendations after appropriate analyses of relevant and reliable information.

Confidentiality

Management accountants have a responsibility to:

- Refrain from disclosing confidential information acquired in the course of their work, except when authorized, unless legally obligated to do so.

- Inform subordinates as appropriate regarding the confidentiality of information acquired in the course of their work and monitor their activities to assure the maintenance of that confidentiality.

- Refrain from using or appearing to use confidential information acquired in the course of their work for unethical or illegal advantage either personally or through third parties.

Integrity

Management accountants have a responsibility to:

- Avoid actual or apparent conflicts of interest and advise all appropriate parties of any potential conflict.

- Refrain from engaging in any activity that would prejudice their ability to carry out their duties ethically.

- Refuse any gift, favor or hospitality that would influence or appear to influence their actions.

- Refrain from either actively or passively subverting the attainment of the organization's legitimate and ethical objectives.

- Recognize and communicate professional limitations or other constraints that would preclude responsible judgment or successful performance of an activity.

- Communicate unfavorable as well as favorable information and professional judgments or opinions.

- Refrain from engaging in or supporting any activity that would discredit the profession.

Objectivity

Management accountants have a responsibility to:

- Communicate information fairly and objectively.

- Disclose fully all relevant information that could reasonably be expected to influence an intended user's understanding of the reports, comments and recommendations presented.

Summary

In this chapter we have discussed the concepts of information and communication and have attempted to relate these concepts to the major financial reports included in the conventional financial statement set. We have, in this context, examined some of the major influences on financial accounting, the objectives of financial accounting, and the basic features and elements of published financial reports. We have also noted, where appropriate, the interrelationships and conflicts that exist between and among these factors.

By way of conclusion, a few points are made here concerning some of the limitations inherent in the conventional financial statement set. An awareness of these limitations is necessary in order that the financial statements not be misinterpreted.

First, the basic elements of the balance sheet, income statement, and statement of changes in financial position are measured and reported primarily in terms of historical exchange prices. Thus, conventional financial statements are predominantly historical in their orientation and do not purport to reflect current or future economic well-being or changes. Furthermore, historical exchange prices are not adjusted for subsequent fluctuations in purchasing power of the measuring unit, money. As a result, unless the reader implicitly or explicitly adjusts for purchasing power changes, the financial statement and its elements are denominated in measuring units of varying sizes, making suspect the meaning of many of the financial statement numbers.

Second, because in many cases alternative accounting procedures are permitted for essentially similar phenomena under generally accepted accounting principles, comparisons between firms are often difficult and must always be made with extreme caution. Measures of both balance sheet and income statement elements may be significantly influenced by adoption of one generally accepted alternative procedure over another. It should be noted that accounting policy disclosures describing all significant accounting procedures employed by the firm are required as an integral part of published financial statements, but dollar amounts of the effects of choosing one alternative over another are not reflected in the statements.

Finally, and perhaps most importantly, financial statements do not pretend to portray all of the information that might be useful to readers in making their economic decisions. Indeed, the things **not** shown in the conventional statements may be as important in evaluating the firm as those things that **are** disclosed. Specifically, in analyzing the operating performance of a firm, information concerning sales **not** made (that is, lost opportunities) is perhaps as important to the analyst—if not more so—as information concerning the net income derived from sales that were made. Yet this information is not to be found in the conventional financial statements. Additionally, certain items that do not meet the generally accepted accounting definitions for assets and liabilities, yet may indeed represent economic resources or obligations of the enterprise, are excluded from the balance sheet or, at best, are relegated to the statement's notes. Examples include: restrictive labor union contracts, purchase commitments, certain lease arrangements, and a highly skilled labor force. Similarly, information regarding employee turnover, absenteeism, and age of management—all of which are relevant to the long-term health of the firm—are not available in published financial statements.

In the following chapters, we shall examine the basic financial statements and reports that are used internally by management in some detail. As we proceed through these chapters, the significance of the general limitations just mentioned should become clear, and some additional limitations will be highlighted.

Problems

1.   Estimated time 5 minutes (June 1978)

1. Although challenged frequently the "historical cost" principle is still widely supported for financial reporting because historical cost

a. is an objectively determinable amount.
b. is a good measure of current value for a going concern.
c. facilitates the calculation of economic income.
d. results in the lowest income tax accruals.
e. facilitates comparisons between years.

2. The most common test of "revenue realization" for most transactions is

a. the receipt of cash.
b. the receipt of a purchase order.
c. the transfer of title for a product or provision of service to a customer.
d. the quotation of value on a market exchange.
e. the point when a product or service is ready for sale.

3. The concept referred to by the term "matching" principle is

a. that net income should be reported on an annual basis

b. that all transactions must refer to a statement of the Accounting Principles Board (APB) or Financial Accounting Standards Board (FASB).

c. that all cash receipts for a period be related to the cash disbursements for the period.

d. that where possible the expenses to be included in the income statement were incurred to produce the revenues.

e. the current liabilities have the same period of existence as the current assets.

4. The concept of "conservatism" often is considered important in accounting. The application of this concept means that in the event there is some doubt as to how a transaction should be recorded it should be recorded so as to

a. understate income and overstate assets.
b. overstate income and overstate assets.
c. understate income and understate assets.
d. overstate income and understate assets.
e. the concept relates to the content of the president's letter which accompanies the statements, not the statements themselves.

5. The internal accounting and reporting system should be designed

a. to meet external reporting requirements.
b. to balance management information needs with the cost of obtaining that information.
c. to eliminate fraud by accounting personnel.
d. by persons not directly involved with the system, such as consultants.
e. for efficiency, not necessarily for effectiveness.

6. Objectivity as used in accounting refers to

a. determining the revenue first, then determining the costs incurred in earning that revenue.
b. the entity giving the same treatment to comparable transactions from period to period.
c. the accountant using data that can be verified by other competent persons.
d. the disclosure of all facts that may influence the judgment of an informed reader.
e. providing for all losses and anticipating no gains.

7. The accounting measurement that is **not** consistent with the "going concern" concept is

a. historical cost.
b. realization.
c. the transaction approach.
d. liquidation value.
e. continuity.

8. Depending upon the circumstances, revenue can be recognized at different times for accounting purposes. Generally accepted revenue recognition methods do **not** include

a. end of production.
b. during production.
c. receipt of cash.
d. point of sale.
e. present value of a contract to sell merchandise.

9. Depreciation expense reported in the income statement represents

a. the process of allocating the cost of long-lived assets to periods benefited.
b. the process of valuing long-lived assets for balance sheet

purposes.
c. the estimated decline in market value of long-lived assets employed by a business.
d. the present value of benefits received from long-lived assets employed by a business.
e. a major source of working capital for most businesses.

---

2. Estimated time 30 minutes (June 1980)

Firms prepare annual financial statements for internal management use and for distribution to outside parties. In addition, many firms prepare some type of summary reports or statements quarterly, monthly, and/or weekly for both internal use and external distribution. The frequency of reporting may affect the cost to prepare and the objectivity of the reports or statements.

Required A. Basic accounting theory assumes the accounting period appropriate for internal and external reporting for most firms is one year. Explain why the year is employed as the basic accounting reporting period.

B. Explain in general terms why summary reports or statements are prepared for shorter reporting periods other than one year. Give an example in your explanation of why (1) internal management and (2) an outside party may want reports or statements which cover a shorter time period than one year.

C. Adjustments to the accounting records are made whenever summary reports or statements are prepared annually, quarterly, or monthly.

1. Explain why these adjustments are needed.
2. Cite specific examples of some adjustments that would have to be made to the accounting records.

D. How is the objectivity of financial information presented in summary reports or statements affected when more frequent reports are prepared? Explain your answer.

---

3. Estimated time 30 minutes (June 1975)

Financial statements are an important means by which entities communicate economic information to interested parties. The objectives of financial statements have received the attention of the accounting profession, the business community, the government and the general public at various times and in various degrees for many years.

In the past five years there has been increased concern and intensive study of financial statement objectives. The objectives recommended range from "the statements are the management's report on its stewardship of the investors' capital" to "the statements provide information to investors for predicting, comparing, and evaluating the economic activities of an enterprise."

The objectives established for financial statements will depend upon whether the statements are prepared by management or some other party, what the statements are to represent (results of past activities or prediction of future actions), for whom the statements are intended, and how the statements will be used.

Required **A.** Discuss the responsibilities of management for the entity's financial statements.

B. Does management prepare financial statements in order to reflect past performance of the business entity or to help predict the future preformance of the entity? Discuss briefly.

C. Discuss briefly how financial statements can be used by investors in making investment decisions.

---

4.   Estimated time 20 minutes (June 1989)

Statement on Management Accounting Number 1B (SMA 1B), "Objectives of Management Accounting," provides basic information about management accounting and guidelines for the management accountant in fulfilling the objectives of providing information and participating actively in the management process. The chart below depicts the objectives, responsibilities, and principal activities involved in the management accounting process. The responsibilities of the management accountant in fulfilling the objectives include: planning the strategic, tactical, and operating aspects of an organization; evaluating historical and expected events; controlling the integrity of financial information; assuring the accountability of resources; and providing external reporting based on generally accepted accounting principles.

Required For each of the five principal activities of the management accountant identified below,

- Reporting
- Resource Management
- Information Systems Development
- Verification
- Administration

1. describe how it relates to the responsibilities of the management accountant, and

2. identify two specific tasks or procedures that would be performed or implemented by the management accountant.

Solutions

1.

1. a. Historical cost is definite and objective, not a matter for conjecture or opinion. Once established, it is fixed as long as the asset remains the property of the company. Historical cost also has disadvantages. During a period when general price levels are changing, cost is said to go "out of date" almost as soon as it is determined. In a pei: ☌ f rising or falling prices, the cost figures of the preceding year are viewed as not comparable with current cost figures. Financial statements that present the cost of fixed assets acquired 20 or 30 years ago may be misleading, because readers of such statements tend to think in terms of current price levels. As depreciation expense, based on

recorded cost, enters into income calculations, even the net income figure is influenced by price level changes.

2. c. Revenue is realized when the earning process is virtually complete and an exchange transaction has occurred. Generally, an objective test, confirmation by a sale to independent interests, is adopted as the test to indicate realization of revenue. Other methods are acceptable when the basic rule is too difficult to apply:

1. percentage-of-completion approach—in certain long-term construction contracts
2. end of production—where the price and amount are certain, as in the mining of certain minerals
3. receipt of cash—as in the installment sales method.

3. d. The matching principle dictates that efforts or expenses be matched with accomplishments or revenues. In its broadest sense, matching refers to the entire process of income determination. Paragraph 147 of *APB Statement No. 4* defines this as "identifying, measuring, and relating revenues and expenses of an enterprise for an accounting period." Matching may also be used in a more limited sense to refer only to the process of expense recognition or in an even more limited sense to refer to the recognition of expenses by associating costs with revenue on a cause-and-effect basis.

4. c. The convention of conservatism says that when in doubt, an accountant should choose the solution that will be least likely to overstate assets and income. Frequently, assets and liabilities are measured in a context of significant uncertainties. Historically, it has been generally preferred that possible errors in measurement be in the direction of understatement rather than overstatement of net income and net assets. This has led to the convention of conservatism, which is expressed in rules adopted by the profession as a whole; such as the rule that inventory should be measured at the lower of cost and market.

5. b. Answer "b" represents the primary objective of the system design. Answers "a" and "c" may influence the components of the system, but are not primary objectives. In fact some companies made the mistake of allowing answer "a" — external reporting requirements — be the most important factor and once the system is operating it fails to meet the needs of management.

6. c. Answer "e" is the result of the concept of conservatism. Answer "b" is consistency. Answer "a" is the matching concept. Answer "d" is full disclosure.

7. d. The use of liquidation values suggests that the entity will not continue as a going concern. It should be also realized that current values may also be consistent with the going concern concept.

8. e. Generally revenue is not realized at the time a sales contract is obtained. Answer "b" — during production — is used where a contract may take several years to complete such as the construction of an office building. Here accountants may use the "percentage complete method."

9. a. Answer "a" is the objective of the depreciation charge against revenue. Depreciation does not attempt to determine the value of the asset.

2.

A. One year is employed as the basic accounting time period because it is the time interval established by common business practice, tradition and government requirement for taxation. The year became the commonly used time period because of agricultural cycles and it was the regular calendar by which people lived. The year covers most operating cycles and seasonal cycles, and allows comparability for equal time periods.

B. Financial information is issued at other, more frequent, intervals than annually because of the need for even more timely information by management, investors, and other external users. The frequency of reporting is a trade-off between the value of information for decision-making purposes and the cost of obtaining the additional information.

1. Internal management may dictate monthly, weekly, and sometimes daily, reporting in order to enable it to react in a timely manner to the business environment.

2. Interim financial information is essential to provide investors and other outside parties with timely information as to the progress of the enterprise. The usefulness of such information rests upon its ability to reflect the annual results of operations.

C. 1. The time period assumption underlies the whole area of accruals and deferrals that distinguishes accrual accounting from cash accounting. Adjustments are made to accounting records whenever reports are issued to satisfy the basic accounting principles of matching revenues and expenses. Because of the artificial and arbitrary delineation of the lifespan of a business into selected shorter intervals, accruals and deferrals of revenue and costs are necessary in order to correctly measure the results of operations and present the financial position of an organization.

2. Some specific accruals that would be needed include bad debts, pension costs, vacation pay, and depreciation. Some examples of deferrals include the capitalization of lump sum payments of taxes, insurance, rentals (either payments made or collection received in advance).

D. The objectivity of financial statements is reduced as more frequent reports are required. The increased frequency of reports requires more allocations of costs and revenues and requires also more estimates of financial data. Further, the chance is greater that an unusual operating circumstance could distort the data. Consistent application of accounting practices may overcome some of the problems due to the reduced objectivity found in more frequent statements.

3.

A. Management is responsible for communicating reliable financial information of the enterprise's business transactions in order to fulfill its stewardship function to stockholders. As a result, management is responsible for preparing financial statements that reflect the firm's operations and financial position. The financial statements should fairly present the firm's past performance and disclose all material facts of interest to present and future stockholders.

B. The financial statements are prepared by management in fulfilling its stewardship function to reflect the past performance of an entity and are not intended to predict a firm's future performance. However, past performance may be a good indicator of future performance. Stockholders, investors, creditors, and government may use the information presented in financial statements in conjunction with prior years' financial statements and industry and general economic data to make forecasts or predictions about an entity's future performance. However, the financial statements themselves are not meant to be management's predictions of future performance.

C. The financial statements provide one source of data investors can use in evaluating a firm before an investment decision is reached. The financial statements furnish investors with information on the firm's business and different product lines of the company. The historical data included in the financial statements can be used in making a detailed financial analysis of a firm (e.g., ratio analysis, sales and cost trends, estimated cash flow statement, etc.) In addition, the historical data can be used in conjunction with other past data, industry data, and general economic data to formulate projections of a firm's future performance upon which the investment can be made.

4.

1. and 2. Management accountants discharge their responsibilities by organizing and implementing activities in seven principal categories. Five of these activities, and how they relate to the responsibilities of the management accountant, are outlined below, along with specific tasks or procedures that are performed or implemented to fulfill these responsibilities.

• Reporting relates to the internal need for information about past and future events and circumstances, to be made available in timely reports, in order to provide the perspective necessary for management to make decisions in a goal-congruent manner. In addition to reporting internally, management accountants make appropriate information available to shareholders, creditors, governmental regulatory agencies, and tax authorities.
  Reporting tasks include
- accumulating, analyzing, preparing, interpreting, and communicating financial information.
- analyses of alternate methods of raising funds.

• Resource management necessitates the establishment of systems which facilitate planning and control of the organization's resources to ensure that their use is consistent with established policies.
  Resource management tasks include
- custody and management of working capital, including credit and collections and inventory management.

- developing and maintaining a system to control plant, property, and equipment.
- insurance management.

• Information systems development calls for the management accountant to interact with the information systems personnel to design and develop the overall management information system.

    Information systems development tasks include
- specifying the data inputs needed to obtain the required output.
- managing and securing databases.

• Verification entails assurance as to the accuracy and reliability of information derived from the accounting system or related sources that is used throughout the organization. Management accountants also must be satisfied that actions taking place throughout the entity are consistent with policies of the organization.

    Verification tasks include
- internal audits.
- general ledger account reconciliations.

• Administration includes development and maintenance of an effective and efficient management accounting organization. This organization addresses and resolves issues relevant to the accounting and financial structure.

    Administrative tasks include
- recruiting, training, developing, and assisting in the on-going maintenance of professional skills of personnel in the various areas of responsibility.
- encouraging management accountants to understand and be conversant with all aspects of the business in order to support other disciplines in the company.

Chapter 2

Cost Concepts and Flows

Grant W. Newton

In this chapter we look at some basic cost concepts by discussing the way costs can be classified and describing the flow of costs through a job order and process cost systems. We also will examine two approaches that are part of the new manufacturing environment—just-in-time and activity-based costing.

Cost Classifications

Cost Classified by Nature

Manufacturing Costs All production costs incurred to complete the product and place it in a salable condition. Manufacturing costs are frequently classified as direct materials, direct labor, and factory overhead. Since costs attach to the product or groups of products as they are manufactured, expenditures, regardless of their nature, usually are capitalized as inventory assets and do not become "expired costs" or "expenses" until the goods are sold. For example, an outlay of $300 for direct labor used to manufacture product X does not appear as an expired cost until X is sold, the rationale being that such costs should not be capitalized until they can be matched with revenue generated (the matching concept).[1]

Direct Materials All raw material costs that become an integral part of the finished product and that can be conveniently and economically assigned to specific units manufactured.

Statement on Management Accounting (SMA) No. 4E covers measurement of direct materials costs. Cost of packaging materials is a part of the materials costs to the extent it is included in the finished product. Also, packaging supplies necessary to deliver goods to customers, to the extent that the goods are packed with these supplies as part of the production process, should be a part of material quantity.

The Statement indicates that materials cost should include scrap, waste, and normally anticipated defective units that occur in the ordinary course of the production process. Unanticipated quantities of scrap, shrinkage, waste, or defective units should be included in manufacturing overhead or expensed in the period incurred. Also routine quality assurance samples that are destroyed as part of testing should be classified as materials. However, nonroutine quality assurance samples taken due to manufacturing problems and cost of marketing samples should not be added to materials costs.

Materials cost includes the invoice price plus other costs paid to the vender, shipping costs, sales taxes, duty, cost of delivery containers and pallets (less net of return refunds), and royalty payments based on direct materials quantities. Trade discounts and cash discounts (if they exceed reasonable interest rates) should reduce materials costs.

The Statement indicates that material-related costs should be allocated to the cost objective in an economically feasible manner. These costs should be allocated on the basis of some measure of direct material quantity or cost rather than a measure related to direct labor. Listed below are some costs that are considered material-related:

- Purchasing
- Receiving
- Receiving inspection
- Material storage costs (prior to entering production)
- Issuing costs for materials entering production

Material storage (after entering production), issuing costs (after production started), production planning and control costs, and internal transportation costs are *not* considered material-related costs.

Direct Labor All labor costs related to time spent on products that can be conveniently and economically assigned to specific units manufactured.

Statement on Management Accounting (SMA) No. 4C in-

---

1. There are certain exceptions, such as occur under percentage-of-completion contract accounting. Also, some service industries use job order costing for billing and control purposes but treat service labor expenses as period expenses not carried to inventories.

dicates that estimates of direct labor quantities and unit prices may be sufficiently accurate to be considered "specifically identified" with a cost object. For example, break time and personal time relate to all productive time in a day. Nevertheless, break time and personal time are assigned to standard labor time as an average percentage of productive time. Also, health insurance premium is added to direct labor cost as a percentage of direct labor cost or as a fixed amount per hour of direct labor.

The Statement lists the following cost elements to be included in cost of labor because they can be both measured and specifically identified with a quantity of labor:

- Basic compensation
- Individual production efficiency bonuses
- Group production efficiency bonuses
- FICA (employer's portion)
- Cost of living allowances

For companies with relatively stable operations, the Statement suggests that the following elements be specifically identified with direct labor quantity over a period of one year or less, even though the relationship is less clear than with those listed above:

- Health insurance
- Group life insurance
- Holiday pay
- Vacation pay
- Pension costs and other post-retirement benefits
- Worker's compensation insurance expense
- Unemployment compensation insurance (state or federal)

Statement No. 4C also suggests that sick leave credit based on time worked, if the credit can be accumulated and taken as vacation or as additional pay after a certain length of time, should be considered part of labor costs. Payroll and personnel department costs and most profit sharing plan costs are not treated as labor costs. In addition, the following items are also not considered to be part of labor costs:

- Wage continuation plans (e.g., separation allowance)
- Contributions to Supplemental Unemployment Benefit (SUB) plans
- Membership dues
- Safety-related items
- Company-sponsored cafeteria
- Recreational facilities

Factory Overhead All manufacturing costs other than direct materials and direct labor. Before computers, factory overhead was not identified with a particular product or group of products; the accounting effort was considered excessive and not cost effective. Now that computer technology is available, it is now economically feasible to physically trace many overhead costs to products. Indirect materials, indirect labor, property taxes, insurance, supervisor's salaries, depreciation of factory building and factory equipment, and power are examples of factory overhead. Indirect materials and indirect labor need some elaborating.

Indirect Materials Indirect materials include materials and supplies used in the manufacturing operation that do not become part of the product, such as oil for the machinery and cleaning fluids for the custodian. Indirect

materials also includes raw materials that are of insignificant cost, such as glue and tacks, that become part of the product.

Indirect Labor Labor costs that cannot be identified or traced to specific units manufactured. Examples include supervision, inspection, maintenance, personnel and material handling.

Prime Costs Total direct materials and direct labor costs.

Conversion Costs Total direct labor and factory overhead costs incurred to convert the direct materials into the finished product.

Nonmanufacturing Costs Includes costs related to selling and other activities not related to the production of goods. Examples include sales commission, freight on goods sold, salary of vice president of finance, and other selling and administrative expenses. Expenses such as insurance on the building where both sales and production activities occur and president's salary benefit both manufacturing and nonmanufacturing activities and should thus be allocated to both.

Common Costs Costs that benefit two or more operations, products, or services. Thus, the electricity used to heat a building where several products are manufactured is a common cost. The costs associated with a group of products produced simultaneously are common costs, but they are generally referred to as **joint-product costs**.

Cost Classified by Variability

Variable Costs Costs that change directly in proportion to changes in activity (volume). Direct labor and direct materials are examples of variable costs.

Fixed Costs Costs that remain unchanged for a given time period regardless of changes in activity (volume). Rent, insurance on property, maintenance and repairs of buildings, and depreciation of factory equipment are examples of fixed costs.

Semivariable Costs Costs that contain both fixed and variable elements. Examples are social security taxes, materials handling, personnel services, heat, light, and power. These cost elements must be divided into their proper elements.

Cost Classified by Types of Inventory

Raw Materials Inventory The cost of all raw material and production supplies that have been purchased but not used at the end of the period.

Work-in-process Inventory The cost associated with goods that are partially complete at the end of the period.

Finished Good Inventory Cost of completed goods that have not been sold at the end of the period.

Cost Classified by Whether or Not Inventoriable

Product Costs All costs that "attach" or "cling" to the units that are produced and are reported as assets until the goods are sold. All manufacturing costs are product costs under an absorption costing system and are carried from one account to another until the goods are sold.

Period Costs   A cost that must be charged against income in the period incurred and cannot be inventoried. Examples of period costs include selling and administrative expenses. Under direct costing, fixed factory overhead is a period cost.

Cost Used for Planning and Control

Budget   A plan of action for a certain time period expressed in dollar values.

Static Budget   A budget prepared for one level of activity. When changes occur in the level of activity, the budget does not adjust to the new volume level.

Flexible Budget   A budget prepared for a range rather than a single activity level. The budget is often expressed in a formula where the budgeted cost = fixed cost + variable cost rate(s) × volume level. The total budgeted costs vary with changes in the level of activity.

Continuous Budget   A twelve-month budget that perpetually adds data for a month or quarter in the future as the data for the just ended month or quarter is deleted.

Standard Costs   A predetermined cost estimate that should be attained; usually expressed in terms of units.

Budgeted Cost   Used to represent the expected/planned cost for a given period. For example, a company that plans to manufacture 1,000 units of product X, which has a standard price per unit of $4, would have budgeted cost for the period of $4,000 for product X.

Direct Costing   A type of product costing where fixed costs are charged against revenue as incurred and are not assigned to specific units of product manufactured. Also, referred to as **variable costing**.

Costs Used for Decision Making

Incremental Costs   The difference in cost between two or more alternatives. In evaluating a given alternative incremental cost is the additional cost expected to be incurred. This cost is compared with the additional revenue to determine the feasibility of this particular alternative. To be an incremental cost, the cost must be a future cost and be different under various alternatives. Also referred to as **relevant costs** and **differential costs**.

Sunk Costs   Past costs that have been incurred and are irrelevant to a future decision.

Opportunity Costs   The value of the best alternative foregone as the result of selecting a different use of resource or by choosing a particular strategy.

Total Cost Management   The process of managing all resources along with the activities that result in use of those resources. Emphasis is placed on actions, conditions or events that drive the cost consuming activities.

Value Added Costs   Costs that add value to the product. These costs result from activities that are necessary to satisfy the requirements of the consumer. Effort should be made to eliminate those costs that do not add value to the product, such as storage and materials handling.

Cost Classified by Type of Cost Systems

Every manufacturing operation needs some type of system to record its production costs. The system used can be classified as job order costing, process costing, or some combination of both and are based on either direct or absorption costing procedures. In addition, management can elect to use standard costs along with actual costs or to rely solely on actual costs. The decision as to whether a job order or process costing system is needed is an important one that requires careful analysis of the nature of the company's operations. In order for a system to provide management with the information it needs to make decisions, it should be selected only after there is a complete understanding of the type of products manufactured, the production methods followed, and the way materials and other costs flow through the departments.

Activity Costing   In addition to a traditional job order or process cost system, a company may use activity costing where product costs and other financial and operation costs are accumulated based on the activities required to manufacture the product or achieve a financial or operational goal.

Objectives of Cost Systems

Cost systems are used for three basic purposes:
   1. Cost management and control
   2. Product cost determination
   3. Inventory valuation and income determination

   The traditional cost system is designed primarily to measure inventory and determine the income for the period. The primary focus has been the measurement of materials and labor costs directly associated with the product, followed by an allocation of all remaining manufacturing costs (overhead), usually based on direct labor dollars or hours. While this process most likely provides a reasonable value for work-in-process and finished goods, it is little help in controlling costs and in determining the actual cost of products.

   In today's manufacturing environment, the traditional cost system is increasingly found to be inadequate. Consumers are demanding higher quality and greater variety in products. Delivery time is decreasing while intolerance of missed delivery dates is growing. Howell and Soucy suggest that traditional cost accounting is seriously deficient in the highly competitive, global markets in which many businesses function. The system has received much criticism lately for failing to provide management with the information it needs to make sound decisions and com-

━━━━━ Example 2-1 ━━━━━

Baker Co., a manufacturer, had these beginning and ending inventories at the end of its current year:

	Beginning	Ending
Raw materials	$22,000	$30,000
Work-in-process	40,000	48,000
Finished goods	25,000	18,000

During the year the following transactions occurred:

1. Raw materials purchased — $300,000
2. Indirect materials and supplies purchased — 50,000
3. Direct labor cost — 120,000
4. Indirect factory labor — 60,000
5. Property taxes on factory building — 15,000
6. Depreciation on factory building — 5,000
7. Property taxes and depreciation on salesroom and office (shared on a 50%-50% basis) — 15,000
8. Utilities (60% to factory, 20% to salesroom, and 20% to office) — 50,000
9. Indirect materials issued to factory — 40,000
10. Unused raw materials returned to storeroom — 10,000
11. Factory overhead applied on the basis of 120% of direct labor costs — ?
12. Sales salaries — 40,000
13. Office salaries — 24,000
14. Sales on account — 730,000

Over- or underapplied overhead is deducted from or added to cost of goods sold.

Required   A. Prepare T accounts and post the data therein.

B. Prepare a cost of goods manufactured statement.

C. Prepare an income statement.

pete successfully.[2]

The material in the following sections will describe the traditional cost accounting systems first. This will be followed by a discussion of the changes which are currently being implemented in cost accounting, and which are beginning to make a great impact on the decision-making process.

Job Order Costing

Job order costing is typically used by industries whose products or services can be easily identified by units or groups of units, or by customers requiring different types of resour-

2. Robert A. Howell and Stephen R. Soucy, "Cost Accounting in the New Manufacturing Environment," *Management Accounting* (August, 1987).

ces and skills. Aircraft construction, ship building, and furniture and building construction are examples of production processes where job order costing is frequently used. This method is also used by service industries such as hospitals, accounting firms, repair shops, and architects. The unit of activity is the job, that is, all costs are accumulated by jobs.

Example 2-1, an adapted CPA examination problem, is a basic type of a job order cost problem. The solution to part A of the problem is in Exhibit 2-1. Note the flow of the costs from raw materials, labor, and overhead to work-in-process, and finished goods inventory accounts, and finally to cost-of-goods sold. This basic flow is the same regardless of the type of system, historical or standard, or the nature of the process, job order or process costing.

A cost-of-goods sold statement for the Baker Company is shown in Exhibit 2-2; Exhibit 2-3 contains the income statement. The underapplied overhead of $6,000 ($150,000 total debit in factory overhead control less $144,000 applied) was added to the cost of goods sold to get the actual cost of goods sold for the current year.

In cost accounting, control accounts are frequently used. **Control accounts** are aggregate summaries of detailed subsidiary ledgers; for example, a control finished goods inventory account summarizes hundreds of subsidiary inventory ledgers by product types. Following is a list of the subsidiary ledgers that support the major manufacturing control accounts.

Control Account	Subsidiary Ledger
Materials (stores)	Materials ledger cards
Work-in-process	Job order system—cost sheets
	Process system—cost of production report
Finished goods	Finished goods ledger cards
Factory overhead	Departmental cost ledger

The job order cost sheet is used to accumulate direct materials, direct labor, and a factory overhead for each job. The total of all the cost sheets for uncompleted jobs should equal the balance in the work-in-process account. If the nature of the process is such that employees from several departments work on the job, the cost sheet will, in addition to presenting the total cost for the job, summarize the cost by departments.

Indirect Cost Allocation

In order to determine the full cost of manufacturing a product, it is necessary to allocate the overhead costs to that product. Many of these overhead costs are indirect fixed and variable costs—those that cannot be traced to a single cost objective but are common to two or more objectives. External financial reporting requires that the cost of manufacturing a product include all manufacturing costs—direct costs, indirect fixed costs, and indirect variable costs. (See Chapter 5.) (Nonmanufacturing selling and administrative expenses need not be capitalized.) Thus, one major purpose of cost allocation is to determine the full cost of manufacturing for external reporting purposes.

For internal managerial accounting purposes the allocation

Exhibit 2-1

Baker Company
T Accounts

Raw materials			
Bal. (1/1)	22,000		
(1)	300,000	(15)	302,000[a]
(10)	10,000		
	332,000		
Bal. (12/31)	30,000		

Work-in-process			
Bal. (1/1)	40,000		
(3)	120,000	(10)	10,000
(11)	144,000	(16)	548,000[b]
(15)	302,000		
	606,000		
Bal. (12/31)	48,000		

Finished goods			
Bal. (1/1)	25,000		
(16)	548,000	(17)	555,000[c]
	573,000		
Bal. (12/31)	18,000		

Accrued payroll			
		(3)	120,000
		(4)	60,000
		(12)	40,000
		(13)	24,000

Factory overhead applied			
		(11)	144,000

Factory overhead control			
(4)	60,000		
(5)	15,000		
(6)	5,000		
(8)	30,000		
(9)	40,000		

Materials and supplies			
(2)	50,000	(9)	40,000

Cost of goods sold			
(17)	555,000		

Sales expense control			
(7)	7,500		
(8)	10,000		
(12)	40,000		

Administrative expense control			
(7)	7,500		
(8)	10,000		
(13)	24,000		

Accounts payable			
		(1)	300,000
		(2)	50,000

Various credits			
		(5)	15,000
		(6)	5,000
		(7)	15,000
		(8)	50,000

Accounts receivable			
(14)	730,000		

Sales			
		(14)	730,000

[a](15) Total debits to raw materials are $332,000. Since $30,000 are still in process, the amount transferred out must be $302,000.

[b](16) Total debits to work-in-process total $606,000, and with a balance of $48,000, this means that $548,000 must have been transferred out after considering the $10,000 return.

[c](17) With total debits of $573,000 and a balance of $18,000 in finished goods, the cost of goods sold is $555,000.

==

Exhibit 2-2

Baker Company
Cost of Goods Manufactured
Current Year

Raw materials:

Raw materials inventory, January 1	$ 22,000	
Purchases	300,000	
Total available	322,000	
Less: Raw materials inventory, December 31	30,000	
Total raw materials used	292,000	
Direct labor	120,000	
Factory overhead applied	144,000	
Total manufacturing costs	556,000	
Add: Work-in-process inventory, January 1	40,000	
Total cost to account for	596,000	
Less: Work-in-process inventory, December 31	48,000	
Total cost of goods manufactured	**$548,000**	

==

Exhibit 2-3

Baker Company
Income Statement (Summary Form)
Current Year

Sales		$730,000
Cost of goods sold:		
Finished goods inventory, January 1	$ 25,000	
Cost of goods manufactured (Exhibit 6-2)	548,000	
Total available	573,000	
Less: Finished goods inventory, December 31	18,000	
Cost of goods sold—normal	555,000	
Add: Underapplied factory overhead	6,000	
Total cost of goods sold—actual		561,000
Gross profit		169,000
Sales expenses	57,500	
Administrative expenses	41,500	99,000
Net income		**$ 70,000**

==

of indirect costs is sometimes misleading for certain types of decision making. The planning and controlling effort for indirect fixed costs must be directed to the source of such costs, which means that cost allocation would not be of any benefit. For decision-making purposes, the important costs are often the incremental costs and not full costs after indirect costs are allocated. **Incremental cost** or **differential cost** is the difference in total cost between two alternatives, that is,

the cost that can be traced directly to a given alternative and that would not be incurred if that alternative were rejected.[3]

Production and Service Departments The nature of the manufacturing process influences the organization of the particular company involved. Many firms find that departments suit their needs best. Departments can be classified as production or service departments. Goods flow through production departments and direct material and/or labor is expended on them in some fashion. Service departments, such as maintenance, contribute in an indirect way to the manufacturing of the products.

For effective control, all costs incurred by a department are accumulated in that department. If the department is classified as a service department, the final cost accumulation is accumulated in the manufacturing overhead control account. In a production department, direct costs are accumulated in work-in-process inventory control. Budgeted direct and indirect costs may be compared with actual costs in order to evaluate departmental efficiency and effectiveness.

Basis for Cost Allocation As mentioned previously, it is necessary to allocate overhead costs to the product in order to determine the cost of the goods manufactured and eventually the cost of goods sold. There are also other reasons for cost allocation. Horngren and Foster list the four following purposes that may be sought by a given cost allocation:

1. **Predicting economic effects of decisions** Estimate the impact of various actions on the total costs of the organization. Examples of such actions are decisions to add or discontinue products.

2. **Determining income and asset valuations** Examples are product costs used for computing cost of goods sold and inventory balances.

3. **Ascertaining a mutually agreeable price** Examples are contracts based on costs instead of market price. Hence, cost allocations can become a means of establishing a mutually satisfactory *price*. A *cost* allocation may be hard to defend on the basis of any cause-effect reasoning. However, an allocation may be a "reasonable" or "fair" *means of establishing a selling price* in the minds of the affected parties.

4. **Obtaining desired motivation** Achieve goal congruence and incentive when other means fail. An example is charging the operating divisions for central costs such as basic research even though cause-and-effect or fairness justifications are weak. On the other hand, some top managers will insist that such allocation practices get division managers to take a desired interest in, say, central research activities.[4]

Under certain conditions it is possible for one allocation to

3. An exception exists especially in situations involving government contracts, where there is no specific market for a given product. This price is based on total costs plus a negotiated profit; to determine the total costs it is necessary to allocate indirect costs.
4. Charles T. Horngren and George Foster, *Cost Accounting: A Managerial Emphasis,* 6th ed. (Englewood Cliffs, N.J.: Prentice-Hall, 1987), p. 412.

accomplish all of these objectives. An example is in the allocation of selected variable factory overhead items. For other costs, accomplishing all these objectives is very difficult, especially for fixed costs, where the decisions about them are made at a high level, and yet many lower segments are affected.

Most of the literature on cost allocation suggests that indirect costs should either be allocated to products and/or departments on the relative benefit received by each or allocated according to the cause-and-effect relationship existing between the indirect costs and the other cost objectives. The cause-and-effect rationale should be used as the key method to judge the vehicle selected to allocate a given cost. Horngren notes that accountants often cite "benefits received" as the best way to allocate costs when the cause-and-effect logic is strained, as if it were a substitute criterion.[5] If a causal relationship cannot be established, the most common basis is the "ability to bear." Thus, sales dollars or profit margins is often selected as the base for cost allocation. There may be causal relationship between sales and cost; however, this should be firmly established and not arbitrarily selected without careful analysis.

The Cost Accounting Standards Board suggests that the allocation be selected according to the following priority list:

1. The base should be a measure of input or other activity in the responsibility center where the cost was incurred and from which it will be allocated. Examples include hours worked by the maintenance department or miles driven for a motor pool.

2. The base should be a measure of the output from the responsibility center where the cost was incurred and from which it will be allocated. The number of repair jobs completed by the maintenance department or the number of trips taken by the motor pool would be the bases used under this criterion.

3. The base should be a measure of inputs or other activity in the responsibility center (production or other service departments) to which the indirect cost will be allocated. Examples would include the number of machine hours in the production department for allocating the maintenance department's cost or the number of individuals working in the production department for allocation of the personnel department's cost.

Allocation Procedure   The basic procedures leading to an allocation of manufacturing costs for the individual products can be summarized as follows:

1. All direct costs should be accumulated by production and service departments.

2. Allocate common or indirect costs to the production and service departments according to benefits received or some other logical basis. Typical costs to be allocated by this step include electric power, depreciation on manufacturing equipment, insurance, and property taxes on the manufacturing plant.

3. Allocate the service department's costs to production

departments.

4. Allocate all production department direct and indirect overhead costs to products and capitalize as inventory assets until the goods are completed and sold.

5. Do not capitalize nonmanufacturing expenses as inventory assets.

Overhead rates are normally determined by following the steps above, using budgeted costs and expected or budgeted volume levels. The overhead rate should then be set at the beginning of the year and applied to products as they are manufactured. Any difference between the actual overhead costs and the applied overhead costs result in the over- or under-applied overhead variance. The use of actual costs and actual volume to determine the rate would delay final allocations to products until all indirect costs had been determined, which may be too slow, especially under job order costing when jobs are completed before all overhead costs are determined.

The overhead application rate can be calculated for each production department in the following way:

$$\frac{\text{Department}}{\text{Overhead rate}} = \frac{\text{Total budgeted overhead costs}}{\text{Activity level}}$$

Activities commonly used to allocate the production department's costs to products are direct labor hours, machine hours, direct labor costs, materials costs, and units produced. It is not necessary to use the same basis for all production departments. For example, a highly automated department may use machine hours, while one that requires a great deal of labor may use direct labor hours. Also, it is even possible to use more than one basis in one department. If we can identify within a department some overhead items that are correlated with machine hours and other items correlated with units of output, then the budgeted overhead costs could be divided into these two groups and separate rates determined.

Most nonmaterials costs do not vary with labor volume but with the diversity of products and the complexity of the process. Thus, the use of direct labor hours to allocate most of the overhead items does not result in an accurate cost for the product. Alternative approaches to handling cost allocation are often used.

In one case,[6] a plumbing manufacturer analyzed its costs and found that a significant number of overhead expenses were generated every time a part was run through a production department. For example, the planning department scheduled the part, warehousing issued the materials, operations set up the machines, and inspection examined the finished job. The company defined a production run of a single part number as a transaction which served as the basis for allocating selected costs. Volume was chosen as another basis because of its "push" on other cost items. The company determined that utilities, supplies, depreciation, maintenance, tooling, scrap (80%) and industrial engineering (process support function) were volume driven. Set-up, supervision, training, materials handling, quality control, manufacturing management, and manufacturing engineering (product support function) were determined by transaction.[7]

5. *Ibid.*, p. 413.

6. Michael O'Guin, "Focus the Factory with Activity-Based Costing," *Management Accounting* (February, 1990), p. 36.
7. *Ibid,* pp. 38-39.

Service Department and Administrative Expenses Service and administrative expenses are those that are incurred by headquarters' staffs or other central units. In order to maintain the company as a functioning entity, administrative expenses are incurred for the benefit of all units of the company. Service units generally exist to provide services to other units and, thus, are not as broad in nature as administrative costs.

An organization's service and administrative costs can be substantial, and some or all of these costs usually are allocated to cost objects. Thus, the allocation of service and administrative costs can have a significant impact on product cost and pricing, asset valuation, and segment profitability.

The National Association of Accountants issued SMA No. 4B, "Allocation of Service and Administrative Costs," to help management accountants deal with the problems associated with the allocation of service and administrative costs. This statement identifies three general types of cost construction or allocation objectives; they are full cost, responsibility cost, and differential cost.

Organizations that follow a **full cost** construction would allocate service and administrative costs to applicable cost objects. A "cost object" can be any physical unit or organizational subset for which costs are measured or estimated. Examples of cost objects include products, contracts, projects, sales territories, or other organizational subdivisions. The full cost of a cost object is the sum of its direct costs plus its fair share of applicable indirect costs, including service and administrative costs. Under the full cost approach, a unit should be assigned cost using the absorption costing approach plus an allocated portion of service and administrative costs.

The circumstances under which the full cost construction may be appropriate include:

- external reporting.

- analysis of the profitability of a business segment or product line.

- measurement of the cost of providing a service.

- calculation of a price to be based on full cost, i.e., rates for regulated companies and cost-type contracts.

When an organization follows a **responsibility cost** construction, service and administrative costs usually are not allocated. However, there may be situations when the allocation of such costs would be appropriate, such as when

- the costs can be influenced by the actions of the responsibility center's manager and managers are to participate in the control of these costs.

- the allocation is helpful in indicating the amount of resources that headquarters provides as support to the responsibility centers and that these costs must be covered.

- the allocation improves performance comparability (relates business unit profit to total company profit).

The reasons why service and administrative costs would not be allocated to responsibility centers include the following.

- Service and administrative costs are not related to individual business units, so allocations are arbitrary and tend to distort divisional profits.

- Business managers object to being charged for costs that are not within their control.

- The cost of making allocations exceeds the potential benefits derived.

Differential cost, as defined previously, involves measuring the cost increase (incremental cost) related to a specific job or project. Any increase in service or administrative costs attributable to an incremental decision would be allocated only to the job in question.

When service and administrative costs are allocated, the costs are first grouped into homogeneous pools and then allocated to cost objects according to some allocation base.

"Homogeneous pools" are collections of costs that are similar in nature and have a presumed causal connection. Examples of homogeneous pools include personnel-related costs, payroll-related costs, space-related costs, and energy-related costs.

Three procedures are used to allocate the service departments' costs to the production departments: direct, step or sequential, and simultaneous. Under the direct method, the total cost of the service departments is allocated directly to the production departments rather than first passing through other service departments. When the step approach is used, service departments receive their share of allocated costs for services rendered by other departments. For example, since the building occupancy and maintenance department serves the engineering department as well as the production department, a part of the building occupancy and maintenance cost should be allocated to engineering. The service department cost that is allocated first is generally that which renders the most service to the other service departments. The disadvantage of this system is that once a service department's costs are allocated, it will not receive any share of subsequent allocations from other service departments. The simultaneous allocation approach eliminates this weakness because the amount allocated from the service departments to each production department is determined by solving a set of simultaneous equations. This process is described in Part 4.

No matter which method of allocation is used, a predetermined rate rather than actual cost is usually charged to the department receiving the services whenever possible. This practice prevents the transfer of responsibility for variations in price or efficiency from the service department to the operating departments.

Before deciding on any procedure for cost allocation, or whether, in fact, costs should be allocated, careful consideration should be given to the impact the decision can have on the attitudes of the employees affected. If their performance report shows direct and indirect costs, including costs over which they have little or no control, will this cause them to have a better understanding of the total cost it takes to manufacture the product? As a result of this will they then be motivated to be more cost conscious? Alternatively, will the added cost lead only to confusion and frustration, causing the affected employee to devote too much concern to the way costs are allocated and not concentrate on the costs which he or she can control?

If it is decided that costs are to be allocated, the departmental performance report should clearly identify those costs for which the manager is directly responsible.

Example 2-2 is an adapted CPA examination problem illustrating the allocation of service department costs by the

Example 2-2

Thomas Manufacturing Company has two producing departments, Fabrication and Assembly, and three service departments, General Factory Administration, Factory Maintenance, and Factory Cafeteria. A summary of costs and other data for each department prior to allocation of service department costs for the year ended June 30, 19X2, follows.

The costs of General Factory Administration, Factory Maintenance, and Factory Cafeteria are allocated on the basis of direct labor hours, square footage occupied, and number of employees, respectively. There are no factory overhead variances. Round all final calculations to the nearest dollar.

Required   A. Assuming that Thomas Manufacturing Company elects to distribute service department costs directly to the producing departments without inter-service department cost allocation, compute the amount of Factory Maintenance costs that would be allocated to production departments.

B. Assuming the same policy of allocating service departments to producing departments only, compute the amount of General Factory Administration costs that would be allocated to production departments.

C. Assuming that Thomas Manufacturing Company elects to distribute service department costs to other service departments (starting with the service department with the greatest total costs) as well as to the producing departments and that once a service department's costs have been allocated, no subsequent service department costs are recirculated back to it, compute the total costs for the production departments after the allocation of service departments costs.

| | Producing Departments | | Service Departments | | |
	Fabrication	Assembly	General Factory Administration	Factory Maintenance	Factory Cafeteria
Direct labor costs	$1,950,000	$2,050,000	$90,000	$82,100	$87,000
Direct materials costs	3,130,000	950,000	–	65,000	91,000
Factory overhead costs	1,650,000	1,850,000	70,000	56,100	62,000
Direct labor hours	562,500	437,500	31,000	27,000	42,000
Number of employees	280	200	12	8	20
Square footage occupied	88,000	72,000	1,750	2,000	4,800

Exhibit 2-4

Part A: Allocation of Factory Maintenance Costs Based on Square Footage.

Total costs to be allocated:

Direct labor	$ 82,100
Direct materials	65,000
Factory overhead	56,100
Total	$203,200

Square footage

Department	Total	Percent
Fabrication	88,000	55%
Assembly	72,000	45
Total	160,000	100%

Allocation of factory maintenance costs

Department	Total costs	Percent	Amount
Fabrication	$203,200	55%	$111,760
Assembly	$203,200	45%	91,440
Total			$203,200

Exhibit 2-5

Part B: Allocation of General Factory Administration Based on Direct Labor Hours.

Total costs to be allocated:

Direct labor	$ 90,000
Factory overhead	70,000
Total	$160,000

Direct labor hours

Department	Total	Percent
Fabrication	562,500	56.25%
Assembly	437,500	43.75
Total	1,000,000	100.00%

Allocation of general factory administration

Department	Total costs	Percent	Amount
Fabrication	$160,000	56.25%	$ 90,000
Assembly	$160,000	43.75%	70,000
Total			$160,000

━━━━━━━━━━━━━ **Exhibit 2-6** ━━━━━━━━━━━━━

Part C.

	Service departments			Production department		
	General factory administration	Factory maintenance	Factory cafeteria	Fabrication	Assembly	Total costs
Direct labor	$ 90,000	$ 82,100	$ 87,000	$1,950,000	$2,050,000	$ 4,259,100
Direct materials	—	65,000	91,000	3,130,000	950,000	4,236,000
Factory overhead	70,000	56,100	62,000	1,650,000	1,850,000	3,688,100
Total direct costs	160,000	203,200	240,000	6,730,000	4,850,000	$12,183,200
Allocation of factory cafeteria[a]	5,760	3,840	(240,000)	134,400	96,000	
	165,760	207,040	$ 0			
Allocation of factory maintenance[b]	2,277	(207,040)		112,630	92,133	
	168,037	$ 0				
Allocation of general factory administration[c]	(168,037)			94,521	73,516	
Total	$ 0			$7,071,551	$5,111,649	$12,183,200

Percent Allocation Schedule

	[a]Number of employees		[b]Square footage		[c]Direct labor hours	
Department	Total	Percent	Total	Percent	Total	Percent
Fabrication	280	56%	88,000	54.4%	562,500	56.25%
Assembly	200	40	72,000	44.5	437,500	43.75
General factory administration	12	2.4	1,750	1.1		
Factory maintenance	8	1.6				
Total	500	100.0%	161,750	100.0%	1,000,000	100.00%

direct and step approaches. The solution to the problem is shown in Exhibits 2-4 to 2-6. Note that in this particular example there are no common costs to be allocated before the service departments' costs are reallocated. The rate in this example is based on actual costs and actual volume.

Allocation of Information Systems Costs SMA No. 4F sets forth guidelines for allocating information systems costs. The Statement indicates that there are three types of information systems costs.

1. Systems Development — includes feasibility analysis, conceptual and detail design, coding, testing, training, and maintenance, all of which are involved when a new system or application is developed.

2. Operating Costs — includes the payroll and expenses incurred in the day-to-day operation of the data processing facility. They include the use of hardware, software, and telecommunications resources.

3. Software Maintenance Costs — includes monitoring of the updating cycle to assure that all valid transactions are processed properly, that corrections to invalid transactions are expedited, and that new procedures are designed, tested, and used.

The Statement indicates that the decision to allocate information systems costs to users is a management accounting decision and depends on the concepts employed and the facts and circumstances of each case. Some advantages of allocation to users are:

1. It increases user involvement. Allocation to users causes

managers to monitor their usage of information systems services and to discuss alternative solutions with the information systems department manager.

2. It encourages efficient operation and allocation of resources, and encourages users to decide which services are worthwhile to use and how extensively they should be used.

3. It motivates information systems managers to monitor costs more closely because costs will be scrutinized by users as well as by the accounting and internal audit departments.

Although generally recommended, SMA No. 4F acknowledges there may be circumstances in which problems arising from such allocations seem to outweigh the benefits. Some reasons for not charging users for information systems services are:

1. Charging discourages development of new computer applications and may create conflict between the information systems department and users.

2. Charging full cost in such situations may seem unfair to users and may discourage them from using a new application.

3. The cost of determining the amount to charge may be greater than the benefits to be derived from charging.

4. Charging involves systems resources that could be used for other purposes.

5. The amount to be charged is not easy to determine, and the allocation procedure may be difficult to explain to users.

6. Charging for information systems services adds another layer of administrative detail to an already complex accounting system.

Allocation methods may include the following:

1. **Full Cost** allocates all information systems costs to the users. However, this method may discourage use of information systems services if rates are high as a result of underutilized facilities.

2. **Variable Cost** (cost less than full cost) encourages the full utilization of information systems facilities. It may lead to the overutilization of facilities, thus creating bottlenecks and delays.

3. **Cost Plus Profit** reflects the concept that the information systems organization should seek to earn an adequate return on the entity's tangible and intangible investments in its facilities.

4. **Market Price** seeks to provide an arm's-length price that would be paid for information systems services if they were provided by outside services. However, this price may be difficult to determine or may not exist.

The allocations may be made using different bases, depending on the costs involved and particular circumstances:

1. A labor-based charge (labor hours, labor cost) may be appropriate in those situations in which labor is a reasonable surrogate for total information system costs.

2. A machine-based charge, or central processing unit (CPU) time, may be appropriate in those situations in which machine usage is a reasonable surrogate for total information system costs. Examples of such situations would include environments in which operations predominate and systems development and maintenance are less significant.

3. A multiple-based charge, such as labor and machine time, or additional factors, also may be deemed appropriate. Such multiple factors are, however, more difficult to develop and support and, thus, should be considered carefully.

4. Allocated charges for recurring services such as payroll, billing, general ledger accounting, and so on may be fixed at the beginning of a period and reviewed at specific intervals. This permits the user to know the allocated charges and gives the provider the incentive to meet the budgeted charges.

The Statement indicates that the amount allocated to users may be based upon a single rate for all services or multiple prices based upon the services actually received by the users. The single-factor approach is the easiest to implement and explain to users. A single-factor-based allocation is most appropriate when the information system is unsophisticated and/or is used primarily to process similar types of data. The Statement suggests that multiple-factor allocation methods usually are more satisfactory than single-factor methods in environments built around mainframes or large minicomputers because users are charged for the specific resources they consume.

Process Costing

Process costing techniques are used when there is usually continuous mass production of like products. Chemicals, food processing, paper, textiles, petroleum, and gas and water utilities are examples of industries where process cost systems are frequently used. Process costing methods are used by both manufacturing and service industries.

In job order costing, costs are accumulated by jobs or orders. In contrast, process costing systems accumulate manufacturing costs by basic processes or process departments for a given time period. The cost per unit for a particular department is determined by dividing the total cost incurred for a given time period, such as a month, by the equivalent whole units produced. Costs flow from one department or process to another as the item being manufactured moves through the processes. The objectives of process costing are to determine the total cost of goods manufactured and the value of ending inventories.

Most process cost problems can be solved in six basic steps:

1. **Units to account for** Identify those units we must account for, such as those started in this period and those still in process from the previous period.

2. **Units accounted for** Account for all units according to whether they were transferred to the next process or to finished goods, are still in process, or were lost. This total must agree with the total in step 1.

3. **Equivalent units** Convert the units accounted for in step 2 into equivalent units of production, which is adjusted for the stage of completion for unfinished units and lost units.

(Note that steps 1 through 3 do not involve dollar amounts.)

4. **Total cost to account for** Identify the cost incurred for direct materials and conversion costs (direct labor and overhead) and the cost transferred in from the previous department.

Example 2-3

The Culver City manufacturing company produces a single product in two production departments—A and B.

The following cost and production data were for the month of July:

	Department A	Department B
PRODUCTION DATA		
Units in process, July 1	2,000	1,000
Units started	6,000	–
Units transferred to B	5,000	–
Units transferred to finished goods	–	4,000
Units in process, July 31	3,000	2,000
COST DATA		
Materials	$24,600	$ –
Labor	18,270	11,250
Factory overhead	5,510	7,875
BEGINNING IN PROCESS COSTS		
Prior department costs	–	8,000
Materials	7,400	–
Labor	2,730	2,250
Factory overhead	1,490	1,125

In department A, the materials are added at the beginning of the process, and the beginning inventory is 60 percent completed as to conversion cost, while the ending inventory is two-thirds complete. No additional materials are added in department B. The beginning inventory in department B is 75 percent complete and the ending is only 25 percent complete as to conversion costs.

Required Determine the value of work-in-process inventories as of July 31 and the cost of the goods transferred to finished goods inventory.

5. Cost per equivalent unit For each cost element, divide the totals in step 4 by the equivalent units calculated in step 3.

6. Total cost accounted for Using the cost information from step 5, determine the cost transferred out and the cost of the work-in-process inventories. The total cost accounted for must agree with the total cost to account for in step 4.

These six steps are frequently presented in one report referred to as the **Cost of Production Report**.

Two methods are commonly used to trace beginning inventories through the process: **weighted-average** and **first-in, first-out** (FIFO). In practice, weighted-average is used most of the time. The FIFO method, however, has appeared frequently on previous CPA examinations and is discussed in most cost texts; as a result we should be familiar with the technique for the CMA examination.

The problem in Example 2-3 will first be used to illustrate the weighted-average method.

Weighted-Average Method

The weighted-average method treats the beginning work-in-process as if it were part of this period's costs. The cost of units still in process is averaged with the current period's costs to secure one average cost calculation. Since the costs are added together, the equivalent units calculation for this period must also include the equivalent whole units of work completed last period and those units still in process.

Six basic steps are used to determine the portion of department A's costs transferred to department B and the value of the units in process, as shown in Exhibit 2-7. This problem is very simple and a short-cut solution could have been used; but in the interest of learning, it is best to follow these six basic steps.

Step 1 determines that we must account for 8,000 units.

Step 2 shows that we accounted for those 8,000 units by transferring out 5,000 and holding 3,000 in ending inventory.

Step 3 calculates the equivalent unit cost for materials, labor, and overhead. Note that 5000 appears on the line labeled "Transferred to department B" in all three columns since the units transferred out were 100 percent complete. Thus, this period's work is considered with the work incurred last period on the units still in process at the beginning of July. Since the materials are added at the beginning of the process, the 3,000 units in ending inventory are 100 percent complete as far as materials are concerned. Notice the 3,000 units under the materials column. The 3,000 were two-thirds complete as to labor and overhead. Thus, 2,000 units (3,000 × 2/3)—the equivalent whole units—appear in the labor and overhead column.

Step 4 summarizes the total cost incurred and the cost for which we must account. The costs in beginning inventory for materials of $7,400; labor of $2,730; and overhead of $1,490 are added to the costs of $24,600; $18,270; and $5,510 for materials, labor, and overhead respectively. The column labeled "Totals" shows that we must account for a total of $60,000.

Step 5 determines the equivalent unit costs. The total cost of $32,000; $21,000; and $7,000 for materials, labor, and overhead is divided by the appropriate equivalent units (calculated in step 3) of 8,000; 7,000; and 7,000 for materials, labor, and overhead respectively to get the equivalent unit costs. Note—do not divide the $60,000 in the totals column. The $8 whole unit cost is determined by adding the equivalent unit costs for materials, labor, and overhead.

Step 6 shows how much of the costs are associated with unit transferred out and how much with those still in process. The transferred-out cost is $40,000 (5,000 units × $8 cost per unit). The work-in-process inventory as of July 31 consists of the following:

━━━━━━━━━━━━━━━━━━━━━━━ **Exhibit 2-7** ━━━━━━━━━━━━━━━━━━━━━━

Culver City Manufacturing
Cost of Production Report (Weighted-Average)
Department A
For the Month of July 19X1

	Totals	Materials	Labor	Overhead
(1) Units to account for:				
In process, July 1	2,000			
Started	6,000			
Total	**8,000**			
(2) Units accounted for:		(3) Equivalent Units		
Transferred to department B	5,000	5,000	5,000	5,000
In process, July 31	3,000	3,000	2,000	2,000
Total	**8,000**	**8,000**	**7,000**	**7,000**
(4) Cost to account for:				
In process, July 1	$11,620	$ 7,400	$ 2,730	$1,490
Cost added	48,380	24,600	18,270	5,510
Total	**$60,000**	32,000	21,000	7,000
(5) Equivalent unit costs:				
Equivalent units		÷8,000	÷7,000	÷7,000
Unit cost	**$8.00**	**$4.00**	**$3.00**	**$1.00**
(6) Cost accounted for:				
Transferred to department B	$40,000		($8.00 × 5,000)	
		($4.00 × 3,000)	($3.00 × 2,000)	($1.00 × 2,000)
In process, July 31	20,000	$12,000	$ 6,000	$2,000
Total	**$60,000**			

Materials:
$4 × 3,000 units (100 percent complete) $12,000

Labor:
$3 × 2,000 units (two-thirds complete)   6,000

Overhead:
$1 × 2,000 units (two-thirds complete)   2,000

Total value of work-in-process inventory   **$20,000**

Exhibit 2-8 shows the results for department B. The Prior Department Costs heading represents the costs from previous departments and can be viewed as the raw materials costs brought into department B. The $40,000 transferred from department A (step 6, Exhibit 2-7) is added to department B as a part of this period's current costs. The beginning work-in-process inventory, which contains $8,000 labeled Prior Department costs, represents the cost associated with 1,000 units transferred in the last period and still in process at the end of last period. These units will, obviously, always be 100 percent

complete as to prior department costs.

As in department A, the beginning inventory costs are added to the costs incurred this period to arrive at the total cost; this is used to calculate the equivalent unit costs. Steps 1 through 6 of Exhibit 2-8 should be studied.

FIFO Method

The FIFO (first-in, first-out) method keeps the opening work-in-process separate from the goods that are started and completed in the current period. Thus, we have two separate types of unit costs: one for opening work-in-process units that were completed and another for the units started and completed during the current period.

To illustrate the FIFO method, we determine the cost of goods transferred to department B and the ending work-in-process inventory for department A, using the information

Exhibit 2-8

Culver City Manufacturing
Cost of Production Report (Weighted-Average)
Department B
For the Month of July 19X1

	Totals	Prior department	Labor	Overhead
(1) Units to account for:				
In process, July 1	1,000			
Started	5,000			
Total	**6,000**			
(2) Units accounted for:		(3) Equivalent units		
Transferred to finished goods	4,000	4,000	4,000	4,000
In process, July 31	2,000	2,000	500	500
Total	**6,000**	**6,000**	**4,500**	**4,500**
(4) Cost to account for:				
In process, July 1	$11,375	$ 8,000	$ 2,250	$1,125
Cost added	59,125	40,000	11,250	7,875
Total	**$70,500**	48,000	13,500	9,000
(5) Equivalent unit costs:				
Equivalent units		÷6,000	÷4,500	÷4,500
Unit cost	**$13.00**	**$ 8.00**	**$ 3.00**	**$ 2.00**
(6) Cost accounted for:				
Transferred to finished goods	$52,000	($13.00 x 4,000)		
In process, July 31	18,500	($8.00 x 2,000) $16,000	($3.00 x 500) $1,500	($2.00 x 500) $1,000
Total	**$70,500**			

given in Example 2-3. As was probably noticed, under the weighted-average method, we did not use the data given in the problem about the state of completion of beginning inventory; however, under FIFO this information is relevant. In contrast, under FIFO we do not need to know the cost elements (materials, labor, and overhead) of the beginning inventory; under the weighted-average method, this information was used.

Exhibit 2-9 presents the solution to Example 2-3 using FIFO. The places where the FIFO technique differs from the weighted-average method are described below:

Step 1 The information is the same; we must account for 8,000 units.

Step 2 The 5,000 units transferred out must be broken down into (1) those 2,000 opening work-in-process units that were completed and (2) the units started and completed in this period (labeled Transferred to Department B: Current Production), which total 3,000.

Step 3 The equivalent units under FIFO represent only the actual amount of work done during the current period. The materials in the opening work-in-process were added last period and, as a result, a zero is placed in the materials column for the In Process, July 1 category. The opening work-in-process inventory was 60 percent complete as to labor and overhead, which means that 40 percent of the work must be done during the current period or the equivalent of 800 units (40 percent × 2,000 units in process, July 1). Of course, the 3,000 units transferred from current production were fully completed this period. The units in ending inventory are treated the same way under FIFO as under weighted-average.

Step 4 Note that the opening inventory costs for materials, labor, and overhead are not entered under the respective headings, only the total cost of $11,620 appears on the schedule.

Exhibit 2-9

Culver City Manufacturing
Cost of Production Report (FIFO)
Department A
For the Month of July 19X1

	Totals	Materials	Labor	Overhead
(1) Units to account for:				
In process, July 1	2,000			
Started	6,000			
Total	**8,000**			
(2) Units accounted for:		(3) Equivalent units		
Transferred to department B				
In process, July 1	2,000	0	800	800
Current production	3,000	3,000	3,000	3,000
Total transferred to B	5,000			
In process	3,000	3,000	2,000	2,000
Total	**8,000**	**6,000**	**5,800**	**5,800**
(4) Cost to account for:				
In process, July 1	$11,620			
Cost added	48,380	$24,600	$18,270	$5,510
Total	**$60,000**	24,600	18,270	5,510
(5) Equivalent unit costs				
Equivalent units		÷6,000	÷5,800	÷5,800
Unit cost	**$8.20**	**$4.10**	**$3.15**	**$ .95**
(6) Cost accounted for:				
Transferred to department B				
In process, July 1	$11,620		($3.15 x 800)	($.95 x 800)
Current cost added	3,280	—	$2,520	$760
Total in process	14,900			
Current production	24,600		($8.20 x 3,000)	
Total transferred to B	39,500	($4.10 x 3,000)	($3.15 x 2,000)	($.95 x 2,000)
In process, July 31	20,500	$12,300	$6,300	$1,900
Total	**$60,000**			

Step 5 The equivalent unit costs consist of only the cost for this period's production (total cost incurred for materials, labor, and overhead ÷ respective equivalent whole units manufactured this period).

Step 6 The units transferred out are broken down into two batches: 2,000 units in opening inventory and 3,000 units started and completed. The total cost of the 2,000 units consists of the beginning inventory cost of $11,620 plus the cost of $3,280 incurred this period to complete the units ($2,520 of

labor and $760 of overhead). The total cost of the 3,000 units from current production is $24,600 (total unit cost of $8.20 × 3,000).

The cost of the 5,000 units transferred to department B is $39,500 ($14,900 for 2,000 units plus $24,600 for 3,000 units). Since this cost is not broken down into components, the unit cost in department B becomes $7.90 ($39,500 ÷ 5,000 units). Thus, the FIFO method is modified in that subsequent departments use weighted-average methods for cost transferred in.

━━━━━━━━━━━━━━━━━━━━━━━━━━━ **Example 2-4** ━━━━━━━━━━━━━━━━━━━━━━━━━━━

The King Process Company manufactures one product, which requires two processes—No. 1 and No. 2—for completion.

For each unit of process No. 1 output, two units of raw material X are put in at the start of the processing. For each unit of process No. 2 output, three cans of raw material Y are put in at the end of processing and two pounds of process No. 1 output are put in at the start.

Spoilage generally occurs in process No. 2 at the start of the process.

In-process accounts are maintained for raw materials, conversion costs, and prior department costs.

The company uses the FIFO basis for inventory valuation for process No. 1 and finished goods, and average cost for inventory valuation for process No. 2.

Required Determine the equivalent units for process No. 1 and process No. 2.

Data for March:

1. Units transferred:

   From process No. 1 to process No. 2: 2,200 pounds
   From process No. 2 to finished goods: 900 gallons
   From finished goods to cost of goods sold: 600 gallons

2. Units spoiled in process No. 2: 100 gallons

3. Inventory data:

	Process No. 1		Process No. 2		Finished Goods	
	Initial	Final	Initial	Final	Initial	Final
Units	200	300	200	300	700	1,000
Fraction complete conversion costs	1/2	1/2	1/2	2/3		

If this modification were not made, it would be very burdensome to trace these costs through several departments since these costs would be accumulated for a large number of batches.

Special Problems

Several special situations often make it difficult for the student to solve process cost problems. For example, materials can be added in the second department causing an increase in output, or units can change in form (that is, from pounds to cartons), or units can be lost.

When materials such as water are added and cause an increase in units of products, this increase should be added in step 1 as Additional Units Placed in Process. This increase in units must be accounted for in step 2. The cost per unit that may have been transferred in from prior departments is automatically reduced since the equivalent unit calculation includes this increase.

To account for any change in form, the units expressed in steps 1 through 3 should be in the form in which the units are transferred out. So, if in a given department, the product enters in pounds and is transferred out in gallons, steps 1 to 3 of the cost of production report should be expressed in gallons and the units transferred in (at the start) should be converted from pounds to gallons. Consider Example 2-4, a modified CPA examination problem that deals with a change in form. Exhibit 2-10 contains the solution for the example.

Lost Units and Spoilage

Any process that operates continuously is subject to inefficiencies that result in lost units. Some processes, by their very nature, will always have some type of loss, such as evaporation loss. These losses, known as normal spoilages, occur even though the process may be operating effectively, and are considered a part of the cost of producing the good units. On the other hand, losses that occur beyond the amount that would be normally expected are classified as abnormal. Abnormal losses often are the result of unusual operating conditions, such as flooding, or because management has defined a precise limit beyond which lost or spoiled units are considered abnormal. Study Example 2-5, a CPA examination question dealing with spoilage units. The solution is given in Exhibit 2-11.

The loss may occur at the beginning, during, or at the end of the process. Most examination problems assume the loss occurs at the beginning, and even if it states that it occurred at some other point, a solution based on the assumption that it occurred at the beginning has been acceptable. For the CMA examination, if a problem does not state where the loss occurred, assume it occurred at the beginning.

Normal Loss Procedures A line is added to step 2 in the Cost of Production Report to account for lost units. If the normal loss occurred at the beginning of the process, enter 0 (zero) in all columns except the first (Totals Column). The cost of the lost units is spread over the units still in process and the units transferred out. Consider Example 2-6, a CPA examination problem dealing with lost units. Then study the solution presented in Exhibit 2-12. The cost of the 5,000 units that were lost is in the total cost of $538,000 transferred out and in the cost of $105,000 still in process at October 31.

Exhibit 2-13 contains the solution to the same problem when the loss occurs at the end of the process. If the loss occurs at any time other than at the beginning of the process, accumulate the costs for the lost units in a separate category and then allocate them in step 6. When the loss is at the end of the process, the entire cost of the units lost should be included in the transferred out costs. Study Exhibit 2-13. Note that the 5,000 lost units appear in all columns in step 3 and

━━━━━━━━━━━━━ **Exhibit 2-10** ━━━━━━━━━━━━━

King Process Company
Equivalent Product Units

Process No. 1

	Totals	Materials	Labor
(1) Units to account for:			
In process, beginning	200		
Started	2,300[a]		
Total	**2,500**		
(2) Units accounted for:		(3) Equivalent units	
Transferred to Process 2			
In process, beginning	200	0[b]	100[c]
Current production	2,000	2,000	2,000
Total transferred	2,200		
In process, ending	300	300	150
Total	**2,500**	**2,300**	**2,250**

Process No. 2

	Totals	Prior department costs	Materials	Conversion costs
(1) Units to account for:				
In process, beginning	200			
Started (from process 1)	1,100[d]			
Total	**1,300**			
(2) Units accounted for:			(3) Equivalent units	
Transferred out	900	900	900	900
Lost units	100[e]	0[f]	0	0
In process	300	200	0[g]	200[h]
Total	**1,300**	**1,100**	**900**	**1,100**

[a]Total units transferred out	2,200
Lost units	0
Increase in inventory level (300—200)	100
Total started	**2,300**

[b]Since these units were started last period and raw materials were added at the beginning of the process these units received no additional materials.

[c]The units were 50 percent complete; consequently, the equivalent of 50 percent must have been done this period.

[d]Note that it takes two pounds of process No. 1 output to get one unit of finished goods. The total pounds transferred in were 2,200; therefore, the total started in terms of units of finished goods is 1,100 (2,200 × 1/2).

[e]Since 900 units were transferred out and only 300 units are still in process, 100 units were lost (1,300 units – 1,200 units).

[f]The loss occurred at the beginning of the process. By placing zeros in the equivalent unit schedule, the cost associated with the lost units is charged to the units transferred out and the good units in process.

[g]Materials are added at the completion of the process.

[h]The units are two-thirds complete as to conversion costs (2/3 × 300).

Example 2-5

The D. Hayes Cramer Company manufactures product C, which has costs per unit of $1 for materials, $2 for labor, and $3 for overhead costs. During the month of May, 1,000 units of product C were spoiled. These units could be sold for scrap at $.60 each.

The accountant said that the entry to be made for these 1,000 lost or spoiled units could be one of the following four:

1. Spoiled goods	600	
Work-in-process—Materials		100
Work-in-process—Labor		200
Work-in-process—Overhead		300
2. Spoiled goods	600	
Manufacturing expenses	5,400	
Work-in-process—Materials		1,000
Work-in-process—Labor		2,000
Work-in-process—Overhead		3,000
3. Spoiled goods	600	
Loss on spoiled goods	5,400	
Work-in-process—Materials		1,000
Work-in-process—Labor		2,000
Work-in-process—Overhead		3,000
4. Spoiled goods	600	
Receivable	5,400	
Work-in-process—Materials		1,000
Work-in-process—Labor		2,000
Work-in-process—Overhead		3,000

Required Indicate the circumstances under which each of the four solutions above would be appropriate.

Example 2-6

The Biltimar Company manufactures gewgaws in three steps, each of which is done by a different department. The Finishing Department is the third and last step before the product is transferred to finished goods inventory.

All materials needed to complete the gewgaws are added at the beginning of the process in the Finishing Department, and lost units, if any, occur only at this point. The company uses the FIFO cost method in its accounting system and has accumulated the following data for October for the Finishing Department:

1. Production of gewgaws:	Units
In process, October 1 (labor and manufacturing expense, three-fourths complete)	10,000
Transferred from preceding departments during October	40,000
Finished and transferred to finished goods inventory during October	35,000
In process, October 31 (labor and manufacturing expense, one-half complete)	10,000

2. Cost of work in process inventory, October 1:

Costs from preceding departments	$ 38,000
Costs added in Finishing Department prior to October 1:	
Materials	21,500
Conversion costs	81,000
	$140,500

3. Gewgaws transferred to the Finished Department during October had costs of $140,000 assigned from preceding departments.

4. During October, the Finishing Department incurred the following production costs:

Material	$ 70,000
Conversion costs	292,500
	$362,500

Required Prepare a cost of production report.

Exhibit 2-11
D. Hayes Cramer Company
Lost Units Analysis

Entry Number	Circumstances under Which the Solution is Appropriate
1	The loss is to be charged to this specific job, probably because of rigid specifications of this particular job order. The 1,000 units spoiled were part of a much larger special order. Other jobs may be in production and should not absorb any of this loss.
2	The loss on spoiled goods is to be prorated over the entire production for this period. This method is used where spoilage occurs on all jobs of this type, but the percentage of spoilage in each lot fluctuates rather widely.

Entry Number	Circumstances under Which the Solution is Applicable
3	This is the treatment for an abnormal loss that is to be charged completely against operations for the period. This method should be employed if the loss could have been prevented.
4	The loss is recoverable either against a customer (special contract), against an insurance company, or perhaps even against the employees causing such loss to occur.

Exhibit 2-12

Biltimar Company
Cost of Production Report (FIFO Method)
Lost Units at Start of Process for the Month of October 19X1

	Totals	Prior department costs	Materials	Conversion costs
(1) Units to account for				
In process, October 1	10,000			
Transferred in	40,000			
Total	**50,000**			
(2) Units accounted for		(3) Equivalent units		
Transferred out				
In process October 1	10,000	0	0	2,500
Current production	25,000	25,000	25,000	25,000
Total	35,000	25,000	25,000	27,500
Lost	5,000	0	0	0
In process, October 31	10,000	10,000	10,000	5,000
Total	**50,000**	**35,000**	**35,000**	**32,500**
(4) Cost to account for				
In process, October 1	$140,500			
Cost added	502,500	$140,000	$70,000	$292,500
Total	**$643,000**	140,000	70,000	292,500
(5) Equivalent unit cost				
Equivalent units		÷35,000	÷35,000	÷32,500
Unit costs	**$15.00**	**$ 4.00**	**$ 2.00**	**$ 9.00**
(6) Cost accounted for				
Transferred out				
In process, October 1	$140,500			
Cost added to in process	22,500	0	0	($9.00 x 2,500) $22,500
Total	163,000			
Current production	375,000		($15 x 25,000)	
Total transferred out	538,000			
In process, October 31	105,000	($4.00 x 10,000) $40,000	($2.00 x 10,000) $20,000	($9.00 x 5,000) $45,000
Total	**$643,000**			

that the cost of the 5,000 units lost ($65,250) is added to the cost of the 35,000 good units transferred to finished goods. The ending work-in-process inventory as shown in Exhibit 2-13 is $13,500 less than the amount determined in Exhibit 2-12 because it does not contain the adjustment for lost unit costs.

If the loss had occurred when the units were 40 percent complete as to conversion costs, the Lost line in step 3 would have shown 2,000 units (5,000 × 0.40) under the conversion cost column and 5,000 units under the other columns. Since the ending inventory is 50 percent complete, the lost unit cost would be allocated to both the 35,000 units transferred out and the 10,000 units in ending inventory, with 35,000 ÷ 45,000 of the lost unit cost being applied to transferred-out units and

Exhibit 2-13

Biltimar Company
Cost of Production Report (FIFO Method)
Lost Units at End of Process for the Month of October 19X1

	Totals	Prior department costs	Materials	Conversion costs
(2) Units accounted for		(3) Equivalent units		
Transferred out				
In process, October 1	10,000	0	0	2,500
Current production	25,000	25,000	25,000	25,000
Total	35,000	25,000	25,000	27,500
Lost	5,000	5,000	5,000	5,000
In process, October 31	10,000	10,000	10,000	5,000
Total	**50,000**	**40,000**	**40,000**	**37,500**
(4) Cost to account for				
In process, October 1	$140,500			
Cost added	502,500	$140,000	$70,000	$292,500
Total	**$643,000**	140,000	70,000	292,500
(5) Equivalent cost				
Equivalent units		÷40,000	÷40,000	÷37,500
Unit costs	**$13.05**	**$ 3.50**	**$ 1.75**	**$ 7.80**
(6) Cost accounted for				
Transferred out				
In process, October 1	$140,500			($7.80 x 2,500)
Cost added to in process	19,500			$19,500
Total	160,000			
Current production	326,250	($13.05 x 25,000)		
Lost unit adjustment	65,250	($13.05 x 5,000)		
Total transferred out	551,500	($3.50 x 10,000)	($1.75 x 10,000)	($7.80 x 5,000)
In process, October 31	91,500	$35,000	$17,500	$39,000
Total	**$643,000**			

10,000 ÷ 45,000 of the lost unit cost being applied to ending inventory.

Abnormal Loss Procedures Although abnormal losses are sometimes spread over good units, assume here that any cost incurred prior to the point where the loss occurs should be removed from the process and reported on the income statement as a special loss. If the loss in Example 2-6 had been abnormal and had occurred at the end of the period, the solution would have been the same as reported in Exhibit 2-13, except for the cost transferred out. This cost would have been $486,250 (total cost of $160,000 for 10,000 units in process and cost of $326,250 for 25,000 units started and completed in July). The cost of the abnormal loss that would have been

reported on the income statement would have been $65,250. If the loss had occurred at the beginning of the process, it would have totaled only $17,500 (5,000 lost units × prior department's unit cost of $3.50). If some work had been done on these units in this period, the cost for such work would also have been included in the abnormal loss.

Activity-Based Costing

As was noted above, activity accounting accumulates product and other costs based on the activities required to manufacture the product. Many companies have concluded that the allocation of all overhead on the basis of direct labor cost or hours is no longer adequate. One problem is that labor cost at one time accounted for the majority of the costs to manufacture the product. This is obviously no longer the case. In many instances, labor costs now represent less than ten percent of the total cost.

Peavey[8] suggests the following steps in the development of an activity-based costing discussed in detail later.

1. Analyze all the production and support activities. For example, the activity of the purchasing department may consist of three activities—purchase of raw materials, purchase of spare parts and special work related to new products.

2. Allocate all costs to the activity. The activities of each segment of the business are examined to determine the costs associated with the activity. For example, in the purchasing department example above it may be determined that 40% of the costs are related to purchasing raw materials, 40 % to purchasing spare parts, and 20% to special work for new products.

3. Ascertain the factor—a measure of activity volume—which most directly determines the cost of the activity. A key element of activity accounting is then to link the activity with the products manufactured by the use of the factor whose occurrence created the costs. Using the purchasing department example, possible factors are as follows:

Activity	Factor
Purchasing raw materials	Quality of materials used in production
Purchasing spare parts	Number of different parts ordered
Special work	Number of new products

4. Finished goods are assigned costs based on the factors included in their production. Thus the costs of purchasing raw materials and doing special work will be allocated directly to the product based on raw materials used and new products. The cost for the purchase of spare parts will be allocated to the machine activity. The cost for machine activity will then be allocated to products based on factors related to the operating of machines such as machine hours used, etc.

Thus, this model attempts to allocate the costs directly to the resources used to produce the products. In contrast, the traditional model would have allocated the overhead to products based on direct labor hours or dollars, which would have failed to relate the allocation directly to the consumption of the individual overhead items. Activity accounting should provide a better estimate of the total costs to manufacture products. Control is also better under activity accounting, in that costs are controlled at the activity level where they are incurred.

Activity accounting is acceptable for GAAP purposes, but a change to activity accounting may cause the company to report the change under APB No. 20. Peavey suggests the GAAP model needs to be modified to facilitate the use of activity accounting:[9]

Once a company has allocated overhead better by using activity accounting, the next logical step may be to change the traditional GAAP model to permit more activities to be allocated to inventory, including some activities usually considered general and administrative expenses. The activities of accounts payable, payroll, and personnel are all part of product cost. Factors that could serve as a basis for allocating these activities might include the number of different raw materials used in a product, number of employees, number of new hires, or number of new products. If the most reasonable factor is selected, the costs of these activities can be allocated to production in a reasonable way. Under activity accounting, the line between product costs and general expenses becomes less clear.

Joint Products

Some production processes create a more difficult type of cost allocation problem because two or more significant products are produced at the same time from the same inputs. The resulting outputs are referred to as "joint products." The difficulty arises from the fact that individual products are not identifiable until they emerge at the split-off point, so there is no real basis on which to allocate the direct and indirect manufacturing costs incurred up to that point.

Joint products are defined as products that receive some pro rata share of joint costs prior to the split, usually on the basis of some arbitrary cost allocation formula. **By-products** are defined as those products emerging from the split that are not assigned any of the prior joint costs. Usually by-products have a much lower value relative to other products at the point of split-off and are often disposed of for scrap value or are recycled in the production process. If by-products incur separable costs after the split, such costs are usually assigned to the by-products. Many products once considered by-products now make significant contributions to the businesses' profits, and their classification has been changed to that of joint products.

Joint Costs

The term **joint cost** is used to refer to the cost incurred up to the point of split-off. Examples of industries where joint costs are common include meat packing, lumber, dairy, canning, petroleum, flour milling, and chemical. Two aspects of joint costs are important for the accountant and will be examined in this section: (1) the method of allocating joint costs to products and (2) the treatment of joint costs for decision-making purposes.

8. Dennis E. Peavey, "Battle at the GAAP? It's Time for a Change" *Management Accounting* (February 1990), pp. 31-32.

9. *Ibid.*, p. 32.

Allocation Methods

At the point of split-off several products emerge and the accountant finds it necessary to allocate the costs incurred up to that time among the joint products. The arbitrary methods most frequently chosen to allocate these costs are based on some type of physical measure or the relative sales value at the point of the split. In practice, many variations of each of these methods are found.

Physical Measure   Under this method the total joint costs are allocated to the joint products on the basis of some unit of product output measurement such as units, pounds, tons, gallons, or square feet. The cost assigned under this procedure may bear no relation to the costs incurred or the revenue generated by the various products.

Relative Sales Value   This method, which is the most widely used, is based on the assumption that costs should be assigned on the basis of a product's ability to absorb them. Thus, products with the largest sales value should absorb more of the costs. The sales value used in this approach is often the value at the point of the split-off. In situations where products are sold without additional processing, the relative sales value is the sales price of each product times the quantity produced. For products that a business elects to process further, even though a market exists for them as they are, the value used for joint costs allocation purposes is the amount that could have been received if the products had been sold before being processed. For joint products that are processed further, and for which there is no market at the point of split-off, a relative value must be assigned at that point. The most frequently used procedure in this instance is to estimate the sales value of the finished product and reduce it by the processing cost needed to complete the product, which was incurred after split-off.

Example 2-7, an adapted CPA examination question, illustrates the use of each of these allocation methods. Exhibit 2-14 shows that the cost per pound for the three products is $3.26, based on the physical measurement approach. Exhibit 2-15 shows the calculations of the cost per pound at the point of split-off using the relative sales value approach. In part B the yield of Bonanyl-X from Bonanyl has to be determined to get the market value of Bonanyl at the split-off since the 2,755 units of Bonanyl-X come from 2,900 units of Bonanyl but only 2,800 units of Bonanyl were produced this period. Thus, what we need is the market value for these 2,800 units. Note that the conversion cost in department 2 is also for 2,755 units and must be adjusted to determine the cost for 2,660 units (2,800 × 0.95). Even though Am-Salt is processed further, a market price of $6.30 per pound exists, which we can use as the relative sales value.

Part C of Example 2-7 is also answered in Exhibit 2-15.

Use of Net Realizable Values   Since both the physical measure and relative sales values have weaknesses, it is difficult to find a basis for allocating joint costs fairly. An alternative to these is to carry all inventories at net realizable values — final sales value less estimated cost after separation and estimated selling expenses. This approach is used to some extent in the meatpacking, canning, and mining industries, but is generally not preferred by most accountants since profits are reported before the sale occurs. To adjust for this problem, however, the inventory can be reduced by a normal profit. An advantage to this method is that it avoids the problems associated with allocating the joint costs.

Use of Joint Costs in Decision Making

The cost allocated to the joint products by the physical measure or relative sales value method described above should not be used to determine whether a product should be sold at the split-off point or should be processed further. The decision should be based on a comparison of additional revenue to be gained and costs associated with the additional processing. This additional revenue is determined by subtracting the revenue available at the time of the split-off from the total amount expected from the sale of the product after additional processing. If the additional revenue exceeds the further processing cost, profits would be maximized by processing further; the amount of joint costs and the method followed in their allocation do not have any impact on the decision. Joint product decisions must usually be made simultaneously rather than separately for individual products.

Study Example 2-8 which deals with joint costs, and the solution, which is presented in Exhibit 2-16.

By-products

By-products, as mentioned, differ from joint products in that they are not assigned joint costs prior to the split. Several methods are used to account for by-products. Example 2-9, previous CPA examination question, deals with the most significant of these methods. The solution follows the example.

The New Manufacturing Environment

Accountants must be aware of and adapt to the major changes occurring in the manufacturing environment. The objective of this section is to discuss a few of the basic developments.

Just-In Time

Just-in-time (JIT) is the philosophy that activities are undertaken only as needed or demanded. Foster and Horngren[10] have identified four characteristics of JIT:

1. Elimination of all activities that do not add value to a product or service.

2. Commitment to a high level of quality.

3. Commitment to continuous improvement in the efficiency of an activity.

4. Emphasis on simplification and increased visibility to identify activities that do not add value.

10. George Foster and Charles T. Horngren, "JIT: Cost Accounting and Cost Management Issues," *Management Accounting* (June 1987), p. 19.

Example 2-7

In its three departments Amaco Chemical Company manufactures several products:

1. In department 1, the raw materials amanic acid and bonyl hydroxide are used to produce Amanyl, Bonanyl, and Am-Salt. Amanyl is sold to others who use it as a raw material in the manufacture of stimulants. Bonanyl is not salable without further processing. Although Am-Salt is a commercial product for which there is a ready market, Amaco does not sell this product, preferring to submit it to further processing.

2. In department 2, Bonanyl is processed into the marketable product, Bonanyl-X. The relationship between Bonanyl used and Bonanyl-X produced has remained constant for several months.

3. In department 3, Am-Salt and the raw material Colb are used to produce Colbanyl, a liquid propellant that is in great demand. As an inevitable part of this process, Demanyl is also produced. Demanyl was discarded as scrap until discovery of its usefulness as a catalyst in the manufacture of glue; for two years Amaco has been able to sell all of its production of Demanyl.

In its financial statements Amaco states inventory at the lower of cost (on the first-in, first-out basis) or market. Unit cost of the items most recently produced must therefore be computed. Costs allocated to Demanyl are computed so that after allowing for packaging and selling cost of $.04 per pound, no profit or loss will be recognized on sales of this product.

Certain data for October 19X2 follow.

Required Prepare for October 19X2 the schedules listed below. Supporting computations should be prepared in good form. Round answers to the nearest cent.

A. Cost per pound of Amanyl, Bonanyl, and Am-Salt produced -average unit cost method.

B. Cost per pound of Amanyl, Bonanyl, and Am-Salt produced-relative sales value method.

C. Cost per pound of Colbanyl produced. Assume that the cost per pound of Am-Salt produced was $3.40 in September 19X2 and $3.50 in October 19X2.

RAW MATERIALS

	Pounds used	Total cost
Amanic acid	6,300	$5,670
Bonyl hydroxide	9,100	6,370
Colb	5,600	2,240

CONVERSION COSTS (labor and overhead)

	Total cost
Department 1	$33,600
Department 2	3,306
Department 3	22,400

PRODUCTS

	Pounds produced	September 30	October 31	Sales price per pound
Amanyl	3,600			$ 6.65
Bonanyl	2,800	210	110	
Am-Saly	7,600	400	600	6.30
Bonanyl-X	2,755			4.20
Colbanyl	1,400			43.00
Demanyl	9,800			.54

Exhibit 2-14

Amaco Chemical Company
Allocation of Joint Costs
Physical Measure Method

Part A.

Joint costs:	
Amanic acid	$ 5,670
Bonyl hydroxide	6,370
Department 1 conversion costs	33,600
Total joint costs	$45,640

Product	Pounds produced	Cost per pound[a]	Total cost
Amanyl	3,600	$3.26	$11,736
Bonanyl	2,800	3.26	9,128
Am-Salt	7,600	3.26	24,776
	14,000		$45,640

[a] Joint costs ($45,640) ÷ pounds produced (14,000)

=================== **Exhibit 2-15** ===================

Amaco Chemical Company
Allocation of Joint Costs
Relative Sales Value Method

Part B.

Relative sales value for Amanyl:

   3,600 pounds produced × $6.65 sales price
per pound is **$23,940**

Relative sales value for Bonanyl:

Beginning inventory Bonanyl	210
Units added	2,800
Total	3,010
Ending inventory	110
Pounds of Bonanyl used	**2,900**

Yield of Bonanyl-X from Bonanyl
is 0.95 (2,755 ÷ 2,900)

Sales value of Bonanyl-X from 2,800 pounds of Bonanyl (2,800 × .95 × $4.20)	$11,172
Conversion cost (department 2) per pound of Bonanyl-X ($3,306 ÷ 2,755) × current yield (2,800 × .95)	3,192
Relative sales value for Bonanyl	**$ 7,980**

Relative sales value for Am-Salt:

   7,600 pounds produced × $6.30 sales price
per pound is **$47,880**

Product	Relative sales value	Allocation percentage	Total joint costs	Total pounds	Cost per pound
Amanyl	$23,940	30.	$13,692	3,600	$3.80
Bonanyl	7,980	10.	4,564	2,800	1.63
Am-Salt	47,880	60.	27,384	7,600	3.60
	$79,800	**100**	**$45,640**		

The calculation for Amanyl cost per pound is:

$$\underbrace{\frac{\$23,940}{\$79,800}}_{\substack{\text{Relative} \\ \text{sales value}}} = 30\% \times \underbrace{\$45,640}_{\substack{\text{Total joint} \\ \text{costs}}} = \$13,692 \div \underbrace{3,600}_{\text{Pounds}} = \$3.80$$

Part C.

Cost of Am-Salt	
400 units in beginning inventory × $3.40	$ 1,360
7,000 units from current production (7,600 − 600 in ending inventory) × $3.50	24,500
Total	25,860
Cost of Colb	2,240
Department 3 processing costs	22,400
Total cost	50,500
Less cost of by-product Demanyl ($.54 sales price − $.04 packaging and selling costs × 9,800 units produced)	4,900
Total cost of Colbanyl	45,600
Units produced	÷1,400
Cost per unit	**$32.57**

━━━━━━━━━━━━━━━━━━━━ **Example 2-8** ━━━━━━━━━━━━━━━━━━━━

The Harbison Company manufactures two sizes of plate glass, which are produced simultaneously in the same manufacturing process. Since the small sheets of plate glass are cut from large sheets which have flaws in them, the joint costs are allocated equally to each good sheet, large and small, produced. The difference in after-split-off costs for large and small sheets is material.

In 19X1 the Company decided to increase its efforts to sell the large sheets because they produced a larger gross margin than the small sheets. Accordingly, the amount of the fixed advertising budget devoted to large sheets was increased and the amount devoted to small sheets was decreased. However, no changes in sales prices were made.

By mid-year the production scheduling department had increased the monthly production of large sheets in order to stay above the minimum inventory level. However, it also had cut back the monthly production of small sheets because the inventory ceiling had been reached.

At the end of 19X1, the net result of the change in product mix was a decrease of $112,000 in gross margin. Although sales of large sheets had increased 34,500 units, sales of small sheets had decreased 40,200 units.

Required   A. Distinguish between joint costs and

1. After-split-off costs
2. Fixed costs
3. Prime costs
4. Indirect costs

B. Discuss the propriety of allocating joint costs for general purpose financial statements on the basis of

1. Physical measures, such as weights or units
2. Relative sales or market value

C. In the development of weights for allocating joint costs to joint products, why is the relative sales value of each joint product usually reduced by its after-split-off costs.

D. Identify the mistake that the Harbison Company made in deciding to change its product mix and explain why it caused a smaller gross margin for 19X1.

━━━━━━━━━━━━━━━━━━━━ **Exhibit 2-16** ━━━━━━━━━━━━━━━━━━━━

A. 1. Joint costs are the costs of a production process that by its basic nature-not by managerial decision-simultaneously manufactures two or more products of significant relative sales value. After-split-off costs, on the other hand, are costs that can be attributed to one of the joint products after it has emerged from the common process.

2. Only some—not all—joint costs are fixed costs, costs that do not vary directly with volume. Many joint costs do vary directly with volume.

3. Only some—not all—joint costs are prime costs, which are defined as direct material and direct labor costs. Some joint costs are overhead costs.

4. Although indirect costs and joint costs include the same cost elements and cannot be identified with a single unit of product or batch, indirect costs can pertain to a process that produces only one product. As mentioned above, joint costs pertain only to a production process that by its basic nature simultaneously manufactures two or more products of significant relative sales value.

B. 1. Physical measures generally can incorporate the relevant characteristics of raw materials and labor inputs, production rate, and output of the production process since joint costs usually are related to these factors.

Since joint products emerge from a single production process, each unit of output might be assigned an equal share of the joint costs by basing the allocation on the number of units of output produced. This measure could be modified to include the rate of production for each joint product. Another modification could include the weight of the output, a factor that would emphasize the amount (and, hence, the cost) of the raw material input that would emerge as output.

In the situation where one physical measure or a combination of physical measures results in allocations related closely to the revenue-producing power of each joint product, the physical measures may be preferred because joint costs are related to physical factors and because the measures were readily available. In other situations where the selling price is not sufficient to recover such an allocation, one may object to the artificial product "losses" that are created by the allocation basis. Any method, however, is essentially arbitrary and is only as valid as the premise which underlies it. The combined revenues and joint costs of the products are unchanged by the selection of an allocation basis.

2. For those situations in which allocations based on physical measures are misleading, the relative sales value method may be used to avoid implying that management has erred in manufacturing a joint product which has an essentially allocated cost per unit in excess of its sales value per unit. Since a joint product can be eliminated only by long-run actions such as altering raw material composition or the manufacturing process itself, in the short run management usually is limited to determining when the joint product can make the greatest contribution to the recovery of joint costs and overhead: at the time of the split-off or after being processed further. The use of the relative sales value method does not make the short-run issue clear, but it does hedge against a very misleading inference. In assigning costs in proportion to the product's ability to absorb the costs, the method presumes that each joint product should yield a profit under typical marketing conditions.

The relative-sales-value method also presumes a direct relationship between selling price and common costs (particularly to raw materials costs), but this relationship may be altered significantly by scarcity, consumer wants, or market strategy. Hence, this presumption may or may not be valid, depending on the situation.

C. In the development of weights for allocating joint costs to joint products, the relative sales values of joint products usually are reduced by after-split-off costs because the contri-

— continued —

Exhibit 2-16, *continued*

bution of each product to the recovery of joint costs and overhead is the best measure of each product's ability to absorb these costs. Only for the situation in which the after-split-off costs are immaterial or are the same for each joint product is the adjustment unnecessary.

D. The Corporation's decision to emphasize sales of large sheets was based upon the relative sizes of the gross margins for large sheets and small sheets. Because every good sheet finished was assigned an equal share of the joint costs, the relatively higher sales price of the large sheet naturally produced a larger gross margin than the relatively lower sales price of the small sheets. Hence an invalid inference about how to increase profits was made.

The Corporation evidently did not realize that as long as the selling price was higher than variable after-split-off costs, as many of the small sheets of plate glass as possible should

have been sold in order to increase the contribution to the recovery of joint costs and overhead.

When the maximum inventory level for small sheets was reached, the production of small sheets was cut back. If the flawed sheets which emerged from the process were not cut into small sheets and polished for sale, the joint costs of the flawed sheets had to be allocated to the good sheets that were finished (a large proportion of which must have been large, perfect sheets of plate glass). The cost of the large sheets was increased and, when matched with revenue earned at the time of sale, resulted in a lower gross margin.

The reallocation of the fixed advertising budget may have contributed to the change in product mix. There is also the possibility that the market for small sheets, at least to some extent, was interrelated with the market for large sheets. In some cases, one may have been a substitute for the other.

Example 2-9

A. Distinguish between the meanings of joint product and by-product.

B. Describe and briefly discuss the appropriateness of two acceptable methods of accounting for the by-product in determination of the cost of the joint products.

C. Assuming proper treatment of the by-product costs, describe two acceptable methods of allocating to joint products the cost of the initial producing department.

Solution A. Joint products represent two or more products separated in the course of the same processing operation (derived from a common source of materials) each usually requiring further processing and each product having such relative value that no one product can be designated as a major product.

By-product is an article relatively minor in terms of value derived incidental to the production or manufacture of one or more major products.

B. Acceptable methods of accounting for the by-product in the determination of the cost of the major products are:

1. To allocate all producing costs to the major products, ignoring the recovery value of the by-product. The recovery value would be treated as "other income," included with major product sales, or as a deduction from cost of sales of the main product. This method would be acceptable only when there would be very little value in the by-product and the use of a more detailed method would entail accounting costs disproportionate to the benefits derived.

2. To treat either the proceeds from the sale of the by-product or the anticipated net yield of residuals (by-products) as a reduction in the total production costs of main products. This method reflects a lower valuation of major product inventories.

3. To assign to the by-product the replacement cost of the by-product. This method is peculiar to those industries that are able to use the by-product produced within the plant, thus eliminating the purchase of materials from outside vendors. Production costs of the main product are relieved by the amount of the replacement cost of the by-product.

C. Acceptable methods of allocating to joint products the cost of the initial producing department are:

1. To allocate joint costs on the basis of the relative selling prices of the end products. The argument is that if one product sells for more than another, it is because it costs more to produce.

2. To allocate joint costs on the basis of some unit of measurement, such as units, pounds, tons or gallons. If the joint products are not measurable, they must be converted to a denominator that is common to all the units produced.

3. To allocate joint costs on the basis of a survey in which consideration is given to factors such as volume, selling price, technical engineering, and marketing processes.

4. To allocate joint costs on the basis of the profit margin for "profit contribution" remaining after deduction of all direct costs and expenses from the selling price. This method is a variation of the market price method described above.

In a cost system where JIT purchasing is adopted, Foster and Horngren[11] suggest five changes that would be realized:

1. Increase in direct traceability of costs. In a traditional cost system many of the materials handling and warehouse costs are incurred for multipurpose facilities that service

many product lines. Thus, these costs are often considered indirect costs. In a JIT environment, warehouse and materials handling facilities would be more decentralized, often serving a single retail or production area. Thus, these costs would now be direct costs of a retail area or production line.

2. Changes in the cost pools used to accumulate costs. For

11. *Ibid.*, p. 21.

example, the pool used to allocate materials handling costs discussed above would be eliminated.

3. Changes in the bases used to allocate indirect costs to production departments. Under the traditional cost system, costs such as materials handling and warehouse costs might be allocated based on warehouse space. Dollar value of materials or number of deliveries may "better capture the cause and effect relationship between purchasing/materials handling activities and indirect cost incurrance."[12]

4. Reduced emphasis on individual purchase price variance information. Companies in a JIT environment often have long term agreements to achieve price reduction. Thus, there is no need to record price variance in the accounts. Emphasis is placed on total cost of operations. Quality and availability are important considerations in selecting a supplier.

5. Need to reduce the frequency or detail of reporting of purchase deliveries in the internal accounting system. The number of deliveries in a JIT environment are large. Foster and Horngren[13] identify two ways that are used to reduce entries. One is to use batching and only record the aggregate of deliveries for a set time period such as weekly. Another is to use an electronic transfer system where the initial purchase order (or delivery schedule) automatically sets up the data transfer at the delivery date and then transfers the funds at the payment date.

In JIT production "each component on a production line is produced immediately as needed by the next step in the production line. . . . The production line is run on a demand-pull basis, so that activity at each work station is authorized by the demand of downstream work stations.[14]

In a JIT environment emphasis is placed on reducing the time it takes once the production has started until it leaves the production line. This is also referred to as cycle time. If a problem develops in the manufacturing process, such as a defective product, the production line is stopped until the problem is corrected. No value is created by building up inventories on the other parts of the production line. Since there are no inventory build-up on the production line, a problem discovered on the production line results in a smaller quantity be reworked or discarded.

Companies that adopt JIT production often rearrange the layout of their plants to provide for very little materials handling. The objective is to eliminate as much as possible of the cost of production that does not add value to the product such as material handling and carrying cost for inventories. The production lines are often "U" shaped where the raw materials are delivered directly to the start of the production line as they are needed. The materials move, often by the use of conveyer belts, from one station to another until the product is finished near the point where the process started. The finished products are then available for direct shipment to the customer.

In summary, a just-in-time production system allows companies to be customer oriented and minimizes non-value added

costs. Orders, not inventory size, drive the production process. Goods are not produced until they are needed for shipment to the customer. Zero inventory should be a major objective of a manufacturing firm because holding inventory adds no value to the product—thus, provides no customer satisfaction.

Activity-Based Costing (ABC)

For years, manufacturing firms used direct labor hours as the primary cost driver to apply overhead costs to products. A **cost driver** is the activity that causes the cost to be incurred. In today's manufacturing process, a single firm produces hundreds or thousands of products. With plants becoming highly automated, direct labor is no longer an adequate cost driver. Direct labor was realistic when labor cost accounted for the majority of the production costs. Currently, labor cost is often less than 10 percent of the total manufacturing cost. Even machine-hours and raw material content, when applied to all parts of the factory, are too simplistic.

To better control cost, many firms have adopted **activity-based costing (ABC)**. Activity-based costing has been designed for firms that manufacture numerous products and want accurate product costing. The emphasis of ABC is to trace the overhead cost to the product that benefited from the cost. Johnson and Kaplan[15] identify activity-based costing as a two-step process. The first step requires tracing costs according to their activities, dividing them into homogeneous pools, and determining appropriate cost drivers. Following are some examples:

Activity	Cost Driver
Material handling	Number of components
Purchasing raw materials	Quality of materials used in production
Production set-up	Number of set-ups
Packing and shipping	Number of orders
Special works	Number of new products

The second step requires applying the costs of these activities to the product by calculating a rate for the cost driver for each pool. To illustrate the second step, assume that Packaging Department uses number of orders processed as a cost driver and that $100,000 was spent for 10,000 orders being processed. The pool rate would be $10 per order processes ($100,000/10,000). Similar calculations would be made for other overhead costs using appropriate cost drivers. To use direct labor hours for packaging results in arbitrary allocation of overhead cost, which often results in inappropriate management decisions.

To contrast activity-based costing with direct labor cost allocation, assume that Oaks Publishing Corporation publishes three books, *Urban Farming, Exercising for Fun,* and *How to Be Your Own Boss.* The following data have been accumulated for each product to estimate setup costs.

---

12. *Ibid.*
13. *Ibid.*, p. 22.
14. *Ibid.*

15. H. Thomas Johnson and Robert S. Kaplan, *Relevance Lost: The Rise and Fall of Management Accounting* (Boston: Harvard Business School Press, 1987), p. 238.

	Urban Farming	Exercising for Fun	How to Be Your Own Boss
Units produced	2,000	40,000	100,000
Typical batch size	200	1,000	20,000
Number of set-ups	10	40	5
Total direct labor hours	400	8,000	18,000

Urban Farming (10 x $300) .... $ 3,000
Exercising for Fun (40 x $300) 12,000
How to Be Your Own Boss (5 x $300) 1,500
Setup Costs $16,500

In this example, direct labor hours for all three books total 28,400 hours; therefore, using direct labor hours as the cost driver results in each unit printed being assigned setup costs at the rate of $.625 direct labor hour ($16,500/26,400 DLH). Using ABC, the setup cost per unit for each book varies from $.015 to $1.50 per unit.

	Urban Farming	Exercising for Fun	How to Be Your Own Boss
Total setup cost (a)	$3,000	$12,000	$1,500
Units produced (b)	2,000	40,000	100,000
Cost per unit (a/b)	$1.50	$.30	$.015

A comparison between total setup costs for the two cost drivers is shown below.

	DLH	ABC
Urban Farming:		
400 DLH @ $.625	$ 250	
10 setups @ $300		$ 3,000
Exercising for Fun:		
8,000 KLH @ $.625	5,000	
40 setups @ $300		12,000
How to Be Your Own Boss:		
18,000 DLH @ $.116	11,250	
5 setups @ 300		1,500
	$16,500	$16,500

Activity-based costing is an effective approach to properly assigning cost and it is not limited to manufacturing overhead. Administrative expenses also can be allocated to the product using this approach. Activity-based costing may help management focus on costs that don't add value.

For example, purchasing could have some of its costs allocated to the product based on the number of unusual parts ordered. This would encourage more standardization of parts. A car manufacturer's engineering department might be influenced to redesign the air filter space so that fewer filter configurations would have to be purchased, if the cost of storage is traced and attached to engineering.

Activity-based costing, like other methods, has its strengths and weaknesses. Kaplan[16], in defending ABC, wrote "ABC systems provide valuable economic information to companies, especially companies active in process improvement and customer satisfaction.' He added,

> ABC models provide an economic model of the organization that enables managers to set priorities, make tradeoffs, determine the extent of the investment they are willing to undertake for improvements, and, at the end of the day... learn whether these programs have increased profits.[17]

In an article criticizing the overselling of ABC, Johnson conceded that ABC succeeded in increasing profits and reducing cost. However, he concluded that ABC failed to make businesses more responsive to their customers, especially in light of what the global competition was doing. In his concluding comments, he summarized his thoughts by writing:

> Activity-based cost drivers information overcomes distortions inherent in traditional cost accounting information... Activity-based information, however, does not help companies achieve continuous improvement of globally competitive operations.[18]

Major Trends

Howell and Soucy[19] identify six major trends that are taking place among leading U.S. manufacturers.

1. Higher quality — Foreign competitors have provided markets with higher quality goods at competitive prices than U.S. manufacturers. U.S. companies have also realized that poor quality is a significant cost driver. For example, poor quality materials, the lack of highly trained employees, and the failure to properly maintain equipment have resulted in lower quality products. At the same time the cost to manufacture these products has been high because of the increased cost of nonquality items such as scrap, rework, excess inventories and equipment breakdowns, field service and product warranty claims.

2. Lower inventory — Inventory has been reduced because it required too much capital, it encouraged inefficiencies and it failed to provide a basis for properly controlling quality.

3. Flexible flow lines — Flexible flow lines represent the path a product takes through the manufacturing process from the receipt of raw materials to the shipment of the product. Manufacturers are shortening cycle time. To accomplish this all of the equipment needed in the manufacturing process are brought together (thus, large groups of similar equipment are split up) and "mini" product lines are created. This layout reduces significantly the materials handling cost and the amount of funds needed for inventory. This process allows the product to flow through the process in a very short time and reinforces quality and employee identification with the end product. With the short cycle time customer demand then is responsible for pulling the product through the process as discussed above.

4. Automation — By developing flexible flow lines, the manufacturer automation, if it is cost effective, is directed toward the part of the process that adds value rather than focusing on items that do not add value such as automation of materials handling. In evaluating automation, the focus, in addition to direct cost savings, should be on improved quality, delivery service and flexibility, reduced product development time, and improved competitive position. In fact, the manufacturer should attempt to quantify these factors in making automation decisions.

5. Product line organization — There should be a scaling down of centralized service departments and reassigning

16. Robert S. Kaplan, "In Defense of Activity-Based Cost Management," *Management Accountant,* November 1992, p. 58.
17. *Ibid,* p. 63.
18. H. Thomas Johnson, "It's Time to Stop Overselling Activity-Based Concepts," *Management Accountant,* September 1992, p.33.
19. Robert A. Howell and Stephen Soucy, *Factory 2000+: Management Accounting's Changing Role* (Montvale, N.J.: National Association of Accountants, 1988) pp. 2-6.

**TABLE 1/
OPERATING MEASURES IN THE NEW
MANUFACTURING ENVIRONMENT**

Quality

Customer complaints
Customer surveys
Warranty claims
Quality audits
Vendor quality
Cost of quality
  Scrap
  Rework
  Returns and allowances
  Field service
  Warranty claims
  Lost business

Inventory

Turnover rates by location
  Raw materials
  Work-in-process
  Finished goods
  Composite
Turnover rates by product
Cycle count accuracy
Space reduction
Number of inventoried items

Material/Scrap

Quality—incoming material inspection
Material cost as a percentage of total cost
Actual scrap loss
Scrap by part/product/operation
Scrap percentage of total cost

Equipment/Maintenance

Equipment capacity/utilization
Availability/downtime
Machine maintenance
Equipment experience

Delivery/Throughput

On-time delivery
Order fill rate
Lead time—order to shipment
Waste time—lead time less process time
Cycle time—material receipt to product shipment
Set-up time
Production backlog (in total and by product)

people directly to the product lines.

6. Efficient use of information technology — Integrated systems are being developed that allow companies to exercise more control over the factory floor. A single data base is needed that allows use for both operating control and financial reporting purposes.

Updated Cost Systems

In the new manufacturing environment, the measures used in the traditional accounting system (labor utilization, standard versus actual performance and overhead absorption) are inadequate. The cost accountant must look at key factors critical to each particular process. These factors will vary from one process to another. The reporting of key factors by the accountant will allow the workers to more efficiently manage the

process for which they are responsible. The operating measures that could serve as the basis for reporting are classified by Howell and Soucy[20] as follows:

1. Quality
2. Inventory
3. Material/Scrap
4. Equipment/Maintenance
5. Delivery/Throughput

These factors along with several measures that might be used to evaluate performance are presented in Table 1.[21]

20. *Ibid*, pp. 15-21.
21. *Ibid*, p. 21.

Problems

1. The term "conversion costs" refers to

a. manufacturing costs incurred to produce units of output.
b. all costs associated with manufacturing other than direct labor costs and raw material costs.
c. costs which are associated with marketing, shipping, warehousing, billing activities.
d. the sum of direct labor costs and all factory overhead costs.
e. the sum of raw material costs and direct labor costs.

2. The term "prime costs" refers to

a. manufacturing costs incurred to produce units of output.
b. all costs associated with manufacturing other than direct labor costs and raw material costs.
c. costs which are predetermined and should be attained.
d. the sum of direct labor costs and all factory overhead costs.
e. the sum of raw material costs and direct labor costs.

3. Costs which are inventoriable are

a. manufacturing costs incurred to produce units of output.
b. all costs associated with manufacturing other than direct labor costs and raw material costs.
c. costs which are associated with marketing, shipping, warehousing, billing activities.
d. the sum of direct labor costs and all factory overhead costs.
e. the sum of raw material costs and direct costs.

4. The term "variable costs" refers to

a. all costs which are likely to respond to the amount of attention devoted to them by a specified manager.
b. all costs which are associated with marketing, shipping, warehousing, billing activities.
c. all costs which do not change in total for a given period of time and relevant range but become progressively smaller on a per unit basis as volume increases.
d. all manufacturing costs incurred to produce units of output.
e. all costs which fluctuate in total in response to small changes in the rate of utilization of capacity.

5. The term "committed costs" refers to those

a. costs which management decides to incur in the current period to enable the company to achieve objectives other than the filling of orders placed by customers.
b. costs which are likely to respond to the amount of attention devoted to them by a specified manager.
c. costs which are governed mainly by past decisions that established the present levels of operating and organizational capacity and which only change slowly in response to small changes in capacity.
d. costs which fluctuate in total in response to small changes in the rate of utilization of capacity.
e. amortization of costs which were capitalized in previous periods.

6. The term "discretionary costs" refers to those

a. costs which management decides to incur in the current period to enable the company to achieve objectives other than the filling of orders placed by customers.
b. costs which are likely to respond to the amount of attention devoted to them by a specified manager.
c. costs which are governed mainly by past decisions that established the present levels of operating and organizational capacity and which only change slowly in response to small changes in capacity.
d. amortization of costs which were capitalized in previous periods.
e. costs which will be unaffected by current managerial decisions.

7. Those costs referred to as "controllable costs" are

a. costs which management decides to incur in the current period to enable the company to achieve objectives other than the filling of orders placed by customers.
b. costs which are likely to respond to the amount of attention devoted to them by a specified manager.
c. costs which are governed mainly by past decisions that established the present levels of operating and organizational capacity and which only change slowly in response to small changes in capacity.
d. costs which fluctuate in total in response to small changes in the rate of utilization of capacity.
e. costs which will be unaffected by current managerial decisions.

The following data apply to items 8–11.

Selected data concerning the past fiscal year's operations (000 omitted) of the Televans Manufacturing Company are presented below:

	Inventories	
	Beginning	Ending
Raw materials	$75	$ 85
Work-in process	80	30
Finished goods	90	110

Other Data

Raw materials used	$326
Total manufacturing costs charged to production during the year (includes raw materials, direct labor, and factory overhead applied at a rate of 60% of direct labor cost)	686
Cost of goods available for sale	826
Selling and general expenses	25

8. The cost of raw materials purchased during the year amounted to

a. $411.
b. $360.
c. $316.
d. $336.
e. some other amount.

9. Direct labor costs charged to production during the year amounted to.

a. $135.
b. $225.
c. $360.
d. $216.
e. some other amount.

10. The cost of goods manufactured during the year was

a. $636.
b. $766.
c. $736.
d. $716.
e. some other amount.

11. The cost of goods sold during the year was

a. $736.
b. $716.
c. $691.
d. $801.
e. some other amount.

The Following Data Apply to Items 12-14.

Marlan Manufacturing produces a product that passes through two departments. The units from the Molding Department are completed in the Assembly Department. The units are completed in Assembly by adding the remaining direct materials when the units are 60 percent complete with respect to conversion costs. Conversion costs are added proportionately in Assembly. The production activity in the Assembly Department for the current month is presented below. Marlan uses the FIFO (first-in, first-out) inventory method in its process cost system.

Beginning inventory units (25% complete with respect to conversion costs)	8,000
Units transferred in from the Molding Department during the month	42,000
Units to account for	50,000
Units completed and transferred to finished goods inventory	38,000
Ending inventory units (40% complete with respect to conversion costs)	12,000
Units accounted for	50,000

12. The equivalent units transferred from the Molding Department to the Assembly Department for the current month would be

a. 30,000 units.
b. 38,000 units.
c. 40,800 units.
d. 42,000 units.
e. 50,000 units.

13. The equivalent units in the Assembly Department for direct materials for the current month would be

a. 30,000 units.
b. 38,000 units.
c. 40,800 units.
d. 42,000 units.
e. 50,000 units.

14. The equivalent units in the Assembly Department for conversion costs for the current month would be

a. 36,800 units.
b. 40,800 units.
c. 42,800 units.
d. 43,200 units.
e. 45,200 units.

15. In recent years, much attention has been placed on product quality and total quality control. Which one of the following items would not normally be considered a cost of quality?

a. Costs incurred in preventing production of defective units.

b. Costs incurred in detecting defective products during production.

c. Costs incurred in detecting defective products produced before they are shipped to customers.

d. Costs incurred after defective products have been shipped to customers.

e. Costs incurred in shortening product lead times and achieving on-time deliveries.

16. Costs are allocated to cost objectives in many ways and for many reasons. Which one of the following is a purpose of cost allocation?

a. Evaluating revenue center performance.
b. Measuring income and assets for external reporting.
c. Budgeting cash and controlling expenditures.
d. Aiding in variable costing for internal reporting.
e. Implementing activity-based costing.

17. In allocating factory service department costs to producing departments, which one of the following items would most likely be used as an activity base?

a. Units of product sold.
b. Salary of service department employees.
c. Units of electric power consumed.
d. Direct materials usage.
e. Units of finished goods shipped to customers.

18. In joint-product costing and analysis, which one of the following costs is relevant when deciding the point at which a product should be sold in order to maximize profits?

a. Separable costs after the split-off point.
b. Joint costs to the split-off point.
c. Sales salaries for the period when the units were produced.
d. Purchase costs of the materials required for the joint products.
e. The company president's salary.

The Following Data Apply to Items 19 - 22.

Levittown Company employs a process cost system for its manufacturing operations. All direct materials are added at the beginning of the process and conversion costs are added proportionately. Levittown's production quantity schedule for November is reproduced below.

	Units
Work-in-process on November 1, 1986	
(60% complete as to conversion costs)	1,000
Units started during November	5,000
Total units to account for	6,000
Units completed and transferred out	
from beginning inventory	1,000
Units started and completed during November	3,000
Work-in-process on November 30, 1986	
(20% complete as to conversion costs)	2,000
Total units accounted for	6,000

19. Using the FIFO method, the equivalent units for direct materials for November are

a. 5,000 units.
b. 6,000 units.
c. 4,400 units.
d. 3,800 units.
e. some amount other than those given above.

20. Using the FIFO method, the equivalent units for conversion costs for November are

a. 3,400 units.
b. 3,800 units.
c. 4,000 units.
d. 4,400 units.
e. some amount other than those given above.

21. Using the weighted-average method, the equivalent units for direct materials for November are

a. 3,400 units.
b. 4,400 units.
c. 5,000 units.
d. 6,000 units.
e. some amount other than those given above.

22. Using the weighted-average method, the equivalent units for conversion costs for November are

a. 3,400 units.
b. 3,800 units.
c. 4,000 units.
d. 4,400 units.
e. some amount other than those given above.

The Following Data Apply to Items 23 and 24.

Pardise Company budgets on an annual basis for its fiscal year. The following beginning and ending inventory levels (in units) are planned for the fiscal year of July 1, 1986, through June 30, 1987.

	July 1, 1986	June 30, 1987
Raw material*	40,000	50,000
Work in process	10,000	10,000
Finished goods	80,000	50,000

*Two (2) units of raw material are needed to produce each unit of finished product.

23. If Pardise Company plans to sell 480,000 units during the 1986-87 fiscal year, the number of units it would have to manufacture during the year would be

a. 440,000 units.
b. 480,000 units.
c. 510,000 units.
d. 450,000 units.
e. some amount other than those given above.

24. If 500,000 finished units were to be manufactured during the 1986-87 fiscal year by Pardise Company, the units of raw material needed to be purchased would be

a. 1,000,000 units.
b. 1,020,000 units.
c. 1,010,000 units.
d. 990,000 units.
e. some amount other than those given above.

The Following Data Apply to Items 25 - 28.

The managers of Rochester Manufacturing are discussing ways to allocate the cost of service departments such as Quality Control and Maintenance to the production departments. To aid them in this discussion, the controller has provided the information on the following page.

25. If Rochester Manufacturing uses the direct method of allocating service department costs, the total service costs allocated to the Assembly Department would be

a. $80,000.
b. $87,500.
c. $120,000.
d. $167,500.
e. $467,500.

	Quality Control	Maintenance	Machining	Assembly	Total
Budgeted overhead costs before allocation	$350,000	$200,000	$400,000	$300,000	$1,250,000
Budgeted machine hours	——	——	50,000	——	50,000
Budgeted direct labor hours	——	——	——	25,000	25,000
Budgeted hours of service:					
Quality Control	——	7,000	21,000	7,000	35,000
Maintenance	10,000	——	18,000	12,000	40,000

26. Using the direct method, the total amount of overhead allocated to each machine hour at Rochester Manufacturing would be

a. $2.40.
b. $5.25.
c. $8.00.
d. $9.35.
e. $15.65.

27. If Rochester Manufacturing decides not to allocate service costs to the production departments, the overhead allocated to each direct labor hour in the Assembly Department would be

a. $3.20.
b. $3.50.
c. $12.00.
d. $16.00.
e. $18.70.

28. If Rochester Manufacturing uses the step-down method of allocating service costs beginning with Quality Control, the Maintenance costs allocated to the Assembly Department would be

a. $70,000.
b. $108,000.
c. $162,000.
d. $200,000.
e. $210,000.

2.   Estimated time 30 minutes (December 1992)

Richport Company manufactures products that often require specification changes or modifications to meet its customers' needs. Consequently, Richport employs a job order cost system for its operations.

While specification changes and modifications are commonplace, Richport still has been able to establish a normal spoilage rate of two and one-half percent (.025) of normal input. Normal spoilage is recognized during the budgeting process and classified as a component of manufacturing over-

head. Thus, the predetermined overhead rate that is used to apply indirect manufacturing costs to jobs includes an allowance for net spoilage cost for normal spoilage. If spoilage on a job exceeds the normal rate, it is considered abnormal. Then the spoilage has to be analyzed, and a report explaining the cause of the spoilage has to be submitted to management.

Rose Duncan, one of Richport's inspection managers, has been reviewing the output of Job No. N1192-122 that has recently been completed. A total of 122,000 units had been started, and 5,000 units were rejected at final inspection yielding 117,000 good units.

Duncan noted that 900 of the first units produced were rejected due to a design defect that was considered very unusual; this defect was corrected immediately, and no further units were rejected for this reason. These units were disposed of at an additional cost of $1,200 to Richport.

Duncan was unable to identify a rejection pattern for the remaining 4,100 rejected units. These units can be sold at a salvage value of $7.00 per unit.

The total costs accumulated for all 122,000 units of Job No. N1192-122 are presented below. While the job has been completed, all of these costs are still in the work-in-process control account, i.e., the cost of the completed job has not been transferred to finished goods.

Direct material	$2,196,000
Direct labor	1,830,000
Applied manufacturing overhead	2,928,000
Total cost of job	$6,954,000

Required   A. Explain the distinction between normal and abnormal spoilage.

B. Distinguish between

1. spoiled units,
2. reworked units, and
3. scrap.

C. Review the results and costs for Job No. N1192-122 of Richport Company.

1. Prepare an analysis showing the breakdown of spoiled units between normal and abnormal spoilage by first determining

the normal input required to yield 117,000 good units.

2. Prepare the appropriate journal entry (or entries) to properly account for Job No. N1192-122 including spoilage, salvage, disposal, and/or transfer of costs to the finished goods control account.

---

3.   Estimated time 30 minutes (June 1991)

Kristina Company, which manufactures quality paint sold at premium prices, uses a single production department. Production begins with the blending of various chemicals, which are added at the beginning of the process, and ends with the canning of the paint. Canning occurs when the mixture reaches the 90 percent stage of completion. The gallon cans are then transferred to the Shipping Department for crating and shipment. Labor and overhead are added continuously throughout the process. Factory overhead is applied on the basis of direct labor hours at the rate of $3.00 per hour.

Prior to May, when a change in the process was implemented, work-in-process inventories were insignificant. The change in the process enables greater production out results in material amounts of work-in-process for the first time. The company has always used the weighted average method to determine equivalent production and unit costs. Now, production management is considering changing from the weighted average method to the first-in, first-out method.

The following data relate to actual production during the month of May.

```
                  Costs for May

Work-in-process inventory, May 1
    (4,000 gallons 25% complete)
    Direct materials-chemicals          $ 45,600
    Direct labor ($10 per hour)            6,250
    Factory overhead                       1,875

May costs added
    Direct materials-chemicals           228,400
    Direct materials-cans                  7,000
    Direct labor ($10 per hour)           35,000
    Factory overhead                      10,500


                  Units for May

                                        Gallons
Work-in-process inventory,
    May 1 (25% complete)                  4,000
Sent to Shipping Department              20,000
Started in May                           21,000
Work-in-process inventory,
    May 31 (80% complete)                 5,000
```

Required   A. Prepare a schedule of equivalent units for each cost element for the month of May using the

1. weighted average method.
2. first-in, first-out method.

B. Calculate the cost (to the nearest cent) per equivalent unit for each cost element for the month of May using the

1. weighted average method.
2. first-in, first-out method.

C. Discuss the advantages and disadvantages of using the weighted average method versus the first-in, first-out method, and explain under what circumstances each method should be used.

---

4.   Estimated time 60 minutes (June 1993)

Franzel Company manufactures several different models of luggage in its four manufacturing departments. These four departments and one service department (Equipment Maintenance) are housed in one facility. Due to the distinctive characteristics of the costs and operations of the different manufacturing departments, departmental manufacturing overhead rates are employed for each manufacturing department.

Franzel has been reviewing its operations and plans to implement some changes in the budgeting and reporting for the manufacturing departments during the next fiscal year. The Molding Department is being reviewed first, and its cost and operating data for six months of the current fiscal year are presented in the chart below.

This information has been accumulated to assist in developing the manufacturing overhead budget for the coming year; all of these costs are traceable (direct) costs of the Molding Department except for a portion of the fixed costs and the equipment maintenance costs. The fixed costs include the common building and operating costs which are allocated to each of the manufacturing departments on the basis of square feet. The Equipment Maintenance Department costs are charged to the operating departments for services rendered. These costs represent the actual cost of parts and supplies ($150,000 current fiscal year) plus a charge of $50 per hour. The manager of the Equipment Maintenance Department determines the preventive maintenance schedule for each of the production departments; all other repairs are made on a "first come, first served" basis.

Management is comfortable with using the six-month data as the basis for the preliminary budget estimates because most of the activity measures and costs appear to be representative. However, the following adjustments will have to be made for the coming year.

Cost Item	Cost Adjustment
Indirect labor	Cost increase of 8 percent
Equipment maintenance	Cost increase of 10 percent for parts, supplies, and the hourly charge
Fixed costs	$360,000 per month

In the past, the overhead application base in the Molding Department has been machine hours for all costs. However, management has used scattergraphs to analyze the behavior of

Molding Department
Manufacturing Overhead Activity Measures and Actual Costs

	January	February	March	April	May	June
Activity measures:						
Pounds of material	25,000	27,000	30,000	24,000	20,000	22,000
Machine hours	11,500	13,500	12,500	8,500	9,500	10,000
Units produced	50,000	45,000	52,000	42,000	48,000	40,000
Machine setups	15	20	16	18	19	21
Material handling						
costs ($1.40/lb.)	$ 35,000	$ 37,800	$ 42,000	$ 33,600	$ 28,000	$ 30,800
Setup costs	11,500	15,250	12,000	14,000	14,500	22,750
Machine hour costs						
Indirect labor						
($5/machine hr.)	57,500	67,500	62,500	42,500	47,500	50,000
Power ($.20/kwhr.)	21,250	24,250	22,750	16,750	18,250	19,000
Equipment maintenance	15,000	18,000	12,000	19,000	16,000	35,000
Fixed costs	335,000	335,000	335,000	335,000	335,000	335,000
Total overhead	$475,250	$497,800	$486,250	$460,850	$459,250	$492,550

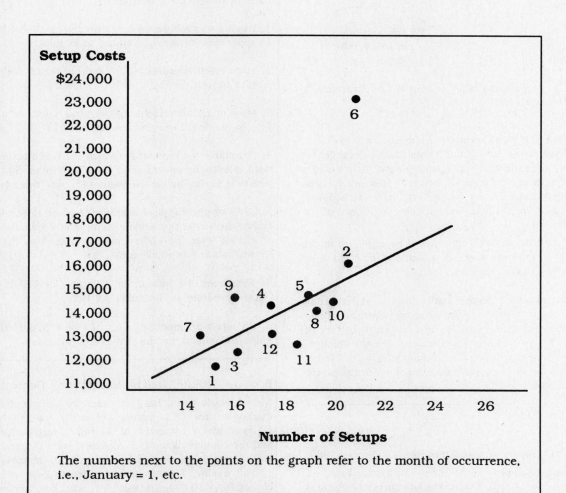

The numbers next to the points on the graph refer to the month of occurrence, i.e., January = 1, etc.

some costs and has concluded that there is more than one cost driver in this department. As shown in the preceding scattergraph which captures data for the 12-month period through June of this year, the number of setups clearly represents the behavior of the setup costs and is now the application base for these costs. Similarly, the cost driver that is most appropriate as an application base for material handlng costs is pounds of material processes. Machine hours will continue to be used as an application base for the remaining costs of the Molding Department.

John Stein, vice president of manufacturing, has indicated that he wants to employ a responsibility accounting system where each manufacturing department will be held accountable for all costs included in its manufacturing overhead budget. Actual monthly costs will be compared to the annual budget, and each department will be expected to come in at or below budgeted monthly costs.

Based on the production budgets, the activity measures for the Molding Department will be at the following levels for the coming fiscal year.

Activity Measure	Estimated Annual Amount
Pounds of material	280,000 pounds
Machine hours	135,000 hours
Units produced	520,000 units
Machine setups	200 setups
Power usage	2.5 kilowatt hours per unit produced
Equipment maintenance	1,600 hours

Required   A. Identify the benefits of using scattergraphs in analyzing cost behavior.

B. 1. Using the cost data presented for the six-month period of the current year, adjusted for the estimated changes expected to occur and the estimated activity measures for the coming year, develop a manufacturing overhead budget for the Molding Department for the coming year. Use the high-low method to determine the fixed and variable components of the setup costs.

2. Develop the overhead rate that should be employed in the Molding Department for the coming year for the costs to be applied on the basis of machine hours.

C. John Stein has recommended that a responsibility reporting system be employed in the manufacturing departments and that departmental managers be held responsible for all manufacturing overhead costs included in the budget. Describe the likely behavior of the manufacturing departmental managers with respect to their accountability for equipment maintenance costs.

---

5.   Estimated time 30 minutes (December 1989)

Valport Company employs a job order cost system based on the full absorption of actual costs. Manufacturing overhead is applied on the basis of machine hours (MH) using a predetermined overhead rate. The current fiscal year rate of $15.00 per MH is based on estimated manufacturing overhead costs of $1,200,000 and an estimated activity level of 80,000 machine hours. Valport's policy is to close the over/under application of manufacturing overhead to the Cost of Goods Sold.

Operations for the year ended November 30, 1989, have been completed, and all of the accounting entries have been made for the year except the application of manufacturing overhead to the jobs worked on during November, the transfer of costs from Work-in-Process to Finished Goods for the jobs completed in November, and the transfer of costs from Finished Goods to Cost of Goods Sold for the jobs that have been sold during November. Summarized data that have been accumulated from the accounting records as of October 31, 1989, and for November 1989, are presented on the next page.

Jobs N11-007, N11-013, and N11-015 were completed during November 1989. All completed jobs except Job N11-013 had been turned over to customers by the close of business on November 30, 1989.

Required   A. Valport Company uses a predetermined overhead rate to apply manufacturing overhead to its jobs. When overhead is accounted for in this manner, there may be over- or underapplied overhead.

1. Explain why a business uses a predetermined overhead rate to apply manufacturing overhead to its jobs.

2. How much manufacturing overhead would Valport have applied to jobs through October 31,1989?

3. How much manufacturing overhead would be applied to jobs by Valport during November 1989?

4. Determine the amount by which the manufacturing overhead is over- or underapplied as of November 30, 1989. Be sure to indicate whether the overhead is over- or underapplied.

5. Over- or underapplied overhead must be eliminated at the end of the accounting period. Explain why Valport's method of closing over- or underapplied overhead to the Cost of Goods Sold is acceptable in this case.

B. Determine the balance in Valport Company's Finished Goods Inventory at November 30, 1989.

C. Prepare a Statement of Cost of Goods Manufactured for Valport Company for the year ended November 30, 1989.

---

6.   Estimated time 30 minutes (December 1990)

Moss Manufacturing has just completed a major change in its quality control (QC) process. Previously, products had been reviewed by QC inspectors at the end of each major process, and the company's ten QC inspectors were charged as direct labor to the operation or job. In an effort to improve efficiency and quality, a computerized video QC system was purchased for $250,000. The system consists of a minicomputer,

Valport Company Data

Work-in-Process		November 1989 Activity		
Job No.	Balance 10/31/89	Direct Materials	Direct Labor	Machine Hours
N11-007	$ 87,000	$ 1,500	$ 4,500	300
N11-013	55,000	4,000	12,000	1,000
N11-015	-0-	25,600	26,700	1,400
D12-002	-0-	37,900	20,000	2,500
D12-003	-0-	26,000	16,800	800
Totals	$142,000	$95,000	$80,000	6,000

Operating Activity	Activity Through 10/31/89	November 1989 Activity
Manufacturing overhead incurred		
Indirect materials	$ 125,000	$ 9,000
Indirect labor	345,000	30,000
Utilities	245,000	22,000
Depreciation	385,000	35,000
Total incurred overhead	$1,100,000	$96,000
Other items		
Material purchases*	$965,000	$98,000
Direct labor costs	$845,000	$80,000
Machine hours	73,000	6,000

Account Balances at Beginning of Fiscal Year	12/01/88
Materials inventory*	$105,000
Work-in-process inventory	60,000
Finished goods inventory	125,000

*Material purchases and materials inventory consist of both direct and indirect materials. The balance of the Materials Inventory account as of November 30, 1989, is $85,000.

15 video cameras, other peripheral hardware, and software.

The new system uses cameras stationed by QC engineers at key points in the production process. Each time an operation changes or there is a new operation, the cameras are moved, and a new master picture is loaded into the computer by a QC engineer. The camera takes pictures of the units in process, and the computer compares them to the picture of a "good" unit. Any differences are sent to a QC engineer who removes the bad units and discusses the flaws with the production supervisors. The new system has replaced the ten QC inspectors with two QC engineers.

The operating costs of the new QC system, including the salaries of the QC engineers, have been included as factory overhead in calculating the company's plant-wide factory overhead rate which is based on direct labor dollars.

The company's president is confused. His vice president of production has told him how efficient the new system is, yet there is a large increase in the factory overhead rate. The com-putation of the rate before and after automation is shown below.

	Before	After
Budgeted overhead	$1,900,000	$2,100,000
Budgeted direct labor	1,000,000	700,000
Budgeted overhead rate	190%	300%

"Three hundred percent," lamented the president. "How can we compete with such a high factory overhead rate?"

Required   A. 1. Define "factory overhead," and cite three examples of typical costs that would be included in factory overhead.

2. Explain why companies develop factory overhead rates.

B. Explain why the increase in the overhead rate should not have a negative financial impact on Moss Manufacturing.

C. Explain, in the greatest detail possible, how Moss Manufacturing could change its overhead accounting system to eliminate confusion over product costs.

D. Discuss how an activity-based costing system might benefit Moss Manufacturing.

---

7.   Estimated time 30 minutes (December 1991)

Princess Corporation grows, processes, packages, and sells three apple products—sliced apples that are used in frozen pies, applesauce, and apple juice. The outside skin of the apple, which is removed in the Cutting Department and processed as animal feed, is treated as a by-product. Princess uses the net realizable (relative sales) value method to assign costs of the joint process to its main products. The by-product is inventoried at its market value, and the net realizable value of the by-product is used to reduce the joint production costs prior to allocation to the main products. Details of Princess' production process are presented below.

• The apples are washed and the outside skin is removed in the Cutting Department. The apples are then cored and trimmed for slicing. The three main products and the by-product are recognizable after processing in the Cutting Department. Each product is then transferred to a separate department for final processing.

• The trimmed apples are forwarded to the Slicing Department where they are sliced and frozen. Any juice generated during the slicing operation is frozen with the slices.

• The pieces of apple trimmed from the fruit are processed into applesauce in the Crushing Department. Again, the juice generated during this operation is used in the applesauce.

• The core and any surplus apple generated from the Cutting Department are pulverized into a liquid in the Juicing Department. There is a loss equal to eight percent of the weight of the good output produced in this department.

• The outside skin is chopped into animal feed and packaged in the Feed Department.

A total of 270,000 pounds of apples were entered into the Cutting Department during November. The schedule presented below shows the costs incurred in each department, the proportion by weight transferred to the four final processing departments, and the selling price of each end product.

Required   A. Princess Corporation uses the net realizable value method to determine inventory values for its main products and by-products. For the month of November 1991, calculate the

1. resulting output for apple slices, applesauce, apple juice, and animal feed, in pounds.

2. net realizable value at the split-off point for each of the three main products.

3. amount of the cost of the Cutting Department assigned to each of the three main products and to the by-product in accordance with corporate policy.

4. gross margins in dollars for each of the three main products.

B. Comment on the significance to management of the gross margin dollar information by main product for planning and control purposes, as opposed to inventory valuation.

---

8.   Estimated time 30 minutes (December 1979)

West Corporation is a divisionalized manufacturing company. A product called Aggregate is manufactured in one department of the California Division. Aggregate is transferred upon completion to the Utah Division at a predetermined price where it is used in the manufacture of other products.

The raw material is added at the beginning of the process. Labor and overhead are added continuously throughout the process. Shrinkage of 10 to 14 percent, all occurring at the beginning of the process, is considered normal. In the California Division all departmental overhead is charged to the departments and divisional overhead is allocated to the departments on the basis of direct labor hours. The divisional overhead rate for 1979 is $2 per direct labor hour.

Processing Data and Costs
November 1991

Department	Costs Incurred	Proportion of Product by Weight Transferred to Departments	Selling Price per Pound of Final Product
Cutting	$60,000	none	none
Slicing	11,280	33%	$.80
Crushing	8,550	30	.55
Juicing	3,000	27	.40
Feed	700	10	.10
Total	$83,530	100%	

The following information relates to production during November 1979:

- Work-in-process, November 1, (4,000 pounds—75% complete):

Raw material	$22,800
Direct labor @ $5.00 per hour	$24,650
Departmental overhead	$12,000
Divisional overhead	$ 9,860

- Raw material:

Inventory, November 1, 2,000 pounds	$10,000
Purchases, November 3, 10,000 pounds	$51,000
Purchases, November 18, 10,000 pounds	$51,500
Released to production during November, 16,000 pounds	

- Direct labor costs @ $5.00 per hour, $103,350.
- Direct departmental overhead costs, $52,000.
- Transferred to Utah Division, 15,000 pounds.
- Work-in-process, November 30, 3,000 pounds, 33⅓% complete.

The FIFO method is used for materials inventory valuation and the weighted average method is used for work-in-process inventories.

Required A. Prepare a cost of production report for the department of California Division producing Aggregate for November 1979 which presents:

1. the equivalent units of production by cost factor of Aggregate (e.g., raw material, direct labor, and overhead).
2. calculates the equivalent unit costs for each cost factor of Aggregate.
3. the cost of Aggregate transferred to the Utah Division.
4. the cost of abnormal shrinkage, if any.
5. the cost of the work-in-process inventory at November 30, 1979.

B. The California Division intends to implement a flexible budgeting system to improve cost control over direct labor and departmental overhead. The basis of the flexible budget will be the production that occurs in the budget period. For the department producing Aggregate, what amount reflects the best measure of production activity for the November 1979 flexible budget? Explain your answer.

---

9.   Estimated time 30 minutes (December 1988)

Wood Glow Manufacturing Co. produces a single product, a wood refinishing kit that sells for $17.95. The final processing of the kits occurs in the Packaging Department. An internal quilted wrap is applied at the beginning of the packaging process. A compartmented outside box printed with instructions and the company's name and logo is added when units are 60 percent through the process. Conversion costs, consisting of direct labor and applied overhead, occur evenly throughout the packaging process. Conversion activities after the addition of the box involve package sealing, testing for leakage, and final inspection. Rejections in the Packaging Department are rare and may be ignored. The following data pertain to the ac-

tivities of the Packaging Department during the month of October.

- Beginning work-in-process inventory was 10,000 units, 40 percent complete as to conversion costs.
- 30,000 units were started and completed in the month.
- There were 10,000 units in ending work-in-process, 80 percent complete as to conversion costs.

The Packaging Department's October costs were

Quilted wrap	$80,000
Outside boxes	50,000
Direct labor	22,000
Applied overhead ($3.00/per direct labor dollar)	66,000

The costs transferred in from prior processing were $3.00 per unit. The cost of goods sold for the month was $240,000, and the ending finished-goods inventory was $84,000. Wood Glow uses the first-in, first-out method of inventory valuation.

Wood Glow's controller, Mark Brandon, has been asked to analyze the activities of the Packaging Department for the month of October. Brandon knows that in order to properly determine the department's unit cost of production, he must first calculate the equivalent units of production.

Required A. Prepare an equivalent units of production schedule for the October activity in the Packaging Department. Be sure to account for the beginning work-in-process inventory, the units started and completed during the month, and the ending work-in-process inventory.

B. Determine the cost per equivalent unit of the October production.

C. Assuming that the actual overhead incurred during October was $5,000 more than the overhead applied, describe how the value of the ending work-in-process inventory would be determined.

---

10.   Estimated time 30 minutes (December 1988)

Romano Foods Inc. manufactures Roman Surprise Fresh Frozen Pizzas that are 12 inches in diameter and retail for $4.69 to $5.99, depending upon the topping. The company employs a process costing system in which the product flows through several processes. Joe Corolla, vice president of Production, has had a long-running disagreement with the controller, Sue Marshall, over the handling of spoilage costs. Corolla resists every attempt to charge production with variance responsibilities unless they are favorable. Spoilage costs have not been significant in the past, but, in November, the Mixing Department had a substantial amount of spoilage. Traditionally, Romano Foods has treated 10 percent of good output as normal spoilage. The department input 120,000 units of ingredients, and 13,000 dough units were rejected at inspection. Marshall is concerned about the abnormal spoilage and wants Corolla to take corrective steps. Corolla, on the other hand, maintains that the Mixing Department is operating properly. He has prepared the following report for the Mixing Department to support his contention.

Romano Foods-Mixing Department
Production Cost Report
Month ended November 30, 1988

Input Units	Total Cost	Good Output Units	10% Normal Spoilage	Abnormal Spoilage	Good Unit Cost
120,000	$45,360	107,000	12,000	1,000	$.42

Budgeted unit cost	$0.435
Actual cost per good unit	0.420
Favorable variance	$0.015

Cost Reconciliation

Cost of 107,000 good units @ $.42 each	$44,940
Abnormal spoilage (charge to purchasing for buying inferior materials): 1,000 units @ $.42 each	420
Total cost	$45,360

Required A. Revise Joe Corolla's Production Cost Report for November 1988 by calculating

1. the number of units of normal spoilage.

2. the number of units of abnormal spoilage.

3. the total and unit costs of the Mixing Department's production of good units in November.

4. the total and unit costs of abnormal spoilage.

B. Prepare the journal entry to transfer costs for the Mixing Department for November to the Assembly Department.

C. Describe how Joe Corolla's Production Cost Report has shown the performance of the Mixing Department to be less favorable than that shown in the revised report.

---

11. Estimated time 30 minutes (December 1987)

Rose Bach has recently been hired as Controller of Empco Inc., a sheet metal manufacturer. Empco has been in the sheet metal business for many years and is currently investigating ways to modernize its manufacturing process. At the first staff meeting Bach attended, Bob Kelley, Chief Engineer, presented a proposal for automating the Drilling Department. Kelley recommended that Empco purchase two robots that would have the capability of replacing the eight direct labor workers in the department. The cost savings outlined in Kelley's proposal included the elimination of direct labor cost in the Drilling Department plus a reduction of manufacturing overhead cost in the department to zero because Empco charges manufacturing overhead on the basis of direct labor dollars using a plant-wide rate.

The president of Empco was puzzled by Kelley's explanation of cost savings, believing it made no sense. Bach agreed, explaining that as firms become more automated, they should rethink their manufacturing overhead systems. The president then asked Bach to look into the matter and prepare a report for the next staff meeting.

To refresh her knowledge, Bach reviewed articles on manufacturing overhead allocation for an automated factory and discussed the matter with some of her peers. Bach also gathered the historical data presented in the next column on the manu-

	Historical Data		
Date	Average Annual Direct Labor Cost	Average Annual Manufacturing Overhead Cost	Average Manufacturing Overhead Application Rate
1940s	$1,000,000	$ 1,000,000	100%
1950s	1,200,000	3,000,000	250
1960s	2,000,000	7,000,000	350
1970s	3,000,000	12,000,000	400
1980s	4,000,000	20,000,000	500

	Annual Averages		
	Cutting Department	Grinding Department	Drilling Department
Direct labor	$ 2,000,000	$1,750,000	$ 250,000
Manufacturing overhead	11,000,000	7,000,000	2,000,000

facturing overhead rates experienced by Empco over the years. Bach also wanted to have some departmental data to present at the meeting and, using Empco's accounting records, was able to estimate the annual averages presented above for each manufacturing department in the 1980s.

Required A. Disregarding the proposed use of robots in the Drilling Department, describe the shortcomings of the system for applying overhead that is currently used by Empco Inc.

B. Explain the misconceptions underlying Bob Kelley's statement that the manufacturing overhead cost in the Drilling Department would be reduced to zero if the automation proposal was implemented.

C. Recommend ways to improve Empco Inc.'s method for applying overhead by describing how it should revise its overhead accounting system:

1. in the Cutting and Grinding Departments.

2. to accommodate the automation of the Drilling Department.

---

12. Estimated time 30 minutes (December 1989)

Alderon Industries is a manufacturer of chemicals for various purposes. One of the processes used by Alderon produces SPL-3, a chemical used in swimming pools; PST-4, a chemical used in pesticides; and RJ-5, a by-product that is sold to fertilizer manufacturers. Alderon uses the net realizable value of its main products to allocate joint production costs, and the first-in, first-out (FIFO) inventory method to value the main products. The by-product is inventoried at its net realizable value, and this value is used to reduce the joint production costs before the joint costs are allocated to the main products. The ratio of output quantities to input quantities of direct material used in the joint process remains consistent from month to month.

Data regarding Alderon's operations for the month of November 1989 are presented on the next page. During this month, Alderon incurred joint production costs of $1,702,000

Alderon Industries
November 1989 Operations

	SPL-3	PST-4	RJ-5
Finished goods inventory in gallons (11/1/89)	18,000	52,000	3,000
November sales in gallons	650,000	325,000	150,000
November production in gallons	700,000	350,000	170,000
Sales value per gallon at split-off	none	$3.80	$.70*
Additional processing costs	$874,000	$816,000	none
Final sales value per gallon	$4.00	$6.00	none

*Disposal costs of $.10 per gallon will be incurred in order to sell the by-product.

in the manufacture of SPL-3, PST-4, RJ-5.

Required   A. Determine Alderon Industries' allocation of joint production costs for the month of November 1989. Be sure to present appropriate supporting calculations.

B. Determine the dollar values of the finished goods inventories for SPL-3, PST-4, and RJ-5 as of November 30, 1989.

C. Alderon Industries has an opportunity to sell PST-4 at the split-off point for $3.80 per gallon. Prepare an analysis showing whether Alderon should sell PST-4 at the split-off point or continue to process this product further.

---

13.   Estimated time 30 minutes (June 1981)

Doe Corporation grows, processes, cans and sells three main pineapple products—sliced pineapple, crushed pineapple, and pineapple juice. The outside skin is cut off in the Cutting Department and processed as animal feed. The skin is treated as a by-product. Doe's production process is as follows:

- Pineapples first are processed in the Cutting Department. The pineapples are washed and the outside skin is cut away. Then the pineapples are cored and trimmed for slicing. The three main products (sliced, crushed, juice) and the by-product (animal feed) are recognizable after processing in the

Cutting Department. Each product is then transferred to a separate department for final processing.

- The trimmed pineapples are forwarded to the Slicing Department where the pineapples are sliced and canned. Any juice generated during the slicing operation is packed in the cans with the slices.

- The pieces of pineapple trimmed from the fruit are diced and canned in the Crushing Department. Again, the juice generated during this operation is packed in the can with the crushed pineapple.

- The core and surplus pineapple generated from the Cutting Department are pulverized into a liquid in the Juicing Department. There is an evaporation loss equal to 8 percent of the weight of the good output produced in this department which occurs as the juices are heated.

- The outside skin is chopped into animal feed in the Feed Department.

The Doe Corporation uses the net realizable value method (relative sales value method) to assign costs of the joint process to its main products. The by-product is inventoried at its market value.

A total of 270,000 pounds were entered into the Cutting Department during May. The schedule presented below shows the costs incurred in each department, the proportion by weight transferred to the four final processing departments, and the selling price of each end product.

Processing Data and Costs
May 1981

Department	Costs Incurred	Proportion of Product by Weight Transferred to Departments	Selling Price per Pound of Final Product
Cutting	$60,000	—	none
Slicing	4,700	35%	$.60
Crushing	10,580	28	.55
Juicing	3,250	27	.30
Animal feed	700	10	.10
Total	$79,230	100%	

Required **A.** The Doe Corporation uses the net realizable value method to determine inventory values for its main products and by-products. Calculate:

1. the pounds of pineapple that result as output for pineapple slices, crushed pineapple, pineapple juice, and animal feed.
2. the net realizable value at the split-off point of the three main products.
3. the amount of the cost of the Cutting Department assigned to each of the three main products and to the by-product in accordance with corporate policy.
4. the gross margins for each of the three main products.

B. Comment on the significance to management of the gross margin information by main product.

C. In the production of joint products either a by-product or scrap could be generated.

1. Distinguish between a by-product and scrap.
2. Would the proper accounting treatment for scrap differ from that for by-products? Explain your answer.

Solutions

1.

1. d.

2. e.

3. a. The answer assumes absorption costing methods are used.

4. e.

5. c.

6. a.

7. b. Controllable costs are those costs that can be influenced by a specified manager within a given time period.

8. d.

Ending inventory, raw materials	$ 85
Raw materials used	326
Total available	411
Beginning inventory, raw materials	75
Raw materials purchased	**$336**

9. b.

Total manufacturing costs	$686
Raw materials used	326
Labor and overhead	360
The $360 total is 1.6 of the labor costs	÷ 1.6
Total labor costs	**$225**

10. c. The cost of goods manufactured represents the cost of goods completed and transferred to finished goods.

Beginning work in process	$ 80
Total manufacturing costs	686
Total costs to account for	766
Ending work in process	30
Cost of goods manufactured	**$736**

or

Total goods available	$826
Less: beginning finished goods	90
Cost of goods manufactured	**$736**

11. b.

Cost of goods available	$826
Less: finished goods inventory (ending)	110
Cost of goods sold	**$716**

12. d. Units transferred in during the month would be considered 100 percent complete during the month transferred in as far as prior department costs are concerned.

13. b. Transferred out:

Beginning inventory	8,000
Current production	30,000
Ending work-in-process	0
	38,000

14. b. Transferred out:

Beginning inventory (75%)	6,000
Current production	30,000
Ending work-in-process (40%)	4,800
	40,800

15. e. All costs except "e" impact the quality of the product. Shortening product lead time improves quality of service but not necessarily quality of product.

16. b. Cost allocation is needed in many companies to determine the income and expense for external reporting purposes. The allocation determines the value of inventories and thus the reported profit. Allocated costs should not impact the evaluation of a revenue center or the cost when variable costing is used.

17. c. Factory service costs would most likely be driven by units of electricity costs consumed rather than units sold, salary of service department employees, direct materials costs or finished goods shipped.

18. a. Costs identified in items "b" through "e" do not impact the decision of sell now or process further. These costs will be the same regardless of the decision to sell or process. Costs incurred after the split-off, if the product is processed further, are relevent.

19. a. Transferred out

Beginning inventory (1,000 × 0)	0
Started and completed	3,000
Ending work-in-process (2,000 × 100%)	2,000
Equivalent units	5,000

20. b. Transferred out

Beginning inventory (1,000 × .40)	400
Started and completed	3,000
Ending work-in-process (2,000 × .20)	400
Equivalent units	3,800

21. d. Transferred out

Transferred out	4,000
Ending work-in-process (2,000 × 100%)	2,000
Equivalent units	6,000

22. d. Transferred out

Transferred out	4,000
Ending work-in-process (2,000 × .20)	400
Equivalent units	4,400

23. d.

Sales, budgeted	480,000
Desired ending inventory	50,000
Goods available, budgeted	530,000
Beginning inventory	80,000
Goods manufactured	450,000

24. c.

Production requirements (500,000 × 2)	1,000,000
Desired ending inventory	50,000
Total needed	1,050,000
Beginning inventory	40,000
Raw material purchases	1,010,000

25. d.

Quality control $350,000 x $7,000/$28,000	87,500
Maintenance $2000,000 x $12,000/$30,000	80,000
Total	167,500

26. e.

Quality control $350,000 x $21,000/28,000	$262,500
Maintenance $200,000 x $18,000/$30,000	120,000
Direct overhead	400,000
Total overhead	$782,500
Machine hours	÷ 50,000
Rate per hour	$15.65

27. c. Direct overhead costs of $300,000 divided by 25,000 direct labor hours.

28. b.

Quality control to maintenance $350,000 x $7,000/$35,000 x $18,000/$30,000	$ 42,000
Maintenance $200,000 x $18,000/$30,000	120,000
Total	$162,000

2.

A. Normal spoilage is the occurence of unacceptable units arising under efficient operating conditions. Normal spoilage is an inherent result of the particular process or operation and is uncontrollable in the short run. The costs associated with normal spoilage are typically viewed as part of the cost of the good units produced.

Abnormal spoilage is spoilage that is not expected to arise under efficient operating conditions and is not an inherent part of the production process. Accordingly, abnormal spoilage is usually considered controllable and is not included as a portion of the cost of good units produced but as an expense of the period.

B. 1. Spoiled units are unacceptable units of production that are either discarded or sold for disposal value.

2. Reworked units are unacceptable units of production that are subsequently reconditioned into good units which can be sold as acceptable finished goods.

3. Scrap represents inputs that do not become part of the output and have minor economic value when compared to the sales value of the completed product.

C. 1. An analysis of the 5,000 units rejected by Richport Company for Job No. N1192-122 yields the following breakdown between normal and abnormal spoilage.

	Units
Normal spoilage*	3,000
Abnormal spoilage:	
Design defect	900
Other [5,000 - (3,000 + 900)]	1,100
Total units rejected	5,000

*Normal spoilage	=	.025 of normal input
Normal input	=	117,000 ÷ (1-.025)
	=	120,000 units
Normal spoilage	=	120,000 x .025
	=	3,000 units

2. The journal entries required to properly account for Job

No. N1192-122 are presented below and use an average cost per unit of $57 ($6,954,000 ÷ 122,000).

	Debit	Credit
Spoiled inventory (or A/R or cash)[1]	$ 28,700	
Abnormal loss[2]	107,500	
WIP control[3]		$135,000
Cash[4]		1,200

To account for 5,000 units rejected.

Finished goods inventory	$6,819,000	
WIP control		$6,819,000

To transfer 117,000 units to finished goods inventory.

Supporting Calculations

[1] Units for sale (4,100) or sold at $7 each.

[2] Loss from abnormal spoilage:

200 units @ $57	$114,000
Disposal cost	1,200
Cost recovery (1100 x $7)	7,700
	$107,500

[3] WIP control:

900 defective units @ $57	$ 51,300
1100 other rejected units @ $57	62,700
300 normal units @ $7	21,000
	$135,000

[4] Additional cost to dispose of 900 units rejected because of design defect.

3.

A. 1. The equivalent units for each cost element, using the weighted average method, are presented below.

	Direct Materials		Conver-
	Chemicals	Cans	sion
Units completed and transferred to Shipping	20,000	20,000	20,000
Work-in-process at 5/31			
Chemicals (100%)	5,000		
Cans (0%)		0	
Conversion costs (80%)			4,000
Equivalent units	25,000	20,000	24,000

2. The equivalent units for each cost element, using the first-in, first-out method, are presented below.

	Direct Materials		Conver-
	Chemicals	Cans	sion
Transferred to Shipping from 5/1 work-in-process (4,000 @ 25%)			
Chemicals (0%)	0		
Cans (100%)		4,000	
Conversion costs (75%)			3,000
Current production transferred to Shipping (100%)	16,000	16,000	16,000
5/31 work-in-process (5,000 @ 80%)			
Chemicals (100%)	5,000		
Cans (0%)		0	
Conversion costs (80%)			4,000
Equivalent units	21,000	20,000	23,000

B. 1. The cost per equivalent unit for each cost element, using the weighted average method, is presented below.

	Direct Materials		Conver-
	Chemicals	Cans	sion*
Work-in-process at 5/1	$ 45,600	$ 0	$ 8,125
May costs added	228,400	7,000	45,500
Total costs	$274,000	$7,000	$53,625
÷			
Weighted average Equivalent units	25,000	20,000	24,000
Cost per Equivalent units	$10.96	$.35	$2.23

*Conversion cost = Direct labor + Factory overhead

2. The cost per equivalent unit for each cost element, using the first-in, first-out method, is presented below.

	Direct Materials		Conver-
	Chemicals	Cans	sion
May costs incurred	$228,400	$7,000	$45,500
÷			
First-in, first-out Equivalent units	21,000	20,000	23,000
Cost per Equivalent units	$10.88	$.35	$1.98

C. The weighted average method is generally easier to use as the calculations are simpler. This method tends to obscure current period costs as the cost per equivalent unit includes both current costs and prior costs that were in the beginning inventory. This method is most appropriate when conversion costs, inventory levels, and raw material prices are stable.

The first-in, first-out method is based on the work done in the current period only. This method is most appropriate when conversion costs, inventory levels, or raw material prices fluctuate. In addition, this method should be used when accuracy in current equivalent unit costs is important or when a standard cost system is used.

4.

A. The benefits of using scattergraphs in analyzing cost behavior include the following.

• Scattergraphs provide a quick way of determining if a causal (linear) relationship exists between costs and activities.

• The use of scattergraphs facilitates the identification of extreme observations (outliers) that may require further analysis. In addition, scattergraphs do not give much weight to outliers when determining the "line of best fit" while other methods may give too much weight to outliers.

• Changes in cost behavior patterns are generally more noticeable when displayed on a scattergraph.

• Scattergraphs can be easily understood as they rely on visual observation and represent a common sense approach.

B. 1. The manufacturing overhead budget for the Molding Department of Franzel Company for the coming year is calculated as follows.

Material handling (280,000 lbs. x $1.40 per lb.)	$ 392,000
Setup costs [($750 x 200 setups) + ($250 x 12 months)][1]	153,000
Indirect labor [135,000 hours x ($5.00 x 1.08)]	729,000
Utilities [(520,000 units x 2.5 kwhr) x $.20 per kwhr]	260,000
Equipment maintenance	
Parts ($150,000 x 1.10)	165,000
Labor [1,600 hours x ($50 x 1.10)]	88,000
Fixed costs (1360,000 per month x 12)	4,320,000
Total manufacturing overhead	$6,107,000

1. Using the high-low method to determine the fixed and variable components of the setup costs, the month of June must be treated as an outlier and dropped from the analysis. Therefore, the high month is February with 20 setups at a cost of $15,250, and the low month is January with 15 setups at a cost of $11,500.

Variable cost

Per setup   = Change in costs ÷ Change in number of setups

            = ($15,250 − $11,500) ÷ (20 − 15)

            = $3,750 ÷ 5

            = $750

Fixed cost

Per month   = Monthly cost − (Setups x $750)

High month = $15,250 − (20 x $750)

              = $250

Low month   = $11,500 − (15 x $750)

              = $250

2. The overhead rate that should be employed in the Molding Department for the coming year for the costs to be applied on the basis of machine hours is $41.20 per machine hour, calculated as follows.

Costs to be applied on the basis of machine hours:

Indirect labor	$ 729,000
Power	260,000
Equipment maintenance	
- Parts	165,000
- Labor	88,000
Fixed costs	4,320,000
Total costs	$5,562,000

C. The basic premise underlying responsibility accounting is that the performance of departmental managers will be judged by how well they manage those items directly under their control. The inclusion of equipment maintenance costs (as well as certain portions of fixed costs) violates this premise as the manager of the Equipment Maintenance Department determines the preventive maintenance schedule for each of the production departments. The inclusion of the equipment costs is likely to affect the behavior of the manufacturing departmental managers in the following ways.

• The managers are likely to become frustrated and dissatisfied with not being able to control all the factors on which their performance will be evaluated.

• Depending on the degree of pressure that is applied by top management to achieve the budget overhead expenses, an atmosphere of hostility could develop between the departmental managers and top management.

• If the departmental managers are having difficulty controlling expenses in other areas, they may ask the manager of the Equipment Maintenance Department to postpone the scheduled maintenance. These delays are likely to be detrimental to overall productivity in the long run, and an adversarial relationship could develop between the manufacturing departmental managers and the manager of the Equipment Maintenance Department.

5.

A. 1. A company will use a predetermined indirect overhead rate to allocate, to production jobs, those overheads which are not directly related to the production of jobs. As a result, management will have timely, accurate job cost information. Predetermined overhead rates are easy to apply and, also, avoid volatility and fluctuations in job costs caused by changes in the production volume and/or overhead costs throughout the year.

2. The manufacturing overhead applied through October 31, 1989 is calculated as follows.

Machine hours used
x a predetermined
hourly overhead rate = overhead applied.
      73,000 x $15 = $1,095,000

3. The manufacturing overhead applied in November 1989 is calculated as follows.

Machine hours used
x a predetermined
hourly overhead rate = overhead applied.
              6,000 x $15 = $90,000

4. Manufacturing overhead underapplied through November 30, 1989 is calculated as follows.

Actual overhead incurred	
($1,100,000 + $96,000)	$1,196,000
Applied overhead	
($1,095,000 + $90,000)	(1,185,000)
Underapplied overhead	$ 11,000

5. The method of closing the over/underapplied overhead to cost of goods sold is not theoretically appropriate, but this method is considered acceptable when the amount is not material and will not distort the financial results. In this case, the amount of underapplied overhead is only 0.9 percent of the incurred overhead, an immaterial amount. Also, most of the jobs worked on have been completed and sold; therefore, closing the underapplied overhead to cost of goods sold would not distort the financial results nor conceal relevant information.

B. The balance in Valport's Finished Goods Inventory at November 30, 1989 is comprised only of Job No. N11-013 and is calculated as follows.

10/31/89 balance for Job No. N11-013	$55,000
November materials	4,000
November direct labor	12,000
November overhead (1,000 x $15)	15,000
Total finished goods inventory	$86,000

C. Valport's Statement of Cost of Goods Manufactured as of November 30, 1989, is constructed in the next column.

6.

A. 1. Factory overhead costs include all indirect costs (all production costs except direct material and direct labor). These costs cannot be practically or economically traced to end products and, therefore, must be assigned by some allocation method. Typical factory overhead costs include

• indirect labor, i.e., lift-truck driver's wages, maintenance and inspection labor, engineering labor, and supervisors.

• other indirect factory costs, i.e., building maintenance, machine and tool maintenance, property taxes, property insurance, pension costs, depreciation on plant and equipment, rent expense, and utility expense.

2. Companies develop factory overhead rates to facilitate the costing of products as they are completed and shipped, rather than waiting until actual costs are accumulated for the period of production.

B. The overhead rate increase should not have a negative impact on Moss Manufacturing because the increase in indirect costs was offset by a decrease in direct labor.

Valport Company
Statement of Cost of Goods Manufactured
For the Year Ended November 30, 1989
($000's omitted)

Materials inventory		
12/1/88		$ 105,000
Material purchases		
($965,000 + $98,000)		1,063,000
Cost of materials available		1,168,000
Less: Indirect materials		
($125,000 + $9,000)	$134,000	
Materials inventory		
11/30/89	85,000	219,000
Direct materials used		949,000
Direct labor		
($845,000 + $80,000)		925,000
Manufacturing overhead		
Indirect materials	$134,000	
Indirect labor		
($345,000 + $30,000)	375,000	
Utilities		
($245,000 + $22,000)	267,000	
Depreciation		
($385,000 + $35,000)	420,000	1,196,000
Manufacturing costs incurred		3,070,000
Add: Work-in-process		
inventory 12/1/88		60,000
Gross Manufacturing costs		3,130,000
Less: Work-in-process 11/30/89*		150,200
Cost of goods manufactured		$2,979,800

* Supporting calculations for
work-in-process 11/30/89

	D12-002	D12-003	Total
Material	$37,900	$26,000	$63,900
Direct labor	20,000	16,800	36,800
Applied overhead			
2,500 x $15	37,500		37,500
800 x $15		12,000	12,000
Totals	$ 95,400	$ 54,800	$150,200

C. Rather than using a universal plant-wide overhead rate, Moss Manufacturing could implement separate overhead pools and allocate the overheads to the activities using the appropriate pools. Examples are as follows.

• Separate costs into departmental overhead accounts (or other relevant pools), with one account for each production and service department. Each department would allocate its overhead to products on the basis that best reflects the use of these overhead services.

• Individual machines (or other more relevant allocation bases) could be treated as separate cost centers with the machine costs collected and charged to the products using the machine(s).

D. An activity-based costing system might benefit Moss Manufacturing because it

• differentiates costs between value adding and non-value adding activities.

• costs products according to the activities involved in the production process.

• considers all organizational expenses as variable.

7.

A. 1. For the month of November 1991, Princess Corporation's resulting pounds of apple slices, applesauce, apple juice, and animal feed were 89,100, 81,000, 67,500, and 27,000, respectively, as calculated in Exhibit 1.

Exhibit 1

Princess Corporation
Product Output in Pounds
November 1991

Product	Input	Proportion	Total Pounds	Pounds Lost	Net Pounds
Slices	270,000	.33	89,100	-	89,100
Sauce	270,000	.30	81,000	-	81,000
Juice	270,000	.27	72,900	5,400	67,500 (1)
Feed	270,000	.10	27,000	-	27,000
		1.00	270,000	5,400	264,600

Note (1)
Net Pounds: = 72,900 - (.08 x net pounds.)
= 72,900 ÷ 1.08
= 67,500 net pounds

---

2. The net realizable value for each of the three main products is calculated below.

Calculation of net Realizable Value
at the Split-off Point

Product	Net Pounds	Price	Selling Revenue	Separable Costs	Net Realizable Value
Slices	89,100	$.80	$ 71,280	$11,280	$ 60,000
Sauce	81,000	.55	44,550	8,550	36,000
Juice	67,500	.40	27,000	3,000	24,000
			$142,830	$22,830	$120,000

3. The net realizable value of the by-product is deducted from the production costs prior to allocation to the main products,

as presented below.

Allocation of Cutting Department Costs
To Main and By-Products

Net realizable value
(NRV) of by-product = By-product revenue - Separable costs

= $.10(270,000 x 10%) - $700

= $2,700 - $700

= $2,000

Costs to be allocated = Joint cost - NRV of by-product

= $60,000 - $2,000

= $58,000

Exhibit 2

Princess Corporation
Gross Margin in Dollars
November 1991

Product	Revenue	Separable Cost	Joint Cost	Gross Margin
Slices	$ 71,280	$11,280	$29,000	$31,000
Sauce	44,550	8,550	17,400	18,600
Juice	27,000	3,000	11,600	12,400
	$142,830	$22,830	$58,000	$62,000

4. The gross margin in dollars for each of Princess Corporation's three main products is reflected in Exhibit 2 above.

B. The gross margin dollar information by main product is determined by the arbitrary allocation of joint production costs. As a result, these cost figures and the resulting gross margin information are of little significance for planning and control purposes. The allocation is made only for purposes of inventory valuation and income determination.

Note: The concepts needed to solve Part B are covered in Chapter 4.

8.

A. See below.

B. The best measure of production activity for direct labor and departmental overhead during a month is the equivalent amount of work done in that month. For November 1979, this amount would be 13,000 equivalent pounds. This amount in-

8. A.

California Division
Cost of Production Report
November, 1979

	Physical Flow	Materials	Direct Labor	Overhead	
			Conversion Costs		
Work in process—Beginning	4,000				
Pounds of material added	16,000				
Production to account for	**20,000**				
Completed pounds transferred	15,000	15,000	15,000	15,000	
Shrinkage (normal)	2,000[1]				
Work in process—End	3,000	3,000	1,000	1,000	
Production accounted for	**20,000**	**18,000**	**16,000**	**16,000**	
					Total
Costs to account for:					
Beginning inventory		$ 22,800	$ 24,650	$ 21,860	$ 69,310
Added costs					
Material (10,000 +					
51,000 + 20,600)		81,600			81,600
Direct labor (given)			103,350		103,350
Overhead (52,000 + 41,340)				93,340	93,340
Total costs		**$104,400**	**$128,000**	**$115,200**	**$347,600**
Equivalent unit costs		**$ 5.80**	**$ 8.00**	**$ 7.20**	**$ 21.00**
Costs distributed:					
To Utah Division 15,000 pounds		$ 87,000	$120,000	$108,000	$315,000
Work in process—Ending		17,400	8,000	7,200	32,600
Total costs accounted for		**$104,400**	**$128,000**	**$115,200**	**$347,600**

[1]The shrinkage is normal because it falls within the allowable limits of 10–14%; 2,000 ÷ 16,000 = 12.5%.

cludes only the work done in the current month. Supporting calculations are as follows:

Work done to complete beginning work in process (4,000 × 25%)	1,000
Units started and completed (15,000 − 4,000)	11,000
Work done on units still in process at the end of the month (3,000 × 33⅓%)	1,000
Total	**13,000**

9.

A. The equivalent units of production schedule for the Packaging Department's October activity is as follows.

	Whole Units	Quilted Wrap	Boxes	Direct Labor	Overhead
To complete beginning WIP inventory	10,000	0	10,000	6,000	6,000
Started and completed	30,000	30,000	30,000	30,000	30,000
Ending WIP inventory	10,000	10,000	10,000	8,000	8,000
Equivalent units of production		40,000	50,000	44,000	44,000

B. Cost per equivalent unit of October production is as follows.

	October Costs +	Equivalent Units =	Unit Costs
Quilted Wrap	$80,000	40,000	$2.00
Boxes	50,000	50,000	1.00
Direct labor	22,000	44,000	.50
Applied overhead	66,000	44,000	1.50
Equivalent unit cost			$5.00

C. If $5,000 is considered an immaterial amount for Wood Glow Manufacturing, the additional overhead incurred would be charged to the cost of goods sold for the month of October. If $5,000 is material, the underapplied overhead should be prorated among the cost of goods sold, work-in-process inventory, and finished goods inventory.

10.

A. The revised cost production report for November 1988 is as follows.

Romano Foods - Mixing Department
Revised Production Cost Report
Month ended November 30, 1988

Total Cost	Input Units	Good Output Units	10% Normal Spoilage	Abnormal Spoilage	Good Unit Cost
120,000	$45,360	107,000	10,700	2,300	$.4158

Budgeted unit cost	$.4350
Actual cost per good unit	.4158
Favorable variance	$.0192

Cost Reconciliation
Cost of 107,000 good units at $.4158	$44,490.60
Abnormal spoilage (2,300 x $.378)	869.40
Total production costs	$45,360.00

Supporting Calculations

1. 10 percent of good output = units of normal spoilage
    .10 x 107,000 units = 10,700 units of normal spoilage

2.
Total spoilage	13,000
Less normal spoilage	10,700
Abnormal spoilage	2,300

3.
Total cost of November production	$45,360
Divide by total input (units)	120,000
Unit cost of production	$ .378

Good units completed (107,000 x $.378)	$40,446.00
Normal spoilage (10,700 x $.378)	4,044.60
Total cost of good units	$44,490.60
Unit cost of good units ($44,490.60 ÷ 107,000)	$ .4158

4.
Abnormal spoilage (units)	2,300
Multiplied by unit cost of production	$ .378
Total cost of abnormal spoilage	$ 869.40

B. The journal entry, required to transfer November costs of the Mixing Department to the Assembly Department, charges the cost of good production to the Assembly Department, charges a loss account for abnormal spoilage, and credits the Mixing Department with the total cost of production.

	Debit	Credit
Work-in-process Assembly	$44,490.60	
Loss from Abnormal Spoilage	869.40	
Work-in-process Mixing		$45,360.00

C. Corolla's report is less favorable than the revised report because he ignored the normal spoilage in calculating the unit cost. In addition, he miscalculated normal spoilage as ten percent of total input rather than ten percent of good output and, thus, miscalculated abnormal spoilage. Corolla divided the November production costs ($45,360) by the good units produced plus the incorrect amount of abnormal spoilage (107,000 + 1,000 = 108,000) to get the $.42 per unit. By ignoring the equivalent units of the normal spoilage, he used a higher base for calculating the unit cost. Normal spoilage should always be incorporated into the equivalent unit calculation to get an accurate representation of the unit cost.

11.

A. Empco Inc. is currently using a plant-wide overhead rate that is applied on the basis of direct labor dollars. In general, a plant-wide manufacturing overhead rate is acceptable only if a similar relationship between overhead and direct labor exists in all departments, or the company manufactures products which receive proportional services from each department. From the departmental data supplied, the relationship in each department between overhead and direct labor appears to be quite different at Empco. Because no information is provided about Empco's products and their direct labor requirements, an evaluation of the company's overhead system on this basis cannot be made.

In most cases, departmental overhead rates are preferable to plant-wide overhead rates because plant-wide overhead rates do not provide:

• an accurate allocation of product costs or a good definition of the cost relationships for each product.

• an accurate basis for product pricing decisions.

• a framework for reviewing overhead costs on a departmental basis, identifying departmental cost overruns, or taking corrective action to improve departmental cost control.

• sufficient information about product profitability, thus, increasing the difficulties associated with management decision-making.

B. Because Empco uses a plant-wide overhead rate applied on the basis of direct labor dollars, the elimination of direct labor in the Drilling Department through the introduction of robots may appear to reduce the overhead cost of the Drilling Department to zero. However, this change will not reduce fixed manufacturing expenses such as depreciation, plant supervision, etc. In reality, the use of robots is likely to increase fixed expenses because of increased depreciation expense. Under Empco's current method of allocating overhead costs, these costs will merely be absorbed by the remaining departments. As a result, the Cutting and Grinding Departments will become more expensive to operate, and costing and pricing decisions will become more distorted if the basis for applying fixed manufacturing overhead is not changed. In addition, the capital budgeting decision to purchase the robots is seriously flawed by this assumption.

C. 1. In order to improve the allocation of overhead costs in the Cutting and Grinding Departments, Empco should

• establish separate overhead rates for each of these departments.

• select an application basis for each of these departments that best reflects the relationship of the departmental activity to the incurring of overhead costs (e.g. direct labor hours, machine hours, etc.)

• separate those costs (e.g., industrial engineering, maintenance) that cannot be specifically identified with one department, collect these costs in a separate pool, and then allocate these costs to the three producing departments.

• identify, if possible, fixed and variable overhead costs and establish fixed and variable overhead rates.

• develop departmental budgets and report monthly variances from these budgets.

2. In order to accommodate the automation of the Drilling Department in its overhead accounting system, Empco should

• establish a separate overhead rate for the Drilling Department.

• apply overhead costs to the Drilling Department on the basis of robot or machine hours.

• identify, if possible, fixed and variable overhead costs and establish fixed and variable overhead rates.

• develop a departmental budget for the Drilling Department and report monthly variances from this budget.

12.

A. Because by-products are assigned an inventory cost equal to their net realizable value (NRV) at the time they are produced, the NRV (assigned cost) of RJ-5 must be deducted from the joint production costs prior to allocation. The allocation of Alderon Industries' November 1989 joint production costs would be $960,000 to SPL-3, $640,000 to PST-4, and $102,000 to RJ-5, as calculated in Exhibit 1.

Alderon Industries
Exhibit 1

Joint production costs to be allocated

Total production costs incurred	$1,702,000
Less NRV of RJ-5 (Note)	102,000
Joint production costs to be allocated	$1,600,000

(Note) NRV of RJ-5
170,000 gallons x ($.70 - $.10) = $102,000

Allocation basis

	SPL-3	PST-4	Total
November gallons produced	700,000	350,000	
Final sales value per gallon	$4.00	$6.00	
Total sales value	$2,800,000	$2,100,000	
Less separable costs	874,000	816,000	
NRV at split-off	$1,926,000	$1,284,000	$3,210,000

SPL-3 allocation = ($1,926,000 ÷ $3,210,000) x $1,600,000
= .60 x $1,600,000
= $960,000

PST-4 allocation = ($1,284,000 ÷ $3,210,000) x $1,600,000
= .40 x $1,600,000
= $640,000

Alderon Industries
Exhibit 2

	SPL-3	PST-4	RJ-5
Joint cost allocation	$960,000	$640,000	$102,000
Additional processing costs	874,000	816,000	
Total costs	$1,834,000	$1,456,000	$102,000
Divide by gallons produced	700,000	350,000	170,000
Cost per gallon	$2.62	$4.16	$.60

Inventory valuation:

11/1/89 inventory gallons	18,000	52,000	3,000
Gallons added	700,000	350,000	170,000
Gallons available	718,000	402,000	173,000
Gallons sold in November	650,000	325,000	150,000
11/30/89 inventory gallons	68,000	77,000	23,000
Cost per gallon	$2.62	$4.16	$.60
Finished goods inventory value	$178,160	$320,320	$13,800

B. The finished goods inventory values at November 30, 1989 are $178,160 for SPL-3, $320,320 for PST-4, and $13,800 for RJ-5, as calculated in Exhibit 2.

C. Alderon Industries should sell PST-4 at the split-off point as the incremental revenue of the sales beyond the split-off point is less than the incremental cost of further processing.

Per gallon sales value beyond the split-off point	$6.00
Per gallon sales value at the split-off point	3.80
Incremental sales value	$2.20
Additional processing costs per gallon ($816,000 ÷ 350,000 gallons)	(2.33)
Per gallon gain (loss) of further processing	$(.13)

13.

A. 1. Product output in pounds

Product	Proportion	Total Pounds	Pounds Lost in Processing	Net Pounds
Slices	.35	94,500	—	94,500
Crushed	.28	75,600	—	75,600
Juice	.27	72,900	5,400	67,500
Animal feed	.10	27,000	—	27,000
		270,000	5,400	264,600

$$72,900 - .08x = X$$
$$72,900 = 1.08x$$
$$67,500 = X$$

2. See below.

3. Allocation of joint costs

Cutting department costs		$60,000
Less net revenue of byproduct		
Sales value	$2,700	
Separable cost	(700)	
Net revenue of animal feed		2,000
Balance of joint cost to be allocated to main products in proportion to net realizable value		**$58,000**

Allocation of joint cost:

Slices	52%	$30,160
Crushed	31%	17,980
Juice	17%	9,860
		$58,000

4. Gross margins for the main products

Product	Sales Revenue	Separable Cost	Joint Cost	Gross Margin
Slices	$ 56,700	$ 4,700	$30,160	$21,840
Crushed	41,580	10,580	17,980	13,020
Juice	20,250	3,250	9,860	7,140
	$118,530	**$18,530**	**$58,000**	**$42,000**

B. Gross margin information by main product is not significant because it is the result of combined sales and costs for each product. The cost figure is determined arbitrarily by allocating a portion of the joint (common) costs to each of the main products, thereby diminishing the value of the gross margin by product. The cost figures are calculated in this manner because they are needed for asset valuation and income determination but the cost figures or the resulting gross margin has little value for planning and control.

C. 1. A byproduct is a product of relatively small total value which is produced simultaneously with a product of greater total value. Scrap is material residue from a manufacturing operation that has measurable but relatively minor recovery value.

2. A byproduct is frequently inventoried at its market value. Costs are assigned to the byproduct equal to the potential sales revenue. These assigned costs will result in a reduction of the manufacturing costs for the main product. Scrap is typically not assigned any cost. The sales value is regarded as an offset to factory overhead which results in a reduction of the costs of the main product.

---

13. **A.**

2. Net realizable value at the splitoff point

Product	Pounds of Production	Selling Price	Sales Revenue	Separable Cost	Net Realizable Value Amount	Percent
Slices	94,500	.60	$ 56,700	$ 4,700	$ 52,000	52%
Crushed	75,600	.55	41,580	10,580	31,000	31
Juice	67,500	.30	20,250	3,250	17,000	17
			$118,530	**$18,530**	**$100,000**	**100%**

Chapter 3

Strategic Planning and Forecasting

Grant W. Newton

During the last ten years, the use of strategic planning has grown dramatically in the United States and elsewhere. Rapid changes in technology, upheavals in the economy, and many other factors have indicated that rigorous planning and analysis is necessary if they are to survive in a changing environment. Strategic planning is geared to such rigorous analysis of a firm's potential. It involves studying the internal strengths and weaknesses of a firm, an assessment of its external threats and opportunities, and finally a determination of which course is best for achieving its predetermined goals.

Anthony defined **strategic planning** as "the process of deciding on changes in the objectives of an organization, in the resources to be used in attaining these objectives, and in the policies that are to govern the acquisition and use of these resources."[1] Thus, the three important aspects of strategic planning are the determination of objectives, the decision as to the best allocation of resources, and the establishment of policies that will achieve the objectives. The success of this planning relies heavily on the ability of the planners to forecast future trends. Without these estimates, it is impossible to deal with even the short-range planning that must be done. For this reason, a discussion of forecasting has also been included in this chapter.

Drucker has aided in the understanding of strategic planning by describing what strategic planning is not:

1. Strategic planning is not forecasting. It is because the future cannot be accurately forecasted that the need for strategic planning exists.

2. Strategic planning is not the process of making future decisions. Decisions can only be made in the present; anything else is "pious intent." The purpose of strategic planning is to enable managers to make better current decisions.

3. Strategic planning does not eliminate risk. In fact, it does not even attempt to reduce risk. Risk is the essence of business; profit is the company's reward for taking the risk. The purpose of strategic planning is to enable the firm to take the right kinds of risk (e.g., those risks with the greatest long-run payoff).[2]

How Are Strategic Plans Established?

The exact procedures used by individual companies in establishing their strategic plans will naturally vary. However, they do tend to have certain elements in common. The model in Exhibit 3-1 developed by Gerstner is a conceptual illustration of the basic strategic planning process.[3]

The model works in this manner:

1. The environmental forces are examined since a business does not operate in a vacuum; it affects, and is affected by, its environment. It should analyze the present environ-

1. Robert N. Anthony, "Framework for Analysis," *Management Services*, (March/April, 1967), 17.

2. Peter F. Drucker, "Long-Range Planning," *Management Science* 5 (April 1959), 238.
3. Louis V. Gerstner, Jr., "Can Strategic Planning Pay Off?" *Business Horizons* 15 (December 1972), 7.

Exhibit 3-1

The Basic Strategic Planning Concept

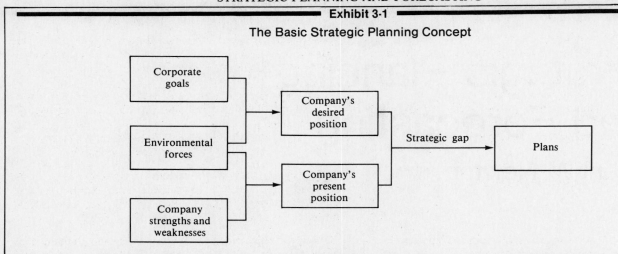

mental conditions and then attempt to forecast future environmental trends.

2. The company's strengths and weaknesses are assessed. In addition to being used in long-range planning, this assessment is also useful to the company in conducting its short-run operations.

3. A statement of the corporate goals is developed.

By analyzing the company's present position in conjunction with these three elements, the desired position is determined. The difference between these two positions is labeled the strategic gap. Strategic plans are simply those plans designed to narrow the gap and bring the two positions closer together.

Environmental Forces

An analysis of the environmental forces relevant to strategic planning can be broken into two parts—the past and present environment and future environmental trends.

Analyzing the past and present environment is relatively easy; the major questions to be answered are:

1. The market—What is total demand? Is it increasing? Is it decreasing?

2. The customers—What are their needs, expectations, values, and resources?

3. The competition—Who? Where? What are their strenghts and limitations?

4. Suppliers—Are they there? For example, sugar beet factories in Maine went bankrupt in part because farmers did not plant enough beets.

5. The industry—Is there surplus capacity? A shortage of capacity? What is the distribution system?

6. Capital market—How and at what costs and conditions can capital be raised?

7. Government and society—What demands are society and govenment making on the firm?[4]

The answers to these questions can be obtained from historical data. However, trying to answer these same questions in terms of the situation five to ten years from now is extremely difficult. The techniques presently used for forecasting environmental factors are extremely weak and thus not highly reliable in terms of accuracy. However, it is generally conceded that it is better to have a somewhat inaccurate prediction of the future environment than no prediction at all.

Company's Strengths and Weaknesses

While appearing to be a simple task, Peter Drucker has observed that evaluating this area requires much thought and study. Further, Drucker also pointed out that the right answer is usually anything but obvious.[5]

With this in mind, the evaluation should include an analysis of the following:

Organizational Structure
- What is the present structure?
- Does this structure lend itself to the creation of new operating divisions and profit centers?
- Is there sufficient depth in top management so that management of new facilities can come from within or will it be necessary to hire outside of the firm?
- Has management policy on recruitment and development of new employees been successful?

Competitive Ability
- Does the firm know who its actual competition is?
- Has past forecasting of the competitor's likely market strategies been accurate?
- How quickly has the firm been able to react to completely unexpected moves by competitors?

Market Capability
- In what market (both geographical and product) has the firm been involved? Is there a pattern of success and failure?
- What promotional activities does the firm utilize?
- What channels of distribution does the firm use?

4. William E. Rothschild, "The C.A.S.E. Approach-A Valuable Aid for Management Development," *California Management Review* 14 (Fall 1971), 34.

5. Peter F. Drucker, *The Practice of Management* (New York: Harper and Row, 1954), p. 49.

Production Facilities
- What types of production processes have been used in the past?
- Where are the facilities located?
- Does surplus capacity exist in the firm?
- What technical skills do the workers possess? Can these skills be applied to other products?
- Are labor relations favorable?

Administration
- Is management given the information it needs?
- Could the present administration handle a major acquisition?
- Are the lines of communication will defined and operational?
- Does the company have a data processing system that is able to handle present needs?
- What changes would be necessary to handle additional requirements?[6]

This checklist is not intended to be all encompassing since each individual company will have differing requirements.[7] The important point is that questions such as these must be answered during the strategic planning process.

In addition to its value in long-range planning, a critical self-analysis has short-run benefits as well since it indicates areas that need improvement and areas of strength that can be used to fuller advantage.

Statement of the Corporate Goals

Corporate goals are those objectives established by top management that give direction to the company's activities. Due to the varied nature of corporate goals, it would be difficult to generalize about them. However, the objectives of many companies would include statements in all or some of the following areas:

1. Desired rate of growth
2. Desired rate of return
3. Desired market share
4. Research and development
5. Employee development
6. Financial policy

While the list could be endless, the important point is that company goals that are accepted as given in the short run are open to change during the strategic planning process.

By analyzing the forecasted environmental trends in conjunction with the firm's corporate goals, the planners can determine the company's desired position. This is one of the most important parts of the planning process since it, in effect, determines the future of the company.

It is in this phase that planners determine new corporate goals (objectives). Scott suggests that the determination of new objectives usually goes through four stages:

1. **Preliminary objectives**   During this stage of the process, the planners begin to formulate some vague and highly generalized notions about what the new objectives should be. These goals may be based on the old corporate goals, but by no means should they be restricted to them.

2. **Tentative objectives**   Here the planners begin to establish working objectives. These objectives reflect attempts by the planners to develop more specific goals than those established in the preliminary stage.

3. **Revised objectives**   During this stage, the planners can take the goals established in stage 2 and adjust, correct, or confirm them in light of subsequent investigation and study. This stage demonstrates the need for flexibility in planning.

4. **Final objectives**   These are the corporate goals that will be written into the strategic plan. Two important things occur here. One, the corporate goals are reviewed for the final time, and two, the planners are forced to choose which goals will go into the plan. During the process of determining objectives, the planners will have undoubtedly determined many objectives; yet not all can go into the plan. Therefore, only the most important ones should be included.[8]

These objectives can be incorporated into the management by objectives (MBO) system in firms that have such a system. See Volume 1, Chapter 10 for a discussion of management by objectives.

Gerstner recommends that the strategic planning process utilize a decision-oriented approach to be successful. To ensure that such an approach is used, emphasis should be placed on three critical aspects: evaluating competitive strategies, assessing environmental forces, and developing contingency plans.[9] While there are many potential contingencies, the planners should take one or two of the events most likely to occur that could significantly affect their strategy and develop a contingency plan for each event. This type of planning causes the company to ask "what if" questions, and should the unexpected changes occur, the company is in a position to act immediately and effectively.

Relationship to Other Planning

The product of the strategic planning process provides the input for the development of a three- to 5-year or longer profit plan and also for the annual profit plan (budget). In some companies, the three- to five-year plan is partially developed while the strategic plans are being established.

6. James McKinnon, "Corporate Planning," *The Accountants' Magazine* 163 (November 1970), 539.
7. For a more detailed list of environmental factors, see Robert E. Jensen, *Phantasmagoric Accounting: Research and Analysis of Economic, Social and Environmental Impact of Corporate Business, Studies in Accounting Research No. 14* (Sarasota, Florida: American Accounting Association, 1976), pp. 197-207.
8. Brian W. Scott, *Long Range Planning in American Industry* (New York: American Management Association, 1965), p. 97.
9. Gerstner, 9-11.

The three- to five-year and annual profit plans comprise the detailed plans for action that will, hopefully, enable the company to accomplish its objectives.

Forecasting

Almost every business decision is based on future expectations. Since management must make decisions today about an uncertain tomorrow, a well-organized system of forecasting helps businesses reduce the uncertainty in those expectations.

Forecasting, expressed in terms of time periods, can be classified into three types. The first deals with the long-range forecast used for revenue planning. The time covered by this forecast, while depending on the nature of the company's operations and the purpose of the forecast, is generally from three to ten years. Management's concern in the long-range forecast is planning for the resources needed to achieve company objectives. Long-range forecasting is the most difficult and relies heavily on "expert opinion," especially with such forecasting techniques as DELPHI and cross-impact analysis.

A second type of forecasting covers the intermediate term. This involves the monthly, quarterly, and yearly operation and control of the business. Stults suggests that the intermediate forecast involves the following:

1. Facilities utilization—how should facilities be used to optimize profits?

2. Labor requirements—what new skilled people will be needed or will a layoff be necessary?

3. Purchasing—what raw materials will be needed?

4. Working capital—how much will be required?

5. Marketing activities—what promotion level, manpower requirements, sales quotas should be established?

6. Inventory planning—are there periods in which a stockpile will be needed to smooth out the manufacturing operation?[10]

The third type is a short-range forecast concerned with the day-to-day and weekly scheduling of production. The determination of cash needs is also a useful forecast.

Since so many aspects of a business center around the sales forecast, we will emphasize it in our discussion. Remember, however, that the business applications of forecasting are virtually limitless.

Importance of Sales Forecasting

Many businesses have found it necessary in today's environment to place much more emphasis than ever on planning the marketing function. Business executives design marketing strategies so that the realistic and predetermined objectives can be achieved. Sales forecasting is the key to management's ability to ensure that the marketing management approach works. Thus, sales forecasting helps management develop a system that coordinates the marketing action with company objectives. These forecasts also serve as the basis for many other decisions that must be made. Sales forecasts are used to:

1. Regulate production

2. Set inventory levels

3. Control purchases

4. Establish sales quotas

5. Direct sales effort

6. Determine advertising budget

7. Estimate working capital and cash needs

8. Plan capital outlay requirements

9. Control expenses

10. Determine if manufacturing and distribution facilities should be expanded or constructed

11. Plan personnel needs

12. Plan and schedule research and development activities

13. Plan maintenance and repair scheduling

The sales forecast is an important control tool. Forecasted sales and actual sales are compared and an attempt is made to determine the reasons for the difference.

Still another aspect of the sales forecast is its use in integrating the external business environment in which the company must operate and translating external environmental factors into company programs. There are controllable, partially controllable, and noncontrollable factors that management must consider in making the sales forecast. The noncontrollable factors determine the environmental limits within which the company will operate. The company has almost no control over such factors as social forces, economic climate, and so on. The objective is to recognize and appraise them. Two external environmental factors that management can have some influence over are technology and competitive climate.

In addition to evaluating the external business climate, management must estimate the impact of internal business factors on potential markets. These are the controllable factors, which consist of financial position, technical know-how, plant and equipment capacity, material and personnel resources, image, and position in the market place.[11]

Stages of Forecasting

The four major stages of forecasting are: (1) collecting information for the forecast, (2) evaluating and projecting the data, (3) operationally applying the forecast, and (4) controlling and auditing the forecast. Before examining each of these stages, it is important to realize that there is a great deal of overlapping and interdependence of one stage with another. For example, the last stage to be discussed will be

10. Fred C. Stults, "What Every Manager Should Know About Sales Forecasting," *Management Review* 57 (November 1968), 36.

11. William Lazar, "Sales Forecasting: Key to Integrated Management," *Business Horizons* 12 (Fall 1969), 61-62.

control, but control always begins at the planning stage where data are collected and projected.

Collecting Information   Information about the company and the business environment must be assembled. Regarding the business environment, it is necessary to identify the non-controllable and partially controllable environmental factors. This is often done through a study of the current or planned operating environment. For example, if it is determined that the economic condition of the economy has an affect on sales, information that could be used to measure this condition would be collected. Sources of information include the government, governmental agencies such as the Federal Reserve Board and National Bureau of Economic Research, industry, university research, and company records.

Information on company operations is usually available from historical records. Sales information is often analyzed in one or more of the following groupings:

1. By product
2. By geographical territory
3. By market (for example, wholesale or retail, type customer)
4. By individual customer
5. By sales unit (for example, division, sales force, sales region, salespeople)

In addition to sales, information about the company's financial position, technological capability, plant capacity, and material and personnel available is extremely valuable for planning purposes.

Evaluating the Data and Making Projections   After the information has been collected, the next step is to analyze the data and then make the sales forecast. In analyzing the data, emphasis is placed on determining trends, patterns, relationships, cycles, and seasonal fluctuations. The analytical tools often used are time series analysis, least squares, simple correlation, multiple correlation, input-output tables, and breakeven charts.[12] These tools for analyzing data will be discussed in relation to the forecasting methods which utilize them.

If all the variations that companies introduce into forecasting were classified as separate methods, the list of forecasting methods would be very large. Probably no two companies use the same method. Nevertheless, forecasting methods can normally be discussed under three general categories. These are (1) qualitative methods, (2) statistical analysis and projection, and (3) causal models.

Qualitative Methods   The objective of this approach is to bring together logically the opinions and judgments of those knowledgable about the factors being estimated. This approach is used in estimating sales in the relative short run, where individual salespeople estimate their own sales for the

next period. The estimates are reviewed by sales managers and then submitted to top management for their consideration. Necessary revisions are made and the estimates become the sales figure used in the profit planning process. Since the individual salespeople have input to the process, it is referred to as the "sales force composite" approach. Companies not involving the sales force may poll executives and use their opinions as a basis for the forecast.

Qualitative approaches are commonly used in estimating sales for new products and in technological forecasting. One popular technique used in the Delphi method, that obtains opinions of a panel of experts through the use of questionnaires and the responses from one questionnaire are used to prepare the next one. The process continues until a consensus is obtained or total disagreement is reached. While the actual application of the specific procedures of Delphi vary, Tersine and Riggs suggest that the following example is typical.

A forecast is initiated by a questionnaire which requests estimates of a set of numerical quantities (dates by which specific technological events will occur, probabilities or occurrence by given dates, event desirability and feasibility, and the like). The results of the first round are summarized, and the median and interquartile range of the responses is computed and fed back to the respondents with a request to revise their first estimates where appropriate. On succeeding rounds, those individuals whose opinions deviate greatly from the majority (outside the interquartile range) are requested to give the reasons for their extreme opinions. A collection of these reasons is presented to each participant, along with a new median and interquartile range, and participants are given another opportunity to reconsider and revise earlier opinions or estimates. The process is continued until a consensus is reached. Instead of starting with a preconceived list of questions, sometimes preliminary questionnaires are used to select and develop questions for which estimates can be obtained.[13]

One modification of the delphi technique that is used is known as cross-impact analysis. "This process takes into consideration the impact of the occurrence of an event or a subsequent event when several events are interrelated. Usually the analysis will develop a series of conditional probabilities for events."[14] An iterative process is used to help ensure that contradicting predictions are eliminated. Another technique used for forecasting is similar to the Delphi method in that it draws on the expertise of informed individuals. Basically, the method involves setting up a scenario (a description of anticipated future conditions) and then logically developing possible outcomes from the conditions given. This method can be particularly useful for long-range planning when there are high levels of uncertainty.

Game theory, another qualitative technique, is used for new product and investment decisions. Game theory assumes two players with opposing interests. Each player has a choice

12. *Ibid.*, 66.

13. Richard J. Tersine and Walter E. Riggs, "The Delphi Technique: A Long-Range Planning Tool," *Business Horizons* 19 (April 1976), 52.
14. *Ibid.*, 55.

of many strategies; however, only one of those may be used. A player attempts to select a strategy that will maximize her or his expected average benefits in each decision-making situation. In forecasting, there is a tendency, once the most likely forecast is selected, to deemphasize other forecast possibilities. Game theory can be used to overcome this tendency.[15]

Market research, where hypotheses about the real market are systematically evaluated and tested, is also used extensively for forecasting new product sales.

Statistical Analysis and Projection The use of statistical techniques is a common means of forecasting sales in many companies. The objective of the forecaster in using these methods is to observe, measure, and project various relationships within a particular company or industry.

Time series analysis is an example of a statistical technique that can be used for long-term sales forecasting. This approach assumes that in the long run, sales are affected by long-term growth trends, cyclical business fluctuations, and seasonal variations. It is difficult to measure the impact of each of the above factors because of chance variations caused by strikes, material shortages, actions of competitor, and changes in business conditions. By removing these chance variations time series analysis facilitates the analysis of underlying factors. The National Industrial Conference Board, in a study of business practices in forecasting, listed two steps usually followed in forecasting sales by this approach:

1. The actual pattern of sales figures over time is broken down or "decomposed" into four components: secular trend, cycle, seasonal, and irregular. This step illustrates what sales volumes would have been during the period being analyzed had each factor been the only one influencing sales.

2. The basic patterns of the trend, cycle, and seasonal forces are then projected forward, making allowances for any conditions that might alter the past patterns. For example, it might be decided that an increase in defense spending or a revision of the tax law would cause a change in the cyclical movement during the forecast period. An appropriate adjustment would then be made in this component before the projection was made.[16]

The use of time series analysis forces the forecaster to consider the underlying trends and seasonal elements in sales. However, it does, also, assume the continuation of historical patterns without giving adequate consideration to outside influences.

Other statistical techniques used include moving averages, exponential smoothing, and trend analysis.

Causal Models The most sophisticated type of forecasting technique is a causal model, that mathematically defines the relevant causal relationships. Common types of causal techniques include regression analysis, econometric models, input-output models, intention-to-buy and anticipation surveys, and the use of leading indicators.

Regression analysis relates sales to one or more independent variables such as economic indicators, competitive conditions, or factors internal to the business. These relationships are incorporated in a regression equation developed by utilizing the least-square technique. The first step in regression analysis is to develop a list of factors that logically affect the sales of the company. These factors are tested through correlation analysis, and those that appear to have the greatest impact on sales are selected. If more than one factor has a substantial impact, the technique used is referred to as multiple regression analysis. This method is considered to be one of the better approaches because it emphasizes those factors that cause sales to vary and because the equations developed can be used in econometric or simulation models. Regression analysis is explained in greater detail in Part 4.

The econometric model is a system of interdependent regression equations that describe some aspect of sales. This approach is sometimes considered excellent for predicting sales for three months to two year periods.[17] (The details of this approach are beyond the scope of this chapter.)

Causal techniques are sometimes used by some companies to identify the variables that influence industry sales. Once the analysis is concluded, industry volume is estimated for the forecast period, and the rate of growth of the company is compared with the growth rate for the industry. This comparison helps establish a target share of the market. Sales estimated with industry analysis is compared with estimates obtained by other approaches to determine which approach is the most satisfactory.

A good planning program does not simply rely on one technique, but uses a combination of techniques.

Operationally Applying and Controlling Forecasts The last two steps in a comprehensive sales forecasting program are applying the forecast operationally and auditing or controlling the forecast. Operationally applying the forecast involves refining the sales estimate, while controlling the forecast involves a comparison of the actual data with the forecasted data. On the basis of this comparison future plans or even the forecasting techniques can, if needed, be modified.

One of the first steps in operationally applying the forecast is to categorize sales by such volume and profit control units, product, geographical territory, market (class of customer, end use, or trade channel), individual customers, and sales unit (division, sales force, company-owned outlet, sales region, sales district, and even sales person). By dividing the forecast into these various groups, management is able to establish specific goals for the sales force. The particular way in which a company decides to refine the forecast

15. S. S. Singhui, "Game Theory Technique in Investment Planning," *Long Range Planning* (August 1974), 59.
16. National Industrial Conference Board, *Forecasting Sales*, Studies in Business Policy, No. 106 (New York: National Industrial Conference Board, 1963), p. 34.
17. John C. Chambers, Satinder K. Mullick, and Donald D. Smith. "How to Choose the Right Forecasting Technique." *Harvard Business Review* 49 (July-August 1971), 55-64 (gatefold chart).

depends on the diversity of product line, extent of geographical sales area, number of markets and customers, and several other factors.[18]

The specific goals or targets determined from refining the forecast are used to establish and coordinate operational plans. These plans consist of production schedules, purchasing plans, financial requirements, personnel needs, plant expansion, capital equipment budget, inventory levels, and marketing plans.

The key to proper sales evaluation and control is the feedback of information on a timely basis. The time period used for comparison depends on the nature of the company and the importance of a fast reply. For some companies, a daily or weekly comparison is needed, while for others, monthly comparisons may be adequate. On-line interactive computer technology has greatly helped many firms have daily or even continuous sales reports.

Feedback, however, is not the controlling device but is rather the basis for action which is the controlling device. Action may be classified as corrective, where an immediate adjustment is made, or as adoptive, where replanning is necessary to regain control over operations. Before any action can be taken, the reason for the difference between the forecast and the actual must be ascertained. The comparison of actual with forecast serves as a danger signal but does not explain the reason for the difference. Once this reason is known, a decision can be made as to the type of action necessary.

Planning often suffers because management does not develop an effective sales forecasting program. Management is reluctant at times to make predictions about future relationships that affect sales; it is easier to direct their attention to operational problems that are more concrete and easier to understand and solve. The manager, however, cannot afford to neglect sales forecasting-the key to effective marketing, planning, and control.

Problems

1. Estimated time 30 minutes (December 1972)

Arment Co. has sales in the range of $25-30 million, has one manufacturing plant, employs 700 people, including 15 national account sales people and 80 traveling sales representatives. The home office and plant is in Philadelphia, and the product is distributed east of the Mississippi River. The product is a line of pumps and related fittings used at construction sites, in homes, and in processing plants. The company has total assets equal to 80 percent of sales. Its capi-

talization is: accruals and current liabilities 30 percent, long-term debt 15 percent, and shareholders' equity 55 percent. In the last two years sales have increased 7 percent each year, and income after tax has amounted to 5 percent of sales.

Required   A. Strategic decisions by top management on a number of important topics serve as a basis for the annual profit plan. What are these topics, and why are they important?

B. What specific procedures will be followed each year in developing the annual profit plan?

2. Estimated time 30 minutes (December 1979)

Deenah Products Inc. is a manufacturer of paper and paper products. The company has never had a formal long-range planning program. Top management believes that a long-range planning program would be beneficial to the company.

Required   A. Identify and discuss the benefits generally attributed to long-range planning.

B. Economic and demographic data are important for long-range planning. List three examples each of (1) economic data and (2) demographic data that Deenah Products Inc. should consider in its long-range planning program. For each example identify the source for the data and explain why it is important to long-range planning.

3. Estimated time 30 minutes (June 1981)

Marval Products manufactures and wholesales several different lines of luggage in two basic types—soft-side and molded. Each luggage line consists of several different pieces all of which are in different sizes. At least one line is a complete set of luggage designed to be used by both men and women, but some lines and styles are designed specifically for men or women. Some lines also have matching attache cases. Luggage lines are discontinued and introduced as tastes change or as product improvements are developed.

Marval Products also manufactures luggage for large retail companies according to each company's specifications. This luggage is marketed under the retail companies' own private label rather than the Marval label.

Marval has been manufacturing several lines of luggage under its own label and private lines for one or more retail companies for the last ten years.

Required   A. Identify and discuss the factors Marval Products needs to consider in its periodic review of long-term product strategy including any decisions with respect to new and/or existing products.

B. Identify and discuss the factors Marval Products needs to consider when developing its sales component of the annual budget.

18. National Industrial Conference Board, p. 37.

4.   Estimated time 30 minutes (June 1982)

Two months ago, Harold Lewis and his son Dan, President and Executive Vice-President respectively of Stop-and-Sip Soft Drink, met to discuss the company's future. The main conclusion from their meeting was that the company had reached the peak of its internal growth, and they should look for some means of external expansion.

Stop-and-Sip Soft Drink was organized and incorporated 15 years ago by Harold Lewis, who is 57. Dan Lewis, who is 31 and has an MBA in Marketing, has worked in the business for seven years.

The firm's one large plant, a warehouse, and administrative offices are located in Vancouver, Washington. The firm also owns warehouses in Spokane, Washington and Salem, Oregon. The soft drinks are sold to local wholesalers throughout Washington and northern Oregon. Stop-and-Sip manufactures soft drink syrup and processes its own products into bottles and cans. The company's products consist of Supercola, Picker-Upper (a cherry-cola blend), Beer-Belly Root Beer, and Goofy-Grape. Supercola and Beer-Belly Root Beer are also manufactured in diet versions. Supercola accounts for about 50 percent of the sales with the rest divided about evenly among the other products. The soda is bottled in one-liter plastic containers, one-quart glass bottles, and 12-ounce metal cans in the respective proportion of sales—30 percent, 20 percent and 50 percent.

The existing plant was built six years ago and is operating at what is considered nearly full capacity, a full one-shift most of the year and a smaller second shift during the late spring and summer months when sales are especially high. The plant is operated by a salaried production manager who supervises the 28 hourly employees. A bookkeeper-office manager and one secretary also work at the administrative offices.

Since their original discussion two months ago, Harold and Dan Lewis have located two firms—Oregon Pop and Canco—which provide a reasonable opportunity for acquisition and merger. The following facts have been accumulated in order to review these two companies as potential acquisitions.

Oregon Pop

Oregon Pop is owned and operated by Douglas Ross, 55, and his son Andy, 27. Ross and his son started the company three years ago when Andy finished his degree in engineering with a minor in chemistry.

Oregon Pop's operations are all located in Eugene, Oregon. Sales are limited to the northern Willamette Valley of Oregon with primary concentration in Eugene, Salem, and Portland. Oregon Pop manufactures soft drink syrup, and processes its own products in bottles and cans. The products consist of Snapper (a lemon-lime drink), Rooty-Toot Root Beer, and Sparkle (a sparkling apple juice that Andy Ross developed last year in Oregon Pop's small lab).

Snapper accounts for 60 percent of the sales, Sparkle 30 percent, and Rooty-Toot 10 percent. The soda is bottled in one-quart glass bottles and 12-ounce metal cans. Sparkle is only available in bottles.

The plant was built specifically for Oregon Pop when the company was formed and includes computerized blending and

bottling operations. The plant operates at nearly full capacity during the peak soft drink months in the summer and during fall when sales of Sparkle are high. During the rest of the year, operations are at about 60 percent of capacity. The plant is managed by Andy Ross and is operated by a staff of 10 hourly employees, including two in the warehouse.

Canco

The second company being considered for acquisition is Canco. Canco is closely held by a small group of diverse investors. The firm operates throughout the northwest states. It manufactures soft drink cans and metal containers for such dairy products as whipped cream, cream cheese and dips. Canco is of special interest to Dan and Harold Lewis because Canco holds a patent on push-top lids. Lids with integral, non-removable openers are mandated by Oregon law.

Canco has manufacturing and storage facilities in Boise, Idaho and Tacoma, Washington. The administrative offices are in Boise. The two plants are about 18 years old and have been fairly well maintained. They operate at around 90 percent of capacity throughout the year with the dairy cans being produced mostly in the fall and winter. Production and sales are about 60 percent to dairy and 40 percent to soft drinks.

The president of Canco, Tim Roberts, is 48 years old. None of the operating management nor the employees own any shares in the company. Canco is decentralized, and each plant has a plant manager. The company employs 32 plant workers, all members of the metalworkers' local of a national union, and an office staff of five.

Financial Data

Harold Lewis has summarized financial data for all three companies as shown on the next page.

Management Conclusions

Harold Lewis believes Stop-and-Sip should consider both firms but he will agree to only one acquisition at this time. Further, he believes they should evaluate the two candidates at this point, without regard to the terms of the acquisition, the manner of payment, or the accounting treatment required. He thinks that those items can be negotiated and handled at a later date.

Required **A.** Specifically identify the overall strengths of each company being considered for merger with Stop-and-Sip, in terms of how the acquired company would be compatible with the parent.

B. Specifically identify the overall weaknesses of each company being considered for merger with Stop-and-Sip in terms of how the acquired company would not be compatible with the parent.

Stop-and-Sip Soft Drink

	Two Years Ago	Last Year	Current Year
Sales	$25,300,000	$28,190,000	$31,326,000
Assets	$11,640,000	$12,870,000	$13,991,000
Net profit margin	3.0%	3.4%	3.6%
Current ratio	1.9 times	2.1 times	2.0 times
Debt/equity ratio	.8 times	.9 times	1.0 times
Times interest	4.4 times	4.6 times	4.7 times
Inventory turnover	7.5 times	7.9 times	8.4 times

Oregon Pop

	Two Years Ago	Last Year	Current Year
Sales	$1,920,000	$3,200,000	$4,110,000
Assets	$1,510,000	$2,160,000	$2,700,000
Net profit margin	negative*	negative*	negative*
Current ratio	1.7 times	1.6 times	1.6 times
Debt/equity ratio	1.2 times	1.3 times	1.5 times
Times interest earned	.8 times	.5 times	.1 times
Inventory turnover	8.6 times	9.4 times	10.1 times

*Oregon Pop has a substantial net operating tax-loss carryforward.

Canco

	Two Years Ago	Last Year	Current Year
Sales	$37,484,000	$40,200,000	$43,200,000
Assets	$14,960,000	$15,800,000	$16,565,000
Net profit margin	3.1%	3.7%	4.0%
Current ratio	2.3 times	2.3 times	2.4 times
Debt/equity	.3 times	.3 times	.2 times
Times interest earned	12.6 times	13.1 times	16.2 times
Inventory turnover	4.5 times	5.4 times	5.8 times

5.　　　　　Estimated time 30 minutes (June 1983)

Unlike many companies in its industry, OreWood Products has the financial resources to endure slow periods in its base market. OreWood owns its own timberlands and has low debt levels that contribute to its strength. Both sales and earnings over the last decade have fluctuated sharply above and below an eight percent compound annual growth trend-line. The fluctuations are characteristic of the industry, but the growth rate is above average for the industry, as is OreWood's return-on-assets.

OreWood's common stock is widely held and traded in the over-the-counter-market. The stock currently is selling for six times earnings. OreWood is the fifth largest wood products company in the United States and is about one-third the size of its biggest competitor. The company is organized into three divisions.

One division is responsible for managing the timberlands that are large enough to meet OreWood's wood fiber needs and for providing surplus logs for sale outside the company. Most of these timberlands were acquired in the early part of this century at a cost which is miniscule compared to current fair market value.

A second division operates three large mills that produce lumber and plywood for the residential and light commercial building markets. Historically sensitive to business cycles, there are now two structural changes that will affect business. New wood technologies enable the production of lumber and plywood from previously unusable tree species grown in the southeastern United States. Sharply higher shipping costs are the second change, putting products from the Pacific northwest at a cost disadvantage in the eastern and midwestern markets.

OreWood's third division operates two paper mills that produce kraft paper for use in making cardboard boxes. This market also is sensitive to business cycles and shipping costs. There are frequent periods of unused production capacity partly due to the huge size of new paper mills. Both paper mills—and the three lumber and plywood mills—were built in the Pacific northwest prior to 1950 and have been expanded regularly since then.

The Board of Directors has been reviewing the long-run direction of OreWood. Several members of the Board have suggested that OreWood consider the acquisition and merger route to growth. The Board concluded that OreWood should formulate a strategy for growth.

Important factors that should be considered in this growth strategy are the company profile (i.e., where it is) and company objectives (i.e., where it wants to be).

Required   A. Identify and discuss the key categories that should be included in the company profile prepared by the management of OreWood Products.

B. Describe specific, important considerations that would lead OreWood Products to consider using acquisition and merger activities as part of its growth strategy.

C. To select an acquisition and merger candidate, OreWood Products probably would employ a screening procedure to evaluate potential candidates and then select a candidate from those that satisfy the screening criteria.

1. Identify significant screening criteria OreWood could use in evaluating merger and acquisition candidates.

2. Discuss criteria OreWood should use to select one candidate from the group of final candidates.

---

6.   Estimated time 30 minutes (December 1990)

Sovera Enterprises, an expanding conglomerate, was founded 35 years ago by Emil Sovera. The company's policy has been to acquire businesses that show significant profit potential; if a business fails to attain projected profits, it is usually sold. Presently, the company consists of eight businesses acquired throughout the years; three of these businesses are described below.

LaBue Videodiscs produces a line of videodisc players. The sale of videodisc players has not met expectations, but the management of LaBue believes that the company will succeed in being the first to develop a moderately priced videodisc recorder/player. Market research predicts that the first company to develop this product will be a star.

Ulysses Travel Agencies also showed potential, and the travel industry is growing. However, Ulysses' market share has declined for the last two years even though Sovera has contributed a lot of money to Ulysses' operations. The travel agencies located in the midwest and eastern sections of the country have been the biggest drain on resources.

Reddy Self-Storage was one of the first self-storage companies to open. For the last three years, Reddy as maintained a large market share while growth in the self-storage market has slowed considerably.

Ron Ebert, chairman of Sovera, prepared the agenda for the company's annual planning meeting where the present businesses were evaluated and strategies for future acquisitions were formulated. The following statements of strategy for each of the subsidiary companies discussed were formulated as the basis for the master plan.

• **LaBue Videodiscs.** Sovera's discretionary resources are to be employed to support the growth of this business. The future officers of Sovera are to be developed here.

• **Ulysses Travel Agencies.** An orderly disposal of the least profitable locations is the initial objective. Once the disposals are complete, an acceptable profit and growth strategy for the remaining locations will be formulated.

• **Reddy Self-Storage.** The strategy for this company is to maintain efficient operations and maximize the generation of cash for use in the further development of Sovera's other companies.

These strategy statements were part of the strategic plan presented to Sovera's Board of Directors. The Directors' only debate was whether Sovera should sell the entire Ulysses organization rather than parts of it. However, the Board approved all three statements as presented and circulated them to managers throughout the three units as the corporation's "new marching orders."

Required   A. Identify corporate policies and practices needed for strategic planning to be effective.

B. Identify at least four general characteristics that differentiate the three businesses identified above, and describe how these characteristics influenced the formation of a different strategy for each business.

C. Discuss the likely effects of the three strategy statements on the behavior of the top management and middle management of each of the three businesses.

Solutions

1.

A. The following topics are among those considered by top management to be strategic planning issues.

1. What are overall objectives of the firm?
2. What markets will be served?
3. What channels of distribution will be utilized?
4. What form of organization structure will be suited to the firm's objectives and activities?
5. What basic financial structure will be employed?
6. What intensity of research and development will be planned?

Decisions with regard to the above and similar topics are important because they give the firm the objectives to be reached and provide the basic methods to be used to reach the objectives. The annual profit plan includes the specific activities required to carry out the required strategic plans and to reach the firm's objectives.

B. The annual profit plan reflects the company's expectations for sales, expenses, profits, and changes in financial position for the budget year.

For Arment Co. it would begin with the sales plans for the year. The company would estimate the sales volume in its several product lines and market segments taking into account (1) the state of the economy and its effect on Arment products, (2) the effect on sales of adjustments in Arment's marketing efforts, (3) the actions by Arment's competitors, and (4) the opinions of Arment's sale people as to the prospects for next year. The result would be a **sales budget** for the several products, customer classes and territories. The sales budget and the various marketing efforts to accomplish the sales budget would be the foundation for development of the **marketing expense budget** (including sales force, advertising, and distribution expenses) broken down as appropriate to the products, customer classes and territories. The sales budget plus decisions with respect to inventory levels would serve as the basis of the **manufacturing and production budget**. This budget would identify quantities of different products to be manufactured and overall requirements for materials, labor and other manufacturing expenses. The overall level of sales and production activity would be used to develop the **administrative expense budget**. This budget would indicate levels of accounting, legal, personnel and general administration to be carried out.

Corporation policies with respect to research and development and current financial status would be used to develop the **research and development budget**.

The impact of the budgets described above plus corporation actions to carry out strategic decisions (e.g., acquire long-term financing, build a plant, etc.) would be used to prepare **cash budgets, capital additions budgets** and to prepare the **budgeted income statement** and **balance sheet** for the year.

2.

A. The benefits of long-range planning include the following:

- requires firms to identify their goals and objectives, strengths, and weaknesses.
- provides a basis for orderly development and growth.
- allows for more effective capital expenditure planning.
- focuses attention on achievement of short-term goals consistent with long-range objectives.
- provides clear standards against which long-range progress can be evaluated and measured.

B. 1. *Economic data*

- Projected market (supply and demand) for sale of paper and paper products and selling prices in both short- and long-term.

  Source: Company and industry market research, government forecasts, and private economic forecasts.

  Importance: Market data identify potentials for growth and reduction in production of specific types of products, need for changes in transportation, storage, and/or marketing strategies, and desirability of change in production capabilities and financing options. Primary use of pricing predictions would be in identifying products which appear to be viable for future production. Pricing policy coupled with cost control on the company level are needed in long-term planning to maintain or improve product profitability.

- Availability and cost of raw materials and labor used in the production of paper and paper products in short- and long-term.

  Source: Company and industry market research, government forecasts, and private economic forecasts.

  Importance: Availability of raw materials needs to be determined to know whether products can be produced. Management needs to know if a sufficient quantity and quality of labor is available in the vicinity of the company's manufacturing plants at a reasonable rate. Cost data is required to determine if products will be profitable to produce and sell.

- Technological advances in the paper and related industries.

  Source: Company and industry research studies, government studies, university research.

  Importance: New technological advances may influence production methods, type and usage of raw materials, and costs of production.

2. *Demographic data*

- Shifts in market dispersion for Deenah products.

  Source: Company and industry research, local and state bureaus' information, paper-user industry data on plant locations and growth in use of products.

  Importance: The location of supply and storage facilities, marketing and transportation channels may have to be changed in the future.

- There are a number of population characteristics which are important, including:
  —distribution of population by age categories.
  —birth rate.

—data on consumer income.

Source: Census Bureau, academic studies, government reports, industry market research.

Importance: Product, age and income characteristics may have impacts on selling and pricing of products.

3.

A. Specific factors which Marval Products needs to consider in its periodic review of long-term product strategy include the following:

• Examine the current state of the economy and its expected future status, and the current and future availability of resources, such as manpower, plant and equipment, and capital.

• Review consumer attitudes with regard to product appeal, changing travel modes and patterns, and changing life styles and affluency.

• Analyze the level of industry sales, Marval's current and projected market share, and Marval's degree of influence or dominance in the industry.

• Examine the product lines with respect to the nature of the production process, length of time the product has been established, and utilization of resources and plant capacity.

B. Factors which Marval Products needs to consider when developing the sales component of its annual budget include the pricing strategy, size of Marval's market share and the relationship to its competitors, sales-mix of products such that contribution can be maximized, available production capacity, effect of advertising on sales volume, and national and international economic conditions.

4.

A. The strengths of Oregon Pop include the following:

• Horizontal integration will broaden the product line to include the complementary products of Snapper and Sparkle.

• The plants use similar bottle and can types and sizes for their products. This could result in some operating efficiencies.

• Oregon Pop has modern facilities including a computerized blending and bottling operation. This technology possibly could be implemented in other plants, if desired.

• The production of Sparkle will help stabilize the seasonal effect of soft drink production throughout the fall.

• Sales are increasing at a faster rate than the rate of sales at Stop-and-Sip (24% for Stop-and-Sip over the two years versus 114% for Oregon Pop).

The strengths of Canco include the following:

• A vertical type of merger would lessen the dependence on a single type of product.

• The merger would provide Stop-and-Sip with direct access to the supplier holding the patent needed to can soda for Oregon

Pop under the mandates of the bottle bill.

• The seasonality of the business would be diminished because of the production of cans for dairy products in the off-season.

• Canco apparently has utilized very little debt as evidenced by a good debt/equity ratio and the high times interest ratio. This combination should provide additional borrowing capacity to finance future expansion.

B. The weaknesses of Oregon Pop include the following:

• Oregon Pop's profitability record is not good and will probably create a drag on overall profits until the high overhead facilities can be utilized more effectively.

• Oregon Pop has a higher debt/equity ratio and a poor times-interest-earned ratio.

• Placement of Douglas Ross could create a management problem. Harold Lewis (Stop-and-Sip) and Douglas Ross (Oregon Pop) serve similar financial and personnel roles. Each is in his late 50s, but not quite at retirement age.

• The sales market territory already is covered by Stop-and-Sip.

The weaknesses of Canco include the following:

• Relocation of central offices could create problems of personnel displacement.

• The Canco plants are fairly old and may be nearing the time for replacement.

• The Canco plant employees are unionized.

• Canco is a larger firm than Stop-and-Sip and is relatively thin with management talent.

5.

A. The key categories that could be included in the company profile of OreWood Products are shown below.

Category	Position of OreWood Products
• Expertise	OreWood has expertise in managing timberlands and operating lumber and paper mills.
• Manufacturing capacity	OreWood has excess capacity in its Pacific northwest, all of which are well over thirty years old.
• Competitive (market) position	OreWood is in a weak competitive position due to higher shipping costs and the new technologies used by other suppliers.
• Financial position	OreWood has low debt levels and above average growth and return-on-assets.

B. The merger and acquisition route probably would be OreWood's best route to growth because internal diversification or growth is slower and may be more expensive in the long-run. Furthermore, merger and acquisition are the fastest ways to deal with the structural changes affecting the business.

Factors that support growth by merger and acquisition include the following.

- OreWood's strengths are all aimed at its present markets; these markets have doubtful growth prospects.

- The acquisition of timberlands and mills close to the eastern and midwestern markets could eliminate the obstacle to growth caused by escalating transportation costs.

- OreWood would become more competitive by acquiring companies in the southeastern United States that have the new wood technologies.

- OreWood presently has the financial strength to diversify through acquisition and merger and could sell off some excess capacity to realize greater and more liquid financial strength.

C. 1. Screening criteria Orewood could use in evaluating merger and acquisition candidates include:

- Reputation and quality of the candidate's owners and management.
- Growth potential of the market in which the candidate operates.
- Size of the candidate.
- Potential synergistic effects of combining with the candidate (e.g., cyclical nature of the candidate).
- Financial condition of the candidate, including any contracts and leases binding on the candidate.

2. Criteria Orewood should use to select one candidate from the group of final candidates include:

- Company history—both operational and financial.
- Legal and tax considerations.
- Ease of integration with parent company.
- Quality of product and market share by product line, including expectation for growth and assessment of competition.

6.

A. The corporate policies and practices that are needed for strategic plans to be effective include

- continued, visible management support for the plan
- clear communication of the plan to all key personnel.
- delegating responsibility for implementing the plan.
- providing the necessary resources to achieve the plan.
- management flexibility to alter the plan should circumstances warrant a change.

B. At least four general characteristics that differentiate the three Sovera Enterprises' subsidiaries include

- growth potential.
- profitability.
- discretionary cash flow.
- level of risk.

These characteristics influenced the formulation of a different strategy for each subsidiary in the following manner.

- LaBue Videodiscs subsidiary has promise to be a leading player in the videodisc market if it can develop a moderately priced videodisc record/player before its competition. Because of LaBue's profit potential, the corporation has placed a high priority on the growth of this subsidiary by allocating discretionary resources to support its product development efforts and growth.

- Ulysses Travel has a high level of risk associated with both profit and growth potential. This is a mature company in a very competitive business. The plan to divest agencies with the biggest drain on resources will reduce the risk.

- Reddy Self-Storage's growth potential is limited as the self-storage market has declined considerably. The subsidiary has predictable profits that will allow it to generate cash (cash cow). In order to maintain profitability, the subsidiary has been directed to maintain efficient operations and maximize cash flow to support the expansion and operating plans of the other subsidiaries.

C. The likely effects of these three strategies on the behavior of the top and middle management of each of the three businesses include the following.

LaBue Videodiscs

- Top management will be challenged to develop a moderately priced unit and to capture market share before the competition enters the market.

- Top management and middle management will view the strategy of developing all future officers as a career opportunity. There will be high morale and loyalty to the group and the company.

Ulysses Travel Agencies

- Top management will be challenged to efficiently dispose of the resource draining agencies, to operate the remaining agencies on a profitable basis, and to grow in geographical areas where there is adequate profit potential.

- Middle managers, particularly those in the least productive agencies, will view their jobs as threatened as the method of their agencies' disposal is not yet defined, i.e., outright closure or sale to another party.

- Top and middle managers will view the strategy of developing all future officers in the videodisc subsidiary as career limiting. Morale and motivation are likely to be low.

Reddy Self-Storage

- Top management will be challenged to operate their subsidiary in an efficient, cash providing manner while taking any opportunity to grow as their market may grow. However, their motivation will be limited as there is little market growth and the excess cash they generate is being diverted to other business units.

- Top and middle managers will view the strategy of developing the corporation's future officers in the videodisc subsidiary as career limiting.

Chapter 4

Profit Planning and Budgetary Control

Grant W. Newton

Almost everyone is familiar with budgets. They are prepared, to varying degrees, by virtually every type of organization, including the family. For businesses, budgets assume a particularly important role as the monetary expression of the objectives of the firm. However, the budget is just one part of a comprehensive planning and control system designed to achieve the ultimate goals of the firm.

In order to have an effective budgeting and control process, the firm should study the relationship between cost, volume, and profit. This would allow it to make a rational analysis of the interplay between changes in these factors. The first part of this chapter covers this analysis; the balance is devoted to a discussion of the annual budgeting process.

Cost-Volume-Profit Analysis

Selling price, the number and type of products to manufacture, the amount to spend on promotion costs, and the type of equipment to buy are decisions that are made after the relationship between cost, volume, and profit has been completely analyzed. The key to establishing this relationship is understanding the value of the contribution margin.

The **contribution margin** is the difference between sale price and variable costs. It is the amount available to cover fixed costs first and then provide for a profit. Contribution margin can be expressed in terms of total dollar values and in terms of contribution margin per unit as shown for sales of 20,000 units:

	Total	Per Unit
Sales	$200,000	$10
Variable costs	120,000	6
Contribution margin	80,000	$ 4
Fixed costs	40,000	
Net income	$ 40,000	

Variable costs are those costs which vary directly with production and can include costs for both manufacturing and selling and administrative activities. Other terms used to refer to the contribution margin include **marginal income** and **marginal contribution**.

Break-even Analysis

The **break-even point** is the point where there is neither a profit nor a loss from sales. It is the point where all fixed and variable costs are covered and nothing is left for profit. The break-even point can be expressed in terms of units or sales dollars.

An Example   The Westwood Lamp Company is a small operation where one type of lamp is produced which sells for $20. The variable manufacturing costs are $11 and the variable selling expenses are $1 per unit. Fixed manufacturing costs are $30,000 and fixed selling and administrative costs total $10,000.

The break-even point expressed in units for Westwood is:

$$\text{BEP in units} = \frac{\text{Fixed costs}}{\text{Contribution margin per unit}}$$

$$= \frac{\$40,000}{\$8^a}$$

$$= 5,000 \text{ units}$$

[a] Sales price of \$20, less variable manufacturing of \$11 and variable selling of \$1.

The analysis can be expanded to include the sales (in units) necessary to earn a desired profit. For example, if Westwood expects to earn \$80,000 in profits, 15,000 units must be sold:

$$\frac{\text{Fixed costs} + \text{Desired profit}}{\text{Contribution margin per unit}} = \frac{\$40,000 + \$80,000}{\$8}$$

$$= 15,000 \text{ units}$$

The contribution margin ratio (contribution margin ÷ sales price) is used in calculating the break-even sales volume.

$$\frac{\text{BEP in}}{\text{sales dollars}} = \frac{\text{Fixed costs}}{1 - \dfrac{V}{S}} = \frac{\text{Fixed costs}}{\text{Contribution margin ratio}}$$

$$= \frac{\$40,000}{.40^a}$$

$$= \$100,000$$

where V = Aggregate variable costs in dollars   S = Aggregate sales in dollars

[a] Contribution margin per unit of \$8 divided by sales per unit of \$20.

To determine the sales volume (in dollars) needed to earn the \$80,000 desired profit, the latter is added to fixed costs:

$$\frac{\text{Fixed costs} + \text{Desired profit}}{\text{Contribution margin ratio}} = \frac{\$40,000 + \$80,000}{.40}$$

$$= \$300,000 \text{ sales dollars}$$

The following equation is an effective way to analyze the relationship between cost, profit, and volume:

Sales = Variable expense + Fixed expense + Net income

This equation can be used to calculate break-even points or to estimate profit at various levels. The break-even point in sales dollars for Westwood is:

Let X = Sales dollars needed to break even
$$X = .60X + \$40,000$$

$$.40X = \$40,000$$
$$X = \$100,000$$

If Westwood desires a net income of 15 percent of sales, the sales volume in units would be:

Let X = Sales volume in units needed to earn the 15 percent

$$\$20X = \$12X + \$40,000 + .15(\$20X)$$
$$\$5X = \$40,000$$
$$X = 8,000 \text{ units}$$

The break-even point in the Westwood example can be graphed as shown in Exhibit 4-1. The fixed costs are placed above the variable costs in order to depict the fact that the contribution margin covers more of the fixed costs as volume increases. Once the break-even sales level of 5,000 units is reached, any contribution from additional sales represents profit.

Study the R. A. Ro and Company problem, a previous CMA problem, in Example 4-1. The solution is presented in Exhibit 4-2. In answering part A, notice how the equation can be used to calculate net income. The profit must be reduced by the taxes for the year at a rate of 40 percent. In answering part C, the fixed cost is increased to \$146,250 (\$135,000 + \$11,250). In answering part D, remember that in any break-even problem, the sales volume is unknown. For part E, notice that last year's profit was \$54,000. Part F is calculated in the following way:

Let Y = Maximum advertising

Desired profit = (Sales − Variable costs − Fixed costs − Additional advertising) × (1 − Tax rate)
$$\$60,000 = [(22,000 \times \$25) - (22,000 \times \$13.75 - \$135,000 - Y] .6$$
$$\$60,000 = (\$550,000 - \$302,500 - \$135,000 - Y] .6$$
$$\$60,000 = (\$67,500 - .6Y)$$
$$.6Y = (\$67,500 - \$60,000)$$
$$Y = \$12,500$$

Assumptions of Break-even Chart   The break-even chart is based on a large number of assumptions. If the assumptions are not true, then the break-even point or desired profit level may vary—to what extent depends on the amount of deviation from the assumed character of the costs and revenues comprising the chart. The assumptions are:

1. All costs are linear and can be divided into either fixed or variable components. Fixed costs remain constant while variable costs change proportionally with variations in volume.

2. The sales price per unit does not change with changes in volume.

Exhibit 4-1

Westwood Lamp Company

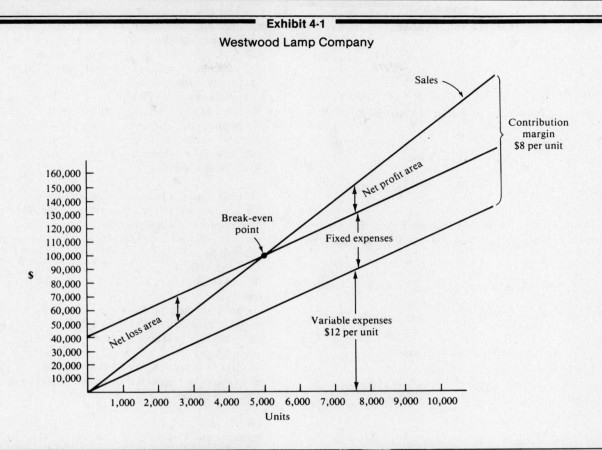

Example 4-1

R. A. Ro and Company, maker of quality handmade pipes, has experienced a steady growth in sales for the past five years. However, increased competition has led Mr. Ro, the president, to believe that an aggressive advertising campaign will be necessary next year to maintain the company's present growth.

To prepare for next year's advertising campaign, the company's accountant has prepared and presented Mr. Ro with the following data for the current year, 19X2:

Required   A. What is the projected after-tax net income for 19X2?

B. What is the break-even point in units for 19X2?

C. Mr. Ro believes an additional selling expense of $11,250 for advertising in 19X3, with all other costs remaining constant, will be necessary to attain the sales target. What will be the after-tax net income for 19X3 if the additional $11,250 is spent?

D. What will be the break-even point in dollar sales for 19X3 if the additional $11,250 is spent for advertising?

E. If the additional $11,250 is spent for advertising in 19X3, what is the required sales level in dollar sales to equal 19X2's after-tax net income?

F. At a sales level of 22,000 units, what is the maximum amount that can be spent on advertising if an after-tax net income of $60,000 is desired?

COST SCHEDULE

Variable costs:	
Direct labor	$ 8.00/ pipe
Direct materials	3.25/pipe
Variable overhead	2.50/pipe
Total variable costs	$13.75/pipe
Fixed costs:	
Manufacturing	$ 25,000
Selling	40,000
Administrative	70,000
Total fixed costs	$135,000

Selling price, per pipe:	$25.00
Expected sales, 19X2 (20,000 units):	$500,000
Tax rate:	40%

Mr. Ro has set the sales target for 19X3 at a level of $550,000 (or 22,000 pipes).

Exhibit 4-2
R. A. Ro and Company

A. (Sales − Variable costs − Fixed costs) × (1 − tax rate)

$$= \text{after-tax net income}$$

$$(\$500,000 - \$275,000 - \$135,000) \times (1 - .40)$$

$$= \text{Projected 19X2 after-tax income} = \$54,000$$

B. $\dfrac{\text{Fixed costs}}{\text{Variable contribution per unit}} = \text{Break-even volume in units}$

$$\frac{\$135,000}{(\$25.00 - \$13.75)} = \frac{\$135,000}{\$11.25} = 12,000 \text{ units}$$

C. $(\$550,000 - \$302,500 - \$146,250) \times (1 - .40)$

$$= \text{Projected 19X3 after-tax income} = \$60,750$$

D. $\dfrac{\text{Fixed costs}}{\text{Variable contribution per dollar sales}} = \text{Break-even volume in dollars}$

$$\frac{\$146,250}{.45} = \$325,000$$

E.

$$X = \text{required 19X3 sales units}$$

$$\$25X = \text{required 19X3 sales dollars}$$

$$\$54,000 = (\$25.00X - \$13.75X - \$146,250)$$

$$\times (1 - .40)$$

$$X = 21,000 \text{ units}$$

$$\$25X = \$525,000$$

3. The sales mix is constant (if multiple products are simultaneously being analyzed).

4. The price of the input factors (materials, labor and so on) does not change.

5. The only factor that influences costs and revenue is changes in the sales volume. No allowance is made for efficiency and increased productivity as volume increases.

Flexible Budgets

Flexible budgets make performance analysis possible when output deviates from planned levels. Consider a situation where 10,000 units were budgeted for and only 8,000 units were actually produced. In a static budget approach, a comparison of planned costs with actual costs would yield a variance. For example, most university departments have a fixed annual budget that does not vary with the number of students processed. The variance under this approach could be interpreted as being favorable when, in fact, the operation was actually very inefficient for the period. This is because we are comparing the actual costs for 8,000 students (or units) with the planned costs for 10,000 students (or units). The **flexible-budgeting** approach suggests that the actual volume be used for cost analysis in determining the efficiency of the department's operations. A comparison of the planned

volume with the actual volume would, however, still be made to evaluate how effective the manager was in attaining the planned output. Both measures are necessary to judge the manager's performance and each must be calculated separately for proper contrast.

In addition to being based on the concept of a common activity, flexible budgeting utilizes cost behavior patterns. To predict cost effectively at any level of output, management must have some understanding of the nature of costs and how they behave. Costs can be classified as variable, fixed, or semivariable.

Variable Costs   Normally, the variable cost, as viewed by the accountant, has a linear relationship. However, if it is determined that the behavior of the variable cost is not linear, but curvilinear or some other nonlinear shape, the cost can still be included in the flexible budget. This can be accomplished by the use of a formula describing the cost function or by using the total cost as shown on a graph of the past costs.

Some cost may be classified as variable yet also increase in steps, as shown in Exhibit 4-3. Note in (a) that the cost as shown by the broken line can be considered variable. The extent, however, to which step-like behavior can be viewed as variable costs depends on the width of the steps. In (b) is an example of step behavior so wide that it must be considered a fixed cost.

Fixed Costs   Fixed costs are created by decisions made by management. Generally, as companies grow, there is a tendency for the percentage of total fixed costs to increase. During such growth management is reducing its variable costs and making long-term commitments, so-called operating leverage. As long as the activity level increases, or at least does not decline, the fixed cost commitment will be profitable. Should the outputs decrease, however, these fixed costs could put a real financial strain on the company provided that they are not already sunk costs. Although these costs are fixed because of management decisions, other decisions can be made to alter their status. Thus, in the long-run, all costs can be viewed as variable.

Fixed costs that are budgeted for one period at a time (usually a year) and are subject to change within the period are called **programmed costs**. Other authors refer to these costs as **managed** or **discretionary costs**. They differ from variable costs in that they are not necessarily correlated with volume of activity. Examples of such costs are research and development costs, training costs, consultant fees, and advertising. Effective planning is critical if maximum benefit is to be obtained from programmed costs. Decisions to incur these costs are normally made at the beginning of a new budget period.

Committed costs, another subdivision of fixed costs, are those where a longer permanent commitment by management is required. Examples of these costs are depreciation, long-term lease agreements, property taxes, and insurance. These costs cannot be eliminated without affecting the long-term goals of the company. The planning period for committed costs is several years, and these costs are much less responsive to monthly and yearly operating decisions. Some committed costs are sunk costs (such as depreciation), whereas others require cash outflows (for example, property taxes and lease payments).

Semivariable Costs   Semivariable (sometimes called "mixed") costs are the most difficult to predict because they contain elements of both fixed and variable costs. This type of cost can be the product of several conditions. One possible situation producing semivariable costs occurs when there is a need to maintain some minimum level of a service or commodity no matter how low the operating level. This minimum level would be considered the fixed portion. As operations increased, quantities in excess of the minimum level would be related to volume. Maintenance is an example of this type of situation. Another circumstance that produces semivariable patterns is the lumping of costs together. Power costs can fit into this category, if the charges for lighting and heating are combined with those for operating the machinery. Several approaches are used to analyze these costs in order to segment them into their fixed and variable components. These approaches are described in Volume 5, Chapter 5. Semivariable costs are shown graphically in Exhibit 4-4.

Note that the total costs at zero volume consist of fixed costs only. This may not, in fact, represent the true level of fixed costs since that volume level is outside the relevant range, which is based on recent experience. The concept of the relevant range is applicable to all types of costs. A volume level below the relevant range may result in much lower fixed costs, while one above the range would result in a substantial rise in fixed costs. For example, if a company were already producing at capacity, increasing production would necessitate the purchase of additional machinery, which would add to the fixed costs. The variable elements may also change outside of the relevant range.

Do Example 4-2, a previous CPA examination problem, which illustrates several types of behavior patterns for various expenses. The answers are given in Exhibit 4-5.

Activity Measurement   When more than one product is manufactured, it is difficult to determine the manner in which activity should be measured. Horngren suggests that when a variety of products or operations exists the following criteria should help in selecting a measure of volume:

1. Cause of Cost Fluctuation.   The activity selected must, at least to some extent, cause the cost to vary or otherwise be associated with cost variation. Examples of commonly used measures include direct labor hours, machine hours, miles traveled, number of calls made, and pages of output.

2. Independence of Activity Unit.   The item selected should be affected primarily by volume. For example, direct labor cost is affected by changes in the wage rate; whereas, direct labor hours are not.

3. Ease of Understanding.   The activity selected should be easily understood and obtained with a minimum of clerical costs.

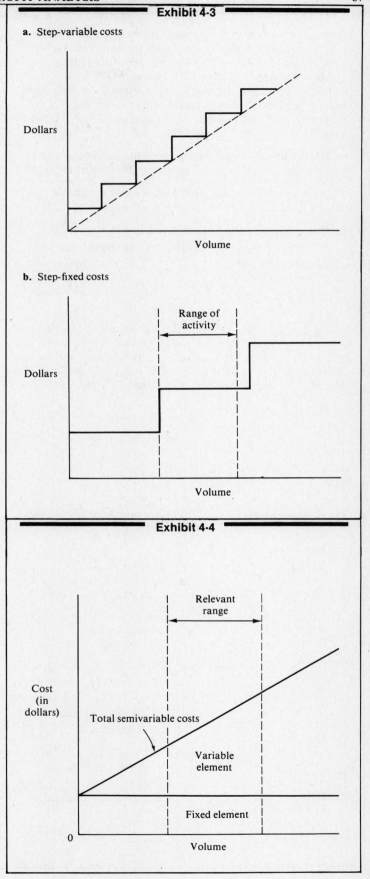

Exhibit 4-3

a. Step-variable costs

Dollars

Volume

b. Step-fixed costs

Range of activity

Dollars

Volume

Exhibit 4-4

Relevant range

Cost (in dollars)

Total semivariable costs

Variable element

Fixed element

0   Volume

Example 4-2

On a lined sheet of paper, number the first ten lines from 1 to 10. Select the graph which matches the numbered factory cost or expense data and write the letter identifying the graph on the appropriate numbered line.

The vertical axes of the graphs represent *total* dollars of expense and the horizontal axes represent production. In each case the zero point is at the intersection of the two axes. The graphs may be used more than once.

1. Depreciation of equipment, where the amount of depreciation charged is computed by the machine hours method.

2. Electricity bill—a flat fixed charge, plus a variable cost after a certain number of kilowatt hours are used.

3. City water bill, which is computed as follows:

First 1,000,000 gallons or less	$1,000 flat fee
Next 10,000 gallons	.003 per gallon used
Next 10,000 gallons	.006 per gallon used
Next 10,000 gallons	.009 per gallon used
etc., etc., etc.	

4. Cost of lubricant for machines, where cost per unit decreases with each pound of lubricant used (for example, if one pound is used, the cost is $10; if two pounds are used, the cost is $19.98; if three pounds are used, the cost is $29.94; with a minimum cost per pound of $9.25).

5. Depreciation of equipment, where the amount is computed by the straight-line method. When the depreciation rate was established, it was anticipated that the obsolescence factor would be greater than the wear and tear factor.

6. Rent on a factory building donated by the city, where the agreement calls for a fixed fee payment unless 200,000 work-hours are worked, in which case no rent need be paid.

7. Salaries of repair crew, where one repair person is needed for every 1,000 hours of machine hours or less (that is, 0 to 1,000 hours requires one repair person, 1,001 to 2,000 hours requires two, and so on).

8. Federal unemployment compensation taxes for the year, where labor force is constant in number throughout year (average annual salary is $10,000 per worker). Only the first $4,200 earned is subject to tax.

9. Cost of raw material used.

10. Rent on a factory building donated by county, where agreement calls for rent $100,000 less $1 for each direct labor hour worked in excess of 200,000 hours, but minimum rental payment of $20,000 must be paid.

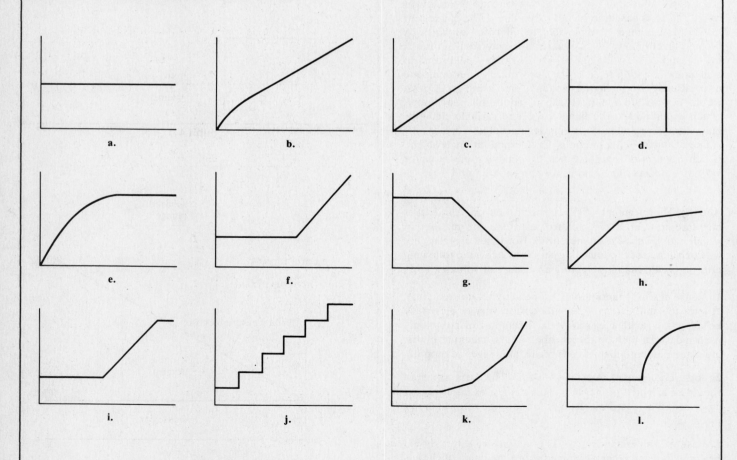

Exhibit 4-5

Cost Behavior Pattern

1. c: The depreciation expense rises directly in relation to the number of machine hours used.

2. f: Through the initial stages of production only a flat fee is charged; after the specified number of kilowatt hours are used up, the expense is related to the units of production.

3. k: The changes in the graph indicate the rate is increasing at an increasing rate.

4. b: The curve of the graph is the result of the decreasing price per unit. Once the $9.25 minimum cost is reached, the expense is directly related to units produced.

5. a: The depreciation expense is the same at all levels of production.

6. d: The fees are fixed until 200,000 work-hours are achieved and at that point they drop to zero.

7. j: This is an example of a step-cost.

8. h: While there is a constant number of employees, they are not necessarily the same employees throughout the year.

9. c: Raw materials used should vary with the units produced.

10. g: The expense is fixed at $100,000 until 200,000 hours of labor are utilized, at which point the expense drops $1 for each additional labor hour used. However, since there is a minimum rental fee of $20,000, the expense would remain at that point for all additional levels of production.

Example 4-3

The Melcher Co. produces farm equipment at several plants. The business is seasonal and cyclical in nature. The company has attempted to use budgeting for planning and controlling activities, but the variable nature of the business has caused some company officials to be skeptical about the usefulness of budgeting to the company. The accountant for the Adrian plant has been using a system she calls "flexible budgeting" to help her plant management control operations.

The company President asks her to explain what the term means, how she applies the system at the Adrian plant, and how it can be applied to the company as a whole. The accountant presents the following data as part of her explanation.

Required **A.** Prepare a budget for January.

B. Prepare a report for January comparing actual and budgeted costs for the actual activity for the month.

C. Can flexible budgeting be applied to the nonmanufacturing activities of the company? Explain your answer.

BUDGET DATA FOR 19X3

Normal monthly capacity of the plant in direct labor hours		10,000 hours
Material costs	6 lbs. @ $1.50	$9.00 unit
Labor costs	2 hours @ $3.00	$6.00 unit

OVERHEAD ESTIMATE
AT NORMAL MONTHLY CAPACITY

Variable (controllable):	
Indirect labor	$6,650
Indirect materials	600
Repairs	750
Total variable	8,000
Fixed (noncontrollable):	
Depreciation	3,250
Supervision	3,000
Total fixed	6,250
Total fixed and variable	$14,250
Planned units for January 19X3	4,000
Planned units for February 19X3	6,000

ACTUAL DATA FOR JANUARY 19X3

Hours worked	8,400
Units produced	3,800
Costs incurred:	
Material (24,000 lbs.)	$36,000
Direct labor	25,200
Indirect labor	6,000
Indirect materials	600
Repairs	1,800
Depreciation	3,250
Supervision	3,000
Total	$75,850

Exhibit 4-6

Melcher Company

A. January volume: Units planned— 4,000

Direct labor hours planned— 8,000

Budgeted January costs based upon planned volume:

Material: 24,000 lbs. @ $1.50/lb.		$36,000
Labor: 8,000 hours @ $3.00/hr.		24,000
Overhead:		
Variable:		
Indirect labor (4,000 × $1.33)	$5,320	
Indirect materials (4,000 × $0.12)	480	
Repairs (4,000 × $0.15)	600	6,400
Fixed:		
Depreciation	3,250	
Supervision	3,000	6,250
Budgeted costs for January		$72,650

B.

	Budget adjusted to actual activity— 3,800 units	Actual costs	Under (over) adjusted budget
Materials (3,800 × $9)	$34,200	$36,000	$(1,800)
Labor (3,800 × $6)	22,800	25,200	(2,400)
Overhead[a]			
Indirect labor (3,800 × $1.33)	5,054	6,000	(946)
Indirect Material (3,800 × $.12)	456	600	(144)
Repairs (3,800 × $.15)	570	1,800	(1,230)
Depreciation	3,250	3,250	–
Supervision	3,000	3,000	–
	$69,330	$75,850	$(6,520)

[a] The overhead portion of flexible budgets are sometimes based on labor hours or labor dollars. If those alternatives had been applied here, the total overhead variance would have been $5,880—the same amount since the budgeted direct labor rate of $3 is equal to the actual rate.

C. Yes. Flexible budgeting is the process of adjusting budgets to reflect actual levels. Comparison of actual costs to budgets adjusted to actual activity levels results in better measures of the cost performances of management units. The concept can be applied to all operations where costs should change as department activity changes. The concept is limited only by the difficulties of identifying the proper activity base for measuring activity change and measuring the cost behavior with respect to this activity unit.

4. Adequacy of Control Over Base. Adequate control must be exercised over the item being used as the basis. Standard hours allowed is better than actual hours. When actual hours are used, managers can increase their budget allowance for overload by taking longer to complete the job; however, if standard hours allowed are used, the inefficiencies could not be hidden.[1]

Illustration of Flexible Budgets Once the cost behavior patterns are determined and the measure of activity selected, a budget can be determined for various output levels. The flexible budget can also be expressed in a formula where budgeted costs for a given volume level will be some fixed amount plus the variable cost rate times the volume:

Budgeted cost = Fixed costs + Variable costs

× Level of output

Example 4-3, a previous CMA examination problem, illustrates how flexible budgeting can be used. Part A requires the construction of a budget for January, which would be prepared based on the planned output of 4,000 units. The information needed to construct the flexible budget is summarized below:

Variable Cost (per unit)		
Materials		$ 9.00
Labor		6.00
Overhead:		
Indirect labor ($6,650 ÷ 5,000)	$1.33	
Indirect materials ($600 ÷ 5,000)	.12	
Repairs ($750 ÷ 5,000)	.15	1.60
Total variable costs		$16.60
Fixed Costs per month		$6,250

Note that the variable overhead rate per unit is determined by taking the budget cost and dividing it by the normal output used to calculate the budget. The normal capacity is 10,000 hours, which represents an output of 5,000 units since it takes two hours to make one unit.

Exhibit 4-6 contains the solution to Example 4-3. In part B, note that the budget is reconstructed to reflect what the cost should be for the actual output of 3,800 units. The variances calculated using 3,800 units as the volume level are much more meaningful than they would be if the actual costs were compared with the budget for 4,000 units.

Flexible Budgets-Other Types Flexible budgets can be prepared for service departments, for marketing areas, and for many administrative functions. In manufacturing operations, the budget is frequently based on direct labor hours, direct labor costs, or machine hours. Commercial areas often use other activity bases, such as miles traveled, invoice lines printed, number of customers, number of transactions, weight of shipment, and gross sales dollars.

1. Charles T. Horngren and George Foster, *Cost Accounting: A Management Emphasis,* 6th ed. (Englewood Cliffs, N.J.: Prentice-Hall, 1987), pp. 223-224.

Example 4-4

The University of Boyne offers an extensive continuing education program in many cities throughout the state. For the convenience of its faculty and administrative staff and also to save costs, the university operates a motor pool. Until February the motor pool operated with 20 vehicles. However, an additional automobile was acquired in February this year, increasing the total to 21 vehicles. The motor pool furnishes gasoline, oil and other supplies for the cars, and hires one mechanic who does routine maintenance and minor repairs. Major repairs are done at a nearby commercial garage. A supervisor manages the operations.

Each year the supervisor prepares an operating budget for the motor pool. The budget informs university management of the funds needed to operate the pool. Depreciation on the automobiles is recorded in the budget in order to determine the cost per mile.

The schedule below presents the annual budget approved by the university. The actual costs for March are compared to one-twelfth of the annual budget.

The annual budget was constructed upon the following assumptions:

1. 20 automobiles in the pool
2. 30,000 miles per year per automobile
3. 15 miles per gallon per automobile
4. $0.60 per gallon of gas
5. $0.006 per mile for oil, minor repairs, parts and supplies
6. $135 per automobile in outside repairs

The supervisor is unhappy with the monthly report comparing budget and actual costs for March. He claims it presents unfairly his performance for March. His previous employer used flexible budgeting to compare actual costs to budgeted amounts.

Required   A. Employing flexible budgeting techniques, prepare a report that shows budgeted amounts, actual costs, and monthly variation for March.

B. Explain briefly the basis of your budget figure for outside repairs.

University Motor Pool
BUDGET REPORT
For March, 19X6

	Annual Budget	One month Budget	March Actual	Over* Under
Gasoline	$24,000	$2,000	$2,800	$800*
Oil, minor repairs, parts and supplies	3,600	300	380	80*
Outside repairs	2,700	225	50	175
Insurance	6,000	500	525	25*
Salaries and benefits	30,000	2,500	2,500	–
Depreciation	26,400	2,200	2,310	110*
	$92,700	$7,725	$8,565	$840*
Total miles	600,000	50,000	63,000	
Cost per mile	$0.1545	$0.1545	$0.1360	
Number of automobiles	20	20	21	

Example 4-4, a previous CMA examination problem, requires the preparation of a flexible budget for a university motor pool. The solution is given in Exhibit 4-7.

The Budgeting Process

Budgeting, the process used to establish plans and budgets, varies among organizations. In some organizations the top executives initiate the process by establishing overall goals—such as a specified rate of return on investment, market position, productivity level, or personnel development—for the organization and for its major operating segments. These goals are then given to subordinate executives for translation into workable plans. In other organizations the process starts with the development of economic forecasts by the headquarters staff personnel. These forecasts are used by the various divisions, with staff assistance, in formulating their own objectives and long-range plans. As these objectives are established, product and operating managers are developing tentative operating budgets. Once the objectives are approved by top management, the operating budgets are finalized and submitted to the headquarters staff for review, coordination with other divisions' budgets, and approval.[2]

Objectives of Budgeting

Shillinglaw suggests that the annual budgetary planning process has at least six major objectives:

1. To force managers to *analyze* the company's activities critically and creatively.

2. To direct some of management's attention from the present to the *future*.

3. To enable management to *anticipate* problems or opportunities in time to deal with them effectively.

4. To reinforce the managers' *motivation* to work to achieve the company's goals and objectives.

5. To give managers a continuing *reminder* of the actions they have decided on.

6. To provide a *reference point* for control reporting.[3]

2. Gordon Shillinglaw, *Managerial Cost Accounting*, 4th ed. (Homewood, Illinois: Richard D. Irwin, 1977), pp. 143-144.
3. *Ibid.*, p. 138.

━━━━━━━━━━━━━━━━━━━━━━━━ **Exhibit 4-7** ━━━━━━━━━━━━━━━━━━━━━━━━

A.

University Motor Pool
MONTHLY BUDGET REPORT
For March, 1976

	Monthly budget	March actual	Over* under
Gasoline	$2,520	$2,800	$280*
Oil, minor repairs, parts and supplies	378	380	2*
Outside repairs	236	50	186
Insurance	525	525	—
Salaries and benefits	2,500	2,500	—
Depreciation	2,310	2,310	—
Totals	$8,469	$8,565	$ 96*
Number of automobiles	21	21	—
Actual miles	63,000	63,000	—
Cost per mile	$0.1344	0.1359	0.0015*

Supporting calculations for monthly budget amounts:

Gasoline: $\dfrac{63,000 \text{ miles}}{15 \text{ miles/gal}} \times \$.60 \text{ per gallon} = \$2,520$

Oil, et al.: $63,000 \text{ miles} \times \$.006 \text{ per mile} = \$378$

Outside repairs: $\dfrac{\$135 \text{ per auto} \times 21 \text{ autos}}{12 \text{ months}} = \$236.25$

Insurance: Annual cost for one auto $= \$6,000 \div 20 \text{ autos}$
$= \$300 \text{ per auto}$
Annual cost for 21 autos $= 21 \times \$300$
$= \$6,300$
Monthly cost $= 6,300/12 = \$525$

Salaries and benefits: No change
$\dfrac{\$30,000 \text{ annual cost}}{12 \text{ months}} = \$2,500/\text{month}$

Depreciation: Annual depreciation per auto $= \$26,400/20 \text{ autos}$
Annual depreciation for 21 autos $= \$1,320/\text{auto} \times 21$
$= 27,720$
Monthly depreciation $= \dfrac{27,720}{12}$
$= \$2,310$

B. Outside automobile repairs are a function of the use of the automobile over its lifetime. However, these repairs occur irregularly throughout the year and the life of the car. A monthly budget figure based on a per mile charge becomes questionable. Therefore, the use of one-twelfth of the estimated annual outside repair costs, adjusted for the number of cars in operation during a month, would appear to be more reasonable.

Thus, budgeting assists in planning, organizing, and controlling the financial and operational activities of the business. However, while budgeting benefits management in many ways, it can also, if used incorrectly, raise resentment and build up unnecessary pressure, resulting in worse rather than better performance. The budget can, at times, cause managers to feel restricted and not as flexible as they should be if they are to adapt to changes occuring in the environment.

Activity Budgeting

While the annual profit plan is developed within the existing structure of the responsibility accounting centers, emphasis must be placed on activities. Each center may be involved with several independent activities, as well as with activities that are an integral part of a program that involves several responsibility centers.

Exhibit 4-8 illustrates a typical organization, which is carrying out several different activities. All of the activities are independent except those that relate to Program A. In preparing the budget for these responsibility centers, emphasis is placed on programs, Program A and the individual separate programs or activities at each center. Placing emphasis on activities in the construction of the budget is referred to as **program planning**. Businesses and many nonprofit organiza-

tions have, for some time, realized the importance of looking at programs. The process, however, received considerable attention with the development of Planning-Programming-Budgeting Systems (PPBS) in the federal government in the 1960s. This system suggests that the benefits of a proposed program should be compared with its costs in determining its acceptability. Although it is impossible to quantify all benefits, the conversion of as many benefits as possible to numbers and an identification of the other benefits should provide information to help the evaluator decide which programs are best.

Another approach used to help management review the various programs and select the combination that appears to maximize its objectives is **zero-base budgeting**. Zero-base budgeting has three main features.

1. The activities of individual responsibility centers are divided into a series of incremental "packages."

2. Each package is ranked ordinally.

3. Managers at higher levels consolidate the proposals submitted by their subordinates, providing their own ordinal rankings.[4]

This budgeting process requires each manager to evaluate the benefits expected from the requested programs and to

4. *Ibid.*, p. 142.

Exhibit 4-8

Illustration of Activities

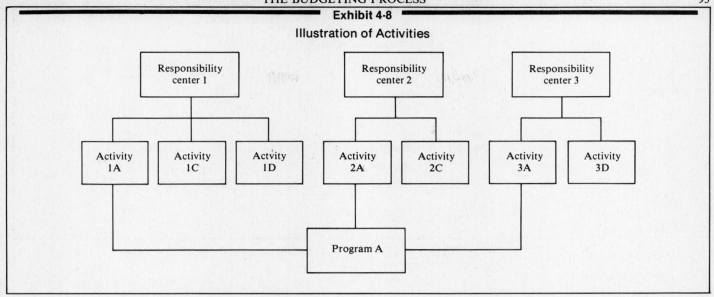

rank them according to their desirability. If, as often occurs, several spending proposals must be rejected, those that are least desirable will go first. Management, of course, must be very careful in using the priority rankings of various centers. A ranking of "4" by a manager in personnel may not have the same priority as a "4" ranking by a manager in the recreation department.

Administration of Budget

Although many aspects of the budgeting process are decentralized, the task of putting the various estimates and plans together into a final financial report must be centralized. This function is usually assigned to an individual within the financial area frequently referred to as the **budget director**. The function of the director, in addition to calculating and coordinating the financial data, is to establish procedures to follow in preparing budget, review information for completeness and relationship to other plans, and to report on performance. To assist the director and his or her staff and to provide advice to individuals with input to the budget, many companies have established a **budget committee**. The budget committee typically consists of the budget director, company economists, the president, and other top-level line executives, and, while operating in a consulting capacity, it does have significant influence on budget preparation. The committee will review economic condition forecasts, long-range goals and policies upon which the budget is to be based, and other information given to various individuals involved in preparing the budget. The committee reviews the actual budgets as they are submitted and makes suggestions. Any inconsistencies between the various budgets and the company goals should be resolved. The committee examines the budget in terms of its feasibility and profitability. Can the projections be reasonably accomplished? And if accomplished, will they provide the desired profits? Finally, the budget committee periodically reviews the comparisons of actual costs with budgeted costs.

It should be emphasized again that although the responsibility for the preparation of the budget lies with line personnel, the director and budget committee do have considerable input to the process.

Illustration of Comprehensive Profit Plan

The Palms Manufacturing Company makes two basic products known as Cee and Dee. Data which have been assembled by the managers follow:

	Cee	Dee
Requirements for finished unit:		
Product information:		
Raw material 1	10 pounds	8 pounds
Raw material 2		4 pounds
Raw material 3	2 units	1 unit
Direct labor	5 hours	8 hours
Product information:		
Sales price	$100	$150
Sales units	12,000	9,000
Estimated beginning inventory	400	150
Desired ending inventory	300	200

Raw material information:

	Raw materials		
	1	2	3
Cost	$2.00 per pound	$2.50 per pound	$.50 per unit
Estimated beginning inventory	3,000	1,500	1,000
Desired ending inventory	4,000	1,000	1,500

Exhibit 4-9

Palms Manufacturing Co.
Sales Forecasts By Products
19X1

	CEE		DEE		Total Dollars
	Units	Dollars	Units	Dollars	
First quarter	2,400	$ 240,000	1,800	$ 270,000	$ 510,000
Second quarter	3,600	360,000	2,700	405,000	765,000
Third quarter	3,000	300,000	2,250	337,500	637,500
Fourth quarter	3,000	300,000	2,250	337,500	637,500
Total	**12,000**	**$1,200,000**	**9,000**	**$1,350,000**	**$2,550,000**

Factory overhead information:

Indirect materials	$10,000
Miscellaneous supplies and tools	5,000
Indirect labor	40,000
Supervision	20,000
Payroll taxes and fringe benefits	75,000
Maintenance costs—fixed	20,000
Maintenance costs—variable	10,000
Depreciation	70,000
Heat, light, and power—fixed	8,710
Heat, light, and power—variable	5,090
Total	**$263,800**

Selling and administrative expense information:

Advertising	$ 60,000
Sales salaries	200,000
Travel and entertainment	60,000
Depreciation—warehouse	5,000
Office salaries	20,000
Executive salaries	250,000
Supplies	4,000
Depreciation—office	6,000
Total	**$605,000**

The direct labor wage rate is $4 per hour. Overhead is applied on the basis of direct labor hours. Tax rate is 40 percent.

The budgeted sales level is divided into quarters. It is estimated that 20 percent of the annual sales will be in the first quarter, 30 percent in the second, and 25 percent in the third and fourth quarters. The beginning inventory of finished products has the same cost per unit as the ending inventory. The work-in-process inventory is negligible.

A comprehensive profit plan for the Palms Manufacturing Company for 19X1 will include the following detailed budgets:

1. Sales budget
2. Production budget

3. Direct materials purchase budget
4. Direct labor budget
5. Factory overhead budget
6. Cost of goods sold budget, with schedule of ending inventory
7. Selling and administrative expenses budget
8. Cash receipts and disbursements budget—including capital outlays (cash budget)
9. Budgeted income statement
10. Budgeted balance sheet
11. Budgeted change in financial position

(The budgeted income statement, the budgeted balance sheet, and the budgeted cash flow statement are summarized in Volume 2. Although cash budgets are discussed in this chapter, previous CMA examination problems are used to illustrate their preparation and so the cash budget for Palms is not presented.)

Sales Budget The sales budget serves as the basis for the preparation of the other budgets. This sales budget must be integrated with the long-range sales plan. The key decisions that establish the long-range sales plan come from the strategic planning process. In many companies the long-range sales plan is completed each year prior to the start of the annual comprehensive profit plan. Any changes necessary in the short-range plan to meet the short-range profit objective should be made in accordance with the underlying assumptions of the long-range plan. For example, a company would want to be careful about deviating from its long-range pricing srategy to meet the short-range budget.

The project sales can be classified in many ways. Among the most common are sales by products, by product lines, by distribution channels, by size of customer, and by territories. The techniques for forecasting sales were described in Chapter 2. The sales forecast by products for Palms Manufacturing Company is presented in Exhibit 4-9. This budget is broken down by quarters.

Production Budget The objective in planning production and inventory levels is to develop a plan that provides for the lowest total costs. For many businesses where seasonal sales are common, production planning is critical. Three possible production patterns are available for companies with seasonal sales.

1. Give precedence to production stability. An inflexible production policy is established, which causes inventories to fluctuate inversely with sales.

2. Give precedence to inventory stability. In this case, production levels will fluctuate directly with sales patterns.

3. Establish inventory and production policies so that an optimum balance—in terms of the effect on profits—among sales, inventory, and production is maintained.[5]

The stable production policy suggested in the first pattern is desirable for several reasons. It provides for stable employment, which should result in better morale, greater productivity, fewer turnovers, fewer layoffs, and more highly qualified employees. Plant facilities are obviously better utilized with stable production. The problem with stable production is that the cost of carrying the inventory and the risk associated with the accumulation of large inventories may be so great that it precludes operating in this manner.

Adoption of the stable inventory pattern does result in much lower inventory costs; however, the fluctuation in production has an adverse effect on employee morale and productivity. In addition, production facilities may not be adequate to meet the sales demand in peak periods.

For most companies, it is advantageous to select a production policy that is between the two extremes. For example, a policy may state that production for any month should not vary more than 20 percent from the yearly average and inventories should not be above or drop below predetermined levels.

Careful planning of sales, production, and inventory levels can result in substantial savings. For example, the development of a product with a different seasonal pattern from other products can cause profits to increase by a larger amount than the increase in contribution margin due to the introduction of a product that causes stable production with improved morale and efficiency.

The production budget is one of the most important parts of the comprehensive profit plan. It is based on the sales forecast and the desired change in inventory levels. The production schedule must be coordinated with sales to maintain a proper balance. Frequently, for example, the sales staff may want to push one product and put less emphasis on others to the extent that sales orders in one month may exceed the productive capacity. Thus, although the sales budget is generally developed first and the other budgets are based on it, there must still be continuous communication between the production and sales areas to ensure that production requirements for various quarters or months do not exceed capacity.

Capacity is more than just the physical plant capabilities. Within a year, capacity can be established by adding second shifts, working weekends, or by subcontracting with outside companies to manufacture part or all of a needed product. A decision is made by management as to how much capacity can and should be expanded in this manner although there is a limit as to how far it can be expanded in the short run. For the long run, new plants can be constructed.

---

5. Glenn A. Welsch, et al, *Budgeting: Profit Planning and Control,* 5th ed. (Englewood Cliffs, N.J.: Prentice-Hall, 1976), p. 216.

Exhibit 4-10

Palms Manufacturing Co.
Production Schedule In Units
19X1

	Product	
	CEE	DEE
Planned sales (Exhibit 8-9)	12,000	9,000
Desired ending inventory	300	200
Total units required	12,300	9,200
Less estimated beginning inventory	400	150
Production in units	**11,900**	**9,050**

The production budget for Palms Manufacturing Co. is shown in Exhibit 4-10.

Direct Materials Purchase Budget   A budget for the direct materials purchase requirement is prepared for each raw material. The budget is based on the following information:

1. The units to be manufactured (from the production budget)

2. The type and quantity of raw materials needed for each kind of product to be manufactured

3. Cost per raw material

4. Desired ending inventory level

5. Estimate of beginning inventory

The materials budget deals only with direct materials. Indirect materials and supplies are frequently provided for in the factory overhead budget. The budget process, however, as used for direct materials, is also applicable to indirect materials and supplies.

Exhibit 4-11 illustrates the direct materials purchase budget for Palms. Example 4-5 is a previous CMA examination problem also dealing with this budget. Do this example now. The solution is given in Exhibit 4-12.

Direct Labor Budget   The direct labor budget benefits management by providing data about the number of hours necessary for the desired output; the data, in turn, indicate the number of employees needed. This information also provides a basis for estimating indirect labor costs.

The responsibility for the development of this budget is assumed by production. The direct labor budget for Palms is presented in Exhibit 4-13. To prepare this budget, data on anticipated production levels, the amount of labor required per unit, and the wage rate is necessary.

Expense Budgets   The emphasis in planning expense budgets should not be on decreasing expenses but rather on better utilization of limited resources. Realistic expense planning and control may result in either decreased or increased expenditures. An increased expenditure, could benefit the busi-

Exhibit 4-11

Palms Manufacturing Co.
Direct Materials Purchase Budget
19X1

	Raw material			Total costs
	1	2	3	
Units required for production (Schedule 1)	191,400	36,200	32,850	
Desired ending inventory	4,000	1,000	1,500	
Total units required	195,400	37,200	34,350	
Less estimated beginning inventory	3,000	1,500	1,000	
Total purchases in units	192,400	35,700	33,350	
Cost per unit	× $2.00	× $2.50	× $ .50	
Total costs of purchases	$384,800	$89,250	$16,675	$490,725

SCHEDULE 1

Raw material	CEE (11,900 units)			DEE (9,050 units)			Total quantity	Total costs
	Per unit	Total quantity	Total costs	Per unit	Total quantity	Total costs		
1 ($2.00/pound)	10	119,000[a]	$238,000[b]	8	72,400	$144,800	191,400	$382,800
2 ($2.50/pound)		—		4	36,200	90,500	36,200	90,500
3 ($.50/unit)	2	23,800	11,900	1	9,050	4,525	32,850	16,425
			$249,900			$239,825		$489,725

[a] Production units of 11,900 × 10 pounds raw material 1.

[b] Cost per pound of $2 × total quantity of 119,000.

Example 4-5

The Press Company manufactures and sells industrial components. The Whitmore Plant is responsible for producing two components referred to as AD-5 and FX-3. Plastic, brass, and aluminum are used in the production of these two products.

Press Company has adopted a thirteen-period reporting cycle in all of its plants for budgeting purposes. Each period is four weeks long and has 20 working days. The projected inventory levels for AD-5 and FX-3 at the end of the current (seventh) period and the projected sales for these two products for the next three four-week periods are presented below.

Past experience has shown that adequate inventory levels for AD-5 and FX-3 can be maintained if 40 percent of the next period's projected sales are on hand at the end of a reporting period. Based on this experience and the projected sales, the Whitmore Plant has budgeted production of 8,000 AD-5 and 6,000 of FX-3 in the eighth period. Production is assumed to be uniform for both products within each four-week period.

The raw material specifications for AD-5 and FX-3 are as follows:

	AD-5	FX-3
Plastic	2.0 lb.	1.0 lb.
Brass	0.5 lb.	—
Aluminum	—	1.5 lb.

	Projected inventory level (in units) end of seventh period	Projected sales (in units)		
		Eighth period	Ninth period	Tenth period
AD-5	3,000	7,500	8,750	9,500
FX-3	2,800	7,000	4,500	4,000

The sales of AD-5 and FX-3 do not vary significantly from month to month. Consequently, the safety stock incorpo-

continued

Example 4-5, *continued*

rated into the reorder point for each of the raw materials is adequate to compensate for variations in the sales of the finished products.

Raw material orders are placed the day the quantity on hand falls below the reorder point. Whitmore Plant's suppliers are very dependable so that the given lead times are reliable. The outstanding orders for plastic and aluminum are due to arrive on the tenth and fourth working days of the eighth period respectively. Payments for all raw material orders are remitted in the month of delivery.

Required Whitmore Plant is required to submit a report to corporate headquarters of Press Company summarizing the projected raw material activities before each period commences. The data for the eighth period report are being assembled. Determine the following items for plastic, brass, and aluminum for inclusion in the eighth period report:

a. Projected quantities (in pounds) of each raw material to be issued to production
b. Projected quantities (in pounds) of each raw material ordered and the date (in terms of working days) the order is to be placed
c. The projected inventory balance (in pounds) of each raw material at the end of the period
d. The payments for purchases of each raw material

	Purchase price per pound	Standard purchase lot (in lbs.)	Reorder point (in lbs.)	Projected inventory status at the end of the seventh period (in pounds)		Lead time in working days
				On hand	On order	
Plastic	$.40	15,000	12,000	16,000	15,000	10
Brass	.95	5,000	7,500	9,000	–	30
Aluminum	.55	10,000	10,000	14,000	10,000	20

Exhibit 4-12

The Press Company

Projected raw material issues:

	Plastic	Brass	Aluminum
AD-5 (8,000 units)	16,000 lb.	4,000 lb.	–
FX-3 (6,000 units)	6,000 lb.	–	9,000 lb.
Projected raw material issues	22,000 lb.	4,000 lb.	9,000 lb.

Projected inventory activity and ending balance:

	Plastic	Brass	Aluminum
Average daily usage (issues ÷ working days)	1,100 lb.	200 lb.	450 lb.
Beginning inventory	16,000 lb.	9,000 lb.	14,000 lb.
Orders received:			
Ordered in 7th period	15,000[d] lb.	–	10,000[b] lb.
Ordered in 8th period	15,000[e] lb.	–	–
Subtotal	46,000 lb.	9,000 lb.	24,000 lb.
Issues	22,000[a] lb.	4,000[c] lb.	9,000[f] lb.
Projected ending inventory balance	**24,000 lb.**	**5,000 lb.**	**15,000 lb.**

[a] Order 15,000 pounds of plastic on fourth working day.
[b] Order for 10,000 pounds of aluminum ordered during seventh period, received on fourth working day.
[c] Ordered 5,000 pounds of brass on eighth working day.
[d] Order for 15,000 pounds of plastic ordered during seventh period, received on tenth working day.
[e] Order for 15,000 pounds of plastic ordered on fourth working day of eighth period, received on fourteenth working day.
[f] No orders for aluminum would be placed during the eighth period.

Projected payments for raw material purchases:

Raw material	Day/period ordered	Day/period received	Quantity ordered	Amount due	Period due
Plastic	20th/Seventh	10th/Eighth	15,000 lb.	$6,000	Eighth
Aluminum	4th/Seventh	4th/Eighth	10,000 lb.	5,500	Eighth
Plastic	4th/Eighth	14th/Eighth	15,000 lb.	6,000	Eighth
Brass	8th/Eighth	Due Ninth	5,000 lb.	4,750	Ninth

Exhibit 4-13

Palms Manufacturing Co.
Direct Labor Budget
19X1

	Products		
	CEE	DEE	Totals
Units to be produced	11,900	9,050	
Hours required per unit	× 5	× 8	
Total hours required	59,500	72,400	131,900
Cost per hour	× $4	× $4	× $4
Total	**$238,000**	**$289,600**	**$527,600**

Exhibit 4-14

Palms Manufacturing Co.
Factory Overhead Budget
19X1

Variable costs:		
Indirect materials	$10,000	
Miscellaneous supplies and tools	5,000	
Indirect labor	40,000	
Payroll taxes and fringe benefits	75,000	
Maintenance costs—variable	10,000	
Heat, light, and power—variable	5,090	
Total variable costs		$145,090
Fixed costs:		
Supervision	20,000	
Depreciation	70,000	
Maintenance costs—fixed	20,000	
Heat, light, and power—fixed	8,710	
Total fixed costs		118,710
Total factory overhead		**$263,800**

Variable overhead rate	($145,090 ÷ 131,900)	$1.10
Fixed overhead rate	($118,710 ÷ 131,900)	.90
Total overhead rate	($263,800 ÷ 131,900)	**$2.00**
Total cost to Cee	(59,500 × $2.00)	$119,000
Total cost to Dee	(72,400 × $2.00)	144,800
Total		**$263,800**

Exhibit 4-15

Palms Manufacturing Co.
Selling and Administrative Expense Budget
19X1

Selling expenses:		
Advertising	$ 60,000	
Sales salaries	200,000	
Travel and entertainment	60,000	
Depreciation	5,000	
Total selling expense		$325,000
Administrative expenses:		
Office salaries	20,000	
Executive salaries	250,000	
Supplies	4,000	
Depreciation	6,000	
Total administrative expenses		280,000
Total selling and administrative expenses		**$605,000**

Exhibit 4-16

Palms Manufacturing Co.
Cost of Goods Sold Statement
19X1

Schedule 1

	Cee	Dee	Total		Cee	Dee
Direct materials used (Exhibit 8-11)	$249,900	$239,825	$ 489,725	Materials cost per unit	$21.00	$26.50
				Direct labor	20.00	32.00
Direct labor (Exhibit 8-13)	238,000	289,600	527,600	Factory overhead—variable	5.50	8.80
Factory overhead (Exhibit 8-14)	119,000	144,800	263,800	Total variable costs	46.50	67.30
				Factory overhead—fixed	4.50	7.20
Total manufacturing costs	606,900	674,225	1,281,125	Total unit costs	$51.00	$74.50
Add beginning inventory (Schedule 1)	20,400	11,175	31,575	Number of units in beginning inventory	400	150
Goods available	627,300	685,400	1,312,700	Number of units in ending inventory	300	200
Less desired ending inventory (Schedule 1)	15,300	14,900	30,200	Beginning inventory value (no. units × unit cost)	$20,400	$11,175
Cost of goods sold	$612,000	$670,500	$1,282,500	Ending inventory value (no. units × unit cost)	$15,300	$14,900

---

ness—for example, through increased profits or improved ROI—by resulting in better quality products, higher productivity, expanded activities, and the like. Thus, the key to effective expense budgeting is to relate the expenditures with the benefits derived from the outlay.

The budgets for factory overhead and selling and administrative expenses are presented in Exhibits 4-14 and 4-15.

Completion of the Comprehensive Profit Plan In order to complete the profit plan, a cost of goods sold budget, cash flow budget, planned statement of change in financial position, planned income statement, and planned balance sheet must be prepared. Once these statements are integrated, the profit plan for the year can be tested to see if it meets all the objectives of the company. Does the plan provide for adequate cash flow? Is the projected profit adequate? Is the plan consistent with the long-term goals and policies of the company? If the plan is not consistent with the company's objectives, then management must find ways to improve the plan by analyzing the possible alternatives.

Since the budget director and the others involved in the preparation of the budget are testing it against the organization's objectives as it is being prepared, it is hoped that many of the problems will be corrected before it reaches the final stage.

The cost of goods sold statement and the income statement for Palms are presented in Exhibit 4-16 and 4-17. For effective planning, it is also helpful to prepare an income statement based on the contribution approach. Such a statement is presented in Exhibit 4-18. The difference in net income before taxes between the absorption approach and the contribution approach is caused by the change in inventory levels that

results in the contribution approach charging less fixed costs against profit for Cee and more for Dee than the absorption approach. The net effect is a $90 larger net income under direct costing.

Increase in profit for Dee under direct costing—decrease in inventory of 100 units (400 beginning and 300 ending) × $4.50 (fixed cost rate)	$450
Decrease in profit for Cee under direct costing—increase in inventory of 50 units (150 beginning and 200 ending) × $7.20 (fixed cost rate)	360
Net difference	$ 90

The difference can also be shown in the following way:

Total fixed costs charge against income under absorption costing:	
Cee: 12,000 units sold × $4.50	$ 54,000
Dee: 9,000 units sold × $7.20	64,800
Total	118,800
Budgeted fixed costs (amount charged against income under direct costing, Exhibit 8-18)	118,710
Net difference	$ 90

To complete the profit plan for Palms Manufacturing, a cash budget, balance sheet, and statement of change in financial position are required. However, these statements are omitted, since previous CMA problems are used to illustrate their preparation (see Example 4-6).

Exhibit 4-17
Palms Manufacturing Co.
Income Statement
19X1

Sales (Exhibit 8-9)	$2,550,000
Cost of goods sold (Exhibit 8-16)	1,282,500
Gross profit	1,267,500
Selling and administrative expenses (Exhibit 8-15)	605,000
Net income	662,500
Income tax (40 percent tax rate)	265,000
Net income after tax	$ 397,500

Exhibit 4-18
Palms Manufacturing Co.
Income Statement
Contribution Approach
19X1

Sales		$2,550,000
Variable cost of goods sold (Schedule 1)		1,163,700
Contribution margin— manufacturing		1,386,300
Variable selling expenses		320,000
Contribution margin—final		1,066,300
Fixed costs:		
Manufacturing (Exhibit 8-14)	$118,710	
Selling expenses	5,000	
Administrative expenses	280,000	403,710
Net income before taxes		$ 662,590

Schedule 1

	Product		
	Cee	Dee	Total
Total units sold	12,000	9,000	
Variable manufacturing cost per unit (Exhibit 8-16)	X $46.50	X 67.30	
Variable cost of goods sold	$558,000	$605,700	$1,163,700

Implementation of Profit Plan   Once the plan receives approval, it must be distributed to the various segments of the organization. Special sessions should be conducted at the various levels of management to assure that each manager understands his or her responsibilities. If these managers were involved in the planning process, then they are already familiar with the nature of their responsibilities and the budget should not contain any major surprises.

The plan serves as the basis for measuring performance so it should include a system of adequate feedback to provide timely evaluation to managers. The budget should also be flexible enough to be adjusted as changing conditions warrant. It should be viewed as an instrument setting forth the goals and objectives of the organization that coordinates and does not restrict the activities of employees.

Cash Budgets

Cash is an asset that must be handled wisely; too much cash on hand may mean that the firm is foregoing profitable investment opportunities, while too little cash can result in the firm's inability to meet its current obligations. Thus, the flow of cash should be carefully monitored and controlled.

The cash budget is an important part of any system designed to control cash. Cash budgeting focuses on the amount and timing of cash flows. It enables a firm to anticipate their cash position and plan accordingly.

The period of time included in the cash budget depends on the needs of the business. A small retailer that does most of its business on the weekend but must pay the employees on Thursday may need daily or weekly cash flow information, as well as longer term budgets. The sales pattern may also place limits on the period covered; firms with widely fluctuating sales may get realistic inflow figures for only short periods. However, even under these conditions some information such as leasing costs, salaries, and so on can be reflected with accuracy.

Cash budgets are normally prepared by using either the cash receipts and disbursements method or the income statement method. When the **cash receipts and disbursements approach** is utilized, a cash budget is constructed from the information contained in the detailed profit plan. The sources of cash include cash sales, collections of accounts receivable, money from the sale of an asset, and any other activity during the period covered that resulted in a cash inflow. Cash disbursements are the result of payments of expenses, capital expenditure outlays, and so on. The receipts and disbursements can then be netted.

The **income statement approach** uses a slightly different method for constructing the budget. It begins with the net income figure for the period and then adjusts it for changes in: accruals, prepaid items, inventories, receivables, and any other expenses that do not require cash, as well as for the revenues that were not in the form of cash (such as an increase in accounts receivable). This method is similar to that used in determining the working capital provided by operations in the statement of changes in financial position (see Part 2). Here, net income is converted from an accrual basis of accounting to a cash basis.

Example 4-6, a previous CMA examination problem, illustrates the preparation of a cash budget using the cash receipts

Example 4-6

The Barker Corporation manufactures and distributes wooden baseball bats. The bats are manufactured in Georgia at its only plant. This is a seasonal business with a large portion of its sales occurring in late winter and early spring. The production schedule for the last quarter of the year is heavy in order to build up inventory to meet expected sales volume.

The company experiences a temporary cash strain during this heavy production period. Payroll costs rise during the last quarter because overtime is scheduled to meet the increased production needs. Collections from customers are low because the fall season produces only modest sales. This year the company concern is intensified because of the rapid increases in prices during the current inflationary period. In addition, the sales department forecasts sales of less than one million bats for the first time in three years. This decrease in sales appears to be caused by the popularity of aluminum bats.

The cash account builds up during the first and second quarters as sales exceed production. The excess cash is invested in U.S. Treasury bills and other commercial paper. During the last half of the year the temporary investments are liquidated to meet the cash needs. In the early years of the company, short-term borrowing was used to supplement the funds released by selling investments, but this has not been necessary in recent years. Because costs are higher this year, the treasurer asks for a forecast for December to judge if the $40,000 in temporary investments will be adequate to carry the company through the month with a minimum balance of $10,000. Should this amount ($40,000) be insufficient, she wants to begin negotiations for a short-term loan.

The unit sales volume for the past two months and the estimate for the next four months are

October (actual) 70,000 January (estimated) 90,000
November (actual) 50,000 February (estimated) 90,000
December (estimated) 50,000 March (estimated) 120,000

The bats are sold for $3 each. All sales are made on account. One-half of the accounts are collected in the month of the sale, 40 percent are collected in the month following the sale, and the remaining 10 percent in the second month following the sale. Customers who pay in the month of the sale receive a 2 percent cash discount.

The production schedule for the six-month period beginning with October reflects the company's policy of maintaining a stable year-round work force by scheduling overtime to meet production schedules:

October (actual) 90,000 January (estimated) 90,000
November (actual) 90,000 February (estimated) 100,000
December (estimated) 90,000 March (estimated) 100,000

The bats are made from wooden blocks that cost $6 each. Ten bats can be produced from each block. The blocks are acquired one year in advance so they can be properly aged. Barker pays the supplier one-twelfth of the cost of this material each month until the obligation is retired. The monthly payment is $60,000.

The plant is normally scheduled for a 40-hour, five-day work week. During the busy production season, however, the work week may be increased to six ten-hour days. Workers can produce 7.5 bats per hour. Normal monthly output is 75,000 bats. Factory employees are paid $4 per hour (up $0.50 from last year) for regular time and time and one-half for overtime.

Other manufacturing costs include variable overhead of $0.30 per unit and annual fixed overhead of $280,000. Depreciation charges totalling $40,000 are included among the fixed overhead. Selling expenses include variable costs of $0.20 per unit and annual fixed costs of $60,000. Fixed administrative costs are $120,000 annually. All fixed costs are incurred uniformly throughout the year.

The controller has accumulated the following additional information:

1. The balances of selected accounts as of November 30, 19X4, are as follows:

Cash	$ 12,000
Marketable securities (cost and market are the same)	40,000
Accounts receivable	96,000
Prepaid expenses	4,800
Account payable (arising from raw material purchase)	300,000
Accrued vacation pay	9,500
Equipment note payable	102,000
Accrued income taxes payable	50,000

2. Interest to be received from the company's temporary investments is estimated at $500 for December.
3. Prepaid expenses of $3,600 will expire during December, and the balance of the prepaid account is estimated at $4,200 for the end of December.
4. Barker purchased new machinery in 19X4 as part of a plant modernization program. The machinery was financed by a 24-month note of $144,000. The terms call for equal principal payments over the next 24 months with interest paid at the rate of 1 percent per month on the unpaid balance at the first of the month. The first payment was made May 1, 19X4.
5. Old equipment, which has a book value of $8,000, is to be sold during December for $7,500.
6. Each month the company accrues $1,700 for vacation pay by charging Vacation Pay Expense and crediting Accrued Vacation Pay. The plant closes for two weeks in June when all plant employees take a vacation.
7. Quarterly dividends of $0.20 per share will be paid on December 15 to stockholders of record. Barker Corporation has authorized 10,000 shares. The company has issued 7,500 shares, and 500 of these are classified as treasury stock.
8. The quarterly income taxes payment of $50,000 is due on December 15, 19X4.

Required A. Prepare a schedule that forecasts the cash position at December 31, 19X4. What action, if any, will be required to maintain a $10,000 cash balance?

B. Without prejudice to your answer in part A, assume Barker regularly needs to arrange short-term loans during the November-to-February period. What changes might Barker consider in its methods of doing business to reduce or eliminate the need for short-term borrowing?

Exhibit 4-19

Barker Corporation
Cash Forecast
For the Month of December

CASH RECEIPTS

Sales and collections on account:

October sales (3 × 70,000 × .10)	$21,000	
November sales (3 × 50,000 × .40)	60,000	
December sales (3 × 50,000 × .50 × .98)	73,500	$154,500
Interest from investments		500
Sale of equipment		7,500
Total cash receipts		162,500

CASH DISBURSEMENTS

Direct labor—regular $\dfrac{90,000 \times 4.00}{7.5}$	48,000	
overtime $\dfrac{15,000 \times 2.00}{7.5}$	4,000	52,000
Variable overhead (.30 × 90,000)		27,000
Fixed overhead [(280,000 − 40,000)/12]		20,000
Variable selling expenses (.20 × 50,000)		10,000
Fixed selling expenses (60,000 / 12)		5,000
Fixed administrative (120,000 / 12)		10,000
Payment of accounts payable (raw materials)		60,000
Cash outlay on prepaid expenses		3,000
Note payment (144,000 / 24)		6,000
Interest on note payable (102,000 × .01)		1,020
Dividend payment (7,000 × .20)		1,400
Income taxes		50,000
Total cash disbursements		245,420
Disbursements over receipts		82,920
Cash balance 12/1/X4		12,000
Cash short before minimum balance		70,920
Minimum cash balance desired		10,000
Cash needed for operations		80,920
Sale of marketable securities		40,000
Cash proceeds required from borrowing		**$ 40,920**

Based on the cash forecast, the treasurer not only will have to sell the temporary investments (marketable securities of $40,000), but also should initiate negotiations for a short-term loan for approximately $41,000.

and disbursements method. The solution is presented in Exhibit 4-19. The steps to follow in solving this, or any other, cash budgeting problem are:

1. Estimate cash receipts.
2. Estimate cash disbursements.
3. Determine cash needs.

Estimate Cash Receipts Several sources of cash were mentioned earlier. In order to calculate the estimated collection of the receivables, the pattern of collection must be analyzed. The accountants at the Barker Corporation have found that:

1. 50 percent of the accounts are collected in the month of sale
2. 40 percent are collected in the month following the sale
3. 10 percent are collected in the second month after the sale.

Since all sales are made on account, the computation is simple. Note, however, that the calculation for December's collection is (3 × 50,000 × .50 × .98). This is price × units × percent collected × 100%-discount. The customers that pay in December receive a 2 percent discount. Other sources of cash include $500 from interest earned and $7,500 from sale of equipment.

Estimate Cash Disbursements Cash disbursements may be the result of many actions, including the payment of dividends or operating expenses and the purchase of marketable securities or assets. In order to determine the cash payments the firm will be making, it is necessary to secure information on the company's policy for payment for purchases, the amount of accruals and prepayments, outlays expected for capital expenditures, and the dividend payments anticipated. In the case of a manufacturing company, such as Barker, outlays for labor and overhead must be determined.

The 90,000 bats that the Barker Corporation must manufacture in December will require the use of overtime. The normal monthly output is 75,000 bats. The direct labor cost is $52,000 as shown in Exhibit 4-19. The fixed portion of overhead is $240,000 ($280,000 − $40,000 depreciation) and the variable overhead is $.30 per bat. The cash disbursed for accounts payable is $60,000. The $3,000 for prepaid expenses is determined as follows:

Balance as of 11/30/X4	$4,800
Amount expiring in December	3,600
Resulting balance	1,200
Balance as of 12/31/X4	4,200
Cash required	**$(3,000)**

The accrued vacation pay does not involve an outlay of cash during December.

Determine Cash Needs   Once the projected cash receipts and disbursements have been calculated, management can assess its cash needs. In the case of the Barker Corporation, an additional cash requirement is made in the form of a minimum cash balance of $10,000. As can be seen in Exhibit 8-19, to achieve this $10,000 ending balance in the cash account, Barker must sell its temporary investments and, in addition, borrow $41,000.

The solution to part B of Example 4-6, which deals with the improvement of cash flows for Barker Corporation, is described below.

B. Possible changes Barker Corporation could adopt in its methods of conducting business to alleviate the need for short-term borrowing include:

1. Action to speed up collection of accounts receivable.

2. Change production policies in a way to alleviate cash flow problems such as hiring part-time employees to reduce overtime costs.

3. Develop a related but alternative type of business for the slack period.

4. Increase amounts of equity capital, and/or long-term debt.

Summary   The cash flow statement may be prepared in the format of the Statement of Cash Flows required by Financial Accounting Standards Board Statement No. 95. Under this standard the cash flows would be divided into three categories — operating, financing and investing. While, most of the focus in the discussion here has been on the operating section of the statement (since an operating budget is being prepared), to complete the cash analysis it is necessary to prepare a capital expenditure budget. Most of the time, items in this budget would be considered investing activities. Finally, a plan must be developed to determine how the resources for the capital expenditure budget and, in some cases, operational activities will be financed.

As stated earlier, the total impact of the proposed budget must be evaluated. The evaluation involves an analysis of the impact the budget has on the company's projected balance sheet and statement of operations. For a discussion of the balance sheet, statement of cash flows, and statement of operations, please refer to Part 2.

Problems

---

1.   **Multiple Choice**

1. Cost-volume-profit analysis is a technique available to management to understand better the interrelationships of several factors which affect a firm's profit. As with many such techniques, the accountant oversimplifies the real world by making assumptions. Which of the following is not a major assumption underlying cost-volume-profit analysis?

a. All costs incurred by a firm can be separated into their fixed and variable components.

b. The product selling price per unit is constant at all volume levels.

c. Operating efficiency and employee productivity are constant at all volume levels.

d. For multiproduct situations the sales mix can vary at all volume levels.

e. Costs vary only with changes in volume.

The following data apply to items 2-6.

Laraby Company produces a single product. It sold 25,000 units last year with the following results:

Sales		$625,000
Variable costs	$375,000	
Fixed costs	150,000	525,000
Net income before taxes		100,000
Income taxes (45%)		45,000
Net income		**$ 55,000**

In an attempt to improve its product, Laraby is considering replacing a component part in its product that has a cost of $2.50 with a new and better part costing $4.50 per unit in the coming year. A new machine would also be needed to increase plant capacity. The machine would cost $18,000 with a useful life of 6 years and no salvage value. The company uses straight line depreciation on all plant assets.

2. What was Laraby Company's breakeven point in number of units last year?

a. 6,000.
b. 15,000.
c. 21,000.
d. 18,000.
e. none of the above.

3. How many units of product would Laraby Company have had to sell in the last year to earn $77,000 in net income after taxes?

a. 29,000.
b. 23,000.
c. 22,700.
d. 29,300.
e. none of the above.

4. If Laraby Company holds the sales price constant and makes the suggested changes, how many units of product must be sold in the coming year to break even?

a. 15,300.
b. 18,750.
c. 19,125.
d. 21,000.
e. none of the above.

5. If Laraby Company holds the sales price constant and makes the suggested changes, how many units of product will the company have to sell to make the same net income after taxes as last year?

a. 31,625.
b. 31,250.
c. 33,500.
d. 25,300.
e. none of the above.

6. If Laraby Company wishes to maintain the same contribution margin ratio, what selling price per unit of product must it charge next year to cover the increased material costs?

a. $27.00.
b. $25.00.
c. $32.50.
d. $28.33.
e. none of the above.

7. The Black Company manufactures and sells a specialty perfume. The company budgets a margin of safety of 20 percent for 1978. Fixed costs are budgeted at $270,000 annually. Variable costs are $6.60 per ounce. If the sales price per ounce is $12, the budgeted level of sales revenue for 1978 is

a. $589,330.
b. $720,000.
c. $480,000.
d. $750,000.
e. none of the above.

8. Region Company sells a product for $35 per unit, and the variable production and sales costs are $21 per unit. If Region Company adopts a 40 percent increase in selling price of its product, how much can unit sales decline before total profits decline?

a. 40 percent.
b. 50 percent.
c. 57 percent.
d. 100 percent.
e. none of the above.

9. Kane Corporation has a practical production capacity of one million units. The current year's master budget was based on the production and sales of 700,000 units during the current year. Actual production for the current year was 720,000 units while actual sales amounted to only 600,000 units. The units are sold for $20 each and the contribution margin ratio is 30 percent. The dollar amount which best quantifies the marketing department's failure to achieve budgeted performance for the current year is

a. $2,400,000 unfavorable.
b. $2,000,000 unfavorable.
c. $720,000 unfavorable.
d. $600,000 unfavorable.
e. some amount other than those given above.

10. Order-filling costs, as opposed to order-getting costs, include all but which one of the following items?

a. Clerical processing of sales orders.
b. Credit check of new customers.
c. Packing and shipping of sales orders.
d. Collection of payments for sales orders.
e. Mailing catalogs to current customers.

11. The control of order-filling costs

a. can be accomplished through the use of flexible budget standards.
b. requires a budget which shows budgeted expenses for the average level of activity.
c. is related to pricing decisions, sales promotion, and customer reaction.
d. is not crucial because they are typically fixed and not subject to frequent changes.
e. is not crucial because the order-filling routine is entrenched and external influences are minimal.

12. Which one of the following will not affect the budgeting of order-getting costs?

a. Market research and tests.
b. Location of distribution warehouses.
c. Policies and actions of competitors.
d. Sales promotion policies.
e. General economic conditions.

13. The report to a territorial sales manager which shows the contribution to profit by each sales person in the territory is called

a. a profit report.
b. an absorption profit report.
c. a gross profit report.
d. a distribution report.
e. a responsibility report.

14. A budget system referred to as the "program planning and budgeting system (PPBS)"

a. drops the current month or quarter and adds a future month or a future quarter as the current month or quarter is completed.
b. consolidates the plans of the separate requests into one overall plan.
c. divides the activities of individual responsibility centers into a series of packages which are ranked ordinally.
d. classifies budget requests by activity and estimates the benefits arising from each activity.
e. presents the plan for a range of activity so that the plan can be adjusted for changes in activity levels.

15. A systemized approach known as zero-base budgeting (ZBB)

a. presents the plan for only one level of activity and does not adjust to changes in the level of activity.
b. presents a statement of expectations for a period of time but does not present a firm commitment.
c. divides the activities of individual responsibility centers into a series of packages which are ranked ordinally.
d. classifies budget requests by activity and estimates the benefits arising from each activity.
e. presents the plan for a range of activity so that the plan can be adjusted for changes in activity levels.

16. A continuous budget

a. drops the current month or quarter and adds a future month or a future quarter as the current month or quarter is completed.

b. presents a statement of expectations for a period of time but does not present a firm commitment.

c. presents the plan for only one level of activity and does not adjust to changes in the level of activity.

d. presents the plan for a range of activity so that the plan can be adjusted for changes in activity levels.

e. classifies budget requests by activity and estimates the benefits arising from each activity.

17. A static budget

a. drops the current month or quarter and adds a future month or a future quarter as the current month or quarter is completed.

b. presents a statement of expectations for a period of time but does not present a firm commitment.

c. presents the plan for only one level of activity and does not adjust to changes in the level of activity.

d. presents the plan for a range of activity so that the plan can be adjusted for changes in activity levels.

e. divides the activities of individual responsibility centers into a series of packages which are ranked ordinally.

18. A flexible budget

a. classifies budget requests by activity and estimates the benefits arising from each activity.

b. presents a statement of expectations for a period of time but does not present a firm commitment.

c. presents the plan for only one level of activity and does not adjust to changes in the level of activity.

d. presents the plan for a range of activity so that the plan can be adjusted for changes in activity levels.

e. divides the activities of individual responsibility centers into a series of packages which are ranked ordinally.

19. When an organization prepares a forecast, it

a. presents a statement of expectations for a period of time but does not present a firm commitment.

b. consolidates the plans of the separate requests into one overall plan.

c. presents the plan for a range of activity so that the plan can be adjusted for changes in activity levels.

d. classifies budget requests by activity and estimates the benefits arising from each activity.

e. divides the activities of individual responsibility centers into a series of packages which are ranked ordinally.

The following data apply to items 20–24

The SAB Company uses a profit-volume graph similar to the one shown below to represent the cost/volume/profit relationships of its operations. The vertical (y-axis) is the profit in dollars and the horizontal (x-axis) is the volume in units. The diagonal line is the contribution margin line.

20. Point A on the profit-volume graph represents

a. the point where fixed costs equal sales.

b. the point where fixed costs equal variable costs.

c. a volume level of zero units.

d. the point where total costs equal total sales.

e. the point where the rate of contribution margin increases.

21. The vertical distance from the dotted line to the contribution margin line denoted as B on the profit-volume graph represents

a. the total contribution margin.

b. the contribution margin per unit.

c. the contribution margin rate.

d. total sales.

e. the sum of the variable and fixed costs.

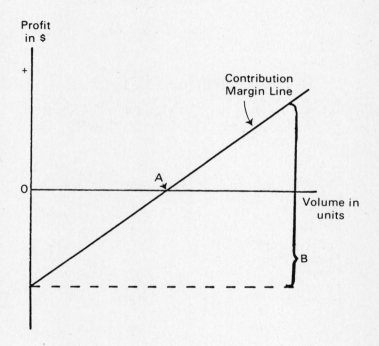

22. If SAB Company's fixed costs were to increase,

a. the contribution margin line would shift upward parallel to the present line.

b. the contribution margin line would shift downward parallel to the present line.

c. the slope of the contribution margin line would be more pronounced (steeper).

d. the slope of the contribution margin line would be less pronounced (flatter).

e. the contribution margin line would coincide with the present contribution margin line.

23. If SAB Company's variable costs per unit were to increase but its unit selling price stays constant,

a. the contribution margin line would shift upward parallel to the present line.

b. the contribution margin line would shift downward parallel to the present line.

c. the slope of the contribution margin line would be more pronounced (steeper).

d. the slope of the contribution margin line would be less pronounced (flatter).

e. the slope of the contribution margin line probably would change but how it would change is not determinable.

24. If SAB Company decided to increase its unit selling price to offset exactly the increase in the variable cost per unit,

a. the contribution margin line would shift upward parallel to the present line.
b. the contribution margin line would shift downward parallel to the present line.
c. the slope of the contribution margin line would be more pronounced (steeper).
d. the slope of the contribution margin line would be less pronounced (flatter).
e. the contribution margin line would coincide with the present contribution margin line.

The Following Data Apply to Items 25-28

The estimated unit costs for a company using full absorption costing and operating at a production level of 12,000 units per month are as follows.

Cost Item	Estimated Unit Cost
Direct material	$32
Direct labor	20
Variable manufacturing overhead	15
Fixed manufacturing overhead	6
Variable selling	3
Fixed selling	4

25. Estimated conversion costs per unit are
a. $35.
b. $41.
c. $44.
d. $48.
e. some amount other than those given above.

26. Estimated prime costs per unit are
a. $73.
b. $32.
c. $67.
d. $52.
e. some amount other than those given above.

27. Estimted total variable costs per unit are
a. $67.
b. $38.
c. $70.
d. $52.
e. some amount other than those given above.

28. Estimated total costs that would be incurred during a month with a production level of 12,000 units and a sales level of 8,000 units are
a. $692,000.
b. $664,000.
c. $960,000.
d. $948,000.
e. some amount other than those given above.

29. Woodman Company applies factory overhead on the basis of direct labor hours. Budget and actual data for direct labor and overhead for 1983 are as follows.

	Budget	Actual
Direct labor hours	600,000	550,000
Factory overhead costs	$720,000	$680,000

The factory overhead for Woodman Company in 1983 is
a. overapplied by $20,000.
b. overapplied by $40,000.
c. underapplied by $20,000.
d. underapplied by $40,000.
e. neither underapplied or overapplied.

30. Carley Products has no work-in-process for finished goods inventories at the close of business on December 31, 1983. The balances of Carley's accounts as of December 31, 1983 are as follows.

Cost of goods sold	$2,040,000
General selling and administrative expenses	900,000
Sales	3,600,000
Factory overhead control	700,000
Factory overhead applied	648,000

Carley Products' income before income taxes for 1983 is
a. $660,000.
b. $608,000.
c. $712,000.
d. $1,508,000.
e. some amount other than those given above.

2.

The Following Data Apply to Items 1-4.

DisKing Company is a retailer for video disks. The projected after-tax net income for the current year is $120,000 based on a sales volume of 200,000 video disks. DisKing has been selling the disks at $16 each. The variable costs consist of the $10 unit purchase price of the disks and a handling cost of $2 per disk. DisKing's annual fixed costs are $600,000, and DisKing is subject to a 40 percent income tax rate.

Management is planning for the coming year when it expects that the unit purchase price of the video disks will increase 30 percent.

1. DisKing Company's breakeven point for the current year in number of video disks is
a. 100,000 units.
b. 150,000 units.
c. 50,000 units.
d. 60,000 units.
e. some amount other than those given above.

2. An increase of 10 percent in projected unit sales volume for the current year would result in an increased after-tax income for the current year of

a. $80,000.
b. $32,000.
c. $48,000.
d. $12,000.
e. some amount other than those given above.

3. The volume of sales in dollars that DisKing Company must achieve in the coming year to maintain the same after-tax net income as projected for the current year if unit selling price remains at $16 is

a. $12,800,000.
b. $14,400,000.
c. $11,520,000.
d. $32,000,000.
e. some amount other than those given above.

4. In order to cover a 30 percent increase in the disk's purchase price for the coming year and still maintain the current contribution margin ratio, DisKing Company must establish a selling price per disk for the coming year of

a. $19.60.
b. $19.00.
c. $20.80.
d. $20.00.
e. some amount other than those given above.

The Following Data Apply to Items 5 and 6.

Berol Company plans to sell 200,000 units of finished product in July of 1984 and anticipates a growth rate in sales of five percent per month. The desired monthly ending inventory in units of finished product is 80 percent of the next month's estimated sales. There are 150,000 finished units in the inventory on June 30, 1984.

Each unit of finished product requires four pounds of direct material at a cost of $1.20 per pound. There are 800,000 pounds of direct material in the inventory on June 30, 1984.

5. Berol's production requirement in units of finished product for the three-month period ending September 30, 1984, is

a. 712,025 units.
b. 630,000 units.
c. 664,000 units.
d. 665,720 units.
e. some amount other than those given above.

6. Without prejudice to your answer for Item 5, assume Berol plans to produce 600,000 units of finished product in the three-month period ending September 30, 1984, and have direct materials inventory on hand at the end of the three-month period equal to 25 percent of the use in that period. The estimated cost of direct materials purchases for the three-month period ending September 30, 1984, is

a. $2,200,000.
b. $2,400,000.
c. $2,640,000.
d. $2,880,000.
e. some amount other than those given above.

7. The Atwood Company uses a performance reporting system that reflects the company's decentralization of decision making. The departmental performance report shows one line of data for each subordinate who reports to the group vice-president. The data presented shows the actual costs incurred during the period, the budgeted costs, and all variances from budget for that subordinate's department. The Atwood Company is using a type of system called

a. flexible budgeting.
b. responsibility accounting.
c. contribution accounting.
d. cost-benefit accounting.
e. program budgeting.

8. Micro Manufacturers uses an accounting system that charges costs to the manager who has been delegated the authority to make the decisions incurring the costs. For example, if the sales manager accepts a rush order that requires the incurrence of additional manufacturing costs, these additional costs are charged to the sales manager because the authority to accept or decline the rush order was given to the sales manager. This type of accounting system is known as

a. functional accounting.
b. contribution accounting.
c. reciprocal allocation.
d. transfer price accounting.
e. profitability accounting.

9. Rough Rapids Manufacturing currently uses the company budget only as a planning tool. Management has decided that it would be beneficial to also use budgets for control purposes. In order to implement this change, the management accountant must

a. organize a budget committee.
b. appoint a budget director.
c. report daily to operating management all deviations from plan.
d. synchronize the budgeting and accounting system with the organizational structure.
e. develop forecasting procedures.

10. When sales volume is seasonal in nature, certain items in the budget must be coordinated. The three most significant items to coordinate in budgeting seasonal sales volume are

a. production volume, finished goods inventory, and sales volume.
b. raw material, work-in-process, and finished goods inventories.
c. raw material inventory, work-in-process inventory, and production volume.
d. direct labor hours, work-in-process inventory, and sales volume.
e. raw material inventory, direct labor hours, and manufacturing overhead costs.

11. The two most appropriate factors for budgeting manufacturing overhead expenses would be

a. management judgment and sales dollars.

b. sales volume and production volume.
c. machine hours and production volume.
d. management judgment and contribution margin.
e. management judgment and production volume.

12. Of the following items, the one item that would **not** be considered in evaluating the adequacy of the budgeted annual operating income for a company is

a. return on investment.
b. long-range profit objectives.
c. industry average for earnings on sales.
d. earnings per share.
e. internal rate of return.

13. Which one of the following sequences for performance reports can best be used in the management control process as a communications tool?

a. Plan approval, feedforward, feedback, corrective action.
b. Plan approval, feedforward, corrective action, feedback.
c. Feedforward, plan approval, feedback, corrective action.
d. Feedforward, plan approval, corrective action, feedback.
e. Feedback, corrective action, plan approval, feedforward.

14. RedRock Company uses flexible budgeting for cost control. RedRock produced 10,800 units of product during March, incurring an indirect materials cost of $13,000. Its master budget for the year reflected an indirect materials cost of $180,000 at a production volume of 144,000 units. A flexible budget for March production would reflect indirect material costs of

a. $13,000.
b. $13,500.
c. $13,975.
d. $11,700.
e. some amount other than those given above.

15. Simson Company's master budget shows straight-line depreciation on factory equipment of $258,000. The master budget was prepared at an annual production volume of 103,200 units of product. This production volume is expected to occur uniformly throughout the year. During September, Simson produced 8,170 units of product, and the accounts reflected actual depreciation on factory machinery of $20,500. Simson controls manufacturing costs with a flexible budget. The flexible budget amount for depreciation on factory machinery for September would be

a. $19,475.
b. $20,425.
c. $20,500.
d. $21,500.
e. some amount other than those given above.

The Following Data Apply to Items 16 and 17.

Esplanade Company has the following historical pattern its credit sales.

70 percent collected in month of sale
15 percent collected in the first month after sale
10 percent collected in the second month after sale

4 percent collected in the third month after sale
1 percent uncollectible

The sales on open account have been budgeted for the last six (6) months of 1986 as shown below.

July	$ 60,000
August	70,000
September	80,000
October	90,000
November	100,000
December	85,000

16. The estimated total cash collections during October 1986 from accounts receivable would be

a. $63,000.
b. $84,400.
c. $89,100.
d. $21,400.
e. some amount other than those given above.

17. The estimated total cash collections during the fourth calendar quarter from sales made on open account during the fourth calendar quarter would be

a. $172,500.
b. $275,000.
c. $230,000.
d. $251,400.
e. some amount other than those given above.

The Following Data Apply to Items 18 and 19.

Information taken from Valenz Company's records for the fiscal year ended November 30, 1986, is as follows.

Direct materials used	$300,000
Direct labor	100,000
Variable factory overhead	50,000
Fixed factory overhead	80,000
Selling and administrative costs-variable	40,000
Selling and administrative costs-fixed	20,000

18. If Valenz Company uses variable (direct) costing, the inventoriable costs for the 1985-86 fiscal year are

a. $400,000.
b. $450,000.
c. $490,000.
d. $530,000.
e. some amount other than those given above.

19. Using absorption (full) costing, inventoriable costs are

a. $400,000.
b. $450,000.
c. $530,000.
d. $590,000.
e. some amount other than those given above.

3.   Estimated time 30 minutes (December 1988)

The Mason Agency, a division of General Service Industries, offers consulting services to clients for a fee. The corporate management at General Service is pleased with the performance of the Mason Agency for the first nine months of the current year and has recommended that the division manager of the Mason Agency, Richard Howell, submit a revised forecast for the remaining quarter, as the division has exceeded the annual plan year-to-date by 20 percent of operating income. An unexpected increase in billed hour volume over the original plan is the main reason for this gain in income. The original operating budget for the first three quarters for the Mason Agency is presented at the top of the next page.

When comparing the actuals for the first three quarters to the original plan, Howell analyzed the variances and will reflect the following information in his revised forecast for the fourth quarter.

• The division currently has 25 consultants on staff, 10 for management consulting and 15 for EDP consulting, and has hired three additional management consultants to start work at the beginning of the fourth quarter in order to meet the increased client demand.

• The hourly billing rate for consulting revenues is market acceptable and will remain at $90 per hour for each management consultant and $75 per hour for each EDP consultant. However, due to the favorable increase in billing hour volume when compared to plan, the hours for each consultant will be increased by 50 hours per quarter. There is no learning curve for billable consulting hours for new employees.

• The budgeted annual salaries and actual annual salaries, paid monthly, are the same at $50,000 for a management consultant and 8 percent less for an EDP consultant. Corporate management has approved a merit increase of 10 percent at the beginning of the fourth quarter for all 25 existing consultants, while the new consultants will be compensated at the planned rate.

• The planned salary expense includes a provision for employee fringe benefits amounting to 30 percent of the annual salaries; however, the improvement of some corporate-wide employee programs will increase the fringe benefit allocation to 40 percent.

• The original plan assumes a fixed hourly rate for travel and other related expenses for each billing hour of consulting. These are expenses that are not reimbursed by the client, and the previously determined hourly rate has proven to be adequate to cover these costs.

• Other revenues are derived from temporary rentals and interest income and remain unchanged for the fourth quarter.

• General and administrative expenses have been favorable at 7 percent below the plan; this 7 percent savings on fourth quarter expenses will be reflected in the revised plan.

• Depreciation for office equipment and microcomputers will stay constant at the projected straight-line rate.

• Due to the favorable experience for the first three quarters and the division's increased ability to absorb costs, the corporate management at General Service Industries has increased the corporate expense allocation by 50 percent.

The Mason Agency
1988-1989 Operating Budget

	First Quarter	Second Quarter	Third Quarter	Total Nine Months
Revenue				
Consulting fees				
Management consulting	$315,000	$315,000	$315,000	$ 945,000
EDP consulting	421,875	421,875	421,875	1,265,625
Total consulting fees	$736,875	$736,875	$736,875	$2,210,625
Other revenue	10,000	10,000	10,000	30,000
Total revenue	$746,875	$746,875	$746,875	$2,240,625
Expenses				
Consultant salary expense	$386,750	$386,750	$386,750	$1,160,250
Travel and related expense	45,625	45,625	45,625	136,875
General and administrative expense	100,000	100,000	100,000	300,000
Depreciation expense	40,000	40,000	40,000	120,000
Corporate allocation	50,000	50,000	50,000	150,000
Total expenses	$622,375	$622,375	$622,375	$1,867,125
Operating income	$124,500	$124,500	$124,500	$ 373,500

Required A. Prepare a revised operating budget for the fourth quarter for the Mason Agency that Richard Howell will present to General Service Industries. Be sure to furnish supporting calculations for all revised revenue and expense amounts.

B. Discuss the reasons why an organization would prepare a revised forecast.

---

4.   Estimated time 20 minutes (June 1976)

All-Day Candy Company is a wholesale distributor of candy. The company services grocery, convenience, and drug stores in a large metropolitan area.

Small but steady growth in sales has been achieved by the All-Day Candy Company over the past few years while candy prices have been increasing. The company is formulating its plans for the coming fiscal year. Presented below are the data used to project the current year's after-tax net income of $110,400.

Average selling price	**$4.00** per box
Average variable costs:	
Cost of candy	$2.00 per box
Selling expenses	.40 per box
Total	**$2.40** per box
Annual fixed costs:	
Selling	$160,000
Administrative	280,000
Total	**$440,000**
Expected annual sales volume (390,000 boxes)	$1,560,000
Tax rate	40%

Manufacturers of candy have announced that they will increase prices of their products an average of 15 percent in the coming year due to increases in raw material (sugar, cocoa, peanuts, and so on) and labor costs. All-Day Candy Company expects that all other costs will remain at the same rates or levels as the current year.

Required A. What is All-Day Candy Company's break-even point in boxes of candy for the current year?

B. What selling price per box must All-Day Candy Company charge to cover the 15 percent increase in the cost of candy and still maintain the current contribution margin ratio?

C. What volume of sales in dollars must the All-Day Candy Company achieve in the coming year to maintain the same net income after taxes as projected for the current year if the selling price of candy remains at $4 per box and the cost of candy increases 15 percent?

5.   Estimated time 30 minutes (December 1990)

Watson Corporation manufacturers and sells extended keyboard units to be used with microcomputers. Robin Halter, budget analyst, coordinated the preparation of the annual budget for the year ending August 31, 1991. The budget was based on the prior year's sales and production activity. The pro forma statements of income and cost of goods sold are presented below.

Watson Corporation
Pro Forma Statement of Income
For the Year Ending August 31, 1991
($000 omitted)

Net sales		$25,550
Cost of goods sold		16,565
Gross profit		8,985
Operating expenses		
Marketing	$3,200	
General and administrative	2,000	5,200
Income from operations		
before income taxes		$ 3,785

Watson Corporation
Pro Forma Statement of Cost of Goods Sold
For the Year Ending August 31, 1991
($000 omitted)

Direct materials:		
Materials inventory, 9/1/90	$ 1,200	
Materials purchased	11,400	
Materials available for use	12,600	
Materials inventory, 8/31/91	1,480	
Direct materials consumed		$11,120
Direct labor		980
Factory overhead:		
Indirect materials	1,112	
General factory overhead	2,800	3,912
Cost of goods manufactured		16,012
Finished goods inventory, 9/1/90		930
Cost of goods available for sale		16,942
Finished goods inventory, 8/31/91		377
Cost of goods sold		$16,565

On December 10, 1990, Halter met with Walter Collins, vice president of finance, to discuss the first quarter's results (the period September 1 to November 30, 1990). After their discussion, Collins directed Halter to reflect the following changes to the budget assumptions in revised pro forma statements.

• The estimated production in units for the fiscal year should be revised from 140,000 to 145,000 units with the balance of production being scheduled in equal segments over the last nine months of the year. The actual first quarter's production was 25,000 units.

• The planned inventory for finished goods of 3,300 units at the end of the fiscal year remains unchanged and will be valued at the average manufacturing cost for the year. The finished goods inventory of 9,300 units on September 1,

1990, had dropped to 9,000 units by November 30, 1990.

• Due to a new labor agreement, the labor rate will increase eight percent effective June 1, 1991, the beginning of the fourth quarter, instead of the previously anticipated effective date of September 1, 1991, the beginning of the next fiscal year.

• The assumptions remain unchanged for direct materials inventory at 16,000 units for the beginning inventory and 18,500 units for the ending inventory. Direct materials inventory is valued on a first-in, first-out basis. During the first quarter, direct materials for 27,500 units of output were purchased for $2,200,000. Although direct materials will be purchased evenly for the last nine months, the cost of the direct materials will increase by five percent on March 1, 1991, the beginning of the third quarter.

• Indirect material costs will continue to be projected at ten percent of the cost of direct materials consumed.

• One-half of general factory overhead and all of the marketing and general and administrative expenses are considered fixed.

Required A. Based on the revised data presented, calculate Watson Corporation's projected sales for the year ending August 31, 1991, in

1. number of units to be sold.
2. dollar volume of net sales.

B. Prepare the pro forma Statement of Costs of Goods Sold for the year ending August 31, 1991.

6. **Estimated time 40 minutes (June 1979)**

Pearsons, a successful regional chain of moderate priced menu restaurants each with a carryout delicatessen department, is planning to expand to a nationwide operation. As the chain gets larger and the territory covered becomes wider, managerial control and reporting techniques become more important.

The company management believes that a budget program for the entire company as well as each restaurant-deli unit is needed. The budget presented below has been prepared for the typical unit in the chain. A new unit once it is in operation is expected to perform in accordance with the budget.

Typical Pearsons Restaurant-Deli
Budgeted Income Statement for the Year
Ending December 31
($000 omitted)

	Delicatessen	Restaurant	Total
Gross Sales	$1,000	$2,500	$3,500
Purchases	600	1,000	1,600
Hourly wages	50	875	925
Franchise fee	30	75	105
Advertising	100	200	300
Utilities	70	125	195
Depreciation	50	75	125
Lease expense	30	50	80
Salaries	30	50	80
Total	960	2,450	3,410
Net income before income taxes	$ 40	$ 50	$ 90

Pearsons Restaurant-Deli
Akron, Ohio
Net Income for the Year Ended
December 31, 1978

	Actual Results			Budget	Over (Under) Budget
	Delicatessen	Restaurant	Total		
Gross sales	$1,200	$2,000	$3,200	$3,500	$(300)
Purchases	780	800	1,580	1,600	(20)
Hourly wages	60	700	760	925	(165)
Franchise fee	36	60	96	105	(9)
Advertising	100	200	300	300	—
Utilities	76	100	176	195	(19)
Depreciation	50	75	125	125	—
Lease expense	30	50	80	80	—
Salaries	30	50	80	80	—
Total	1,162	2,035	3,197	3,410	(213)
Net income before income taxes	$ 38	$ (35)	$ 3	$ 90	$(87)

All units are of approximately the same size with the amount of space devoted to the carryout delicatessen similar in each unit. The style of the facilities and the equipment used are uniform in all units. The unit operators are expected to carry out the advertising program recommended by the corporation. The corporation charges a franchise fee which is a percentage of gross sales for the use of the company name, the building and facilities design, and the advertising advice.

The Akron, Ohio unit was selected to test the budget program. The Akron, Ohio restaurant-deli performance for the year ended December 31, 1978 compared to the typical budget is presented at the bottom of the preceeding page.

A careful review of the report and a discussion of its meaning was carried out by the company management. One conclusion was that a more meaningful comparison would result if a flexible budget analysis for each of the two lines were performed rather than just the single budget comparison as in the test case.

Required   A. Prepare a schedule which compares a flexible budget for the deli line of the Akron restaurant-deli to its actual performance.

B. Would a complete report, comparing a flexible budget to the performance of each of the two operations, make the problems of the Akron operation easier to identify? Explain, using an example from the problem and your answer to Requirement A.

C. Should a flexible budget comparison to actual performance become part of the regular reporting system

1. for the annual review?
2. for a monthly review?

Explain your answer.

___

7.   Estimted time 30 minutes (December 1980)

The Triple-F Health Club (Family, Fitness, and Fun) is a non-profit family oriented health club. The club's Board of Directors is developing plans to acquire more equipment and expand the club facilities. The Board plans to purchase about $25,000 of new equipment each year and wants to begin a fund to purchase the adjoining property in four or five years. The adjoining property has a market value of about $300,000.

The club manager, Jane Crowe, is concerned that the Board has unrealistic goals in light of its recent financial performance. She has sought the help of a club member with an accounting background to assist her in preparing a report to the Board supporting her concerns.

The club member reviewed the club's records, including the cash basis income statements presented in the next column. The review and disussions with Jane Crowe disclosed the following additional information.

• Other financial information as of October 31, 1980
   —Cash in checking account, $7,000.
   —Petty cash, $300.

—Outstanding mortgage balance, $390,000.
—Accounts payable arising from invoices for supplies and utilities which are unpaid as of October 31, 1980, $2,500.

• No unpaid bills existed on October 31, 1979.

• The club purchased $25,000 worth of exercise equipment during the current fiscal year. Cash of $10,000 was paid on delivery and the balance was due on October 1 but has not been paid as of October 31, 1980.

• The club began operations in 1974 in rental quarters. In October of 1976 it purchased its current property (land and building) for $600,000, paying $120,000 down and agreeing to pay $30,000 plus 9% interest annually on November 1 until the balance was paid off.

• Membership rose three percent during 1980. This is approximately the same annual rate the club has experienced since it opened.

• Membership fees were increased by 15 percent in 1980. The Board has tentative plans to increase the fees by 10 percent in 1981.

• Lesson and class fees have not been increased for three years. The board policy is to encourage classes and lessons by keeping the fees low. The members have taken advantage of this policy and the number of classes and lessons have grown significantly each year. The club expects the percentage growth experienced in 1980 to be repeated in 1981.

• Miscellaneous revenues are expected to grow at the same percentage as experienced in 1980.

Triple-F Health Club Statement of Income (Cash Basis) *For Years Ended October 31* ($000 omitted)		
	1980	1979
Cash revenues		
Annual membership fees	$355.0	$300.0
Lesson and class fees	234.0	180.0
Miscellaneous	2.0	1.5
Total cash received	591.0	481.5
Cash expenses		
Manager's salary and benefits	36.0	36.0
Regular employees' wages and benefits	190.0	190.0
Lesson and class employee wages and benefits	195.0	150.0
Towels and supplies	16.0	15.5
Utilities (heat and light)	22.0	15.0
Mortgage interest	35.1	37.8
Miscellaneous	2.0	1.5
Total cash expenses	496.1	445.8
Cash income	**$ 94.9**	**$ 35.7**

• Operating expenses are expected to increase. Hourly wage rates and the manager's salary will need to be increased 15 percent because no increases were granted in 1980. Towels and supplies, utilities, and miscellaneous expenses are expected to increase 25 percent.

Required A. Construct a cash budget for 1981 for the Triple-F Health Club.

B. Identify any operating problem(s) that this budget discloses for the Triple-F Health Club. Explain your answer.

C. Is Jane Crowe's concern that the Board's goals are unrealistic justified? Explain your answer.

---

8. Estimated time 30 minutes (December 1982)

Small businesses are usually the first organizations to feel the effects of a recessionary economy and are generally the last to recover. Two major reasons for small business financial difficulties are managerial inexperience and inadequate financing or financial management.

Small business managers frequently have problems in planning and controlling profits including revenue generation and cost reduction activities. These important financial methods are especially critical during a recessionary time period. The financial problems of small businesses are further compounded when there are poor accounting records and inexperience in the management of money.

Required A. Profit planning is critical for the planning and controlling of profits of a small business. Identify key features that need to be considered when developing a profit plan.

B. The management accountant can help assure that good accounting records exist in an organization. Discuss the key features which form the basis for a good accounting system that will support management decisions.

C. Explain how the management accountant can assist an organization in adopting measures to assure appropriate money management.

---

9. Estimated time 30 minutes (June 1991)

CrossMan Corporation, a rapidly expanding crossbow distributor to retail outlets, is in the process of formulating plans for 1992. Joan Caldwell, director of marketing, has completed her 1992 forecast and is confident that sales estimates will be met or exceeded. The following sales figures show the growth expected and will provide the planning basis for other corporate departments.

Month	Forcasted Sales	Month	Forecasted Sales
January	$1,800,000	July	$3,000,000
February	2,000,000	August	3,000,000
March	1,800,000	September	3,200,000
April	2,200,000	October	3,200,000
May	2,500,000	November	3,000,000
June	2,800,000	December	3,400,000

George Brownell, assistant controller, has been given the responsibility for formulating the cash flow projection, a critical element during a period of rapid expansion. The following information will be used in preparing the cash analysis.

• CrossMan has experienced an excellent record in accounts receivable collection and expects this trend to continue. Sixty percent of billings are collected in the month after the sale and 40 percent in the second month after the sale. Uncollectible accounts are nominal and will not be considered in the analysis.

• The purchase of the crossbows is CrossMan's largest expenditure; the cost of these items equals 50 percent of sales. Sixty percent of the crossbows are received one month prior to sale and 40 percent are received during the month of sale.

• Prior experience shows that 80 percent of accounts payable are paid by CrossMan one month after receipt of the purchased crossbows, and the remaining 20 percent are paid the second month after receipt.

• Hourly wages, including fringe benefits, are a factor of sales volume and are equal to 20 percent of the current month's sales. These wages are paid in the month incurred.

• General and administrative expenses are projected to be $2,640,000 for 1992. The composition of the expenses is given below. All of these expenses are incurred uniformly throughout the year except the property taxes. Property taxes are paid in four equal installments in the last month of each quarter.

Salaries	$ 480,000
Promotion	660,000
Property taxes	240,000
Insurance	360,000
Utilities	300,000
Depreciation	600,000
Total	$2,640,000

• Income tax payments are made by CrossMan in the first month of each quarter based on the income for the prior quarter. CrossMan's income tax rate is 40 percent. CrossMan's net income for the first quarter of 1992 is projected to be $612,000.

• CrossMan has a corporate policy of maintaining an end-of-month cash balance of $100,000. Cash is invested or borrowed monthly, as necessary, to maintain this balance.

• CrossMan uses a calendar year reporting period.

Required A. Prepare a Pro Forma Schedule of Cash Receipts and Disbursements for CrossMan Corporation, by month, for the second quarter of 1992. Be sure that all receipts, disbursements, and borrowing/investing amounts are presented on a monthly basis. Ignore the interest expense and/or interest income associated with the borrowing/investing activities.

B. Discuss why cash budgeting is particularly important for a rapidly expanding company such as CrossMan Corporation.

10.   Estimated time 30 minutes (June 1985)

WestWood Corporation is a woodstove manufacturer located in southern Oregon. WestWood manufactures three models—small stoves for heating a single room, medium-sized units for use in mobile homes and as a supplement to central heating systems, and large stoves with the capacity to provide central heating.

The manufacturing process consists of shearing and shaping steel, fabricating, welding, painting, and finishing. Molded doors are custom built at an outside foundry in the state, brass plated at a plater, and fitted with custom etched glass during assembly at WestWood's plant. The finished stoves are delivered to dealers either directly or through regional warehouses located throughout the western United States. WestWood owns the three tractor trailers and one large truck used to ship stoves to dealers and warehouses.

The budget for the year ending February 28, 1986, was finalized in January of 1985 and was based upon an-assumption of the continuation of the 10 percent annual growth rate that WestWood had experienced since 1980.

Stove sales are seasonal, and the first quarter of WestWood's fiscal year is usually a slack period. As a consequence, inventory levels were down at the start of the current fiscal year on March 1, 1985.

WestWood's sales orders for the first quarter ended May 31, 1985, were up 54 percent over the same period last year and 40 percent above the first quarter budget. Unfortunately, not all of the sales orders could be filled due to the reduced inventory levels at the beginning of the quarter. WestWood's plant was able to increase production over budgeted levels, but not in sufficient quantity to compensate for the large increase in orders. Therefore, there is a large backlog of orders. Furthermore, preliminary orders for the busy fall season are 60 percent above the budget and the projections for the winter of 1985-86 indicate no decrease in demand. WestWood's President attributes the increase to effective advertising, the products' good reputation, the increased number of installations of woodstoves in new houses, and the bankruptcy of WestWood's principal competitor.

Required   **A.** WestWood Corporation's sales for the remainder of the 1985-86 fiscal year will be much greater than were predicted five months ago. Explain the effect this increase will have on the operations in the following functional areas of WestWood.

1. Production.
2. Finance and accounting.
3. Marketing.
4. Personnel.

B. Some companies follow the practice of preparing a continuous budget.

1. Explain what a continuous budget is.
2. Explain how WestWood Corporation could benefit by the preparation of a continuous budget.

11.   Estimated time 30 minutes (June 1988)

Bob Bingham is the controller of Atlantis Laboratories, a manufacturer and distributor of generic prescription pharmaceuticals. He is currently in the process of preparing the annual budget and reviewing the current business plan. The business unit managers of Atlantis prepare and assemble the detailed operating budgets, with technical assistance from the corporate accounting staff. The final budgets are then presented by the business unit managers to the corporate executive committee for approval. The corporate accounting staff reviews the budgets for adherence to corporate accounting policies, but no detailed review for reasonableness of the line items within the budget is done.

Bingham is aware that the upcoming year for Atlantis may be a difficult one due to the expiration of a major patent and the loss of a licensing agreement for another product line. He also knows that during the budgeting process, "budgetary slack" is created in varying degrees throughout the organization. Bingham believes this slack has a negative effect on the overall business objectives of Atlantis Laboratories and should be eliminated where possible.

Required   **A.** Define "budgetary slack."

B. Explain the advantages and disadvantages of "budgetary slack" from the point of view of

1. the business unit manager who must achieve the budget.
2. corporate management.

C. Bob Bingham is considering implementing zero-based budgeting at Atlantis Laboratories.

1. Define zero-based budgeting.

2. Describe how zero-based budgeting could be advantageous to Atlantis Laboratories in controlling budgetary slack.

3. Discuss the disadvantages Atlantis Laboratories might encounter from using zero-based budgeting.

12.   Estimated time 35 minutes (December 1991)

Bee-Line Toys manufactures inexpensive skateboards for distribution to national discount chains. The Company has a comprehensive annual budgeting process that ends with the preparation of a pro forma income statement and a pro forma statement of financial position. All of the underlying budget schedules have been completed for the year ending December 31, 1992, and selected data from these schedules are presented in the next column. Also shown on the next page are Bee-Line's pro forma Statement of Cash Receipts and Disursements for the year ending December 31, 1991. Bee-Line uses the accrual basis of accounting.

In order to facilitate the budgeting process, Bee-Line accumulates all raw material, direct labor, manufacturing overhead (with the exception of depreciation), selling, and administrative costs in an account called *Expenses Payable*. The company's income tax rate is 40 percent, and income tax expense is classified as current income taxes payable.

1992 Selected Data

- *Sales*

Unit Sales	Unit Price	Total Revenue
9,500,000	$5.50	$52,250,000

The majority of sales are on account.

- *Production*

Production Units	Unit Cost	Total Manu-facturing Cost
9,640,000	$4.75	$45,790,000

- *Raw Material Purchases*

Item	Quantity	Cost	Total Cost
Board	9,600,000	$.80	$7,680,000
Wheel Assembly*	18,800,000	.30	5,640,000

*Each unit requires two wheel assemblies.

- *Direct Labor Cost*

Production Hours	Cost per Hour	Total Cost
2,410,000	$9.00	$21,690,000

Each unit of production requires 15 minutes of direct labor.

- *Manufacturing Overhead*

Variable overhead	$ 5,790,000
Supervisory salaries	1,250,000
Depreciation	724,000
Other fixed costs	2,840,000
Total manufacturing overhead	$10,604,000

The manufacturing overhead rate is $4.40 per direct labor hour ($10,604,000 ÷ 2,410,000 hours).

- *Selling and Administrative Expense*

Selling expense	$1,875,000
Administrative expense	3,080,000
Total expense	$4,955,000

- *Mortgage Payable*

Each semi-annual payment consists of interest plus an even principal reduction of $100,000. Interest payments for 1992 are $250,000.

Required Complete the budgeting process at Bee-Line Toys by preparing the pro forma Statement of Financial Position as of December 31, 1992. Be sure to support the statement with appropriate calculations.

Bee-Line Toys
Pro Forma Statement of Cash Receipts and Disbursements
For the Year Ending December 31, 1992
(in thousands)

Cash balance 1/1/92 (estimated)	$	565
Cash receipts		
Cash sales		5,300
Collection of accounts receivable		46,600
Proceeds from sale of additional common stock (20,000 shares)		420
Total cash available		52,885
Cash disbursements		
Raw material		13,380
Direct labor		21,640
Manufacturing overhead		9,650
Selling/administrative expense		4,980
Income taxes		860
Purchase of equipment		1,200
Cash dividends		320
Mortgage payment		450
Total disbursements		52,480
Projected cash balance 12/31/92	$	405

Bee-Line Toys
Pro Forma Statement of Financial Position
as of December 31, 1991
(in thousands)

Assets

Cash	$	565
Accounts receivable		825
Raw material inventory*		301
Finished goods inventory **		608
Total current assets		2,299
Land		1,757
Plant and equipment		12,400
Less accumulated depreciation		2,960
Total long-term assets		11,197
Total assets		$13,496

Liabilities and Shareholders' Equity

Expenses payable	$	690
Mortgage payable		200
Income taxes payable		356
Total current liabilities		1,246
Long-term mortgage payable		2,700
Total liabilities		3,946
Common stock (500,000 shares authorized, 300,000 shares outstanding, $10 par value)		3,000
Paid-in capital in excess of par		5,400
Retained earnings		1,150
Total shareholders' equity		9,550
Total liabilities and shareholders' equity		$13,496

*65,000 Boards @ $.80 each
830,000 Wheel Assemblies @ $.30 each

**128,000 units @ $4.75 each

Solutions

1.

1. d. The sales mix is assumed to remain constant for all volume levels.

2. b.

Sales price per unit ($625,000 ÷ 25,000)	$25
Variable costs ($375,000 ÷ 25,000)	15
Contribution margin	**$10**

$$BEP = \frac{Fixed\ costs}{Contribution\ margin/unit} = \frac{\$150,000}{\$10}$$

$$= \textbf{15,000 units}$$

3. a.

$$Number\ of\ units = \frac{Fixed\ costs + desired\ profit/(1-t)}{Contribution\ margin/unit}$$

$$= \frac{\$150,000 + \dfrac{\$77,000}{1-.45}}{\$10}$$

$$= \textbf{29,000 units}$$

4. c.

$$BEP = \frac{\$150,000 + \$18,000/6}{\$10 + \$2.50 - \$4.50} = \frac{\$153,000}{\$8}$$

$$= \textbf{19,125 units}$$

5. a.

$$Number\ of\ units = \frac{\$153,000 + \dfrac{\$55,000}{1-.45}}{\$8}$$

$$= \textbf{31,625 units}$$

6. d.

	Per unit	Percent
Sales	$25	100%
Variable costs	15	60%
Contribution margin	**$10**	**40%**

Variable costs were 60 percent of sales. The variable costs have increased to $17 ($15 − $2.50 + $4.50). Thus, the new sales price is $28.33 ($17 ÷ .60).

7. d.

$$BEP\ (Sales\ \$) = \frac{Fixed\ costs}{1 - \dfrac{Variable\ costs}{Sales}} = \frac{\$270,000}{\dfrac{\$6.60}{\$12.00}}$$

$$1 - \frac{Variable\ costs}{Sales} = 1 - \frac{\$6.60}{\$12.00}$$

$$= \$600,000$$

$$Margin\ of\ safety = \frac{Budgeted\ sales - breakeven\ sales}{Budgeted\ sales}$$

Let X = Budgeted sales

$$.20 = \frac{X - \$600,000}{X}$$

$$.2X = X - \$600,000$$

$$.8X = \$600,000$$

$$X = \$750,000$$

8. b. The contribution margin was $14 ($35 − $21) without this price increase and $28 ($35 × 1.4 − $21) with the increase. Thus, sales volume could decline by 50 percent before profits would fall below profit level without sales increase.

9. d.

Budgeted sales	700,000 × $20 =	$14,000,000
Actual sales	600,000 × $20 =	$12,000,000
Amount by which sales less than budget		**$ 2,000,000** U
Contribution margin (30%)		$ 600,000 U

Contribution margin is a preferable measure to sales dollars because it indicates the amount contributed to fixed costs.

10. e. This is a form of solicitation for orders. The cost is incurred before any orders are received.

11. a. These costs vary directly with unit sales.

12. b. The location of distribution warehouses will affect delivery costs, which are order-filling costs.

13. e. It shows the costs and revenues for which each sales person is responsible.

14. d. The comparison of costs and benefits determines the acceptability of proposed programs.

15. c. Managers at higher levels consolidate the proposals submitted by their subordinates, providing their own ordinal rankings. Where several spending proposals must be rejected, those that are marked the lowest will go first.

16. a. This process allows continuous updating of the budget. The budget may be static or flexible.

17. c.

18. d. The budget is often expressed as a formula where the budgeted cost = fixed cost + variable cost rate × volume level.

19. a. The forecast is valid only so long as the assumptions and expectations on which it was based are unchanged. Items b, c, d, e are types of profit planning and budgeting.

20. d. The point where the company has no profit—sales equals total costs or contribution margin equals fixed costs.

21. a. The line referred to in the problem is a contribution line. As volume increases, the total contribution margin increased. The distance labelled B represents total contribution margin.

22. b. An increase in fixed costs will cause the loss to be greater at zero volume and it will take a larger volume to breakeven. The slope of the contribution margin line, however, will not change.

23. d. An increase in the variable costs with no change in sales will result in a decrease in the contribution and cause the line to slope more to the right.

24. e. There would be no change in the contribution margin per unit; thus, no change in the contribution margin line.

25. b. Conversion cost is direct labor plus overhead.

26. d. Prime costs consist of the direct materials and direct labor costs.

27. c. Direct materials, direct labor, variable overhead, and variable selling expenses are the variable costs that are associated with each unit.

28. d.
Direct materials ($32 × 12,000)	= $384,000
Direct labor ($20 × 12,000)	= 240,000
Variable overhead ($15 × 12,000)	= 180,000
Fixed overhead ($6 × 12,000)	= 72,000
Variable selling ($3 × 8,000)	= 24,000
Fixed selling ($4 × 12,000)	= 48,000
Total	$948,000

29. c.
Applied overhead $\left(\dfrac{\$720,000}{600,000} \times 550,000\right)$ $660,000

Actual 680,000

Underapplied $ 20,000

30. b. Factory overhead applied is included in cost of goods sold. The difference between the amount applied and the control account must be deducted to determine net income:

Sales	$3,600,000
Less: Cost of goods sold	$2,040,000
General selling and administrative	900,000
Volume variance	52,000
Net income	$608,000

2.

1. b. BEP $= \dfrac{FC}{C/M \text{ per unit}}$

$= \dfrac{600,000}{16-12}$

$= 150,000$ units

2. c. $[(\$4 \times 200,000 \times 1.1) - \$600,000] \times .60 - \$120,000 = \$48,000$

3. a.
Sales − VC − FC	= $120,000/.6
$16X − ($10 × 1.3 + $2)X − $600,000	= $200,000
16X − 15X − $600,000	= $200,000
X	= 800,000
$16X	= $12,800,000

4. d. current C/M ratio is $4/$16 = .25

Sales Price $= \dfrac{\$10 \times 1.3 + \$2}{1 - .25} = \$20$

5. d.
	August	September	October
Sales	$210,000	$220,500	$231,525

	July	August	September
Ending inventory	$168,000	$176,400	$185,220
Sales	200,000	210,000	220,500
	$368,000	$386,400	$405,720
Beg. inventory	150,000	168,000	176,400
Production	$218,000	$218,400	$229,320

Total for quarter is $665,720.

6. c.
Production	600,000
Raw material per unit	× 4
	2,400,000
Ending inventory	600,000
	3,000,000
Beginning inventory	800,000
Unit purchases	2,200,000
Cost per unit	× $1.20
Cost of purchases	$2,640,000

7. b.

8. e.

9. d. The accounting system must capture the results of operations in terms of the budgeted costs for the budget to be used as a planning tool.

10. a.

11. e. Production volume, not sales volume, along with management judgment are the most appropriate factors. Machine hours in a highly automated operation would be important but should also be related to production volume.

12. e. The internal rate of return is used to evaluate long-term projects. All of the other ratios (items) mentioned are used to evaluate the budgeted income.

13. a. First, the plan must be approved and then it is communicated to the appropriate party (feedforward). After the results occur, this information is given to the employees (feedback) so that corrective action can be taken.

14. b. Total budgeted cost of $180,000 divided by budgeted units of 144,000 results in a unit cost of $1.25. The budgeted cost for March is 10,800 units times $1.25, or $13,500.

15. d. Total cost of $258,000 divided by twelve is $21,500.

16. b.

October, $90,000 × .70	=	$63,000
September, $80,000 × .15	=	12,000
August, $70,000 × .10	=	7,000
July, $60,000 × .04	=	2,400
Total October collections		$84,400

17. c.

October ($90,000 × .95)	$ 85,500
November ($100,000 × .85)	85,000
December ($85,000 × .70)	59,500
	$230,000

18. b. Inventoriable costs consist of direct materials used, direct labor and variable overhead. Fixed costs and selling and administrative costs are not included in inventory.

19. c. Fixed factory overhead costs of $80,000 are added to the variable manufacturing costs.

3.

A. The revised operating budget for the Mason Agency for the fourth quarter is presented in the next column.

The Mason Agency
Revised Operating Budget
Fourth Quarter 1988 - 1989

Revenues
Consulting fees	
Management consulting	$468,000
EDP consulting	478,125
Total consulting revenue	946,125
Other revenue	10,000
Total revenue	956,125

Expenses
Consulting salary expense	510,650
Travel and related expense	57,875
General and administrative expense	93,000
Depreciation expense	40,000
Corporate allocation	75,000
Total expenses	776,525
Operating income	$179,600

Supporting Calculations

- Schedule of projected revenues for fourth quarter 1988-1989.

	Management Consulting	EDP Consulting
Third Quarter		
Revenues	$315,000	$421,875
Hourly billing rate	÷ $90	÷ $75
Billable hours	3,500	5,625
Number of consultants	÷ 10	÷ 15
Hours per consultant	350	375
Fourth Quarter		
Planned increase	50	50
Billable hours per consultant	400	425
Number of consultants	x 13	x 15
Billable hours	5,200	6,375
Billing rate	x $90	x $75
Projected revenue	$468,000	$478,125

- Schedules of projected salaries, travel, general and administrative, and allocated corporate expenses.

Compensation	Management Consulting	EDP Consulting
Existing consultants		
Annual salary	$ 50,000	
($50,000 x 92%)		$ 46,000
Quarterly salary	12,500	11,500
Planned increase (10%)	1,250	1,150
Total	$ 13,750	$ 12,650
Number of consultants	x 10	x 15
Total	$137,500	$189,750

New consultants (3)
  at old salary
  (3 x $12,500)   37,500

Total   175,000   189,750
    Benefits (40%)   70,000   75,900
    Total   245,000 $265,650
                               265,650
Total compensation $510,650

Travel expense
  Management consultants
    (400 hrs x 13)   5,200
  EDP consultants
    (425 hrs x 15)   6,375
    Total hours   11,575
  Rate per hour*   x $5
    Total travel expense $57,875

*Third quarter travel expense ÷ hours = Rate
$45,625 ÷ 9,125 = $5.00

General and administrative
($100,000 x 93%) $93,000

Corporate allocation
($50,000 x 150%) $75,000

B. An organization would prepare a revised forecast when the assumptions underlying the original forecast are no longer valid. The assumptions may involve factors outside or inside the company. Changes in assumptions involving external factors may include changes in demand for the company's products or services, changes in the cost of various inputs to the company, or changes in the economic or political environment in which the company operates. Changes in assumptions involving internal factors may include changes in company goals or objectives by management or stockholders.

4.

A.

$$\text{Breakeven point in boxes of candy} = \frac{\text{Annual fixed costs}}{\text{Contribution margin per box}}$$

$$= \frac{\$440,000}{(\$4.00 - 2.40)}$$

$$= \frac{\$440,000}{\$1.60 \text{ per box}}$$

$$= 275,000 \text{ boxes}$$

B.

	Current year	
	Dollars	Percent
Selling price	$4.00	100%
Variable costs	2.40	60
Contribution margin	**$1.60**	**40%**

$$\text{Contribution margin rate} = \frac{\text{Selling price} - \text{Variable costs}}{\text{Selling price}}$$

$$\text{Selling price} = \frac{\text{Variable costs}}{1 - \text{Contribution margin rate}}$$

$$= \frac{(\$2.00 \times 1.15) + \$.40}{1 - .40}$$

$$= \frac{\$2.70}{.60} = \$4.50$$

C.

$$\begin{matrix}\text{Sales volume necessary} \\ \text{to earn a} \\ \text{designated net} \\ \text{income after taxes}\end{matrix} = \frac{\text{Fixed costs} + \dfrac{\text{Net income after taxes}}{1 - \text{Tax rate}}}{\text{Contribution margin rate}}$$

$$\begin{matrix}\text{Sales volume necessary to earn} \\ \$110,400 \text{ after taxes}\end{matrix} = \frac{\$440,000 + \left(\dfrac{110,400}{1 - .4}\right)}{\left(\dfrac{\$4.00 - 2.70}{\$4.00}\right)}$$

$$= \frac{\$624,000}{.325} = \$1,920,000$$

5.

A. 1. Based on the revised data presented, Watson Corporation's projected unit sales for the year ending August 31, 1991, are 151,000 units calculated as follows.

Beginning inventory - finished goods	9,300
Planned production	145,000
Units available for sale	154,300
Ending inventory - finished goods	3,300
Units to be sold	151,000

2. Based on the revised data presented, Watson Corporation's projected dollar volume of net sales for the year ending August 31, 1991, is $26,425,000 calculated as follows.

Selling price per unit	= Original projected sales dollars

$$\text{Selling price per unit} = \frac{\text{Original projected sales dollars}}{\text{Original projected unit sales}}$$

$$= \frac{\$25,550,000}{(9,300 + 140,000 - 3,300)}$$

$$= \$175 \text{ per unit}$$

Dollar volume of projected net sales
$$= \$175/\text{unit} \times 151,000 \text{ units}$$
$$= \$26,425,000$$

B. Based on the revised data presented, Watson Company's pro forma Statement of Costs of Goods Sold for the year ending August 31, 1991, is presented on the following page.

```
                 Watson Corporation
    Pro Forma Statement of Cost of Goods Sold
      For the Year Ending August 31, 1991

Direct materials
  Materials inventory, 9/1/90      $ 1,200,000
  Materials purchased¹              12,120,000
  Materials available for use       13,320,000
  Materials inventory, 8/31/91²      1,554,000
    Direct materials consumed       11,766,000

Direct labor³                        1,037,400

Factory overhead
  Indirect material⁴    $1,176,600
  General factory
  overhead⁵              2,850,000
    Factory over-
      head applied                    4,026,600

Cost of goods manufactured          16,830,000

Finished goods inventory, 9/1/90       930,000

Cost of goods available for sale    17,760,000

Finished goods inventory, 8/31/91⁶     383,028

    Cost of goods sold             $17,376,972
```

Supporting Calculations

¹ Material purchased:
  27,500 units @ $80 per unit* $ 2,200,000
  40,000 units @ $80 per unit   3,200,000
  80,000 units @ $84 per unit**   6,720,000
                                  $12,120,000
  * $2,200,000 ÷ 27,500 units
  ** $80.00 x 1.05

² Materials inventory, 8/31/91:
  18,500 units x $84 $1,554,000

³ Direct labor:
  25,000 units @ $7 per unit* $ 175,000
  80,000 units @ $7 per unit   560,000
  40,000 units @ $7.56 per unit**   302,400
                                   $1,037,400
  * $980,000 ÷ 140,000 units
  ** $7.00 x 1.08

⁴ Indirect material:
  $11,766,000 x .10 $1,176,600

⁵ General factory overhead:
  $2,800,000 ÷ 2 $1,400,000

  $1,400,000 x 145,000 units   1,450,000
  140,000 units
                                   $2,850,000

⁶ Finished goods inventory, 8/31/91:
  Average cost per unit
  $16,830,000 = $116.07 per unit
  145,000 units

  Finished goods
  3,300 x $116.07 $383,028

6.

A.

	% to Sales		Akron Deli only ($000s omitted)	
		Actual	Budget	Over (Under) Budget
Gross sales	100%	$1,200	$1,200	$ —0—
Variable expenses:				
Purchases	60%	$ 780	$ 720	$ 60
Hourly wages	5%	60	60	—0—
Franchise fee	3%	36	36	—0—
Utilities	7%	76	84	(8)
Total variable expenses		952	900	52
Contribution margin		248	300	(52)
Fixed expenses:				
Advertising		100	100	—0—
Depreciation		50	50	—0—
Lease		30	30	—0—
Salaries		30	30	—0—
Total fixed expenses		210	210	—0—
Net income before income taxes		$ 38	$ 90	$ (52)

	Actual Results	Static Budget	Flexible Budget	Variations-over/(under)			
				Static		Flexible	
				Amount	%	Amount	%
Purchases	$780	$600	$720	$180	30	$60	8
Hourly wages	60	50	60	10	20	—0—	—
Franchise fee	36	30	36	6	20	—0—	—
Utilities	76	70	84	6	9	(8)	(10)

B. Yes, a complete report which compares the performance of each operation with a flexible budget for each operation would make the identification of problems easier.

If activity for the period is different from that originally budgeted, a flexible budget for the level of activity achieved is more useful for control purposes than the original budget. The use of a flexible budget enables management to compare performance with a budget prepared for that same activity. This helps managers to identify areas which need managerial attention.

In addition, the flexible budget amounts and actual costs for the deli and restaurant operations need to be reported separately if control is to be exercised over the individual expenses of each operation. Variations from budgeted amounts for individual items in each operation are needed to identify those areas needing management attention. The separation also eliminates the possibilities of a negative variation from budget for an individual item of one operation being hidden by a positive variation in the other operation for the same item.

Good examples of variations which are misstated if actual performance is compared to the static budget are purchases, hourly wages, franchise fees, and utilities as shown in the above schedule for the Deli operation. The variations in purchases and utilities are hidden in the combined report. A cost overrun exists with purchases (8%) while utilities are almost 10% below budget.

C. 1. Yes, a comparison of the flexible budget with actual performance would give management a means of evaluating the budgeting and control processes of the firm on an annual basis. This would provide management with:

- a basis for budgeting future periods.
- a means of evaluating performance for the concluded fiscal year.
- a means for identifying those special areas which may need close management scrutiny.

2. Yes, the monthly review provides for frequent reports. This leads to timely identification of problems and ongoing performance evaluation.

7.

A. (See next column)

B. Operating problems which Triple-F Health Club could experience in 1981 include:

Triple-F Health Club
Budgeted Statement of Income (Cash Basis)
For the Year Ended October 31, 1981
($000 omitted)

Cash revenue	
Annual membership fees $355 \times 1.1 \times 1.03$	$402.2
Lesson and class fees $\frac{234}{180} = 1.3 \times \$234$	304.2
Miscellaneous $\frac{2.0}{1.5} \times \$2$	2.7
Total cash received	$709.1
Cash expenses	
Manager's salary and benefits 36×1.15	41.4
Regular employees' wages and benefits 190×1.15	218.5
Lesson and class employee wages and benefits $195 \times 1.3 \times 1.15$	291.5
Towels and supplies 16×1.25	20.0
Utilities (heat and light) 22×1.25	27.5
Mortgage interest $360 \times .09$	32.4
Miscellaneous 2×1.25	2.5
Total cash expenses	633.8
Cash income	75.3
Cash payments	
Mortgage payment	30.0
Accounts payable balance at 10/31/80	2.5
Accounts payable on equipment at 10/31/80	15.0
Planned new equipment purchase	25.0
Total cash payments	72.5
Cash surplus	2.8
Beginning cash balance	7.3
Cash available for working capital and to acquire property	**$10.1**

• Lessons and classes contribution to cash decreased because the projected wage increase for lesson and class employees is not made up by the increased volume of lessons and classes.

• Operating expenses are increasing faster than revenues from membership fees.

• Triple-F seems to have a cash management problem. Although there appears to be enough cash generated for the club to meet its obligations, there are past due amounts on equipment and regular accounts. Perhaps the cash balance may not be large enough for day to day operating purposes.

C. Jane Crowe's concern with regard to the Board's expansion goals are justified. The 1981 budget projections show only a minimal increase of $2.8 in the cash balance. The total cash available is well short of the $60.0 annual additional cash needed for the land purchase over and above the club's working capital needs. However, it appears that the new equipment purchases can be made on an annual basis. If the Board desires to purchase the adjoining property, it is going to have to consider significant increases in fees or other methods of financing such as membership bonds, or additional mortgage debt.

8.

A. The profit plan for a small business may not need to contain the same level of detail as a large business. The key features of the small business profit plan would include estimates of key factors such as revenues (sales demand, sales price) and expenses for the plan period, systematic evaluation of the available resources (raw materials, labor, financing) and their use, coordination of related functions or elements, such as scheduling production to meet sales or sufficient productive capacity to meet sales demand.
The period covered by the profit plan in a small business may not be as long as in a large business. A quarterly, or even seasonal, plan may be adequate and certainly preferable to no plan. Use of a shorter period will tend to encourage longer planning in the future. The plan should project reasonable profit goals and evaluate competition as part of a sales forecast.

B. The management accountant must exercise care to ensure that the small business does not suffer from an information overload (strive for simplicity). A cost system should be established that captures sufficient data on a timely basis to allow a reasonable level of operations evaluation without becoming too costly or too sophisticated for the business. To the extent possible, the system should capture data by cost element, i.e., direct material and labor costs, and should segregate an account for overhead items. Emphasis should be placed on the reasons for the information gathering and its use rather than on the collection system or the profit plan being an end in itself.

C. The management accountant can insist upon and assist in the preparation of regular cash budgets. These cash flow reports should identify the major sources and uses of cash and point out the periods of potential cash shortage or surplus. This will enable arrangements for borrowing or short-term investment.

9.

A. A Pro Forma Schedule of Cash Receipts and Disbursements for CrossMan Corporation, by month, for the second quarter of 1992, is presented on the next page. (For Pro Forma Schedule purposes, interest expenses and/or interest income associated with the borrowing/investing activities have not been considered.)

B. Cash budgeting is particularly important for a rapidly expanding company such as CrossMan Corporation because as sales grow rapidly so do expenditures for product purchases. These expenditures generally precede cash receipts, often by a considerable time period, and a growing company must be prepared to finance this increasing gap between expenditures and receipts.

CrossMan Corporation
Pro Forma Schedule of Cash Receipts and Disbursements
Second Quarter 1992
(in thousands)

	April	May	June
Beginning cash balance	$ 100	$ 100	$ 100
Accounts receivable collections			
Prior month's sales (60%)	1,080	1,320	1,500
Two months' prior sales (40%)	800	720	880
Total collections	1,880	2,040	2,380
Cash available	1,980	2,140	2,480
Disbursements			
Material purchases[1]	1,004	1,156	1,310
Wages (20% of current sales)	440	500	560
General & administrative[2]	150	150	210
Income taxes[3]	408	-	-
Total disbursements	2,002	1,806	2,080
Net cash flow	(22)	334	400
Cash borrowed	122	-	-
Cash invested	-	(234)	(300)
Ending cash balance	$ 100	$ 100	$ 100

Notes

[1]Material purchases:

	Feb	Mar	April	May	June	July
Sales	$2,000	$1,800	$2,200	$2,500	$2,800	$3,000
Material cost (50%)	1,000	900	1,100	1,250	1,400	1,500
Material receipts						
Next month's material costs (60%)	540	660	750	840	900	
This month's material costs (40%)	400	360	440	500	560	
Total receipts	$ 940	$1,020	$1,190	$1,340	$1,460	
Material payments						
Prior month's receipts (80%)			$ 816	$ 952	$1,072	
Two months' prior receipts (20%)			188	204	238	
Total payments			$1,004	$1,156	$1,310	

[2]General & Administrative expense:

	April	May	June
Salaries (1/12 of annual)	$ 40	$ 40	$ 40
Promotion (1/12 of annual)	55	55	55
Property taxes (1/4 of annual)	-	-	60
Insurance (1/12 of annual)	30	30	30
Utilities (1/12 of annual)	25	25	25
Depreciation (non-cash item)	-	-	-
Total expense	$150	$150	$210

[3]Income tax expense:

First quarter pre-tax income	=	Net income + (1-tax rate)
	=	$612 + .6
	=	$1,020
Tax expense	=	.4 x $1,020
	=	$408

10.

A. 1. The increase in sales could have the following effects on production.

• Production capacity may have to be reallocated to the three models based upon the composition of the sales increase.

• Some parts, in addition to the molded doors, may have to be purchased from outside suppliers.

• Depending upon the ability to purchase parts from outside suppliers and the long-term sales projections, additional capacity may be required.

• Additional labor in the form of additional shifts, overtime, or new hires may be required.

2. The increase in sales could have the following effects on finance and accounting.

• Short-term financing may be needed to finance increased receivable levels and for the replacement of depleted inventories.

• Long-term financing may be needed to expand production capacity.

• Budgeting may have to be revised because sales volume is probably beyond the relevant range assumed for the current budget.

3. The increase in sales could have the following effects on marketing.

• The need to advertise will probably decrease.

• Investigation into the credit-worthiness of potential credit customers may need to become more thorough and the number of investigations will probably increase.

• Collection efforts may have to be increased unless credit granting is tightened.

• Customers may have to accept extended shipping dates or may receive units on some rational basis of output allocation.

4. The increase in sales could have the following effects on personnel.

• There may be increased instances of having to deal with existing workers because of the stress created by the greatly increased volume.

• If additional shifts or overtime are scheduled, personnel would be required to explain why it is needed and convince the employees that it is necessary and beneficial for the company.

• Any additional workers needed to meet the increased demand would be hired through personnel.

B. 1. A continuous (rolling/cycle) budget is the preparation of a new twelve-month budget as each period (e.g., month, quarter) is completed. At the end of each period, the budget amounts for the period just completed are deleted, the amounts for the remaining periods of the old budget are revised as necessary, and budget amounts for the new period are added. Thus, a twelve-month budget is rolled forward as each period is completed.

2. The preparation of a continuous budget would force West-Wood's management to engage in planning on an almost continuous basis. Shorter planning cycles increase the chances that management will anticipate and give attention to problem situations earlier than would otherwise have been the case. Thus, planning would be enhanced in all of the functional areas and there would not be any periods when a budget did not exist.

11.

A. Budgetary slack is a planned difference between budgeted revenue and expected revenue and/or budgeted expenditures and expected expenditures. Budgetary slack describes the tendency of managers to underestimate revenues and overestimate expenditures during the budgetary process in order to build in allowances for unexpected declines in revenue and/or unforeseen expenses. Budgetary slack occurs because of conflicts between a manager's personal interests and the interests of the organization. These conflicts include pressure from management to achieve budgets and the desire on the manager's part to look favorable in the eyes of management.

B. 1. From the point of view of the business unit manager, budgetary slack provides

• flexibility under unexpected circumstances.

• managers with the opportunity to show consistent performance despite variations in departmental resources and workloads.

• a blending of personal and organization goals.

However, the use of budgetary slack limits the objective evaluation of a business unit and therefore, limits the objective evaluation of the performance of the unit manager. It also becomes more difficult for the business unit manager to evaluate the performance of subordinates and to use the budget as a control mechanism over subordinate performance. Therefore, inefficient spending may result, especially if expenditures are less than the budget.

There may be advantages and disadvantages of budgetary slack from the point of view of business unit managers other than those mentioned above.

2. From the perspective of corporate management, the use of budgetary slack increases the probability that budgets will be achieved. This increased dependability enhances the overall corporate budgeting process. Corporate management may also allow budgetary slack as a form of reward to managers for previous good performance.

From the point of view of corporate management, the use of budgetary slack

• increases the likelihood of inefficient allocation of scarce corporate resources.

• decreases the effectiveness of the corporate planning process.

• decreases the ability to identify potential weaknesses or trouble spots in the budgeting process and take corrective action.

• decreases the objectivity of performance evaluations.

• is a source of inefficiency in an organization and is detrimental to organizational goals as it may hide waste.

C. 1. Zero-base budgeting is a planning and budgeting technique that evaluates all proposed operating and administrative expenditures as though they were being initiated for the first time. Each manager must evaluate each expenditure, investigate alternative means of conducting each activity, evaluate alternative budget amounts for various levels of service, justify each expenditure, and finally rank expenditures in order of importance.

2. Atlantis Laboratories could benefit from zero-base budgeting as each of the business unit managers would be required to specifically identify and justify all proposed expenditures for the upcoming year. Rather than focus on the incremental changes in activities from the previous year, the unit managers would be required to evaluate each expenditure as if it were being initiated as a new expenditure. This increased evaluation of expenditures would make it difficult to include budgetary slack in the budget for the upcoming year. Contingency planning would also be enhanced because all expenditures would be ranked on a priority basis, thus allowing Atlantis to eliminate those expenditures with low priorities should the need arise.

3. The biggest disadvantage of using zero-base budgeting is the significant amount of time and cost involved in its implementation. In addition, the concept of zero-base budgeting may be difficult for management to learn and accept. Atlantis must be sure that the benefits of zero-base budgeting outweigh the associated costs. In addition, morale may be low because the specification of service levels, particularly minimum levels, may be threatening to managers as budgeting at these levels can result in personnel reductions. The corporate management of Atlantis may also find it difficult to determine satisfactory performance measures for the various business units.

12.

Bee-Line Toys pro forma Statement of Financial Position as of December 31, 1992 is presented in the next column.

Bee-Line Toys
Pro Forma Statement of Financial Position
as of December 31, 1992
(in thousands)

Cash		$ 405
Accounts receivable[1]		1,175
Raw materials inventory[2]		125
Finished goods inventory[3]		1,273
Total current assets		2,978
Land		1,757
Plant and equipment[4]	$13,600	
Accumulated depreciation[5]	3,684	9,916
Total assets		$14,651
Expenses payable[6]		$ 885
Mortgage payable		200
Income taxes payable[7]		264
Total current liabilities		1,349
Long-term mortgage[8]		2,500
Total liabilities		3,849
Common stock[9]		3,200
Paid-in capital in excess of par[10]		5,620
Retained earnings[11]		1,982
Total shareholders' equity		10,802
Total liabilities and shareholders' equity		$14,651

Supporting Calculations are presented on the next page.

Supporting Calculations:

¹Accounts receivable:

Beginning accounts receivable		$ 825
Total sales	$52,250	
Less cash sales	5,300	46,950
Sub-total		47,775
Less collections		46,600
Ending accounts receivable		$ 1,175

²Raw material inventory:

Beginning raw material inventory	$ 301
Purchases: Boards	7,680
Wheels	5,640
Less Production:	
Boards (9,640 x $ .80)	(7,712)
Wheels (9,640 x 2 x $ .30)	(5,784)
Ending raw material inventory	$ 125

³Finished goods inventory:

Beginning finished goods inventory	$ 608
Units completed (9,640 x $4.75)	45,790
Cost of goods sold (9,500 x $4.75)	(45,125)
Ending finished goods inventory	$ 1,273

⁴Plant and equipment:

Beginning balance	$12,400
Purchase of equipment	1,200
Ending balance	$13,600

⁵Accumulated depreciation:

Beginning balance	$ 2,960
1992 depreciation	724
Ending balance	$ 3,684

⁶Expenses payable:

Beginning balance	$ 690
Raw material purchases ($7,680 + $5,640)	13,320
Labor usage 21,690	
Overhead incurred ($10,604 - $724)	9,880
Selling & administrative expense	4,955
Raw material paid	(13,380)
Labor paid	(21,640)
Overhead paid	(9,650)
Selling & administrative paid	(4,980)
Ending balance	$ 885

⁷Income taxes payable:

Beginning balance	$ 356
1992 tax expense*	768
Taxes paid	(860)
Ending balance	$ 264

⁸Long-term mortgage payable:

Beginning balance	$ 2,700
Amount to current portion payable	(200)
Ending balance	$ 2,500

⁹Common stock:

Beginning balance	$ 3,000
Common stock issued (20,000 x $10)	200
Ending balance	$ 3,200

¹⁰Paid-in capital in excess of par:

Beginning balance	$ 5,400
Excess from stock issuance ($420 - $200)	220
Ending balance	$ 5,620

¹¹Retained earnings:

Beginning balance	$ 1,150
1992 net income*	1,152
Dividends	(320)
Ending balance	$ 1,982

*1992 pro forma income

Sales	$52,250
COGS (9,500 x $4.75)	$45,125
Selling expense	1,875
Administrative expense	3,080
Operating income	2,170
Interest expense	250
Income before taxes	1,920
Income tax (40%)	768
Net income	$ 1,152

Chapter 5

Direct Costing and the Contribution Approach

Grant W. Newton

Direct costing is a tool used to provide management with information about cost, volume, and profit relationships in a form that is easy to understand. Built into the accounts of a direct costing system is the information needed to prepare break-even analysis, flexible budgets, and contribution margin analysis. Under direct costing, only the variable costs— direct materials, direct labor, and variable overhead—are assigned to finished goods, work-in-process inventories, and to the cost of goods sold. All fixed manufacturing costs are considered period costs and are charged against profits as incurred. The key advantage of direct costing is not that it omits fixed costs from inventory but that the concept facilitates profit planning, cost control, and other aspects of decision making.

Absorption and Direct Costing

The difference, conceptually, between direct and absorption costing centers around the way fixed manufacturing costs are treated; this difference is based on timing—when costs are charged against profits. Under direct costing, these costs are expensed when incurred as period costs. Under absorption costing, they are absorbed into inventory assets and are written off when the goods are sold.

Example 5-1, a previous CMA examination problem, is designed to show the differences between the two approaches. Study the problem and attempt to work parts A, B, and C. Exhibit 5-1 contains the solution to part A, an income state-

ment based on direct costing. Note that the cost of the beginning inventory, $15 per unit, consists of only variable manufacturing costs. The inventory under the absorption costing approach is $3 more, due to the inclusion of fixed costs as shown in Exhibit 5-2. The problem states that practical capacity is used to determine the fixed cost rate. The volume variance should be added to (subtracted from if the variance is favorable) the standard cost of goods sold. The variance is the difference between the practical capacity of 30,000 units and the actual production of 24,000 units times the $3 rate or $18,000.

Part C of Example 5-1 asks for an explanation of the difference in net income. The difference in net income is $12,000 ($118,000 under absorption costing from Exhibit 5-2 and $106,000 under direct costing from Exhibit 5-1). Absorption costing profit is greater since the number of units produced this period exceeds the units sold. The number of units in ending inventory is higher than in beginning inventory, which means that more fixed costs have accumulated in inventories. The difference in profit of $12,000 is simply the increase in the inventory level of 4,000 units (6,000 units ending − 2,000 units beginning) times the fixed cost rate of $3 (6,000 − 2,000 × $3 = $12,000). If sales had exceeded production, the direct costing approach would have yielded the larger profit. Assuming everything else constant, profits are a function of sales volume under direct costing, whereas under absorption costing, profits are a function of both sales and production. If the Shire Company in the example had operated at full practical capacity with no change in units sold, the net income under direct costing would still have been only $106,000. But under absorption costing the profits would have been $18,000 more than the $118,000 net income shown in Exhibit 5-2. Under these conditions, the inventory

Example 5-1

The S. T. Shire Company uses direct costing for internal management purposes and absorption costing for external reporting purposes. Thus, at the end of each year financial information must be converted from direct costing to absorption costing in order to satisfy external requirements.

At the end of 19X1 it was anticipated that sales would rise 20 percent the next year. Therefore, production was increased from 20,000 units to 24,000 units to meet this expected demand. However, economic conditions kept the sales level at 20,000 units for both years.

The following data pertain to 19X1 and 19X2.

The overhead rate under absorption costing is based upon practical plant capacity which is 30,000 units per year. All variances and under- or overabsorbed overhead are taken to Cost of Goods Sold.

All taxes are to be ignored.

Required   A. Present the income statement based on direct costing for 19X2.

B. Present the income statement based on absorption costing for 19X2.

C. Explain the difference, if any, in the net income figures. Give the entry necessary to adjust the book figures to the financial statement figure, if one is necessary.

D. The company finds it worthwhile to develop its internal financial data on a direct cost basis. What advantages and disadvantages are attributed to direct costing for internal purposes?

E. There are many who believe that direct costing is appropriate for external reporting and there are many who oppose its use for external reporting. What arguments for and against the use of direct costing are advanced for its use in external reporting?

Data for Shire Company

	19X1	19X2
Selling price per unit	$ 30	$ 30
Sales (units)	20,000	20,000
Beginning inventory (units)	2,000	2,000
Production (units)	20,000	24,000
Ending inventory (units)	2,000	6,000
Unfavorable labor, materials and variable overhead variances (total)	$ 5,000	$ 4,000

Standard variable costs per unit for 19X1 and 19X2

Labor	$7.50
Materials	4.50
Variable overhead	3.00
	$15.00

Annual fixed costs for 19X1 and 19X2 (Budgeted and Actual)

Production	$ 90,000
Selling and administrative	100,000
	$190,000

level would be increased to 12,000 units from 2,000 units and the absorption costing profits would be $30,000 more than those under direct costing (12,000 units − 2,000 units times $3 fixed costs per unit).

Summary of Relationship Between Direct and Absorption Costing

A comparison of direct costing with absorption costing leads to the following generalizations:

1. When sales and production are in balance, direct and absorption costing methods yield the same profits. Under either method fixed costs incurred are charged against revenue for that period.

2. When production exceeds sales (that is, when work-in-process and finished goods inventories are increasing), absorption costing shows a higher profit. This type of condition is described in the Shire Company example.

3. When sales exceed production (that is, when work-in-process and finished goods inventories are decreasing), absorption costing shows a lower profit. Fixed costs previously deferred in inventory under absorption costing are charged against revenue in the period in which the goods are sold. Thus, total fixed charges against revenue exceed the amount of fixed costs incurred this period.

4. When sales volume is constant but production fluctuates, direct costing yields a constant profit figure because profit is not affected by inventory changes. Under the same circumstances, absorption costing yields a fluctuating profit figure. The profit may go up or down depending on the nature of the changes in inventories. Note that when production was changed from 20,000 to 24,000 units in the Shire Company example, net income rose as inventories increased.

5. If production volume is constant, profits will vary as sales change under both direct and absorption costing. The profit figures will move in the same direction, but will not necessarily be the same amount. Generally, direct cost profits will vary more than absorption because under absorption more of the production costs are charged to inventories.

6. The divergence between periodic profit figures computed by direct and absorption costing methods tends to be smaller for long periods than for short periods because differences

Exhibit 5-1
S.T. Shire Company
Income Statement, Direct Costing
For Year 19X2

Sales (20,000 × $30)		$600,000
Less: variable cost of goods sold		
Beginning inventory (2,000 × $15)	$ 30,000	
Production (24,000 × $15)	360,000	
Available for sale	390,000	
Ending inventory (6,000 × $15)	90,000	
Standard variable cost of goods sold	300,000	
Manufacturing variances (variable)	4,000	
Variable cost of goods sold		304,000
Contribution margin		296,000
Less fixed costs:		
Production	$ 90,000	
Selling and administration	100,000	190,000
Net income		**$106,000**

Exhibit 5-2
S.T. Shire Company
Income Statement, Absorption Costing
For Year 19X2

Sales (20,000 × $30)			$600,000
Less: cost of goods sold			
Beginning inventory (2,000 × $18[a])		$ 36,000	
Production (24,000 × $18)		432,000	
Available for sales		468,000	
Ending inventory (6,000 × $18)		108,000	
Standard cost of goods sold		360,000	
Manufacturing variances			
Variable	$ 4,000		
Volume	18,000[b]	22,000	
Cost of goods sold			382,000
Gross profit			218,000
Less selling and administrative costs			100,000
Net income			**$118,000**

[a] Beginning inventory consists of variable costs of $15 + fixed cost of $3 (fixed production costs of $90,000 divided by practical plant capacity of 30,000 units).

[b]
Budgeted production costs	$90,000
Applied production costs (24,000 units × $3.00 per unit)	72,000
Volume variance	**$18,000**

between production and sales volume tend to approach equality over a long period.[1]

7. Direct costing is not accepted for income tax accounting or financial reporting to the public. Therefore, it is used mainly for internal management purposes.

8. Direct costing requires the separation of fixed and variable production costs, which is often a very complicated task, especially when these costs are semifixed step functions.

Adjusting Inventories

For the reasons just discussed, management may find it desirable to maintain all records on a direct costing basis and use direct costing for decision-making purposes. At year end, the inventories are adjusted to include the fixed overhead costs for external financial purposes.

Assuming the beginning inventory includes the fixed cost as a result of an adjustment last period, the entry to adjust the books, as required by part C of Example 5-1, so that the inventories reflect the fixed costs is:

Inventory (4,000 × $3)	12,000	
Cost of goods sold (20,000 × $3)	60,000	
Unabsorbed fixed overhead (volume variance)	18,000	
Fixed production costs		90,000

In making the entry, it is presumed that the books are maintained on a direct costing basis and the adjustment is made so the ending inventory reflects the fixed production costs. If an adjustment was not made for the 2,000 units in beginning inventory, then the entry would be:

Inventory (6,000 × $3)	18,000	
Cost of goods sold (20,000 × $3)	60,000	
Unabsorbed fixed overhead	18,000	
Fixed production costs		90,000
Retained earnings		6,000

Internal Use of Direct Costing

Accountants provide information to management to assist them in planning, organizing, and controlling their operations. A system must provide the type of information management needs in a useful form. For many companies, the use of direct costing in the information system facilitates product pricing, the planning of future profits, and the controlling of costs.

Pricing Decisions

All costs must be recovered in the long run if a company is to stay in business, yet pricing is much more difficult than just

1. Adapted from "Direct Costing," *NAA Research Report No. 23* (New York: National Association of Accountants, 1953), pp. 38-39.

determining the "full" costs and adding a set profit to determine the proper price. The fact that many fixed costs are joint or common costs, that it takes a large number of products to even recover the fixed costs from some operations, and that the profit margin varies from one product to another all make the pricing decision difficult. We do know that in order to maximize profits, the proper sales price that should be selected is the one that, when multiplied by the number of units expected to sell at that price, will result in the largest contribution margin. Direct costing, by establishing the relationship between fixed and variable costs, does provide cost information that facilitates the pricing decision.

Economists suggest that for firms operating under conditions of monopolistic competition the optimum output is the volume level at which the increase in marginal cost (due to the production of one additional unit) equals the increase in total revenue. The contribution margin approach is more consistent with economic realities than is the net income per unit derived from absorption costing. In a highly competitive market, where prices are regulated through supply and demand, the company may have little control over the price, but it can control the quantity it produces. Again, under these conditions, the contribution margin analysis afforded by direct costing is better than that of the absorption costing approach in determining the quantity to produce.

Planning and Decision Making

It is important that the relationship between cost, volume, and profits be ascertained before most managerial decisions are made. For companies using direct costing, this information is, for the most part, immediately available. These data facilitate such decisions as: pricing special orders, planning operations for a short time period, cost-volume-profit relationships (break-even analysis), and determining the contribution margin by segments, make or buy, product mix, and discontinuance or expansion of product line. Also, flexible budgets can be readily prepared with the information provided by direct costing.

Companies participating in *NAA Research Report No. 37* felt that direct costing's major use was in forecasting and reporting income for internal management purposes. The report states that:

> The marginal income (contribution margin) figure, which results from the first step in matching costs and revenues in the direct costing income statement, is reported to be a particularly useful figure to management because it can be readily projected to measure increments in net income that accompany increments in sales. The theory underlying this observed usefulness of the marginal income figure in decision making rests upon the fact that, within a limited volume range, period costs tend to remain constant in total when volume changes occur. Under such conditions, only the direct costs are relevant in costing increments in volume.

> The tendency of net income to fluctuate directly with sales volume was reported to be an important practical advantage possessed by the direct costing approach to income determination because it enables management to trace changes in sales to their consequence in net income. Another advantage attributed to the direct costing income statement was that management has a

better understanding of the impact that period costs have on profits when such costs are brought together in a single group.[2]

Control Tool

Direct costing facilitates the preparation of reports on a responsibility accounting basis. The income statement prepared on this basis is much more meaningful from the viewpoint of both the marketing and production managers. The statement the marketing manager receives would clearly show the contributions the various products or product lines make to cover fixed costs and provide profit. Differences between planned sales and actual sales caused by changes in sales price, sales mix, or sales volume are detailed so that the marketing manager responsible for these differences can analyze the report and take the necessary corrective action.[3] For the production manager control is made easier by the separation of costs into their fixed and variable components and by the clear identification of these costs for which the individual manager is responsible.

Example 5-2 is an adapted CMA examination problem illustrating how direct costing is a better tool for control than absorption. Part A asks for an explanation of why profits declined while sales increased and control was exercised over costs. The solution follows:

Because Sun Company uses absorption costing, the net income is influenced by both sales volume and production volume. Sales volume was increased in the November 30, 19X4 forecast, and at standard gross profit rates this would increase earnings before taxes by $5,600. However, during this same period, production volume was below the January 1, 19X4 forecast, causing an unplanned volume variance of $6,000. The volume variance and the increased selling expenses (due to the 10 percent increase in sales) overshadowed the added profits from sales as shown below:

Increased sales		$26,800
Increased cost of sales at standard		21,200
Increased gross margin at standard		5,600
Less:		
Volume variance	6,000	
Increased selling expenses	1,340	7,340
Decrease in earnings		$(1,740)

Part B asks for the action Sun Company could take to improve their reported profit.

Solution: The answer, based on the assumption that the absorption costing approach will continue to be used by Sun, is to increase production if raw materials can be acquired. Even if Sun has to pay more for the raw materials, it would still increase this year's net income, providing the increase in

---

2. "Applications of Direct Costing," *NAA Research Report No. 37* (New York: National Association of Accountants, 1961), pp. 84-85.
3. Adolph Matz and Milton F. Usry, *Cost Accounting: Planning and Control*, 6 th ed. (Cincinnati: South-Western Publishing Co., 1976), p. 684.

━━━━━━━━━━━━━━━━━━━━━━ **Example 5-2** ━━━━━━━━━━━━━━━━━━━━━━

Sun Company, a wholly owned subsidiary of Guardian, Inc., produces and sells three main product lines. The company employs a standard cost accounting system for record keeping purposes.

At the beginning of 19X4, the president of Sun Company presented the budget to the parent company and accepted a commitment to contribute $15,800 to Guardian's consolidated profit in 19X4. The president has been confident that the year's profit would exceed budget target since the monthly sales reports that she has been receiving have shown that sales for the year will exceed budget by 10 percent. The president is both disturbed and confused when the controller presents an adjusted forecast as of November 30, 19X4, indicating that profit will be 11 percent under budget. The two forecasts are presented.

There have been no sales price changes or product mix shifts since the 1/1/X4 forecast. The only cost variance on the income statement is the underabsorbed manufacturing overhead. This arose because the company produced only 16,000 standard machine hours (budgeted machine hours were 20,000) during 19X4 as a result of a shortage of raw materials while its principal supplier was closed by a strike. Fortunately Sun Company's finished goods inventory was large enough to fill all sales orders received.

Required   A. Analyze and explain why the profit has declined in spite of increased sales and good control over costs.

B. What plan, if any, could Sun Company adopt during December to improve their reported profit at year end? Explain your answer.

C. Illustrate and explain how Sun Company could adopt an alternative internal cost reporting procedure that would avoid the confusing effect of the present procedure.

Sun Company
FORECASTS OF OPERATING RESULTS

	Forecasts as of	
	1/1/X4	11/30/X4
Sales	$268,000	$294,800
Cost of sales at standard	212,000ª	233,200
Gross margin at standard	56,000	61,600
Over- (under-) absorbed fixed manufacturing overhead	–	(6,000)
Actual gross margin	56,000	55,600
Selling expenses	13,400	14,740
Administrative expenses	26,800	26,800
Total operating expenses	40,200	41,540
Earnings before tax	$ 15,800	$ 14,060

ª Includes fixed manufacturing overhead of $30,000.

cost is less than $1.50 times the standard machine hours required to make each unit (total fixed cost of $30,000 divided by 20,000 standard machine hours equals $1.50). While the increase in production may increase this period's profits, the decision to increase production, if it results in a higher price for raw materials, may cause future period's profits to be less.

The answer to part C is given in Exhibit 5-3 which contains an income statement based on direct costing that would avoid the confusing effect of the present procedure and not lead to an illogical increase in production this period.

Advantages and Disadvantages

Part D of Example 5-1 requests the candidate to list the advantages and disadvantages attributed to direct costing for internal purposes. They are:
   Advantages

1. The fixed costs are reported at incurred values (and not absorbed), thus increasing the likelihood of better control of those costs.

2. Profits are directly influenced by changes in sales volume (and not influenced by changing inventory levels).

3. The impact of fixed costs on profits is emphasized.

4. The income statements are in the same form as the cost-volume-profit relationship.

5. Marginal contributions by product line, territory, and so on is emphasized and more readily ascertainable.

Disadvantages

1. Total costs may be overlooked when making decisions.

2. The distinction between fixed and variable cost is often arbitrary for many costs.

3. Many costs are semifixed, that is, not entirely fixed or variable.

4. Emphasis on variable cost may cause managers to ignore fixed costs.

5. It is not accepted for tax reporting and external reporting; thus, additional record keeping costs are required.

For a company that has adopted a JIT inventory system, variable costing for control and cost reduction purposes may be adopted. Since inventory balances are significantly reduced under JIT, there may not be any need to allocate the fixed cost to the product during the manufacturing of the product. Variable costing, thus, may be used to avoid the cost of allocating fixed costs to the manufacturing process.

━━━━━━━━━━━━━━━━━━━━━━━━━━━━━━━

External Use of Direct Costing

Direct costing is not acceptable for external reporting according to the AICPA, Internal Revenue Service, and SEC. In

Accounting Research Bulletin No. 43, the AICPA states that cost is the primary basis of accounting for inventories where cost is the price paid or consideration given to acquire an asset. For inventories, cost is the sum of the applicable expenditures and charges directly or indirectly incurred in bringing an article to its existing condition and location. The bulletin does not mention direct costing, but states that "the exclusion of all overheads from inventory costs does not constitute an acceptable accounting procedure."[4]

The 1957 pronouncement of the Committee on Concepts and Standards of the American Accounting Association likewise opposes direct costing. It states that "the cost of a manufactured product is the sum of the acquisition costs reasonably traceable to that product and should include both direct and indirect factors. The omission of any element of manufacturing cost is not acceptable."[5]

The SEC takes the position that direct costing for external reporting is not a generally accepted accounting procedure and does not allow financial statements to show inventories valued according to the direct costing approach. Thus, inventories must be adjusted to reflect the fixed costs, as would be included under absorption costing.

The Internal Revenue Service will not allow the use of direct costing in determining the income subject to tax. Section 471 of the Internal Revenue Code specifically states that the direct costing method is not in accord with the regulations.

Those who favor the use of direct costing for external reporting purposes believe that this method presents a more meaningful and better understood income statement. They also advocate that the variable costs assigned to inventories should reflect the savings incurred as a result of producing the unsold units this period.

Part E of Example 5-1 asks for the arguments for and against the use of direct costing in external reporting. The arguments for are:

1. Statements would readily reflect the direct impact of sales volume on profits.

2. The consequences of fixed costs would be more obvious.

3. Inventory fluctuations would not influence profits.

Arguments against include:

1. Costs are not matched to revenues.

2. The difficulty in separating fixed and variable costs might cause statements to be misleading.

3. Statements would confuse investors accustomed to absorption costing statements.

4. Confidential information (on the nature of costs) could be disclosed to competitors.

Variable Costing and JIT

As noted above variable and absorptions costing will provide different net income figures whenever the number of units pro-

duced is different from the number of units sold. Also, absorption costing net income can be erratic and move in a direction that is different from the movement of sales. JIT inventory methods reduces erratic behavior under absorption costing net income because there are no fluctuations levels of inventory which created the differences between net income under absorption and variable costing. Under JIT goods are produced for specific customers' orders resulting in low or no inventories. Thus, there is no need to trace fixed costs through work-in-process and finished goods inventories.

Though there will still remain a difference in the cost of a unit of product when one used variable costing, as opposed to absorption costing, JIT will cause the differences in net income to disappear. Since absorption costing is required for external reporting, the net income under JIT will be more representative of economic reality.[6]

Contribution Approach

An income statement based on direct costing with contribution margins for divisions, products, product lines, or other segments, can be very helpful in planning future profits, selecting the proper sales mix, controlling costs, and making other decisions. Its use as a device for segments and total company planning and control and analyzing the sales mix will be discussed in the following sections. A more extended discussion of the use of the contribution approach is covered in the "Incremental Cost" Chapter of Part 4.

Exhibit 5-3

Sun Company
Forecast of Operating Results

	Forecasts as of	
	1/1/X4	11/30/X4
Sales	$268,000	$294.800
Variable costs		
Manufacturing	182,000	200,200
Selling expenses	13,400	14,740
Total variable costs	195,400	214,940
Contribution margin	72,600	79,860
Fixed costs		
Manufacturing	30,000	30,000
Administration	26,800	26,800
Total fixed costs	56,800	56,800
Earnings before taxes	$ 15,800	$ 23,060

4. Committee on Accounting Procedure, *Restatement and Revision of Accounting Research Bulletin No. 43* (New York: American Institute of Certified Public Accountants, 1953), pp. 28-29.

5. American Accounting Association, "Accounting and Reporting Standards for Corporate Financial Statements, 1957 Revision," *Accounting Review 32* (October 1957), 539.

6. Garrison, *Managerial Accounting,* 6th edition (Homwood, Ill.: Irwin, 1990) p. 277.

Exhibit 5-4

	Contribution approach	Divisional performance		
	Total for the firm	Division A	Division B	Division C
Total sales	$2000	$700	$500	$800
Less: variable manufacturing costs	1000	325	250	425
Manufacturing contribution margin	1000	375	250	375
Less: variable selling and administrative costs	300	125	75	100
Contribution margin	700	250	175	275
Less: the various fixed costs which should be the responsibility of division managers (supervisor and sales force salaries, some types of advertising and promotion, R & D, and other discretionary fixed costs)	200	75	50	75
Amount contributed to profit by division managers	500	175	125	200
Less: the fixed costs which are controllable by others (including depreciation and insurance)	150	75	25	50
Amount contributed to profit by the segments	350	$100	$100	$150
Less: costs that cannot be allocated equitably to particular segments	125			
Income before taxes	$ 225			

Example 5-3

The Scent Company sells men's toiletries to retail stores throughout the United States. For planning and control purposes the Scent Company is organized into twelve geographic regions with two to six territories within each region. One sales person is assigned to each territory and has exclusive rights to all sales made in that territory. Merchandise is shipped from the manufacturing plant to the twelve regional warehouses, and the sales in each territory are shipped from the regional warehouse. National headquarters allocates a specific amount at the beginning of the year for regional advertising.

The net sales for the Scent Company for the year ended September 30, 19X4 totaled $10 million. Costs incurred by national headquarters for national administration, advertising, and warehousing are summarized as follows:

National administration	$250,000
National advertising	125,000
National warehousing	175,000
	$550,000

The results of operations for the South Atlantic Region for the year ended September 30, 19X4 are on the next page.

The South Atlantic Region consists of two territories— Green and Purple. The salaries and employee benefits consist of the following items:

Regional vice president	$24,000
Regional marketing manager	15,000
Regional warehouse manager	13,400
Sales personnel (one for each territory with all receiving the same salary base)	15,600
Employee benefits (20 percent)	13,600
	$81,600

The sales personnel receive a base salary plus a 4 percent commission on all items sold in their territory. Bad debt expense has averaged 0.4 percent of net sales in the past. Travel and entertainment costs are incurred by the sales personnel calling upon their customers. Freight-out is a function of the quantity of goods shipped and the distance shipped. Thirty percent of the insurance is expended for protection of the inventory while it is in the regional warehouse, and the remainder is incurred for the protection of the warehouse. Supplies are used in the warehouse for packing the merchandise that is shipped. Wages relate to the hourly paid employees who fill orders in the warehouse. The warehouse operating costs account contains such costs as heat, light, and maintenance.

The following cost analyses and statistics by territory for the current year are representative of past experience and are representative of expected future operations.

continued

Example 5-3, *continued*

Cost Analysis by Territory

	Green	Purple	Total
Sales	$300,000	$600,000	$900,000
Cost of sales	$184,000	$276,000	$460,000
Advertising fees	$ 21,800	$ 32,900	$ 54,700
Travel and entertainment	$ 6,300	$ 7,800	$ 14,100
Freight-out	$ 9,000	$ 13,600	$ 22,600
Units sold	150,000	350,000	500,000
Pounds shipped	210,000	390,000	600,000
Sales personnel miles traveled	21,600	38,400	60,000

Required **A.** The top management of Scent Company wants the regional vice presidents to present their operating data in a more meaningful manner. Therefore, management has requested that the regions separate their operating costs into the fixed and variable components of order-getting, order-filling, and administration. The data are to be presented in the following format:

	Territory costs		Regional costs	Total costs
	Green	Purple		
Order-getting				
Order-filling				
Administration				

Using management's suggested format, prepare a schedule that presents the costs for the region by territory with the costs separated into variable and fixed categories by order-getting, order-filling, and administrative functions.

Scent Company   STATEMENT OF OPERATIONS • SOUTH ATLANTIC REGION
For the Year Ended September 30, 19X4

Net sales	$900,000
Costs and expenses	
Advertising fees $ 54,700	
Bad debt expense 3,600	
Cost of sales 460,000	
Freight-out 22,600	
Insurance 10,000	
Salaries and employee benefits 81,600	
Sales commissions 36,000	
Supplies 12,000	
Travel and entertainment 14,100	
Wages and employee benefits 36,000	
Warehouse depreciation 8,000	
Warehouse operating costs 15,000	
Total costs and expenses	753,600
Territory contribution	**$146,400**

B. Suppose the top management of Scent Company is considering splitting the Purple Territory into two separate territories (Red and Blue). From the data that have been presented, identify what data would be relevant to this decision (either for or against) and indicate what other data you would collect to aid top management in its decision.

C. If Scent Company keeps its records in accordance with the classification required in part A, can standards and flexible budgets be employed by the company in planning and controlling marketing costs? Give reasons for your answer.

Segment Reporting

To evaluate the performance of any division or segment effectively, all costs and revenues for which the division manager is responsible must be clearly identified. In addition to variable costs, other costs, especially discretionary fixed costs, might be influenced by the manager. These latter types of costs also influence the variable cost. Renting machinery to perform a task previously handled by workers reduces labor costs but increases the discretionary fixed costs (assume only one machine is needed to produce all the units that can be sold).

A cost that is common to all segments, and over which the manager of the segment has no control, should be excluded for certain types of decisions, especially performance evaluation. The extent to which certain costs are assigned to segments depends on company policy and the way in which the segment is organized. For example, in some cases, depreciation of equipment used by a segment may be a segment cost. In other cases, where the managers were not responsible

for the acquisition of the assets, it would not be assigned. An advertisement in a local newspaper for a product could easily be assigned to the sales manager of the territory where the ad appeared and also to that product. If the advertisement referred to several products, the cost could still be assigned to the relative territory but very little would be gained by allocating it to the various products. Likewise, if the ad were in a national magazine, the costs generally would not be allocated to territories. Joint costs can be a special problem, especially when the decisions of various managers interactively affect these costs.

An income statement can be easily converted to reflect various measures of performance as shown in Exhibit 5-4. The amount contributed to profit by division managers is an important measure because it shows the segment contribution controllable by the manager. If it is desirable to calculate the final contribution made by the segment after the cost directly related to the segment but which the manager cannot control is subtracted, the third item (amount contributed to profit by segments) would be included. This entire breakdown could

Exhibit 5-5

Scent Company
Cost by Regions
19X4

	Territory costs		Regional Cost	Total costs
	Green	Purple		
ORDER-GETTING				
Variable:				
Sales commissions (0.04 × sales)	$ 12,000	$ 24,000		$ 36,000
Bad debt (0.004 × sales)	1,200	2,400		3,600
Total variable	13,200	26,400		39,600
Fixed:				
Advertising fees	21,800	32,900		54,700
Travel and entertainment	6,300	7,800		14,100
Salaries	7,800	7,800	$15,000	30,600
Employee benefits (0.20 × salaries)	1,560	1,560	3,000	6,120
Total fixed	37,460	50,060	18,000	105,520
Total order-getting	**$ 50,660**	**$ 76,460**	**$18,000**	**$145,120**
ORDER-FILLING				
Variable:				
Cost of sales	$184,000	$276,000		$460,000
Freight-out	9,000	13,600		22,600
Supplies[a] ($.02 × pounds shipped)	4,200	7,800		12,000
Wages & employment benefits[a] ($.06 × pounds shipped)	12,600	23,400		36,000
Insurance (on inventory)[b]	1,200	1,800		3,000
Total variable	211,000	322,600		533,600
Fixed:				
Warehouse operating costs			$15,000	15,000
Insurance (on warehouse)			7,000	7,000
Depreciation			8,000	8,000
Salary			13,400	13,400
Employee benefits			2,680	2,680
Total fixed	—0—	—0—	46,080	46,080
Total order-filling	**$211,000**	**$322,600**	**$46,080**	**$579,680**
ADMINISTRATIVE				
Fixed:				
Salary			$24,000	$ 24,000
Employee benefits			4,800	4,800
Total administrative			**$28,800**	**$ 28,800**
Total costs				**$753,600**

[a] Allocated on basis of pounds shipped.

[b] Allocated on basis of cost of goods sold dollars ($0.30 \times \$10,000 = \$3,000$ to be allocated;

$\$3,000 \times \dfrac{184,000}{460,000} = \$1,200$ to Green; $\qquad \$3,000 \times \dfrac{276,000}{460,000} = \$1,800$ to Purple).

Example 5-4

The Manhattan Company manufactures products A and B. After the first weeks of the quarter, management decided to reduce the sales price of B and increase sales volume to use some of the idle capacity. The price of A was increased at the same time since management did not expect a major reduction in volume as the result of a price change. The budget for the first quarter along with the average results are presented below.

Required Analyze the impact of these changes on the contribution margin for Manhattan Company.

Budget

	A		B		Total	
Sales	10,000 × $10 =	$100,000	6,000 × $12 =	$72,000	16,000 × $10.75 =	$172,000
Variable costs	10,000 × $ 6 =	60,000	6,000 × $ 6 =	36,000	16,000 × $ 6.00 =	96,000
Contribution margin	10,000 × $ 4 =	**$ 40,000**	6,000 × $ 6 =	**$36,000**	16,000 × $ 4.75 =	**$ 76,000**

Actual

	A		B		Total	
Sales	9,000 × $12 =	$108,000	11,000 × $11 =	$121,000	20,000 × $11.45 =	$229,000
Variable costs	9,000 × $ 6.40 =	57,600	11,000 × $ 6.20 =	68,200	20,000 × $ 6.29 =	125,800
Contribution margin	9,000 × $ 5.60 =	**$ 50,400**	11,000 × $ 4.80 =	**$ 52,800**	20,000 × $ 5.16 =	**$103,200**

be extended to the various products or product lines of the division for the purpose of analysis.

The costs classified as unallocable could be assigned by some arbitrary method to the other divisions and even to products. If such an assignment is made, it should be done only after segment contribution is properly determined, and the report should clearly indicate these costs for which the managers of the various segments are not responsible. Generally, no benefit is gained by the allocation; it is frequently confusing to managers, resulting in more harm than good.

Example 5-3 contains a previous CMA examination problem requiring the reporting of operating costs by segments. The solution to part A is given in Exhibit 5-5. The supplies are used to pack the goods that are shipped. A reasonable way to allocate this cost to the territories would be to base it on the pounds shipped. The total cost for the South Atlantic region for supplies is $12,000 divided by 600,000 pounds shipped, resulting in a cost of $.02 per pound. Wages relate to the hourly paid employees who fill orders in the warehouse. Again, the pounds shipped would be the most reasonable way to allocate the wages and related benefits. The rate is $.06 per pound ($36,000 ÷ 600,000). The cost of insurance on the inventory would be a variable order-filling cost while the insurance on the warehouse would be considered fixed. Since the insurance cost on inventory varies with the dollar value of inventory, the cost of goods sold would be a reasonable basis for allocating this cost.

The items that make up the fixed order-filling costs are not controllable by the managers of the Green and Purple Territories. Thus, no useful purpose would be served by allocating these costs to the territories. They are, however, a direct cost of the region.

For part B of the example, the data Scent Company should consider collecting to aid in this decision include a breakdown of present sales and sales personnel miles traveled in Purple Territory according to the proposed separate territories (that is, Red and Blue), a forecast of the sales potential of Red and Blue Territories, and an estimate of increased costs arising from the split. In addition, the current territorial data given in the problem—sales volume, advertising fees, sales personnel, miles traveled—provide evidence that the Purple Territory is quite a bit larger than the Green Territory. The schedule prepared in part A would help confirm that the only increase in cost from the territorial division is the sales personnel's salaries and fringe benefits.

Part C asks if standards and flexible budgets can be employed by the company in planning and controlling marketing costs. Standards and flexible budgets can be used whenever there is a measurable activity base. In order-filling activities, there is a measurable activity base (units, pounds shipped, pounds handled, and so on). It would be difficult to establish standards for order-getting activities because of the nature of the costs and the lack of a measurable activity base; however, a company can still establish a budget for planning and controlling these costs.

Contribution Margin Analysis

The causes of an increase or decrease in the budgeted contribution margin can be isolated by analyzing the variance. The contribution margin variance is caused by a change in sales price or variable costs, change in quantity sold, or change in mix of products sold.

Consider Example 5-4. The increase in the contribution margin of $27,200 is caused by four factors:

1. Change in sales prices
2. Change in variable costs
3. Change in quantities sold
4. Change in sales mix

■ **Example 5-5** ■

Mill Company manufactures and sells two similar types of industrial components which are substitutes for each other. One component is manufactured from plastic, while the other uses metal. Both components are manufactured in the same plant but in separate production departments. The budgeted and actual income statements for Mill Company for the 19X4 fiscal year are presented on the next page.

The 19X4 sales mix was different from that which was budgeted. More metal components were sold than planned because of reduced availability of plastic components. Some increase in the volume of metal components was also due to the lower than budgeted price. The sales volume of plastic components was down because of lost production. A general shortage of plastic required Mill Company to use an inferior grade. This plastic cost $0.05 more per pound than the standard plastic, and 10 percent of the material released to production was not suitable for use in production. The plastic shortage is expected to ease in 19X5, and the regular plastic will be available in adequate quantities at $0.45 per pound.

A 10 percent increase over 19X4 planned volume is estimated for 19X5 with the sales mix remaining the same as that planned for 19X4. The plan also calls for a $0.50 per unit price reduction from 19X4's actual price on the metal component.

Manufacturing Operation

The company coordinates its raw materials purchases and production schedules with sales so that changes in inventory levels are insignificant and inventories of raw materials and finished goods are very low. Production equalled the actual sales volume during 19X4. The purchases and use of raw materials in 19X4 were as follows:

Plastic

Purchases	620,000 lbs. @$0.45 = $279,000
Charged to production	600,000 lbs. @$0.40 = $240,000

Metal

Purchases	550,000 lbs. @$1.40 = $770,000
Charged to production	525,000 lbs. @$1.40 = $735,000

The production required the following amounts of direct labor hours and total direct labor wages in 19X4.

	Direct labor hours	Average wage rate	Total wage
Department 1	72,000	$5.75	$414,000
Department 2	125,000	$6.20	$775,000

A large proportion of the workers in Department 1 were inexperienced and average wages were therefore lower than standard. However, the inexperience resulted in nonproductive time equal to 10 percent of standard hours of production and in material scrap equal to 3 percent of the standard material quantities.

The actual manufacturing overhead incurred during 19X4 was

	Department 1	Department 2
Variable overhead		
Supplies	$ 26,000	$ 55,000
Indirect labor	14,000	45,000
Other	40,000	80,000
	$ 80,000	$180,000
Fixed overhead	$120,000	$200,000

The company uses a current standard full cost system to aid in controlling costs and preparing timely reports. The standard costs for 19X4 were

	Plastic	Metal
Raw materials	2 lbs. @$0.40 = $0.80	2 lbs. @$1.40 = $2.80
Direct labor	.25 hrs. @$6.00 = 1.50	.5 hrs. @$6.00 = 3.00
Variable overhead	.25 hrs. @$1.20 = 0.30	.5 hrs. @$1.40 = 0.70
Fixed overhead	.25 hrs. @$1.60 = 0.40	.5 hrs. @$2.00 = 1.00
	$3.00	$7.50

The budgeted overhead costs for the planned level of activities for 19X4 were as follows:

	Department 1 (plastic)		Department 2 (metal)	
	Total	Per DHL	Total	Per DHL
Variable overhead				
Supplies	$ 30,000	$ .40	$ 40,000	$ .40
Indirect labor	15,000	.20	40,000	.40
Other	45,000	.60	60,000	.60
	$ 90,000	$1.20	$140,000	$1.40
Fixed overhead	$120,000	$1.60	$200,000	$2.00

A review of the manufacturing standards and operations for 19X5 discloses that metal prices and quality will remain the same as in 19X4. Plastic of regular quality will be available but at $0.45 per pound. The workers in the plastic component department will have developed the skills necessary to produce at standard production rates. Wage rates will remain the same as in the 19X4 standard. Variable overhead will remain at the 19X4 budgeted rates, but fixed overhead will increase 10 percent in both departments.

— continued —

Operating Expenses

The company has divided its market area into twelve territories. The twelve territorial salesmen are paid a salary of $4,000 plus a 3 percent commission on net sales. Salesmen are reimbursed for the allowable travel and entertainment costs they incur. The company's experience with uncollectible accounts justifies a bad debt estimate of one-tenth of one percent of net sales. The sales administration and promotion account includes all costs to administer, process and promote sales, except salaries. Warehouse employees are paid on an hourly basis. Shipping and packing costs average $0.30 per component sold (for both plastic and metal). The warehouse operating costs include such items as depreciation, utilities, insurance, and property taxes. General administrative expenses include all costs incurred for the overall administration of the company.

The following changes from 1974 budgeted levels are expected for 1975:

1. Each salesman will receive a $500 increase in annual salary.

2. Warehouse employees will receive a 10 percent wage increase.

3. Employee benefits will increase to 20 percent of salaries and wages from the present 15 percent level.

4. Sales administration and promotion costs and sales administration salaries are expected to rise 15 percent.

5. Travel and entertainment costs are expected to increase $12,000.

The remaining operating expense items are expected to be at the 1974 budgeted rates or levels.

Required   A. Mill Company has adopted direct costing for internal reporting purposes. Prepare a projected income statement for the company for the 19X5 fiscal year on a direct costing basis (round calculations to the nearest thousand dollars).

B. The management of Mill Company would like a detailed explanation of why gross margin before manufacturing variances was $100,000 less than originally budgeted for 19X4. Calculate a sales price variance, a quantity variance and a mix variance to explain the $100,000.

C. Explain the significance of quantity and mix variances and the conditions which must exist for this type of variance analysis to be meaningful.

Mill Company   BUDGETED AND ACTUAL INCOME STATEMENTS
For the Fiscal Year Ending December 31, 19X4 (000 omitted)

	Budget			Actual results			Over (under) budget
	Plastic	Metal	Total	Plastic	Metal	Total	
Net sales in units	**300**	**200**	**500**	**260**	**260**	**520**	**20**
Revenue from net sales	$1,800	$2,000	$3,800	$1,560	$2,470	$4,030	$ 230
Cost of sales at standard	900	1,500	2,400	780	1,950	2,730	330
Gross margin before manufacturing variances	900	500	1,400	780	520	1,300	(100)
Manufacturing variances:							
Raw materials	—	—	—	63	7	70	70
Direct labor	—	—	—	24	(5)	19	19
Variable overhead	—	—	—	2	(2)	—	—
Fixed overhead	—	—	—	16	(60)	(44)	(44)
Total variances	—	—	—	105	(60)	45	45
Gross margin after manufacturing variances	$ 900	$ 500	$1,400	$ 675	$ 580	$1,255	$(145)

continued

Example 5-5, *continued*

OPERATING EXPENSES

Selling expenses:

Personnel costs:

Sales commissions	$ 114		$ 121	$ 7
Sales personnel salaries	48		48	—
Warehouse wages	40		41	1
Sales administrative salaries	43		43	—
Employee benefits	37		39	2
Sales administration and promotion	110		115	5
Bad debt allowance	4		4	—
Travel and entertainment	75		80	5
Shipping and packing costs	150		156	6
Warehouse operating costs	85		87	2
Total selling expenses	706		734	28
General administrative expenses	194		191	(3)
Total operating expenses	900		925	25
Net income before income taxes	500		330	(170)
Income taxes (40%)	200		132	(68)
Net income	$ 300		$ 198	$(102)

The first step in solving this example is to isolate the sales price and cost changes. These two variances are similar to the price variance in a standard cost system.

1. Sales Price Variance

Product	(Actual sales price	–	Standard sales price)	×	Actual quantity sold	=	Sales price variance
A	($12	–	$10)	×	9,000	=	$18,000 F
B	($11	–	$12)	×	11,000	=	–11,000 UF
			Net sales price variance				$ 7,000 F

2. Sales Cost Variance

Product	(Standard costs	–	Actual costs)	×	Actual quantity sold	=	Variable cost variance
A	($6	–	$6.40)	×	9,000	=	–$3,600 UF
B	($6	–	$6.20)	×	11,000	=	– 2,200 UF
			Net variable cost variance				–$5,800 UF

The net change in sales price and variable costs is $1,200 favorable and represents the increase in contribution margin caused by price changes (sales and variable costs). Some problems may ask only for the calculation of the net change in contribution margin per unit. That variance is:

Product	(Actual contribution margin	–	Standard contribution margin)	×	Actual quantity sold	=	Contribution margin price change
A	($5.60	–	$4.00)	×	9,000	=	$14,400 F
B	($4.80	–	$6.00)	×	11,000	=	– 13,200 UF
			Contribution price variance			=	$ 1,200 F

Once the price variances have been isolated the next step involves the calculation of the sales quantity and mix variances.

3. Quantity Variance

Product	(Actual quantity	–	Budgeted quantity)	×	Budgeted average contribution margin per unit	=	Quantity variance
A	(9,000	–	10,000)	×	$4.75	=	–$ 4,750 UF
B	(11,000	–	6,000)	×	$4.75	=	23,750 F
			Total quantity variance				$19,000 F

4. Mix Variance

Product	(Actual quantity	–	Budgeted quantity)	×	(Budgeted contribution margin for each product	–	Budgeted average contribution margin per unit)	=	Mix variance

Exhibit 5-6

Mill Company
Projected Income Statement
For Fiscal Year Ending December 31, 19X5
(000 omitted)

	Plastic		Metal		Total
Net sales in units	(300 × 1.10)	330	(200 × 1.10)	220	550
Revenue from net sales	(330 × $6)	$1,980	(220 × $9)	$1,980	$3,960
VARIABLE COSTS					
Manufacturing:					
Raw materials	(330 × 2 × $.45)	297	(220 × 2 × $1.40)	616	913
Direct materials	(330 × .25 × $6)	495	(220 × .5 × $6)	660	1,155
Variable overhead	(330 × .25 × $1.20)	99	(220 × .5 × $1.40)	154	253
Total		891		1,430	2,321
Manufacturing contribution margin		**$1,089**		**$ 550**	$1,639
Nonmanufacturing:					
Sales commissions			($3,960 × .03)		119
Warehouse wages			($40 × 1.10 × 1.10)		48
Employee benefits			($167 × .20)		33
Bad debt allowance			($3,960 × .001)		4
Shipping and packing			(550 × $.30)		165
Total					369
Contribution margin					1,270
FIXED COSTS					
Manufacturing overhead			[($120 + $200) × 1.10]		352
Sales salaries			[($4 + $.50) × 12]		54
Sales administration salaries			($43 × 1.15)		49
Employee benefits			[($54 + $49) × .20]		21
Sales administration and promotion			($110 × 1.15)		127
Travel and entertainment			($75 + $12)		87
Warehouse operating costs					85
General administrative expenses					194
Total fixed costs					969
Projected net income before income taxes					301
Income taxes (40%)					120
Projected net income					**$ 181**

A (9,000 − 10,000) × ($4.00 − $4.75) = $ 750 F

B (11,000 − 6,000) × ($6.00 − $4.75) = 6,250 F

         Total mix variance   **$7,000 F**

The total difference between the budgeted contribution margin and the actual contribution margin is summarized below.

Sales price variance	$ 7,000 F
Variable cost variance	5,800 UF
Quantity variance	19,000 F
Mix variance	7,000 F
Net change in contribution margin	**$27,200 F**

Exhibit 5-7
Mills Company
Analysis of Price, Quantity, and Mix Variances
19X4 (000 omitted)

Price variance

Product	$\left(\begin{array}{c}\text{Actual}\\\text{price}\end{array}\right.$	−	$\left.\begin{array}{c}\text{Standard}\\\text{price}\end{array}\right)$	×	Actual quantity	=	Price variance	Total
Plastic	($6.00	−	$ 6.00)	×	260	=	$ 0	
Metal	($9.50	−	$10.00)	×	260	=	130 UF	$130 UF

Quantity variance

Product	$\left(\begin{array}{c}\text{Actual}\\\text{quantity}\end{array}\right.$	−	$\left.\begin{array}{c}\text{Budgeted}\\\text{quantity}\end{array}\right)$	×	Budgeted contribution margin	=	Quantity variance	
Plastic	(260	−	300)	×	$2.80	=	$112 UF	
Metal	(260	−	200)	×	$2.80	=	168 F	56 F

Mix variance

Product	$\left(\begin{array}{c}\text{Actual}\\\text{quantity}\end{array}\right.$	−	$\left.\begin{array}{c}\text{Budgeted}\\\text{quantity}\end{array}\right)$	×	$\left(\begin{array}{c}\text{Budgeted}\\\text{contribution}\\\text{for each}\\\text{product}\end{array}\right.$	−	$\left.\begin{array}{c}\text{Budgeted}\\\text{contribution}\\\text{margin}\end{array}\right)$	=	Mix variance	
Plastic	(260	−	300)	×	($3.00	−	$2.80)	=	$ 8 UF	
Metal	(260	−	200)	×	($2.50	−	$2.80)	=	18 UF	26 UF

Total variance (price, quantity, and mix) **$100 UF**

There are many ways to compute the quantity and mix variances. The method just used, as suggested by some, is recommended because a manager's performance report for a specific product is not affected by the performance of another product. The manager can exercise some control over an individual product's price, cost, and even the quantity sold, but has very little control over the mix of products sold.

Note that the weighted-average contribution margin is used to calculate the quantity variance. Any future quantity variance for the Manhattan Company will be calculated at the $4.75 average contribution margin per unit. The mix variance measures the impact of any deviations from the $4.75 average contribution margin. Thus, any change in quantity from the budgeted amount will be assessed in terms of the impact it had on the change in contribution margin from the average of $4.75.

A mix variance is useful only when one product is substituted for another. Under conditions where market or production restrictions do not exist, the only quantity variance calculated would be in which, for each individual product, the difference between the actual quantities and budgeted quantities is multiplied by the budgeted contribution margin per unit. This amount represents the profit lost if quantity is less than planned, or, if quantity is greater, it represents the addition to profit caused by selling a greater quantity than that planned.

It should be recognized that the variances are interrelated. In our example, the lowering of the price of B resulted in an unfavorable sales price variance but a very favorable quantity variance.

Industry Variances When data are available, some companies like to compare their results with that of their industry. For some, such as the automobile and steel industries, data are available on a timely basis making the analysis more helpful. For other products, data are either not available or cannot be determined early enough to be used effectively. Two industry variances that are typically calculated are market size variance and market share variance. These two variances are actually subdivisions of sales quantity variances. To illustrate the calculation of these two variances, assume the following data for the Manhatten Company:

Product	Estimated Industry Market (units)	Budgeted Market Share	Actual Industry Sales (units)
A	200,000	5%	200,000
B	150,000	4%	200,000

The actual market share for A was 4.5% (9,000/200,000) and for B, 5.5% (11,000/200,000). The variances are calculated as follows:

Market Size Variance

Product	Budgeted market-share percentage	×	$\left(\begin{array}{c}\text{Actual}\\\text{industry}\\\text{sales}\\\text{volume}\end{array}\right.$	−	$\left.\begin{array}{c}\text{Budgeted}\\\text{industry}\\\text{sales}\\\text{volume}\end{array}\right)$	×	Budgeted average contribution margin per unit	=	Market size variance
A			5% × (200,000 — 200,000) × 4.75					=	$ 0
B			4% × (200,000 − 150,000) × 4.75					=	9,500F
			Total market size variance						$9,500F

Market Share Variance

Product	(Actual market share percentage	—	Budgeted market share percentage)	×	Actual industry sales volume	×	Budgeted average contribution margin per unit	=	Market share variance
A			(4.5% − 5%) × 200,000 × 4.75					=	$ 4,750UF
B			(5.5% − 4%) × 200,000 × 4.75					=	14,250F
			Total market share value variance						$ 9,500

	Total	
	Per unit	Amount
Budgeted sales	$7.60	$3,800
Cost of sales	4.80	2,400
Gross margin	$2.80	$1,400

Note that the total quantity variance of $19,000 is not divided into parts — market size and market share — that add up to the $19,000 total. The quantity variance of Product A is due solely to a decline in market share while the favorable sales volume variance for B is due both to an increase in the industry market for Product B and to an increase in the market share.

Example 5-5, an adapted CMA examination problem, illustrates the preparation of an income statement based on direct costing and the analysis of the gross margin. The solution to part A is shown in Exhibit 5-6. Part B requires an analysis of the $100,000 gross margin variance. Before determining the causes of the variances, we should note that even though the analysis is based on gross margin and not contribution margin, the same steps should be followed, simply substituting gross for contribution margin. Since the costs are at standard, there will not be any cost variances to calculate. The budgeted average gross margin per unit is $2.80.

	Plastic		Metal	
	Per unit	Amount	Per unit	Amount
Budgeted sales	$6.00	$1,800	$10.00	$2,000
Cost of sales	3.00	900	7.50	1,500
Gross margin	$3.00	$ 900	$ 2.50	$ 500

The price, quantity, and mix variances are calculated in Exhibit 5-7. The solution is based on the procedure previously described and differs somewhat from the solution published by the Institute of Management Accounting. The total price, quantity, and mix variances, however, are the same; it is only the variance for the individual products that differs. As discussed, this approach was selected because it provides for the calculation of a quantity variance for each product regardless of the quantities of other products that were sold.

The solution to part C is as follows: Computation of quantity and mix variances provides management with additional information for analyzing why actual sales differed from budgeted sales. The quantity variances measure a change in volume (while holding the mix constant), and the mix variance measures the effect of a change in the product mix (while holding the volume constant). This type of variance analysis is useful when the products are substitutes for each other or when products, not necessarily substitutes for each other, are marketed through the same channels.

Problems

1.   Multiple Choice

INSTRUCTIONS: Select the BEST answer for each of the questions below.

1. Which of the following statements is true for a firm that uses "direct" (variable) costing?

a. the cost of a unit of product changes because of changes in number of units manufactured.
b. profits fluctuate with sales.
c. an idle facility variation is calculated by a direct cost system.
d. product costs include "direct" (variable) administrative costs.
e. none of the above.

2. When a firm prepares financial reports by using absorption costing, it may find that

a. profits will always increase with increases in sales.
b. profits will always decrease with decreases in sales.
c. profits may decrease with increased sales even if there is no change in selling prices and costs.
d. decreased output and constant sales result in increased profits.
e. none of the above.

3. An accountant would typically have the following in mind when referring to the "margin of safety":

a. the excess of budgeted or actual sales over the variable costs and the fixed costs at breakeven.
b. the excess of budgeted or actual sales revenue over the fixed costs.
c. the excess of actual sales over budgeted sales.
d. the excess of sales revenue over the variable costs.
e. none of the above.

4. Which of these alternatives would decrease contribution per unit margin the most?

a. a 15 percent decrease in selling price.
b. a 15 percent increase in variable expense.
c. a 15 percent increase in selling price.
d. a 15 percent decrease in variable expense.
e. a 15 percent decrease in fixed expenses.

5. If fixed costs decrease while variable cost per unit remains constant, the new variable contribution margin in relation to the old will be

a. unchanged.
b. higher.
c. lower.
d. indeterminate.
e. none of the above.

The graph below applies to questions 6. and 7. only.

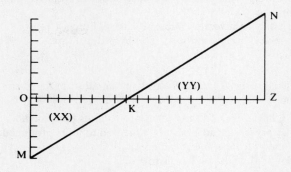

6. On the Profit/Volume chart above

a. the areas XX and YY and the point K represent profit, loss, and volume of sales at break-even point, respectively.
b. the line O-Z represents the volumes of sales.
c. the two lines O-M and N-Z represent fixed costs.
d. the line M-N represents total costs.
e. none of the above is true.

7. The vertical scale represents

a. volume of sales.
b. units produced.
c. profit above O and loss below O.
d. contribution margin.
e. none of the above.

8. In breakeven analysis, a number of assumptions typically are made. Which of the following assumptions typically is not made?

a. volume is the only relevant factor affecting cost.
b. no change between beginning and ending inventory.
c. the sales mix will be maintained as volume changes.
d. prices of cost factors fluctuate proportionally with volume.
e. none of the above.

9. To which of these independent variable would "setup" expense probably have the closest relationship?

a. machine hours.
b. direct labor hours.
c. number of shop orders.
d. direct labor cost.
e. number of employees.

10. Which of the following expenses should not be on a monthly cost control report of a department manager?

a. department labor costs.
b. department supplies costs.
c. depreciation cost on department equipment.
d. cost of material used in the department.
e. none of the above.

11. A management purpose for allocating joint costs of a processing center to the various products produced is

a. to develop accurate processing cost variances by product.
b. to report more correct standard product costs for comparative analysis.
c. to establish inventory values for unsold units.
d. to record accurate cost of sales by product line.
e. none of the above.

12. Unabsorbed overhead costs in an absorption costing systems are

a. fixed factory costs not allocated to units produced.
b. factory overhead costs not allocated to units produced.
c. excess variable overhead costs.
d. costs that cannot be controlled.
e. none of the above.

13. Which of these variances is least significant for cost control?

a. labor price variance.
b. material quantity variance.
c. overhead budget variance.
d. overhead volume variance.
e. labor quantity variance.

The following statement applies to questions 14 to 18:
In analyzing the relationship of total factory overhead with changes in direct labor hours, the following relationship was found to exist:

$$Y = \$1000 + \$2X$$

14. The above equation was probably found through the use of which of the following mathematical techniques?

a. linear programming.
b. multiple regression analysis.
c. simple regression analysis.
d. dynamic programming.
e. none of the above.

15. The relationship as shown above is

a. parabolic.
b. curvilinear.
c. linear.
d. probabilistic.
e. none of the above.

16. Y in the above equation is an estimate of

a. total variable costs.
b. total factory overhead.
c. total fixed costs.
d. total direct labor hours.
e. none of the above.

17. The $2 in the equation is an estimate of

a. total fixed costs.
b. variable costs per direct labor hour.
c. total variable costs.
d. fixed costs per direct labor hour.
e. none of the above.

18. The use of such a relationship of total factory overhead to changes in direct labor hours is said to be valid only within the relevant range. The phrase "relevant range" means

a. within a reasonable dollar amount for labor costs.
b. withing the range of observations of analysis.
c. within the range of reasonableness as judged by the department supervisor.
d. within the budget allowance for overhead.
e. none of the above.

The Following Data Apply to Items 19-22.

Denham Company began operations on January 3, 1983. Standard costs were established in early January assuming a normal production volume of 160,000 units. However, Denham produced only 140,000 units of product and sold 100,000 units at a selling price of $180 per unit during 1983. Variable costs totalled $7,000,000 of which 60 percent were manufacturing and 40 percent were selling. Fixed costs totalled $11,200,000 of which 50 percent were manufacturing and 50 percent were selling. Denham had no raw materials or work-in-process inventories at December 31, 1983. Actual input prices per unit of product and actual input quantities per unit of product were equal to standard.

19. Denham's cost of goods sold at standard cost for 1983 using full absorption costing is

a. $8,200,000.
b. $7,200,000.
c. $6,500,000.
d. $7,000,000.
e. some amount other than those given above.

20. The value assigned to Denham's December 31, 1983 inventory using variable (direct) costing is

a. $2,800,000.
b. $1,200,000.
c. $2,000,000.
d. $3,000,000.
e. some amount other than those given above.

21. Denham's manufacturing overhead volume variance in 1983 using full absorption costing is

a. $800,000 unfavorable.
b. $800,000 favorable.
c. $700,000 unfavorable.
d. $700,000 favorable.
e. some amount other than those given above.

22. Denham's 1983 income from operations using variable (direct) costing is

a. $3,400,000.
b. $1,800,000.
c. $2,600,000.
d. $1,000,000.
e. some amount other than those given above.

The Following Data Apply to Items 23-27.

Folsom Fashions sells a line of women's dresses. Folsom's performance report for November 1984 is as follows.

	Actual	Budget
Dresses sold	5,000	6,000
Sales	$235,000	$300,000
Variable costs	145,000	180,000
Contribution margin	$ 90,000	$120,000
Fixed costs	84,000	80,000
Operating income	$ 6,000	$ 40,000

The company uses a flexible budget to analyze its performance and to measure the effect on operating income of the various factors affecting the difference between budgeted and actual operating income.

23. The effect of the sales volume variance on the contribution margin for November is

a. $30,000 unfavorable.
b. $18,000 unfavorable.
c. $20,000 unfavorable.
d. $15,000 unfavorable.
e. $65,000 unfavorable.

24. The sales price variance for November is

a. $30,000 unfavorable.
b. $18,000 unfavorable.
c. $20,000 unfavorable.
d. $15,000 unfavorable.
e. $65,000 unfavorable.

25. The variable cost flexible budget variance for November is

a. $5,000 favorable.
b. $5,000 unfavorable.
c. $4,000 favorable.
d. $4,000 unfavorable.
e. $6,000 favorable.

26. The fixed cost variance for November is

a. $5,000 favorable.
b. $5,000 unfavorable.
c. $4,000 favorable.
d. $4,000 unfavorable.
e. $1,000 favorable.

27. The following additional information would be needed for Folsom to calculate the dollar impact of a market unit share change on operating income for November 1984.

a. Folsom's budgeted market share and the budgeted total market size.
b. Folsom's budgeted market share, the budgeted total market size, and average market selling price.
c. Folsom's budgeted market share and the actual total market size.
d. Folsom's actual market share and the actual total market size.
e. There is no information that would make such a calculation possible.

2.   Estimted time 30 minutes (December 1973)

The Arsco Co. makes three grades of indoor-outdoor carpets. The sales volume for the annual budget is determined by estimating the total market volume for indoor-outdoor carpet, and then applying the company's prior year market share, adjusted for planned changes due to company programs for the coming year. The volume is apportioned between the three grades based upon the prior year's product mix, again adjusted for planned changes due to company programs for the coming year.

Given on the next page are the company budget for 19X3 and the results of operations for 19X3.

Industry volume was estimated at 40,000 rolls for budgeting purposes. Actual industry volume for 19X3 was 38,000 rolls.

Required   A. Calculate the profit impact of the unit sales volume variance for 19X3 using budgeted variable margins.

B. What portion of the variance, if any, can be attributed to the state of the carpet market?

C. What is the dollar impact on profits (using budgeted variable margins) of the shift in product mix from the budgeted mix?

---

3.   Estimated time 30 minutes (December 1988)

The financial results for the Continuing Education Department of BusEd Corporation for November 1988 are presented at the top of the next page. Mary Ross, president of BusEd, is pleased with the final results but has observed that the revenue and most of the costs and expenses of this department exceeded the budgeted amounts. Barry Stein, vice president of the Continuing Education Department, has been requested to provide an explanation of any amount that exceeded the budget by five percent or more.

Stein has accumulated the following facts to assist in his analysis of the November results.

1. The budget for calendar year 1988 was finalized in December 1987, and at that time, a full program of continuing education courses was scheduled to be held in Chicago during the first week of November 1988. The courses were scheduled so that eight courses would be run on each of the five days during the week. The budget assumed that there would be 425 participants in the program and 1,000 participant days for the week.

2. BusEd charges a flat fee of $150 per day of course instruction, i.e., the fee for a three-day course would be $450. BusEd grants a 10 percent discount to persons who subscribe to its publications. The 10 percent discount is also granted to second and subsequent registrants for the same course from the same organization. However, only one discount per registration is allowed. Historically, 70 percent of the participant day registrations are at the full fee of $150 per day and 30 percent of the participant day registrations receive the discounted fee of $135 per day. These percentages were used in developing the November 1988 budgeted revenue.

Arsco Company

	Budget			
	Grade 1	Grade 2	Grade 3	Total
Sales—units	1,000 rolls	1,000 rolls	2,000 rolls	4,000 rolls
Sales—dollars (000 omitted)	$1,000	$2,000	$3,000	$6,000
Variable expenses	700	1,600	2,300	4,600
Variable margin	300	400	700	1,400
Traceable fixed expense	200	200	300	700
Traceable margin	$ 100	$ 200	$ 400	700
Selling and administrative expense				250
Net income				$ 450

	Actual			
	Grade 1	Grade 2	Grade 3	Total
Sales—units	800 rolls	1,000 rolls	2,100 rolls	3,900 rolls
Sales—dollars (000 omitted)	$810	$2,000	$3,000	$5,810
Variable expenses	560	1,610	2,320	4,490
Variable margin	250	390	680	1,320
Traceable fixed expanse	210	220	315	745
Traceable margin	$ 40	$ 170	$ 365	575
Selling and administrative expense				275
Net income				$ 300

3. The following estimates were used to develop the budgeted figures for course related expenses.

Food charges per participant day (lunch/coffee breaks)	$ 27
Course materials per participant	8
Instructor fee per day	1,000

4. A total of 530 individuals participated in the Chicago courses in November 1988, accounting for 1,280 participant days. This included 20 persons who took a new, two-day course on pension accounting that was not on the original schedule; thus, on two of the days, nine courses were offered, and an additional instructor was hired to cover the new course. The breakdown of the course registrations was as follows.

Full fee registrations	704
Discounted fees	
Current periodical subscribers	128
New periodical subscribers	128
Second registrations from the same organization	320
Total participant day registrations	1,280

5. A combined promotional mailing was used to advertise the Chicago program and a program in Cincinnati that was scheduled for December 1988. The incremental costs of the combined promotional piece was $5,000, but none of the promotional expenses ($20,000) budgeted for the Cincinnati program in December will have to be incurred. This earlier than normal promotion for the Cincinnati program has resulted in early registration fees collected in November as follows (in terms of participant days).

Full fee registrations	140
Discounted registrations	60
Total participant day registrations	200

6. BusEd continually updates and adds new courses, and includes $2,000 in each monthly budget for this purpose. The additional amount spent on course development during November was for an unscheduled course that will be offered in February for the first time.

Barry Stein has prepared the quantitative analysis of the November 1988 variances shown at the bottom of the next page.

Required After reviewing Barry Stein's quantitative analysis of the November variances, prepare a memorandum addressed to Mary Ross explaining the following.

1. The cause of the revenue mix variance.

BusEd Corporation
Statement of Operations - Continuing Education Department
November 1988

	Budget	Actual	Favorable/ (Unfavorable) Dollars	Favorable/ (Unfavorable) Percent
Revenue				
Course fees	$145,500	$212,460	$66,960	46.0
Expenses				
Food charges	$ 27,000	$ 32,000	$ (5,000)	(18.5)
Course materials	3,400	4,770	(1,370)	(40.3)
Instructor fees	40,000	42,000	(2,000)	(5.0)
Instructor travel	9,600	9,885	(285)	(3.0)
Staff salaries and benefits	12,000	12,250	(250)	(2.1)
Staff travel	2,500	2,400	100	4.0
Promotion	20,000	25,000	(5,000)	(25.0)
Course development	2,000	5,000	(3,000)	(150.0)
Total expenses	$116,500	$133,305	$(16,805)	(14.4)
Revenues over expenses	$ 29,000	$ 79,155	$ 50,155	172.9

BusEd Corporation
Analysis of November 1988 Variances

Budgeted revenue			$145,500
Variances:			
Quantity variance			
[(1,280-1,000) x $145.50]	$40,740	F	
Mix variance [($143.25-$145.50) x 1,280]	2,880	U	
Timing difference ($145.50 x 200)	29,100	F	66,960 F
Actual revenue			$212,460
Budgeted expenses			$116,500
Quantity variances			
Food charges [(1,000-1,280) x $27]	$ 7,560	U	
Course materials [(425-530) x $8]	840	U	
Instructor fees (2 x $1,000)	2,000	U	10,400 U
Price variances			
Food charges [($27.00-$25.00) x 1,280]	$ 2,560	F	
Course materials [($8.00-$9.00) x 530]	530	U	2,030 F
Timing differences			
Promotion	$ 5,000	U	
Course development	3,000	U	8,000 U
Variances not analyzed (5 percent or less)			
Instructor travel	$ 285	U	
Staff salaries and benefits	250	U	
Staff travel	100	F	435 U
Actual expenses			$133,305

2. The implication of the revenue mix variance.

3. The cause of the revenue timing difference.

4. The significance of the revenue timing difference.

5. The primary cause of the unfavorable total expense variance.

6. How the favorable food price variance was determined.

7. The impact of the promotion timing difference on future revenues and expenses.

8. Whether or not the course development variance has an unfavorable impact on the company.

---

4.   Estimated time 30 minutes (June 1979)

CLK Co. is a manufacturer of electrical components. The company maintains a significant inventory of a broad range of finished goods because it has built its business upon prompt shipments of any stock item.

The company manufactured all items it sold until recently when it discontinued the manufacturing of five items. The items were dropped from the manufacturing process because the unit costs computed by the company's full cost system did not provide a sufficient margin to cover shipping and selling costs. The five items are now purchased from other manufacturers at a price which allows CLK to make a very small profit after shipping and selling costs. CLK keeps these items in its product line in order to offer a complete line of electrical components.

The President is disappointed at recent profitability performance. He thought that the switch from manufacture to purchase for the five items would improve profit performance. However, the reverse has occurred. All other factors affecting profits—sales volume, sales prices, and incurred selling and manufacturing costs—were as expected so the profit problem can be traced to this decision. The President has asked the Controller's department to re-evaluate the financial effects of the decision.

The task was assigned to a recently hired assistant controller. She has reviewed the data used to reach the decision to purchase rather than manufacture. Her conclusion is that the company should have continued to manufacture the item. In her opinion the incorrect decision was made because full (absorption) cost data rather than direct (variable cost) data was used to make the decision.

Required   **A.** Explain what features of direct (variable) costing as compared to full (absorption) costing make it possible for her conclusion to be correct.

B. For internal measurement purposes compare the income, return on investment, and inventory values under full (absorption) costing and direct (variable) costing for periods where

1. inventory quantities are rising.

2. inventory quantities are declining.

3. inventory quantities are stable.

C. What advantages are said to accrue to decision making if direct (variable) costing is used?

---

5.   Estimated time 60 minutes (June 1980)

The Markley Division of Rosette Industries manufactures and sells patio chairs. The chairs are manufactured in two versions—a metal model and a plastic model of a lesser quality. The company uses its own sales force to sell the chairs to retail stores and to catalog outlets. Generally, customers purchase both the metal and plastic versions.

The chairs are manufactured on two different assembly lines located in adjoining buildings. The division management and

Markley Division
Operating Results for the First Quarter

	Actual	Budget	Favorable (unfavorable) relative to the budget
Sale in units			
Plastic model	**60,000**	**50,000**	**10,000**
Metal model	**20,000**	**25,000**	**(5,000)**
Sales revenue			
Plastic model	$630,000	$500,000	$130,000
Metal model	300,000	375,000	(75,000)
Total sales	930,000	875,000	55,000
Less variable costs			
Manufacturing (at standard)			
Plastic model	480,000	400,000	(80,000)
Metal model	200,000	250,000	50,000
Selling			
Commissions	46,500	43,750	(2,750)
Bad debt allowance	9,300	8,750	(550)
Total variable costs (except) variable manufacturing variances)	735,800	702,500	(33,300)
Contribution margin (except variable manufacturing variances)	194,200	172,500	21,700
Less other costs			
Variable manufacturing costs variances from standards	49,600	—	(49,600)
Fixed manufacturing costs	49,200	48,000	(1,200)
Fixed selling & admin. costs	38,500	36,000	(2,500)
Corporation offices allocation	18,500	17,500	(1,000)
Total other costs	155,800	101,500	(54,300)
Divisional operational income	**$ 38,400**	**$ 71,000**	**$ (32,600)**

sales department occupy the third building on the property. The division management includes a division controller responsible for the divisional financial activities and the preparation of reports explaining the differences between actual and budgeted performances. The controller structures these reports such that the sales activities are distinguished from cost factors so that each can be analyzed separately.

The operating results for the first three months of the fiscal year as compared to the budget are presented in the schedule on the preceeding page. The budget for the current year was based upon the assumption that Markley Division would maintain its present market share of the estimated total patio chair market (plastic and metal combined). A status report had been sent to corporate management toward the end of the second month indicating that divisional operating income for the first quarter would probably be about 45 percent below budget; this estimate was just about on target. The division's operating income was below budget even though industry volume for patio chairs increased by 10 percent more than was expected at the time the budget was developed.

The manufacturing activities for the quarter resulted in the production of 55,000 plastic chairs and 22,500 metal chairs. The costs incurred by each manufacturing unit are presented below.

			Plastic Model	Metal Model
Raw materials (stated in equivalent finished chairs)				
	Quantity	Price		
Purchases				
Plastic	60,000	$5.65	$339,000	
Metal	30,000	$6.00		$180,000
Usage				
Plastic	56,000	$5.00	280,000	
Metal	23,000	$6.00		138,00
Direct labor				
9,300 hours @ $6.00 per hour			55,800	
5,600 hours @ $8.00 per hour				44,800
Manufacturing overhead				
Variable				
Supplies			43,000	18,000
Power			50,000	15,000
Employee benefits			19,000	12,000
Fixed				
Supervision			14,000	11,000
Depreciation			12,000	9,000
Property taxes and other items			1,900	1,300

The standard variable manufacturing costs per unit and the budgeted monthly fixed manufacturing costs established for the current year are presented below.

	Plastic Model	Metal Model
Raw material	$5.00	$6.00
Direct labor		
1/6 hour @ $6.00 per DLH	1.00	
1/4 hour @ $8.00 per DLH		2.00
Variable overhead		
1/6 hour @ $12.00 per DLH	2.00	
1/4 hour @ $8.00 per DLH		2.00
Standard variable manufacturing cost per unit	**$8.00**	**$10.00**

	Plastic Model	Metal Model
Budgeted fixed costs per month		
Supervision	$4,500	$3,500
Depreciation	4,000	3,000
Property taxes and other items	600	400
Total budgeted fixed costs for month	**$9,100**	**$6,900**

Required   A. Explain the variance in Markley Division's contribution margin attributable to sales activities by calculating the:

1. sales price variance.
2. sales mix variance.
3. sales volume variance.

B. What portion of sales volume variance, if any, can be attributed to a change in Markley Divison's market share?

C. Analyze the variance in Markley Division's variable manufacturing costs ($49,600) in as much detail as the data permit.

D. Based upon your analyses prepared for Requirements A, B, and C:

1. Identify the major cause of Markley Division's unfavorable profit performance.
2. Did Markley's management attempt to correct this problem? Explain your answer.
3. What other steps, if any, could Markley's management have taken to improve the division's operating income? Explain your answer.

---

6.   Estimated time 30 minutes (December 1982)

BBG Corporation is a manufacturer of a synthetic element. Gary Voss, President of the company, has been eager to get the operating results for the just completed fiscal year. He was surprised when the income statement revealed that income before taxes has dropped to $885,000 from $900,000 even though sales volume had increased 100,000 kg. This drop in net income had occurred even though Voss had implemented the following changes during the past 12 months to improve the profitability of the company.

• In response to a 10 percent increase in production costs, the sales price of the company's product was increased by 12 percent. This action took place on December 1, 1981.

• The managements of the selling and administrative departments were given strict instructions to spend no more in fiscal 1982 than in fiscal 1981.

BBG's Accounting Department prepared and distributed to top management the comparative income statements presented below. The accounting staff also prepared related

BBG Corporation
Statements of Operating Income
For the years ended November 30, 1981 and 1982
($000 omitted)

	1981	1982
Sales revenue	$9,000	$11,200
Cost of goods sold	$7,200	$ 8,320
Manufacturing volume variance	(600)	495
Adjusted cost of goods sold	$6,600	$ 8,815
Gross margin	$2,400	$ 2,385
Selling and administrative expenses	1,500	1,500
Income before taxes	$ 900	$ 885

BBG Corporation
Selected Operating and Financial Data
for
1981 and 1982

	1981	1982
Sales price	$ 10/kg.	$11.20/kg.
Material cost	$1.50/kg.	$ 1.65/kg.
Direct labor cost	$2.50/kg.	$ 2.75/kg.
Variable overhead cost	$1.00/kg.	$ 1.10/kg.
Fixed overhead cost	$3.00/kg.	$ 3.30/kg.
Total fixed overhead costs	$3,000,000	$3,300,000
Selling and administrative (all fixed)	$1,500,000	$1,500,000
Sales volume	900,000 kg.	1,000,000 kg.
Beginning inventory	300,000 kg.	600,000 kg.

financial information that is presented in the schedule in the box above to assist management in evaluating the company's performance. BBG uses the FIFO inventory method for finished goods.

Required   A. Explain to Gary Voss why BBG Corporation's net income decreased in the current fiscal year despite the sales price and sales volume increases.

B. A member of BBG's Accounting Department has suggested that the company adopt variable (direct) costing for internal reporting purposes.

1. Prepare an operating income statement through income

before taxes for the year ended November 30, 1982, for BBG Corporation using the variable (direct) costing method.

2. Present a numerical reconciliation of the difference in income before taxes using the absorption costing method as currently employed by BBG and the variable (direct) costing method as proposed.

C. Identify and discuss the advantages and disadvantages of using the variable (direct) costing method for internal reporting purposes.

---

7.   Estimated time 30 minutes (June 1991)

Portland Optics Inc. specializes in manufacturing lenses for large telescopes and cameras used in space exploration. As the specifications for the lenses are determined by the customer and vary considerably, the company uses a job order cost system. Factory overhead is applied to jobs on the basis of direct labor hours, utilizing the absorption (full) costing method. Portland's predetermined overhead rates for 1989 and 1990 were based on the following estimates.

	1989	1990
Direct labor hours	32,500	44,000
Direct labor cost	$325,000	$462,000
Fixed factory overhead	130,000	176,000
Variable factory overhead	162,500	198,000

Jim Bradford, Portland's controller, would like to use variable (direct) costing for internal reporting purposes as he believes statements prepared using variable costing are more appropriate for making product decisions. In order to explain the benefits of variable costing to the other members of Portland's management team, Bradford plans to convert the company's Income Statement from absorption costing to variable costing and has gathered the following information for this purpose, along with a copy of Portland's 1989-90 Comparative Income Statement.

Portland Optics Inc.
Comparative Income Statement
For the Years 1989-90

	1989	1990
Net sales	$1,140,000	$1,520,000
Cost of goods sold:		
Finished goods at January 1	16,000	25,000
Cost of goods manufactured	720,000	976,000
Total available	736,000	1,001,000
Finished goods at December 31	25,000	14,000
Cost of goods sold before overhead adjustment	711,000	987,000
Overhead adjustment	12,000	7,000
Cost of goods sold	723,000	994,000
Gross profit	417,000	526,000
Selling expense	150,000	190,000
Administrative expense	160,000	187,000
Operating income	$ 107,000	$ 149,000

• Portland's actual manufacturing data for the two years are presented below.

	1989	1990
Direct labor hours	30,000	42,000
Direct labor cost	$300,000	$435,000
Raw materials used	140,000	210,000
Fixed factory overhead	132,000	175,000

• The company's actual inventory balances were:

	12/31/88	12/31/89	12/31/90
Raw material	$32,000	$36,000	$18,000
Work-in-process			
Costs	$44,000	$34,000	$60,000
Direct labor hours	1,800	1,400	2,500
Finished goods			
Costs	$16,000	$25,000	$14,000
Direct labor hours	700	1,080	550

• For both years, all administrative costs were fixed, while a portion of the selling expense resulting from an eight percent commission on net sales was variable. Portland reports any over- or underapplied overhead as an adjustment to the cost of goods sold.

Required **A.** For the year ended December 31, 1990, prepare the revised Income Statement for Portland Optics Inc. utilizing the variable costing method. Be sure to include the contribution margin on the revised income statement.

B. Describe two advantages of using variable costing rather than absorption costing.

The following data are used for both Questions 8 and 9. Refer to these data for each question. Each question is independent and not affected by the solution to the other question. The specific questions follow the data.

Caprice Company manufactures and sells two products—a small portable office file cabinet that it has made for over 15 years and a home/travel file introduced in 1981. The files are made in Caprice's only manufacturing plant. Budgeted variable production costs per unit of product are as follows.

	Office File	Home/Travel File
Sheet metal	$ 3.50	—
Plastic	—	$3.75
Direct labor (@ $8 per DLH)	4.00	2.00
Variable manufacturing overhead (@ $9 per DLH)	4.50	2.25
	$12.00	$8.00

Variable manufacturing overhead costs vary with direct labor hours. The annual fixed manufacturing overhead costs are budgeted at $120,000. A total of 50 percent of these costs are directly traceable to the Office File Department and 22 percent of the costs are traceable to the Home Travel File Department. The remaining 28 percent of the costs are not traceable to either department.

Caprice employs two full-time salespersons—Pam Price and Robert Flint. Each salesperson receives an annual salary of $14,000 plus a sales commission of 10 percent of his/her total gross sales. Travel and entertainment expense is budgeted at $22,000 annually for each salesperson. Price is expected to sell 60 percent of the budgeted unit sales for each file and Flint the remaining 40 percent. Caprice's remaining selling and administrative expenses include fixed administrative costs of $80,000 that cannot be traced to either file plus the following traceable selling expenses.

	Office File	Home/Travel File
Packaging expenses per unit	$ 2.00	$ 1.50
Promotion	$30,000	$40,000

Data regarding Caprice's budgeted and actual sales for the fiscal year ended May 31, 1984, are presented in the schedule below. There were no changes in the beginning and ending balances of either finished goods or work-in-process inventories.

	Office File	Home/Travel File
Budgeted sales volume in units	15,000	15,000
Budgeted and actual unit sales price	$29.50	$19.50
Actual unit sales		
Pam Price	10,000	9,500
Robert Flint	5,000	10,500
Total units	15,000	20,000

Data regarding Caprice's operating expenses for the year ended May 31, 1984, follow.

• There were no increases or decreases in raw materials inventory for either sheet metal or plastic and there were no usage variances. However, sheet metal prices were six percent above budget and plastic prices were four percent below budget.

• The actual direct labor hours worked and costs incurred were as follows.

	Hours	Amount
Office file	7,500	$ 57,000
Home/Travel file	6,000	45,600
	13,500	$102,600

• Fixed manufacturing overhead costs attributable to the office file department were $8,000 above the budget. All other fixed manufacturing overhead costs were incurred at the same amounts as budgeted, and all variable manufacturing overhead costs were incurred at the budgeted hourly rates.

• All selling and administrative expenses were incurred at budgeted rates or amounts except the following items.

Non-traceable admin-		
istrative expenses		$ 34,000
Promotion		
Office files	$32,000	
Home/Travel files	58,000	90,000
Travel and entertainment		
Pam Price	$24,000	
Robert Flint	28,000	52,000
		$176,000

8.   Estimated time 30 minutes (June 1984)

Required   A. Prepare a segmented income statement of Caprice Company's actual operations for the fiscal year ended May 31, 1984. The report should be prepared in a contribution margin format by product and should reflect total income (loss) for the company before income taxes.

B. Identify and discuss any additional analyses that could be made of the data presented that would be of value to Caprice Company.

9.   Estimated time 30 minutes (June 1984)

Required   A. Prepare a performance report for the year ended May 31, 1984, that would be useful in evaluating the performance of Robert Flint.

B. Discuss the effects of Robert Flint's sales mix on Caprice Company's

1. manufacturing operations.
2. profits.

10.   Estimated time 30 minutes (December 1986)

Jack Stern is a successful investor whose specialty is revitalizing failed businesses. His goal is to maximize his profits within

---

The Edge Company Inc.
Statement of Financial Position
as of January 1, 1987
($000 omitted)

Assets	
Cash	$ 450
Accounts receivable	0
Inventory	100
Plant and equipment	2,000
Total assets	$2,550
Liabilities and Equities	
Accounts payable	$ 0
Current portion of	
long-term debt	90
Long-term debt	1,610
Common stock (no par value)	850
Retained earnings	0
Total liabilities and equities	$2,550

---

the limits of careful use of external financing which usually means limiting growth rates and foregoing some potential profit. Stern believes this is the key to his success and that unlimited growth can easily lead to fatal financing problems. Stern is once again set to test his approach.

Five years ago, Robert West perfected a technique for joining the edges of laminated plastic parts so that the edges of subsurface layers were not visible. Since subsurface layers are a different color than the surface layer, West's edges greatly improved the appearance of the finished product. West then designed equipment that permitted large volume production of the edges. West's product was unique, and sales and production levels grew rapidly. Rapid growth, however, soon exceeded West's management ability and his ability to obtain financing. A few months ago, West's firm closed, leaving a regional bank holding the plant, equipment, and some inventory.

Stern believes that the product has sales and profit potential and has offered the bank $400,000 in cash plus assumption of the loan for the plant, equipment, and inventory. The bank was only too happy to accept Stern's offer.

Stern has established Edge Company and contributed to it the acquired assets and $450,000 in cash. Edge Company's Statement of Financial Position at the start of business is presented above.

To implement his goal of making conservative use of external financing, Stern has established the following financial objectives:

● paying no dividends, thus keeping all cash generated within the company.

● issuing no additional capital stock.

● incurring no new long-term debt while servicing current interest and $90,000 of principal annually on the existing bank loan.

● keeping the cash balance at no less than $50,000.

● taking advantage of supplier credit but not allowing accounts payable to exceed $100,000.

The bank's loan officer had commented that West was unable to control costs and working capital, and Stern agreed. He plans to hold variable costs at 75 percent of sales. Even though the existing plant and equipment have a capacity of $12,000,000 in annual sales, Stern's plan is to budget a lump-sum of $500,000 per year for fixed costs, including both depreciation and interest. Depreciation of plant and equipment is $100,000 per year.

In making his plans, Stern has used 20 percent as the average income tax rate applicable to Edge Company. Because some of the firms he acquires have been in income tax trouble, Stern makes a point of keeping tax payments current and aims to finish each year with no tax liability on the books.

Customers for products of this kind are notoriously slow payers; however, Stern is confident that accounts receivable can be kept at 15 percent of annual sales. He also believes that inventories can be maintained at 20 percent of annual variable costs.

Some of West's former sales people have been rehired, and they feel that Edge Company's first year sales could easily reach $5,000,000. But, Stern believes that managing growth is the most important part of the plan, and he plans to limit first year sales to $2,100,000.

Required A. Determine whether Jack Stern's financial objectives can be achieved by preparing a Pro Forma Income Statement in a variable (direct) costing format for the Edge Company for the year ending December 31, 1987 and a Pro Forma Statement of Financial Position for the Edge Company as of December 31, 1987. Assume that Jack Stern's projections occur and sales are limited to $2,100,000.

B. Without prejudice to Requirement A above, assume that the following results from the company's first fiscal year ending December 31, 1987 occurred, and that Jack Stern's financial objectives were met.

● Sales: $2,000,000

● Net income: $0

● Cash balance at December 31, 1987: $60,000
● Accounts payable at December 31, 1987: $100,000
● Net working capital at December 31, 1987: $470,000

Compute the maximum amount by which Edge Company could increase dollar sales in its second year (ending December 31, 1988) and still achieve Jack Stern's financial objectives.

---

11. Estimated time 30 minutes (June 1987)

Stratford Corporation is a diversified company whose products are marketed both domestically and internationally. The company's major product lines are pharmaceutical products, sports equipment, and household appliances. At a recent meeting of Stratford's Board of Directors, there was a lengthy discussion on ways to improve overall corporate profitability without new acquisitions as the company is already heavily leveraged. The members of the Board decided that they required additional financial information about individual corporate operations in order to target areas for improvement.

Dave Murphy, Stratford's Controller, has been asked to provide additional data that would assist the Board in its investigation. Stratford is not a public company and, therefore, has not prepared complete income statements by segment. Murphy regularly has prepared an income statement by product line through contribution margin. However, Murphy now believes that income statements prepared through operating income along both product lines and geographic areas would provide the Directors with the required insight into corporate operations. Murphy has the following data available to him.

Murphy had several discussions with the Division Managers for each product line and compiled the following information from these meetings.

● The Division Managers concluded that Murphy should allocate fixed factory overhead on the basis of the ratio of the variable costs expended per product line or per geographic area to total variable costs.

● Each of the Division Managers agreed that a reasonable basis for the allocation of depreciation on plant and equipment would be the ratio of units produced per product line or per geographical area to the total number of units produced.

● There was little agreement on the allocation of administrative and selling expenses so Murphy decided to allocate only those expenses that were directly traceable to the segment being delineated; i.e., manufacturing staff salaries to product lines and sales staff salaries to geographic areas. Murphy used the data in the next column for this allocation.

	Product Lines			
	Pharmaceutical	Sports	Appliances	Total
Production/Sales in units	160,000	180,000	160,000	500,000
Average selling price per unit	$8.00	$20.00	$15.00	
Average variable manufacturing cost per unit	4.00	9.50	8.25	
Average variable selling expense per unit	2.00	2.50	2.25	
Fixed factory overhead excluding depreciation				$500,000
Depreciation of plant and equipment				400,000
Administrative and selling expense				1,160,000

Stratford Corporation
Statement of Income by Product Lines
For the Fiscal Year Ended April 30, 1987

	Pharmaceutical	Sports	Appliances	Unallocated	Total
	Product Lines				
Sales in units	160,000	180,000	160,000		
Sales	$1,280,000	$3,600,000	$2,400,000	—	$7,280,000
Variable manufacturing and selling costs	960,000	2,160,000	1,680,000	—	4,800,000
Contribution margin	$ 320,000	$1,440,000	$ 720,000	—	$2,480,000
Fixed costs					
Fixed factory overhead	$ 100,000	$ 225,000	$ 175,000	$ —	$ 500,000
Depreciation	128,000	144,000	128,000	—	400,000
Administrative and selling expense	120,000	140,000	80,000	820,000	1,160,000
Total fixed costs	$ 348,000	$ 509,000	$ 383,000	$ 820,000	$2,060,000
Operating income (loss)	$ (28,000)	$ 931,000	$ 337,000	$(820,000)	$ 420,000

Manufacturing Staff		Sales Staff	
Pharmaceutical	$120,000	U.S.	$ 60,000
Sports	140,000	Canada	100,000
Appliances	80,000	Europe	250,000

• The Division Managers were able to provide reliable sales percentages for their product lines by geographical area.

Percentage of Unit Sales

	U.S.	Canada	Europe
Pharmaceutical	40%	10%	50%
Sports	40%	40%	20%
Appliances	20%	20%	60%

Murphy prepared the product line income statement shown above based on this data.

Required   **A.** Prepare a segmented income statement for Stratford Corporation based on the company's geographic areas of sales. The statement should be in good form and show the operating income for each segment.

B. As a result of the information disclosed by both segmented income statements (by product line and by geographic area), recommend areas where Stratford Corporation should focus its attention in order to improve corporate profitability.

Solutions

1.

1. b. Under direct costing, profits are a function of sales volume and are not influenced by changes in production volumes.

2. c. The profits could decrease under conditions where production was less than sales.

3. e. The excess of budgeted or actual sales over the sales at breakeven point. While the sales at breakeven point does equal the variable and fixed costs, it is assumed by the suggested answer that the accountant "typically" has in mind the sales, not costs.

4. a. The decrease in selling price would be the answer, assuming the variable cost is less than the sales price, and if it was not, it would not be profitable to produce units.

5. a. Changes in fixed costs do not affect the contribution margin.

6. b. A. is incorrect because XX represents loss area. Lines OM and N2 represent loss and profit respectively. The line MN represents net income.

7. c. See 6. above.

8. d. It is assumed that the cost factors remain constant.

9. c. The more orders, the greater the "set up" cost would generally be.

10. c. The manager does not generally have control over the purchase of equipment.

11. c. Since the joint cost is allocated on some arbitrary basis it is not useful for determining variances, for comparative analysis, or for decision making.

12. a. The unabsorbed overhead costs in an absorption costing system is the difference between actual cost and the cost applied to units produced.

13. d. The volume variance is caused by the failure to produce at the denominator level volume. To change the volume variance, the activity level used to calculate the fixed overhead rate is all that needs to be changed. Thus, the volume variance is a function of activity level used, and not how effectively costs were controlled.

14. c. Simple regression or least squares analysis.

15. c. Limar: y = a + bx.

16. b. Y is the total costs.

17. b. b is the rate of change or the variable cost per unit.

18. b. Since the company has not experienced cost behavior outside the observed values, the analysis must be restricted to this area.

19. c.
Variable costs
($7,000,000 × .60 × (100,000 ÷ 140,000))= $3,000,000
Fixed costs
(11,200,000 × .50 × (100,000 ÷ 160,000)) = 3,500,000
$6,500,000

Note that fixed cost is based on the applied rate determined using 160,000 units (normal volume).

20. b.
Variable costs
($7,000,000 × .60 × (40,000 ÷ 140,000)) . = $1,200,000

21. c.
Fixed cost rate is 11,200,000 × .50 ÷ 160,000 = $35
Volume variance = Actual quantity produced (140,000) – normal volume (160,000) × standard applied rate ($35), or $700,000 UF.

22. d.

Sales	$18,000,000
Variable costs—manufacturing	3,000,000
Contribution margin—manufacturing	15,000,000
Variable cost—selling	2,800,000
Contribution margin	12,200,000
Fixed costs	11,200,000
Net income	1,000,000

23. c. Sales Volume variance = CM × (Actual – Budgeted volume)
= $20 × (5,000 – 6,000)
= 20,000 UF

24. d. Sales price variance = AQ × (ASP* – BSP)
= 5,000 × [($235,000/5,000) – ($300,000/6,000)]
= 5,000 × (47 – 50)
= 15,000 UF
*Actual standard price

25. a. Variable cost variance = AQ × (BUC – AUC)
= 5,000 × [($180,000/6,000) – ($145,000/5,000)]
= 5,000 × ($30 – $29)
= 5,000 F

26. d. $84,000 Actual – $80,000 Budget

27. c. With Folsom's budgeted market share, Folsom's actual sales, and the actual market total sales the impact of a change in the market could be calculated.

2.

A. Volume variance

19X3 Budgeted Volume	4,000 rolls
19X3 Actual Volume	3,900 rolls
Volume Below Budget	**100 rolls**
1973 Budgeted variable margin	$1,400,000 ÷ 4,000 rolls = $350

Volume variance 100 × $350 = $35,000 below budget

B. Arsco Co. expected to have a 10% share of a 40,000 roll market. Carrying this relationship to the actual industry results, Arsco would expect a 3,800 roll volume for 19X3. Using the notion of a flexible budget, the company should have expected a $70,000 unfavorable margin ([4,000 – 3,800] × $350) rather than $35,000. Arsco has a favorable volume variance of $35,000 when its results are compared to a budget adjusted for industry volume.

C. Mix Variance

	Actual quantities at actual mix	Actual quantities at budgeted mix		Budgeted margin	
Grade 1	800 rolls	975	(175)	@ $300	$(52,500)
Grade 2	1,000 rolls	975	25	@ $400	10,000
Grade 3	2,100 rolls	1950	150	@ $350	52,500
	3,900 rolls	**3,900 rolls**		favorable	**$10,000**

3.

To: Mary Ross   December 16, 1988
From: Barry Stein
Subject: Explanation of November 1988 Variances

1. The revenue mix variance resulted from a higher proportion of participants being eligible for discounts. The budgeted revenue was based on 30 percent of the participants taking the discount; but, during November, 45 percent of those attending the courses received discounts. As a result, the weighted average fee dropped from $145.50 to $143.25.

2. The most significant implication of the revenue mix variance is that the proportion of discount fees has increased by 50 percent. If the increase represents a trend, the implications for future profits could be serious as revenues per participant day will decline while costs are likely to remain steady or increase.

3. The revenue timing difference was caused by early registrations for the December program to be held in Cincinnati. The early registrations resulted from the combined promotional mailing for both the Chicago and Cincinnati programs. These early registrations have been prematurely recognized as revenue during November.

4. The revenue recognition in November of early registrations for the December courses is inappropriate, and, consequently, revenues during the month of December may be lower than expected.

5. The primary causes of the unfavorable total expense variance were additional food charges, course materials, and instructor fees. Although these quantity variances are unfavorable, the increased costs of $10,400 are more than offset by the additional revenues of $40,740 with which these items are associated.

6. The favorable food price variance was determined by multiplying the difference between the budgeted and actual price per participant day times the actual participant days. The actual price per participant day was determined by dividing the actual food charges by the total participant days ($32,000 ÷ 1,280).

7. While the combined promotional piece had a $5,000 unfavorable impact on November expenses, there will be no need for further promotion of the Cincinnati program. Therefore, the $20,000 budgeted for this purpose in December will not be expended, lowering planned expenses for the month.

The promotion timing difference represents an incorrect matching of costs and revenue. The costs allocated to the Cincinnati program should be reflected on the December statement of operations to be matched against the December program.

8. The course development variance is unfavorable to the November budget, but its overall impact on the company cannot be determined until such time as the level of acceptance of the new course is experienced.

4.

A. Full (absorption) costing assigns both variable and fixed manufacturing costs to the units produced. With direct (variable) costing only the variable manufacturing costs are assigned to the units produced and the fixed manufacturing costs are treated as period costs.

When CLK Co. decided to purchase rather than manufacture the five items, it compared the outside purchase price with the full cost to manufacture the items. The full cost included an allocated portion of the fixed manufacturing costs. The total fixed costs would not be affected by this decision and would continue to be incurred even though the five items were discontinued. In decisions of this type dealing with marginal production (and sales) only those costs which are relevant should be considered. They are more likely to be the variable costs. Hence, the direct cost approach would have been the more useful costing approach because it emphasizes the variable costs which are the relevant costs to be compared with the outside purchase price.

B. A portion of the fixed manufacturing costs in addition to the variable manufacturing costs are inventoried under the full (absorption) costing method while only variable manufacturing costs are inventoried under the direct (variable) costing method. Consequently, the inventory values are always higher in full (absorption) costing regardless of whether the physical quantities of inventory are rising, falling, or stable. The effects on net income and return on investment are explained as follows.

1. Inventory quantities are rising.

Under absorption costing a portion of the fixed manufacturing costs would be inventoried and identified with the inventory build-up during the period. This would result in lower cost of goods sold and a higher net income than under direct costing.

Under direct costing the fixed costs would flow through to the income statement resulting in the lower net income figure.

The ROI comparison is not as easily made. Without specific data one cannot determine which method's ROI will be higher during a period in which inventory quantities rise. The absorption costing income will be higher but its investment base also will be higher. The investment base will be higher by the amount of the inventoried fixed costs, including the fixed costs associated with the current increase in inventory quantity. If the amount of the difference in incomes is large relative to the income amount and the amount of fixed costs added to the inventory is small relative to the investment, the absorption costing ROI is likely to be higher than the direct costing ROI. If the income difference is small relative to the income and the effect on the investment base is also small the absorption costing ROI will be lower than the direct costing ROI.

2. Inventory quantities are declining.

Absorption costing would release fixed costs previously inventoried as inventories decline, thus resulting in higher cost of goods sold for the period and lower net income than under direct costing. Under direct costing only current period fixed costs would be charged against income resulting in the higher net income. The higher net income divided by the lower investment base (because direct cost inventories do not include assigned fixed costs) will result in a higher ROI for direct costing than for absorption costing.

3. Inventory quantities are stable.

When inventory quantities are stable, net income is the same for both methods. The ROI will be higher under direct costing.

C. The emphasis of direct (variable) costing is on cost behavior and the identification of costs which vary as activity levels change. Managers tend to think in direct costing terms, i.e., as activity increases costs increase. Managers key upon the relevant costs in decision making which means they are interested in the change in contribution margin and the change in total fixed costs. Direct costing is useful for decision making because the relevant costs are more easily identifiable—i.e., the variable costs are separated from the fixed and the changes in fixed costs are highlighted.

5.

A. 1. *Sales price variance*

The sales price variance should incorporate the changes for sales commissions and bad debts which amount to 5% (46,500/930,000; 43,750/875,000) and 1% (9,300/930,000; 8,750/875,000) respectively.

(Actual sales price — Budgeted sales price)(1 — Selling expense) (Actual sales volume)

Plastic	($10.50−$10.00) (1−.06) (60,000) =	$28,200
Metal	($15−$15) (1−.06) (20,000) =	0
Total		**$28,200** F

2. *Sales mix variance*

$$\begin{array}{l}\text{Budgeted weighted} \\ \text{average contri-} \\ \text{bution margin} \\ \text{per unit}\end{array} = \frac{\text{Budgeted contribution margin}}{\text{Budgeted sales}}$$

$$= \frac{\$172,500}{75,000}$$

$$= \$2.30/\text{unit}$$

$$\begin{array}{l}\text{Actual weighted} \\ \text{average contri-} \\ \text{bution margin} \\ \text{per unit}\end{array} = \frac{\text{Actual contribution margin} -}{\text{Favorable price variance}}{\text{Actual total unit sales}}$$

$$= \frac{\$194,200 - \$28,200}{80,000}$$

$$= \frac{\$166,000}{80,000}$$

$$= \$2.075/\text{unit}$$

(Actual weighted ave. contribution margin per unit — Budgeted weighted ave. contribution margin per unit) (Actual total unit sales)
($2.075 − $2.30) 80,000 = $18,000 U

3. *Sales volume variance*

(Actual unit sales—Budgeted unit sales) (Budgeted weighted ave. contribution margin per unit)

(80,000 − 75,000) $2.30 = $11,500 F

Summary of variances

Price		
Plastic	$28,200 F	
Metal	0	$28,200 F
Mix		18,000 U
Volume		11,500 F
Total Contribution Margin Variance		**$21,700 F**

B.
Markley Division's expected sales	75,000 units
Extra 10% industry increase	7,500 units
Sales volume required to retain market share	82,500 units
Actual sales volume	80,000 units
Loss in market share	2,500 units
Weighted average contribution margin per unit	$2.30
Sales volume variance attributable to a reduction in the market share	**$ 5,750 U**

C. *Price variance*

(Actual price − Standard price) (Actual quantity purchased)

Plastic	($5.65/unit − $5/unit) 60,000 =	$39,000 U
Metal	($6/unit − $6/unit) 30,000 =	0
Total		**$39,000 U**

Material usage variance

(Actual quantity used − Standard quantity allowed) (Standard price)

Plastic	(56,000 − 55,000) $5 =	$5,000 U
Metal	(23,000 − 22,500) $6 =	3,000 U
Total		**$8,000 U**

Labor rate variance
(Actual rate − Standard rate) (Actual hours worked)

Plastic	($6/hour − $6/hour) 9,300 =	$0
Metal	($8/hour − $8/hour) 5,600 =	0
Total		**$0**

Labor efficiency variance

(Actual hours − Standard hours) (Standard rate)

Plastic	(9,300 − 9,166⅔) $6/hr. =	$800 U
Metal	(5,600 − 5,625) $8/hr. =	200 F
Total		**600 U**

Variable overhead spending variance

(Actual variable overhead) − (Standard VOH rate × Actual labor hours worked)

Plastic	$112,00 − ($12/hr. × 9,300 hrs.) =	$400 U
Metal	45,000 − ($8/hr. × 5,600 hrs.) =	200 U
Total		**$600 U**

Variable overhead efficiency variance

(Actual labor hours worked − Standard labor hours allowed) (Standard VOH rate)

Plastic	(9,300 − 9,166⅔) $12/hr. =	$1,600 U
Metal	(5,600 − 5,625) $8/hr. =	200 F
Total		**$1,400 U**

Summary of variances

Material price—plastic		$39,000 U.
Material usage—plastic	$5,000 U	
—metal	3,000 U	8,000 U
Labor efficiency—plastic	$ 800 U	
—metal	200 F	600 U
Variable overhead		
spending—plastic	$ 400 U	
—metal	200 U	600 U
Variable overhead		
efficiency—plastic	$1,600 U	
—metal	200 F	1,400 U
Total variable		
manufacturing cost		
variance		**$49,600** U

D. 1. The major cause of Markley Division's unfavorable profit performance is the large material price variance in the production of the plastic model—The company paid $5.65 for plastic material per chair versus the standard price of $5.00. Considering that the company is exceeding budgeted sales of plastic chairs, plus the fact they have a lower budgeted contribution margin per unit, this excess price variance has a significant impact on company profits.

2. The company attempted to meet this problem by raising the prices of plastic chairs. However, the price increase was only $.50. This is a relatively low increase in light of the cost change and may have contributed the shift in sales mix to the plastic chairs.

3. Steps Markley's management might have taken to improve the division's operating income include:

- increasing the sales price of the plastic model to fully compensate for the increase in raw material cost (i.e., at least $.65 rather than $.50).

- attempting to improve sales mix by increased sales effort being devoted to the metal model.

- attempting to maintain market share by increased sales effort.

- reviewing all cost control procedures to be sure they are functioning as planned.

6.

A. In absorption (full) costing, as currently employed by BBG Corporation, fixed manufacturing overhead is considered a product cost rather than a period cost. Fixed manufacturing overhead is applied to production based upon a normal production volume of 1,000,000 kg. Thus, the fixed manufacturing overhead is applied to products in the same manner as variable costs even though they do not vary with production. In addition, if production and sales are not equal during the year, fixed manufacturing overhead costs are deferred as part of inventory costs (production exceeds sales) or released upon sale of inventory (sales exceed production).

During 1981 production exceeded sales resulting in a portion of the fixed manufacturing overhead costs being inventoried in finished goods rather than being recognized as an expense of the period. This resulted in 1981 income before taxes being higher than might be expected. Then in 1982, sales exceeded production resulting in more fixed manufacturing overhead costs being recognized as an expense of the period rather than being incurred. First, finished goods were sold out of inventory which meant that the fixed overhead costs that were incurred in 1981 and inventoried were released as period costs in 1982. Secondly, fixed manufacturing overhead was underapplied in 1982 because only 850,000 units were produced. This gave rise to an unfavorable volume variance that was charged to Cost of Goods Sold. Both of these occurrences increased Costs of Goods Sold and resulted in a reduction of gross margin and income before taxes in 1982.

B. 1.

BBG Corporation
Operating Income Statement
For the Year Ended November 30, 1982
($000s omitted)

Sales		$11,200
Variable cost of goods sold:		
600,000 units at $5.00	$3,000	
400,000 units at $5.50	2,200	5,200
Contribution margin		$ 6,000
Fixed cost of operation:		
Factory overhead	$3,300	
Selling and administrative	1,500	4,800
Income before taxes		$ 1,200

2.   *Reconciliation*

Net Income 1982—Direct Costing	$ 1,200
Net Income 1982—Absorption Costing	885
Difference	$ 315
Accounted for as follows:	
Beginning inventory reduction:	
600,000 units at $3.00	$ 1,800
Ending inventory:	
450,000 units at $3.30	1,485
Difference	$ 315

C. The advantages of direct (variable) costing for internal reporting include the following.

- Direct costing aids in forecasting and reporting income for internal management purposes.

- Fixed costs are reported at incurred values (and not absorbed), increasing the opportunity for more effective control of these costs.

- Profits vary directly with sales volume and are unaffected by changes in inventory levels.

- Analysis of the cost/volume/profit relationship is facilitated and management is able to determine the breakeven point and total profit for a given volume of production and sales.

The disadvantages of direct (variable) costing for internal reporting include the following.

• Management may fail to consider properly the fixed cost elements and their impact in the decision-making process.

• Direct costing lacks acceptability for external financial reporting or as the basis for income tax calculation. As a result, additional record keeping costs are required.

• The distinction between fixed and variable costs is often arbitrary.

7.

A. The revised Income Statement for Portland Optics Inc. for the year ended December 31, 1990, using the variable costing method, is presented below.

```
            Portland Optics Inc.
          Revised Income Statement
      For the Year Ended December 31, 1990

Net sales                        $1,520,000
Variable costs:
  Finished goods
    inventory 1/1      $ 20,680
  Work-in-process
    inventory 1/1        28,400
  Manufacturing costs
    incurred            834,000
      Total available   883,080
  Finished goods
    inventory 12/31     (11,800)
  Work-in-process
    inventory 12/31     (50,000)
  Variable manu-
    facturing costs     821,280
  Variable selling costs 121,600
      Total variable costs         942,880
Contribution margin                577,120
Fixed costs:
  Fixed factory overhead $175,000
  Fixed selling expense    68,400
  Administrative expense  187,000
      Total fixed expense          430,400
Operating income                 $ 146,720
```

Supporting Calculations

Finished goods inventory 1/1:

Inventory using full cost	$25,000
Less: Fixed overhead (1,080 hrs. x $4*)	4,320
	$20,680

*Fixed overhead rate:
1989: $130,000 ÷ 32,500 = $4.00/hr.
1990: $176,000 ÷ 44,000 = $4.00/hr.

Work-in-process inventory 1/1:

Inventory using full cost	$34,000
Less: Fixed overhead (1,400 hrs. x $4)	5,600
	$28,400

Manufacturing costs:

Materials	$210,000
Direct labor	435,000
Variable overhead (42,000 hrs. x $4.50*)	189,000
	$834,000

*Variable overhead rate:
$198,000 ÷ 44,000 = $4.50/hour

Finished goods inventory 12/31:

Inventory at full cost	$14,000
Less: Fixed overhead (550 hrs. x $4)	2,200
	$11,800

Work-in-process inventory 12/31:

Inventory at full cost	$60,000
Less: Fixed overhead (2,500 hrs. x $4)	10,000
	$50,000

Variable selling costs:

Net sales x Commission rate ($1,520,000 x .08)	$121,600

Fixed selling expense:

Total selling expense	$190,000
Less: Variable selling costs	121,600
	$ 68,400

B. Two of the several advantages of using variable costing rather than absorption costing are as follows:

• Financial statements using variable costing are more easily understood because they show that profits move in the same direction as sales. This effect is more logical than that shown with absorption costing, where profit is affected by changes in inventory.

• Variable costing facilitates the analysis of cost-volume-profit relationships by separating fixed and variable costs on the income statement.

8.

A.

Caprice Company
Segment Contribution Operating Statement
For the Year Ended May 31, 1984

	Office File	Home/Travel File	Total
Sales in units	15,000	20,000	
Sales revenue	$442,500	$390,000	$832,500
Variable manufacturing costs			
Raw materials	$ 55,650	$ 72,000	$127,650
Direct labor	57,000	45,600	102,600
Variable overhead	67,500	54,000	121,500
Total variable manufacturing costs	$180,150	$171,600	$351,750
Manufacturing contribution margin	$262,350	$218,400	$480,750
Variable selling costs			
Packaging	$ 30,000	$ 30,000	$ 60,000
Commissions	44,250	39,000	83,250
Total variable selling costs	$ 74,250	$ 69,000	$143,250
Contribution margin	$188,100	$149,400	$337,500
Traceable fixed costs			
Manufacturing overhead	$ 68,000	$ 26,000	$ 94,400
Promotion	32,000	58,000	90,000
Total traceable fixed costs	$100,000	$ 84,400	$184,400
Product segment margin	$ 88,100	$ 65,000	$153,100
Non-traceable fixed costs			
Manufacturing overhead			$ 33,600
Travel and entertainment			52,000
Sales salaries			28,000
Administrative			34,000
Total non-traceable fixed costs			$147,600
Income before income taxes			$ 5,500

B. The following additional analyses that would be of value to Caprice Company that could be made from the data presented include the following.

• A flexible budget could be prepared based on budgeted data for the actual level of sales activity achieved. A flexible budget would facilitate performance evaluation through a comparison of actual results with the budgeted amounts that should have been achieved at the actual level of sales activity. The flexible budget is helpful in assessing how efficient the company was in its operations.

• Cost/volume/profit relationships are evident from contribution margin format. This facilitates the evaluation of operating leverage, the determination of margin of safety, and the calculation of impact on profits arising from changes in costs and/or volumes.

9.

A. (See next page.)

B. 1. The large increase in sales of the home/travel file could have caused emergency purchases of plastic at higher than normal prices. Plastic prices were four percent below budget but may have been even lower with better production planning.

Flint's large increase in the sales of the home/travel file may have caused some production problems. The actual labor hours worked in the manufacture of the home/travel file (6,000) exceeded the hours allowed (20,000 units × .25 DLH/unit = 5,000) by 1,000 DLH giving rise to an $8,000 unfavorable labor efficiency variance [(5,000 – 6,000 DLH) × $8.00/DLH]. The unfavorable labor efficiency variance for the home/travel file could be the result of the increased pressure to produce more units or a shift of workers from the manufacture of office files to the home/travel files.

2. Robert Flint's increased sales of the home/travel file had a net positive effect on profits. While his sales efforts emphasized the home/travel file, the product with the smaller contribution margin per unit, this product also had the greater contribution margin per direct labor hour (see schedule below). The increase in sales quantity of the home/travel file more than compensates for the decreased sales quantity of the office file.

	Office File	Home/Travel File
Selling price/unit	$29.50	$19.50
Unit variable costs		
Manufacturing (at budget)	$12.00	$ 8.00
Packaging	2.00	1.50
Commissions	2.95	1.95
Total variable costs per unit	$16.95	$11.45
Contribution margin per unit	$12.55	$ 8.05
Units produced per DLH	2	4
Contribution margin per DLH	$25.10	$32.20

Flint's actions may have had some negative impacts on profits. For instance, his travel and entertainment expenses were $6,000 above budget. If his increased sales effort had been better planned for, production problems could have been mitigated, the favorable price variance for plastic might have been larger and the unfavorable labor efficiency variance might have been smaller.

9. A.

Caprice Company
Performance Report — Robert Flint
For the Year Ended May 31, 1984

	Office File			Home/Travel File			Total		
	Budget	Actual	Variance*	Budget	Actual	Variance*	Budget	Actual	Variance*
Sales in units	6,000	5,000	1,000 U	6,000	10,500	4,500 F	—	—	—
Sales revenue	$177,000	$147,500	$29,500 U	$117,000	$204,750	$87,750 F	$294,000	$352,250	$58,250 F
Variable costs									
Manufacturing (at budgeted rates)	$ 72,000	$ 60,000	$12,000 F	$ 48,000	$ 84,000	$36,000 U	$120,000	$144,000	$24,000 U
Packaging	12,000	10,000	2,000 F	9,000	15,750	6,750 U	21,000	25,750	4,750 U
Commissions	17,700	14,750	2,950 F	11,700	20,475	8,775 U	29,400	35,225	5,825 U
Total variable costs	$101,700	$ 84,750	$16,950 F	$ 68,700	$120,225	$51,525 U	$170,400	$204,975	$34,575 U
Contribution margin	$ 75,300	$ 62,750	$12,550 U	$ 48,300	$ 84,525	$36,225 F	$123,600	$147,275	$23,675 F
Fixed costs									
Travel and entertainment							$ 22,000	$ 28,000	$ 6,000 U
Salary							14,000	14,000	—
Total fixed costs							$ 36,000	$ 42,000	$ 6,000 U
Salesperson contribution							$ 87,600	$105,275	$17,675 F

* F — favorable
  U — unfavorable

10.

A. Jack Stern's financial objectives for Edge Company can be achieved as shown in the following financial statements.

The Edge Company Inc.
Pro Forma Income Statement
For the Year Ended December 31, 1987
($000 omitted)

Sales	$2,100
Variable costs (75% of sales)	1,575
Contribution margin	525
Fixed costs	500
Income before taxes	25
Income taxes (20%)	5
Net income	$ 20

The Edge Company Inc.
Pro Forma Statement of Financial Position
as of December 31, 1987
($000 omitted)

Assets
Cash*		$ 50
Accounts receivable (15% of sales)		315
Inventory (20% of variable costs)		315
Plant and equipment	$2,000	
Accumulated depreciation	(100)	1,900
Total assets		$2,580

Liabilities and Equities
Accounts payable (maximum allowed)	$ 100
Current portion of long-term debt	90
Long-term debt ($1,610 - 90)	1,520
Common stock (no par value)	850
Retained earnings	20
Total liabilities and equities	$2,580

*See supporting calculations

B. The maximum amount of sales that Edge Company can generate during 1988 can be derived by developing a formula for the change in the cash balance in terms of sales as follows:

Beginning cash - Ending cash = Net income + Depreciation + Δ Accounts payable + Δ Inventory + Δ Accounts receivable - Loan payment

where net income, inventory change and accounts receivable change can be defined in terms of sales as follow.

$$\text{Net income} = \text{C/M rate} \times \text{S} - \text{Tax rate} \times \text{C/M rate} \times \text{S} - \text{Fixed cash expense}$$

$$= .25 \text{ S} - .20(.25)\text{S} - 400$$

$$= .20\text{S} - 400$$

$$\text{Inventory} = \text{Opening balance} - \text{Closing balance}$$

$$= 300 - .20(.75)\text{S}$$

$$= 300* - .15\text{S}$$

Accounts
receivable = Opening balance - Closing balance

= 300* - .15S

*1987 sales of $2,000,000 yields balances of $300,000 for both inventory (.20 × .75 × $2,000,000) and accounts receivable (.15 × $2,000,000)

Assuming Jack Stern will maintain the objective of keeping the cash balance at no less than $50,000, substitution can be made as follows ($000 omitted).

$50 - 60 = .20S - $400 + $100 + 0 + (300 - .15S) + (300 - .15S) - $90

- $10 = - .10S + $210

.10S = $220

S = $2,200

The maximum amount that Edge Company's sales could increase in 1988 and still maintain Stern's objectives is

$2,200,000 - 2,000,000 = $200,000

Supporting Calculations

Pro Forma Cash Flow Statement
($000 omitted)

Beginning cash			$450
Sources of cash from operations			
Sales		$2,100	
Less			
Variable costs	$1,575		
Fixed costs excluding depreciation (500-100)	400		
Income taxes	5	1,980	
Sources from operations			120
Other sources of cash			
Increase in accounts payable			100
Cash available			670
Applications of cash			
Increase in inventory		$ 215	
Increase in accounts receivable		315	
Payment of loan		90	620
Ending cash			$ 50

Stratford Corporation
Statement of Income by Geographic Area
For the Fiscal Year Ended April 30, 1987

11. A.

	Geographic Areas				
	United States	Canada	Europe	Unallocated	Total
Sales in units[1]					
Pharmaceutical	64,000	16,000	80,000		160,000
Sports	72,000	72,000	36,000		180,000
Appliances	32,000	32,000	96,000		160,000
Total unit sales	168,000	120,000	212,000		500,000
Revenue[2]					
Pharmaceutical	$ 512,000	$ 128,000	$ 640,000		$1,280,000
Sports	1,440,000	1,440,000	720,000		3,600,000
Appliances	480,000	480,000	1,440,000		2,400,000
Total revenue	$2,432,000	$2,048,000	$2,800,000		$7,280,000
Variable costs[3]					
Pharmaceutical	$ 384,000	$ 96,000	$ 480,000		$ 960,000
Sports	864,000	864,000	432,000		2,160,000
Appliances	336,000	336,000	1,008,000		1,680,000
Total variable costs	$1,584,000	$1,296,000	$1,920,000		$4,800,000
Contribution margin	$ 848,000	$ 752,000	$ 880,000		$2,480,000
Fixed Costs					
Factory overhead[4]	$ 165,000	$ 135,000	$ 200,000		$ 500,000
Depreciation[5]	134,400	96,000	169,600		400,000
G&A/Selling expense	60,000	100,000	250,000	$ 750,000	1,160,000
Total fixed costs	$ 359,400	$ 331,000	$ 619,600	$ 750,000	$2,060,000
Operating Income (loss)	$ 488,600	$ 421,000	$ 260,400	$ (750,000)	$ 420,000

Supporting Calculations

[1]Sales in Units

	Total Units	× % of Sales	= Units Sold
United States			
Pharmaceutical	160,000	.40	64,000
Sports	180,000	.40	72,000
Appliances	160,000	.20	32,000
Canada			
Pharmaceutical	160,000	.10	16,000
Sports	180,000	.40	72,000
Appliances	160,000	.20	32,000
Europe			
Pharmaceutical	160,000	.50	80,000
Sports	180,000	.20	36,000
Appliances	160,000	.60	96,000

[2]Revenue

	Units Sold	Unit Price	Revenue
United States			
Pharmaceutical	64,000	$ 8.00	$ 512,000
Sports	72,000	20.00	1,440,000
Appliances	32,000	15.00	480,000
Canada			
Pharmaceutical	16,000	8.00	128,000
Sports	72,000	20.00	1,440,000
Appliances	32,000	15.00	480,000
Europe			
Pharmaceutical	80,000	8.00	640,000
Sports	36,000	20.00	720,000
Appliances	96,000	15.00	1,440,000

[3]Variable Costs

	Units Sold (1)	Variable Mfg Cost/Unit (2)	Variable Selling Cost/Unit (3)	Total Variable Cost (1)×[(2)+(3)]
United States				
Pharmaceutical	64,000	$ 4.00	$ 2.00	$ 384,000
Sports	72,000	9.50	2.50	864,000
Appliances	32,000	8.25	2.25	336,000
Canada				
Pharmaceutical	16,000	4.00	2.00	96,000
Sports	72,000	9.50	2.50	864,000
Appliances	32,000	8.25	2.25	336,000
Europe				
Pharmaceutical	80,000	4.00	2.00	480,000
Sports	36,000	9.50	2.50	432,000
Appliances	96,000	8.25	2.25	1,008,000

[4]Factory overhead

	Total Factory Overhead	Area Variable Costs	Proportion of Total	Allocated Factory Cost
United States	$500,000	$1,584,000	33%	$165,000
Canada	500,000	1,296,000	27%	$135,000
Europe	500,000	1,920,000	40%	$200,000
		$4,800,000		$500,000

[5]Depreciation expense

	Total Depreciation	Area Units Sold	Proportion of Total	Allocated Depreciation
United States	$400,000	168,000	33.6%	$134,400
Canada	400,000	120,000	24.0	96,000
Europe	400,000	212,000	42.4	169,600
		500,000		$400,000

B. Areas where Stratford Corporation should focus its attention in order to improve corporate profitability include the following.

• The income statement by product line shows that the pharmaceutical product line may not be profitable. The pharmaceutical product line does have a positive contribution. However, the fixed costs assigned to the product line result in a loss. Stratford should investigate:

— the possibility of increasing the selling price of these products.

— cutting variable costs associated with this product line.

— discontinuing the manufacture of pharmaceuticals and concentrating on the other product lines that are more profitable.

• The income statement by geographic area shows that the European market is the least profitable sales area. In order to improve the profit margin in the European market, Stratford should

— investigate the selling and administrative expenses in this area as they are considerably higher than those in other areas.

— consider increasing the sales of product lines other than pharmaceuticals as this product line makes the smallest contribution to profit.

• Stratford should review the unallocated expenses in an attempt to reduce these costs and improve overall profitability.

Chapter 6

Standard Costs and Variance Analysis

Grant W. Newton

The use of actual costs as a management tool has many weaknesses, especially in providing a standard against which performance can be measured. Costs can be compared with those of previous periods, but this information is of questionable value since it is unknown if previous periods' costs were too high, too low, or reasonable relative to efficiency standards. What is needed is some target value—a standard—to which these costs can be related. Even if we found that prior periods' operations were efficient, current costs may reflect changes in technology, or may reflect other factors and thus, the two still would not be comparable. Budgeted costs are performance evaluation targets, but they may differ from standard costs. The distinction between budgeted and standard costs lies mainly in how such targets are estimated. **Standard costs** are targeted costs usually based on engineering studies of efficient labor and material usage. **Budgeted costs** are target costs established by a variety of methods, such as expenditure allowances established by top management.

To manage and control almost any business effectively, advanced indications of costs are required. Management needs predetermined standard or budgeted costs to plan future operations, control costs, evaluate performance, and price products. Whether the predetermined costs are a mental guess by an individual manager, a formal estimate used to compare with actual results at some future date, or complete standards incorporated into the records, there is general agreement that advance cost information is desirable, if not essential, to successful business management.[1]

---

1. National Association of Accountants, *Standard Costs and Variance Analysis* (New York: Institute of Management Accountants, 1974), p. 2.

Types of Standards

Since the tightness of the standards may influence the extent to which employees are motivated, this factor must be carefully considered in establishing standard times, quantities, and costs. Standards are frequently classified in four ways according to how tight they are:

1. Basic standards These standards do not change over time, and the efficiency of operations is measured by trends. This type is not used frequently.

2. Theoretical or ideal standards These minimum standards are based on the best performance possible under existing operating conditions and with existing equipment.

3. Currently attainable standards Under these standards, some allowance is made for selected types of losses, idle time, and machine breakdowns to the extent that management considers them reasonable. To meet these standards, however, operations must be efficient. They are within the accomplishment range of the worker, yet difficult enough that—when met—the worker feels as though something of value has been accomplished.

4. Average past performance standards What has been done in the past serves as the basis for these standards. They allow for very little improvement and, as a result, are frequently not effective in motivating employees to improve performance. Standards established this way are often referred to as estimated costs since they are developed without any scientific effort.

The most frequently used standards are those designated as "currently attainable." They provide goals the employees can, with effort, attain. Thus, while being acceptable for motivating employees, they can also be used for product costing and budgeting purposes.

Uses of Standard Costs

As noticed above, standard costs have certain advantages over historical costs. Several of these major benefits are summarized here.

1. Cost control Procedures for cost control are designed to produce the product at the specified quality standards with the lowest possible cost under existing operating conditions. To have an effective cost control system, there is a need for some basic guide or standard that specifies how the job is to be done and how much it should cost. As the products are being manufactured, comparisons are made between the actual costs and the predetermined standard. When discrepancies are noticed, some type of corrective action may be required. In addition, standards may help develop a cost-conscious attitude on the part of managers. When individuals responsible for certain costs receive feedback information about the status of the cost of their operation and its relationship to a basic guide, they do tend to become more cost-conscious.

2. Establishing budgets Standard costs are a source of information for estimating raw material, labor, and overhead requirements. If the standards are currently attainable, it would appear that the standard cost and the budgeted costs would be the same. In practice, however, the term **budget** is often used to refer to aggregate costs while **standard** is a unit concept. If standards are not currently attainable, it may be necessary to budget a variance for profit planning purposes. When a normal volume level is used for calculating the fixed overhead cost rate, any expected, significant volume variance should be budgeted.

3. Inventory costing Generally accepted accounting principles for external reporting require that historical actual costs be used for inventory purposes in most instances. However, currently attainable standards may be more desirable for inventory purposes under certain conditions. If unfavorable variances represent waste and other types of inefficiencies, it may be appropriate to charge them against income in the period incurred rather than allocate them. Any favorable variances due to exceptional efficiencies would be treated in a consistent manner. If currently attainable standards are not used and the variances are significant, they are normally prorated among costs of goods sold, finished goods, and work-in-process inventories.

4. Product pricing The National Association of Accountants (NAA), in one of its research studies, suggests that standard costs are more easily adjusted and projected into the future than are past actual costs for the following reasons:

a. Standard costs are based upon a carefully determined usage of material and labor and thus are free from distortions caused by excess spoilage, reoperations, and so on. To the extent that these inefficiencies are avoidable by competitors, they are probably not recoverable from the selling price.

b. Standards can easily be adjusted to reflect changes in materials and labor prices.

c. Standard overhead rates based on a normal activity level are an acceptable basis for pricing that provides for the full recovery of overhead costs in the long run.

d. Standard costs for marketing activities can easily be assigned to the product, although not entered in the inventory records.[2]

5. Motivating employees A standard cost developed jointly by management and the individual responsible for the costs, if accepted by the individual as her or his personal goal, can be a motivating influence for the employee and result in higher productivity. See Chapter 8 for a discussion of the behavioral aspects of standard costs.

6. Reducing paperwork costs Record keeping costs can be reduced since the inventory ledger is kept only in terms of quantity. The use of standards can result in additional savings in both the creation and analysis of reports. Less time is required to prepare budgets and production reports when standard costs are used. Deviations from standard are highlighted in the reports, making analysis both easier and faster.

Standard Cost Problem

Example 6-1 contains the results of one period's operations for the Connecticut Company. The facts in the problem will be used throughout our discussion of standard costs. Read the problem and become familiar with its contents.

Direct Materials

The responsibility for direct materials is split between the purchasing and production managers. The purchasing manager has the responsibility of acquiring the proper quantity of raw materials at the time needed and at the correct price. The production manager must see that the materials are used efficiently. It is important that each manager be responsible for only the factors over which he or she has control. Thus, the production manager should not be responsible for the variances in price and other activities of the purchasing department. The use of price and quantity standards help in assigning responsibility to the individual in a position to exercise control over the costs.

---

2. *Ibid.*, p. 18.

Price Standards

Materials price standards are usually based on either the expected price during the period the standards are in effect or on the price existing at the time the standards were established. The purchasing department, in conjunction with the cost accounting department, establishes the standards.

While it is true that the prices are mostly influenced by activities, there are several ways in which the purchasing department can exert some control over the price. For example, purchases can be made in large quantities to obtain discounts, the least costly mode of transportation can be selected, and quotations from several suppliers can be obtained.

Usage Standards

The materials quantity or usage standards are usually based on engineering studies. The standards specify the kind of material to be used as well as the quantities needed. The product specifications allow for an acceptable amount of spoilage, waste, evaporation, and so on. In addition to the engineering studies, test runs under controlled conditions and past experience may also be considered in establishing quantity standards. These standards are normally established by the department responsible for product design, with the assistance of the production and cost accounting departments. The standards must be acceptable to the production department if members of this department are going to use them as realistic goals.

Materials Price Variance

A **price variance** occurs if the actual price differs from the established standard price. In our Connecticut Company example the price variance is:

Actual quantity purchased X actual price:

$$2,200 \times \$2.10 = \$4,620$$

Actual quantity purchased X standard price:

$$2,200 \times \$2.00 = 4,400$$

Total purchase price variance $ 220 UF

Notice that the variance is simply the difference between the actual price and the standard price times the actual quantity. The quantity used in this illustration is the quantity purchased—not the quantity requisitioned. Thus, the price variance is isolated at the time the materials are purchased. Another alternative is to delay the calculation until the materials are issued to production. For control purposes, however, it is much better to isolate the variance at the time of purchase so that if corrective action is necessary it will be undertaken immediately. The variance can be isolated at the time of issuance for situations where the materials price is fairly stable and the amount of inventories carried is very low. If isolated at the time of purchase, the variance is known as a **purchase price variance**, otherwise, it is simply referred to as a **price variance**.

Example 6-1

The Connecticut Company manufactures a basic product that is used by several electronic firms. The standard costs for one unit are summarized below:

Standard cost per unit:

Materials	2 units @ $2.00	$4.00
Labor	1/2 unit @ $4.00	2.00
Variable overhead		1.00
Fixed overhead		2.00
Total standard cost per unit		**$9.00**

Overhead is correlated with direct labor hours. Additional information follows:

Expected actual output	1,000 units
Schedule production	925 units
Actual units manufactured	900
Practical capacity	1,500 units

Actual costs:

Material purchased	2,200 units @ $2.10	$4,620
Labor	440 hours @ $4.10	1,804
Variable overhead		950
Fixed costs		2,100
Units of material used		2,000

Price variances are caused by unexpected changes in the price of raw materials; by purchasing a different grade; by purchasing in larger or smaller quantities than normal; by purchasing goods from a different location than usual, resulting in a different transportation cost; by rush orders; or other-related causes.

Materials Usage Variance

The **materials usage variance**—also referred to as a **quantity variance**—is determined by comparing the actual quantity used at the standard price with the quantity that should have been used (for the actual quantity produced) at the standard price. The quantity variance for the Connecticut Company is:

Actual quantity X standard price:

$$2,000 \times \$2.00 = \$4,000$$

Standard quantity allowed X standard price:

$$1,800 \times \$2.00 = 3,600$$

Materials usage variance $ 400 UF

An important point to remember in calculating the quantity variance is that the standard quantity allowed is the actual units produced times the standard quantity allowed per unit, so this figure may be different from the budgeted production for the period. Note that the expected output was 1,000 units, but only 900 units were produced. Thus, the standard allowed is 1,800 (900 X 2) units of materials times the standard price of $2.

There are many types of inefficiencies, or efficiencies in the case of a favorable variance, that can cause a usage variance. Among the causes for favorable variances are: new employees or employees not familiar with the process to which they are assigned, the use of a poor quality of materials, machine breakdowns, fatigue, pressure to get the rush job completed, or other related human factors that cause employees not to work as efficiently as normal. Notice that the cause may not be under the control of the production department; an unfavorable variance caused by the use of an inferior grade of materials that was ordered in error is the responsibility of the purchasing department.

General Ledger Entries

There are two methods for recording materials purchases. One is to isolate the variance at the time of purchase; the other is to record it at the time of issuance. Using the Connecticut Company example, each method is illustrated below:

Method 1 — Isolate price variance at time of purchase

Materials (actual quantity purchased X standard price)	4,400	
Materials purchase price variance	220	
Accounts payable (actual quantity purchased X actual price)		4,620

To record direct materials purchased.

Work-in-process (standard quantity X standard price)	3,600	
Materials usage variance	400	
Materials (actual quantity issued X standard price)		4,000

To record the issuance of direct materials.

Method 2 — Isolate price variance at time of issuance

Materials (actual quantity purchased X actual price)	4,620	
Accounts payable (actual quantity purchased X actual price)		4,620

Work-in-process (standard quantity X standard price)	3,600	
Materials price variance	200	
Materials usage variance	400	
Materials (actual quantity issued X actual price)		4,200

The materials price variance under method 2 is the actual quantity issued (2,000) times the difference in the actual price ($2.10) and standard price ($2.00). Under method 1, the materials are recorded at standard in the materials accounts; under method 2 they are recorded at actual costs. The $20 difference in the two price variances is due to the increase in inventory of 200 units times the $.10 price variance per unit.

Method 1 is better for control purposes. It also has the advantage of simplifying the inventory accounting process since all goods are at standard price.

There are two procedures for isolating the materials usage variance. Under one method, the variance is determined as excess materials are requisitioned even though the goods are still in process; under the other procedure the variance is isolated after the goods are completed. Although it is generally best to isolate the variance as soon as possible for control purposes, the nature of some processes is such that the quantity variance cannot be determined until the actual goods produced for a given time period are counted and the in-process inventory is determined. Under these conditions, the second method must be used.

Method 1—Isolate quantity variance at time of excess usage

Work-in-process (standard quantity X standard price)	3,600	
Materials usage variance	400	
Materials (actual quantity X standard price)		4,000

To record issuance of materials.

Method 2—Isolate quantity variance after goods completed

Work-in-process (actual quantity X standard price)	4,000	
Materials (actual quantity X standard price)		4,000
Finished Goods (standard quantity X standard price)	3,600	
Materials usage variance	400	
Work-in-process		4,000

Note that under method 2 the work-in-process account contains actual quantities rather than the standard quantities used in method 1. The same procedures apply in accounting for the labor efficiency variance. Also, notice that the variances under method 1 and method 2 are the same.

In working a problem that may appear on the CMA examination, the variances should be isolated as soon as possible according to the nature of the problem, unless the instructions to the problem require otherwise. Thus, it is best to use method 1 for the materials price variance and method 1 for quantity variances (material usage and labor efficiency) if possible.

Direct Labor Standards

Direct Labor Rate Standards

Rates for labor are determined by union negotiations or by the prevailing rate in the area where the company is located. As with materials prices, management does normally have some control over the rate. Examples of variances for which management should be held accountable include using a worker with the wrong rate for a particular job or using day rate when workers should be on incentive piece rates.

The rate standards are usually changed as wage rates change. These rates are normally set by the division of the business that has the information from which standards are developed. Frequently, this is the cost accounting department.

Labor Efficiency Standards

A widely used method for establishing performance standards for labor is time and motion studies. In addition, other factors should be taken into consideration such as work layout, condition of equipment, availability of materials, nature of operating instructions, and assistance in materials handling. Past performance and the opinion of an experienced supervisor are also frequently used in setting time standards.

Standards for time are normally established by the methods engineer working with the production department. Standards are established for each operation and are then combined to give the standard for a given product. To be effective as a motivating factor, the standards must be perceived as reasonable and attainable by the workers in the production department. Often, if workers have some input in the standards setting process, they are more willing to accept them as personal goals.

Normally the standards should make some allowance for fatigue, poor quality of materials, and some personal time for workers. Provision is often made for rework costs and breakdowns, along with other factors that cause idle time in the overhead budget; when these types of costs are incurred, they are charged against the overhead account.

Labor Rate Variance

The labor rate variance—similar to the materials price variance—is the difference between the actual labor rate and the standard rate times the actual hours worked. In our example the rate variance is as follows:

Actual hours worked × actual rate:

$$440 \times \$4.10 = \$1,804$$

Actual hours worked × standard rate:

$$440 \times \$4.00 = 1,760$$

Labor rate variance $\quad\quad\quad\quad\quad\quad$ \$ 44 UF

Labor rate variances are typically caused by changes in the wage rates and by using the incorrect mix of labor. Assigning employees to an operation where they have more training and experience than the job requires will result in an unfavorable wage rate variance because they will receive more per hour than the standard allows.

Labor Efficiency Variance

The efficiency variance for the Connecticut Company is favorable:

Actual hours worked × standard rate:

$$440 \times \$4.00 = \$1,760$$

Standard hours allowed × standard rate:

$$450 \times \$4.00 = 1,800$$

Labor efficiency variance $\quad\quad\quad\quad$ \$ 40 F

The standard hours allowed was determined by multiplying the labor standard of one-half hour per unit times the actual units produced ($\frac{1}{2} \times 900 = 450$).

Using a lesser grade of material than the standard, and fatigue, carelessness or other inefficiencies by workers all cause unfavorable labor efficiency variances.

Format for Variance Analysis

There are many short-cut techniques available for variance analysis; however, one of the most useful is the columnar technique suggested by Horngren.[3] The material and labor variances for the Connecticut Company, using this procedure, are shown in Exhibit 6-1. This method is easy to learn and a very valuable technique for solving standard cost problems.

Factory Overhead Analysis

As discussed in Chapter 4, because of the nature of fixed costs, it is necessary to break the overhead costs into two parts—fixed and variable—in order to estimate them accurately for any given output level. Here, the variable portion of overhead cost will be analyzed separately from the fixed, and then they will be combined and analyzed.

Variable Overhead Costs

The variable overhead cost fluctuates proportionally with changes in activity levels. The variable rate is developed after analyzing the past behavior patterns of the overhead costs and by considering expected changes in those costs. This rate is correlated with an activity variable such as direct labor hours, direct labor costs, machine hours, materials costs, or units produced. If the costs are based on an input activity, two variable overhead variances can be calculated: spending and efficiency. If the variable overhead costs are correlated with some measure of outputs (for example, units, pounds and so on), then only a budget variance can be determined.

The **spending variance** is the difference between the actual costs incurred and the budgeted overhead costs based on an input activity. This variance is the responsibility of the department manager. These expenses should be in line with the costs budgeted, based on the direct labor hours worked. For the Connecticut Company example the variable spending variance is:

3. Charles T. Horngren, et al. *Cost Accounting: A Managerial Emphasis* (Englewood Cliffs, N.J.: Prentice-Hall, 1994), p. 279.

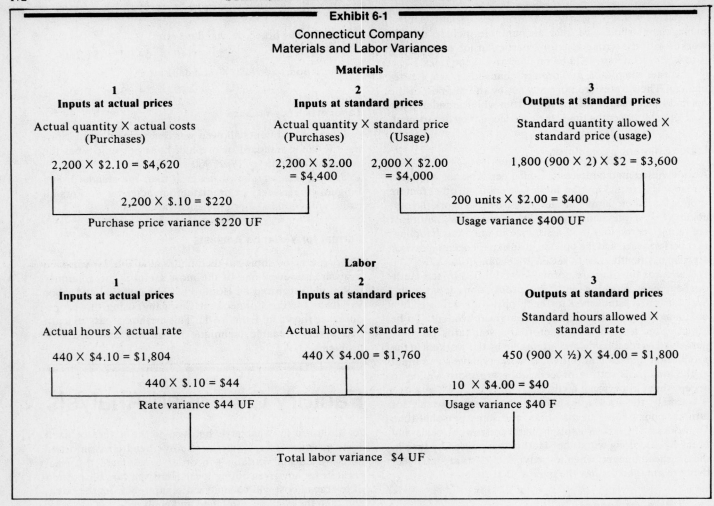

Exhibit 6-1

Connecticut Company
Materials and Labor Variances

Materials

1	2	3
Inputs at actual prices	**Inputs at standard prices**	**Outputs at standard prices**
Actual quantity × actual costs (Purchases)	Actual quantity × standard price (Purchases) (Usage)	Standard quantity allowed × standard price (usage)
2,200 × $2.10 = $4,620	2,200 × $2.00 = $4,400 2,000 × $2.00 = $4,000	1,800 (900 × 2) × $2 = $3,600

2,200 × $.10 = $220

Purchase price variance $220 UF

200 units × $2.00 = $400

Usage variance $400 UF

Labor

1	2	3
Inputs at actual prices	**Inputs at standard prices**	**Outputs at standard prices**
Actual hours × actual rate	Actual hours × standard rate	Standard hours allowed × standard rate
440 × $4.10 = $1,804	440 × $4.00 = $1,760	450 (900 × ½) × $4.00 = $1,800

440 × $.10 = $44

Rate variance $44 UF

10 × $4.00 = $40

Usage variance $40 F

Total labor variance $4 UF

Actual variable costs	$950
Budgeted cost based on actual hours worked (440 × $2)	880
Variable spending variance	$ 70 UF

The spending variance is caused by price changes in indirect labor, supplies, and other items that make up the total variable overhead. In addition, the variance can be caused by the inefficient use of overhead items or can simply be due to a poor budget estimate. An inherent difficulty is the fact that many overhead costs are incurred at various intervals not necessarily related to the chosen activity (for example, direct labor hours) being used to calculate the rate.

The **efficiency variance** is the difference between the budgeted variable overhead cost based on actual hours and the costs based on standard hours allowed. Whenever actual hours differ from the standard hours allowed, there is a variable overhead efficiency variance. Whether the deviation is favorable or unfavorable, the responsibility for this variance lies with the manager in charge of labor for the period. Input bases other than direct labor hours can also be used to

determine the efficiency variance. The efficiency variance for the Connecticut Company is $20 favorable:

Budgeted cost based on actual hours worked	$880
Budgeted cost based on standard hours allowed (450 × $2)	900
Total efficiency variance	$ 20 F

The variances are illustrated in columnar form in Exhibit 6-2. Note that the total budget variance of $50 unfavorable is the only variance that would be calculated if the variable overhead were correlated only with units produced.

Fixed Overhead

The budgeted fixed overhead costs do not change as the activity level changes within a given range. The two variances normally determined in fixed overhead costs analysis are a budget and a volume variance. The **budget** or **spending variance** is the difference between the actual fixed overhead costs and the budgeted fixed costs. The budgeted cost for the Connecticut Company was $2,000, which resulted in the following variance:

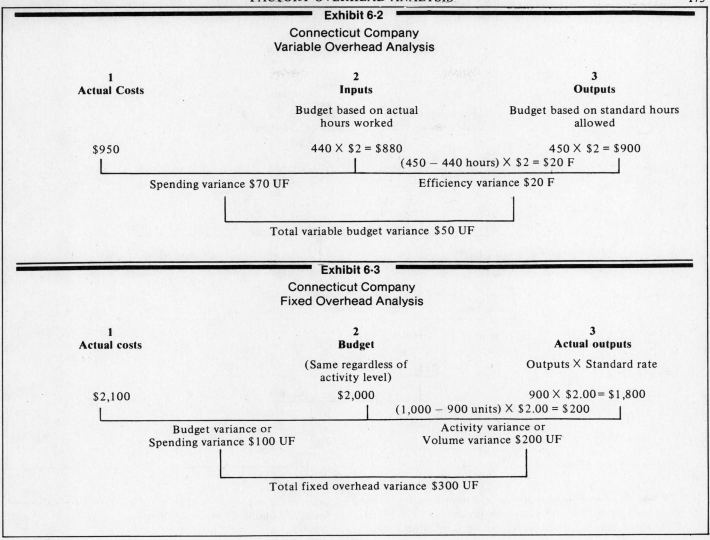

Exhibit 6-2

Connecticut Company
Variable Overhead Analysis

1 **Actual Costs**	**2** **Inputs**	**3** **Outputs**
	Budget based on actual hours worked	Budget based on standard hours allowed
$950	440 × $2 = $880	450 × $2 = $900

(450 − 440 hours) × $2 = $20 F

Spending variance $70 UF   Efficiency variance $20 F

Total variable budget variance $50 UF

Exhibit 6-3

Connecticut Company
Fixed Overhead Analysis

1 **Actual costs**	**2** **Budget**	**3** **Actual outputs**
	(Same regardless of activity level)	Outputs × Standard rate
$2,100	$2,000	900 × $2.00 = $1,800

(1,000 − 900 units) × $2.00 = $200

Budget variance or   Activity variance or
Spending variance $100 UF   Volume variance $200 UF

Total fixed overhead variance $300 UF

Actual budgeted fixed costs	$2,100
Budgeted fixed costs	2,000
Budget variance	$ 100 UF

The variance of $100 is the responsibility of the individual who has control over the items that make up the total budgeted fixed costs. Although the variance involves fixed costs, it is still controllable at some level in the organization.

Activity Level For direct materials, direct labor, and variable overhead, the level of activity used in establishing the standard is not too critical as long as operations are within a reasonable range; however, this is not true for fixed overhead. Two activity levels are frequently used: expected annual and normal. The **expected annual level** is simply the activity level anticipated for the next year while the **normal level** represents the average output expected over a long enough time period to incorporate sales trends. In order to use the normal approach, management must be able to forecast sales with a reasonable degree of accuracy for a

period longer than one year. Since this is not an easy task for many businesses, the expected annual output is the more frequently used activity level.

It would appear that volume variances resulting from the use of the normal approach should be carried forward in the balance sheet at year end. The accounting profession and the Internal Revenue Service, however, have not allowed this. Under normal and expected annual output, the variance is frequently charged to cost of goods sold, as described later. While this may appear to make the two methods, in the final analysis, result in the same net income per year, it does not, since the amount of fixed costs in inventory is different.

Volume Variance A **volume variance** occurs when there is a difference between the planned and actual production levels and the fixed costs are applied to the units as they are produced. Thus, a process that uses a direct cost system does not have a volume variance. The volume variance is also referred to as **capacity**, **idle capacity**, or **denominator variance**.

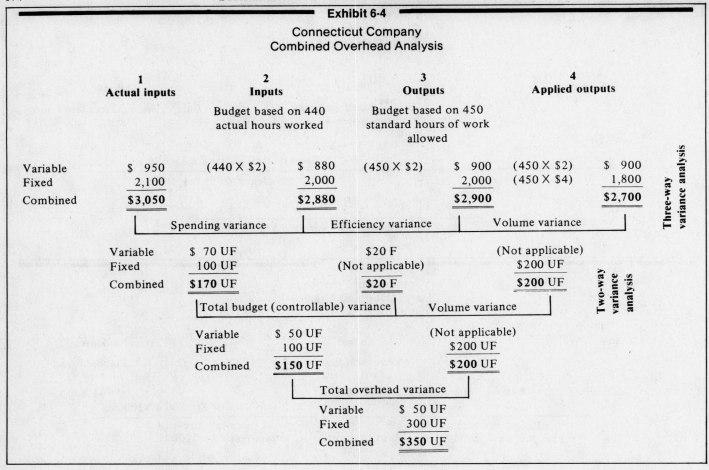

The fixed overhead cost rate is determined by dividing the budgeted fixed costs by the planned activity level—expected actual for the next year or normal output. The overhead rate may be stated in terms of some standard input for a desired output or simply in terms of units of output. In the Connecticut Company example, which uses the expected annual output approach, the rate is:

$$\frac{\text{Budgeted fixed costs, \$2,000}}{\text{Expected output, 1,000 units}} = \$2 \text{ per unit}$$

or

$$\frac{\text{Budgeted fixed costs, \$2,000}}{\text{Standard hours allowed for expected output, 500 hours}}$$

$$= \$4 \text{ per standard hour allowed}$$

The volume variance is $200 unfavorable:

Budgeted fixed costs	$2,000
Applied fixed costs (900 units × $2)	1,800
Volume variance	$ 200 UF

Note that the volume variance is the difference between the expected output of 1,000 units and the actual output of 900 units times the standard rate of $2 per unit (1,000 − 900 × $2 = $200) or the difference between the standard hours

allowed for expected output and the standard hours allowed for actual output times the standard rate per hour (500 − 450 × $4 = $200).

The volume variance is the amount of over- or under-absorbed fixed overhead cost. It is known as the uncontrollable variance and is simply caused by the fact that the actual output does not equal the planned output. If it had been known in advance that only 900 units would be produced, this volume level would have been used in determining the overhead rate and there would have been no volume variance. If the actual volume level is less than planned, the variance will be unfavorable and if the level is greater, the variance will be favorable.

Exhibit 6-3 presents the fixed overhead analysis in columnar form.

Combined Analysis

If the actual cost in a given problem is not broken down into its fixed and variable components, it will be necessary to use the combined analysis. The Connecticut Company overhead variances are analyzed in Exhibit 6-4. Note that the budgeted fixed cost from column 2 of Exhibit 6-3 appears in both the input and output columns (2 and 3) of Exhibit 6-4, and that the budget variable overhead cost based on standard hours allowed in column 3 of Exhibit 6-2 is also the applied cost (column 4 of Exhibit 6-4). Thus, there is no volume variance for variable costs.

When only budget (controllable) and volume are calculated, the method is referred to as the "two-variance method." If the budget variance is broken down into two components, spending and efficiency, these, along with the volume variance, provide the "three-variance analysis."

General Ledger Entries

The entries to record the overhead cost incurred and applied for the Connecticut Company would be:

Factory overhead control	3,050	
Various credits		3,050

To record actual cost incurred:

Work-in-process	2,700	
Factory overhead applied		2,700

To record the applied overhead for 900 units produced (450 standard hours allowed $\times$ variable cost rate of $2 + fixed cost rate of $4).

The general ledger procedures used in practice are not all the same. In processes where the actual yield from a given input is not known until the end of the period, when the work-in-process inventory is examined, the overhead may be applied on the basis of actual hours worked. Company policy regarding the point in time when the variances are isolated and the way in which they are broken down influences the way in which the transactions are recorded.

If the Connecticut Company elects to enter the overhead variances in the accounts, the following entry would be made:

Factory overhead applied	2,700	
Factory overhead volume variance	200	
Factory overhead spending variance	170	
Factory overhead efficiency variance		20
Factory overhead control		3,050

To isolate overhead variances in accounts.

Analyzing the Variance Account

One of the important objectives of a standard cost system is to provide a way to establish responsibility and exercise control over costs. At times, it is difficult to accomplish this objective. It was noted earlier that the purchasing manager has the responsibility for acquiring the quality of raw materials and the production manager for using the materials efficiently. It is difficult, however, to establish the exact responsibility as to the timing of the purchase and the assignment of the responsibility for inventory holding costs.

In order for the variance to provide a basis for corrective action, it must be analyzed in terms of responsibility. Several parts of previous CMA problems dealt with the assignment of responsibility in selected areas. As you work through the problems at the end of the chapter, note any similar situations.

Calculating a total variance and then subdividing it into its three or four parts is not adequate for effective control. Each item that makes up the total actual and budgeted costs must be analyzed. Even a total variance of zero should be examined since there could be counterbalancing variances in the account. If this is known, corrective action will, hopefully, be taken.

The flexible budget for the Connecticut Company appears in Exhibit 6-5. Based on this budget an analysis of overhead is presented in Exhibit 6-6. Note that the variable variance is broken down into its two components, spending and efficiency. The only way to determine why the actual costs do not agree with the flexible budget is to investigate each item in the overhead budget where there is a material variance. An explanation column could be added to the schedule in Exhibit 6-6 to identify the cause for each of these variances.

Variance analysis is an important part of the control process in that it alerts the user to the existence of areas where further investigation is needed.

Illustrative Problem

Example 6-2 is a good problem to work to check your understanding of standard cost accounting. Study the problem and prepare a schedule analyzing the variances. Note that the number of units produced during December was 1,200, as given along with the actual overhead. The overhead rates are $.75 for fixed and $1.50 for variable. The rates can be determined by analyzing the flexible budget information:

Total cost at	5,200 hours	$10,800
Total cost at	4,000 hours	9,000
Total difference	1,200 hours	$ 1,800

$$\text{Variable cost rate} = \frac{\text{Change in total cost}}{\text{Change in volume}}$$

$$= \frac{\$1,800}{1,200 \text{ hours}} = \$1.50 \text{ per hour}$$

Total cost at	4,000 hours	$9,000
Variable costs	4,000 hours $\times$ $1.50	6,000
Total fixed cost		$3,000

$$\text{Fixed cost rate} = \frac{\$3,000}{4,000 \text{ hours}} = \$.75 \text{ per hour}$$

The overhead rates per hour could also have been determined by dividing the cost per unit of $3 fixed and $6 variable by the four hours required to produce one unit.

Exhibit 6-7 presents the variance analysis for this CPA problem.

Exhibit 6-5

Connecticut Company
Flexible Budget
Machining Department

					Variable cost/hour
Units	800	900	1,000	1,100	—
Standard hours allowed	400	450	500	550	—
Variable overhead					
Indirect labor	$ 480	$ 540	$ 600	$ 660	$1.20
Clerical costs	80	90	100	110	.20
Maintenance	160	180	200	220	.40
Supplies	80	90	100	110	.20
Total variable	$ 800	$ 900	$1,000	$1,100	$2.00
Fixed costs					
Supervision	800	800	800	800	
Property taxes	200	200	200	200	
Insurance	100	100	100	100	
Depreciation	900	900	900	900	
Total fixed	2,000	2,000	2,000	2,000	
Total overhead costs	$2,800	$2,900	$3,000	$3,000	

Exhibit 6-6

Connecticut Company
Detailed Analysis of Overhead

	(1) Actual	(2) Budget based on actual hours worked	(3) Budget based on standard hours worked	(4) Spending variance (1) – (2)	(5) Efficiency variance (2) – (3)	(6) Total budget variance
Variable costs						
Indirect labor	$ 580	$ 528	$ 540	$52 UF	$12 F	$ 40 UF
Clerical costs	80	88	90	8 F	2 F	10 F
Maintenance	165	176	180	11 F	4 F	15 F
Supplies	125	88	90	37 UF	2 F	35 UF
Total variable costs	950	880	900	$70 UF	$20 F	50 UF
Fixed costs						
Supervision	880	800	800			80 UF
Property taxes	230	200	200			30 UF
Insurance	90	100	100			10 F
Depreciation	900	900	900			—
Total fixed costs	2,100	2,000	2,000			100 UF
Total overhead costs	$3,050	$2,880	$2,900			$150 UF

Example 6-2

The Jones Furniture Company uses a standard cost system in accounting for its production costs. The standard cost of a unit of furniture follows:

Lumber, 100 feet @ $150 per 1,000 feet		$15.00
Direct labor, 4 hours @ $2.50 per hour		10.00
Manufacturing overhead:		
Fixed (30% of direct labor)	$3.00	
Variable (60% of direct labor)	6.00	9.00
Total unit cost		$34.00

The flexible monthly overhead budget in effect and the actual unit costs for December are shown in the next column.

Required Prepare a schedule which shows an analysis of each element of the total variance from standard cost for the month of December.

Flexible Overhead Budget

Direct labor hours	Estimated overhead
5,200	$10,800
4,800	10,200
4,400	9,600
4,000 (normal capacity)	9,000
3,600	8,400

Cost for December

Lumber used (110 feet @ $120 per 1,000 feet)	$13.20
Direct labor (4¼ hours @ $2.60 per hour)	11.05
Manufacturing overhead ($10,560 ÷ 1,200 units)	8.80
Total actual unit cost	$33.05

Exhibit 6-7

Jones Company
Analysis of Variances

Materials

Actual	Inputs at standard price	Outputs at standard price
[132,000 feet (1,200 units × 110 feet per unit) × $.12 per foot]	(132,000 × $.15 per foot)	[120,000 (1,200 units × 100 feet) × $.15 per foot]
$15,840	$19,800	$18,000

132,000 × $.03 = $3,960 F — Price variance

12,000 × $.15 = $1,800 UF — Usage variance

Labor

Actual	Inputs at standard price	Outputs at standard price
[5,100 hours (1,200 units × 4¼) × $2.60 per hour]	(5,100 hours × $2.50 per hour)	[4,800 hours (1,200 units × 4) × $2.50 per hour]
$13,260	$12,750	$12,000

5,100 × $.10 = $510 UF — Rate variance

300 × $2.50 = $750 UF — Efficiency variance

Overhead

Actual	Budget Based on actual hours	Budget Based on standard hours allowed	Applied
	Var. 5,100 × $1.50 = $ 7,650	4,800 × $1.50 = $ 7,200	(4,800 × $2.25 or 1,200 × $9
	Fixed 3,000	3,000	
$10,560	$10,650	$10,200	$10,800

$90 F — Spending variance

300 × $1.50 = $450 UF — Efficiency variance

(4,800 − 4,000) × $.75 = $600 F — Volume variance

$360 UF — Budget variance

$600 F — Volume variance

$240 F — Total overhead variance

Exhibit 6-8

Connecticut Company
Selected Account Balances
Year Ending December 31, 19X1

Cost of goods sold	$90,000
Raw materials inventory	5,600
Total purchases	56,000
Finished goods inventory	18,000
Work-in-process inventory	12,000
Materials purchase price variance	2,000 UF
Materials usage variance	2,700 UF
Labor rate variance	600 UF
Labor efficiency variance	800 F
Overhead budget variance	1,700 UF
Overhead volume variance	3,000 UF

Disposition of Variances

For interim financial statements, the variances can either be carried forward to the next period or closed into the income of the current period. Variances are carried forward as an adjustment to inventories or as a deferred charge or credit. When net income is adjusted by the amount of the variance, the variances are either added (substracted for net favorable variance) to cost of goods sold or subtracted (added for net favorable variance) directly from net income.

Variances existing at year end are not normally carried forward, but are disposed of in one of three ways: (1) by adjusting net income as described above, (2) by adjusting ending finished goods and work-in-process inventories so that the balances reflect the standards as adjusted at year end and any balance in the net variance account is included in this period's income, or (3) by adjusting inventories and cost of goods sold to reflect the actual costs. If the standards are reasonable and realistic, then the procedure of closing the variance account to net income is in line with the basic objectives of standard costing theory. On the other hand, if for some reason the standards are not reasonable, then they should either be adjusted according to the second alternative, or the variances should be prorated among the work-in-process, finished goods, and cost of goods sold so that these accounts reflect some approximation of the actual costs for the year.

Even if there are large unfavorable variances, it does not necessarily mean that the standards are not reasonable. The variances may be caused by waste or inactivity, which means that they should be written off as losses and part of the variances should not be added to inventories.

To illustrate the procedures for disposing of the variances at year end, selected account balances at year end for the Connecticut Company are presented in Exhibit 6-8. The balances are at standard for all accounts except, of course, the variances.

Under alternative one, where the entire variance is charged against this period's net income, the following entry would be made:

Variance summary	9,200	
Labor efficiency variance	800	
Materials purchase price variance		2,000
Materials usage variance		2,700
Labor rate variance		600
Overhead budget variance		1,700
Overhead volume variance		3,000

To close variances to summary account.

Cost of goods sold	9,200	
Variance summary		9,200

To adjust profits for net unfavorable variance.

The alternate treatment involves closing all of the variances directly to the income summary account.

If the decision is made to prorate the variances among the inventories and the cost of goods sold, the first step is to remove from the materials purchase price variance the portion that should be added to raw materials inventory. The purchase at the standard price for materials were $56,000 and the balance in inventory is $5,600, which is 10 percent of the total purchases for the year. Thus, 10 percent of the price variance of $200 (10 percent × $2,000) should be added to the raw materials inventory. The balance of $1,800 and the other variance of $7,200 for a total of $9,000 should be prorated to cost of goods sold, work-in-process, and finished goods.

Account	Amount	Percent of total amount	Total variance to be allocated	Amount of variance allocated
Cost of goods sold	$ 90,000	75	$9,000	$6,750
Finished goods	18,000	15	9,000	1,350
Work-in-process	12,000	10	9,000	900
Total	$120,000	100		$9,000

The entry to record the adjustment is:

Cost of goods sold	6,750	
Finished goods inventory	1,350	
Work-in-process inventory	900	
Raw materials inventory	200	
Variance summary		9,200

To prorate variances.

In practice, the adjustment to raw materials inventory is frequently not made since the amount involved is, in many cases, immaterial.

Learning Curve

Standards that are at one time correct may become inaccurate due to a learning or familiarity experience. As a worker performs a certain task, productivity increases. The impact of this learning process, which is especially obvious in new products or processes, is predicted by a **learning curve**. The curve was first used during World War II by aircraft manufacturers. Case studies have shown that learning often follows a pattern: as the cumulative number of units manufactured is doubled, the cumulative average time that it takes to make a unit is reduced by a constant percentage. If the rate of reduction is 20 percent, the learning curve is referred to as an 80 percent curve. The learning curve is a power function, and if plotted on double logarithmic paper will appear as a straight line.

Crowningshield and Gorman list several ways in which learning curves can be used:

1. Preparing cost estimates: the seller may use the learning curve in submitting bids; the buyer may use it in evaluating bids if he has reason to believe that the bidder can apply the learning curve; unit costs on repeat orders should be lower.

2. Setting standards and budget allowances; it is easy to see the over-allowances which would result if the learning curve were disregarded, particularly on the early performances.

3. Scheduling labor requirements.

4. Evaluating performances by comparing progress reports with the accomplishments anticipated under the learning curve.

5. Setting incentive wage rates with due consideration for the fact that labor times will normally be reduced as the workman becomes more experienced.[4]

Study Example 6-3. In solving learning curve problems, there are three steps that must be remembered:

1. Double the cumulative quantity.

2. Multiply the cumulative average by the learning curve percentage.

3. Multiply the cumulative average by the cumulative quantity.

Following these steps, part (a) of Exhibit 6-9 is constructed. The results tell us that it will take 32,768 hours to make the modifications for 16 jets. Notice that Venice has already made the modification on 2 jets; therefore, the time required for the next 14 would be 24,768 (32,768 total for 16 − 8,000 required for first two jets). If Venice wanted to modify only 6 jets, the time required would be 12,480 (20,480 − 8,000) hours. The cumulative average represents the average time it takes to modify each jet if the quantity in column one is modified. If 16 are improved, the average is

4. Gerald R. Crowningshield and Kenneth A. Gorman, *Cost Accounting* (Boston: Houghton Mifflin Co., 1974), p. 698.

Example 6-3

The Venice Aircraft Corporation modified two private jets for one of its customers so they would meet the local airport pollution requirements. The costs were:

Materials	$ 30,000
Labor (8,000 hours)	80,000
Variable overhead[a]	25,000
Total costs	$135,000

[a]It is estimated that 80 percent of the overhead varies with labor.

The modifications have worked successfully and Venice expects to redo 14 other jets for three other customers. Venice allows a 40 percent mark-up on costs to cover fixed costs and profits. What price should be established per jet for the modifications with an 80 percent learning curve?

Exhibit 6-9

Venice Corporation
Learning Curve Analysis

Part (a): Learning Curve Effect

(Step 1) Cumulative quantity	(Step 2) Cumulative average hours per jet	(Step 3) Cumulative hours
2	4,000[a]	8,000
4	3,200 (4,000 × .80)	12,800
8	2,560 (3,200 × .80)	20,480
16	2,048 (2,560 × .80)	32,768

[a] 8,000 hours ÷ 2 jets

Part (b): Minimum Bid Price per Jet

Materials cost [14 × ($3,000 ÷ 2)]		$210,000
Labor (32,768 hours − 8,000 hours × $10 per hour[a])		247,680
Variable overhead:		
Part that varies with labor (32,768 hours −8,000 hours × $2.50 per hour[b])	$61,920	
Part that does not vary with labor (5,000 ÷ 2 × 14)	35,000	96,920
Total costs		554,600
Mark-up on cost of 0.40 percent		221,840
Total sales price		$776,440
Sales price per jet $776,440 ÷ 14		$ 55,460

[a]Cost per hour is $10 for labor ($80,000 ÷ 8,000 hours)

[b]Cost per hour is $2.50 for variable overhead ($25,000 x 0.80 ÷ 8,000 hours).

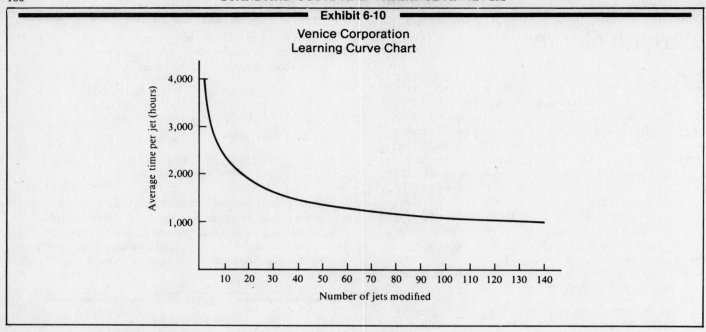

Exhibit 6-10

Venice Corporation
Learning Curve Chart

2,048 hours. The final 8 units require an average of only 1,536 hours [(32,768 – 20,480) ÷ 8].

Part (b) of Exhibit 6-9 shows that each jet will cost $39,614, which is considerably less than the $67,500 per jet for the first two. Notice that the materials cost does not change as a result of the learning curve, and 20 percent of the overhead ($5,000) is not affected. The impact of the learning curve on the reduction in average time to modify each jet is shown in Exhibit 6-10. Once 32 jets have been modified, the change is considerably less.

Most manufacturing operations are subject to the learning effect; however, the impact varies considerably. For a production process that has been in operation for several years, the learning effect, while there, may be so small that it is almost impossible to measure. However, for a new process the learning effect must definitely be considered before any reasonable cost estimate is made. Summers and Welsch list the following activities as those most subject to learning curve analysis:

1. Activities which have not been performed or not performed in their present operational form.

2. Activities being performed by new employees and others not familiar with the operations.

3. Activities which involve the use of a given raw material for the first time or which involve a change in the way the material is used.

4. Production runs of short duration, especially if these runs are repeated.[5]

---

5. Edward L. Summers and Glenn A. Welsch, "How Learning Curves Can Be Applied to Profit Planning," *Management Services 7* (March/April 1970), 46.

Mix and Yield Variance

The materials usage variance can be broken down into two basic parts—mix and yield—where the final product consists of different kinds or different grades of the same product. If a combination of materials placed in process differs from the standard mix, a **mix variance** results. If the quantity produced differs from the expected output based on the total quantities of materials placed in the process, a **yield variance** occurs. Using more of grade B material because it is cheaper and less of grade A will cause a favorable mix variance; however, this change could cause the yield to be considerably less than expected. In situations where the mix of raw materials placed in process can be altered, it is important to break the usage variance down into its mix and yield components to determine the real cause of the variance so corrective action can be taken.

Mix Variance

Study Example 6-4, which is an illustration of a situation where a mix and yield variance can be calculated. Note that 125 pounds are used for a standard yield of 80 percent or 100 pounds. The actual pounds placed in process were 120,000; thus, the yield should have been 96,000 pounds (120,000 × 0.8).

The mix variance is shown in part (a) of Exhibit 6-11. It is the difference between the actual pounds of each raw material that were used at the standard price and the pounds of each that should have been used based on the total pounds placed in process at the standard price. The standard ratio that should be placed in process is 2/5 (50/125) of A, 2/5 (50/125) of B, and 1/5 (25/125) of C. Thus, for a total

Beverly Hills Company manufactures one basic product, which consists of three types of materials. The standard cost for 100 pounds of output is shown at right.

A 20 percent shrinkage occurs shortly after the raw materials are placed in process.

During the past week 120,000 pounds consisting of 47,000 pounds of A, 43,000 pounds of B, and 30,000 pounds of C were placed in process. The pounds produced totaled 90,000.

Type material	Pounds	Standard costs/pounds	Total costs
A	50	$4	$200
B	50	8	400
C	25	2	50
	125		$650
Standard cost per pound of input ($650 ÷ 125)			$5.20
Standard cost per ount of output ($650 ÷ 100)			$6.50

━━━━━━━━━━━━━━ Exhibit 6-11 ━━━━━━━━━━━━━━

Beverly Hills Company
Analysis of Mix and Yield Variance

Part (a): Mix variance

Actual quantity at standard price	−	Standard mix for actual input at standard price	=	Mix variance
A [47,000 × $4 = $188,000]	−	[48,000 (120,000 × 2/5) × $4 = $192,000]	=	$ 4,000 F
B [43,000 × $8 = $344,000]	−	[48,000 (120,000 × 2/5) × $8 = $384,000]	=	40,000 F
C [30,000 × $2 = $ 60,000]	−	[24,000 (120,000 × 1/5) × $2 = $ 48,000]	=	12,000 UF
Total mix variance				$32,000 F

$$\begin{pmatrix} A - 47,000 \times \$4 = \$188,000 \\ B - 43,000 \times \$8 = \ 344,000 \\ C - 30,000 \times \$2 = \ 60,000 \\ \text{Total} \quad \$592,000 \end{pmatrix} - \begin{pmatrix} 120,000 \text{ pounds started} \times \text{standard} \\ \text{cost per pound of } \$5.20 \text{ or } \$624,000 \end{pmatrix} = \$32,000\ F$$

Part (b): Yield variance

Standard mix for actual input at standard price	−	Standard mix for actual output at standard price	=	Yield variance
A [48,000 × $4 = $192,000]	−	[45,000 (112,500 × 2/5) × $4 = $180,000]	=	$12,000 UF
B [48,000 × $8 = $384,000]	−	[45,000 (112,500 × 2/5) × $8 = $360,000]	=	24,000 UF
C [24,000 × $2 = $ 48,000]	−	[22,500 (112,500 × 1/5) × $2 = $ 45,000]	=	3,000 UF
Total yield mix				$39,000 UF

$$\begin{pmatrix} 120,000 \text{ pounds started} \times \\ \text{standard input cost per} \\ \text{pound of } \$5.20 \text{ or } \$624,000 \end{pmatrix} - \begin{pmatrix} 90,000 \text{ pounds of output} \times \\ \text{standard per pound of output} \\ \text{of } \$6.50 \text{ or } \$585,000 \end{pmatrix} = \$39,000\ UF$$

input of 120,000 pounds, 48,000 (120,000 × 2/5); 48,000 (120,000 × 2/5); and 24,000 (120,000 × 1/5) pounds of A, B, and C, respectively, should have been placed in process. However, less than the required amounts of A and B and too much of C were actually placed in process, resulting in a favorable variance of $32,000. Another way to calculate the mix variance is to multiply the standard price per pound of input of $5.20 ($650 ÷ 125 pounds) times the 120,000 pounds placed in process and subtract this from the actual quantities

used for each raw material times the standard price, as shown in part (a) of Exhibit 6-11.

Yield Variance

The second part of the quantity variance, known as a **yield variance**, is the difference between the standard mix for actual input times the standard price and the standard mix for the actual output at the standard price. The standard price for the latter calculation is the standard after any adjustment made for anticipated shrinkage. In Example 6-4 there is a 20 percent shrinkage, thus, the standard is not $5.20, but $6.50 ($5.20 ÷ 0.8 or the standard cost of $650 divided by the expected output of 100 pounds). The yield variance for Example 6-4 is presented in part (b) of Exhibit 10-11. Note that the variance can be calculated by analyzing each raw material or by taking the total volumes for input and output and multiplying them times the respective standard prices.

The total mix variance of $32,000 F plus the yield variance of $39,000 UF gives us the total usage variance of $7,000 UF as shown below:

Actual quantity X standard price:

A 47,000 X $4 =	$188,000	
B 43,000 X $8 =	344,000	
C 30,000 X $2 =	60,000	$592,000

Standard quantity allowed for actual output X standard price (90,000 X $6.50)   585,000

Total usage variance $ 7,000 UF

Labor Yield Variance

Assume for the Beverly Hills Company (Example 6-4) that the standard labor cost for 100 pounds of output was $250, which consisted of 25 hours (0.25 of an hour per pound) at $10 per hour. The hours worked totaled 23,000. The traditional efficiency is:

Actual hours X standard rate	$230,000
Standard hours allowed for actual output X standard rate (90,000 X 0.25 X $10)	225,000
Total efficiency variance	$ 5,000 UF

This variance can be divided into two parts: one is caused by factors other than yield and the other is caused by yield. The nonyield part of the efficiency variance is:

Actual hours X standard rate (23,000 X $10)	$230,000
Standard hours allowed based on expected output X standard rate (120,000 X 0.80 X 0.25 X $10)	240,000
Labor efficiency variance (nonyield part)	$ 10,000 F

The yield part of efficiency variance is:

Standard hours allowed based on expected output X standard rate	$240,000
Standard hours allowed for actual output	225,000
Labor efficiency (yield part) variance	$ 15,000 UF

This additional analysis illustrates that the operations this period were efficient—favorable variance of $10,000—when expressed in terms of the pounds started. The unfavorable efficiency variance is caused by the poor yield. If this yield variance were primarily caused by the change in mix of the products, individuals responsible for labor costs would not be held accountable for the inefficiency. However, it is possible that the low yield from this period's production was caused by operating the equipment poorly, failure to handle the raw materials carefully, or other related inefficiencies.

Impact of New Manufacturing Environment

Companies operating under the "new manufacturing environment" will need to make major changes in the cost accounting system. Howell and Soucy[6] suggest that companies that are moving toward world class manufacturing can be classified in terms of six major trends:

1. Higher quality
2. Lower inventory
3. Flexible flow lines
4. Automation
5. Product line organization
6. Effective use of information.

In chapter 2 we discussed these trends in some detail. The question that we want to examine now is, what impact will these changes have on standard cost systems? Howell and Soucy[7] suggest the following:

1. Standards for planning purposes will still be needed — Companies need to have an estimate of the cost that should be incurred to manufacture a product. This should include material from a bill of material, labor, and other identifiable and allocated costs.

2. Standards for control purposes will be less important — Actual cost incurred should, if the manufacturing process is of high quality, approximate the standard estimate. Thus variances should be small and are probably unnecessary to track for accounting purposes. They may, however, be tracked for operational purposes. For example, variances from plant production performances such as scrap and rework should be tracked for operational purposes.

3. Tracking of variances at the operational level should be on a real time basis rather than on a delayed basis — For example, variances from plant production performances such as scrap need to be reported as soon as the variance occurs rather than on a delayed basis.

4. Less emphasis is placed on labor efficiency variance — To the extent that the direct labor component of product cost is less significant and is in many cases fixed, labor efficiency variance is no longer relevant.

6. Robert A. Howell and Stephen Soucy, *Factory 2000+: Management Accounting's Changing Role* (Montvale, N.J.: National Association of Accountants, 1988), p. 2.
7. *Ibid.*, pp. 13-14.

5. Emphasis is on actual cost and cost trends — What is important is how much is being spent for materials, labor and other manufacturing and non manufacturing costs and the trends of these costs over time.

6. Emphasis on full costing for inventory valuation and financial reporting will no longer be necessary — In the new manufacturing environment with the use of just-in-time receipt of raw material or purchased parts, raw material inventories will be very low. With tight flow lines, work-in-process inventories will be insignificant. Fast response time will reduce significantly the need to keep finished goods inventory. With these changes there will be high inventory turnovers and low inventory levels and thus no need to track costs under the current full costing approach.

7. Emphasis will be placed on the various layers that constitute a product's total costs and the cost characteristics, both in the short and long run — In the short run, few costs are variable (for example, labor often will be considered fixed) and contribution margins will be high. In the long run, all costs are variable. Emphasis is on costs either as variable or avoidable and on full costs, including nonmanufacturing as well as manufacturing costs. All assets are relevant to each individual unit produced, thus there should be a return to job costing practices.

As a result of the above changes, recording information in a standard cost system will be significantly different. Entries may be made to record the purchase of raw materials and the next entry would be to record the completion of the order by debiting finished goods inventory. Thus, there are no work-in-process accounts. In some situations where the raw materials inventory is taken directly to the job and finished goods are shipped to customers as soon as they are completed, materials and conversion costs would be charged directly to the cost of goods sold account. The nature of the process would determine the extent to which inventories should be reflected in the accounts.

Problems

1. Multiple Choice

The data presented below apply to Items 1–8, which follow the data. These items are related to the facts presented in the data and should be answered on the basis of those facts.

Eastern Company manufactures special electrical equipment and parts. Eastern employs a standard cost accounting system with separate standards established for each product.

A special transformer is manufactured in the transformer department. Production volume is measured by direct labor hours in this department and a flexible budget system is used to plan and control department overhead.

Standard costs for the special transformer are determined annually in September for the coming year. The standard cost of a transformer for 1977 was computed at $67 as shown in the next column.

Direct materials			
Iron	5 sheets	@ $2.00	$10.00
Copper	3 spools	@ $3.00	9.00
Direct labor	4 hours	@ $7.00	28.00
Variable overhead	4 hours	@ $3.00	12.00
Fixed overhead	4 hours	@ $2.00	8.00
Total			**$67.00**

Overhead rates were based upon normal and expected monthly capacity for 1977, both of which were 4,000 direct labor hours. Practical capacity for this department is 5,000 direct labor hours per month. Variable overhead costs are expected to vary with the number of direct labor hours actually used.

During October, 1977, 800 transformers were produced. This was below expectations because a work stoppage occurred during contract negotiations with the labor force. Once the contract was settled, the department scheduled overtime in an attempt to catch up to expected production levels.

The following costs were incurred in October, 1977:

Direct material	Direct materials purchased	Materials used
Iron	5,000 sheets @ $2.00 per sheet	3,900 sheets
Copper	2,200 spools @ $3.10 per spool	2,600 spools

Direct labor
Regular time: 2,000 hours @ $7.00
1,400 hours @ $7.20

Overtime: 600 of the 1,400 hours were subject to overtime premium. The total overtime premium of $2,160 is included in variable overhead in accordance with company accounting practices.

Variable overhead: $10,000
Fixed overhead: $ 8,800

Answer the following items:

1. The most appropriate time to record any variation of actual material prices from standard is

a. at year end, when all variations will be known.
b. at the time of purchase.
c. at the time of material usage.
d. as needed to evaluate the performance of the purchasing manager.
e. some time other than those shown above is appropriate.

2. The total material quantity variation is

a. $200 favorable.
b. $400 favorable.
c. $600 favorable.
d. $400 unfavorable.
e. some amount other than those shown above.

3. The labor rate (price) variation is

a. $280 unfavorable.

b. $340 unfavorable.

c. $1,680 unfavorable.

d. $2,440 unfavorable.

e. none of the above responses is correct.

4. The variable overhead spending variation is

a. $200 favorable.

b. $400 unfavorable.

c. $600 unfavorable.

d. $1,600 unfavorable.

e. some amount other than those shown above.

5. The efficiency variation in variable overhead is the standard variable overhead rate times the difference between standard labor hours of output and

a. 2,000 hours.

b. 2,600 hours.

c. 2,800 hours.

d. 3,400 hours.

e. some amount other than those shown above.

6. The budget (spending) variation for fixed overhead is

a. $2,400 unfavorable.

b. $0.

c. $800 unfavorable.

d. not calculable from the problem.

e. some amount other than those shown above.

7. The fixed overhead volume variation is

a. $400 unfavorable.

b. $2,200 unfavorable.

c. $2,400 unfavorable.

d. $1,600 unfavorable.

e. some amount other than those shown above.

8. An unfavorable fixed overhead volume variation is most often caused by

a. actual fixed overhead incurred exceeding budgeted fixed overhead.

b. an over-application of fixed overhead to production.

c. a decrease in the level of the finished inventory of transformers.

d. production levels exceeding sales levels.

e. normal capacity exceeding actual production levels.

The Following Data Apply to Items 9-13.

Edney Company employs a standard absorption system for product costing. The standard cost of its product is as follows.

Raw materials		$14.50
Direct labor	2DLH @ $8	16.00
Manufacturing overhead	2DLH @ $11	22.00
Total standard cost		$52.50

The manufacturing overhead rate is based upon a normal annual activity level of 600,000 direct labor hours. Edney planned to produce 25,000 units each month during 1983. The budgeted manufacturing overhead for 1983 is as follows.

Variable	$3,600,000
Fixed	3,000,000
	$6,600,000

During November of 1983, Edney Company produced 26,000 units. Edney used 53,500 direct labor hours in November at a cost of $433,350. Actual manufacturing overhead for the month was $260,000 fixed and $315,000 variable. The total manufacturing overhead applied during November was $572,000.

9. The variable manufacturing overhead spending variance for November is

a. $9,000 unfavorable.

b. $4,000 unfavorable.

c. $11,350 unfavorable.

d. $9,000 favorable.

e. $6,000 favorable.

10. The variable manufacturing overhead efficiency variance for November is

a. $3,000 unfavorable.

b. $9,000 unfavorable.

c. $1,000 favorable.

d. $12,000 unfavorable.

e. zero.

11. The fixed manufacturing overhead spending (budget) variance for November is

a. $10,000 favorable.

b. $10,000 unfavorable.

c. $6,000 favorable.

d. $4,000 unfavorable.

e. zero.

12. The fixed manufacturing overhead volume variance for November is

a. $10,000 favorable.

b. $10,000 unfavorable.

c. $3,000 favorable.

d. $22,000 favorable.

e. zero.

13. The total variance related to efficiency of the manufacturing operation for November is

a. $9,000 unfavorable.

b. $12,000 unfavorable.

c. $21,000 unfavorable.

d. $11,000 unfavorable.

e. $25,000 unfavorable.

14. Each finished unit of Product DX-25 has 60 pounds of raw material. The manufacturing process must provide for a 20 percent waste allowance. The raw material can be purchased for $2.50 a pound under terms of 2/10, n/30. The company takes all cash discounts. The standard direct material cost for each unit of Product DX-25 is.

a. $180.00.

b. $187.50.

c. $183.75.

d. $176.40.

e. some amount other than those given above.

Each unit of Product XK-46 requires three direct labor hours. Employee benefit costs are treated as direct labor costs. Data on direct labor are as follows.

Number of direct employees	25
Weekly productive hours per employee	35
Estimated weekly wages per employee	$245
Employee benefits (related to weekly wages)	25%

15. The standard direct labor cost per unit of Product XK-46 is

a. $21.00.

b. $26.25.

c. $29.40.

d. $36.75.

e. some amount other than those given above.

The Following Data Apply to Items 16-19.

Arrow Industries employs a standard cost system in which direct materials inventory is carried at standard cost. Arrow has established the following standards for the prime costs of one unit of product.

	Standard Quantity	Standard Price	Standard Cost
Direct materials	8 pounds	$1.80 per pound	$14.40
Direct labor	.25 hour	$8.00 per hour	2.00
			$16.40

During May, Arrow purchased 160,000 pounds of direct material at a total cost of $304,000. The total factory wages for May were $42,000, 90 percent of which were for direct labor. Arrow manufactured 19,000 units of product during May using 142,500 pounds of direct material and 5,000 direct labor hours.

16. The direct material purchase price variance for May is

a. $16,000 favorable.

b. $16,000 unfavorable.

c. $14,250 favorable.

d. $14,250 unfavorable.

e. some amount other than those given above.

17. The direct material usage (quantity) variance for May is

a. $14,400 unfavorable.

b. $1,100 favorable.

c. $17,100 unfavorable.

d. $17,100 favorable.

e. some amount other than those given above.

18. The direct labor price (rate) variance for May is

a. $2,200 favorable.

b. $1,900 unfavorable.

c. $2,000 unfavorable.

d. $2,090 favorable.

e. some amount other than those given above.

19. The direct labor usage (efficiency) variance for May is

a. $2,200 favorable.

b. $2,000 favorable.

c. $2,000 unfavorable.

d. $1,800 unfavorable.

e. some amount other than those given above.

The Following Data Apply to Items 20-24.

Dori Castings is a job order shop that uses a full absorption, standard cost system to account for its production costs. The overhead costs are applied on a direct labor hour basis.

20. Dori's choice of a production volume as a denominator for calculating its factory overhead rate

a. has no effect on the fixed factory overhead rate for applying costs to production.

b. has an effect on the variable factory overhead rate for applying costs to production.

c. has no effect on the fixed factory overhead budget variance.

d. has no effect on the fixed factory overhead production volume variance.

e. has no effect on the overall (net) fixed factory overhead variance.

21. A production volume variance will exist for Dori in a month where

a. production volume differs from sales volume.

b. actual direct labor hours differ from standard allowed direct labor hours.

c. there is a budget variance in fixed factory overhead costs.

d. the fixed factory overhead applied on the basis of standard allowed direct labor hours differs from actual fixed factory overhead.

e. the fixed factory overhead applied on the basis of standard allowed direct labor hours differs from the budgeted fixed factory overhead.

22. Which of the following costs does Dori's system treat as variable when determining the inventory value of manufactured products?

a. Only variable manufacturing costs.

b. Only variable manufacturing costs and variable selling costs.

c. Only variable manufacturing costs and semi-variable (mixed) manufacturing costs.

d. All manufacturing costs and no selling costs.

e. All manufacturing costs and variable selling costs.

23. The amount of fixed factory overhead that Dori would apply to finished production would be

a. the actual direct labor hours times the standard fixed factory overhead rate per direct labor hour.

b. the standard allowed direct labor hours for the actual units of finished output times the standard fixed factory overhead rate per direct labor hour.

c. the standard units of output for the actual direct labor hours worked times the standard fixed factory overhead rate per unit of output.

d. the actual fixed factory overhead cost per direct labor hour times the standard allowed direct labor hours.

e. the actual fixed factory overhead cost per direct labor hour times the actual direct labor hours worked on finished production.

24. The year-end balances in the factory overhead variance accounts generated in Dori's standard cost system should be prorated to

a. raw materials, work-in-process, and finished goods.
b. raw materials, work-in-process, finished goods, and cost of goods sold.
c. work-in-process and finished goods.
d. work-in-process, finished goods, and cost of goods sold.
e. work-in-process and cost of goods sold.

---

2.   Estimated time 30 minutes (June 1988)

ColdKing Company is a small producer of fruit-flavored frozen desserts. For many years, ColdKing's products have had strong regional sales on the basis of brand recognition; however, other companies have begun marketing similar products in the area, and price competition has become increasingly important. John Wakefield, the company's controller, is planning to implement a standard cost system for ColdKing and has gathered considerable information from his co-workers on production and material requirements for ColdKing's products. Wakefield believes that the use of standard costing will allow ColdKing to improve cost control and make better pricing decisions.

ColdKing's most popular product is raspberry sherbet. The sherbet is produced in ten-gallon batches, and each batch requires six quarts of good raspberries. The fresh raspberries are sorted by hand before entering the production process. Because of imperfections in the raspberries and normal spoilage, one quart of berries is discarded for every four quarts of acceptable berries. Three minutes is the standard direct labor time for sorting that is required to obtain one quart of acceptable raspberries. The acceptable raspberries are then blended with the other ingredients; blending requires 12 minutes of direct labor time per batch. After blending, the sherbet is packaged in quart containers. Wakefield has gathered the following pricing information.

• ColdKing purchases raspberries at a cost of $.80 per quart. All other ingredients cost a total of $.45 per gallon.

• Direct labor is paid at the rate of $9.00 per hour.

• The total cost of material and labor required to package the sherbet is $.38 per quart.

Required   A. Develop the standard cost for the direct cost components of a ten-gallon batch of raspberry sherbet. The standard cost should identify the

1. standard quantity,
2. standard rate, and
3. standard cost per batch

for each direct cost component of a batch of raspberry sherbet.

B. As part of the implementation of a standard cost system at ColdKing, John Wakefield plans to train those responsible for maintaining the standards in the use of variance analysis. Wakefield is particularly concerned with the causes of unfavorable variances.

1. Discuss the possible causes of unfavorable material price variances and identify the individual(s) who should be held responsible for these variances.

2. Discuss the possible causes of unfavorable labor efficiency variances and identify the individual(s) who should be held responsible for these variances.

---

3.   Estimated time 30 minutes (December 1984)

The Salter Division of Fleming Corporation specializes in the manufacturing of computer diskettes. The retail price of these floppy disks range from $3 to $140 each, and they are normally sold in boxes of ten. The Salter Division has a single department production process and employs a standard process cost system on a variable (direct) costing basis.

Model B, a five-inch multipurpose diskette, is Salter's most popular product. Over one million units have been produced and sold in each of the past two years. Demand was expected to continue to increase in 1984, and 100,000 units were scheduled for production each month.

The quantity, time, and cost standards in effect for the Model B diskette for 1984 are given below. The raw material is added at the beginning of the process while conversion costs are incurred uniformly throughout the process.

Raw materials:	2 oz./diskette @ $8/lb.	$1.00
Direct labor:	4DLH/100 diskettes @ $18/DLH	.72
Variable overhead:	150 percent of direct labor cost	1.08
Standard variable cost per diskette		$2.80

The balance of Salter Division's Work-in-Process Inventory account at the beginning of each month is the standard cost of the incomplete equivalent units still in production. The actual costs incurred during the month for raw materials, direct labor, and variable overhead are entered into the Work-in-Process Inventory account. The completed units (finished goods) are transferred out at standard. The manufacturing variances are computed and closed out from the Work-in-Process Inventory account leaving the account valued at standard for the start of the next month.

Data regarding the operations for November 1984 are presented in the next column. The variances have not yet been closed out of the Work-in-Process Inventory account.

		Equivalent Units	
	Total Units	Raw Materials	Conversion Costs
Units completed From beginning inventory (40% complete)	14,600	—	8,760
Started and completed	91,800	91,800	91,800
Work-in-Process, November 30 (70% complete)	11,200	11,200	7,840
Total	117,600	103,000	108,400

A summary of costs for November 1984 is presented below.

Work in Process, November 1—	
at standard	$ 25,112
Raw materials purchased and used—$13,000 pounds	98,800
Direct labor—4,390 hours	76,825
Variable overhead	117,675
Total costs to account for	$318,412
Cost of units completed and transferred out—at standard (106,400 units)	297,920
Balance of Work-in-Process, November 30—before close out of variances	$ 20,492

Required   A. The manufacturing variances must be removed from Salter Division's Work-in-Process Inventory account so that the inventory account will be stated at standard as of November 30, 1984.

1. Determine the standard cost of the Work-in-Process Inventory account at November 30, 1984.
2. Identify and calculate the applicable raw material, direct labor, and variable overhead variances for November 1984.

B. Discuss the benefits of a standard process cost system.

---

4.   Estimated time 60 minutes (CPA)

Melody Corporation is a manufacturing company that produces a single product known as "Jupiter." Melody uses the first-in, first-out (FIFO) process costing method for both financial statement and internal management reporting.

In analyzing production results, standard costs are used, whereas actual costs are used for financial statement reporting. The standards, which are based upon equivalent units of production, are as follows:

Raw material per unit	1 pound at $10 per pound
Direct labor per unit	2 hours at $4 per hour
Factory overhead per unit	2 hours at $1.25 per hour

Budgeted factory overhead for standard hours allowed for April production is $30,000.

Data for the month of April 1977 are presented below:

• The beginning inventory consisted of 2,500 units which were 100 percent complete as to raw material and 40 percent complete as to direct labor and factory overhead.

• An additional 10,000 units were started during the month.

• The ending inventory consisted of 2,000 units which were 100 percent complete as to raw material and 40 percent complete as to direct labor and factory overhead.

• Costs applicable to April production are as follows:

	Actual cost	Standard cost
Raw material used (11,000 pounds)	$121,000	$100,000
Direct labor (25,000 hours actually worked)	105,575	82,400
Factory overhead	31,930	25,750

Required A. For each element of production for April (raw material, direct labor, and factory overhead) compute the following:

1. equivalent units of production.
2. cost per equivalent unit or production at actual and at standard.

Show supporting computations in good form.

B. Prepare a schedule analyzing for April production the following variances as either favorable or unfavorable:

1. total materials.
2. materials price.
3. materials usage.
4. total labor.
5. labor rate.
6. labor efficiency.
7. total factory overhead.
8. factory overhead volume.
9. factory overhead budget.

Show supporting computations in good form.

---

5.   Estimated time 30 minutes (December 1979)

The Lenco Co. employs a standard cost system as part of its cost control program. The standard cost per unit is established at the beginning of each year. Standards are not revised during the year for any changes in material or labor inputs or in the manufacturing processes. Any revisions in standards are deferred until the beginning of the next fiscal year. However, in order to recognize such changes in the current year, the company includes planned variances in the monthly budgets prepared after such changes have been introduced.

The following labor standard was set for one of Lenco's products effective July 1, 1979, the beginning of the fiscal year.

Class I labor	4 hrs.	@ $ 6.00	$24.00
Class II labor	3 hrs.	@ 7.50	22.50
Class V labor	1 hr.	@ 11.50	11.50
Standard labor cost per 100 units			**$58.00**

The standard was based upon the quality of material that had been used in prior years and what was expected to be available for the 1979–80 fiscal year. The labor activity is performed by a team consisting of four persons with Class I skills, three persons with Class II skills and one person with Class V skills. This is the most economical combination for the company's processing system.

The manufacturing operations occurred as expected during the first five months of the year. The standard costs contributed to effective cost control during this period. However, there were indications that changes in the operations would be required in the last half of the year. The company had received a significant increase in orders for delivery in the spring. There were an inadequate number of skilled workers available to meet the increased production. As a result, the production teams, beginning in January, would be made up of more Class I labor and less Class II labor than the standard required. The teams would consist of six Class I persons, two Class II persons and one Class V person. This labor team would be less efficient than the normal team. The reorganized teams work more slowly so that only 90 units are produced in the same time period that 100 units would normally be produced. No raw materials will be lost as a result of the change in the labor mix. Completed units have never been rejected in the final inspection process as a consequence of faulty work; this is expected to continue.

In addition, Lenco was notified by its material supplier that a lower quality material would be supplied after January 1. One unit of raw material normally is required for each good unit produced. Lenco and its supplier estimated that 5% of the units manufactured would be rejected upon final inspection due to defective material. Normally, no units are lost due to defective material.

Required   A. How much of the lower quality material must be entered into production in order to produce 42,750 units of good production in January with the new labor teams? Show your calculations.

B. How many hours of each class of labor will be needed to produce 42,750 good units from the material input? Show your calculations.

C. What amount should be included in the January budget for the planned labor variance due to the labor team and material changes? What amount of this planned labor variance can be associated with the (1) material change; and (2) the team change? Show your calculations.

---

6.   Estimated time 30 minutes (June 1982)

Energy Products Company produces a gasoline additive, *Gas Gain*. This product increases engine efficiency and improves gasoline mileage by creating a more complete burn in the combustion process.

Careful controls are required during the production process to ensure that the proper mix of input chemicals is achieved and that evaporation is controlled. If the controls are not effective, there can be loss of output and efficiency.

The standard cost of producing a 500-liter batch of *Gas Gain* is $135. The standard materials mix and related standard cost of each chemical used in a 500-liter batch are as follows.

Chemical	Standard Input Quantity in Liters	Standard Cost per Liter	Total Cost
Echol	200	$.200	$ 40.00
Protex	100	.425	42.50
Benz	250	.150	37.50
CT-40	50	.300	15.00
	600		$135.00

The quantities of chemicals purchased and used during the current production period are shown in the schedule below. A total of 140 batches of *Gas Gain* were manufactured during the current production period. Energy Products determines its cost and chemical usage variations at the end of each production period.

Chemical	Quantity Purchased	Total Purchase Price	Quantity Used
Echol	25,000 liters	$ 5,365	26,600 liters
Protex	13,000 liters	6,240	12,880 liters
Benz	40,000 liters	5,840	37,800 liters
CT-40	7,500 liters	2,220	7,140 liters
Total	85,500 liters	$19,665	84,420 liters

Required   A. Calculate the purchase price variances by chemical for Energy Products Company.

B. Calculate the total material usage variance related to *Gas Gain* for Energy Products Company and then analyze this total usage variance into the following two components:

1. total mix variance.
2. total yield variance.

---

7.   Estimated time 30 minutes (June 1985)

NuLathe Co. produces a turbo engine component for jet aircraft manufacturers. A standard cost system has been used for years with good results.

Unfortunately, NuLathe has recently experienced production problems. The source for its direct material went out of business. The new source produces a similar but higher quality material. The price per pound from the original source had averaged $7.00 while the price from the new source is $7.77. The use of the new material results in a reduction in scrap. This scrap reduction reduces the actual consumption of direct material from 1.25 to 1.00 pounds per unit. In addition, the direct labor is reduced from 24 to 22 minutes per unit because there is less scrap labor and machine setup time.

The direct material problem was occurring at the same time that labor negotiations resulted in an increase of over 14 percent in hourly direct labor costs. The average rate rose from $12.60 per hour to $14.40 per hour. Production of the main product requires a high level of labor skill. Because of a continuing shortage in that skill area, an interim wage agreement had to be signed.

NuLathe started using the new direct material on April 1, the same date that the new labor agreement went into effect.

NuLathe Co.—Analysis of Prime Costs

Standard Cost Variance Analysis for April 1985

	Standard	Price Variance		Quantity Variance		Actual
Direct materials	$ 8.16	($.97 × 1.0)	$.97 U	($6.80 × .2)	$1.36 F	$ 7.77
Direct labor	4.10	($2.10 × $\frac{22}{60}$)	.77 U	($12.30 × $\frac{2}{60}$)	.41 U	5.28
	$12.26					$13.05

Comparison of 1985 Actual Costs

	First Quarter Costs	April Costs	Percentage Increase (Decrease)
Direct materials	$ 8.75	$ 7.77	(11.2)%
Direct labor	5.04	5.28	4.8 %
	$13.79	$13.05	(5.4)%

NuLathe has been using standards that were set at the beginning of the calendar year. The direct material and direct labor standards for the turbo engine component are as follows.

Direct material	1.2 lbs. @ $6.80/lb.	$ 8.16
Direct labor	20 min. @ $12.30/DLH	4.10
Standard prime cost per unit		$12.26

Howard Foster, Cost Accounting Supervisor, had been examining the performance report (see above) that he had prepared at the close of business on April 30. Jane Keene, Assistant Controller, came into Foster's office, and Foster said, "Jane, look at this performance report. Direct material price increased 11 percent and the labor rate increased over 14 percent during April. I expected greater variances, yet prime costs decreased over five percent from the $13.79 we experienced during the first quarter of this year. The proper message just isn't coming through."

"This has been an unusual period," said Keene. "With all the unforeseen changes, perhaps we should revise our standards based on current conditions and start over."

Foster replied, "I think we can retain the current standards but expand the variance analysis. We could calculate variances for the specific changes that have occurred to direct material and direct labor before we calculate the normal price and quantity variances. What I really think would be useful to management right now is to determine the impact the changes in direct material and direct labor had in reducing our prime costs per unit from $13.79 in the first quarter to $13.05 in April—a reduction of $.74."

Required   A. Discuss the advantages of:

1. immediately revising the standards.
2. retaining the current standards and expanding the analysis of variances.

B. Prepare an analysis that reflects the impact the new direct material and new labor contract had on reducing NuLathe Co.'s prime costs per unit from $13.79 in the first quarter to $13.05 in April. The analysis should show the changes in prime costs per unit that are due to the:

1. use of new direct material.
2. new labor contract.

This analysis should be in sufficient detail to identify the changes due to:

- direct material price.
- direct labor rate.
- the effect of direct material quality on direct material usage.
- the effect of direct material quality on direct labor usage.

8.   Estimated time 30 minutes (June 1986)

Allglow Company is a cosmetics manufacturer specializing in stage makeup. The company's best selling product is SkinKlear, a protective cream used under the stage makeup to protect the skin from frequent use of makeup. SkinKlear is packaged in three sizes—8 ounces, one pound, and three pounds—and regularly sells for $21.00 per pound. The standard cost per pound of SkinKlear, based on Allglow's normal monthly production of 8,000 pounds, is as follows.

Based on these standard costs, Allglow prepares monthly budgets. Presented below are the budgeted performance and the actual performance for May 1986 when the company produced and sold 9,000 pounds of SkinKlear.

Barbara Simmons, Allglow's President, was not pleased with these results; despite a sizeable increase in the sales of SkinKlear, there was a decrease in the product's contribution to the overall profitability of the firm. Simmons has asked Allglow's Cost Accountant, Brian Jackson, to prepare a report that identifies the reasons why the contribution margin for SkinKlear has decreased. Jackson has gathered the information presented below to help in the preparation of the report.

While doing his research, Jackson discovered that the Manufacturing Department had mechanized one of the manual operations in the compounding process on an experimental basis. The mechanized operation replaced manual operations that represented 40 percent of the compounding process.

The workers' inexperience with the mechanized operation caused increased usage of both the cream base and the moisturizer; however, Jackson believed these inefficiencies would be negligible if mechanization became a permanent part of the

Cost Item	Quantity	Standard Cost	Total Cost
Direct materials			
Cream base	9.0 oz.	$ .05/oz.	$ .45
Moisturizer	6.5 oz.	.10/oz.	.65
Fragrance	.5 oz.	1.00/oz.	.50
			$ 1.60
Direct labor*			
Mixing	.5 hr.	$4.00/hr.	$2.00
Compound-ing	1.0 hr.	5.00/hr.	5.00
			7.00
Variable overhead**	1.5 hr.	$2.10/hr.	3.15
Total standard cost per pound			$11.75

*Direct labor dollars include employee benefits.
**Applied on the basis of direct labor hours.

Contribution Report for SkinKlear
For the Month of May 1986

	Budget	Actual	Variance
Units	8,000	9,000	1,000F
Revenue	$168,000	$180,000	$12,000F
Direct material	12,800	16,200	3,400U
Direct labor	56,000	62,500	6,500U
Variable overhead	25,200	30,900	5,700U
Total variable costs	$ 94,000	$109,600	$15,600U
Contribution margin	$ 74,000	$ 70,400	$ 3,600U

process and the workers' skills were improved. The idle time in compounding was traceable to the fact that fewer workers were required for the mechanized process. During this experimental period, the idle time was charged to direct labor rather than

May 1986 Usage Report for SkinKlear

Cost Item	Quantity	Actual Cost
Direct materials		
Cream base	84,000 oz.	$ 4,200
Moisturizer	60,000 oz.	7,200
Fragrance	4,800 oz.	4,800
Direct labor		
Mixing	4,500 hr.	18,000
Compounding—manual	5,300 hr.	26,500
Compounding—mechanized	2,700 hr.	13,500
Compounding—idle	900 hr.	4,500
Variable overhead		30,900
Total variable cost		$109,600

overhead. The excess workers could either be reassigned or laid off in the future. Jackson also was able to determine that all of the variable manufacturing overhead costs over standard could be traced directly to the mechanization process.

Required **A.** Prepare an explanation of the $3,600 unfavorable variance between the budgeted and actual contribution margin for SkinKlear during May 1986 by calculating the following variances.

1. Sales price variance.
2. Material price variance.
3. Material quantity variance.
4. Labor efficiency variance.
5. Variable overhead efficiency variance.
6. Variable overhead spending variance.
7. Contribution margin volume variance.

B. Allglow Company must decide whether or not the compounding operation in the SkinKlear manufacturing process that was mechanized on an experimental basis should continue to be mechanized. Calculate the variable cost savings that can be expected to arise in the future from the mechanization. Explain your answer.

9.   Estimated time 60 minutes (June 1977)

The Justin Company has recently installed a standard cost system to simplify its factory bookkeeping and to aid in cost control. The company makes standard items for inventory, but because of the many products in its line, each is manufactured periodically under a production order. Prior to the installation of the system, job order cost sheets were maintained for each production order. Since the introduction of the standard costs system, however, they have not been kept.

The fabricating department is managed by a general supervisor who has overall responsibility for scheduling, performance and cost control. The department consists of four machine/work centers. Each work center is manned by a four-person work group or team and the centers are aided by a 12-person support group. Departmental practice is to assign a job to one team and expect the team to perform most of the work necessary to complete the job, including acquisition of materials and supplies from the stores department and machining and assembling. This has been practical and satisfactory in the past and is readily accepted by the employees.

Information regarding production cost standards, products produced, and actual costs for the fabricating department in March is presented on the next page.

Required **A.** Justin Company assumes that its efforts to control costs in the fabricating department would be aided if variances were calculated by jobs. Management intends to add this analysis next month. Calculate all the variances by job that might contribute to cost control under this assumption.

B. Do you agree with the company's plan to initiate the calculation of job variances in addition to the currently calculated departmental variances? Explain your answer.

Unit standard costs

	Part		
	A7A	C6D	C7A
Material	$2.00	$ 3.00	$1.50
Direct labor	1.50	2.00	1.00
Overhead (per direct labor dollar)[a]			
Variable	3.00	4.00	2.00
Fixed	.75	1.00	.50
	$7.25	$10.00	$5.00

[a] The departmental standard overhead rates are applied to the products as a percentage of direct labor dollars. The labor base was chosen because nearly all of the variable overhead costs are caused by labor activity. The departmental overhead rates were calculated at the beginning of the year as follows:

	Variable (including indirect labor)	Fixed
Estimated annual cost	$360,000	$ 90,000
Estimated annual department direct labor dollars	$180,000	$180,000
Overhead rate	200%	50%

10. Estimated time 30 minutes (December 1983)
Requirement D (June 1993)

Maidwell Company manufactures washers and dryers on a single assembly line in its main factory. The market has deteriorated over the last five years and competition has made cost control very important. Management has been concerned about the materials cost of both washers and dryers. There have been no model changes in the past two years and economic conditions have allowed the company to negotiate price reductions in many key parts.

Maidwell uses a standard cost system in accounting for materials. Purchases are charged to inventory at a standard price with purchase discounts considered an administrative cost reduction. Production is charged at the standard price of the materials used. Thus, the price variance is isolated at time of purchase as the difference between gross contract price and standard price multiplied by the quantity purchased. When a substitute part is used in production rather than the regular part, a price variance equal to the difference in the standard prices of the materials is recognized at the time of substitution in the production process. The quantity variance is the actual quantity used compared to the standard quantity allowed with the difference multiplied by the standard price.

The materials variances for several of the parts Maidwell uses are unfavorable. Part No. 4121 is one of the items that has an unfavorable variance. Maidwell knows that some of these parts will be defective and fail. The failure is discovered during production. The normal defective rate is five percent of normal input. The original contract price of this part was $.285 per unit;

Analysis of the Fabricating Department Account for March

Charges		
Materials		
Job No. 307-11	$ 5,200	
Job No 307-12	2,900	
Job No. 307-14	9,400	$17,500
Labor charges		
Job No. 307-11	4,000	
Job No. 307-12	2,100	
Job No. 307-14	6,200	
Indirect labor	12,200	24,500
Variable overhead costs (e.g., supplies, electricity, etc.)		18,800
Fixed overhead costs (e.g., supervisor's salary, depreciation, property tax and insurance, etc.)		7,000
Total charges to department for March		$67,800

Credits		
Completed Jobs		
Job No. 307-11 2000 units part A7A @ 7.25	$14,500	
Job No. 307-12 1000 units part C6D @ 10.00	10,000	
Job No. 307-14 6000 units part C7A @ 5.00	30,000	$54,500
Variances transferred to the factory variance account		
Materials[a]	1,500	
Direct labor[b]	1,300	
Variable overhead	9,000	
Fixed overhead	1,500	13,300
Total credits		$67,800

[a] Material price variances are isolated at acquisition and charged to the Stores Department.

[b] All direct labor was paid at the standard wage rate during March.

thus, Maidwell set the standard unit price at $.285. The unit contract purchase price of Part No. 4121 was increased $.04 to $.325 from the original $.285 due to a parts specification change. Maidwell chose not to change the standard, but treat the increase in price as a price variance. In addition, the contract terms were changed from n/30 to 4/10, n/30 as a consequence of negotiations resulting from changes in the economy.

Data regarding the usage of Part No. 4121 during December are as follows.

- Purchases of Part No. 4121   150,000 units
- Unit price paid for purchases of Part No. 4121 $.325
- Requisitions of Part No. 4121 from stores for use in products   134,000 units
- Substitution of Part No. 5125 for Part No. 4121 to use obsolete stock (standard unit price of Part No. 5125 is $.35)   24,000 units
- Units of Part No. 4121 and its substitute (Part No. 5125) identified as being defective   9,665 units
- Standard allowed usage (including normal defective units) of Part No. 4121 and its substitute based upon output for the month   153,300 units

Maidwell's material variances related to Part No. 4121 for December were reported as follows.

Price variance	$7,560.00 U
Quantity variance	1,339.50 U
Total material variances for Part No. 4121	$8,899.50 U

Bob Speck, the Purchasing Director, claims the unfavorable price variance is misleading. Speck says that his department has worked hard to obtain price concessions and purchase discounts from suppliers. In addition, Speck has indicated that engineering changes have been made in several parts increasing their price even though the part identification has not changed. These price increases are not his department's responsibility. Speck declares that price variance simply no longer measures the Purchasing Department's performance.

Jim Buddle, the Manufacturing Manager, thinks that responsibility for the quantity variance should be shared. Buddle states that manufacturing cannot control quality arising from less expensive parts, substitutions of material to use up otherwise obsolete stock, or engineering changes that increased the quantity of materials used.

The Accounting Manager, Mike Kohl, has suggested that the computation of variances be changed to identify variations from standard with the causes and functional areas responsible for the variances. The following system of materials variances and the method of computation for each was recommended by Kohl.

Variance	Method of Calculation
Economics variance	Quantity purchased times the changes made after setting standards that were the result of negotiations based on changes in the general economy.
Engineering change variance	Quantity purchased times change in price due to part specifications changes.
Purchase price variance	Quantity purchased times change in contract price due to changes other than parts specifications or the general economy.
Substitutions variance	Quantity substituted times the difference in standard price between parts substituted.
Excess usage variance	Standard price times the difference between the standard quantity allowed for production minus actual parts used (reduced for abnormal scrap).
Abnormal failure rate variance	Abnormal scrap times standard price.

Required   **A.** Discuss the appropriateness of Maidwell Company's current method of variance analysis for materials and indicate whether the claims of Bob Speck and Jim Buddle are valid.

B. Compute the materials variances for Part No. 4121 for December using the system recommended by Mike Kohl.

C. Indicate who would be responsible for each of the variances in Mike Kohl's system of variance analysis for materials.

D. A problem similar to this one was on the June 1993 examination. This question also asked the candidate to describe the likely behavior of Speck and Buddle.

---

11.   Estimated time 45 minutes (June 1992)

Alaire Corporation manufactures several different types of printed circuit boards; however, two of the boards account for the majority of the company's sales. The first of these boards, a television (TV) circuit board, has been a standard in the industry for several years. The market for this type of board is competitive and, therefore, price-sensitive. Alaire plans to sell 65,000 of the TV boards in 1993 at a price of $150 per unit. The second high-volume product, a personal computer (PC) circuit board, is a recent addition to Alaire's product line. Because the PC board incorporates the latest technology, it can be sold at a premium price; the 1993 plans include the sale of 40,000 PC boards at $300 per unit.

Alaire's management group is meeting to discuss strategies for 1993, and the current topic of conversation is how to spend the sales and promotion dollars for next year. The sales manager believes that the market share for the TV board could be expanded by concentrating Alaire's promotional efforts in this area. In response to this suggestion, the production manager said, "Why don't you go after a bigger market for the PC board? The cost sheets that I get show that the contribution from the PC board is more than double the contribution from the TV board. I know we get a premium price for the PC board; selling it should help overall profitability."

Alaire uses a standard cost system, and the following data apply to the TV and PC boards.

	TV Board	PC Board
Direct material	$80	$140
Direct labor	1.5 hours	4 hours
Machine time	.5 hours	1.5 hours

Variable factory overhead is applied on the basis of direct labor hours. For 1993, variable factory overhead is budgeted at $1,120,000, and direct labor hours are estimated at 280,000. The hourly rates for machine time and direct labor are $10 and

Budgeted Cost		Cost Driver	Annual Activity for Cost Driver
Material overhead:			
Procurement	$ 400,000	Number of parts	4,000,000 parts
Production scheduling	220,000	Number of boards	110,000 boards
Packaging and shipping	440,000	Number of boards	110,000 boards
	$1,060,000		
Variable overhead:			
Machine set-up	$ 446,000	Number of set-ups	278,750 set-ups
Hazardous waste disposal	48,000	Pounds of waste	16,000 pounds
Quality control	560,000	Number of inspections	160,000 inspections
General supplies	66,000	Number of boards	110,000 boards
	$1,120,000		
Manufacturing:			
Machine insertion	$1,200,000	Number of parts	3,000,000 parts
Manual insertion	4,000,000	Number of parts	1,000,000 parts
Wave soldering	132,000	Number of boards	110,000 boards
	$5,332,000		

Required per unit	TV Board	PC Board
Parts	25	55
Machine insertions	24	35
Manual insertions	1	20
Machine set-ups	2	3
Hazardous waste	.02 lb.	.35 lb.
Inspections	1	2

$14, respectively. Alaire applies a material handling charge at 10 percent of material cost; this material handling charge is not included in variable factory overhead. Total 1993 expenditures for material are budgeted at $10,600,000.

Ed Welch, Alaire's controller, believes that before the management group proceeds with the discussion about allocating sales and promotional dollars to individual products, it might be worthwhile to look at these products on the basis of the activities involved in their production. As Welch explained to the group, "Activity-based costing integrates the cost of all activities, known as cost drivers, into individual product costs rather than including these costs in overhead pools." Welch has prepared the schedule shown below to help the management group understand this concept.

"Using this information," Welch explained, "we can calculate an activity-based cost for each TV board and each PC board and then compare it to the standard cost we have been using. The only cost that remains the same for both cost methods is the cost of direct material. The cost drivers will replace the direct labor, machine time, and overhead costs in the standard cost."

Required   A. Identify at least four general advantages that are associated with activity-based costing.

B. On the basis of standard costs, calculate the total contribution expected in 1993 for Alaire Corporation's

1. TV board.
2. PC board.

C. On the basis of activity-based costs, calculate the total contribution expected in 1993 for Alaire Corporation's

1. TV board.
2. PC board.

D. Explain how the comparison of the results of the two costing methods may impact the decisions made by Alaire corporation's management group.

---

12.   Estimated time 30 minutes (December 1992)

Talbot Company manufactures shirts which are sold to customers for embossing with various slogans and emblems. Bob Ricker, manufacturing supervisor, recently received the following November Production Report; the November budget is based on the manufacture of 80,000 shirts.

November 1992 Production Report

	Budget	Actual	Variance
Direct materials	$160,000	$162,000	$ (2,000)
Direct labor	240,000	246,000	(6,000)
Factory overhead	200,000	241,900	(41,900)

Ricker was extremely upset by the negative variances in the November report as he has worked very closely with his people for the past two months to improve productivity. He immediately asked to meet with his boss, Chris Langdon, to discuss the report and express his disappointment. Langdon, also disturbed by the November results, suggested that Ricker meet with Sheryl Johnson, Talbot's manager of cost accounting, to see if he can gain further insight into the production problems. Johnson was extremely helpful and provided Ricker with the additional information on the annual budget and the November actuals shown below and in the next column.

Variable Overhead Expenditures

	Annual	Per Unit	November
Indirect material	$ 450,000	$ .45	$36,000
Indirect labor	300,000	.30	33,700
Equipment repair	200,000	.20	16,400
Equipment power	50,000	.05	12,300
Total	$1,000,000	$1.00	$98,400

Fixed Overhead Expenditures

	Annual	November
Supervisory salaries	$ 260,000	$ 22,000
Insurance	350,000	29,500
Property taxes	80,000	6,500
Depreciation	320,000	34,000
Heat, light, telephone	210,000	21,600
Quality inspection	280,000	29,900
Total	$1,500,000	$143,500

• Factory overhead at Talbot includes both variable and fixed components and is applied on the basis of direct labor hours. The company's 1992 budget includes the manufacture of one million shirts and the expenditure of 250,000 direct labor hours.

• The standard labor rate at Talbot is $12.00 per hour, and the standard material cost per shirt is $2.00.

• Actual production for November was 82,000 shirts.

With this data, Johnson and Ricker prepared to analyze the November variances, paying particular attention to the factory overhead variance because of its significance. Johnson knows that part of the problem is caused by the fact that Talbot does not use flexible budgeting, and she will be able to explain this to Ricker as they analyze the data.

Required   A. By calculating the four variances listed below, prepare an explanation of the $41,900 unfavorable variance between budgeted and actual factory overhead during the month of November 1992.

1. Volume (flexible budget) variance for total factory overhead.
2. Variable overhead efficiency variance.
3. Variable overhead spending variance.
4. Fixed overhead spending variance.

B. Describe the likely behavioral impact on Bob Ricker of the information provided by the calculations required in Requirement A. Be sure to make specific reference to the variances calculated, indicating Ricker's responsibility in each case.

Solutions

1.

1. b. For control purpose it is best to ascertain variances from standard as soon as possible. At the time of purchase is the earliest time the purchase variance can generally be determined.

2. d.

Iron
Standard quantity allowed for actual output (800 × 5)	4,000
Actual quantity used	3,900
Favorable quantity variance	100 F
Standard cost per unit	$ 2
Total Iron variance	$ 200 F

Copper
Standard quantity allowed for actual output (800 × 3)	2,400
Actual quantity used	2,600
Unfavorable quantity variance	200 UF
Standard cost per unit	$ 3
Total Copper variance	600 UF
Total Iron and Copper variance	$ 400 UF

3. a.
Actual hours × standard rate (3,400 × $7)	$23,800
Actual hours × actual rate (2,000 × $7 + 1,400 × $7.20)	24,080
Unfavorable labor rate variance	$ (280) UF

4. a. Variable overhead analysis:

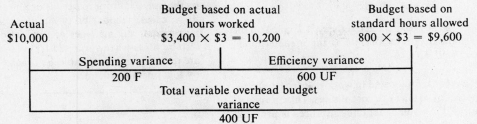

Actual	Budget based on actual hours worked	Budget based on standard hours allowed
$10,000	$3,400 × $3 = 10,200	800 × $3 = $9,600

Spending variance	Efficiency variance
200 F	600 UF

Total variable overhead budget variance

400 UF

5. d. See the analysis above.

6. c. Fixed overhead analysis:

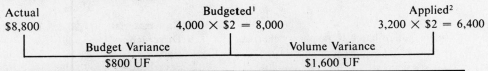

Actual	Budgeted[1]	Applied[2]
$8,800	4,000 × $2 = 8,000	3,200 × $2 = 6,400

Budget Variance	Volume Variance
$800 UF	$1,600 UF

[1]Normal and expected capacity in hours × fixed overhead cost rate.
[2]Standard hours allowed for actual output × fixed overhead cost rate.

7. d. See the question above.

8. e. The volume (denominator) variance is caused by the actual production level differing from the normal (expected actual) capacity. If the actual production level is less than normal capacity, the variance is unfavorable; if it is greater, the variance is favorable.

9. e.

Variable overhead rate $= \dfrac{\$3,600,000}{600,000 \text{ hrs}} = \$6$ per hour

Budgeted overhead based on actual hours (53,500 × $6)	$321,000
Actual variable overhead	315,000
Overhead spending variance	$ 6,000 F

10. b.

Budgeted overhead based on standard hours allowed (26,000 × 2 × $6)	$312,000
Budgeted overhead based on actual hours	321,000
Overhead efficiency variance	$ 9,000 UF

11. b.

Budgeted fixed overhead ($3,000,000 ÷ 12)	$250,000
Actual fixed overhead	260,000
Fixed overhead spending variance	$ 10,000 UF

12. a.

Applied fixed overhead (26,000 × 2 × $5)	$260,000
Budgeted fixed overhead	250,000
Fixed overhead volume variance	$ 10,000 F

13. c. The total labor hours in excess of standard allowed for actual output is 1,500. These hours times the standard labor rate and the standard variable overhead rate produce an amount representing the variance associated with labor inefficiency. Inefficiency of labor may also create material variances (1,500 × ($8 + $6)) = $21,000 UF.

14. c. 60 pounds ÷ (1 – .20 waste) × $2.50 × .98 = $183.75

15. b. 3 hours × $245/35 × 1.25 = $26.25

16. b. Purchase price variance = AQ purchased × (SP – AP)
= 160,000 × ($1.80 – $1.90) = 16,000 UF
(A = actual, Q = qty., S = standard, P = price)

17. d. Usage variance = SP × (SQ allowed – AQ)
= $1.80 × [(19,000 × 8) – 142,500]
= $1.80 × 9,500 = $17,100 F

18. a. DL rate (price) variance = AH × (SR – AR)
= 5,000 × [8 – ($42,000 × .90 – 5,000)]
= 5,000 × ($8.00 – $7.56) = $2,200 F
(R = rate, H = hours)

19. c. Usage variance = SR × (SH allowed – AH)
= $8 × [(19,000 × .25) – 5,000]
= $8 × (4,750 – 5,000) = $2,000 UF

20. c. The budget for fixed factory overhead is the estimated fixed costs for the period which do not relate to the production volume in the short-run.

21. e. Answer "e" provides the definition for the volume variance. If the values (fixed factory overhead applied on the basis of standard allowed direct labor hours and budgeted fixed factory overhead) are equal, then the production volume that was used as the denominator to calculate the fixed cost rate equals the actual production volume.

22. d. Since Dori has a full absorption costing system all fixed and variable manufacturing costs are included in inventory.

23. b. As answer "b" suggests fixed overhead is applied on the basis of standard hours allowed at the predetermined fixed overhead rate.

24. d. Overhead costs are allocated to work-in-process, finished goods inventories and to cost of sales. Thus, any variance unless due to unusual circumstances is prorated among the three accounts. Also, in practice the total variance is often charged to cost of goods sold.

2.

A. Standard cost for ten-gallon batch of raspberry sherbet.

Direct material
Raspberries (7.5 qts.* × $.80)	$6.00	
Other ingredients (10 gal. × $.45)	4.50	$10.50

Direct labor
Sorting	$\frac{[(3 \text{ min} \times 6 \text{ qts.}) \times \$9.00]}{60}$	$2.70	
Blending	(12 min ÷ 60) × $9.00	1.80	4.50
Packaging	(40 qts.** × $.38)		$15.20
Standard cost per ten-gallon batch			$30.20

* 6 quarts × (5 ÷ 4) = 7.5 quarts required to obtain 6 acceptable quarts.

** 4 quarts per gallon × 10 gallons = 40 quarts

B. 1. In general, the purchasing manager is held responsible for unfavorable material price variances. Causes of these variances include the following.

• Failure to correctly forecast price increases.

• Purchasing in nonstandard or uneconomical lots.

• Failure to take purchase discounts available.

• Failure to control transportation costs.

• Purchasing from suppliers other than those offering the most favorable terms.

However, failure to meet price standards may be caused by a rush of orders or changes in production schedules. In this case, the responsibility for unfavorable material price variances should rest with the sales manager or the manager of production planning. There may also be times when variances are caused by external events and are therefore uncontrollable, e.g., a strike at a supplier's plant.

2. In general, the production manager or foreman is held responsible for unfavorable labor efficiency variances. Causes of these variances include the following.

• Poorly trained labor.

• Substandard or inefficient equipment.

• Inadequate supervision.

• Machine breakdowns from poor maintenance.

• Poorly motivated employees/absenteeism.

Failure to meet labor efficiency standards may also be caused by the use of inferior materials or poor production planning. In these cases, responsibility should rest with the purchasing manager or the manager of production planning. There may also be times when variances are caused by external events and are therefore uncontrollable, e.g., lack of skilled workers caused by low unemployment.

3.

A. 1.

	Equivalent Units	Standard Cost per Equivalent Unit	Total Standard Cost
Raw materials	11,200	$1.00	$11,200.00
Direct labor	7,840	.72	5,644.80
Variable overhead	7,840	1.08	8,467.20
			$25,312.00

2. Raw material purchase price variance

(SP – AP)   × AQ purchased
($8.00 – 7.60[1]) × 13,000 = $5,200 F

Raw material usage (quantity) variance

(Q used – Q allowed) × SP
(13,000 – 12,875[2])   × $8.00 = $1,000 U

Direct labor rate (price) variance

(S rate – A rate)× Actual hours
($18.00 – 17.50[3])× 4,390 = $2,195 F

Direct labor usage (efficiency) variance

(Actual hours – Allowed hours) × Standard rate
(4,390 – 4,336[4])   × $18 = $972 U

Variable overhead spending variance

(Standard overhead rate × Actual hours worked) – Actual variable overhead incurred
($27.00[5] × 4,390) – 117,675
$118,530 – 117,675 = $855 F

Variable overhead efficiency variance

(Actual hours – Allowed hours) × Standard rate
(4,390 – 4,336[4])   × ($18.00 × 150%)
54   × $27.00 = $1,458 U

Total variance is $4,820 F

[1] $\frac{\$98,800}{13,000 \text{ pounds}}$ = $7.60/pound

[2] 103,000 equivalent units × 2 ounce/equivalent unit × 1/16 pounds/ounce = 12,875 pounds

[3] $\frac{\$76,825}{4,390 \text{ hours}}$ = $17.50/hour

[4] 108,400 equivalent units × 4DLH/100 equivalent units = 4,336 DLH

[5] $18.00 × 1.5 of DL cost = $27/DLH

B. The following benefits accrue from the use of a standard process cost system.

- Standard cost per unit and equivalent units can be used to prepare budgets.

- The variances generated from the comparison of standard cost and actual cost can be used in performance evaluation.

- A standard cost system provides predetermined product costs that are not affected by monthly volume changes.

- The use of standard costs eliminates the conflict between the weighted-average method and the first-in, first-out method of process costing.

4.

A.

Computation of Equivalent Units—Materials

	Actual units	Completed in current period(%)	Equivalent units
Beginning work-in-process inventory	2,500	0	0
Started and completed during the month	8,000	100	8,000
Ending work-in-process inventory	2,000	100	2,000
Total	12,500		10,000

Computation of Cost Per Equivalent Unit—Materials

Current costs ÷ equivalent units:
Actual = $121,000 ÷ 10,000 = **$12.10**

Standard = $100,000 ÷ 10,000 = **$10.00**

Computation of Equivalent Units—Labor

	Actual units	Completed in current period(%)	Equivalent units
Beginning work-in-process inventory	2,500	60	1,500
Started and completed during the month	8,000	100	8,000
Ending work-in-process inventory	2,000	40	800
Total	12,500		10,300

Computation of Cost Per Equivalent Unit—Labor

Current costs ÷ equivalent units
Actual = $105,575 ÷ 10,300 = **$10.25**

Standard = $ 82,400 ÷ 10,300 = **$ 8.00**

Computation of Equivalent Units—Combined Factory Overhead

	Actual units	Completed in current period(%)	Equivalent units
Beginning work-in-process inventory	2,500	60	1,500
Started and completed during the month	8,000	100	8,000
Ending work-in-process inventory	2,000	40	800
Total	12,500		10,300

Computation of Cost per Equivalent—Combined Factory Overhead

Current cost per equivalent units:
Actual   = $31,930 ÷ 10,300 = **$3.10**

Standard = $25,750 ÷ 10,300 = **$2.50**

B.

1.   Total Materials Variance

Actual purchases	$121,000
Standard production	100,000
Unfavorable	**$ 21,000**

2.   Materials Price Variance

Actual quantity used at actual (11,000 lbs. × $11)	$121,000
Actual quantity used at standard (11,000 lbs × $10)	110,000
Unfavorable	**$ 11,000**

3.   Materials Usage Variance

Actual quantity used at standard (11,000 lbs. × $10)	$110,000
Standard quantity allowed (10,000 lbs. × $10)	100,000
Unfavorable	**$ 10,000**

4.   Total Labor Variance

Actual labor cost	$105,575
Standard labor cost	82,400
Unfavorable	**$ 23,175**

5.   Labor Rate Variance

Actual hours worked at actual rate (25,000 hours)	$105,575
Actual hours worked at standard rate (25,000 × $4)	100,000
Unfavorable	**$ 5,575**

6.   Labor Efficiency Variance
Actual hours worked at standard rate
   (25,000 × $4) $100,000
Standard hours worked at standard
   rate (20,600 × $4)   82,400
                            Unfavorable   **$ 17,600**

7.   Total Factory Overhead Variance
Actual factory overhead $ 31,930
Factory overhead applied at standard   25,750
                            Unfavorable   **$ 6,180**

8.   Factory Overhead Volume Variance
Budgeted factory overhead $ 30,000
Factory overhead applied at standard   25,750
                            Unfavorable   **$ 4,250**

9.   Factory Overhead Budget Variance
Actual factory overhead $ 31,930
Budgeted factory overhead   30,000
                            Unfavorable   **$ 1,930**

5.

A. Material needed for 42,750 units:
42,750 finished units ÷ 95% good units from production =
45,000 units of direct material

B. Hours needed to produce 42,750 finished units:
45,000 direct material units ÷ 90 labor efficiency = 50,000
equivalent material units of labor

(Problem 5 solution continued on next page.)

6.

A.

	Actual	Standard Price x Actual Quantity Purchased		Price Variance
Echol	$ 5,365	($ .20 × 25,000)	$ 5,000	$365 U
Protex	6,240	($.425 × 13,000)	5,525	715 U
Benz	5,840	($ .15 × 40,000)	6,000	160 F
CT-40	2,220	($ .30 × 7,500)	2,250	30 F
Total	**$19,665**		**$18,775**	**$890 U**

B. Standard cost of entire output ($135 × 140) $18,900

Standard Cost of Actual Quantity Used

Echol	($.20 × 26,600)	$ 5,320
Protex	($.425 × 12,880)	5,474
Benz	($.15 × 37,800)	5,670
CT-40	($.30 × 7,140)	2,142
Total usage variance		18,606
		$ 294 F

Material mix and yield variances

1. Material mix variance
   Standard cost of actual quantity used $18,606.00

   Standard weighted average cost
     of actual quantity used
     ($.225/liter* × 84,420) $18,994.50

   Material mix variance $388.50 F

2. Material yield variance
   Standard weighted average cost
     of actual quantity used
     ($.225/unit* × 84,420) $18,994.50

   Standard cost of entire output $18,900.00

   Material yield variance $ 94.50 U

   Total usage variance $294.00 F

*Standard weighted average cost $\frac{\$135}{600}$ liters = $.225/liter

Class I labor: 6 hours $\times$ $\dfrac{50,000}{100}$ = 3,000 hours

Class II labor: 2 hours $\times$ $\dfrac{50,000}{100}$ = 1,000 hours

Class V labor: 1 hour $\times$ $\dfrac{50,000}{100}$ = 500 hours

C. Planned Labor Variance

Normal labor cost 42,750 @ $58.00/100		$24,795
Expected labor cost		
Class I Labor 3000 DLH @ $ 6.00 =	$18,000	
Class II Labor 1000 DLH @ $ 7.50 =	7,500	
Class V Labor 500 DLH @ $11.50 =	5,750	
		31,250
Total planned labor variance		**$6,455**

Material change:

Normal material	42,750	
New material	45,000	
Extra material	**2,250**	
	@ $58/100	$1,305

Labor

Equivalent material units	50,000	
New material	45,000	
Extra team time	**5,000**	
	@ $58/100	2,900
Actual team cost/100	$62.50/100	
Standard team cost/100	58.00/100	
Extra team cost/100	$ 4.50/100	
Equivalent material		
units of labor	$\times$ 50,000	2,250
		5,150
Total variance		**$6,455**

7.

A. 1. Revising the standards immediately would facilitate their use in a master budget. Use of revised standards would minimize production coordination problems and facilitate cash planning. Revised standards would facilitate more meaningful cost-volume-profit (C/V/P) analysis and result in simpler, more meaningful variance analysis. Standards are often used in decision analysis such as make-or-buy, product pricing, or product discontinuance. The use of obsolete standards would impair the analysis.

2. Standard costs are carried through the accounting system in a standard cost system. Retaining the current standards and expanding the analysis of variances would eliminate the need to make changes in the accounting system.

Changing standards could have an adverse psychological impact on the persons using them. Retaining the current standards would preserve the well known benchmarks and allow for consistency in reporting variances throughout the year.

Variances are often computed and ignored. Retaining the current standards and expanding the analysis of variances would force a diagnosis of the costs and would increase the likelihood that significant variances would be investigated.

B. 1. Changes in prime costs per unit due to the use of new direct material.

● Changes due to direct material price

(New material price – Old material price) × (New material quantity)

($7.77 – $7.00) × 1 pound = $ .77 U

● Changes due to the effect of direct material quality on direct material usage

(Old material quantity – New material quantity) × (Old material price)

(1.25 pounds – 1.00) × $7.00 = 1.75 F

● Changes due to the effect of direct material quality on direct labor usage

(Old labor time – New labor time) × (Old labor rate)

$\left(\dfrac{24}{60} - \dfrac{22}{60}\right) \times \$12.60$ = .42 F

Total changes in prime costs per unit due to the use of new direct material $1.40 F

2. Changes in prime costs per unit due to the new labor contract

(New labor rate – Old labor rate) × (New labor time)

($14.40 – $12.60) × $\dfrac{22}{60}$ = .66 U

Reduction of prime costs per unit ($13.79 – $13.05) $ .74 F

8.

A.
1. Sales price variance		$9,000 U
2. Material price variance		1,200 U
3. Material quantity variance		600 U
4. Labor efficiency variance		500 F
5. Variable overhead efficiency variance		210 F
6. Variable overhead spending variance		2,760 U
7. Contribution margin volume variance		9,250 F
Contribution margin variance		**$3,600 U**

Supporting Calculations

1. Actual sales price = $\dfrac{\text{Actual revenue}}{\text{Actual units}}$

= $\dfrac{\$180,000}{9,000}$

= $20 per unit

Budgeted sales price = $\dfrac{\text{Budgeted revenue}}{\text{Budgeted units}}$

= $\dfrac{\$168,000}{8,000}$

= $21 per unit

Sales price variance   = Actual units × (Actual price-
Budgeted price)

                          = 9,000 units × ($20-$21)

                          = $9,000 U

2. Material price variance= Actual quantity × (Standard
price-Actual price)

Calculation of actual prices:
Cream base $4,200 ÷ 84,000 oz. = $ .05/oz.
Moisturizer $7,200 ÷ 60,000 oz. = $ .12/oz.
Fragrance $4,800 ÷ 4,800 oz. = $1.00/oz.

Calculation of variance:
Cream base 84,000 oz. × ($ .05-$ .05) =$ -0-
Moisturizer 60,000 oz. × ($ .10-$ .12) =$1,200U
Fragrance   4,800 oz. × ($1.00-$1.00) =$ -0-
      Total material price variance $1,200 U

3. Material quantity variance = Standard price × (Standard
quantity—Actual quantity)

Calculation of standard quantities for 9,000 units:
Cream base 9,000 units × 9.0 oz./unit = 81,000 oz.
Moisturizer 9,000 units × 6.5 oz./unit = 58,500 oz.
Fragrance   9,000 units × .5 oz./unit = 4,500 oz.

Calculation of variance:
Cream base $ .05/oz. × (81,000 oz.-84,000 oz.) =$150U
Moisturizer $ .10/oz. × (58,500 oz.-60,000 oz.) = 150U
Fragrance $1.00/oz. × (4,500 oz.- 4,800 oz.) = 300U
      Total material quantity variance $600U

4. Labor efficiency variance = Standard rate × (Standard
hours—Actual hours)

Calculation of standard hours for 9,000 units:
Mixing   9,000 units × .5 hr./unit = 4,500 hrs.
Compounding 9,000 units × 1 hr./unit = 9,000 hrs.

Calculation of variance:
Mixing
   $4.00/hr. × (4,500 hrs.-4,500 hrs.)   = $ -0-
Compounding-manual (60%)
   $5.00/hr. × [(.6) (9,000) - 5,300 hrs.] =   500 F
Compounding-mech. (40%)
   $5.00/hr. × [(.4) (9,000) - 2,700 hrs.] = 4,500 F
Compounding idle
   $5.00/hr. × (0-900)   = 4,500 U
      Total labor efficiency variance $ 500 F

5. $\begin{bmatrix}\text{Variable overhead} \\ \text{efficiency variance}\end{bmatrix} = \begin{bmatrix}\text{Standard rate} \times \text{(Standard hours-} \\ \text{Actual hours)}\end{bmatrix}$

$2.10 × [(1.5 hrs./unit) (9,000 units)   = $210 F
- 13,400 hrs.]

6. Variable overhead = (Actual hours × Standard overhead
   spending variance   rate)—Actual variable overhead
                = (13,400 × $2.10) - $30,900
                = $28,140 - $30,900
                = $2,760 U

7. Budgeted unit contribution= $\dfrac{\text{Total budgeted contribution}}{\text{Budgeted units}}$

                          = $\dfrac{\$74,000}{8,000}$

                          = $9.25/unit

Contribution margin
volume variance   = Budgeted unit contribution ×
(Actual units—Budgeted
units)

                          = $9.25 × (9,000-8,000)

                          = $9,250 F

B. Allglow Company should continue to mechanize a portion of the compounding operation in the SkinKlear manufacturing process because of the variable cost savings that can be expected to arise in the future.

Elimination of idle hours due to reassignment of workers (900 hrs. × $5.00)	$4,500
Elimination of variable overhead applied to idle hours (900 hrs. × $2.10)	1,890
Variable overhead spending variance traceable to mechanization [$30,900-(13,400 × $2.10)]	(2,760)
Variable cost savings for 9,000 units	$3,630

Material inefficiencies caused by the mechanization will be neglible when the process is permanent and the workers' skills are improved.

9.

A. The variances Justin Company can calculate by job which can contribute to cost control are material quantity, direct labor efficiency, and variable overhead efficiency. These three variances are usage variances which are based upon the quantity of material or labor used on a specific job. The schedule on the next page presents these three variances by job.

B. Yes, the company's plan to calculate variances by job in addition to department variances is a good idea. Each job is assigned to a team, and therefore, many of the costs are controllable at the team level. By calculating the variances by job, Justin Company could evaluate the teams to determine if they are handling their responsibilities. The variances by job would be an additional and different signal from departmental variances to management that investigation may be needed. In addition, if large variances occur by job, the information obtained from the variances by job may serve as the basis for the revision of standards. The price variance for materials and the spending variance for variable overhead and the fixed overhead would not be included in the evaluation, because they would not be controllable at the team level.

9. A.

	Job number		
	307-11	307-12	307-14
Material quantity variance			
Actual costs	$5,200	$2,900	$ 9,400
Standard costs			
Job 307-11 2,000 units × $2.00	4,000		
Job 307-12 1,000 units × $3.00		3,000	
Job 307-14 6,000 units × $1.50			9,000
Variance	1,200 U	100 F	400 U
Direct labor efficiency variance			
Actual costs	4,000	2,100	6,200
Standard costs			
Job 307-11 2,000 units × $1.50	3,000		
Job 307-12 1,000 units × $2.00		2,000	
Job 307-14 6,000 units × $1.00			6,000
Variance	1,000 U	100 U	200 U
Variable overhead efficiency variance			
Applied costs (200% of standard direct labor cost)	8,000	4,200	12,400
Standard			
Job 307-11 2,000 units × $3.00	6,000		
Job 307-12 1,000 units × $4.00		4,000	
Job 307-14 6,000 units × $2.00			12,000
Variance	2,000 U	200 U	400 U
Total variances by job	**$4,200 U**	**$ 200 U**	**$ 1,000 U**

10.

A. Isolation of the material price variance at the time of purchase is appropriate because it records the entire amount of the variance in the correct period. The claims of Bob Speck and Jim Buddle, however, are all valid.

Speck is correct in stating that the price variance is misleading and does not measure his department's performance. Purchase discounts are price concessions obtained by the Purchasing Department for which the Purchasing Department should receive credit.

Buddle is correct in stating that the responsibility for the quantity variance should be shared. An analysis of increased quantities may indicate that there has been a purchase of inferior parts. This is the responsibility of the Purchasing Department. The substitution of materials to use up otherwise obsolete stock is the result of actions or decisions of Purchasing, Engineering, or both and should be charged to the responsible department(s).

B.

Economic variance = (Quantity purchased) × (Negotiation changes - contract terms)
= 150,000 × [($.285 + $.04) × .04]
= $1,950 favorable

Engineering change variance = (Quantity purchased) × (Price change from specifications)
= 150,000 × $.04
= $6,000 unfavorable

Purchase price variance = (Quantity purchased) × (Other price changes)
= 150,000 × $0 = $0

Substitutions variance = (Quantity substituted) × (Difference in standard price)
= 24,000 × ($.35 – $.285)
= $1,560 unfavorable

Excess usage variance = (Standard price) × [(Standard quantity allowed) – (Actual usage reduced for normal scrap)]
= $.285 × [153,300 – (158,000 – 2,000*)]
= $769.50 unfavorable

Abnormal failure rate variance = (Abnormal spoilage) × (Standard price)
= 2,000* × $.285
= $570 unfavorable

	Units
*Total spoilage	9,665
Normal spoilage (153,300 × .05)	7,665
Abnormal spoilage	2,000

C. The following persons would be responsible for the variances in Mike Kohl's system of variance analysis.

Variance	Person Responsible
Economics	Purchasing
Engineering change	Engineering
Purchase price	Purchasing - generally Sales - in the case of a rush order Manufacturing - in the case of poor production planning
Substitutions	Engineering - in the case of poor design or choice of parts Manufacturing - in case of failing to notify Purchasing of planned usage to be sure that a sufficient supply of a part is on hand when needed
Excess usage	Manufacturing
Abnormal failure rate	Manufacturing - in the case of carelessness Purchasing - in the case of the purchase of inferior parts

D. Vantage Manufacturing's current method of variance analysis is an adequate method for isolating the basic price and quantity variances. However, this method fails to identify the causes of the variances and properly assign responsibility.

Both Bob Speck and Jim Buddle are likely to be demotivated if the current system of variance analysis is retained.

The proposed variance analysis refines the current analysis by separating the price variance into several components. This new analysis allows management to trace the variance to a cause and facilitates the assignment of responsibility.

Speck would be pleased and motivated with the proposed variance analysis as his department will receive credit for negotiating favorable contract terms and would not be penalized for the price increases caused by the engineering change.

Buddle is also likely to be pleased and motivated with the proposed system as it does not automatically assume that all quantity variances are the responsibility of manufacturing. The new system recognizes the fact that some quantity variances result from inferior parts and are, therefore, the responsibility of the Purchasing Department. [Adapted]

11.

A. At least four general advantages associated with activity-based costing include the following.

• Provides management with a more thorough understanding of complex product costs and product profitability for improved resource management and pricing decisions.

• Allows management to focus on value-added and nonvalue-added activities so that nonvalue-added activities can be controlled or eliminated, thus streamlining production processes.

• Highlights the interrelationship (cause and effect) of activities which identifies opportunities to reduce costs, i.e., designing products with fewer parts in order to reduce the cost of the manufacturing process.

• Provides more appropriate means of charging overhead costs to products.

B. 1. Using standard costs, the total contribution expected in 1993 by Allaire Corporation from the TV Board is $1,950,000, calculated as follows.

	Per Unit	Totals for 65,000 units
Revenue	$150	$ 9,750,000
Direct material	80	5,200,000
Material overhead (10% of material)	8	520,000
Direct labor ($14 x 1.5 hours)	21	1,365,000
Variable overhead ($4 x 1.5 hours)*	6	390,000
Machine time ($10 x .5)	5	325,000
Total cost	120	7,800,000
Unit contribution	$ 30	
Total contribution (65,000 x $30)		$ 1,950,000

*Variable overhead rate
$1,120,000 ÷ 280,000 hours = $4 per hour.

2. Using standard costs, the total contribution expected in 1993 by Allaire Corporation from the PC Board is $2,360,000, calculated as follows.

	Per Unit	Totals for 40,000 units
Revenue	$300	$12,000,000
Direct material	140	5,600,000
Material overhead (10% of material)	14	560,000
Direct labor ($14 x 4 hours)	56	2,240,000
Variable overhead ($4 x 4 hours)*	16	640,000
Machine time ($10 x 1.5)	15	600,000
Total cost	241	9,640,000
Unit contribution	$ 59	
Total contribution (65,000 x $30)		$ 2,360,000

*Variable overhead rate
$1,120,000 ÷ 280,000 hours = $4 per hour.

C. Shown below are the calculations of the cost drivers which apply to both C. 1. and C. 2.

Procurement
$400,000 ÷ 4,000,000 = $ .10 per part

Production scheduling
$220,000 ÷ 110,000 = $2.00 per board

Packaging & shipping
$440,000 ÷ 110,000 = $4.00 per board

Machine set-ups
$446,000 ÷ 278,750 = $1.60 per board

Hazardous waste disposal
$48,000 ÷ 16,000 = $3.00 per pound

Quality control
$560,000 ÷ 160,000 = $3.50 per inspection

General supplies
$66,000 ÷ 110,000 = $ .60 per board

Machine insertion
$1,200,000 ÷ 3,000,000 = $ .40 per part

Manual insertion
$4,000,000 ÷ 1,000,000 = $4.00 per part

Wave soldering
$132,000 ÷ 110,000 = $1.20 per board

1. Using activity-based costing, the total contribution expected in 1993 by Allaire Corporation from the TV Board is $2,557,100 calculated as follows.

	Per Unit	Totals for 65,000 units
Revenue	$150.00	$9,750,000
Direct material	80.00	5,200,000
Material overhead		
Procurement ($.10 x 25)	2.50	162,500
Production scheduling	2.00	130,000
Packaging & shipping	4.00	260,000
Variable overhead		
Machine set-ups ($1.60 x 2)	3.20	208,000
Waste disposal ($3 x .02)	.06	3,900
Quality control	3.50	227,500
General supplies	.60	39,000
Manufacturing		
Machine insertion ($.40 x 24)	9.60	624,000
Manual insertion	4.00	260,000
Wave soldering	1.20	78,000
Total cost	110.66	7,192,900
Unit contribution	$ 39.34	
Total contribution		$2,557,100

2. Using activity-based costing, the total contribution expected in 1993 by Allaire Corporation from the PC Board is $1,594,000 calculated as follows.

	Per Unit	Totals for 40,000 units
Revenue	$300.00	$12,000,000
Direct material	140.00	5,600,000
Material overhead		
Procurement		
($.10 x 55)	5.50	220,000
Production scheduling	2.00	80,000
Packaging & shipping	4.00	160,000
Variable overhead		
Machine set-ups		
($1.60 x 3)	4.80	192,000
Waste disposal		
($3 x .35)	1.05	42,000
Quality control		
($3.50 x 2)	7.00	280,000
General supplies	.60	24,000
Manufacturing		
Machine insertion		
($.40 x 35)	14.00	560,000
Manual insertion		
($4 x 20)	80.00	3,200,000
Wave soldering	1.20	48,000
Total cost	260.15	10,406,000
Unit contribution	$ 39.85	
Total contribution		$ 1,594,000

D. The analysis using standard costs shows that the unit contribution of the PC Board is almost double that of the TV Board. On this basis, Alaire's management is likely to accept the suggestion of the production manager and concentrate promotional efforts on expanding the market for the PC Boards.

However, the analysis using activity-based costs does not support this decision. This analysis shows that the unit dollar contribution from each of the boards is almost equal, and the total contribution from the TV Board exceeds that of the PC Board by almost $1,000,000. As a percentage of selling price, the contribution from the TV Board is double that of the PC Board, e.g., 26 percent versus 13 percent.

12.

A. Calculations of the four variances covered in items 1-4 provide the bases for a reconciliation, presented below, of the $41,900 variance between budgeted and actual factory overhead during the month of November 1992.

1. Volume (Flexible budget) variance

$= $ (Budgeted units-Actual units) x Standard variable overhead rate

$= $ (80,000 - 82,000) x $1

$= $ $2,000 unfavorable

2. Variable overhead efficiency variance

$= $ (Standard hours required for output-Actual hours) x Standard variable overhead rate

Standard hours required for output

$= $ 82,000 x .25

$= $ 20,500 hours

Actual hours

$= $ $246,000 ÷ $12

$= $ 20,500 hours

$= $ 0 hours of variance

3. Variable overhead spending variance

$= $ (Actual units x Standard variable overhead rate) - Actual variable overhead

$= $ (82,000 x $1) - $98,400

$= $ $16,400 unfavorable

4. Fixed overhead spending variance

$= $ Budgeted fixed overhead-Actual fixed overhead

$= $ [$200,000 - (80,000 x $1)] -$143,500

$= $ $23,500 unfavorable

- Reconciliation of overhead variance

Flexible budget variance	$ 2,000 U
Variable overhead efficiency variance	—
Variable overhead spending variance	16,400 U
Fixed overhead spending variance	23,500 U
Total overhead variance	$41,900 U

B. Bob Ricker is likely to be pleased with some of the information provided by the analysis and should be motivated to seek new productivity improvements. Some of the information may be confusing and cause him to be concerned about some of the budget areas.

- The volume (flexible budget) variance shows that $2,000 of the total variance was due to the increase in production from 80,000 to 82,000 units; if Ricker was authorized to produce 82,000 units, this variance is strictly a budgeting problem.

- The variable overhead efficency variance, which is zero, is clearly Ricker's responsibility and shows that direct labor has been productive.

- The variable overhead spending variance, from the information provided, shows that most of the variance is due to overspending on indirect labor and power usage. Ricker may be responsible for indirect labor and should be concerned about looking for the causes of the overspending and implementing corrective action.

- The fixed overhead spending variance reflects items in fixed overhead that would not generally be under Ricker's control. However, there is a significant increase in quality inspection expenses. As the quality of the work that Ricker is responsible for may affect expenditures in this area, he may wish to investigate this area more thoroughly.

Chapter 7

Divisional Performance Evaluation[1]

Grant W. Newton

The trend in business toward larger firms and divisionalization has led to an increased emphasis on the need for techniques and accounting systems that enable top management to evaluate the various facets of the operation. The ability to measure performance is crucial since it provides the feedback necessary to make predictions for future decisions, appraise the abilities of managers, and assess the profitability of the investment made in each subunit of the company.[2]

Selection of the method used to evaluate a manager is important since it may significantly influence his or her behavior. One of the basic tenets of performance evaluation is the concept of responsibility accounting, which recognizes various decision centers throughout an organization and traces costs (and revenues, assets, and liabilities where pertinent) to the individual managers who are primarily responsible for making decisions about the costs in question."[3] This means managers are held responsible only for those items that are actually controllable by them. This accountability can be established as a cost center, profit center, or an investment center. **Cost centers** refer to responsibility centers for cost control and are usually departments or, in some cases, processes. **Profit centers** include various segments of the business where the manager is responsible for revenue as well as expenses. What distinguishes a profit center from an **investment center** is that the latter includes the responsibility for the profitable use of assets.

To facilitate accountability, both the accounting system and the method of performance evaluation should reflect the actual structure of the firm. The accounting system should be designed in conjunction with the organizational structure so that it measures and reports the type of information management needs.

Nature of Decentralization

As organizations grow, top management must make decisions as to the division of activities and responsibilities and the coordination of subunits. During this growth process the power to make decisions must be given to others in the organization.[4] Clayden suggests that there are two main categories of reasons for decentralization:

1. *Operational*—At times technological or geographical specialties necessitate divisions. For example, in conglomerate acquisitions it may be best, at least for a time, to keep the present organizational structure and decision-making authority.

2. *Motivational*—Long chains of command in large companies can result in an impersonal organizational structure. Decentralization provides local motivation and encourages internal competition.[5]

1. See Chapter 8 for a discussion of the behavioral aspects of divisional performance evaluation.
2. Charles T. Horngren, et al., *Cost Accounting: A Managerial Emphasis*, 8th ed., (Englewood Cliffs, N.J.; Prentice-Hall, 1994), p. 890.
3. *Ibid.*

4. *Ibid.*
5. Roger Clayden, "A New Way to Measure and Control Divisional Performance," *Management Services* 7 (September-October, 1970), 22.

In addition, giving managers the authority to make decisions provides them the opportunity to grow and develop personally and acquire necessary experience for future advancement.

The basis of decentralization is a breakdown of responsibilities according to function, market distribution, geographic area, or other logical plan. When complete decentralization exists, the manager of the individual entity possesses virtually total freedom to make decisions for the operation; the opposite is true if there is complete centralization—there, all decisions are made at the top. Most organizations are somewhat between these two extremes. In essence, the degree to which the manager is allowed to make decisions is an indication of the extent to which the organization is decentralized. It is important to make a distinction between "divisionalization" and "decentralization." Decentralization is the process of giving others the authority to make decisions. This authority can be granted without a business being divisionalized. A **division**, as referred to in this chapter, is a segment of a company where responsibility for profit has been assigned; examples include companies that have divided their operations into profit or investment centers.

Certain conditions must be present for divisionalization to succeed. Solomons suggests that the most important factor is that "each division should be sufficiently independent of other divisions, both in respect to its production facilities and its marketing organization, to make its separate profit responsibility a reality.[6] This does not mean that divisions must be totally independent—if they were, they would be separate companies and not divisions of the same company. For obvious reasons there must be considerable cooperation between various divisions. For example, they may share the results of research or production and marketing information. Another condition for the success of divisionalization is "a degree of self-restraint on the part of the corporate administration in issuing directives to the divisions".[7]

For many companies, divisionalization may not be the best solution even though the conditions for success are satisfied. Some possible reasons for this are: the company is too small, the costs involved exceed the expected benefits, or the managers may lack the experience and financial know-how necessary to run a division successfully.

ROI Analysis

Many approaches are used to measure the performance of divisions and among the most widely used of these is return on investment (ROI):

$$ROI = \frac{Net\ income}{Sales} \times \frac{Sales}{Total\ investment}$$

This formula or a similar variation of it has achieved popularity because it succeeds in integrating the important and

6. David Solomons, *Divisional Performance: Measurement and Control* (Homewood, Ill.; Richard D. Irwin, 1968), pp. 10-11.
7. *Ibid.*, p. 12.

meaningful aspects of a firm's objectives in one single figure. This figure, expressed as a percentage, can be used to compare one division with other divisions or with operations of outside companies. Using ROI as an evaluation tool gives individual managers broad control in that they do not have to abide by a budget. Although a projected rate of return must be earned, managers can use their judgment as to how that is done. The ROI is favored by many because it measures how well managers use the assets over which they have control.

DuPont was one of the first companies to adopt the ROI approach for its decentralized operations, and many other companies have since adopted some form of it. The DuPont Company made quarterly evaluations by comparing the actual ROI with the ROI objective. In this comparison each component of the ROI was analyzed by DuPont by the use of the chart presented in Exhibit 7-1.

Difficulties of ROI Analysis

Decentralized companies encounter several difficulties in using ROI for performance evaluation. One problem deals with properly defining net income and investments.

Net Income   The net income figure used in the ROI formula could represent the contribution margin, net profit before taxes and interest, final net income, or some modification of one of these. The net income figure most suitable for measuring the performance of the manager should include only the revenue and costs over which the manager has control. For example, taxes would not be included unless the manager is responsible for tax planning. Costs allocated from the corporate office would be omitted.

Investments   Two important decisions must be made regarding the investment base: which items to include and how to value those items. Possible alternatives to consider in selecting the base are total assets, total assets employed, total assets minus current liabilities, total assets minus total liabilities (owners' equity), fixed assets, or some other combination consisting of modifications of these. In general, the investment base should include those accounts—assets and liabilities—over which the division has responsibility. For example, if the division is responsible for the payment of current liabilities and for managing other items that comprise the working capital, total assets minus current liabilities may possibly be the best combination. Using total assets as the base would encourage the manager to reduce the asset base and improve the ROI by paying the liabilities as soon as they are incurred. (This action, however, would not be consistent with the goal of most companies to manage cash effectively.) A division that does not have any control over payments to creditors or short-term bank credit would want to exclude all liabilities from the base and use total assets as the investment figure. Also, there may be a question as to whether certain investments not typically accounted for as "assets," such as investments in training programs and research and development, should be included.

The total assets employed approach excludes idle assets

Exhibit 7-1
The Dupont System of Financial Control
(An adaptation)

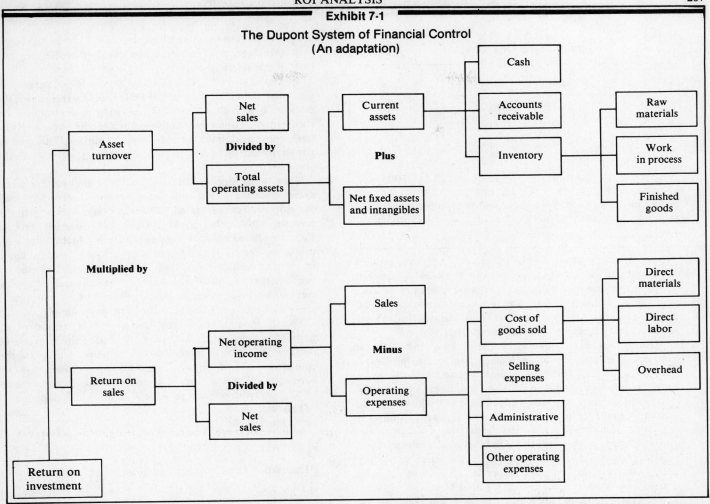

from the base. If top management insists that certain idle assets be retained in a given division even though they are not being utilized, then it may be best to remove these assets from the investment base. However, if the objective of ROI is to encourage divisions to use all assets under their control effectively, then all such assets should be included.

Thus, for control and motivational purposes, the base should include all investment items—but only those items— the manager can control.

Another factor to consider is whether the investment base should consist of the beginning balance, ending balance, or an average of the investments for the period. Use of the beginning or ending balances would encourage managers to adjust the investment base at year end; in addition, this approach would not take into consideration the change in investments during the period due to seasonal influences. Monthly or quarterly averages should eliminate these discrepancies.

Another problem lies with the selection of a method to value assets. Possible methods include gross book value, net book value, and some type of economic value or replacement costs. Since assets are recorded at historical cost for financial statement purposes, most companies also use these values for performance evaluation. However, neither gross book value nor net book value are completely satisfactory. The use of gross book value (original cost) encourages managers

to discard still useful, but unprofitable assets. If these assets are almost fully depreciated or if composite depreciation methods are used, no capital loss will result from the disposition. Yet, the sale of these assets can be a real drain on the firm since very little may be received on their disposal, and when volume increases again, a large outlay may be necessary to obtain the needed replacements. Thus, this type of action may be temporarily beneficial to the division, but in the long-run detrimental to the company.

Net book value (cost minus accumulated depreciation) provides a division manager with a method whereby the disposal of an asset reduces the investment base only by the amount of the undepreciated value of the fixed asset. Therefore, net book value eliminates the desire to discard some useful assets; however, the declining investment base creates another problem. Since the investment base decreases as the asset ages, automatically increasing the rate of return, some divisions become reluctant to invest in newer, more productive assets because the rate of return will decrease. This disadvantage could be eliminated by using the compound interest method of depreciation. Under this method, which is just the opposite of accelerated depreciation, a small amount is charged to depreciation the first year, and as the asset ages, more is charged, causing a constant ROI. Since this approach cannot be used for income tax purposes or for external reporting purposes and because it is more difficult to understand than the more commonly used depreciation methods,

---

Exhibit 7-2

**ROI Using
Straight-Line Depreciation**

Year	Average investment	Profits	ROI
1	$108.000[a]	$12,000	11.1%
2	84,000	12,000	14.3
3	60,000	12,000	20.0
4	36,000	12,000	33.3
5	12,000	12,000	100.0

[a] Beginning investment of $120,000 plus investment at year end ($120,000 − $24,000 of depreciation) divided by two.

---

the compound interest method has received very little support.

Economic values would seem to be the ideal measure to use for performance evaluation. However, because of their high degree of subjectivity, they are not practical. A reasonable substitute for the economic value approach, and one that is more objective, is replacement cost.

During periods of rising prices, the ROI will be higher than in periods of constant or decreasing prices. The increase in profits, a result of rising prices, is contrasted with the investment base which changes only when new assets are acquired. With this discrepancy, comparison of one division with another is not very meaningful since assets are acquired at different times; and even though the assets are identical, they have different cost bases. Using indexes to adjust the base of fixed assets would do for changes in the value of money; however, to adjust for the changes in the relative values of individual assets, replacement costs must be used.

Many accountants prefer to use replacement cost over historical cost. Replacement cost allows financial reporting to be more of a science, rather than an art; also, they know that for investing purposes replacement cost is far more superior. In light of so much evidence, why do so many accountants prefer to use the historical cost rather than the replacement cost? Horngren, et al., have concluded the following:[8]

• Using net book value is easy

• Net book value is consistent with total assets shown on the conventional balance sheet.

• Net book value is consistent with deduction from income, such as depreciation.

• Net book value can be useful for auditing past decisions, if all assets have been recorded in a consistent manner.

Goal Congruence   The ROI approach may encourage divisional managers to increase their division's return at the expense of the total company's profits. For example, if the company's overall rate of return is 15 percent and a division's average rate of return is 24 percent, an opportunity to earn a return of 20 percent on an investment would be rejected. Such an investment would reduce the division's ROI although

it would increase the overall return for the company. Thus, managers may concentrate on a relative profit and not maximize absolute profits.

At times the use of ROI may encourage managers to maximize their short-run return while ignoring the impact the decision has on the future ROI. In order to accomplish the short-run ROI objective, a manager may reduce research and development, training, or maintenance outlays. This type of action would definitely not be in the best interest of the company.

Thus, while decentralization and ROI analysis are advocated as means of motivating employees and providing goals for individual managers and divisions that coincide with the company's goals, they could produce quite different results.

Relationship to Capital Investment Analysis   Many companies use some form of discounted cash flows to make capital investment decisions. A decision to make a capital investment because the rate of return is greater than the cost of capital can cause a division's ROI to go down, especially in the early years of the project. Consider the following example.

The Brentwood Company has a cost of capital of 12 percent; any proposal with a time-adjusted return in excess of this rate would be accepted by the company. A proposal the company is considering would have a cash inflow of $44,000 over a period of five years. The cost of the investment would be $120,000 with no salvage value. The tax rate is 40 percent.

The cash inflow needed to calculate the TAR (time-adjusted rate of return) is:

Cash inflow per year	$44,000
Depreciation (straight-line, $120,000 ÷ 5)	24,000
Net income	20,000
Tax (40 percent)	8,000
Net income after tax	12,000
Depreciation	24,000
Cash inflow per year	**$36,000**

The TAR for $120,000 investment for five years with an annual cash inflow of $36,000 is approximately 15¼ percent.

Using the straight-line method of depreciation the ROI based on the gross investment would be:

$$ROI = \frac{\text{Net cash savings} - \text{Depreciation}}{\text{Investment}}$$

$$= \frac{\$36,000 - \$24,000}{\$120,000} = 10\%$$

Based on net book value (the average investment) the ROI would be 20 percent:

$$ROI = \frac{\text{Net cash savings} - \text{Depreciation}}{\text{Investment} / 2}$$

$$= \frac{\$36,000 - \$24,000}{\$120,000 / 2} = 20\%$$

Exhibit 7-3

ROI Using
Sum-of-Years-Digits Depreciation

(1)	(2)	(3)	(4)	(5)	(6)	(7)
Year	Average investment	Cash savings	Sum-of-years-digits depreciation	Net profit (Col. 3 − Col. 4)	Net profit after taxes (Col. 5 × .60)	ROI (Col. 6 ÷ Col. 2)
1	$100,000[a]	$44,000	$40,000	$ 4,000	$ 2,400	2.4%
2	64,000	44,000	32,000	12,000	7,200	11.3
3	36,000	44,000	24,000	20,000	12,000	33.3
4	16,000	44,000	16,000	28,000	16,800	105.0
5	4,000	44,000	8,000	36,000	21,600	540.0

[a] Beginning investment of $120,000 plus investment at year end ($120,000 − $40,000 depreciation) divided by two.

Exhibit 7-4

ROI Using
Compound Interest Depreciation

(1)	(2)	(3)	(4)	(5)
Year	Cash savings	Return at 15¼ (0.1525 × book investment[a])	Capital recovery (Col. 2 − Col. 3)	Investment balance, end of year (investment − capital recovery)
1	36,000	18,300	17,700	102,300
2	36,000	15,601	20,399	81,901
3	36,000	12,490	23,510	58,391
4	36,000	8,905	27,095	31,296
5	36,000	4,773	31,227	69[b]

[a] At beginning of year (year 1, $120,000 × .1525; year 2, $102,300 × .1525 and so on)

[b] Due to rounding

These returns are the average return over the life of the investment and do not agree with the discounted rate of return of 15¼ percent. Using net book values the rate of return will show considerable variation over the life of the project. Exhibit 7-2 shows that the rate of return using the average net book value and straight-line depreciation will result in an ROI that ranges from 11 percent in the first year to 100 percent in year five. Using the sum-of-years-digits depreciation, the return varies from 2 percent to 540 percent as shown in Exhibit 7-3. These variances occur for an investment that earns a time-adjusted return of 15¼ percent. Only by using the compound interest method of depreciation would ROI agree with the capital investment time-adjusted return.

The compound interest method of depreciation provides for a constant rate of return on the net book value, with the balance of the cash flow being charged as depreciation and representing a recovery of the capital investment. Exhibit 7-4 shows the return and capital recovery for each of the five years. This example is based on the assumption that straight-line depreciation is used for tax purposes and that the annual cash inflow is $36,000 per year. If the tax inflow for year three dropped to $30,000 after taxes, the ROI for that year would be only 7.9 percent.

$$ROI = \frac{\text{Net income (cash flow − depreciation)}}{\text{Net book value of investment}}$$

$$= \frac{\$30,000 − \$23,510}{\$81,901} = 7.9\%$$

Any cash inflow in a given year that is less than the amount planned will cause the ROI to go below the stipulated rate and indicate that plans are not actually being met. The use of the compound interest method of depreciation provides an evaluation system where the basis for performance evaluation is consistent with the criterion used to make investment decisions. However, this approach is seldom used by decentralized companies. No doubt one reason for this is that it requires records for performance evaluation purposes that differ from those used for financial reporting. Generally, managers have been reluctant to adopt procedures that require such a modification. Also, some writers believe it would be difficult for divisional managers to understand the system and, not knowing how it works, these managers would not have the needed confidence in the system for it to function effectively.

Matz and Usry summarized the advantages and limitations

of the use of ROI for internal profit measurement.[9]

Advantages:

1. Focus management's attention upon earning the best profit possible on the capital (total assets) available.
2. Serve as a yardstick in measuring management's efficiency and effectiveness in managing the company as a whole and its major divisions or departments.
3. Tie together the many phases of financial planning, sales objectives, cost control, and the profit goal.
4. Afford comparison of managerial results both internally and externally.
5. Develop a keener sense of responsibility and team effort in divisional and departmental managers by enabling them to measure and evaluate their own activities in the light of the results achieved by other managers.
6. Aid in detecting weaknesses with respect to the use or nonuse of individual assets particularly in connection with inventories.

Limitations:

1. Lack of agreement on the right or optimum rate of return might discourage managers whose opinion is that the rate is set at an unfair level.
2. Proper allocation requires certain data regarding sales, costs, and assets. The accounting and cost system might not give such needed details.
3. Values and valuations of assets, particularly with regard to jointly used assets, might give rise to difficulties and misunderstandings.
4. Excessive preoccupation with financial factors due to constant attention to ratios and trends might distract management's interest from technical and other responsibilities. Product research and development, managerial development, progressive personnel policies, good employee morale, and good customer and public relations are just as important in earning a greater profit and assuring continuous growth.
5. Managers may be influenced to make decisions that are not the best for the long-run interests of the firm merely for the sake of making the current period rate of return on capital employed "look good."
6. A *single* measure of performance (for example, return on capital employed) may result in a fixation on improving the components of the one measure to the neglect of needed attention to other desirable activities—both short- and long-run.

Residual Income

The ROI approach can cause a profitable division to reject an alternative which, while reducing that division's ROI, would have been advantageous to the company. To eliminate this problem and to stress the dollar return, the residual income approach is used by several companies including General Electric. Residual income is the net income of a division less the deduction for the cost of capital. Consider

the following two examples:

	Division A	Division B
Investment base	**$100,000**	**$600,000**
Net income	$ 20,000	$ 90,000
Cost of capital—10 percent	10,000	60,000
Residual income	**$ 10,000**	**$ 30,000**
ROI	20%	15%

Note that Division A has the higher ROI but the residual income is $20,000 less than that of Division B. Under the residual income approach, Division B would be considered the most profitable. Once the cost of capital has been recovered, emphasis is placed on the maximum dollar profit. Improvements in dollar values are stressed rather than improvements in the ratio of net income to the investment. Note that as the cost of capital exceeds 10 percent, the difference in the residual income becomes less and less. When the rate rises to 14 percent, the residual income is the same for both divisions as shown below:

	Residual Income	
Cost of Capital	Division A	Division B
10%	$10,000	$30,000
11	9,000	24,000
12	8,000	18,000
13	7,000	12,000
14	6,000	6,000
15	5,000	–0–
16	4,000	–6,000

Transfer Pricing

If the ROI is to be an effective measuring device, the revenue and costs for each division must be clearly defined, and the managers must be in a position to exercise control over these items. In essence, each of these divisions is a separate financial entity, and when divisions buy from and sell to one another, some price must be established for these transfers. It is important that the transfer price be carefully selected. The pricing system selected should provide for (1) **goal congruence**, (2) **performance evaluation**, and (3) **autonomy**.[10] Goal congruence suggests that the goals of the division should coincide with those of the company as a whole. The benefits from performance evaluation were discussed at the beginning of this chapter. Regarding autonomy, each subunit, if it is to remain a decentralized unit, must be free from constant inter-

---

9. Adolph Matz and Milton F. Usry, *Cost Accounting: Planning and Control,* 6th ed., (Cincinnati: South-Western Publishing Co., 1976), pp. 879-880.

10. Joshua Ronen and George McKinney, "Transfer Pricing for Divisional Autonomy," *Journal of Accounting Research 8* (Spring 1970), '00-101.

ference by top management.

The establishment of a transfer price is an important part of the process of assessing a division's performance. It is imperative, however, that the approach used in establishing the price does not lead to divisions attempting to enhance their own performance at the cost of the company. Since a single method of transfer pricing that will accomodate all the demands imposed upon it has not yet been developed, several approaches are currently in use.

Current Practices

Sharav suggests that the market price, or some approximation thereof, is more likely to be used as the corporation approaches complete decentralization.[11] Divisional autonomy allows buying and selling managers to make their own decisions as to the price at which the product will be transferred. Of course, the availability of an outside market will make it easier to establish greater decentralization and to use a market-oriented price. Under conditions where decentralization is limited and many decisions are made for the division by top management, "while the market-influenced prices are not excluded, some variation or modification of cost is likely to serve as a basis for the transfer."[12]

Market Price   Under this approach, divisions buy and sell to one another at the price used for transactions with outsiders. The advantages of this method from a behavioral standpoint are:

1. It is determined independently of the buyer, thus avoiding conflict among managers.

2. Individual managers have some authority to influence the price. The selling division can change the price on interdivision sales in the same way external prices are changed. The buying division has the option to purchase outside if it can obtain a better price.

3. It gives the selling division an incentive to minimize costs since any savings become profit for the division.

The limitations of this approach are:

1. Market price may not be best for the firm as a whole. For example, Division A elects to purchase externally rather than buy from Division B because the price is $3 per unit less. This decision would not result in the maximization of firm profit if the selling costs of Division B were in excess of $3 per unit and these costs would not be incurred for intracompany transfers. To alleviate this situation, a discount could be allowed for selling expenses. This modification allows the selling division to make the same profit, and it would now be profitable for the buying division to purchase from the selling division.

11. Itzhak Sharav, "Transfer Pricing—Diversity of Goals," *Journal of Accountancy 137* (April 1974), 58.
12. *Ibid.*

2. Even though the buying division is willing to pay market price, the selling division may refuse to sell because current external customers will be turned away, destroying goodwill previously built up.

3. The selling division may lose its competitive advantage, market share, or even monopoly power if a substantial number of external sales are eliminated by divisional sales.

4. It is difficult to determine what the market price is. For example, a division needs to purchase an item that is similar, but not identical, to products sold in the open market. Yet, a significant variation in price exists for this line of similar products. The divisions must now decide on a price to use. Many alternatives are available, including an average sales price, but each of them can cause behavioral problems. One possibility is to have the purchasing division obtain an outside quote and use it. This may work once or twice, but once the outside seller realizes that his estimation is for internal uses, subsequent quotations, even if obtained, will not be very reliable.

Negotiated Price   The use of a negotiated price is one way to overcome some of the problems associated with determining the market price. This method assumes that since divisions possess autonomy, they should be allowed to arrive at a price agreement among themselves. The environment under which the negotiations take place should be similar to the competitive market and a competitive incentive to the division managers should be created. These negotiations may lead to cooperative efforts in certain purchasing and shipping activities that result in cost savings for both divisions.

Unfortunately, negotiated pricing policies can also produce negative effects. If managers insist on an optimum advantageous price for them, the lengthy process may create hostility between divisions. Such dysfunctional behavior may ultimately be to the disadvantage of the corporation as a whole although it still may be less than under alternative methods.

Selling Division's Costs

The use of cost as a basis for a transfer price conceptually places emphasis on product profitability rather than divisional profitability. Among the advantages frequently cited for the use of cost are its ease of administration, its availability, and its potential for reducing the conflict between divisional managers. Several types of costing are used in practice.

Full Costs   Transfer of the product at the actual full cost transfers the inefficiencies of the selling division to the buying division by eliminating the selling division's incentive to reduce costs. To encourage cost reductions, standard full cost could be used as the transfer price. This allows the selling division to benefit from any cost reductions incurred.

However, standard costs do not provide the type of information necessary for decision making and can lead to decisions that will not result in maximum profit for the corporation. Consider a selling division that is not operating at full capacity

Example 7-1

The Ajax division of Gunnco, operating at capacity, has been asked by the Defco division of Gunnco Corp. to supply it with electrical fitting number 1726. Ajax sells this part to its regular customers for $7.50 each. Defco, which is operating at 50 percent capacity, is willing to pay $5 each for the fitting. Defco will put the fitting into a brake unit which it is manufacturing on essentially a cost plus basis for a commercial airplane manufacturer.

Ajax has a variable cost of producing fitting number 1726 of $4.25. The cost of the brake unit as being built by Defco is as follows:

Purchased parts—outside vendors	$22.50
Ajax fitting—1726	5.00
Other variable costs	14.00
Fixed overhead and administration	8.00
	$49.50

Defco believes the price concession is necessary to get the job.

The company uses return on investment and dollar profits in the measurement of division and division manager performance.

Required   **A.** Consider that you are the division controller of Ajax. Would you recommend that Ajax supply fitting 1726 to Defco? (Ignore any income tax issues.) Why or why not?

B. Would it be to the short-run economic advantage of the Gunnco Corporation for the Ajax division to supply Defco division with fitting 1726 at $5 each? (Ignore any income tax issues.) Explain your answer.

C. Discuss the organizational and manager behavior difficulties, if any, inherent in this situation. As the Gunnco controller, what would you advise the Gunnco Corporation president to do in this situation?

and has variable cost of $15 and fixed costs of $5 per unit. If the buying division has the opportunity to purchase externally at $18, it would so elect. This decision would allow the buying division to minimize its costs, but it would cost the corporation $3 for each unit purchased. The reason for this is that the only incremental cash outlays required for the selling division are $15, but for the buying division to go outside it must pay $18. To prevent this difficulty, top management would have to either request that the selling division lower its price or insist that the buying division pay the full price. The behavioral implications of management's decision should also be considered; divisional managers are going to view it as a reduction in their authority.

Full cost pricing does not accomplish the desired results in terms of motivating managers, providing for goal congruence, or giving the managers more autonomy. To mitigate these problems, several writers have suggested the use of marginal, variable, or incremental costs.

Marginal Costs Under this approach, division managers accept additional orders as long as the amount received from sales is greater than the marginal cost of all divisions involved in making the product. A list stating the marginal costs for each product at various volume levels is given to each divisional manager. This price list is then used both to determine which orders to accept and also to decide when to purchase from other divisions and when to buy from outside sources.

Shillinglaw lists the following weaknesses in the marginal cost approach.

1. It is difficult to develop marginal cost and revenue schedules that change with volume.

2. In many cases the system cannot be administered without abrogating the decision-making autonomy of divisions.

3. It ignores the performance measurement aspects of internal profit reporting.[13]

Because of the difficulty in determining the marginal costs, variable costs are frequently used. Under certain conditions, especially when operating at less than full capacity, the variable costs may serve as a good approximation for marginal costs.

Cost Plus Profit Adding a profit to the cost can give the selling division an opportunity to earn a profit on transfers. The profit, if expressed as a percentage of costs, may encourage the division to raise the costs. This problem can be countered by the use of standard costs and by giving the profit in the form of a monthly subsidy. The standard cost could be variable or full. The use of variable costs eliminates the problems associated with the selection of an activity level to allocate fixed costs. This approach might be an acceptable substitute for market price where part of a division's sales are final product sales. Problems easily develop when the demand for outside and divisional sales is increasing and the division is nearing full capacity.

Opportunity Costs

The emphasis of this approach is toward goal congruence. Horngren suggests that if an optimal economic decision is wanted in a particular situation, the first step in the analysis would be to base the transfer price on the additional outlay costs incurred to the point of transfer plus the opportunity costs for the firm as a whole.[14] The opportunity cost would represent the next best alternative for the firm. If the selling division was operating at less than full capacity, the opportunity cost would be zero; at full capacity the opportunity costs would represent the lost contribution margin resulting from giving up outside sales to sell to another division. For example, the incremental cost to produce a product for Division B is $4. The same product with a minor modification that does not require additional time could be sold outside for

13. Gordon Shillinglaw, *Managerial Cost Accounting*, 4th ed., (Homewood, Ill.: Richard D. Irwin, Inc. 1977), pp. 863-864.

14. Horngren and Foster, *Cost Accounting: A Managerial Emphasis*, 6th ed., p. 845.

$6.50 and costs $4.40 to make. The transfer price would be $4 plus the opportunity cost of $2.20 ($6.60 minus $4.40) or $6.20. If the total additional outlays to make this product plus the $2.20 opportunity cost are less than the revenue per unit from sales of the final product, it would be best for the company as a whole if B did purchase the part from the selling division. To illustrate this point consider Example 7-1, a previous CMA examination problem.

The solution to part A and part B is as follows:

A. Ajax should not supply Defco with fitting 1726 for the $5 per unit price. Ajax is operating at capacity and would lose $2.50 ($7.50 − $5.00) for each fitting sold to Defco. The management performance of Ajax is measured by return on investment and dollar profits; selling to Defco at $5 per unit would adversely affect those performance measures.

B. Gunnco would be $5.50 better off in the short run if Ajax supplied Defco the fitting for $5 and the brake unit was sold for $49.50. Assuming the $8 per unit for fixed overhead and administration represents an allocation of cost Defco incurs regardless of the brake unit order, Gunnco would lose $2.50 in cash flow for each fitting sold to Defco but gain $8 from each brake unit sold by Defco.

It should be noted that even if Defco had to pay $7.50 for the part, it would still be better off paying $7.50 and selling the part for an amount in excess of $44 ($36.50 variable costs plus $7.50 for fitting 1726). However, the problem states that the job is on a cost plus basis and Defco believes the cost concession is necessary to get the job. For this problem it appears this alternative does not exist.

The solution to part C follows:

In the short run Gunnco gains an advantage by transferring the fitting at the $5 price and thus selling the brake unit for $49.50. In order to make this happen, Gunnco will have to overrule the decision of the Ajax management.

This action would be counter to the purposes of decentralized decision making. If such action were necessary on a regular basis, the decentralized decision making inherent in the divisionalized organization would be a sham, and the organizational structure would be inappropriate for the situation.

On the other hand, if this were an occurrence of relative infrequency, the intervention of corporate management would not indicate inadequate organization structure. It might, however, create problems with division managements. In the case at hand, if Gunnco management requires that the fitting be transferred at $5, the result will be to enhance Defco's operating results at the expense of Ajax. This certainly is not in keeping with the concept that a manager's performance should be measured by the results achieved by the decisions he controls.

In this case, it appears that Ajax and Defco serve different markets and do not represent closely related operating units. Ajax operates at capacity, Defco does not; no mention is made of any other interdivisional business. Therefore, the Gunnco controller should recommend that each division be free to act in accordance with its best interests. The company is better served in the long run if Ajax is permitted to continue dealing with its regular customers at the market price. If Defco is having difficulties, the solution does not lie with temporary help at the expense of another division but with a more substantive course of action.

One of the most extensive studies to determine the methods of transfer pricing used in practice was made in 1967 by the National Industrial Conference Board. The study was based on the experience of 190 companies in making transfers to domestic divisions. The study revealed that two-thirds of the companies used some form of a cost-based transfer, while over half of those responding used market prices. Thus, some companies used both methods.

Transfer prices can, therefore, vary from the extreme where the price is determined in a competitive market environment to the extreme where the price is simply the manufacturing cost.

Problems

1.   Estimated time 45 minutes (December 1973)

A. R. Oma, Inc. manufactures a line of men's perfumes and after-shaving lotions. The manufacturing process is basically a series of mixing operations, with the addition of certain aromatic and coloring ingredients; the finished product is packaged in a company-produced glass bottle and packed in cases containing six bottles.

A. R. Oma feels that the sale of its product is heavily influenced by the appearance and appeal of the bottle and has, therefore, devoted considerable managerial effort to the bottle production process. This has resulted in the development of certain unique bottle production processes in which management takes considerable pride.

The two areas (that is, perfume production and bottle manufacture) have evolved over the years in an almost independent manner; in fact, a rivalry has developed between management personnel as to "which division is the more important" to A. R. Oma. This attitude is probably intensified because the bottle manufacturing plant was purchased intact ten years ago and no real interchange of management personnel or ideas (except at the top corporate level) has taken place.

Since the acquisition, all bottle production has been absorbed by the perfume manufacturing plant. Each area is considered a separate profit center and evaluated as such. As the new corporate controller you are responsible for the definition of a proper transfer value to use in crediting the bottle production profit center and in debiting the packaging profit center.

At your request, the Bottle Division General Manager has asked certain other bottle manufacturers to quote a price for the quantity and sizes demanded by the perfume division. These competitive prices are:

Volume	Total price	Price per case
2,000,000 eq. cases[a]	$ 4,000,000	$2.00
4,000,000	$ 7,000,000	$1.75
6,000,000	$10,000,000	$1.67

[a] An "equivalent case" represents six bottles each.

A cost analysis of the internal bottle plant indicates that they can produce bottles at these costs.

Volume	Total price	Cost per case
2,000,000 eq. cases	$3,200,000	$1.60
4,000,000	$5,200,000	$1.30
6,000,000	$7,200,000	$1.20

(Your cost analysts point out that these costs represent fixed costs of $1,200,000 and variable cost of $1 per equivalent case.)

These figures have given rise to considerable corporate discussion as to the proper value to use in the transfer of bottles to the perfume division. This interest is heightened because a significant portion of a division manager's income is an incentive bonus based on profit center results.

The perfume production division has the following costs in addition to the bottle costs:

Volume	Total cost	Cost per case
2,000,000 cases	$16,400,000	$8.20
4,000,000	$32,400,000	$8.10
6,000,000	$48,400,000	$8.07

After considerable analysis, the marketing research department has furnished you with the following price-demand relationship for the finished product:

Sales volume	Total sales revenue	Sales price per case
2,000,000 cases	$25,000,000	$12.50
4,000,000	$45,600,000	$11.40
6,000,000	$63,900,000	$10.65

Required **A.** The A. R. Oma Company has used market price transfer prices in the past. Using the current market prices and costs, and assuming a volume of 6,000,000 cases, calculate the income for

1. the bottle division
2. the perfume division
3. the corporation

B. Is this production and sales level the most profitable volume for the following?

1. the bottle division
2. the perfume division
3. the corporation

Explain your answer.

C. The A. R. Oma Company uses the profit center concept for divisional operation.

1. Define a "profit center."
2. What conditions should exist for a profit center to be established?
3. Should the two divisions of the A. R. Oma Company be organized as profit centers?

---

2.   Estimated time 40 minutes (June 1978)

The Barr Food Manufacturing Company is a medium-sized publicly held corporation, producing a variety of consumer food and specialty products. Current year data were prepared (see next page) for the salad dressing product line using 5 months of actual expenses and a 7-month projection. These data were prepared for a preliminary 1979 budget meeting between the specialty products division president, marketing vice president, production vice president, and the controller. The current year projection was accepted as being accurate, but it was agreed that the projected income was not at a satisfactory level.

The division president stated he wanted, at a minimum, a 15 percent increase in gross sales dollars and not less than 10 percent before-tax profit for 1979. He also stated that he would be responsible for a $200,000 reduction in the general and administrative expenses to help achieve the profit goal.

Both the vice president—marketing and the vice president—production felt that the president's objectives would be difficult to achieve. However, they offered the following suggestions:

1. *Sales volume.* The current share of the salad dressing market is 15 percent and the total salad dressing market is expected to grow 5 percent for 1979. Barr's current market share can be maintained by a marketing expenditure of $4.2 million. The two vice presidents estimated that the market share could be increased by additional expenditures for advertising and sales promotion. For an additional expenditure of $525,000 the market share can be raised by one percentage point until the market share reaches 17 percent. To get further market penetration an additional $375,000 must be spent for each percentage point until the market share reaches 20 percent. Any advertising and promotion expenditures beyond this level are not likely to increase the market share to more than 20 percent.

2. *Selling price.* The selling price will remain at $6 per gallon. The selling price is very closely related to the costs of the ingre-

Projected Income Statement
For the year ended December 31, 1978
(5 months actual; 7 months projected)
($000 omitted)

Volume in gallons	**5,000**
Gross sales	$30,000
Freights, allowances, discounts	3,000
Net sales	27,000
Less manufacturing costs	
Variable	13,500
Fixed	2,100
Depreciation	700
Total manufacturing costs	16,300
Gross profit	10,700
Less expenses	
Marketing	4,000
Brokerage	1,650
General and administrative	2,100
Research and development	500
Total expenses	8,250
Income before taxes	**$ 2,450**

dients, which are not expected to change in 1979 from the costs experienced in 1978.

3. *Variable manufacturing costs.* Variable manufacturing costs are projected at 50 percent of the net sales dollar (gross sales less freight, allowances and discounts).

4. *Fixed manufacturing costs.* An increase of $100,000 is projected for 1979.

5. *Depreciation.* A projected increase in equipment will increase depreciation by $25,000 over the 1978 projection.

6. *Freight, allowances and discounts.* The current rate of 10 percent of gross sales dollars is expected to continue in 1979.

7. *Brokerage expense.* A rate of 5 percent of gross sales dollars is projected for 1979.

8. *General and administrative expense.* A $200,000 decrease in general and administrative expense from the 1978 forecast is projected; this is consistent with the president's commitment.

9. *Research and development expense.* A 5 percent increase from the absolute dollars in the 1978 forecast will be necessary to meet divisional research targets.

Required **A.** The controller must put together a preliminary profit plan from the facts given. Can the president's objectives be achieved? If so, present the profit plan which best achieves them. If not, present the profit plan which most nearly meets the president's objectives.

B. The president's objectives, as described in the case, were stated in terms of a percentage increase in gross sales and the percentage return on sales.

1. What other measures of performance (other than sales dollars and return on sales percentage) could be used in setting objectives?

2. Discuss the advantages or disadvantages of the measures you present in relation to those in the case.

---

3.   Estimated time 40 minutes (December 1980)

Darmen Corporation is one of the major producers of prefabricated houses in the home building industry. The corporation consists of two divisions: (1) Bell Division, which acquires the raw materials to manufacture the basic house components and assembles them into kits, and (2) the Cornish Division, which takes the kits and constructs the homes for final home buyers. The corporation is decentralized and the management of each division is measured by its income and return on investment.

Bell Division assembles seven separate house kits using raw materials purchased at the prevailing market prices. The seven kits are sold to Cornish for prices ranging from $45,000 to $98,000. The prices are set by corporate management of Darmen using prices paid by Cornish when it buys comparable units from outside sources. The smaller kits with the lower prices have become a larger portion of the units sold because the final house buyer is faced with prices which are increasing more rapidly than personal income. The kits are manufactured and assembled in a new plant just purchased by Bell this year. The division had been located in a leased plant for the past four years.

All kits are assembled upon receipt of an order from the Cornish Division. When the kit is completely assembled, it is loaded immediately on a Cornish truck. Thus, Bell Division has no finished goods inventory.

The Bell Division's accounts and reports are prepared on an actual cost basis. There is no budget and standards have not been developed for any product. A factory overhead rate is calculated at the beginning of each year. The rate is designed to charge all overhead to the product each year. Any under- or over-applied overhead is allocated to the cost of goods sold account and work in process inventories.

Bell Division's annual report is presented on the next page. This report forms the basis of the evaluation of the division and its management by the corporation management.

Additional information regarding corporate and division practices is as follows:

- The corporation office does all the personnel and accounting work for each division.

- The corporate personnel costs are allocated on the basis of number of employees in the division.

- The accounting costs are allocated to the division on the basis of total costs excluding corporate charges.

- The division administration costs are included in factory overhead.

- The financing charges include a corporate imputed interest charge on division assets and any divisional lease payments.

- The division investment for the return on investment calculation includes division inventory and plant and equipment at gross book value.

Required **A.** Discuss the value of the annual report presented for the Bell Division in evaluating the division and its management in terms of:

1. The accounting techniques employed in the measurement of division activities.
2. The manner of presentation.
3. The effectiveness with which it discloses differences and similarities between years.

Use the information in the problem to illustrate your discussion.

B. Present specific recommendations you would make to the management of Darmen Corporation which would improve its accounting and financial reporting system.

Bell Division
Performance Report
For the Year Ended December 31, 1980

	1980	1979	Increase or (decrease) from 1979 Amount	Increase or (decrease) from 1979 Percent Change
Summary data				
Net income ($000 omitted)	$ 34,222	$ 31,573	$ 2,649	8.4
Return on investment	37%	43%	(6)%	(14.0)
Kits shipped (units)	2,000	2,100	(100)	(4.8)
Production data (in units)				
Kits started	2,400	1,600	800	50.0
Kits shipped	2,000	2,100	(100)	(4.8)
Kits in process at year-end	700	300	400	133.3
Increase (decrease) in kits in process at year end	400	(500)	—	—
Financial data ($000 omitted)				
Sales	$138,000	$162,800	$(24,800)	(15.2)
Production costs of units sold				
Raw material	32,000	40,000	(8,000)	(20.0)
Labor	41,700	53,000	(11,300)	(21.3)
Factory overhead	29,000	37,000	(8,000)	(21.6)
Cost of units sold	102,700	130,000	(27,300)	(21.0)
Other costs				
Corporate charges for				
Personnel services	228	210	18	8.6
Accounting services	425	440	(15)	(3.4)
Financing costs	300	525	(225)	(42.9)
Total other costs	953	1,175	(222)	(18.9)
Adjustments to income				
Unreimbursed fire loss	—	52	(52)	(100.0)
Raw material losses due to improper storage	125	—	125	—
Total adjustments	125	52	73	(140.4)
Total deductions	103,778	131,227	(27,449)	(20.9)
Division income	**$ 34,222**	**$ 31,573**	**$ 2,649**	**8.4**
Division investment	$ 92,000	$ 73,000	$ 19,000	26.0
Return on investment	37%	43%	(6)%	(14.0)

4.   Estimated time 30 minutes (June 1992)

The success of a business enterprise is generally evaluated by the enterprise's degree of accomplishment in attaining its goals. Management must develop the goals and initiate and control the enterprise's activities to reach these goals. The management planning and control process can be described as a series of related functions that are concurrently and continuously being performed. These functions can be described as (1) planning, (2) organizational adaptation for implementation of the plans, (3) resource management and interpersonal influence, and (4) controlling.

Required   A. For each of the four functions of the management planning and control process, describe at least three activities necessary to successfully accomplish each respective function.

B. Identify and describe three types of responsibility centers that management can utilize to measure and control performance.

---

5.   Estimated time 30 minutes (December 1990)

The National Association of Accountants has issued **Statements on Management Accounting Number 4D,** "Measuring Entity Performance," to help management accountants deal with the issues associated with measuring entity performance. Managers can use these measures to evaluate their own performance or the performance of subordinates, to identify and correct problems, and to discover opportunities. To assist management in measuring achievement, there are a number of performance measures available. To present a more complete picture of performance, it is strongly recommended that several of these performance measures be utilized and that they be combined with nonfinancial measures such as market share, new product development, and human resource utilization. Five commonly used performance measures that are derived from the traditional historical accounting system are listed below.

- Gross profit margin (percent)
- Cash flows
- Return on the investment in assets
- Residual income
- Total asset turnover

Required   For each of the five performance measures identified above,

1. describe how the measure is calculated,
2. describe the information provided by the measure, and
3. explain the limitations of this information.

---

6.   Estimated time 30 minutes (June 1992)

Jump-Start Co. (JSC), a subsidiary of Mason Industries, manufactures go-carts and other recreational vehicles. Family recreational centers that feature not only go-cart tracks but miniature golf, batting cages, and arcade games as well, have increased in popularity. As a result, JSC has been receiving some pressure from the Mason management to diversify into

some of these other recreational areas. Recreational Leasing Inc. (RLI), one of the largest firms that leases arcade games to these family recreational centers, is looking for a friendly buyer. Mason's top management believes that RLI's assets could be acquired for an investment of $3.2 million and has strongly urged Bill Grieco, division manager of JSC, to consider acquiring RLI.

Greico has reviewed RLI's financial statements with his controller, Marie Connelly, and they believe that the acquisition may not be in the best interest of JSC. "If we decide not to do this, the Mason people are not going to be happy," said Grieco. "If we could convince them to base our bonuses on something other than return on investment, maybe this acquisition would look more attractive. How would we do if the bonuses were based on residual income using the company's 15 percent cost of capital?"

Mason has traditionally evaluated all of its divisons on the basis of return on investment which is defined as the ratio of operating income to total assets; the desired rate of return for each division is 20 percent. The management team of any division reporting an annual increase in the return on investment is automatically eligible for a bonus. The management of divisions reporting a decline in the return on investment must provide convincing explanations for the decline to be eligible for a bonus, and this bonus is limited to 50 percent of the bonus paid to divisions reporting an increase.

Presented below are condensed financial statements for both JSC and RLI for the fiscal year ended May 31, 1992.

	JSC	RLI
Sales revenue	$10,500,000	—
Leasing revenue	—	$2,800,000
Variable expenses	7,000,000	1,000,000
Fixed expenses	1,500,000	1,200,000
Operating income	$ 2,000,000	$ 600,000
Current assets	$ 2,300,000	$1,900,000
Long-term assets	5,700,000	1,100,000
Total assets	$ 8,000,000	$3,000,000
Current liabilities	$ 1,400,000	$ 850,000
Long-term liabilities	3,800,000	1,200,000
Shareholders' equity	2,800,000	950,000
Total liabilities and shareholders' equity	$ 8,000,000	$3,000,000

Required   A. If Mason Industries continues to use return on investment as the sole measure of division performance, explain why Jump-Start Co. (JSC) would be reluctant to acquire Recreational Leasing Inc. (RLI). Be sure to support your answer with appropriate calculations.

B. If Mason Industries could be persuaded to use residual income to measure the performance of JSC, explain why JSC would be more willing to acquire RLI. Be sure to support your answer with appropriate calculations.

C. Discuss how the behavior of division managers is likely to be affected by the use of

1. return on investment as a performance measure.
2. residual income as a performance measure.

---

7.   Estimated time 30 minutes (December 1981)

Peterdonn Corporation made a capital investment of $100,000 in new equipment two years ago. The analysis made at that time indicated the equipment would save $36,400 in operating expenses per year over a five year period, or a 24 percent return on capital before taxes per year based upon the internal rate of return analysis.

The department manager believed that the equipment had "lived up" to its expectations. However, the departmental report showing the overall return on investment (ROI) rate for the first year in which this equipment was used did not reflect as much improvement as had been expected. The department manager asked the accounting section to "break out" the figures related to this investment to find out why it did not contribute more to the department's ROI.

The accounting section was able to identify the equipment and its contribution to the department's operations. The report presented to the department manager at the end of the first year is shown below.

Reduced operating expenses due to new equipment	$ 36,400
Less: Depreciation—20% of cost	20,000
Contribution before taxes	$ 16,400
Investment—beginning of year	$100,000
Investment—end of year	$ 80,000
Average investment for the year	$ 90,000

$$\text{ROI} = \frac{16,400}{90,000} = 18.2\%$$

The department manager was surprised that the ROI was less than 24 percent because the new equipment performed as expected. The staff analyst in the accounting section replied that the company ROI for performance evaluation differed from that used for capital investment analysis. The analyst commented that the discrepancy could be solved if the company used the compound interest method of depreciation for its performance evaluation reports.

Required   A. Discuss the reasons why the return on investment of 18.2 percent for the new equipment as calculated in the department's report by the accounting section differs from the 24 percent internal rate of return calculated at the time the machine was approved for purchase.

B. Will the use of the compound interest method of depreciation solve the discrepancy as the analyst claims? Explain your answer.

C. Explain how Peterdonn Corporation might restructure the data from the discounted cash flow analysis so that the expected performance of the new equipment is consistent with the operating reports received by the department manager.

---

8.   Estimated time 30 minutes (December 1973)

DePaolo Industries manufactures carpets, furniture, and foam in three separate divisions. DePaolo's operating statement for 1983 is reproduced on the next page.

Additional information regarding DePaolo's operations are as follows:

- Included in Foam's sales revenue is $500,000 in revenue that represents sales made to the Furniture Division that were transferred at manufacturing cost.
- The cost of goods sold is comprised of the following costs.

	Carpet	Furniture	Foam
Direct material	$ 500,000	$1,000,000	$1,000,000
Direct labor	500,000	200,000	1,000,000
Variable overhead	750,000	50,000	1,000,000
Fixed overhead	250,000	50,000	—0—
Total cost of goods sold	$2,000,000	$1,300,000	$3,000,000

- Administrative expenses include the following costs.

	Carpet	Furniture	Foam
Segment expenses			
Variable	$ 85,000	$140,000	$ 40,000
Fixed	85,000	210,000	120,000
Home office expenses (all fixed)			
Directly traceable	100,000	120,000	200,000
General (allocated on sales dollars)	30,000	30,000	40,000
Total	$300,000	$500,000	$400,000

- Selling expense is all incurred at the segment level and is 80 percent variable for all segments.

John Sprint, Manager of the Foam Division, is not pleased with DePaolo's presentation of operating performance. Sprint claimed, "The Foam Division makes a greater contribution to the company's profits than what is shown. I sell foam to the Furniture Division at cost and it gets our share of the profit. I can sell that foam on the outside at my regular markup, but I sell to Furniture for the well-being of the company. I think my division should get credit for those internal sales at market. I think we should also revise our operating statements for internal purposes. Why don't we consider preparing these internal statements on a contribution approach reporting formal showing internal transfers at market?"

Required   A. John Sprint believes that the intra-company transfers from Foam Division to the Furniture Division should be at market rather than manufacturing cost for divisional performance measurement.

1. Explain why Sprint is correct.

2. Identify and describe two approaches used for setting transfer prices other than manufacturing cost used by DePaolo Industries and market price as recommended by Sprint.

DePaolo Industries
Operating Statement
For the Year Ended December 31, 1983

	Carpet Division	Furniture Division	Foam Division	Total
Sales revenue	$3,000,000	$3,000,000	$4,000,000	$10,000,000
Cost of goods sold	2,000,000	1,300,000	3,000,000	6,300,000
Gross profit	$1,000,000	$1,700,000	$1,000,000	$ 3,700,000
Operating expenses				
Administrative	$ 300,000	$ 500,000	$ 400,000	$ 1,200,000
Selling	600,000	600,000	500,000	1,700,000
Total operating expenses	$ 900,000	$1,100,000	$ 900,000	$ 2,900,000
Income from operations before taxes	$ 100,000	$ 600,000	$ 100,000	$ 800,000

B. Using the contribution approach and market based transfer prices, prepare a revised operating statement by division for DePaolo Industries for 1983 that will promote the evaluation of divisional performance.

C. Discuss the advantages of the contribution reporting approach for internal reporting purposes.

9.   Estimated time 30 minutes (December 1989)

Raddington Industries produces tool and die machinery for manufacturers. The company expanded vertically in 1984 by acquiring one of its suppliers of alloy steel plates, Reigis Steel Company. In order to manage the two separate businesses, the operations of Reigis are reported separately as an investment center.

Raddington monitors its divisions on the basis of both unit contribution and return on average investment (ROI), with investment defined as average operating assets employed. Management bonuses are determined on ROI. All investments in operating assets are expected to earn a minimum return of 11 percent before income taxes.

Reigis' cost of goods sold is considered to be entirely variable while the division's administrative expenses are not dependent on volume. Selling expenses are a mixed cost with 40 percent attributed to sales volume. Reigis' ROI has ranged from 11.8 to 14.7 percent since 1984. During the fiscal year ended November 30, 1989, Reigis comtemplated a capital acquisition with an estimated ROI of 11.5 percent; however, division management decided against the investment because it believed that the investment would decrease Reigis' overall ROI.

The 1989 operating statement for Reigis is presented below. The division's operating assets employed were $15,750,000 at November 30, 1989, a five percent increase over the 1988 year-

Reigis Steel Division
Operating Statement
For the Year Ended November 30, 1989
($000 omitted)

Sales revenue		$25,000
Less expenses		
Cost of goods sold	$16,500	
Administrative expenses	3,955	
Selling expenses	2,700	23,155
Income from operations before income taxes		$ 1,845

Required   A. Calculate the unit contribution for Reigis Steel Division if 1,484,000 units were produced and sold during the year ended November 30, 1989.

B. Calculate the following performance measures for 1989 for the Reigis Steel Division.

1. Pretax return on average investment in operating assets employed (ROI).

2. Residual income calculated on the basis of average operating assets employed.

C. Explain why the management of the Reigis Steel Division would have been more likely to accept the contemplated capital acquisition if residual income rather than ROI was used as a performance measure.

D. The Reigis Steel Division is a separate investment center within Raddington Industries. Identify several items that Reigis should control if it is to be evaluated fairly by either the ROI or residual income performance measures.

Solutions

1. The bottle division profits

Revenue	$10,000
Cost	7,200
Profit	$ 2,800

2. The perfume division profits

Revenue	$63,900	
Cost	58,400	($48,400 + $10,000)
Profit	$ 5,500	

3. The corporation profits

Revenue	$63,900	
Cost	55,600	($48,400 + $7,200)
	$ 8,300	

B. **1.** Yes

		Volume	
Cases	**2,000**	**4,000**	**6,000**
Revenue	$ 4,000	$ 7,000	$10,000
Cost	3,200	5,200	7,200
Profit	$ 800	$ 1,800	$ 2,800*

2. No

		Volume	
Cases	**2,000**	**4,000**	**6,000**
Revenue	$25,000	$45,600	$63,900
Cost	20,400	39,400	58,400
Profit	$ 4,600	$ 6,200*	$ 5,500

3. Yes

		Volume	
Cases	**2,000**	**4,000**	**6,000**
Revenue	$25,000	$45,600	$63,900
Cost	19,600	37,600	55,600
Profit	$ 5,400	$ 8,000	$ 8,300*

This apparent inconsistency, where the bottle division and the corporation are the most profitable at 6,000,000 volume and the perfume division is most profitable at 4,000,000 volume, comes from the cost and revenues changing differently for the bottle division, perfume division, and the total coporation as volume changes. Based on market price transfer value, the divisions achieve maximum profit for themselves at different levels of sales based on the market price at the various levels relative to the division cost at these various levels. The corporation achieves maximum profit based on the selling price to outsiders relative to the total cost of making the product.

C. 1. A segment of a business that is responsible for both revenues and expenses and whose performance is measured by profits.

Profit Plans for Alternative Market Shares
(000 omitted)

	Market Shares of					
	15%	16%	17%	18%	19%	20%
Volume in gallons	5,250	5,600	5,950	6,300	6,650	7,000
Contribution margin per gallon[1]	$2.40	$2.40	$2.40	$2.40	$2.40	$2.40
Total contribution margin	$12,600	$13,440	$14,280	$15,120	$15,960	$16,800
Fixed costs except marketing[2]	5,350	5,350	5,350	5,350	5,350	5,350
Marketing base	4,200	4,200	4,200	4,200	4,200	4,200
For 16–17% share		525	1,050	1,050	1,050	1,050
For 18–20% share				875*	1,750	2,625
Total fixed costs	9,550	10,075	10,600	11,475	12,350	13,225
Income before taxes	$ 3,050	$ 3,365	$ 3,680	$ 3,645	$ 3,610	$ 3,575
Gross Sales	$31,500	$33,600	$35,700	$37,800	$39,900	$42,000
% Return on gross sales	9.7%	10.0%	10.3%	9.6%	9%	8.5%
% Growth of gross sales	5%	12%	19%	26%	33%	40%

[1]The contribution margin per unit is calculated as follows:

Sales price per gallon		$6.00
Less variable costs		
Freight allowances, discounts—10%	$ .60	
Variable manufacturing—50% of net sales or $13,500 ÷ 5,000	2.70	
Brokerage—5%	.30	3.60
Contribution margin per gallon		$2.40

[2]Fixed costs

Fixed manufacturing	$2,200
Depreciation	725
General and administrative	1,900
Research and development	525
Total fixed costs	$5,350

2. Some of the conditions that should exist are:

a. Proper organization attitudes for decentralized operations.

b. The division level (or segment) must have freedom and independence so that it can buy outside the company when it is to its advantage to do so.

c. Other sources that are willing to quote a price for the quantity and sizes demanded.

d. Freedom to sell to outside parties.

e. Revenues and costs of the segment must be distinguishable from revenues and costs of other segments.

3. The division should not be organized as a profit center. The bottle division makes special bottles for the perfume division and, therefore, it does not have an opportunity to sell to outside parties.

The perfume division could be treated as a profit center. There are other manufacturers that are willing to quote a price for the quantity and sizes demanded by the perfume division and the perfume division sells to the outside.

2.

A. The president's objectives can be achieved by selling 5,950 gallons of salad dressing which represents a 17 percent share of the market. The sales volume of 5,950 gallons will maximize Barr Food Manufacturing Company's income before taxes. At this volume the return on sales would be 10.3 percent and a sales growth of 19 percent would be experienced. The supporting calculations are given below.

B. 1. and 2. Other alternative measures of performance that could have been used in setting objectives include:

- *Emphasis on dollar profits.* This objective would emphasize the importance of profits, but it may discourage growth in sales volume and in market share.

- *Return on assets.* This objective encourages profitability and is a good measure of assets employed. However, this objective can discourage new investment if the current return on assets exceeds the expected return on new investment. In addition, returns may be overstated because the asset base may not reflect the effects of inflation or the costs to replace assets.

3.

A. 1. The following accounting techniques employed by Darmen for the Bell division reduce the report's effectiveness:

- Controllable vs. uncontrollable costs—The accounting techniques do not remove costs uncontrollable by the division for the report.

- The allocated corporate charges for personnel and accounting are assigned upon more or less an arbitrary basis, especially the accounting costs. Further, actual costs rather than "standard or budgeted" costs are charged. These costs are not controllable by division management.

- The division uses a full cost approach. A standard full cost system would highlight the efficiency of the operation. The

variable costing/contribution margin approach probably would contribute to better management.

- The assets are understated by the value of the leased assets.

2. The manner of presentation is poor and could be improved with the following revisions:

- The report is not organized so as to display controllable income, investment and return on investment.

- There is no presentation which identifies the causes of the differences (i.e., price related, volume related or mix related) displayed in the increase or (decrease) section.

- If the performance report is to compare activities of two different years, the effect of differing practices (lease vs. ownership) should be noted.

3. The differences and similarities between years are not well identified because:

- The change in salesmix is not disclosed.

- The change from leased buildings to owned buildings is not disclosed.

- The allocated costs may be changed at different rates between the years because of the allocation procedures—not the actual costs incurred.

B. Recommendations for improvement of the accounting and financial reporting system include:

- Separate the costs into their fixed and variable components and indicate which costs are controllable or uncontrollable.

- Use a flexible budget format and compare actual results with a flexible budget.

- Calculate and present variances for manufacturing costs.

- Calculate and present the sales price, mix and volume variances.

4.

A. For each of the four functions of the management planning and control process, descriptions of at least three activities necessary to successfully accomplish each respective function are as follows.

Planning:
- Strategic planning includes
  - establishing the enterprise's objectives.
  - developing premises about the environment, including corporate strengths and weaknesses, in which they are to be accomplished.
  - making decisions on the courses of action for accomplishing the objectives.
- Continuous replanning includes
  - correcting current performance deficiencies.
  - coping with unanticipated events that are both favorable

and unfavorable.

- Budgeting includes

    - revenue projections (based on both optimistic and pessimistic scenarios) and detailed estimates of expenses.

    - capital investments and facilities requirements associated with the various projection levels.

Organizational Adaption for Implementation Plans:

- Communicating to and coordinating group and individual activities.

- Establishing managerial authority.

Resource management and interpersonal influences:

- Assuring that competent employees are selected, developed, and rewarded for accomplishing the enterprise's objectives.

- Motivating individuals, peers, supervisors, subordinates, and non-subordinates, as well as groups, to accomplish the enterprise's objectives.

- Interdepartmental communication and sharing of information.

Controlling:

- Establishing goals and standards.

- Comparing and analyzing measured performance against established goals and standards.

- Determining areas that need to be changed or strengthened.

B. Descriptions of three types of responsibility centers that management can utilize to measure and control performance are as follows.

- Cost center. A responsibility center for which a manager is responsible for the controllable costs incurred in the unit.

- Revenue center. A responsibility center for which the manager is responsible for revenues, e.g., a sales district.

- Profit center. A responsibility center for which the manager is responsible for costs, revenues, and profits of the particular center; the focus is on the center's profit.

5.

The calculations of each of the five performance measures, as well as the information provided by each measure and the limitations of the information, are presented below.

Gross Profit Margin (percent)

1. Gross profit margin is determined by dividing gross profit by net sales. Gross profit is determined by subtracting cost of goods sold from net sales.

2. Gross profit margin is a measure of profitability and indicates how much is left of each sales dollar to cover operating expenses and profit.

3. Gross profit margin is a good measure for trend analysis of a particular company, but variable ways of calculating cost of goods sold limit its usefulness for comparative analysis.

Cash Flows

1. Cash flow is determined by adding net cash flows from operating activities to the net cash flows from investing activities and financing activities for a period of time. This information is generally presented as part of the primary financial statements of a company.

2. Cash flow can be used to evaluate cash management performance and measure a company's ability to remain solvent during a particular period.

3. Cash flow date states what happened during a particular period but is not an indicator of future performance.

Return on the Investment in Assets

1. Return on the investment in assets is determined by dividing net income (before nonrecurring items) by average total assets.

2. Return on assets is a profitability measure and can be used to evaluate the efficiency of asset usage and management, and the effectiveness of business strategies to create profits.

3. The calculation of return on assets can be affected by varying accounting assumptions which effect the calculation of net income.

Residual Income

1. Residual income is operating income less an imputed interest for invested capital. This imputed interest is calculated by multiplying net assets times the firm's required rate of return or cost of capital.

2. Residual income measures the amount of operating income earned above the imputed cost of capital for the operating unit. If the measure is positive, returns exceed the cost of financing the operating unit.

3. Because of differing costs of capital, the measure cannot be effectively used for comparative analysis.

Total Asset Turnover

1. Total asset turnover is determined by dividing net sales by average total assets.

2. Total asset turnover measures asset activity and the ability of the firm to generate sales through the use of assets. Generally, the more sales dollars generated per dollar of assets used, the better the net income of an entity.

3. When calculating the turnover, total assets may need to be refined by the elimination of assets that do not relate to sales as the inclusion of these items could distort the measure.

6.

A. If Mason Industries continues to use return on investment as the sole measure of division performance, Jump-Start Co. (JSC) would be reluctant to acquire Recreational Leasing Inc. (RLI) because the post-acquisition combined return on investment would decrease as presented in Exhibit 3 on the next page.

This would result in JSC's management either losing or having their bonuses limited to 50% of the eligible amounts, which assumes management could provide convincing explanations for the decline in return on investment.

Exhibit 3	Return on Investment		
	JSC	RLI	Combined
1. Operating income	$2,000,000	$ 600,000	$ 2,600,000
2. Total assets	8,000,000	3,000,000	11,000,000
3. Return on investment (1 ÷ 2)	25%	20%	23.6%

B. Residual income is the profit earned that exceeds an amount charged for funds committed to a business unit. The amount charged for funds is equal to a specified rate of return times the asset base. The residual income computation is as follows.

Residual Income = Income − (Target Rate × Asset Base)

Consequently, if Mason Industries could be persuaded to use residual income to measure performance, JSC would be more willing to acquire RLI because the residual income of the combined operations would increase, as repesented in Exhibit 4 below.

Exhibit 4	Residual Income		
	JSC	RLI	Combined
1. Total assets	$8,000,000	$3,200,000[1]	$11,200,000
2. Income	2,000,000	600,000	2,600,000
3. Charge for funds (Total assets at 15%)	1,200,000	480,000	1,680,000
4. Residual income (2-3)	$ 800,000	$ 120,000	$ 920,000

[1] Cost to acquire RLI

C. The likely affect on the behavior of division managers whose performance is measured by

1. return on investment includes considerations to

• put off capital improvements/modernization to avoid capital expenditures.

• shy away from profitable opportunities/ investments that would yield more than the company's cost of capital but which may lower overall ROI.

2. residual income includes considerations to

• seek any opportunity/investment that will earn more than the cost of capital target rate.

• seek to reduce the level of assets employed in the business.

7.

A. The rate of return on the investment of 18.2% differs from the internal rate of return of 24% because the methods used to measure the returns are different.

The return on investment (18.2%) calculation is based upon accrual accounting concepts. If the reduced operating expenses

less depreciation remain constant as planned, the numerator in the return on investment fraction will not change over the life of the investment. The denominator in the fraction, the investment base, decreases each year by the amount of the annual depreciation. Consequently, the rate of return calculated will increase each year over the life of the investment.

The internal rate of return calculation (24%) is based upon discounted cash flow concepts. This measure of return on investment presents a percentage which is constant for each year of life of the investment so long as the annual operating expenses are constant and the return of capital (depreciation) implicit in the calculation increases each year. Consequently, the decrease of the return of capital charge is such that the numerator and the denominator change at a rate which keeps the annual return on investment ratio constant.

B. The use of compound interest depreciation could solve the discrepancy between accounting income associated with the return on investment and the discounted cash flow computations associated with rate of return.

A characteristic of the compound interest method of depreciation is that it yields a constant return on investment throughout the life of an investment. The revenue less out-of-pocket operating expenses produces a constant cash flow contribution before depreciation. The cost of the depreciable asset is allocated over time in such a way that the remaining income after asset depreciation is a constant percentage of the unrecovered investment (the book value) at the beginning of each fiscal period. The return on investment will equal the internal rate of return provided the investment value used is the book value of the investment at the beginning of each applicable year.

C. Peterdonn Corporation can restructure the data from the cash flow analysis to make it consistent with the accounting reports (which contain straight-line depreciation) received by the department manager. Once the investment is accepted on the basis of its internal rate of return, the data can be converted into the format consistent with the accounting basis used for reporting. The annual contribution from the new investment would be calculated by subtracting the straight-line depreciation from the net cash operating savings. The accounting book value for each of the years of the investment life would also be calculated. The annual contribution would be divided by the investment base (book value) for each year to obtain the rates of return. This would then present the manager with the different rates of return for each of the years of the investment's life. Thus, the rates would be more comparable with the actual return on investment rates experienced each year.

8.

A. 1. Sprint is correct in believing that the intra-company transfers from the Foam Division to the Furniture Division should be at market rather than manufacturing cost because transfers at market promote goal congruence. Divisional managers seek to maximize divisional profits, and a market based transfer price will lead to buying and selling decisions at the divisional level that will accomplish this goal. In addition, transfers at market promote divisional performance measurement. A market based transfer price dovetails with the profit center concept and makes profit-based performance evaluation feasible.

2. Two possible approaches used for setting transfer prices other than manufacturing cost and market price include the following.

- **Full cost plus a markup.** This approach attempts to approximate an outside market price when market prices are not available because the transferred product or service differs from that available from outside sources. The firm would use its full manufacturing cost plus a set markup. The markup could be the gross profit percentage on outside sales.

- **Adjusted market price.** Market price is adjusted for selling and administrative expenses that are avoided through intracompany transfers, by quantity discounts if the size of the intracompany transfer is sufficiently large, or by any other relevant factor to which the buyer and seller can agree.

8. B.

DePaolo Industries
Segment Contribution Operating Statement
For the Year Ended December 31, 1983

	Total	Carpet	Furniture	Foam
Sales revenue	$10,200,000	$3,000,000	$3,000,000	$4,200,000[1]
Variable manufacturing cost of goods sold	6,200,000	1,750,000	1,450,000[2]	3,000,000
Manufacturing contribution margin	$ 4,000,000	$1,250,000	$1,550,000	$1,200,000
Variable selling and administrative expenses				
Variable selling expense	$ 1,360,000	$ 480,000	$ 480,000	$ 400,000
Variable administrative expense	265,000	85,000	140,000	40,000
Total variable selling and administrative expenses	$ 1,625,000	$ 565,000	$ 620,000	$ 440,000
Contribution margin	$ 2,375,000	$ 685,000	$ 930,000	$ 760,000
Discretionary fixed costs				
Manufacturing overhead	$ 300,000	$ 250,000	$ 50,000	$ --
Selling expenses	340,000	120,000	120,000	100,000
Administrative expenses	415,000	85,000	210,000	120,000
Total discretionary fixed costs	$ 1,055,000	$ 455,000	$ 380,000	$ 220,000
Contribution controllable by division managers	$ 1,320,000	$ 230,000	$ 550,000	$ 540,000
Traceable home office expenses	420,000	100,000	120,000	200,000
Division segment margin	$ 900,000	$ 130,000	$ 430,000	$ 340,000
General home office expenses	100,000			
Income from operations before taxes	$ 800,000			

[1]Foam's outside sales	($4,000,000 – $500,000)	$3,500,000
Foam's cost of outside sales	($3,000,000 – $500,000)	2,500,000
Foam's profit on outside sales		$1,000,000

$$\frac{\$1,000,000}{\$2,500,000} = 40\% \text{ markup on manufacturing cost}$$

Intracompany transfer ($500,000 × 1.4)		$ 700,000
Foam's total sales	($3,500,000 + $700,000)	$4,200,000

[2]Furniture's variable manufacturing cost of sales
($1,300,000 – $50,000 – $500,000 + $700,000 = $1,450,000)

C. The contribution reporting approach for internal reporting purposes separates costs by behavior (variable versus fixed) and assigns costs to segments only if the costs can be traced directly to the segment. Thus, the arbitrary allocation of common costs to segments is avoided. The contribution approach provides data that are useful for analysis and decision-making.

9.

A. The calculation of the unit contribution for Reigis Steel Division, assuming 1,484,000 units were produced and sold during the year ended November 30, 1989, is presented below.

Reigis Steel Division Unit Contribution Margin For the Year Ended November 30, 1989 ($000 Omitted)		
Sales		$25,000
Less variable costs:		
Cost of goods sold	$16,500	
Selling expenses ($2,700 x 40%)	1,080	17,580
Contribution margin		$7,420
Unit contribution margin (000 omitted)		
$7,420 + 1,484 units = $5.00 per unit		

B. Calculations of selected performance measures for 1989 for Reigis Steel Division are presented below.

1. The pretax return on average investment in operating assets employed is 12%, calculated as follows.

ROI = Income from operations before taxes
+ average operating assets
= $1,845,000 + $15,375,000[1]
= .12 or (12%)

[1]Average operating assets employed:
($15,750,000 + 15,000,000[2]) + 2 = $15,375,000

[2]November 30, 1988 operating assets:
$15,750,000 + 1.05 = $15,000,000

2. The calculation of residual income on the basis of average operating assets employed is as follows.

Residual
income = Income from operations before
taxes - minimum required
return on average assets
= $1,845,000 - ($15,375,000 x .11)
= $1,845,000 - $1,691,250
= $153,750

C. The management of Reigis Steel would have been more likely to accept the contemplated capital acquisition if residual income was used as the performance measure because the investment would have increased both the division's residual income and the management bonuses. Using residual income, management would accept all investments with a return higher than 11 percent as these investments would all increase the dollar value of residual income. When using ROI as a performance measure, Reigis' management is likely to reject any investment that would lower the overall ROI (12 percent for 1989), even though the return is higher than the required minimum, as this would lower bonus awards.

D. Reigis must be able to control all items related to profits and investment if it is to be evaluated fairly as an investment center using either ROI or residual income as performance measures. Reigis must control all elements of the business except the cost of invested capital, that being controlled by Raddington Industries.

Chapter 8

Behavioral Aspects of Accounting

Grant W. Newton

This chapter describes the following topics dealing with the applications of behavioral concepts in management accounting:

- Classical vs. behavioral view of the accountant's role
- Responsibility accounting
- Accounting reports and motivation
- Behavioral aspects of budgets
- Behavioral factors in standard cost systems
- Behavioral factors in cost allocation
- Behavioral factors in divisional performance evaluation
- Human resource accounting
- Behavioral aspects of external reports and audits.

Classical vs. Behavioral View of the Role of the Management Accountant

The development of management accounting was largely influenced by the economic principle of profit maximization and the concepts of classical management theory. Guided by such works as *The Adjustment of Wages to Efficiency* by Frederick W. Taylor, the view of the worker as being motivated by economic rewards was built into an accounting system that emphasized meeting predetermined goals. More recently, a group of what have come to be known as behavioral accountants has begun to study the behavioral implications of management accounting. The influence of their ideas on management accounting has yet to be fully realized.

Traditional Theory

One of the earliest schools of management thought as discussed in Chapter 1 was developed by an American engineer, Frederick W. Taylor, around 1900. While working as a gang boss in a steel mill, Taylor recognized the need for a standard of performance by which a worker could be judged. His experimental work resulted in theories that became known as scientific management. His advocacy of such techniques as time-and-motion studies to determine performance standards, and his use of bonuses as a reward for exceeding the standard, served as the basis for the development of standard costs.

Other early writers were concerned with organizing the activities of a business so as to minimize operating costs while providing a coordinated system of administration that would promote the smooth operation of a business. They developed the concepts of lines of responsibility and authority, the span of control, and the unity of command, all of which are still to be found in most management texts. These ideas can be found in management accounting in the procedure of having internal accounting reports follow the preestablished lines of authority and responsibility in order to reflect the manager's accountability.

Modern Theory

The classical management theories offer a different view of human behavior than those more recently developed. As mentioned earlier, the classicists shared the view that people were motivated primarily by economic rewards. The newer theories involve a much more complex set of influences that determine behavior. The impact of this change on management accounting can be significant indeed.

It is felt by some that behavior is influenced by two general factors: the personal characteristics of the individual (for example, abilities, needs, past experience, and expectations) and the environment in which the individual operates (for example, challenges, rewards offered, and so on). Thus, if management accountants seek to bring about changes in behavior (for example, reducing costs) through the accounting information they provide, a thorough understanding of behavioral theory is necessary.

Edwin H. Caplan feels that behavioral theory assumes an important role in the development of both managerial accounting theory and practice. He argues that:[1]

1. The management accounting function is essentially a behavioral function and the nature and scope of management accounting systems is materially influenced by the view of human behavior that is held by the accountants who design and operate these systems.

2. It is possible to identify a "traditional" management accounting model of the firm and to associate with this model certain fundamental assumptions about human behavior. These assumptions are presented in Exhibit 8-1.

3. It is also possible to postulate behavioral assumptions based on modern organization theory and to relate them to the objective of management accounting. A tentative set of such assumptions appears in Exhibit 8-2.

4. Research directed at testing the nature and validity of accounting assumptions with respect to human behavior in business organizations can be useful in evaluating and, perhaps, improving the effectiveness of management accounting systems.

Today, many firms are giving consideration to the modern organizational theories. Caplan selected the **decision-making approach** as the basis for the development of Exhibit 8-2. Note that this model is concerned with the processes of communication and decision making. Summarizing this model, Caplan stated that:

the basic element of organization study is the decision. The objective of managerial decision making is to secure and coordinate effectively the contributions of other participants. This is accomplished by influencing, to the extent possible, their perception of alternatives and consequences of choice and their value structures, so that the resulting decisions are consistent with the current objectives of the dominant members of the organization.[2]

As you can see from the last sections of Exhibits 8-1 and 8-2, the role of the management accountant under the classical and modern organizational theories is vastly different. The classical view ignores the personal goals of the accountant and assumes that only objective information designed to maximize profits will come forth from the accounting system; whereas the modern view recognizes that accountants have needs and desires, which means that the accounting system is not necessarily neutral since it is influenced by the personal and departmental goals of the accountant.

Exhibit 8-1

Behavioral Assumptions of "Traditional" Management Accounting Model of the Firm*

Assumptions with Respect to Organization Goals

A. The principal objective of business activity is profit maximization (economic theory).

B. This principal objective can be segmented into subgoals to be distributed throughout the organization (principles of management).

C. Goals are additive—what is good for the parts of the business is also good for the whole (principles of management).

Assumptions with Respect to the Behavior of Participants

A. Organization participants are motivated primarily by economic forces (economic theory).

B. Work is essentially an unpleasant task that people will avoid whenever possible (economic theory).

C. Human beings are ordinarily inefficient and wasteful (scientific management).

Assumptions with Respect to the Behavior of Mangement

A. The role of the business manager is to maximize the profits of the firm (economic theory).

B. In order to perform this role, management must control the tendencies of employees to be lazy, wasteful, and inefficient (scientific management).

C. The essence of management control is authority. The ultimate authority of management stems from its ability to affect the economic reward structure (scientific management).

D. There must be a balance between the authority a person has and his/her responsibility for performance (principles of management).

Assumptions with Respect to the Role of Management Accounting

A. The primary function of management accounting is to aid management in the process of profit maximization (scientific management).

B. The accounting system is a "goal-allocation" device that permits management to select its operating objectives and to divide and distribute them throughout the firm, that is, assign responsibilities for performance. This is commonly referred to as "planning" (principles of management).

C. The accounting system is a control device that permits management to identify and correct undesirable performance (scientific management).

D. There is sufficient certainty, rationality, and knowledge within the system to permit an accurate comparison of responsibility for performance and the ultimate benefits and costs of that performance (principles of management).

E. The accounting system is "neutral" in its evaluations—personal bias is eliminated by the objectivity of the system (principles of management).

*Source: Caplan, p. 497.

---

1. Edwin H. Caplan, "Behavioral Assumptions of Management Accounting," *Accounting Review,* 41 (July, 1966), 496.

2. Ibid., p. 503.

Exhibit 8-2

Some Behavioral Assumptions from Modern Organization Theory*

Assumptions with Respect to Organization Goals

A. Organizations are coalitions of individual participants. Strictly speaking, the organization itself, which is "mindless," cannot have goals—only the individuals can have goals.

B. Those objectives that are usually viewed as organizational goals are, in fact, the objectives of the dominant members of the coalition, subject to whatever constraints are imposed by the other participants and by the external environment of the organization.

C. Organization objectives tend to change in response to: (1) changes in the goals of the dominant participants; (2) changes in the relationships within the coalition; and (3) changes in the external environment of the organization.

D. In the modern complex business enterprise, there is no single universal organization goal such as profit maximization. To the extent that any truly over-all objective might be identified, that objective is probably organization survival.

E. Facing a highly complex and uncertain world and equipped with only limited rationality, members of an organization tend to focus on "local" (that is, individual and departmental) goals. These local goals are often in conflict with each other. In addition, there appears to be no valid basis for the assumption that they are homogeneous and thus additive—what is good for the parts of the organization is not necessarily good for the whole.

Assumptions with Respect to the Behavior of Participants

A. Human behavior within an organization is essentially an adaptive, problem-solving, decision-making process.

B. Organization participants are motivated by a wide variety of psychological, social, and economic needs and drives.

C. The decision of an individual to join an organization, and the separate decision to contribute her/his productive efforts once a member, are based on the individual's perception of the extent to which such action will further the achievement of his/her personal goals.

D. The efficiency and effectiveness of human behavior and decision making within organizations is constrained by: (1) the inability to concentrate on more than a few things at a time; (2) limited awareness of the environment; (3) limited knowledge of alternative courses of action and the consequences of such alternatives; (4) limited reasoning ability; and (5) incomplete and inconsistent preference systems. As a result of these limits on human rationality, individual and organizational behavior is usually directed at attempts to find satisfactory—rather than optimal—solutions.

Assumptions with Respect to the Behavior of Management

A. The primary role of the business manager is to maintain a favorable balance between (1) the contributions required from the participants and (2) the inducement (that is, perceived need satisfactions) that must be offered to secure these contributions.

B. The management role is essentially a decision-making process subject to the limitations on human rationality and cognitive ability. The manager must make decisions him/herself and must effectively influence the decision premises of others so that their decisions will be favorable for the organization.

C. The essence of management control is the willingness of other participants to *accept* the authority of management. This willingness appears to be a nonstable function of the inducement-contribution balance.

D. Responsibility is assigned from "above" and authority is accepted from "below." It is, therefore, meaningless to speak of the balance between responsibility and authority as if both of these were "given" to the manager.

Assumptions with Respect to the Role of Accounting

A. The management accounting process is an information system whose major purposes are: (1) to provide the various levels of management with data that will facilitate the decision-making functions of planning and control; and (2) to serve as a communications medium within the organization.

B. The effective use of budgets and other accounting control techniques requires an understanding of the interaction between these techniques and the motivations and aspiration levels of the individuals to be controlled.

C. The objectivity of the management accounting process is largely a myth. Accountants have wide areas of discretion in the selection, processing, and reporting of data.

D. In performing their function within an organization, accountants can be expected to be influenced by their own personal and departmental goals in the same way as other participants are influenced.

*Source: Caplan, p. 498.

With the newer theories gaining in acceptance, what about the traditional theores? Are they to be discarded? Caplan feels that:

> One should not infer that the traditional assumptions considered here are completely invalid. The very fact that they have endured for so long suggests that this is not the case. It should at least be recognized, however, that in many respects the extent of their validity may be subject to question. Also, it is not argued that all accountants limit themselves at all times to this traditional view. Rather, the two sets of behavioral assumptions discussed might be considered as extreme points on a scale of many possible views. The significance of the traditional point on such a scale appears to be twofold: (a) it is likely that the traditional model represents a view of behavior which is relatively common in practice; and (b) this view seems to underlie much of what is written and taught about accounting.[3]

3. Ibid., p. 509.

Responsibility Accounting

Responsibility accounting is a system of reporting revenue and cost information to the individual managers who are primarily responsible for the revenue-causing or cost-incurring function. Under certain conditions the manager may also be responsible for assets and liabilities over which control is exercised. Revenue and costs under a responsibility accounting system are classified according to lines of responsibility within a firm. The reports prepared from this system not only identify the revenue earned or the cost incurred, but indicate who is responsible for these items.

An important part of responsibility accounting is identifying those costs that are controllable at various levels of responsibility within an organization. According to Horngren and Foster, a cost is controllable if it can be directly influenced by a given manager within a given time span.[4] Since all costs are controllable at some level within an organization, it is important to identify the level of activity in dealing with costs. Maintenance costs may not be controllable at the factory foreman level, even though part of this cost may be identified with this process. It would, however, be fully controllable at the factory manager's level. At times it may be difficult to identify the manager actually responsible for the costs. Horngren suggests that in most cases the one responsible will be the executive who most closely supervises the day-to-day activities that influence that cost.[5]

Performance Report

Exhibit 8-3 presents an example of reports prepared from a responsibility accounting system. The report is based on the organizational chart for La Canada Company presented in Exhibit 8-4. Note that only the costs over which the manager is responsible are in the performance report. Thus in the supervisor's department, rent, property taxes, and maintenance costs are not in the report. These uncontrollable costs are omitted because the supervisor cannot control them, and to include them would only confuse the performance of the foreman. Others, however, suggest that they should be included but shown separately and clearly identified as uncontrollable. They reason that the manager should be aware of the costs that are indirectly caused by the existence of the supervisor operations. By being aware of these costs the supervisor may be able to influence the individual who has control over them. Note that the supervisor's costs become the responsibility of the vice president for production and that the vice president's costs are the responsibility of the president.

Illustration of Responsibility Accounting

A previous CMA examination question asked for the conditions that must exist for there to be an effective responsibility accounting system. The conditions are:

1. Areas of responsibility and authority should be well defined.

2. Standards of performance including the time dimension for

which the standards apply should be predetermined.

3. Managers must be trained to use the results of this reporting system.

4. Reports must be available to managers on a timely basis.

5. General content and details of the reports must be relevant to the manager's responsibility and authority.

6. The reports should highlight items requiring management attention including evidence of good performance and improving performance as well as performance below acceptable levels.

Another question asked for the benefits that result from responsibility accounting. Some of them are:

1. It requires an organization to define its overall objectives and define and communicate its operational goals as they apply to its subunits.

2. It permits effective utilization of the management by exception concept.

3. It provides immediate performance feedback, which permits prompt corrective action to be taken.

4. It provides an objective measure of an individual's performance.

5. It facilitates the decentralization of decision making and fully utilizes the expertise of all managers.

A part of one CMA problem contained the following:

Listed below are three charges found on the monthly report of a division that manufactures and sells products primarily to outside companies. Division performance is evaluated by the use of Return on Investment. You are to state which, if any, of the following charges are consistent with the responsibility accounting concept. Support each answer with a brief explanation.

1. A charge for general corporation administration at 10% of division sales.

The answer is no because the charge is an arbitrary allocation of costs. It cannot be influenced directly by actions of the division management.

2. A charge for the use of the corporate computer facility. The charge is determined by taking actual annual computer department costs and allocating an amount to each user on the ratio of its use to total corporation use.

The answer is no and yes. The amount of computer service used is within the control of the division management. However, the cost per unit of service varies with the efficiency of the computer facility and the amount of use by other division management.

3. A charge for goods purchased from another division. The charge is based upon the competitive market price for the goods.

The answer is yes, provided the quantity of goods purchased is controllable by the division management and the price is a market price.

4. Charles T. Horngren and George Foster, *Cost Accounting: A Managerial Emphasis,* 6th ed. (Englewood Cliffs, New Jersey: Prentice-Hall, 1987), p. 160.
5. *Ibid.,* p. 161.

Exhibit 8-3

La Canada Company
President's Performance Report
July 19X1

	Budget		Variance Favorable (Unfavorable)	
	July	Year to Date	July	Year to Date
President's office	$ 30,000	$ 210,000	$ 4,000	$ 9,200
V.P. Production	170,000	954,000	14,700	(35,000)
V.P. Sales	45,000	330,000	(4,000)	(20,000)
V.P. Finance	20,000	140,000	—	2,000
Total	$265,000	$1,634,000	$14,700	$(43,000)

V.P. Production
Performance Report
July 19X1

	Budget		Variance Favorable (Unfavorable)	
	July	Year to Date	July	Year to Date
V.P. Production's office	$ 20,000	$140,000	$(4,200)	$(20,000)
Plating Department	65,000	325,000	13,200	1,000
Drill Press Department	70,000	369,000	4,500	(19,000)
Assembly Department	15,000	120,000	1,200	3,000
Total	$170,000	$954,000	$14,700	$(35,000)

Supervisor, Drill Press
Performance Report
July 19X1

	Budget		Variance Favorable (Unfavorable)	
	July	Year to Date	July	Year to Date
Direct materials	$20,000	$110,000	$ 3,000	$(16,000)
Direct labor	35,000	170,000	(2,000)	(15,000)
Supplies	6,000	37,000	1,000	4,000
Rework	8,000	45,000	3,000	9,000
Small tools	1,000	7,000	(500)	(1,000)
Totals	$70,000	$369,000	$ 4,500	$(19,000)

Exhibit 8-4

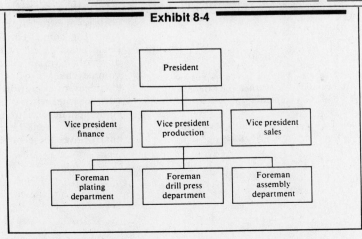

Accounting Reports and Motivation

Various reports prepared by the accountant are designed to communicate information to managers to assist them in the control of their operations.

These reports as well as budgets can be used for motivation. These reports motivate because they provide managers with knowledge about their performance. Properly designed performance reports based on the concepts of responsibility accounting can help motivate managers to accomplish their goals. R. B. Ammons reached the following conclusions regarding performance and knowledge:

• Knowledge of performance affects rate of learning and level reached by learning.

• Knowledge of performance affects motivation. The most common effect of knowledge of performance is to increase motivation.

• The more specific the knowledge of performance, the more rapid the improvement and the higher the level of performance.

• The longer the delay in giving knowledge of performance, the less effect the given knowledge has.

• When knowledge of performance is decreased, performance drops.[6]

It should be pointed out that overemphasis on performance reports may result in undesirable actions. George J. Benston concludes that when reports become the sole criteria for performance evaluation, "managers resort to such anti-productive techniques as delayed maintenance, bickering over cost allocations, and even falsification of inventories" and that "people's needs are too diverse and changeable to be satisfied by any single device or mechanically applied procedure."[7]

Performance reports should:

1. relate to the organizational structure and responsibility centers.

2. clearly identify for the manager the controllable cost and revenue items.

3. facilitate management by exception.

4. identify causes of deviations.

5. be easily understood.

6. contain only relevant information.

7. be timely.

---

6. R.B. Ammons, "Effects of Knowledge of Performance: A Survey and Tentative Theoretical Information," *Journal of General Psychology,* 54 (April, 1956), 283-290. (Emphasis appears in the original.)

7. George J. Benston, "The Role of the Firm's Accounting System for Motivation," *The Accounting Review,* 38 (April, 1963), 354.

8. be prepared and presented with the attitude of "helping" rather than "finding fault."

9. be given to the individual manager directly responsible for costs before submitting to his/her superiors.

Consider Example 8-1, a CMA examination problem. Note that suggestions 2, 3, 4, 6, and 8 above were not followed. This report would not be expected to provide information to motivate the manager. The suggested solution follows:

A. The hospital administrator constructed a static budget. His budget was not representative because he took one-fourth of the annual budget for the summer months. Argon Hospital experiences increased activity during the summer, and, as a result, the budget should have reflected this increased activity.

The cost figures for the budget were not developed properly. Cost estimates should be developed from the underlying activities, including planned changes, valued at current prices. The estimates in this case were based solely upon past costs adjusted downward by a percentage apparently not related in any way to cost reduction procedures or price changes due to inflation.

The administrator also should have considered inviting the department heads to participate in the budgeting procedure. The budget figures might have been more accurate, and the participation might have motivated the department heads to cooperate in both accepting the new system and achieving budget goals.

B. Budget variations should identify costs needing the manager's attention because they are different from the expected amounts (properly adjusted for the time period and level of activity). The causes of the variations (excess prices, excess use of resources, unexpected change in operating procedure, and so on) are not communicated directly by the variations. Analysis of the variations is necessary to determine the cause and identify possible corrective action.

The total variation from budget and the pattern of variations over time provide some of the evidence necessary to judge the effectiveness and efficiency of the manager.

C. The performance report is ineffective in communicating efficiency. The comparison of actual and budgeted costs is not meaningful because two different activity levels are being compared. A more meaningful comparison could be achieved by using a flexible budget. A breakdown of the variances into variations due to spending and volume changes would provide more insight into the efficiency of operations. In addition, it is questionable whether supervisor's salary, administrative costs, and equipment depreciation should be included in the report, because the department head does not exercise any control over these costs.

Example 8-1

The Argon County Hospital is located in the county seat. Argon county is a well known summer resort area. The county population doubles during the vacation months (May–August) and hospital activity more than doubles during these months. The hospital is organized into several departments. Although it is a relatively small hospital, its pleasant surroundings have attracted a well-trained and competent medical staff.

An administrator was hired a year ago to improve the business activities of the hospital. Among the new ideas he has introduced is responsibility accounting. This program was announced along with quarterly cost reports supplied to department heads. Previously, cost data were presented to department heads infrequently. Excerpts from the announcement and the report received by the laundry supervisor are presented in the adjacent column.

The annual budget for 1973 was constructed by the new administrator. Quarterly budgets were computed as one-fourth of the annual budget. The administrator compiled the budget from analysis of the prior three years' costs. The analysis showed that all costs increased each year with more rapid increases between the second and third year. He considered establishing the budget at an average of the prior three years' costs hoping that the installation of the system would reduce costs to this level. However, in view of the rapidly increasing prices he finally chose 1972 costs less 3 percent for the 1973 budget. The activity level measured by patient days and pounds of laundry processed was set at 1972 volume, which was approximately equal to the volume of each of the past three years.

Required **A.** Comment on the method used to construct the budget.
B. What information should be communicated by variations from budgets?
C. Does the report effectively communicate the level of efficiency of this department? Give reasons for your answer.

The hospital has adopted a "responsibility accounting system." From now on you will receive quarterly reports comparing the costs of operating your department with budgeted costs. The reports will highlight the differences (variations) so you can zero in on the departure from budgeted costs (this is called "management by exception"). Responsibility accounting means you are accountable for keeping the costs in your department within the budget. The variations from the budget will help you identify what costs are out of line and the size of the variation will indicate which ones are the most important. Your first such report accompanies this announcement.

Argon County Hospital
Performance Report—Laundry Department
July–September 1973

	Budget	Actual	(Over) Under Budget	Percent (Over) Under Budget
Patient Days	9,500	11,900	(2,400)	(25)
Pounds Processed— Laundry	125,000	156,000	(31,000)	(25)
Costs				
Laundry labor	$ 9,000	$12,500	$(3,500)	(39)
Supplies	1,100	1,875	(775)	(70)
Water, Water Heating and Softening	1,700	2,500	(800)	(47)
Maintenance	1,400	2,200	(800)	(57)
Supervisor's Salary	3,150	3,750	(600)	(19)
Allocated Administration Costs	4,000	5,000	(1,000)	(25)
Equipment Depreciation	1,200	1,250	(50)	(4)
	$21,550	$29,075	$(7,525)	(35)

Administrator's Comments: Costs are significantly above budget for the quarter. Particular attention needs to be paid to labor, supplies, and maintenance.

The reports must be arranged in such a way that the information needed can be easily obtained by the manager. A previous CMA examination problem, shown in Example 8-2, asks for an assessment of the reaction of management to information overload and the type of correction necessary to prevent recurrence of dysfunctional behavior.

The solution follows:

A. 1. Delaying action on certain reports during periods of peak activity could be dysfunctional. If the reports contain information that requires immediate attention, any delay in action would have to be dysfunctional. If the reports continue to accumulate with no action taking place (that is, the department heads do not catch up during the lulls), this definitely is dysfunctional behavior.

2. Having too many reports so that no action or the wrong action is taken is a dysfunctional response and a good example of information overload. The department heads were unable to assimilate the supplied information properly, and therefore they either did not use it or used it incorrectly.

3. Delaying action until reminded by someone can be dysfunctional. If delays continually take place and result in complications and/or delays in other departments, this lack of action is dysfunctional.

Example 8-2

Wright Company employs a computer-based data processing system for maintaining all company records. The present system was developed in stages over the past five years and has been fully operational for the last 24 months.

When the system was being designed, all department heads were asked to specify the types of information and reports they would need for planning and controlling operations. The systems department attempted to meet the specifications of each department head. Company management specified that certain other reports be prepared for department heads. During the five years of systems development and operation there have been several changes in the department head positions due to attrition and promotions. The new department heads often made requests for additional reports according to their specifications. The systems department complied with all of these requests. Reports were discontinued only upon request by a department head, and then only if it was not a standard report required by top management. As a result, few reports were in fact discontinued. Consequently, the data processing system was generating a large quantity of reports each reporting period.

Company management became concerned about the quantity of information that was being produced by the system. The internal audit department was asked to evaluate the effectiveness of the reports generated by the system. The audit staff determined early in the study that more information was being generated by the data processing system than could be used effectively. They noted the following reactions to this information overload:

1. Many department heads would not act on certain reports during periods of peak activity. The department head would let these reports accumulate with the hope of catching up during a subsequent lull.
2. Some department heads had so many reports that they did not act at all upon the information or they made incorrect decisions because of misuse of the information.
3. Frequently, action required by the nature of the report data was not taken until the department head was reminded by someone who needed the decision. These department heads did not appear to have developed a priority system for acting on the information produced by the data processing system.
4. Department heads often would develop the information they needed from alternative, independent sources, rather than utilizing the reports generated by the data processing system. This was often easier than trying to search among the reports for the needed data.

Required **A.** Indicate, for each of the observed reactions, whether they are functional or dysfunctional behavioral responses. Explain your answer in each case.
B. Assuming one or more of the above were dysfunctional, recommend procedures the company could employ to eliminate the dysfunctional behavior and to prevent its recurrence.

---

4. The department head's actions can be considered both functional and dysfunctional. The development of information from alternative sources is dysfunctional to the firm because the formal system is not producing the information in a usable form and the process of developing information from other sources probably has a cost. However, the fact that the department head was able to generate the needed information from other sources in order that action could be taken is a functional response to the problem.

B. The dysfunctional behavior that occurred in Wright Company was a direct result of management's failure to recognize that information systems are dynamic. Once a system is designed and implemented, it should be continually reviewed to acknowledge and incorporate any changes. A systems study committee composed of both systems staff and users should be established to review the present system and to educate users as to information needs and the use of information.

During the systems review, the committee's attention should be directed toward the information that is needed by department heads, the form of the information, and the timing of the information. Unnecessary reports should be eliminated, and individual reports should be redesigned so that only relevant information is included. Once the reporting system is revised, the system should be periodically reviewed to see that it is functioning smoothly and to make any necessary corrections.

In concluding the discussion of accounting reports and motivation, it should be pointed out that performance reports are primarily concerned with explaining the final results, while managerial activity is concerned with the process that gives rise to the final outcome. Anthony G. Hopwood suggests that "if there are environmental or technological factors, or indeed the behaviors of other managers, which constrain the reported efficiency of the process despite the quality of the manager's own efforts, the accounting reports will give an inadequate reflection of his performance."[8] Since the report does stress final outcomes, it would appear that for fair evaluation the accountant should at least highlight the part of the report for which the manager has control. This seems simple, yet it is very difficult to do.

---

8. Anthony G. Hopwood, *An Accounting System and Managerial Behavior* (Lexington, Massachusetts: Lexington Books, 1973), p. 13.

Behavioral Considerations in Budgeting

Various studies have shown that the reactions budgets generate can be positive or negative. Since those reactions translate into profitability, it is desirable that the budget process elicit the kind of responses that promote the interests of the firm. The questions is how this can best be done.

Budgets can be very valuable tools for the firm since they serve three decision-making functions: planning, control, and motivation.[9]

1. Planning—During this phase of the process, goals of the firm are converted into figures. Since these figures become the standard by which performance of individuals is judged their accuracy is crucial.

2. Control—The comparison of planned levels with those actually achieved enables the firm to locate deviations from the plan, and depending on the nature of the deviation, to react appropriately. The control mechanism is usually a series of reports, issued periodically, that indicates the results of operation and how they compare to the plan.

3. Motivation—The entire budgeting process is so intimately linked with human behavior that there are endless motivational opportunities that must be considered.

The entire budgetary process is a communication network for transmitting the needs of the business to, and from, the decision makers. Throughout this system are the human beings whose psychological needs must be met if the firm is to operate efficiently. Herbert J. Weiser states that:

> Through the process of motivation an individual will attempt to satisfy a particular need. One of the higher-level needs is that of self-fulfillment. Thus, if one has a say in establishing standards which will later serve to measure his own performance, and if he feels such standards are reasonable and attainable, he will be motivated to that end.[10]

Accountants are in a position to greatly influence the kinds of behavior that will result from their work. They should, therefore, be cognizant of the motivational factors so that they can be used to advantage. For example, in the creation of accounting reports:

> The data included in the report format, and the timing of the report issuance all must be designed to cause the report recipient to take the action desired by the report preparer. The accountant cannot say that this job is merely to report the facts, because the facts he reports and the way he reports them determine the actions that the company managers will take. Consequently, the

accountant must consider the recipient action he wants to evoke before he can design an effective accounting report.[11]

A firm that is able to successfully incorporate behavioral concepts into its budgeting system has the potential for improved planning, better decision making, increased control, and motivated employees.

Dysfunctional Aspects of Some Common Budget Practices

As noted above, budgets can provoke negative reactions and are at times even ignored. There are a number of reasons why this occurs, but most of them come to the failure of business to include the behavioral factors in the budget system. Four behavioral areas are described below:

1. Use of Budgets as a Pressure Device to Raise Performance Levels Traditionally, the view has been that the control function served very well to aid performance, so constant pressure was applied to obtain higher levels of achievement. The traditional approach is explained by Harold Bierman and Thomas R. Dyckman as involving

> the comparison of actual results with budgeted or standard amounts that represent goals for management. For many years considerable attention has been given to improving the means by which such analyses could be used. Standards and the analysis of variances were used to increase the ability of management to exercise control over performance. The development of cost centers and decentralization of decision making were in large part responses to the need for subcomponents within a firm that had control of specific resources and could therefore be evaluated in light of their utilization of these resources. Central to these developments was the assumption that the more sophisticated the system, the greater the likelihood in success in controlling costs and improving performance.[12]

When Chris Argyris studied factory personnel, he found that the use of the budget for pressure was one of the major reasons for the strained relations throughout the factory. The factory personnel viewed the budgets as the means management had developed to put pressure on them.[13] The result of this situation was the creation of groups to fight the pressure by such means as stabilizing production levels. The effects of the pressure on the supervisors manifested itself in other ways, such as in friction between themselves or other staff members.

Aside from the reactions mentioned above, setting unattainable standards can result in the lowering of the aspiration level, since "the statement can be made that generally the level of aspiration will be raised and lowered respectively as

---

9. J. Ronen and J.L. Livingston, "An Expectancy Theory Approach to the Motivational Impacts of Budgets," *Accounting Review*, 50 (October, 1975), 671.

10. Herbert J. Weiser, "The Accounting Function and Motivation," *MSU Business Topics*, 16 (Winter, 1968), 32-38.

11. Germain Boer, *Direct Cost and Contribution Accounting* (New York: John Wiley and Sons, 1974), pp. 202-203.

12. Harold Bierman and Thomas R. Dyckman, *Managerial Cost Accounting*, 2nd ed. (New York: Macmillan Co., 1971), p. 127.

13. Chris Argyris, "Human Problems with Budgets," *Harvard Business Review*, 31 (January-February, 1953), 98-103.

the performance (attainment) reaches or does not reach the level of aspiration."[14]

G. H. Hofstede found that up to a certain limit of tightness, budgets became stronger motivators. As they become tighter, motivation is thereafter poor again.[15] This limit is based on the factors in the situation, in management, and in the personalities of the individuals. Thus, the limit is not an objectively determined limit but varies depending on the nature of the individual involved and his/her perception of the situation.

2. Emphasis on Negative Results Management by exception is a prime example of this problem. Kurt Lewin and his associates noted that a person will cope with failure by trying to avoid those feelings.[16] This can lead a person to link the failure to the fault of forces outside of her/his control such as the standards set by the firm. This is exactly the kind of situation that management by exception encourages. As Jacob G. Birnberg and Raghu Nath pointed out,

> Traditionally, managements practice management by exception. The emphasis in the feedback received is thus punishment rather than some mixture of punishment and reward. The manager, as the result of this reporting system, may find himself preoccupied with the time he missed the standard by a significant amount rather than how well he has done over the long run. And the worker who feels he is doing the best he can may experience a degree of anxiety because management by exception highlights only his mistakes. In order to resolve the conflict generated by the reporting system, he may doubt the validity of the standard or budget that management has set. Thus in resolving the dissonance he will reject or discredit management's standard.[17]

The person who feels no allegiance to a standard will certainly not be motivated to achieve it. In fact, it would be in keeping with her/his needs to make sure that he/she did not achieve it.

3. Overuse of the Budget as an Evaluation Tool Ostensibly, the control reports are designed to alert management to the need for corrective action. In most cases, these reports end up doing double-duty as an evaluation form. The attraction is that figures are a concrete form of evidence as to the performance of the individual in quesion. Anthony G. Hopwood conducted a study on the use of accounting data in performance evaluations. He concluded that the problems with this practice are that

1. not all relevant dimensions of managerial performance are included.

2. an organization's cost function is rarely known.

3. accounting data is concerned with outcomes, while managerial activity is concerned with the detailed process

giving rise to final income.

4. the main emphasis of accounting reports is on the short term while management considers the long term.[18]

Hopwood found that managers who were judged primarily on their ability to meet assigned budgets were more likely to have job-related tensions and poor relations with supervisors and peers than managers who were not judged solely on this basis. It was also found that these managers would be more likely to falsify accounting data and to make decisions that were to the detriment of the organization, but beneficial to their unit.[19]

The implications of Hopwood's research are clear. When the firm chooses to emphasize the short-term goals of the budget, it is taking a chance on the achievement of its long-term goals, which are presumably more important.

4. Underutilization of the System for Communication Argyris found that while controllers were inviting lower-rank supervisors to participate in the budget-making process, little information was being exchanged.[20] Argyris suggested that to overcome some of these problems management should consider participative budgeting and increase the training in human relations.

One other situation involving the transfer of information will serve to indicate the possible behavioral consequences of communication problems. R. Beresford Dew and Kenneth P. Gee found that a major reason for the nonuse of control information was that it was too out-of-date by the time it arrived to be used effectively.[21] What does this mean in terms of motivation? V. Bruce Irvine illustrated the problem via a chart that indicated that delays in communication of these data resulted in (1) an inability to relate that information to current decisions and actions, (2) little or no learning taking place, and (3) little improvement in performance.[22]

Participative Budgeting

Participative budgeting is viewed by many as an effective means for alleviating the negative reactions and pressures generated by the budget. In this technique, those who will be affected by the proposed budget take an active part in its creation.

The major advantage cited by various advocates is the internalization of the budget by the individual. This results in goal congruence, where the goals of the individual are the same as those of the firm. This condition will also, it is hoped, bring about increased aspiration levels, better morale, and increased production.

The participation of those actually involved with the implementation of the budget should allow realistic, achievable goals to be established as well as increase the participants' desire to achieve the goals they set. Meeting goals is important in

14. Kurt Lewin, et al., "Level of Aspiration," in *Personality and the Behavior Disorders,* Vol. 1, ed. T. Mc. V. Hunt (New York: Ronald Press Co., 1944), p. 337.

15. G. H. Hofstede, *The Game of Budget Control* (The Netherlands: Koninklijke Van Gorcum and Co., 1968), p. 144.

16. Lewin, p. 375.

17. Jacob G. Birnberg and Raghu Nath, "Implications of Behavioral Accounting for Management Accounting," *Accounting Review,* 42 (July, 1967), p. 478.

18. Anthony G. Hopwood, "An Empirical Study of the Role of Accounting Data in Performance Evaluation," *Empirical Research in Accounting: Selected Studies 1972,* Nicholas Dupuch, ed. (Chicago: Institute of Professional Accounting, Graduate School of Business, University of Chicago, 1974), pp. 157-158.

19. Ibid., pp. 162-163.

20. Argyris, p. 108.

21. R. Beresford Dew and Kenneth P. Gee, *Management Control and Information* (New York: John Wiley and sons, 1973), p. 46.

22. V. Bruce Irvine, "Budgeting: Functional Analysis and Behavioral Implciations," *Cost and Management,* 44 (March-April, 1970), 14.

terms of raising aspiration levels, since the level of aspiration will be raised as the performance (attainment) reaches the established level and the level of aspiration will be lowered as the performance fails to reach the established level. Hofstede found, as described above, that the goals should be "tight," but attainable, for purposes of motivation.

Feedback is very important in establishing future levels of aspiration. Selwyn Becker and David Green, Jr., found that whether future goals are higher or lower is a factor of the feedback received.[23]

In evaluating the effectiveness of participative budgeting, two factors should be considered:[24]

1. Impact on the implementation of decisions—As noted above, the theory suggests that the probability of the decision being effectively implemented is greater if subordinates can participate in the process. Research does not, however, fully support this idea. Under certain situations, participative budgeting may work more effectively than others. The following items should at least be evaluated in considering the prospects for successful results.

• nature of individual—highly authoritarian people may not be affected by participating in the decisions.

• nature of organization and environment—Hopwood suggests that: "In highly programmed, environmentally and technologically constrained areas, where speed and detailed control are essential for efficiency, participative approaches may have much less to offer from the point of view of morale. In contrast, in areas where flexibility, innovation, and the capacity to deal with unanticipated problems are important, participation in decision making may offer a more immediate and more narrowly economic payoff than more authoritarian styles."[25]

• social relationships and patterns of beliefs and expectations—national and cultural differences may affect the effectiveness of participative budgeting.

2. Impact on the quality of decisions—There is no conclusive evidence to suggest that the participative budgeting results in higher quality decisions. Again, Hopwood suggests that to answer this question the factors that influence the impact of participation should be considered, but in relation to the conditions needed for high quality decisions. Some of these factors follow:[26]

• access to relevant information—if a manager has all necessary information to make the decision and knows how to use it, asking subordinates to help will not likely improve the decision. At the other extreme, if the information is equally dispersed among all members of the group, their participation should definitely help.

• nature of environment—participation should offer a greater advantage in situations of change and uncertainty where new information is needed frequently.

• motivation to use information—accuracy of information gained by participation depends on the motives of the subordinates. W. H. Read found that there was a significant negative relationship between a manager's desire for promotion and the accuracy of his/her communication about major job problems.[27] Information from lower management may totally conflict with major goals of organization.

A previous CMA Question contained the following statement:

Modern companies have found that the annual profit plan is an important operating tool. the preparation and adoption of the annual profit plan is a significant vehicle for communication within a company.

Part A asked: Explain whether the annual profit plan represents a formal or informal communication channel within a company.

The solution states:

The annual profit plan represents a formal communication channel within a company for the following reasons:

• Profit plans involve a formal commitment on the par of management to take positive actions to make actual events correspond to the formal plan.
• Profit plans are usually reviewed and approved by a higher authority and, once approved, are changed only in unusual specified circumstances.
• Profit plans contain explicit statements of the implementations of management objectives for a period of time which are published to all parties with control responsibility.
• Comparison of actual results with the profit plan forms the basis for management control, motivation, and performance evaluation.

Part B asks: When a company employs a bottom-up approach for developing the annual profit plan, the process is composed of a series of significant steps.

1. List the significant steps that take place from the inception to the conclusion of the profit planning process.
2. For each step listed, identify the management level involved in the step, and the nature and direction(s) of the communication which takes place.

The solution states:

The following steps are employed in the development of an annual profit plan using a bottom-up approach. Identified with each step are the level of management involved in the activity and the nature and direction(s) of communication process.

• Top management identifies and states planning guidelines. All levels of management are involved and communication is downward.

• A general operating budget or profit plan is prepared

23. Selwyn Becker and David Green, Jr., "Budgeting and Employee Behavior," *Journal of Business,* 35 (October 1962), 399-400.

24. For a detailed discussion of these factors see Anthony Hopwood, *Accounting and Human Behavior* (London: Haymarket Publishing Limited, 1974), pp. 75-87.

25. Ibid., p. 80.

26. Ibid., pp. 84-87.

27. W. H. Read, "Upward Communication in Industrial Hierarchies." *Human Relations,* 15 (February, 1962), 3-16.

beginning with a sales budget. Planning guidelines and sales targets are disseminated downward to the lower level of management. The preparation of the production budget and other components are performed at the lower level of management. However, as with the sales budget, there may be the need for consultation with a higher (middle) management level in order to arrive at certain aspects of the specific manager's budget. The communication activity is primarily lateral with some upward communication possible.

• Negotiation may be required to evolve final plans for each component. Middle management formally presents the plan to top management for its review and suggestions. Communication is upward.

• Coordination and review of the profit plan takes place during the process. Top-level management makes recommendations and returns the various plans to middle-level management. Middle-level management incorporates the recommended changes in the budgets, and re-submits them for approval. Communication is downward. There may be some lateral communication during the adjustment phase as attempts are made to coordinate recommendations and develop feasible solutions.

• Final approval and distribution is made of the formal plan. Top management makes the final approval and transmits its decision downward to all levels of management. Communication is downward.

Pseudo-Participation

That those involved in the budgeting process consider their participation to be genuine is critical to the effective use of this technique. Argyris found that while controllers were inviting lower-rank supervisors to participate in budget-making, it was their endorsement of an established budget rather than their opinion that was being sought.[28] Argyris deemed this activity to be "pseudo-participation" and concluded that this had little value. The idea of participation is to encourage the acceptance of the budget as a goal, and a forced "acceptance" would not produce the desired result. Instead, he envisions the use of budgets acquired in this way as a pressure device to achieve the targeted budgetary goals.

Budgetary Slack

One difficulty encountered in participative budgeting and also in nonparticipative systems is the inclusion of slack in the budget. Slack is a cushion built into the budget figures that allows for variance in actual performances. This cushion may b. a substantial amount, possibly as much as 20 to 25 percent of a division's operating expenses. While slack is not restricted to companies where participative budgeting is used, Michael Schiff and Arie Y. Lewin suggest that it is very prevalent at the . . . .! level in decentralized corporations, which are g. . rally most receptive to participation in the budgeting process.[29]

Slack is created deliberately by those involved, according to Schiff and Lewin:

We believe as does Williamson—contrary to Cyert and March—that managers consciously and intentionally create and bargain for organizational slack. Managers are motivated to achieve two sets of goals—the firm's goals and their personal goals. Personal goals are directly related to income (salary and bonuses), size of staff, and control over allocation of resources. To maximize personal goals while achieving the goals of the firm requires a slack environment. This suggests that managers intentionally create slack.[30]

Mohamed Onsi, in a study of 32 managers, found that 80 percent of those interviewed stated explicitly that they bargained for slack.[31] The reasons they gave for its creation were pressure from top management to attain the budget and show yearly profit growth, and a need for a hedge against uncertainty. Schiff and Lewin also point to management by exception, where the organization reward structure places too much emphasis on underachievement of objectives, as a reason managers want to have slack in their budgets.

Schiff and Lewin's study provided insight into a variety of   ck could be incorporated into the budget. Some of the techniques observed were postponing hiring of personnel whose salaries were already budgeted; the use of a low expected sales price, to ensure achieving or exceeding the budgeted contribution margin; manipulation of standard costs by holding off introducing an improvement in production so that efficiency variances could be produced when needed; using accounting adjustments such as capitalizing a new piece of equipment mid-year rather than when purchased to save one-half year's depreciation charges; and a great deal of leeway in discretionary expenditures such as advertising.[32]

While management must be aware of the existence of slack, little is done about it. Onsi reported that management felt they had a "ballpark" estimate of slack but feels this information is not utilized. He and Schiff and Lewin mention the "cooperation the divisional controller" in the use of slack. Onsi says, "there i. vidence controllers are 'considerate' to departmental heads i: using slack to attain their budget."[33] Schiff and Lewin point to the divisional controller as an active participant in the incorporation of slack in the budget. Ostensibly a member of the corporate headquarters "team," the divisional controller in the decentralized firm actually has more incentive to promote t : interests of the division rather than of the corporate controller—his/her boss. As Schiff and Lewin point out, it is 'y logical that the divisional controller, who has intimate owledge of the operation and whose bonus, prestige, and so are tied to the success of the division, would become involved with the setting and achievement of goals.[34] In a centralized company, the controller is far removed from the actual creation of slack. Because the controller is less informed, Schiff and   conclude that slack will permeate all levels of management in the division.

28. Argyris, p. 108.
29. Michael Schiff and Arie Y. Lewin, "Where Traditional Budgeting ....," *Financial Executive,* 35 (May, 1968), 62.

30. Ibid., p. 51.
31. Mohamed Onsi, "Factor Analysis of Behavioral Variables Affecting Budgetary Slack," *Accounting Review,* 48 (July, 1973), 539.
32. Schiff and Lewin, pp. 51-62.
33. Onsi, p. 546.
34. Michael Schiff and Arie Y. Lewin, "The Impact of People on Budgets," *Accounting Review,* 45 (April, 1970), 263-264.

The pervasiveness of slack makes it extremely difficult to eliminate. The use of the budget in performance evaluations gives everyone too much interest in seeing that the targeted goals are achieved. Therefore, some new tactics must be introduced into the budgeting process.

Schiff and Lewin emphasize the need to question the underlying assumptions on which the budget is based.[35] They suggest that task forces be created to review all facets of the operation. The use of outside consultants or recently hired MBA's in studying these groups is preferred, since they can provide more objective evaluation.

A previous CMA examination problem, part of which deals with slack, is presented in Example 8-3. In examining the solution, note how the discussion centers on the facts presented in the problem. The solution follows:

A. The manufacturing manager's views can be separated into two arguments—the use of the same improvement targets for all plants and inconsistent application of target revisions. In both cases the manufacturing manager's arguments are valid.

The manufacturing manager claims that the use of the same improvement targets for all plants fails to recognize the different abilities of plants to achieve targets. His criticism is valid because plants do have different opportunities for improvement and this should be recognized in establishing improvement targets. While his arguments to support his view that older plants have less opportunity for improvement may be valid, there is insufficient data presented to verify his claim.

The manufacturing manager objects to the newer plants obtaining revised targets and then being able to perform better than the revised target. The modification of targets in light of new information is an appropriate budgeting technique. Newer plants may need such revisions because their inexperience makes it more difficult to set parameters and exercise control. However, the manufacturing manager's argument is valid because adjustments have not been available to all plants, and furthermore, the adjustments granted to new plants appear to make it easier for them to achieve targets.

The resulting treatment in establishing and revising targets, when coupled with a performance appraisal and reward system, does appear to discriminate in favor of the newer plants. This would apparently lead to lower bonuses, appraisals, and morale among management of the older plants.

B. Both old and new plants have the capability of concealing slack in their budgets. The older plants cannot introduce budgetary slack through their cost estimates, because their costs have established a pattern over the years. However, the plant management knows those areas of operations where changes and improvements can be initiated. These operating changes can be initiated after the budget is adopted.

The newer plants can incorporate budgetary slack in other ways. Their cost estimates are more uncertain because the plants are newer. The plant operations have not stabilized so that management may be able to inflate costs slightly above what can be realistically expected by them. There may be more opportunities for improved operations, which may not be recognized at the time the budget is adopted. In addition, there is some lag in incorporating the cost savings of the increased experience

Example 8-3

The Noton Company has operated a comprehensive budgeting system for many years. This system is a major component of the company's program to control operations and costs at its widely scattered plants. Periodically the plants' general managers gather to discuss the overall company control system with the top management.

At this year's meeting the budgetary system was severely criticized by one of the most senior plant managers, who said that the system discriminated unfairly against the older, well-run and established plants in favor of the newer plants. The impact was lower year-end bonuses and poor performance ratings. In addition, there were psychological consequences in the form of lower employee morale. In this manager's judgment, revisions in the system were needed to make it more effective. The basic factors of Noton's budget include:
1. announcement of an annual improvement percentage target established by top management.
2. plant submission of budgets implementing the annual improvement target.
3. management review and revision of the proposed budget.
4. establishment and distribution of the final budget.

To support these arguments, the senior manager compared the budget revisions and performance results. The older plants were expected to achieve the improvement target but often were unable to meet it. On the other hand, the newer plants were often excused from meeting a portion of this target in their budgets. However, their performance was usually better than the final budget.

The senior manager further argued that the company did not recognize the operating differences that made attainment of the annual improvement factor difficult, if not impossible. The manager's plant has been producing essentially the same product for its 20 years of existence. The machinery and equipment, which underwent many modifications in the first five years, have had no major changes in recent years. Because they are old, repair and maintenance costs have increased each year, and the machines are less reliable. The plant management team has been together for the last ten years and works well together. The labor force is mature, with many of the employees having the highest seniority in the company. In the manager's judgment, the significant improvements have been "wrung out" of the plant over the years and merely keeping even is difficult.

For comparison the manager noted that one plant opened within the past four years would have an easier time meeting the company's expectations. The plant is new, containing modern equipment that is in some cases still experimental. Major modifications in equipment and operating systems have been made each year as the plant management has obtained a better understanding of the operations. The plant's management, although experienced, has been together only since its opening. The plant is located in a previously nonindustrial area and therefore has a relatively inexperienced work force.

Required   A. Evaluate the manufacturing manager's views. **B.** Equitable application of a budget system requires the ability of corporate management to remove "budgetary slack" in plant budgets. Discuss how each plant could conceal "slack" in its budget.

35. Ibid., pp. 265-267.

of the workers and the efficiency in functioning of the equipment and machinery into the budget.

Behavioral Factors in Standard Cost Systems

Standard costs are precomputed or targeted costs that should be attained under normal conditions. These standards are usually based on inputs from accountants, engineers, and market researchers. The final responsibility for setting the standard should rest with line personnel.

Development of Standard Costs

The idea of standard costs was an outgrowth of the scientific management movement. Taylor and his supporters were interested in making production more efficient. By experimenting with alternate methods of performing tasks, the best method was determined and then used as a standard. This practice of careful measurement and the setting of a standard eventually resulted in standard costs.

Motivational and Aspirational Levels

The setting of a standard at a particular level requires careful consideration of the possible motivational impact. Setting a standard at too high or too low a level normally generates negative results in terms of motivation. Therefore, gauging the desirable level is extremely important.

The ideal standard is one that is achievable under conditions that do not allow for any inefficiencies. Thus, these standards are not generally attainable under normal operating conditions. Consistently failing to achieve a goal can frustrate workers and often leads to their ignoring the goal. An attainable goal, on the other hand, can motivate a worker to achieve that goal.

Andrew C. Stedry studied another aspect of motivation, the individual's aspiration level. He conducted an experiment using college students, in which he attempted to determine the extent of the relationship between the individual's aspiration level (determined by the student), the budgeted performance level (assigned to the student), and the actual level of performance that was attained. The idea behind this was that budgets (which are simply a standard) traditionally involve the imposition of a level of achievement on an individual that is eventually compared to actual performance. The individual, in turn, has a level of performance to which she aspires. Failing to recognize the interaction of this aspiration level with the budgeted amount can result in dysfunctional behavior on the part of the individual.[36]

One suggestion that provides answers to many of the problems of motivation is to allow the employee to participate, at least to some extent, in the setting of the standards. Being involved in setting the standards means the individual is more likely to accept them as being legitimate goals and to adopt them as his personal goals.

Participation is not the total answer to the problem of motivation. Raymond E. Miles and Roger C. Vergin have gleaned the following requirements for a successful control system from the writings of behaviorists. They concluded that:

• Standards must be established in such a way that they are recognized as legitimate. This requires that the method of deriving standards be understood by those affected, and that standards reflect the actual capabilities of the organizational process for which they are established.

• The individual organization member should feel that he has some voice or influence in the establishment of his own performance goals. Participation of those affected in the establishment of performance objectives helps establish legitimacy of these standards.

• Standards must be set in such a way that they convey "freedom to fail." The individual needs assurance that he will not be unfairly censured for an occasional mistake or for variations in performance that are outside his control.

• Feedback, recognized as essential in traditional control designs, must be expanded. Performance data must not only flow upward for analysis by higher echelons, but they must also be summarized and fed back to those directly involved in the process.[37]

It should be realized that the standards alone do not motivate. Individuals are motivated by their own needs and by their perception as to whether meeting a given standard will allow them to satisfy their needs. Edward E. Lawler, III, and John Grant Rhode suggest that good job performance leads to feelings of accomplishment and satisfaction, which is an intrinsic reward that cannot be given by the organization but must originate and be experienced within the individual.[38] The organization can, however, by the way it structures the work environment, influence intrinsic motivation.

Lawler and Rhode also cite several studies that suggest that "intrinsic motivation is most likely to be present when standards or budgets are set that have somewhat less than a 50/50 chance of being attained."[39] The standards that are difficult to attain will have a positive effect on performance only if they are accepted as goals. Very low standards do not have a significant positive effect because their attainment does not result in a significant feeling of satisfaction and accomplishment.

Based on his investigation of the behavioral implications of cost accounting, Caplan stated:

1. Actual cost systems, although important for the purpose of financial accounting, have little value for management control purposes.

2. The proper use of standard costing fits very nicely into the overall concept of the "decision-making" model of behavior.

36. A. C. Stedry, *Budget Control and Cost Behavior* (Englewood Cliffs, New Jersey: Prentice-Hall, 1960).

37. Raymond E. Miles and Roger C. Vergin, "Behavioral Properties of Variance Control," *California Management Review*, 8 (Spring, 1966), 59-60.

38. Edward E. Lawler, III, and John Grant Rhode, *Information and Control in Organizations* (Pacific Palisades, California: Goodyear Publishing Co., 1976), p. 65.

39. Ibid., p. 71.

Example 8-4

Harden Company has experienced increased production costs. The primary area of concern identified by management is direct labor. The company is considering adopting a standard cost system to help control labor and other costs. Useful historical data are not available because detailed production records have not been maintained.

Harden Company has retained Finch & Associates, an engineering consulting firm, to establish labor standards. After a complete study of the work process, the engineers recommended a labor standard of one unit of production every 30 minutes or 16 units per day for each worker. Finch further advised that Harden's wage rates were below the prevailing rate of $3 per hour.

Harden's production vice president thought this labor standard was too tight and the employees would be unable to attain it. From his experience with the labor force, he believed a labor standard of 40 minutes per unit or 12 units per day for each worker would be more reasonable.

The president of Harden Company believed the standard should be set at a high level to motivate the workers, but he also recognized the standard should be set at a level to provide adequate information for control and reasonable cost comparisons. After much discussion, the management decided to use a dual standard. The labor standard recommended by the engi-

neering firm of one unit every 30 minutes would be employed in the plant as a motivation device, and a cost standard of 40 minutes per unit would be used in reporting. Management also concluded that the workers would not be informed of the cost standard used for reporting purposes. The production vice president conducted several sessions prior to implementation in the plant informing the workers of the new standard cost system and answering questions. The new standards were not related to incentive pay but were introduced at the time wages were increased to $3 per hour.

The new standard cost system was implemented on January 1, 1974. At the end of six months of operation, the statistics below on labor performance were presented to top management.

Raw material quality, labor mix, and plant facilities and conditions have not changed to any great extent during the six-month period.

Required   A. Discuss the impact of different types of standards on motivation, and specifically discuss the effect on motivation in Harden Company's plant of adopting the labor standard recommended by the engineering firm.
B. Evaluate Harden Company's decision to employ dual standards in their standard cost system.

	Jan.	Feb.	Mar.	Apr.	May	June
Production (units)	5100	5000	4700	4500	4300	4400
Direct labor hours	3000	2900	2900	3000	3000	3100
Variance from Labor Standard	$1350U	$1200U	$1650U	$2250U	$2550U	$2700U
Variance from Cost Standard	$1200F	$1300F	$700F	$-0-	$400U	$500U

3. Standard cost systems have the potential to be used in one of two ways—either as aids in increasing motivation and goal congruence or as devices to achieve high levels of autocratic and coercive control.[40]

Consider the CMA examination problem in Example 8-4. The solution to Part A follows:

Standards are often classified into three types—ideal (tight), attainable (reasonable), or easy (loose). Standards that are too loose or too tight will generally have a negative impact on worker motivation. If standards are too loose, workers will tend to set their goals at this low rate, thus reducing productivity below what is obtainable. If the standard is too tight, workers will realize that it is impossible to attain the standard. They will become frustrated and will not attempt to meet the standard. An attainable or reasonable standard, which can be achieved under normal working conditions, is likely to contribute to the workers' motivation to achieve the designated level of activity.

The plant management can participate in the setting of standards, or they can be imposed on the plant by top management. Workers and plant management will tend to react negatively in the long run to imposed standards, because they will feel threatened. If they participate in setting the standard, they can identify with the standard procedure and the standard could become one of their personal goals.

In the case of Harden, it appears that the standard was imposed on the plant. In addition, management used an ideal standard to measure performance. Both of these actions appear to have had a negative impact on output over the first six months.

Some writers have suggested that the use of dual standards, one for the setting of goals and one for realistic planning and control, would achieve the maximum motivation level. Harden Company is considering adopting such an approach. The solution to part B deals with dual standards. It states:

Harden made a poor decision to use dual standards. When the workers learn of the dual standard, the company's entire measurement system will become suspect and credibility will be lost. Company morale could suffer because the workers would not know for sure how the company evaluates their performance. As a result, total disregard for the present and any future cost control system is likely to develop.

40. Edwin H. Caplan, *Management Accounting and Behavioral Science* (Reading, Massachusetts: Addison-Wesley Publishing Company, 1971), p. 70.

Behavioral Factors in Cost Allocation

Cost allocation is used by management to make economic decisions, control costs and motivate employees to accomplish management objectives. Cost allocations often are used in establishing prices, especially where interdivisional and/or multinational transfers are involved. Management may allocate the cost of a service area such as the computer operations in an attempt to control the cost in this department. Research and development costs may be allocated to operating units for the purpose of getting them to take a direct interest in the central research activities. The extent to which these objectives can be accomplished varies from one situation to another and also varies among managers, depending on their managerial background and philosophy.

Volume 4 covers the technique of cost allocation. Here we are interested primarily in the behavioral factors associated with cost allocation. Generally, costs that a particular manager can control to some extent can be justifiably allocated. It is those costs for which a cause-and-effect relationship cannot be established that pose the real problem in cost allocation.

Arbitrary Allocations

It can be argued that arbitrarily allocated costs do make managers aware of these costs and that they will therefore make some effort to control them, even though their effectiveness may be limited. Also, managers are not likely to be upset by the allocation of these costs as long as all other divisions or subunits receive comparable allocations. Horngren and Foster state that:

> Some managers maintain that the morale effects of allocation procedures on the production departments are given too much attention. There are also important effects on the morale of the service-department employees. That is, if the other departments are not charged with service-department costs, the service-department staff is likely to feel that it lacks the status of first-class citizenship as an integral part of the organization.[41]

On the other hand, managers suggest that since the individual to which the costs are assigned cannot control them, the cost of making the allocation exceeds its benefits. They also contend that entering these items on performance reports is confusing and diverts attention from areas which can be controlled.

Caplan and Champaux[42] in an N.A.A. Research Study of one company, make the following statement regarding overhead allocation:

> The company's practice of allocating corporate overhead to the division is questionable from a behavioral standpoint. There is a great deal of debate among man-

agement accountants with respect to the advisability of this practice on the grounds that it violates a primary rule of responsibility accounting—"never charge a manager with a cost over which he has no control." The experiences of the Ralin Company seem to support this responsibility accounting view. We are not certain what advantages top management thinks it realizes from the allocation of corporate overhead. But, we are certain from our interviews that such allocations create a considerable amount of anger and resentment among division management. Not only do the annual allocations appear to be made arbitrarily—often without consulting the divisions—but sometimes there are changes in the middle of the year—also without consultation. Because the divisions already are under pressure to meet a budget they feel was imposed on them in the first place, having to absorb additional overhead not in the original plan is viewed by division management as an injustice of major proportion. This situation provides an excellent example of an accounting technique that serves no particularly useful managerial function but has been perpetuated over time by accountants to the detriment of the organizations they serve.[43]

Bodnar and Lusk[44] suggest that the cost allocation process provides an additional source for motivating particular behavior relative to a set of goals established for a division or other subunit. They suggest that to develop a method to allocate cost that will be most effective for motivation, management should specify a set of performance measures, a set of bases for cost allocation and an allocation criterion functional, such as fairness or ability to bear. During the period under study, data about performance and activity relative to the set of allocation bases would be accumulated. Alternative cost allocations would be made based on the results (activity data accumulated) for the period. Based on this analysis management would select the specific allocation method, taking into consideration the allocation criteria previously established.[45] In using this approach Bodnar and Lusk suggest the following:

1. The operational statistics (allocation bases) to be used in the modeling process should be reviewed periodically to ensure subsequent appropriateness.

2. The operant model requires careful specification of (1) the set of goal measures, (2) their measurement surrogates, (3) the definition of periodic responses and (4) the process by which responses are evaluated relative to the allocation criterion functional. It is recommended that each subunit have some form of participation in specification of these four elements. Participation itself generally is considered to be a source of control and reinforcement, hence, a positive factor in the implementation of a control technique. Agreement on the evaluative dimension of the control system should enhance its effectiveness since organizational control inevitably involves manipulation of human behavior.

3. It is recommended that simple, objective (that is, easily quantifiable) measures be used and that these measures be unitized or normalized to account for subunit size differences. Subjective measures should be considered to be inappropriate for this application owing to the disagreement which often accompanies

41. Charles T. Horngren and George Foster, *Cost Accounting: A Managerial Emphasis,* 6th ed. (Englewood Cliffs, N.J.: Prentice-Hall, 1987), p. 511.

42. Edwin H. Caplan and Joseph E. Champaux, *Cases in Management Accounting: Context and Behavior/The Ralin Company—An Exploratory Study* (New York: National Association of Accountants, 1978).

43. Ibid., pp. 53-54.

44. George Bodnar and Edward J. Lusk, "Motivational Considerations in Cost Allocation Systems: A Conditioning Theory Approach," *Accounting Review* (October 1977), pp. 857-868.

45. Ibid., pp. 859-860.

measurement of subjective evaluative indices.

4. It is recommended that the assignment of behavioral weights be done centrally, based upon management's perception of the overall state of the organization, behavioral disposition of the decentralized units, and the desired expansion path of the organization.[46]

Behavioral Factors in Divisional Performance Evaluation

Chapter 7 of this volume describes the divisional performance evaluation and should be studied in conjunction with this part. The objective here is to identify several behavioral factors that influence division performance measurement.

Ability to Exercise Control

Only the items the manager can control should be included in the base for performance evaluation. If the manager has no control over accounts receivable, they should not be in the asset base. Study Example 8-5, a CMA examination problem. Note that George Johnson is responsible for the operations of his division and has input into the capital investment program and is responsible for its implementation. In order for inventory, accounts receivable, and accounts and wages payable to be included it is assumed he is responsible for these items. The solution to Part A follows:

Mr. Johnson is responsible for the current operating results of his division; this includes revenue development, pricing and physical volume; cost incurrence for manufacturing and distributing the product, for maintenance of the facilities, and for development of work force. He is also responsible for contributing to the capital investment program for his division and for implementing the approved capital programs. The inclusions of certain balance sheet items, inventory, accounts receivable, and accounts and wages payable and the contribution return on division net investment imply responsibility for the management of some assets and liabilities.

Attempts may be made to establish divisions when the necessary conditions do not exist to give managers the responsibility to control the items over which they are held accountable. David Solomons suggests that "each division should be sufficiently independent of other divisions, both in respect of its production facilities and its marketing organization, to make its separate profit responsibility a reality."[47] While it may be possible that several functions are centralized, such as cash management and collection and purchasing, the important aspects of production and marketing generally must be centralized.

---

46. Ibid., pp. 866-867.
47. David Solomons, *Divisional Performance: Measurement and Control* (Homewood, Illinois: Richard D. Irwin, Inc., 1965), pp. 9-10.

Placing Emphasis on All Goals

In many companies there is a tendency to place too much emphasis on some short-run profitability measure such as return on investment (ROI) and ignore the others. General Electric has stated that organizational performance will be measured in eight areas, thus stressing the importance of multiple goals. The areas are:

1. profitability
2. market position
3. productivity
4. product leadership
5. personal development
6. employee attitudes
7. public responsibility
8. balance between short-range and long-range goals.

Part B of Example 8-5 asks for an appraisal of Mr. Johnson's performance. In response, it is important to look beyond the fact that the 32 percent return significantly exceeded the budgeted return. The answer follows:

The first impression is that Mr. Johnson has done a fine job. His return is 32 percent compared to a budgeted return of 25 percent for the four year period of 1969-1971. Careful analysis of the data suggests that this result was achieved by manipulation of activities, which results in an overstatement of division net contribution and an understatement of division net investment.
1. Items affecting contribution:
   a. sales—$200,000 below budget.
   b. repairs—$40,000 below its normal relationship to sales.
   c. managed costs—$35,000 below budgeted amounts and $25,000 below last year.
   d. depreciation and rent below budget amounts (see item a below).
2. Items affecting investment:
   a. fixed assets $580,000 below budget—capital plan not implemented (note rent also low suggesting leased capacity not acquired according to plan).
   b. accounts and wages payable $70,000 above normal relationship to material and labor.
   c. inventory $90,000 below normal relationship with sales.
   All the normal items within his control (sales excepted) varied from normal relationships (relationships he accepted and embodies in the budgets he recommended) in directions that enhanced his division return. This suggests he took action to improve the return in the short run at the expense of the longer run. He appears to have deferred repairs, maintenance, employee training and capital improvements. Each should have detrimental effects upon future performance of the division and firm.

The system used by Botel Division places too much emphasis on the ROI and short-run profitability. Part C requires a discussion of changes that could be made to improve the system. The solution follows:

The responsibilities of Mr. Johnson seem quite appropriate for a manager of an autonomous division.

Example 8-5

George Johnson was hired on July 1, 1969, as assistant general manager of the Botel Division of Staple, Inc. It was understood that he would be elevated to general manager of the division on January 1, 1971, when the then current general manager retired and this was duly done. In addition to becoming acquainted with the division and the general manager's duties, Mr. Johnson was specifically charged with the responsibility for development of the 1970 and 1971 budgets. As general manager in 1971, he was, obviously, responsible for the 1972 budget.

The Staple Corporation is a multiproduct company that is highly decentralized. Each division is quite autonomous. The corporation staff approves division prepared operating budgets but seldom makes major changes in them. The corporate staff actively participates in decisions requiring capital investment (for expansion or replacement) and makes the final decisions. The division management is responsible for implementing the capital program. The major method used by the Staple Corporation to measure division performance is contribution return on division net investment. The budgets presented below were approved by the corporation. Revision of the 1972 budget is not considered necessary even though 1971 actual departed from the approved 1971 budget.

Required A. Identify Mr. Johnson's responsibilities under the management and measurement program described above. **B.** Appraise the performance of Mr. Johnson in 1971. **C.** Recommend to the president any changes in the responsibilities assigned to managers or in the measurement methods used to evaluate division management based upon your analysis.

BOTEL DIVISION
(in thousands of $)

Accounts	Actual			Budget	
	1969	1970	1971	1971	1972
Sales	1,000	1,500	1,800	2,000	2,400
Less division variable costs:					
Material and labor	250	375	450	500	600
Repairs	50	75	50	100	120
Supplies	20	30	36	40	48
Less division managed costs:					
Employee training	30	35	25	40	45
Maintenance	50	55	40	60	70
Less division committed costs:					
Depreciation	120	160	160	200	200
Rent	80	100	110	140	140
Total	600	830	871	1,080	1,223
Division net contribution	**400**	**670**	**929**	**920**	**1,177**
Division investment:					
Accounts receivable	100	150	180	200	240
Inventory	200	300	270	400	480
Fixed assets	1,590	2,565	2,800	3,380	4,000
Less accounts and wages payable	(150)	(225)	(350)	(300)	(360)
Net investment	**1,740**	**2,790**	**2,900**	**3,680**	**4,360**
Contribution return on net investment	23%	24%	32%	25%	27%

The use of the contribution return on division net investment for overall performance measurement is a good start for autonomous divisions. In addition to this measure, additional activites should be reported:

1. budget for implementation of capital programs compared to actual implementation;
2. budgeted operating costs and revenues compared to the actual figures;
3. comparison of level of controlled assets to budgeted levels.

The reports should be accompanied by explanations of significant differences. This information plus the return on investment would provide a good measure of the division manager's performance.

Some goals are easily quantified, while others are very difficult to quantify. For those goals that have been quantified, it is much easier to develop a system for evaluation. Thus, in the General Electric list, more emphasis may be placed on profitability (easily quantified) than on public responsibility. It is important for any company to develop guards against these tendencies and give consideration to all of the goals.

Another problem that causes some goals to be stressed over others is the time that elapses between the expenditures and the benefits. In the area of personnel development it will take several years to receive the full benefit from the cash outlay, yet the entire amount was reported as an expense for the period in which the cash outlay was made. Other expenditures result in immediate benefits, and these are obviously preferred by the managers. Again, it is not to the long-run benefit of the company if too much emphasis is placed on decisions that provide immediate results.

Conflict Between Goals

It is easy to see that of General Electric's eight goals, several could conflict with each other. Effort toward the accomplishment of the profitability goal may have an unfavorable effect on employee attitude or public responsibility.

The problem is further complicated by the fact that some goals can be easily quantified and others cannot be. Some have suggested composite weighting systems where each variable is assigned a weight according to its relative importance. There are two basic problems with the use of weights: (1) weights are implicit rather than explicit and thus are very difficult to translate into numerical form, and (2) the implicit weights refuse to stay constant.[48]

There is, in fact, no simple solution for any organization attempting to solve this type of conflict. Caplan suggests that organizations should observe two basic principles:[49]

1. Make every effort to develop the best possible set of goals and criteria.
2. Recognize that the evaluation process is imperfect.

Restraint by Top Management

To have any type of decentralized operations there must be a

willingness for top management not to interfere with the division's operations but to allow division managers to make decisions. The essence of decentralization is giving to the individuals in charge the responsibility to make decisions. At times it is necessary for top management to interfere with a division's operations. Yet each time this occurs there is a cost. This cost must be compared with the benefits gained by such action. Interference is generally resisted by the managers in charge, and it can easily create conflict between divisions because one manager may see the interference as hurting her division and helping the others. The number of times that management interferes must be kept at a minimum.

There must, however, also be considerable cooperation among divisions. David Solomons suggests that if independence of division is "carried to the limit it would destroy the very idea that such divisions are integral parts of any single business. The divisions would then become so many unrelated businesses."[50] Solomon further suggests:[51]

Divisions should be more than investments, for they should contribute not only to the success of the corporation but to the success of each other. They may do this by using a common raw material, and therefore making it possible to buy it more cheaply in bulk. They may, by product transfers, help each other to complete a product line.

A CMA examination problem dealing with intervention by top management is presented in Example 8-6. Note that Part A deals with the economic effect on the company as a whole. The suggested solution is in Exhibit 8-5. Part B asks for a discussion of the advisability of intervention by top management. The solution follows.

Intervention by top management generally is not advisable except in unusual circumstances, because it takes away the delegated decision power given to division management and influences the measures used to judge the performance of division management. It conflicts with important objectives of decentralization—division autonomy over operating decisions and decisions made by those closest to the operating scene. Such interference can result in lower morale and poorer performance by division management because they will be evaluated using measures that are not substantially within their control.

The described policy would avoid the need for intervention by top management or an arbitration committee. However, the policy is undesirable because other unfavorable consequences outweigh this benefit.

There would be no analysis to determine the most profitable use of an item required to be transferred at marginal cost with the described policy. In addition, managers would find that they had reduced control over their operations and that there would be an "uncontrollable" influence on their performance measure; this could result in lower morale for managers.

Over-Emphasis of Indexes

V. F. Ridgeway suggests there are three types of quantitative indexes that can be used: (1) **single criterion** index using only

48. Gordon Shillinglaw, *Managerial Cost Accounting* (Homewood, Illinois: Richard D. Irwin, Inc., 1977). p. 653.
49. Caplan, *Management Accounting and Behavioral Science*, p. 103.
50. Solomons, p. 10.
51. Ibid., pp. 10-11.

Example 8-6

The Lorax Electric Company manufactures a large variety of systems and individual components for the electronics industry. The firm is organized into several divisions with division managers given the authority to make virtually all operating decisions. Management control over divisional operations is maintained by a system of divisional profit and return on investment measures that are reviewed regularly by top management. The top management of Lorax has been quite pleased with the effectiveness of the system they have been using and believe that it is responsible for the company's improved profitability over the last few years.

The Devices Division manufactures solid-state devices and is operating at capacity. The Systems Division has asked the Devices Division to supply a large quantity of integrated circuit IC378. The Devices Division currently is selling this component to its regular customers at $40 per hundred.

The Systems Division, which is operating at about 60 percent capacity, wants this particular component for a digital clock system. It has an opportunity to supply large quantities of these digital clock systems to Centonic Electric, a major producer of clock radios and other popular electronic home entertainment equipment. This is the first opportunity any of the Lorax divisions have had to do business with Centonic Electric. Centonic Electric has offered to pay $7.50 per clock system.

The Systems Division prepared an analysis of the probable costs to produce the clock systems. The amount that could be paid to the Devices Division for the integrated circuits was determined by working backward from the selling price. The cost estimates employed by the division reflected the highest per unit cost the Systems Division could incur for each cost component and still leave a sufficient margin so that the division's income statement could show reasonable improvement. The cost estimates are summarized below.

As a result of this analysis, the Systems Division offered the Devices Division a price of $20 per hundred for the integrated circuit. This bid was refused by the manager of the Devices Division because he felt the Systems Division should at least meet the price of $40 per hundred that regular customers pay. When the Systems Division found that it could not obtain a comparable integrated circuit from outside vendors, the situation was brought to an arbitration committee that had been set up to review such problems.

The arbitration committee prepared an analysis that showed that $.15 would cover variable costs of producing the integrated circuit, $.28 would cover the full cost including fixed overhead, and $.35 would provide a gross margin equal to the average gross margin on all of the products sold by the Devices Division. The manager of the Systems Division reacted by stating, "They could sell us that integrated circuit for $.20 and

Proposed selling price		$7.50
Costs excluding required integrated circuits (IC378)		
Components purchased from outside suppliers	$2.75	
Circuit board etching— labor and variable overhead	.40	
Assembly, testing, packaging —labor and variable overhead	1.35	
Fixed overhead allocations	1.50	
Profit margin	.50	6.50
Amount that can be paid for integrated circuits IC378 (5 @ $20 per hundred)		$1.00

still earn a positive contribution toward profit. In fact, they should be required to sell at their variable cost—$.15 and not be allowed to take advantage of us."

Lou Belcher, manager of Devices, countered by arguing that, "It doesn't make sense to sell to the Systems Division at $20 per hundred when we can get $40 per hundred outside on all we can produce. In fact, Systems could pay us up to almost $60 per hundred and they would still have a positive contribution to profit."

The recommendation of the committee, to set the price at $.35 per unit ($35 per hundred), so that Devices could earn a "fair" gross margin, was rejected by both division managers. Consequently, the problem was brought to the attention of the vice president of operations and the vice president's staff.

Required **A.** What is the immediate economic effect on the Lorax Company as a whole if the Devices Devision were required to supply IC378 to the Systems Division at $.35 per unit—the price recommended by the arbitration committee? Explain your answer.

B. Discuss the advisability of intervention by top management as a solution to transfer pricing disputes between division managers such as the one experienced by Lorax Electric Company.

C. Suppose that Lorax adopted a policy of requiring that the price to be paid in all internal transfers by the buying division would be equal to the variable costs per unit of the selling division for that product and that the supplying division would be required to sell if the buying division decided to buy the item. Discuss the consequences of adopting such a policy as a way of avoiding the need for the arbitration committee or for intervention by the vice president.

one quantity; (2) **multiple criteria** where several quantities are measured simultaneously; and (3) **composite criteria** where several quantities are measured, weighted, and then averaged.[52]

52. V. F. Ridgeway, "Dysfunctional Consequences of Performance Measurements," *Administrative Science Quarterly*, 1 (September, 1956), 240-247.

As mentioned above, the problem with using a single quantitative index such as ROI is that it is stressed and the quality factors are ignored. Using multiple goals has its weaknesses also. The objectives may contradict each other. In addition, managers must, before making a decision that will result in the accomplishment of one goal, assess the impact of the decision on other goals and try to determine if the benefit derived from

Exhibit 8-5

The Lorax Electric Company will earn higher profits if the necessary integrated circuits (ICs) are sold to the Systems Division rather than to regular customers. The improved profit will be $1.00 per clock system as shown below.

Contribution margin from system:		
Proposed selling price		$7.50
Less variable production costs:		
Integrated circuits (IC378) 5 @ $.15	$ .75	
Outside components	2.75	
Circuit board etching	.40	
Assembly, testing, packaging	1.35	5.25
Contribution margin per unit of clock system		$2.25
Contribution margin foregone in Devices Division:		
Selling price of IC378	.40	
Variable production costs	.15	
Contribution margin per circuit	.25	
Units for clock system	5	
Contribution margin lost		1.25
Net advantage to Lorax Company if clock system is produced by Systems Division (per unit):		$1.00/unit

the first outweighs the reduction in the second. With a large number of goals, this decision process becomes very involved. Under the composite approach, weights would be assigned according to the relative importance of the goal. Again, problems develop in how to assign weights and keep them current.

The behavioral impact of any index is, according to Caplan, determined by two factors.[53]

1. the variable it measures—its content

2. the force with which it is applied—the rewards and punishments associated with it.

The content of most indexes involves at least some problems. Accountants must "continually inquire into the validity and appropriateness of the indexes that are being used" and must be "constantly aware of the possibility of unintended and undesired behavior responses to their performance measurement."[54] Thus, excessive force should not be used in applying a specific index.

53. Caplan, *Management Accounting and Behavioral Science*, p. 105.
54. Ibid., pp. 105-106.

Consider this introduction to a CMA question:

The Jackson Corporation is a large, divisionalized manufacturing company. Each division is viewed as an investment center and has virtually complete autonomy for product development, marketing and production.

Performance of division managers is evaluated periodically by senior corporate management. Divisional return on investment is the sole criterion used in performance evaluation under current corporate policy. Corporate management believes return on investment is an adequate measure because it incorporates quantitative information from the divisional income statement and balance sheet in the analysis.

Some division managers complained that a single criterion for performance evaluation is insufficient and ineffective. These managers have compiled a list of criteria which they believe should be used in evaluating division manager's performance. The criteria include profitability, market position, productivity, product leadership, personnel development, employee attitudes, public responsibility, and balance between short-range and long-range goals.

The requirement for Part A states: Jackson management believes that return on investment is an adequate criterion to evaluate division management performance. Discuss the shortcomings or possible inconsistencies of using return on investment as the sole criterion to evaluate divisional management performance. The solution indicates:

The shortcomings or possible inconsistencies of using return on investment as the sole criterion to evaluate divisional management performance include the following:

• ROI tends to emphasize short-run performance at the possible expense of long-run profitability.

• ROI is not consistent with cash flow models used for capital exenditure analysis.

• ROI frequently is not controllable by the division manager because many components included in the computation are committed in amount or are the responsibility of other parties.

• Reliance on ROI as the only measurement indicator could lead to an inaccurate decision or investment at either the divisional or corporate level.

Part B asked the candidate to discuss the advantages of using a multiple criteria to evaluate divisional management performance. They include:

• Multiple performance measures provide a more comprehensive picture of performance by considering a wider range of responsibilities.

• Multiple performance measures emphasize both the short-term and long-term results thereby emphasizing the total performance of the division.

• Multiple performance measures may highlight non-quantitative as well as quantitative-oriented aspects.

• Multiple performance criteria will enhance goal congruence and reduce the importance of the dysfunctional short-run goal of profit maximization.

Part C asked for a description of problems or disadvantages of implementing the multiple performance criteria measurement system suggested to Jackson Corporation by its division managers. They include:

• The measurement criteria are not all equally quantifiable.

• Management may have difficulty applying the criteria on a consistent basis, some criteria may be subjectively more heavily weighted than other criteria, and some criteria may be in conflict with each other.

• A multiple performance measurement system may be confusing to division management.

• Over-emphasis on multiple evaluation criteria may lead to diffusion of effort and the failure to perform as well as expected in any one area.

Human Resource Accounting

There are a growing number of persons in management accounting who feel that present methods used to evaluate performances fail to include a significant factor—the value of human resources. Cost for human-related activities such as hiring and training are expensed as incurred, and yet these costs benefit the future in the same way the purchase of a piece of equipment would. This logic has caused several writers to advocate that companies treat human resources as an integral part of the accounting system.

Human resource accounting has been defined as "the measurement and reporting of the cost and value of people as organization resources."[55] By acknowledging the fact that employees do have an intrinsic value to the firm, and that this value has the potential to appreciate or depreciate, an entire new consideration is included in the measurement process.

Eric G. Flamholtz, one of the major contributors to this area, has identified three fundamental notions that underlie human resource accounting:[56]

1. people are valuable organizational resources—they are capable of providing current and future services to organizations and these expected future services have economic value to the enterprise;

2. human resource value is influenced by management style—management may increase the value of human resources by

proper training or these resources can become depleted through technological obsolescence;

3. human resource accounting information is needed—information about human resource cost and value is necessary to facilitate the effective and efficient management of people as an organizational resource.

At present, the accounting profession does not recognize human resource accounting for accounting purposes. This does not, however, prevent its use as a management tool. As with decision making involving any other type of investment, accounting for human resources necessitates an assessment of the costs and potential values associated with the assets.

In determining costs of human assets, there are actual cash outlays such as payment for moving costs of a new employee, the cost of training programs, and the salaries earned by the trainee, and indirect costs, such as the loss of effectiveness of a supervisor during on-the-job familiarization. These costs can be accumulated and then amortized over the employee's expected life with the firm (based on the turnover rate) or the expected life of the investment, whichever is shorter.[57]

There are treatments other than historical cost for dealing with the investment in and evaluation of human assets. Some of these entail replacement costs, opportunity cost, expected realizable value, and so on.[58] Whatever methods are used, it is important that human resources become a factor in decision making. As R. Lee Brummet observed:

It is likely that managers are inadvertently motivated to act in a way contrary to the best interest of the organization as a result of the deficiency in measurements now being used. They are encouraged to meet targets stated in terms of costs, revenues, or profits measured without regard to the changing condition of human resources.[59]

For example, since employee training costs are not capitalized, a manager might postpone or curtail training in an effort to reduce expenses. While such a move could be as detrimental to the organization as failing to maintain its machinery and equipment, this kind of decision is likely to be made as long as the accounting system fails to reflect the intrinsic value of human resources.

Dahl[60] suggests that four basic principles should be followed in making decisions about human resources:

1. Invest in human resources only when a good return is expected. The long-term investment in employees and the expected return require a scrutiny as involved and methodical as that accompanying the much smaller capital investment.

2. Always consider alternative kinds of human resources that give the best return. For example, certain services might be contracted out at a worthwhile savings to the company.

55. Eric G. Flamholtz, "Human Resource Accounting: An Introduction," *The Lester Witte Report,* 7, No. 3 (1977), p. 4.
56. Ibid.
57. Michael O. Alexander, "Investments in People," *Canadian Chartered Accountant,* 89 (July, 1971), 41.
58. Edwin H. Caplan and Stephen Landekich, *Human Resource Accounting: Past, Present and Future* (New York: National Association of Accountants, 1974), pp. 75-85.
59. R. Lee Brummet, "Accounting for Human Resources," *New York Certified Public Accountant,* 40 (July, 1970), 550.
60. Henry L. Dahl, Jr. "Measuring the Human R.O.I.," *Management Review* (January 1979), pp. 44-50.

3. Invest in capital resources that improve the return on investment on both capital and human resources. Examples include computers, duplicating machinery, automatic manufacturing equipment, constructed for special use, etc. Managerial performance evaluations should include measurements of both return on capital and return on human resources.

4. Improve the use and performance of currently employed human resources. The following may help insure that management makes the best use of human resources:

- Be certain that every job is needed and optimally structured to accomplish the objectives of the individual as well as the company.

- Be sure that every job is filled by a person who can satisfactorily perform the required tasks both now and for some time to come.

- Provide a climate that encourages, permits, and rewards people for making significant contributions.

- Price jobs properly so that neither overpaying nor underpaying occurs. Overpaying tends to increase costs and diminish return on investment, while underpaying is likely to induce increased turnover, which also drives down return on investment.[61]

Dahl also suggests that individual managers might use the following checklist of questions to rate themselves on how well they are presently using available human resources:

1. Are the purposes and desired results in the unit both written and understood by each employee in the unit?

2. Are the jobs in the unit designed to optimally accomplish the objectives of the employee and the unit?

3. Are the jobs within the unit optimally structured to obtain the best return on investment on people?

4. Is the right person on the right job?

5. Does each employee possess the basic knowledge and skills needed to accomplish the present job and that job as it might be in five to ten years?

6. How well are the dissatisfactions of employees minimized? (The work of Scott Myers and Fred Herzberg is important here. They describe situations—unpleasant working environment, cafeteria food, low pay, and so on—that create dissatisfaction in employees. These can and should be corrected.)

7. How well are motivators used? (According to Myers and Herzberg, only four motivators exist: opportunities to grow and develop, recognition for work well done, unexpected rewards, and meaningful and challenging work.)

8. Is each job being satisfactorily performed?

9. Is a greater return on investment in people realized than last year or five years ago?

10. Will the unit have the kinds of people it needs to do the job in the next five to ten years?[62]

Behavioral Aspects of External Reports and Audits

Management is well aware of the significance of financial statements and the audits that accompany them. It recognizes that to a certain extent investors and lenders will use these reports in assessing the condition of the firm and the competence of management itself. The financial well-being of the firm could rest on the outcome of that evaluation. Thus, this subject matter is of interest from a behavioral standpoint because of its implications for the conduct of audits (internal as well as external), the actions of management, and the influence on investors' decisions.

Audits are a particularly interesting area for analysis. Even in the most favorable situations, there is bound to be some stress because of the nature of the task and the importance of the outcome to the auditee. Internal and external auditors must recognize the importance of incorporating behavioral considerations into their work. Failure to do so can cause problems. A study conducted by the Institute of Internal Auditors found that 75 percent of the audit managers in the study indicated they had encountered "active resentment" on the part of auditees.[63] Forty percent of the managers who experienced this resentment indicated that there had been attempts to mislead them or conceal facts.[64]

Behavioral problems in audits can be dealt with by many of the techniques discussed earlier in the chapter. Participation, less negative feedback, and so on, could all be put to use in building a stronger relationship between the auditor and the auditee.

Behavioral considerations for external reports apply to those within the firm as well as without. One is not simply interested in the decisions of investors; the decisions of management, as reflected in the financial statements can also provide insights into behavior. Management is normally concerned with projecting an attractive financial image for the firm in order to appeal to investors. Accomplishing this could result in suboptimization. Fortunately, firms are aided in their efforts by the variety of accounting treatments available. For example, the use of two methods of depreciation; one for financial statement and one for tax purposes.

One of the manifestations of management's preoccupation with pleasing investors—at least on the financial statements—is the practice of "smoothing" earnings. A stream of steady earnings is almost universally heralded as an attraction to investors. Indeed, it would be, if these earnings were not simply a product of manipulation. A recent article by John K. Shank and A. Michael Burnell revealed some of the methods used by firms to ensure the stability of their earnings. One oil company sold enough land each year to achieve its projected growth rate, while a conglomerate, upon winning a law suit, immediately set up a reserve for losses on a product; naturally, the reserve was equal to the amount of the settlement.[65] Such manipulations of

61. Ibid., p. 50.
62. Ibid.

63. *Research Committee Report 17: Behavioral Patterns in Internal Audit Relationships* (New York: Institute of Internal Auditors, 1972), p. 79.
64. Ibid.
65. John K. Shank and A. Michael Burnell, "Smooth Your Earnings Growth," *Harvard Business Review,* 52 (January-February, 1974), 136.

earnings are not always easy to detect, but the sophisticated investor will not rely on a single decisionary measure such as the price-earnings ratio.

Problems

1.   Estimated time 30 minutes (June 1981)

Classical management theory was developed from the input of many theoreticians and gained widespread acceptance in the early 1900s. Classical management theory emphasizes that economic factors are the primary means of motivation. The development of the classical management theory was strongly influenced by classical economists. While times and circumstances have changed dramatically since the early 1900s, many features of this approach, such as the primary functions of management, have withstood the test of time and are accepted today.

Modern organization theory has evolved from the contributions of the earlier theoreticians as well as more contemporary theoreticians. The modern organization theory is generally considered to have come into prominence by the 1930s. A basic component of modern organization theory is that an individual's behavior is adaptive and that a variety of needs and drives are the means of motivation.

While both the classical management theory and modern organization theory are accepted and followed, there are specific basic conflicts between the two schools of thought. These conflicts can be elaborated upon in the areas of organization goals, behavior of employees, behavior of management, and role of accounting.

Required Contrast the classical management theory and the modern organization theory in each of the following four areas:

1. Organization goals.
2. Employee behavior.
3. Management behavior.
4. Role of accounting.

2.   Estimated time 30 minutes (December 1973)

The classical economic model of competition assumed that the objective of measuring the ownership interest in and changes in fundamental elements of accounting theory are based on the objective of measuring the ownership interest in and changes in the amount of the ownership interest (for example, profits) in the financial resources in the firm.

Required Discuss and compare the above paragraph with the views of current organization theorists on
1. the nature of organization goals, and
2. how such goals are established.

3.   Estimated time 30 minutes (June 1981)
Similar question (December 1991)

Denny Daniels is production manager of the Alumalloy Division of WRT Inc. Alumalloy has limited contact with outside customers and has no sales staff. Most of its customers are other divisions of WRT. All sales and purchases with outside customers are handled by other corporate divisions. Therefore, Alumalloy is treated as a cost center for reporting and evaluation purposes rather than as a revenue or profit center.

Daniels perceives the accounting department as a historical number generating process that provides little useful information for conducting his job. Consequently, the entire accounting process is perceived as a negative motivational device that does not reflect how hard or how effectively he works as a production manager. Daniels tried to discuss these perceptions and concerns with John Scott, the Controller for the Alumalloy Division. Daniels told Scott, "I think the cost report is misleading. I know I've had better production over a number of operating periods, but the cost report still says I have excessive costs. Look, I'm not an accountant, I'm a production manager. I know how to get a good quality product out. Over a number of years, I've even cut the raw materials used to do it. But the cost report doesn't show any of this. Basically, it's always negative, no matter what I do. There's no way you can win with accounting or the people at corporate who use those reports".

Scott gave Daniels little consolation. Scott stated that the accounting system and the cost reports generated by headquarters are just part of the corporate game and almost impossible for an individual to change. "Although these accounting reports are pretty much the basis for evaluating the efficiency of your divison and the means corporate uses to determine whether you have done the job they want, you shouldn't worry too much. You haven't been fired yet! Besides, these cost reports have been used by WRT for the last 25 years."

Daniels perceived from talking to the production manager of the Zinc Division that most of what Scott said was probably true. However, some minor cost reporting changes for Zinc had been agreed to by corporate headquarters. He also knew from the trade grapevine that the turnover of production managers was considered high at WRT even though relatively few were fired. Most seemed to end up quitting, usually in disgust, because of beliefs that they were not being evaluated fairly. Typical comments of production managers who have left WRT are

● "Corporate headquarters doesn't really listen to us. All they consider are those misleading cost reports. They don't want them changed and they don't want any supplemental information."

● "The accountants may be quick with numbers but they don't know anything about production. As it was, I either had to ignore the cost reports entirely or pretend they are important even though they didn't tell how good a job I had done. No matter what they say about not firing people, negative reports mean negative evaluations. I'm better off working for another company."

A recent copy of the cost report prepared by Corporate headquarters for the Alumalloy division is shown below. Daniels does not like this report because he believes it fails to reflect the division's operations properly, thereby resulting in an unfair evaluation of performance.

Allumalloy Division
Cost Report
for the Month of April, 1980
($000 omitted)

	Master Budget	Actual Cost	Excess Cost
Aluminum	$ 400	$ 437	$ 37
Labor	560	540	(20)
Overhead	100	134	34
Total	$1060	$1111	$ 51

Required   A. Comment on Denny Daniels' perception of:

1. John Scott, the controller;
2. corporate headquarters;
3. the cost report; and
4. himself as a production manager

and discuss how his perception affects his behavior and probable performance as a production manager and employee of WRT.

B. Identify and explain three changes that could be made in the cost information presented to the production managers that would make the information more meaningful and less threatening to them.

---

4.   Estimated time 30 minutes (June 1982)

Scott Weidner, the Controller in the Division of Social Services for the state, recognizes the importance of the budgetary process for planning, control and motivation purposes. He believes that a properly implemented participative budgeting process for planning purposes and a management by exception reporting procedure based upon the participative budget will motivate his subordinates to improve productivity within their particular departments. Based upon this philosophy, Weidner has implemented the following budget procedures.

• An appropriation target figure is given to each Department Manager. This amount is the maximum funding that each department can expect to receive in the next fiscal year.

• Department Managers develop their individual budgets within the following spending constraints as directed by the controller's staff.
(1) Expenditure requests cannot exceed the appropriation target.

(2) All fixed expenditures should be included in the budget. Fixed expenditures would include such items as contracts and salaries at current levels.
(3) All government projects directed by higher authority should be included in the budget in their entirety.

• The controller's staff consolidates the departmental budget requests from the various departments into one budget that is to be submitted for the entire division.

• Upon final budget approval by the legislature, the controller's staff allocates the appropriation to the various departments on instructions from the Division Manager. However, a specified percentage of each department's appropriation is held back in anticipation of potential budget cuts and special funding needs. The amount and use of this contingency fund is left to the discretion of the Division Manager.

• Each department is allowed to adjust its budget when necessary to operate within the reduced appropriation level. However, as stated in the original directive, specific projects authorized by higher authority must remain intact.

• The final budget is used as the basis of control for a management by exception form of reporting. Excessive expenditures by account for each department are highlighted on a monthly basis. Department Managers are expected to account for all expenditures over budget. Fiscal responsibility is an important factor in the overall performance evaluation of Department Managers.

Weidner believes his policy of allowing the Department Managers to participate in the budget process and then holding them accountable for their performance is essential, especially during these times of limited resources. He further believes the Department Managers will be motivated positively to increase the efficiency and effectiveness of their departments because they have provided input into the initial budgetary process and are required to justify any unfavorable performances.

Required A. Explain the operational and behavioral benefits that generally are attributed to a participative budgeting process.
B. Identify deficiencies in Scott Weidner's participative budgetary policy for planning and performance evaluation purposes. For each deficiency identified, recommend how the deficiency can be corrected. Use the following format in preparing your response.

Deficiencies	*Recommendations*
1.	1.

---

5.   Estimated time 30 minutes (December 1981)

Lymar Products is a divisionalized corporation in the agribusiness industry with its corporate headquarters in Philadelphia. The R & D Division is located in central Illinois and is responsible for all of the corporation's seed, fertilizer, and insecticide research and development. The research and development is conducted primarily for the benefit of Lymar's other operating divisions. The R & D Division conducts contract research for outside firms when such research does not interfere with the division's regular work or does not represent work which is directly competitive with Lymar's interests.

Lymar's annual budget preparation begins approximately five months before the beginning of the fiscal year. Each division manager is responsible for developing the budget for his/her division within the guidelines provided by corporate headquarters. Once the annual budget procedure is completed and the budget is accepted and approved, the division managers have complete authority to operate within the limits prescribed by the budget.

The budget procedures apply to the R & D Division. However, because this division does work for other Lymar divisions and for the corporate office, careful coordination between the R & D Division and the other units is needed to construct a good budget for the R & D Division. Further, the costs associated with the contract research require special consideration by Lymar's management. In the past, there has been good cooperation which has resulted in sound budget preparation.

R & D's management always has presented well documented budgets for both the internal and contract research. When the submitted budget has been changed, the revisions are the result of review, discussion, and agreement between R & D's management and corporate management.

Staff travel is a major item included in R & D's budget. Some 25-35 trips are made annually to corporate headquarters for meetings by R & D's employees. In addition, the division's technical staff makes trips related to their research projects and are expected to attend professional meetings and seminars. These trips always have been detailed in a supporting schedule presented with the annual budget.

Lymar's performance for the current year is considered reasonable in light of current and expected future poor economic conditions, but corporate management has become extremely cost conscious in order to maintain corporate performance at the best possible level. Divisions have been directed to cut down on any unnecessary spending. A specific new directive has been issued stating that any travel in excess of $500 must now be approved in advance by corporate headquarters. In addition, once a division's total dollar amount budgeted for travel has been spent, no budget overruns would be allowed. This directive is effective immediately, and corporate management has indicated that it will continue to be in effect for at least the next two years.

The R & D Division Manager is concerned because this directive appears to represent a change in budget policy. Now, travel which was thought already approved because it was included in the annual budget must be reapproved before each trip. In addition, some scheduled trips previously approved may have to be cancelled because travel funds are likely to run out before the end of the year. R & D staff members already have had to make five special trips to corporate headquarters which were not included in the current year's budget.

The new directive probably will increase costs. The approval process may delay the purchase of airline tickets thus reducing the opportunity to obtain the lowest fares. Further, there will be a major increase in paper work for the R & D Division because virtually every trip exceeds the $500 limit.

Required   A. The directive requiring "the reapproval of all travel in excess of $500" could have far reaching effects for Lymar products.

1. Explain how this directive could affect the entire budget process, especially the validity of the annual budget.
2. Explain what effect this directive is likely to have on the care with which divisions prepare their annual travel budgets in the future.

B. Explain what effect the directive on "reapproval of travel costs" is likely to have on the morale and motivation of the Division Manager and research staff of the R & D Division.

---

6.   Estimated time 30 minutes (December 1978)

Tom Emory and Jim Morris strolled back to their plant from the administrative offices of Ferguson & Son Mfg. Company. Tom was manager of the machine shop in the company's factory; Jim was manager of the equipment maintenance department.

The men had just attended the monthly performance evaluation meeting for plant department heads. These meetings had been held on the third Tuesday of each month since Robert Ferguson, Jr., the president's son, had become plant manager a year earlier.

As they were walking Tom Emory spoke. "Boy, I hate those meetings! I never know whether my department's accounting reports will show good or bad performance. I'm beginning to expect the worst. If the accountants say I saved the company a dollar, I'm called 'Sir,' but if I spend even a little too much— boy, do I get in trouble. I don't know if I can hold on until I retire."

Tom had just received the worst evaluation he had ever received in his long career with Ferguson & Son. He was the most respected of the experienced machinists in the company. He had been with Ferguson & Son for many years and was promoted to supervisor of the machine shop when the company expanded and moved to its present location. The president (Robert Ferguson, Sr.) had often stated that the company's success was due to the high quality of the work of machinists like Emory. As supervisor, Tom stressed the importance of craftsmanship and told his workers that he wanted no sloppy work coming from his department.

When Robert Ferguson, Jr., became the plant manager, he directed that monthly performance comparisons be made between actual and budgeted costs for each department. The departmental budgets were intended to encourage the supervisors to reduce inefficiencies and to seek cost reduction opportunities. The company controller was instructed to have his staff "tighten" the budget slightly whenever a department attained its budget in a given month; this was done to reinforce the plant supervisor's desire to reduce costs. The young plant manager often stressed the importance of continued progress toward attaining the budget; he also made it known that he kept a file of these performance reports for future reference when he succeeded his father.

Tom Emory's conversation with Jim Morris continued as follows:

Emory: "I really don't understand. We've worked so hard to get up to budget and the minute we make it they tighten the budget on us. We can't work any faster and still maintain quality. I think my men are ready to quit trying. Besides, those reports don't tell the whole story. We always seem to be interrupting the big jobs for all those small rush orders. All that setup and machine adjustment time is killing us. And quite frankly, Jim, you were no help. When our hydraulic press broke down last month, your people were nowhere to be found. We had to take it apart ourselves and got stuck with all that idle time."

Morris: "I'm sorry about that, Tom, but you know my department has had trouble making budget, too. We were running well beyond at the time of that problem, and if we'd spent a day on that old machine, we would have never have made it up. Instead we made the scheduled inspections of the fork-lift trucks because we knew we could do those in less than the budgeted time."

Emory: "Well, Jim, at least you have some options, I'm locked into what the scheduling department assigns to me and you know they're being harassed by sales for those special orders. Incidentally, why didn't your report show all the supplies you guys wasted last month when you were working in Bill's department?"

Morris: "We're not out of the woods on that deal yet. We charged the maximum we could to our other work and haven't even reported some of it yet."

Emory: "Well, I'm glad you have a way of getting out of the pressure. The accountants seem to know everything that's happening in my department, sometimes even before I do. I thought all that budget and accounting stuff was supposed to help, but it just gets me into trouble. It's all a big pain. I'm trying to put out quality work; they're trying to save pennies."

Tom Emory's performance report for the month in question is reproduced below. Actual production volume for the month was at the budgeted level.

Machine Shop—October 1978
T. Emory, Supervisor

	Budget	Actual	Variances
Direct labor	$ 39,600	$ 39,850	$ 250 U
Direct materials	231,000	231,075	75 U
Depreciation— equipment	3,000	3,000	0
Depreciation— buildings	6,000	6,000	0
Power	900	860	40 F
Maintenance	400	410	10 U
Supervision	1,500	1,500	0
Idle-time	0	1,800	1,800 U
Set-up labor	680	2,432	1,752 U
Miscellaneous	2,900	3,300	400 U
	$285,980	$290,227	$4,247 U

Required   A. Identify the problems which appear to exist in Ferguson & Son Mfg. Company's budgetary control system and explain how the problems are likely to reduce the effectiveness of the system.

B. Explain how Ferguson & Son Mfg. Company's budgetary control system could be revised to improve its effectiveness.

7.   Estimated time 30 minutes (June 1980)

RV Industries manufactures and sells recreation vehicles. The company has eight divisions strategically located to be near major markets. Each division has a sales force and two to four manufacturing plants. These divisions operate as autonomous profit centers responsible for purchasing, operations, and sales.

John Collins, the Corporate Controller, described the divisional performance measurement system as follows. "We allow the divisions to control the entire operation from the purchase of raw materials to the sale of the product. We, at corporate headquarters, only get involved in strategic decisions, such as developing new product lines. Each division is responsible for meeting its market needs by providing the right products at a low cost on a timely basis. Frankly, the divisions need to focus on cost control, delivery, and services to customers in order to become more profitable.

"While we give the divisions considerable autonomy, we watch their monthly income statements very closely. Each month's actual performance is compared with the budget in considerable detail. If the actual sales or contribution margin is more than 4 or 5 percent below the budget, we jump on the division people immediately. I might add that we don't have much trouble getting their attention. All of the management people at the plant and division level can add appreciably to their annual salaries with bonuses if actual net income is considerably greater than budget."

The budgeting process begins in August when division sales managers, after consulting with their sales personnel, estimate sales for the next calendar year. These estimates are sent to the plant managers who use the sales forecasts to prepare production estimates. At the plants, production statistics, including raw material quantities, labor hours, production schedules and output quantities, are developed by operating personnel. Using the statistics prepared by the operating personnel, the plant accounting staff determines costs and prepares the plant's budgeted variable cost of goods sold and other plant expenses for each month of the coming calendar year.

In October, each division's accounting staff combines plant budgets with sales estimates and adds additional division expenses. "After the divisional management is satisfied with the budget," said Collins, "I visit each division to go over their budget and make sure it is in line with corporate strategy and projections. I really emphasize the sales forecasts because of the volatility in the demand for our product. For many years, we lost sales to our competitors because we didn't project high enough production and sales, and we couldn't meet the market demand. More recently, we were caught with large excess inventory when the bottom dropped out of the market for recreational vehicles.

"I generally visit all eight divisions during the first two weeks in November. After that the division budgets are combined and reconciled by my staff, and they are ready for approval by the Board of Directors in early December. The Board seldom questions the budget.

"One complaint we've had from plant and division management is that they are penalized for circumstances beyond their control. For example, they failed to predict the recent sales decline. As a result, they didn't make their budget and, of course, they received no bonuses. However, I point out that they are well rewarded when they exceed their budget. Furthermore, they provide most of the information for the budget, so it's their own fault if the budget is too optimistic."

Required A. Identify and explain the biases the corporate management of RV Industries should expect in the communication of budget estimates by its division and plant personnel.

B. What sources of information can the top management of RV Industries use to monitor the budget estimates prepared by its division plants?

C. What services could top management of RV Industries offer the divisions to help them in their budget development, without appearing to interfere with the division budget decisions?

D. The top management of RV Industries is attempting to decide whether it should get more involved in the budget process. Identify and explain the variables management needs to consider in reaching its decision.

8. Estimated time 30 minutes (June 1975)

In late 1971 Mr. Sootsman, the official in charge of the State Department of Automobile Regulation, established a system of performance measurement for the department's branch offices. He was convinced that management by objectives could help the department reach its objective of better citizen service at a lower cost. The first step was to define the activities of the branch offices, to assign point values to the services performed, and to establish performance targets. Point values, rather than revenue targets, were employed because the department was a regulatory agency, not a revenue-producing agency. Further, the specific revenue for a service did not adequately reflect the differences in effort required. The analysis was compiled at the state office, and the results were distributed to the branch offices.

The system has been in operation since 1972. The performance targets for branches have been revised each year by the state office. The revisions were designed to encourage better performance by increasing the target or reducing resources to achieve targets. The revisions incorporated non-controllable events, such as population shifts, new branches, and changes in procedures.

The Barry County branch is typical of many branch offices. A summary displaying the budgeted and actual performance for three years is presented on the next page.

Mr. Sootsman has been disappointed in the performance of branch offices because they have not met performance targets or budgets. He is especially concerned because the points earned from citizens' comments are declining.

Required A. Does the method of performance measurement properly capture the objectives of this operation? Justify your answer.

B. The Barry County branch office came close to its target for 1975. Does this constitute improved performance compared to

1973? Justify your answer.

9. Estimated time 30 minutes (June 1976)

Drake Inc. is a multiproduct firm with several manufacturing plants. Management generally has been pleased with the operation of all the plants but the Swan Plant. Swan Plant's poor operating performance has been traced to poor control over plant costs and expenses. Four plant managers have resigned or been terminated during the last three years.

David Green was appointed the new manager of the Swan Plant on February 1, 1976. Green is a young and aggressive individual who had progressed rapidly in Drake's management development program, and he performed well in lower-level management positions.

Green had been recommended for the position by Steve Bradley, Green's immediate supervisor, Bradley was impressed by Green's technical ability and enthusiasm. Bradley explained to Green that his assignment as Swan Plant manager was approved despite the objections of some of the other members of the top management team. Bradley told Green that he had complete confidence in him and his ability and was sure that Green wanted to prove that he had made a good decision. Therefore, Bradley expected Green to have the Swan Plant on expenses controlled but he expected Swan Plant to be on budget by June 30.

As a result of Swan Plant's past difficulties, Steve Bradley has had responsibility for formulating the last four annual budgets for the plant. The 1976 budget was prepared during the last six months of 1975 before Green had been appointed plant manager. The budget report covering the three-month period ending March 31 showed that Swan's costs and expenses were slightly over budget. At a meeting with Bradley, Green described the changes he had instiued the last month. Green was confident that the costs and expenses would be held in check with these changes and the situation would get no worse for the rest of the year.

Bradley repeated that he not only wanted the cost and expenses controlled but he expected Swan Plant to be on budget by June 30. Green pointed out that Swan Plant had been in poor condition for three years. He further stated that, while he appreciated the confidence Bradley had in him, he had only been in charge two months.

Steve Bradley then replied, "I am expected to meet my figures. The only way that can occur is if my subordinates exercise control over their costs and expenses and achieve their budgets. Therefore, to assure that I achieve my goals, get the Swan Plant on budget by June 30 and keep it on budget for the rest of the year."

Required A. Present a critical evaluation of the budget practices described in the problem.

B. What are the likely immediate and long-term effects on David Green and Drake Inc. if the present method of budget administration is continued? Justify your answer.

10. Estimated time 30 minutes (December 1981)

The Kristy Company has grown from a small operation of 50

Barry County Branch Performance Report

	1972		1973		1974	
	Budget	Actual	Budget	Actual	Budget	Actual
Population served	38,000		38,500		38,700	
Number of employees						
Administrative	1	1	1	1	1	1
Professional	1	1	1	1	1	1
Clerical	3	3	2	3	1½	3
Budgeted Performance Points*						
1. Services	19,500		16,000		15,500	
2. Citizen comments	500		600		700	
	20,000		16,600		16,200	
Actual Performance Points*						
1. Services	14,500		14,600		15,600	
2. Citizen comments	200		900		200	
	14,700		15,500		15,800	
Detail of Actual Performance*						
1. New drivers licenses						
a. Examination and road tests (3 points)	3,000		3,150		3,030	
b. Road tests repeat—failed prior test (2 points)	600		750		1,650	
2. Renew drivers licenses (1 point)	3,000		3,120		3,060	
3. Issue license plates (.5 points)	4,200		4,150		4,100	
4. Issue titles						
a. Dealer transactions (.5 points)	2,000		1,900		2,100	
b. Individual transactions (1 point)	1,700		1,530		1,660	
	14,500		14,600		15,600	
5. Citizen comments						
a. Favorable (+.5 points)	300		1,100		800	
b. Unfavorable (-.5 points)	100		200		600	
	200		900		200	

*The budget performance points for services are calculated using 3 points per available hour. The administrative employee devotes ½ time to administration and ½ time to regular services. The calculations for the services point budget are as follows:

1972 4½ people × 8 hours × 240 days × 3 points × 75% productive time = 19,440 rounded to 19,500
1973 3½ people × 8 hours × 240 days × 3 points × 80% productive time = 16,128 rounded to 16,000
1974 3   people × 8 hours × 240 days × 3 points × 90% productive time = 15,552 rounded to 15,500

The comments targets are based upon rough estimates by department officials.
The actual point totals for the branch are calculated by multiplying the weights shown in the report in parentheses by the number of such services performed or comments received.

people in 1970 to 200 employees in 1981. Kristy designs, manufactures and sells environmental support equipment. In the early years each item of equipment had to be designed and manufactured to meet each customer's requirements. The work was challenging and interesting for the employees as innovative techniques were often needed in the production process to complete an order according to customers' requirements. In recent years the company has been able to develop several components and a few complete units which can be used to meet the requirements of several customers.

The early special design and manufacture work has given the Kristy Company a leadership position in its segment of the pollution control market. Kristy takes great pride in the superior quality of its products and this quality has contributed to its dominant role in this market segment. To help ensure high quality performance, Kristy hires the most highly skilled personnel available and pays them above the industry average. This policy has resulted in a labor force that is very efficient, stable, and positively motivated toward company objectives.

The recent increase in government regulations requiring private companies to comply with specific environmental standards has made this market very profitable. Consequently, several competitors have entered the market segment once controlled by Kristy. While Kristy still maintains a dominant position in its market, it has lost several contracts to competitors that offer similar equipment to customers at a lower price.

The Kristy manufacturing process is very labor intensive. The production employees played an important role in the early success of the company. As a result, management gave employees a great deal of freedom to schedule and manufacture customers' orders. For instance, when the company increased the number of orders accepted, more employees were hired rather than pressuring current employees to produce at a faster rate. In management's view, the intricacy of work involved required employees to have ample time to ensure the work was done right.

Management introduced a standard cost system which they believed would be beneficial to the company. They thought it would assist in identifying the most economical way to manufacture much of the equipment, would give management a more accurate picture of the costs of the equipment, and be used in evaluating actual costs for cost control. Consequently, the company should become more price competitive. Although the introduction of standards would likely lead to some employee discontent, management was of the opinion that the overall result would be beneficial. The standards were introduced on June 1, 1981.

During December, the production manager reported to the president that the new standards were creating problems in the plant. The employees had developed bad attitudes, absenteeism and turnover rates had increased, and standards were not being met. In the production manager's judgement, employee dissatisfaction has outweighed any benefits management thought would be achieved by the standard cost system. The production manager supported this contention with the data presented below for 1981, during which monthly production was at normal volume levels.

Required   A. Explain the general features and characteristics associated with the introduction and operation of a standard cost system that make it an effective cost control tool.

B. Discuss the apparent impact of Kristy Company's cost system on:
1. cost control.
2. employee motivation.

C. Discuss the probable causes for employee dissatisfaction with the new cost system.

---

11.   Estimated time 30 minutes (June 1983)

The B&B Company manufactures and sells chemicals for agricultural and industrial use. The company has grown significantly over the last ten years but has made few changes in its information gathering and reporting system. Some of the managers have expressed concern that the system is essentially the same as it was when the firm was only half its present size. Others believe that much of the information from the system is not relevant and that more appropriate and timely information should be available.

Dora Hepple, Chief Accountant, has observed that the actual monthly cost data for most production processes are compared with the actual costs of the same processes for the previous year. Any variance not explained by price changes requires an explanation by the individual in charge of the cost center. She believes that this information is inadequate for good cost control.

George Vector, one of the production supervisors, contends that the system is adequate because it allows for explanation of discrepancies. The current year's costs seldom vary from the previous year's costs (as adjusted for price changes). This indicates that costs are under control.

Vern Hopp, General Manager of the Fine Chemical Division, is upset with the current system. He has to request the same information each month regarding recurring operations. This is a problem that he believes should be addressed.

Walter Metts, President, has appointed a committee to review the system. The charge to this "System Review Task Force" is to determine if the information needs of the internal management of the firm are being met by the existing system. Specific modifications in the existing system or implementation of a new system will be considered only if management's needs are not being met. William Afton, Assistant to the President, has been put in charge of the task force.

Shortly after the committee was appointed, Afton overheard one of the cost accountants say, "I've been doing it this way for 15 years, and now Afton and his committee will try to eliminate

						1981					
	J	F	M	A	M	J	J	A	S	O	N
Absenteeism rates:	1%	1%	1%	1%	.5%	1%	2%	4%	6%	8%	11%
Turnover rate:	.2%	.5%	.5%	.5%	.3%	.8%	.7%	1.4%	1.9%	2.5%	2.9%
Direct labor efficiency variance: (unfavorable)	—	—	—	—	—	$(10,000)	$(11,500)	$(14,000)	$(17,000)	$(20,500)	$(25,000)
Direct materials usage variance: (unfavorable)	—	—	—	—	—	$(4,000)	$(5,000)	$(6,500)	$(8,200)	$(11,000)	$(14,000)

my job." Another person replied, "That's the way it looks. John and Brownie in general accounting also think that their positions are going to be eliminated or at least changed significantly." Over the next few days, Afton overheard a middle management person talking about the task force saying, "That's all this company thinks about—maximizing its profits—not the employees." He also overheard a production manager in the Mixing Department say that he believed the system was in need of revision because the most meaningful information he received came from Brad Cummings, a salesperson. He stated, "After they have the monthly sales meeting, Brad stops by the office and indicates what the sales plans and targets are for the next few months. This sure helps me in planning my mixing schedules."

Afton is aware that two problems of paramount importance to be addressed by his "System Review Task Force" are: (1) to determine management's information needs for cost control and decision making purposes; and (2) to meet the behavioral needs of the company and its employees.

Required **A.** Discuss the behavioral implications of having an accounting information system that does not appear to meet the needs of management.

B. Identify and explain the specific problems B&B Company appears to have with regard to the perception of B&B's employees concerning:

1. the accounting information system.
2. the firm.

C. Assume that the initial review of the System Review Task Force indicates that a new accounting information system should be designed and implemented.

1. Identify specific behavioral factors that B&B's management should address in the design and implementation of a new system.
2. For each behavioral factor identified, discuss how B&B's management can address the behavioral factor.

---

12. Estimated time 30 minutes (December 1983)
Similar question (December 1991)

John Arnston recently has been appointed Chief Operating Officer of Parton Co. Arnston has a manufacturing background and most recently managed the heavy machinery segment of the company. The business segments of Parton range from heavy machinery to consumer foods.

In a recent conversation with the company's chief financial officer, Arnston suggested that segment managers be evaluated on the basis of the segment data appearing in Parton's annual financial report. This report presents revenues, earnings, identifiable assets, and depreciation for each segment for a five-year period. He raised this issue because he thought that evaluating segment managers by using the same type of information often used to evaluate the company's top management would be appropriate.

Parton's chief financial officer has expressed his reservations to Arnston about using segment information from the annual financial report for this purpose. He has suggested that Arnston

consider other ways to evaluate segment management performance.

Required **A.** Identify the characteristics of segment information in the annual financial report that would lead Parton's chief financial officer to have reservations about its use for the evaluation of segment management performance.

B. Are the best interests of the company likely to be served if segment managers are evaluated on the basis of segment information in the annual financial report? Explain your answer.

C. Identify and explain the financial information you would recommend Arnston obtain when evaluating segment management performance.

---

13. Estimated time 30 minutes (June 1989)

Reid Corporation, a diversified manufacturing firm, has been experiencing decreasing profits and market share for the past two years. The company president, Arthur Johnson, has hired a consultant to report on the operations of three of Reid's manufacturing plants. The consultant has made several visits to each of the plants and has recently compiled his findings in a report to Johnson. The consultant observed that the levels of employee participation vary considerably throughout the organization and presented the following examples.

• At the western plant, where small appliances are manufactured, a standard cost system was recently implemented. The steps used by the plant manager to establish the standards provided for employee participation at all points during the process. Despite these efforts, the employee perception is that the final standards were imposed by top management to satisfy some overall corporate goal.

• At the southern plant, where heavy equipment is assembled, stop buttons have been installed on the assembly line to allow workers to correct problems immediately. This enables the employees to have greater control over their work, and, as a consequence, the workers perceive greater involvement in all facets of decision-making.

• At the northern plant, a metal-stamping facility, costs have risen and product quality has declined to the point where the products are no longer competitive. The employees have little sense of commitment to the company as most jobs are routine and uninteresting. There is high employee turnover and excessive absenteeism. Some plant workers have suggested that the formation of quality circles might improve the situation.

Required **A.** Describe four factors that generally determine the level of employee participation in an organization's control systems.

B. Recommend ways to modify the standard cost system at the western plant in order to increase employee participation and gain wider acceptance of the standards.

C. Other than those mentioned above, describe the benefits that have accrued to the southern plant from the installation of the stop buttons on the assembly line.

D. Explain how the northern plant and its employees could benefit from the introduction of quality circles.

---

14.   **Estimated time 30 minutes (December 1989)**

EGA Inc., an international holding company, specializes in electronic and computer applications. At the beginning of the year, EGA acquired Bradley Resources, a financial services company, in an attempt to diversify its portfolio of companies. Bradley was to be treated as a subsidiary of EGA. However, because of time constraints, EGA decided not to train the employees of Bradley in the corporate budgeting process, and instead had the EGA corporate budget department prepare Bradley's annual budget for the current operating year.

The management team at Bradley has received financial reports from EGA that compare actual performance against the original budget. Each month, these managers are required to explain and defend the variances between actual and budget. Six months after the acquisition, Sarah Tremaine, the manager of Bradley's Marketing Department, was reviewed. Her review reflected an unacceptable performance because actual sales were 20 percent below budgeted sales. Consequently, when the third quarter results were released, Tremaine announced her resignation. The remaining departmental managers at Bradley appear to be doing their jobs as expected but have not recently developed any new ideas. In addition, there has been increased absenteeism, tardiness, and turnover among the Bradley employees below the managerial level.

In an attempt to remedy the situation at Bradley, EGA has decided to train the Bradley managers in the corporate budgeting process and to encourage their participation in the preparation of the budget for the upcoming year.

Required   A. Besides saving time, explain several advantages that EGA Inc. might have realized from using an imposed budgetary approach for Bradley Resources.

B. Communication plays an important role in the budgeting process. How could EGA Inc. have used communication to better advantage in implementing the imposed budgetary system?

C. Describe at least four advantages and four disadvantages of the participatory budget system that EGA Inc. is now proposing for Bradley Resources.

---

15.   **Estimated time 30 minutes (June 1989)**

Spiral Laboratories Inc. manufactures and distributes generic pharmaceuticals for sale to customers through retail outlets. Spiral is organized along product lines, with profit and loss responsibilities assigned to the unit manager of each product line. The unit managers receive incentive compensation based on product-line performance.

Currently, Spiral is reviewing its policies regarding the use of legal services. Historically, the company has utilized various outside legal firms, as needed by the unit managers and members of the corporate staff. The cost of legal services to the corporation has been increasing. Recently, the decision was made to hire an in-house attorney to better coordinate and assist in the legal matters of the corporation. The goal is to lower the overall costs of legal services by reducing the use of outside legal services; however, the unit managers still have the option of using outside legal services. Legal services are anticipated to be a continuing need at the corporate level and a periodic need at the unit level.

The corporate controller has identified the following four alternatives for allocating the cost of corporate legal services provided by the in-house attorney.

1. An annual charge to each product-line unit based on the budgeted sales volume of the unit. There would also be a fixed, annual charge to corporate headquarters based on a percentage of total legal costs.

2. No charge to the product-line units with corporate headquarters absorbing all costs for in-house legal services.

3. A fixed, hourly charge for the actual services required by each product-line unit. This hourly charge would be determined on the basis of comparative costs for services obtained from external sources.

4. A fixed, hourly charge for actual services required by product-line units that is based on full recovery of the cost of the corporate legal services. Under- or over-absorption of in-house legal costs would be charged to the product-line units at year-end.

Required   A. Describe the probable behavioral effects on the product-line unit managers of Spiral Laboratories caused by the use of each of the four cost allocation methods.

B. Describe the possible effects on the adequacy and quality of legal services to be provided and/or utilized under each of the four cost allocation methods.

C. Describe the probable effects caused by the use of each of the four cost allocation methods on the behavior of Spiral Laboratories' corporate attorney.

---

16.   **Estimated time 30 minutes (June 1988)**

Some executives believe that it is extremely important to manage "by numbers." This form of management requires that all employees with departmental or divisional responsibilities spend time understanding the company's operations and how they are reflected by the company's financial reports. Because of the manager's increased comprehension of the financial reports and the activities that they represent, his or her subordinates will become more attuned to the meaning of financial reports and the important signposts that can be detected in these reports. Companies utilize a variety of numerical measurement systems including standard costs, financial ratios, human resource forecasts, and operating budgets.

Required   A. 1. Discuss the characteristics that should be present in a standard cost system in order to encourage positive employee motivation.

2. Discuss how a standard cost system should be implemented

to positively motivate employees.

B. The use of variance analysis often results in "management by exception."

1. Explain the meaning of "management by exception."
2. Discuss the behavioral implications of "management by exception."

C. Explain how employee behavior could be adversely affected when "actual to budget" comparisons are used as the basis for performance evaluation.

---

17.   Estimated time 30 minutes (June 1982)

Productivity and cost control can be improved by introducing cost standards in business operations. However, standards must be properly installed and administered to be effective. Consequently, careful attention must be paid to developing the standards. This includes the selection of the operational activities for which performance is to be measured, the levels of performance required, the degree of participation by various departments, and the support of top management for this effort.

Required   A. Discuss the criteria to be used when selecting the operational activities for which performance measures are to be established.
B. Discuss the behavioral issues to be considered when selecting the level of performance to be incorporated into the cost standard.
C. Discuss the role that each of the following departments should play in establishing the standards.
1. Accounting Department.
2. The department whose performance is being measured.
3. The Industrial Engineering Department.

---

18.   Estimated time 30 minutes (December 1992)

Extra Strength Materials (ESM) is a four-year-old company founded by Art Mallory and several associates who developed a process to produce steel-like strength materials of lighter weights than traditional steels and plastics. With government pressure on the automobile industry to produce vehicles capable of higher gas mileage, ESM has had some success in penetrating the automobile industry.

ESM's management and employees have operated in an entrepreneurial spirit, pursuing manufacturing process changes and markets with few controls on spending. As the costs of operations have been exceeding revenues during this start-up phase, ESM recently sought an established partner with the financial resources to expand the company. Mid-America Steel Inc., seeking to diversify its business, bought ESM with the understanding that it would continue to operate as an independent subsidiary with existing management running the company. However, Mid-America's corporate headquarters would exercise oversight of ESM's operations.

Dave Johnson, chief financial officer of Mid-America, requested that his staff review ESM's financial reporting system.

They noted that, in accordance with the entrepreneurial culture, the overall company budget was developed each year by Mallory and his controller so that his staff could concentrate on production, research, and marketing. With the anticipated growth of ESM, Johnson recommended to Mallory that ESM adopt and implement a departmental budgeting system. Mallory announced to his associates and departmental managers that ESM was planning to accept Johnson's recommendation.

Johnson's budget director presented to ESM's managers an overview of the departmental budgeting system and the participation in the process that would be expected of them. Mallory then requested the managers to review the procedures and make suggestions regarding the implementation of the budgeting system. Mallory further advised that since this would be their first exposure to budgeting within ESM, they should raise any questions they might have with regards to budgeting and how operations would be conducted as a result of the changeover.

Required   A. Describe the benefits, other than better cost control, that are likely to accrue to ESM from the implementation of departmental budgeting.

B. Discuss the behavioral issues that the introduction of a departmental budgeting system is likely to raise with ESM's department managers.

C. Discuss the behavioral issues that the introduction of a departmental budgeting system is likely to raise with ESM's production workers.

D. Discuss the likely reactions of ESM's employees after several months of being confronted with the pressures of comparing actual results to budgeted expectations.

---

19.   Estimated time 30 minutes (December 1988)

Terry Travers is the manufacturing supervisor of the Aurora Manufacturing Company which produces a variety of plastic products. Some of these products are standard items that are listed in the company's catalog, while others are made to customer specifications. Each month, Travers receives a performance report displaying the budget for the month, the actual activity for the period, and the variance between budget and actual. Part of Travers' annual performance evaluation is based on his department's performance against budget. Aurora's purchasing manager, Bob Christensen, also receives monthly performance reports, and is evaluated in part on the basis of these reports.

The most recent monthly reports had just been distributed, on the 21st of the following month, when Travers met Christensen in the hallway outside their offices. Scowling, Travers began the conversation, "I see we have another set of monthly performance reports hand-delivered by that not very nice junior employee in the budget office. He seemed pleased to tell me that I was in trouble with my performance again."

Christensen: "I got the same treatment. All I ever hear about are the things I haven't done right. Now, I'll have to spend a lot of time reviewing the report and preparing explanations. The worst part is that the information is almost a month old, and we spend all this time on history."

Travers: "My biggest gripe is that our production activitiy varies a lot from month to month, but we're given an annual budget that's written in stone. Last month, we were shut down for three days when a strike delayed delivery of the basic ingredient used in our plastic formulation, and we had already exhausted our inventory. You know that, of course, since we had asked you to call all over the country to find an alternate source of supply. When we got what we needed on a rush basis, we had to pay more than we normally do."

Christensen: "I expect problems like that to pop up from time to time—that's part of my job—but now we'll both have to take a careful look at the report to see where charges are reflected for that rush order. Every month, I spend more time making sure I should be charged for each item reported than I do making plans for my department's daily work. It's really frustrating to see charges for things I have no control over."

Travers: "The way we get information doesn't help, either. I don't get copies of the reports you get, yet a lot of what I do is affected by your department, and by most of the other departments we have. Why do the budget and accounting people assume that I should only be told about my operations even though the president regularly gives us pep talks about how we all need to work together, as a team?"

Christensen: "I seem to get more reports than I need, and I am never getting asked to comment until top management calls me on the carpet about my department's shortcomings. Do you ever hear comments when your department shines?"

Travers: "I guess they don't have time to review the good news. One of my problems is that all the reports are in dollars and cents. I work with people, machines, and materials. I need information to help me this month solve this month's problems—not another report of the dollars expended last month or the month before."

Required   A. Based upon the conversation between Terry Travers and Bob Christensen, describe the likely motivation and behavior of these two employees resulting from Aurora Manufacturing Company's variance reporting system.

B. When properly implemented, both employees and companies should benefit from variance reporting systems.

1. Describe the benefits that can be realized from using a variance reporting system.

2. Based on the situation presented above, recommend ways for Aurora Manufacturing Company to improve its variance reporting system so as to increase employee motivation.

---

20.   Estimated time 30 minutes (June 1985)

The Motor Works Division of Roland Industries is located in Fort Wayne, Indiana. A major expansion of the division's only plant was completed in April of 1984. The expansion consisted of an addition to the existing building, additional new equipment, and the replacement of obsolete and fully depreciated equipment that was no longer efficient or cost effective.

Donald Futak became the Division Manager of the Motor Works Division effective May 1, 1984. Futak had a brief meeting with John Poskey, Vice-President of Operations for Roland Industries, when he assumed the Division Manager position. Poskey told Futak that the company employed return on gross assets (ROA) for measuring performance of divisions and division managers. Futak asked whether any other performance measures were ever used in place of or in conjunction with ROA. Poskey replied, "Roland's top management prefers to use a single performance measure. There is no conflict when there is only one measure. Motor Works should do well this year now that it has expanded and replaced all of that old equipment. You should have no problem exceeding the division's historical rate. I'll check back with you at the end of each quarter to see how you are doing."

Poskey called Futak after the first quarter results were complete because the Motor Works' ROA was considerably below the historical rate for the division. Futak told Poskey at that time that he did not believe that ROA was a valid performance measure for the Motor Works Division. Poskey indicated that he would get back to Futak. Futak did receive perfunctory memorandums after the second and third quarters, but there was no further discussion on the use of ROA. Now Futak has received the memorandum reproduced below.

May 24, 1985

TO: Donald Futak, Manager—Motor Works Division
FROM: John Poskey, Vice-President of Operations
SUBJECT: Division Performance

The operating results for the fourth quarter and for our fiscal year ended on April 30 are now complete. Your fourth quarter return on gross assets was only nine percent, resulting in a return for the year of slightly under 11 percent. I recall discussing your low return after the first quarter and reminding you after the second and third quarters that this level of return is not considered adequate for the Motor Works Division.

The return on gross assets at Motor Works has ranged from 15 percent to 18 percent for the past five years. An 11 percent return may be acceptable at some of Roland's other divisions, but not at a proven winner like Motor Works—especially in light of your recently improved facility.

I would like to meet with you at your office on Monday, June 3, to discuss ways to restore Motor Works' return on gross assets to its former level. Please let me know if this date is acceptable to you.

Futak is looking forward to meeting with Poskey. He knows the division's ROA is below the historical rate but the dollar profits for the year are greater than prior years. He plans to explain to Poskey why he believes return on gross assets is not an appropriate performance measure for the Motor Works Division. He also plans to recommend that ROA be replaced with three measures—dollar profit, receivables turnover, and inventory turnover. These three measures would constitute a set of multiple criteria that would be used to evaluate performance.

Required   A. On the basis of the relationship between John Poskey and Donald Futak as well as the memorandum from Poskey, identify apparent weaknesses in the performance evaluation process of Roland Industries. Do not include in your answer any discussion on the use of return on assets (ROA) as a performance measure.

B. From the information presented, identify a possible explanation of why Motor Works Division's ROA declined in the fiscal year ended April 30, 1985.

C. Identify criteria that should be used in selecting performance measures to evaluate operating managers.

D. If John Poskey does agree to use multiple criteria for evaluating the performance of the Motor Works Division as Donald Futak has suggested, discuss whether the multiple criteria of dollar profit, receivables turnover, and inventory turnover would be appropriate.

---

21.   Estimated time 30 minutes (June 1985)

The Arvee Corporation has manufactured recreational vehicles for nearly 10 years. During this time Arvee bought existing older buildings near the founder's home to expand its facilities as needed. Now, new competition and rapid sales growth to an annual level of nearly $300 million has made management realize that the company needs to consolidate its locations, reorganize its operations, and modernize its equipment in order to bring costs into line and to maintain traditional profit margins.

Five existing plant locations service the three operating divisions—Van Division (small motorized travel vans), Home Division (large motorized homes), and Trailer Division (nonmotorized hitch-on trailers). Several warehouses service the various plant locations, and the corporate office is at a location separate from the production and warehouse facilities. All buildings are within a five-mile radius. Some plant locations include production facilities for two divisions; the overlap that has developed is creating inefficiencies and additional costs. Corporate management has decided that it should take one of the following two courses of action.

• Alternative No. 1 is to consolidate the facilities into fewer existing locations.

• Alternative No. 2 is to consolidate all facilities into a new location.

With either of these two alternatives, each division would have exclusive management, production, and warehouse areas. A central warehouse would house common production materials and components; each division's production locations would house other inventories unique to its vehicle models.

The manufacturing operations at most of the plant locations need to be reorganized for greater production efficiency. Frequently, the planning for the production facilities required to meet the increased sales was not well conceived. This is now adversely affecting the current work activities as well as materials and production flow. Moreover, the technology for this kind of production is changing. Thus, many of the equipment items need to be replaced because they are obsolete or worn out. In general, management has come to realize that a complete plant modernization is needed to survive the emerging market challenges.

Tony Pratt, Corporate Controller, is charged with the responsibility for presenting a summary report on the proposed plant modernization project for an upcoming meeting of the Modernization Committee that will oversee the implementation of the project. One of the staff accountants, Donna Wessman, was assigned the responsibility of preparing the summary report. Her report is reproduced below. Pratt commended Wessman for getting the report done so promptly and is now studying the report in order to be able to explain it to the Modernization Committee. Pratt had planned to distribute

Arvee Corporation
Proposed Plant Modernization Project
($000 omitted)

	Present Operations	Proposed Operations	Additional Investment
Alternative No. 1:			
Use existing building (1)	$10,500	$10,500	
Repair buildings		1,300	$ 1,300
Revise production as layout		850	850
Upgrade equipment		3,500	3,500
Additional overhead		150	150
Total Alternative No. 1	$10,500	$16,300	$ 5,800
Alternative No. 2:			
New land & buildings		$15,000	$15,000
Production layout		300	300
New equipment		2,500	2,500
Net new factory overhead		600	600
Net direct labor savings (2)		(200)	(200)
Total Alternative No. 2	-0-	$18,200	$18,200

Notes and additional information:

(1) Historical cost used to compare with new investment.

(2) Direct labor savings come from addition of new equipment.

(3) Expected savings from new facilities are projected to be eight percent of current selling price of each of the respective units, or an overall average of $1,200 per unit.

(4) Backup schedules of the current average production costs per unit are available upon request.

(5) There may be logistics problems with some materials and components resulting from the modernization actions.

(6) The straight-line method will be used to depreciate any new buildings and equipment because this method is used for financial reporting purposes.

(7) No salvage values of replaced facilities are included because these are sunk costs and irrelevant.

(8) The tax effects from the modernization are omitted because management is committed to do the project.

(9) The plant layout and net direct labor savings were estimated without the help of the production people; they were very uncooperative in supplying information because they fear losing their jobs.

the report to the committee after making a few supporting comments, and then let the members discuss the report and ask questions.

Required Identify the desirable and undesirable features of Donna Wessman's report as a means of communication in terms of:

1. its form and appearance in presenting the information requested.

2. its content in providing useful information for the Modernization Committee as a basis for its making a choice between the two modernization alternatives.

---

22.   Estimated time 30 minutes (June 1986)

Western Corporation is a holding company with three subsidiaries—an electric utility, a natural resource development company, and an electronics manufacturer. Western is regarded as a utility because the utility subsidiary accounts for over 65 percent of revenues and net income. Virtually all of Western's officers and top executives have risen through the utility. The presence of the other subsidiaries is unusual for a utility. The diversification plus perceptive management have served Western well. The recent hard times for utilities had some impact on Western, but the company emerged in sound condition.

Western's diversification is a coincidental result arising from its policy of acquiring other electric utilities. One utility acquisition included a coal deposit, and from that beginning, other deposits and development activities were added to form the natural resource subsidiary. Similarly, another acquisition included a telephone company that provided the basis for the electronics manufacturing subsidiary.

The acquisition of other electric utilities no longer presents the growth opportunities it did in the past. Western has already acquired virtually all of the smaller utilities in its region that make a reasonable fit with Western. A proposed merger with another large utility would face strong opposition from state and federal regulators. Future economic expansion within Western's territory is now the main growth opportunity for the electric utility. However, the region's economy has been depressed, and the five-year forecast is not optimistic.

Western's strategy for expanding the other two subsidiaries has been to respond to offers initiated by sellers rather than to actively seek acquisitions. This strategy has resulted in the expansion and profitability of the electronics subsidiary. However, the natural resource subsidiary is another matter. Heavily dependent on coal, it has closely tracked the coal market's recent boom and bust. The coal market's future is uncertain. As the result of top management's dismay over the depressed coal market, Western has completed its initial strategic planning exercise. The following statements of strategy for each subsidiary were developed to formulate the basis for the master plan.

• *Electric Utility.* The key variables for this subsidiary are efficient operations and effective relations with regulators. Maximum generation of cash for use in further diversification by the corporation's other subsidiaries is the principal objective for the electric utility.

• *Natural Resources.* An orderly divestiture of low potential

assets is the initial objective. Once the divestitures are accomplished, formulating an acceptable profit and growth strategy for the remaining units is the main objective of the natural resource subsidiary.

• *Electronics.* The corporation's discretionary resources are to be employed to support the growth and diversification of this subsidiary. The future officers of Western are to be developed here.

These strategy statements were part of the strategic plan presented to Western's Board of Directors. The Directors' only debate was whether Western should sell the entire natural resource subsidiary rather than parts of it. In the end, the statements, as presented, received the Board's approval. Following the Board's action, all three statements were circulated to managers throughout the three units and described as the corporation's "new marching orders."

Required **A.** Identify corporate practices or policies that must be present within Western Corporation for the strategic plan to be effective.

B. Several important characteristics differentiate Western Corporation's three subsidiaries.

1. Identify these distinguishing characteristics.

2. Describe how these characteristics influenced the formation of a different strategy for each subsidiary.

C. Discuss the likely effects of the three strategy statements on the behavior of both the top management and the middle management of the electric utility subsidiary of Western Corporation.

---

23.   Estimated time 30 minutes (June 1986)

Galaxy Inc. is a multi-division organization offering a diversified line of products and services. A brief synopsis of Galaxy's four divisions is presented below.

• Star Manufacturing is a maker of athletic equipment that currently is enjoying steady growth. Its market is very competitive and dependent on the economy.

• Sun Appliances is the holder of exclusive patents on medical equipment. The market has monopolistic characteristics and is limited. The division is highly profitable but has little potential for growth. Considerable investments have been made in research and development.

• Venus Services is a newly acquired division that offers financial services and is geared to capture the market for the expanding financial needs of professional women. It has strong growth and profit potential.

• Comet Engineering is a civil engineering firm. A majority of its contracts are with state and local governments. Profit margins are restricted by cost plus fixed fee contracts.

James Wright, Galaxy's President, would like to introduce an incentive plan that would reward the performance of key personnel. He knows, however, that these plans can fail if they are not carefully formulated and properly implemented. Wright's previous employer had an incentive plan based on corporate profit improvement that resulted in "managed" earnings and a seesaw record of "good" and "bad" years.

In order to study the feasibility of an incentive plan for Galaxy, Wright has asked Alice Fischer, Manager of Budgets and Standards, to draft a proposal. Fischer's incentive plan proposal for Galaxy contains the following conditions and guidelines.

• The performance of the manager and key personnel of each division would be measured against the division's annual operating plan. The division operating plan would have been prepared by the division manager and approved by corporate management during the annual budgeting process.

• The minimum acceptable level of performance would be 90 percent of the division's budgeted operating income prior to corporate and capital allocations; no bonuses would be paid for performance below this level. For every percentage point achieved above the minimum acceptable level of performance, one percent of the division's operating income would be put into the division's bonus fund. The maximum bonus fund contribution any division can receive without the review of the Compensation Committee of the Board of Directors is 20 percent of divisional budgeted operating income (for achieving 100 percent of the budgeted operating income).

• The performance of each division would be reviewed by the Compensation Committee of the Board of Directors prior to distribution of the bonus funds. The committee would have the authority to adjust the bonus funds on its judgment of the following factors.

1. Nonquantitative achievements such as planning, executive development, and community relations.

2. Decisions to incur major expenses in the current year that will benefit only future profits, or conversely, the avoidance of expenses that should have been incurred.

3. Uncontrollable external influences such as regulatory actions, strikes, material shortages, and accounting and tax changes.

The adjustment of any bonus fund upward or downward may not exceed 15 percent of the fund.

Required A. Discuss the advantages and disadvantages generally associated with the use of incentive plans.

B. For the incentive plan proposal prepared by Alice Fischer for Galaxy:

1. evaluate the provisions included in the proposal.

2. discuss how the plan provisions could be expected to influence the behavior of the key management personnel in each of Galaxy's four divisions.

---

24. Estimated time 30 minutes (June 1975)

John Knight founded the Newworld Co. over thirty years ago. Although he has relied heavily upon advice from other members of management, he has made all of the important decisions for the company. Newworld has been successful, experiencing steady growth in its early years and very rapid growth in recent years. During this period of rapid growth

Knight has experienced difficulty in keeping up with the many decisions that needed to be made. He feels that he is losing "control" of the company's progress.

Regular discussions regarding his concern have been held with George Armet, the company executive vice president. As a result of these discussions, Armet has studied possible alternative organizational structures to the present highly centralized functional organization.

In a carefully prepared proposal he recommends that the company reorganize according to its two product lines because the technology and marketing methods are quite different. The plastic products require different manufacturing skills and equipment from the brass products. The change could be easily accomplished because the products are manufactured in different plants. The marketing effort is also segregated along product lines within the sales function. The number of executive positions would not change, although the duties of the positions would change. There would no longer be the need for a vice president for manufacturing or a vice president for sales. Those positions would be replaced with a vice president for each of the two product lines. Armet acknowledges that there may be personnel problems at the top management level because the current vice presidents may not be competent to manage within the new structure.

The proposal also contained the recommendations that some of the decision-making power, long held by John Knight, be transferred to the new vice presidents. He argued that this would be good for the company. They would be more aware of the problems and solution alternatives of their respective product lines because they are closer to the operations. Fewer decisions will be required of each person than now are required of John Knight; this would reduce the time between problem recognition and implementation of the solution. Armet further argued that distributing the decision-making power would improve the creativity and spirit of company management.

Knight is intrigued by the proposal and the prospect that it would make the company more manageable. However, the proposal did not spell out clearly which decisions should be transferred and which should remain with the president. He requested Armet to prepare a supplemental memorandum specifying the decisions to be delegated to the vice presidents.

The memorandum presented the recommended decision areas, explaining in each case how the new vice presidents would be closer to the situation and thereby be able to make prompt, sound decisions. The following list summarizes Armet's recommendations:

1. Sales
• Price policy
• Promotional strategy
• Credit policy

2. Operations
• Manufacturing procedures
• Labor negotiations

3. Development of existing product lines

4. Capital investment decisions—up to amounts not exceeding the division "depreciation flow" plus 25 percent of its "after-tax income" (excluding ventures into new fields).

The corporate management would be responsible for overall corporate development. Also, they would allocate the remaining available cash flow for dividends, for investment projects above the limits prescribed, and for investment into new ventures.

Required A. Does the company have the characteristics needed for decentralized profit centers? Briefly explain your answer.

B. Mr. Knight believes that the proposal, as presented, will not work. In his judgment the corporate level management will be unable to control effectively the destiny of the firm because the proposal grants too much investment freedom to the new divisions. Do you agree with Mr. Knight that effective control over the future of the firm cannot be maintained at the corporate level if the capital rationing is shared in the manner specified in the proposal? Support your answer with appropriate discussion including a recommended alternative procedure if you agree with Mr. Knight.

---

25.   Estimated time 45 minutes (December 1974)

Clarkson Company is a large multi-division firm with several plants in each division. A comprehensive budgeting system is used for planning operations and measuring performance. The annual budgeting process commences in August five months prior to the beginning of the fiscal year. At this time the division managers submit proposed budgets for sales, production and inventory levels, and expenses. Capital expenditure requests also are formalized at this time. The expense budgets include direct labor and all overhead items which are separated into fixed and variable components. Direct materials are budgeted separately in developing the production and inventory schedules.

The expense budgets for each division are developed from its plants' results, as measured by the percent variation from an adjusted budget in the first six months of the current year, and a target expense reduction percentage established by the corporation.

To determine plant percentages the plant budget for the just completed half-year period is revised to recognize changes in operating procedures and costs outside the control of plant management (e.g., labor wage rate changes, product style changes, etc.). The difference between this revised budget and the actual expenses is the controllable variance, and is expressed as a percentage of the actual expenses. This percentage is added (if unfavorable) to the corporate target expense reduction percentage. A favorable plant variance percentage is subtracted from the corporate target. If a plant had a 2 percent unfavorable controllable variance and the corporate target reduction was 4 percent, the plant's budget for the next year should reflect costs approximately 6 percent below this year's actual costs.

Next year's final budgets for the corporation, the divisions, and the plants are adopted after corporate analysis of the proposed budgets and a careful review with each division manager of the changes made by corporate management. Division profit budgets include allocated corporate costs, and plant profit budgets include allocated division and corporate costs.

Return on assets is used to measure the performance of divisions and plants. The asset base for a division consists of all assets assigned to the division, including its working capital, and an allocated share of corporate assets. For plants the asset base includes the assets assigned to the plant plus an allocated portion of the division and corporate assets. Recommendations for promotions and salary increases for the executives of the divisions and plants are influenced by how well the actual return on assets compares with the budgeted return on assets.

The plant managers exercise control only over the cost portion of the plant profit budget because the divisions are responsible for sales. Only limited control over the plant assets is exercised at the plant level.

The manager of the Dexter Plant, a major plant in the Huron division, carefully controls his costs during the first six months so that any improvement appears after the target reduction of expenses is established. He accomplishes this by careful planning and timing of his discretionary expenditures.

During 1973 the property adjacent to the Dexter Plant was purchased by Clarkson Company. This expenditure was not included in the 1973 capital expenditure budget. Corporate management decided to divert funds from a project at another plant since the property appeared to be a better long-term investment.

Also during 1973 Clarkson Company experienced depressed sales. In an attempt to achieve budgeted profit, corporate management announced in August that all plants were to cut their annual expenses by 6 percent. In order to accomplish this expense reduction, the Dexter Plant manager reduced preventive maintenance and postponed needed major repairs. Employees who quit were not replaced unless absolutely necessary. Employee training was postponed whenever possible. The raw materials, supplies and finished goods inventories were reduced below normal levels.

Required A. Evaluate the budget procedure of Clarkson Company with respect to its effectiveness for planning and controlling operations.

B. Is the Clarkson Company's use of return on assets to evaluate the performance of the Dexter Plant appropriate? Explain your answer.

C. Analyze and explain the Dexter Plant Manager's behavior during 1973.

---

26.   Estimated time 30 minutes (June 1981)

Divisional managers of SIU Incorporated have been expressing growing dissatisfaction with the current methods used to measure divisional performance. Divisional operations are evaluated every quarter by comparison with the static budget prepared during the prior year. Divisional managers claim that many factors are completely out of their control but are included in this comparison. This results in an unfair and misleading performance evaluation.

The managers have been particularly critical of the process used to establish standards and budgets. The annual budget, stated by quarters, is prepared six months prior to the beginning of the operating year. Pressure by top management to reflect increased earnings has often caused divisional managers to overstate revenues and/or understate expenses. In addition, once the budget has been established, divisions were required to "live with the budget." Frequently, external factors such as the state of the economy, changes in consumer preferences, and actions of competitors have not been adequately recognized in the budget parameters that top management supplied to the divisions. The credibility of the performance review is curtailed when the budget can not be adjusted to incorporate these changes.

Top management, recognizing the current problems, has agreed to establish a committee to review the situation and to make recommendations for a new performance evaluation system. The committee consists of each division manager, the Corporate Controller, and the Executive Vice President who serves as the chairman. At the first meeting, one division manager outlined an Achievement of Objectives System (AOS). In this performance evaluation system, divisional managers would be evaluated according to three criteria:

● Doing better than last year—Various measures would be compared to the same measures of the prior year.

● Planning realistically—Actual performance for the current year would be compared to realistic plans and/or goals.

● Managing current assets—Various measures would be used to evaluate the divisional management's achievements and reactions to changing business and economic conditions.

A division manager believed this system would overcome many of the inconsistencies of the current system because divisions could be evaluated from three different viewpoints. In addition, managers would have the opportunity to show how they would react and account for changes in uncontrollable external factors.

A second division manager was also in favor of the proposed AOS. However, he cautioned that the success of a new performance evaluation system would be limited unless it had the complete support of top management. Further, this support should be visible within all divisions. He believed that the committee should recommend some procedures which would enhance the motivational and competitive spirit of the divisions.

Required A. Explain whether or not the proposed AOS would be an improvement over the measure of divisional performance now used by SIU Incorporated.

B. Develop specific performance measures for each of the three criteria in the proposed AOS which could be used to evaluate divisional managers.

C. Discuss the motivational and behavioral aspects of the proposed performance system. Also, recommend specific programs which could be instituted to promote morale and give incentives to divisional management.

---

27. Estimated time 30 minutes (December 1978)

MBR, Inc., consists of three divisions that formerly were three independent manufacturing companies. Bader Corporation and Roach Company merged in 1975 and the merged corporation acquired Mitchell Co. in 1976. The name of the Corporation was subsequently changed to MBR, Inc., and each company became a separate division retaining the name of its former company.

The three divisions have operated as if they were still independent companies. Each division has its own sales force and production facilities. Each division management is responsible for sales, cost of operations, acquisition and financing of divisional assets, and working capital management. The corporate management of MBR evaluated the performance of the divisions and division managements on the basis of return on investment.

Mitchell Division has just been awarded a contract for a product which uses a component that is manufactured by the Roach Division as well as by outside suppliers. Mitchell used a cost figure of $3.80 for the component manufactured by Roach in preparing its bid for the new product. This cost figure was supplied by Roach in response to Mitchell's request for the average variable cost of the component and represents the standard variable manufacturing cost and variable selling and distribution expense.

Roach has an active sales force that is continually soliciting new prospects. Roach's regular selling price for the component Mitchell needs for the new product is $6.50. Sales of this component are expected to increase. However, the Roach management has indicated that it could supply Mitchell with the required quantities of the component at the regular selling price less variable selling and distribution expenses. Mitchell's management has responded by offering to pay standard variable manufacturing cost plus 20 percent.

The two divisions have been unable to agree on a transfer price. Corporate management has never established a transfer price policy because interdivisional transactions have never occurred. As a compromise, the corporate vice president of finance has suggested a price equal to the standard full manufacturing cost (that is, no selling and distribution expenses) plus a 15 percent markup. This price has also been rejected by the two division managers, because each considered it grossly unfair.

The unit cost structure for the Roach component and the three suggested prices are shown below.

Regular selling price	**$6.50**
Standard variable manufacturing cost	$3.20
Standard fixed manufacturing cost	1.20
Variable selling and distribution expenses	.60
	$5.00
Regular selling price less variable selling and distribution expenses (6.50 — .60)	**$5.90**
Variable manufacturing plus 20% ($3.20 × 1.20)	**$3.84**
Standard full manufacturing cost plus 15% ($4.40 × 1.15)	**$5.06**

Required A. Discuss the effect each of the three proposed prices might have on the Roach division management's attitude toward intracompany business.

B. Is the negotiation of a price between the Mitchell and Roach Divisions a satisfactory method to solve the transfer price problem? Explain your answer.

C. Should the corporate management of MBR, Inc. become involved in this transfer price controversy? Explain your answer.

28.   Estimated time 30 minutes (June 1978)

The Consumer Products Division of the Liberty Manufacturing Company experienced reduced sales in the first quarter of 1978 and has forecasted that the decline in sales will continue through the remainder of the year. The profit budgeted in the original 1978 profit plan was about 40 percent less than that of the prior year. Fortunately, Liberty's other divisions budgeted improved profits in 1978 over 1977.

The top management of Liberty believes in a decentralized organization, and division managers have considerable latitude in managing the operations of their divisions. Division managers receive bonuses of a specified percentage of division profits in addition to their annual salaries.

At the end of the first quarter of 1978, John Spassen, the manager of the Consumer Products Division, felt that drastic action was needed to reduce costs and improve the performance of his division. Consequently he dismissed twenty highly trained, skilled employees as one step to reduce costs. Only five of them are expected to be available for reemployment when business returns to normal in 1979.

The top management, upon reviewing the steps taken by Spassen, was concerned about the consequences of releasing the twenty skilled employees. The company officials had recently attended seminars on human resource accounting and wondered if Spassen would have taken that particular action had a cost-based human resource accounting system been in operation.

Required A. Explain what is accounted for in a cost-based human resource accounting system.

B. Explain how the information generated by a company's cost-based human resource accounting system might apply to the decision to dismiss the twenty skilled employees.

C. What alternative information system might a company develop to evaluate the decision to dismiss the twenty skilled employees?

29.   Estimated time 30 minutes (December 1982)

Kelly Petroleum Company has a large oil and natural gas project in Oklahoma. The project has been organized into two production centers (Petroleum Production and Natural Gas Production) and one service center (Maintenance).

Maintenance Center Activities and Scheduling

Don Pepper, Maintenance Center Manager, has organized his maintenance workers into work crews that serve the two production centers. The maintenance crews perform preventive maintenance and repair equipment both in the field and in the central maintenance shop.

Pepper is responsible for scheduling all maintenance work in the field and in the central shop. Preventive maintenance is performed according to a set schedule established by Pepper and approved by the production center managers. Breakdowns are given immediate priority in scheduling so that downtime is minimized. Thus, preventive maintenance occasionally must be postponed, but every attempt is made to reschedule it within three weeks.

Preventive maintenance work is the responsibility of Pepper. However, if a significant problem is discovered during preventive maintenance, the appropriate production center supervisor authorizes and supervises the repair after checking with Pepper.

When a breakdown in the field occurs, the production centers contact Pepper to initiate the repairs. The repair work is supervised by the production center supervisor. Machinery and equipment sometimes need to be replaced while the original equipment is repaired in the central shop. This procedure is followed only when the time to make the repair in the field would result in an extended interruption of operations. Replacement of equipment is recommended by the maintenance work crew supervisor and approved by a production center supervisor.

Routine preventive maintenance and breakdowns of automotive and mobile equipment used in the field are completed in the central shop. All repairs and maintenance activities taking place in the central shop are under the direction of Pepper.

Maintenance Center Accounting Activities

Pepper has records identifying the work crews assigned to each job in the field, the number of hours spent on the job, and parts and supplies used on the job. In addition, records for the central shop (jobs, labor hours, parts and supplies) have been maintained. However, this detailed maintenance information is not incorporated into Kelly's accounting system.

Pepper develops the annual budget for the Maintenance Center by planning the preventive maintenance that will be needed during the year, estimating the number and seriousness of breakdowns, and estimating the shop activities. He then

Oklahoma Project
Maintenance Center Cost Report
For the Month of November 1982
(in thousands of dollars)

	Budget	Actual	Petroleum Production	Natural Gas Production
Shop hours	2,000	1,800	—	—
Field hours	8,000	10,000	6,000	4,000
Labor-electrical	$ 25.0	$ 24.0	$ 14.4	$ 9.6
Labor-mechanical	30.0	35.0	21.0	14.0
Labor-instrumentation	18.0	22.5	13.5	9.0
Labor-automotive	3.5	2.8	1.7	1.1
Labor-heavy equipment	9.6	12.3	7.4	4.9
Labor-equipment operation	28.8	35.4	21.2	14.2
Labor-general	15.4	15.9	9.6	6.3
Parts	60.0	86.2	51.7	34.5
Supplies	15.3	12.2	7.3	4.9
Lubricants and fuels	3.4	3.0	1.8	1.2
Tools	2.5	3.2	1.9	1.3
Accounting and data processing	1.5	1.5	.9	.6
Total	$213.0	$254.0	$152.4	$101.6

bases the labor, part, and supply costs on his plans and estimates and develops the budget amounts by line item. Because the timing of the breakdowns is impossible to plan, Pepper divides the annual budget by 12 to derive the monthly budget.

All costs incurred by the work crews in the field and in the central shop are accumulated monthly and then allocated to the two production cost centers based upon the field hours worked in each production center. This method of cost allocation has been used on Pepper's recommendation because he believed that it was easy to implement and understand. Furthermore, he believed that a better allocation system was impossible to incorporate into the monthly report due to the wide range of salaries paid to maintenance workers and the fast turnover of materials and parts.

The November cost report provided by the Accounting Department is shown on the previous page.

Production Center Manager's Concerns

Both production center managers have been upset with the method of cost allocation. Furthermore, they believe the report is virtually useless as a cost control device. Actual costs always seem to deviate from the monthly budget and the proportion charged to each production center varies significantly from month to month. Maintenance costs have increased substantially since 1980, and the production managers believe that they have no way to judge whether such an increase is reasonable.

The two production managers, Pepper, and representatives of corporate accounting have met to discuss these concerns. They concluded that a responsibility accounting system could be developed to replace the current system. In their opinion, a responsibility accounting system would alleviate the production managers' concerns and accurately reflect the activity of the Maintenance Center.

Required   A. Explain the purposes of a responsibility accounting system, and discuss how such a system could resolve the concerns of the production center managers of Kelly Petroleum Company.

B. Describe the behavioral advantages generally attributed to responsibility accounting systems that the management of Kelly Petroleum Company should expect if the system were effectively introduced for the Maintenance Center.

C. Describe a report format for the Maintenance Center that would be based upon an effective responsibility accounting system, and explain which, if any, of the Maintenance Center's costs should be charged to the two production centers.

---

30.   **Estimated time 30 minutes (June 1984)**

Company annual reports have become large documents. They now include such sections as letters to the stockholders, descriptions of the business, operating highlights, financial review, management discussion and analysis, segment reporting, and inflation data as well as the basic financial statements. The expansion has been due, in part, to a general increase in degree of sophistication and complexity in accounting standards and disclosure requirements for financial reporting. The expansion also is reflective of the change in the composition and level of

sophistication of its users. Current users include not only stockholders, but financial and securities analysts, potential investors, lending institutions, stockbrokers, customers, employees, and, whether the reporting company likes it or not, competitors. Thus, a report that was designed as a device for communicating basic financial information has increased its scope to either meet the needs of an expanding audience or meet the need to expand the audience.

There are now conflicting views on the value of annual reports ranging from failing to provide adequate data to meet the intent of the report, to providing an unfathomable information overload.

Required   A. The task of the preparer of an annual report is the communication of information from the corporation to targeted users.

1. Identify and discuss the basic factors of communication that must be considered in the presentation of this information.

2. Discuss the communication problems a corporation faces in preparing the annual report that result from the diversity of the users being addressed.

B. Evaluate the effectiveness of current annual reports as communication devices for each of the following users:

1. Current and potential stockholders.
2. Financial analysts.
3. Employees.

C. Discuss the effect on the communication of information to all users as a consequence of knowing that competitors will read and analyze the annual report.

---

31.   **Estimated time 45 minutes (June 1992)**

Lynsar Corporation started as a single plant that produced the major components and then assembled them into electric motors—the company's main product. Lynsar later expanded by developing outside markets for some of the components used in its motors. Eventually, Lynsar reorganized into four manufacturing divisions: Bearing, Casing, Switch, and Motor. Each of the four manufacturing divisions operates as an autonomous unit, and divisional performance is the basis for year-end bonuses.

Lynsar's transfer pricing policy permits the manufacturing divisions to sell externally to outside customers as well as internally to the other divisions. The price for goods transferred between divisions is to be negotiated between the buying and selling divisions without any interference from top management.

Lynsar's profits have dropped for the current year even though sales have increased, and the drop in profits can be traced almost entirely to the Motor Division. Jere Feldon, Lynsar's chief financial officer, has determined that the Motor Division has purchased switches for its motors from an outside supplier during the current year rather than buying them from the Switch Division. The Switch Division is at capacity and has refused to sell the switches to the Motor Division because it can sell them to outside customers at a price higher than the actual full (absorption) manufacturing cost that has always been negotiated in the past with the Motor Division. When the

Motor Division refused to meet the price the Switch Division was receiving from its outside buyer, the Motor Division had to purchase the switches from an outisde supplier at an even higher price.

Feldon is reviewing Lynsar's transfer pricing policy because he believes that sub-optimization has occurred. While the Switch Division made the correct decision to maximize its divisional profit by not transferring the switches at actual full manufacturing cost, this decision was not necessarily in the best interest of Lynsar. The Motor Division paid more for the switches than the selling price the Switch Division charged its outside customer. The Motor Division has always been Lynsar's largest division and has tended to dominate the smaller divisions. Feldon has learned that the Casing and Bearing Divisions are also resisting the Motor Division's desire to continue using actual full manufacturing cost as the negotiated price.

Feldon has requested that the corporate Accounting Department study alternative transfer pricing methods that would promote overall goal congruence, motivate divisional management performance, and optimize overall company performance. Three of the transfer pricing methods being considered are listed below. If one of these methods should be selected, it would be applied uniformly across all divisions.

• Standard full manufacturing costs plus markup.
• Market selling price of the products being transferred.
• Outlay (out-of-pocket) costs incurred to the point of transfer plus opportunity cost per unit.

Required   A. 1. Discuss both the positive and negative behavioral implications that can arise from employing a negotiated transfer price system for goods that are exchanged between divisions.

2. Explain the behavioral problems which can arise from using actual full (absorption) manufacturing costs as a transfer price.

B. Discuss the behavioral problems that could arise if Lynsar Corporation decides to change from its current policy covering the transfer of goods between divisions to a revised transfer pricing policy that would apply uniformly to all divisions.

C. Discuss the likely behavior of both "buying" and "selling" divisional managers for each of the following transfer pricing methods being considered by Lynsar Corporation.

1. Standard full manufacturing costs plus markup.
2. Market selling price of the products being transferred.
3. Outlay (out-of-pocket) costs incurred to the point of transfer plus opportunity cost per unit.

---

32.   **Estimated time 30 minutes (June 1993)**

Ajax Consolidated has several divisions; however, only two divisions transfer products to other divisions. The Mining Division refines toldine which is then transferred to the Metals Division. The toldine is processed into an alloy by the Metals Division and is sold to customers at a price of $150 per unit. The Mining Division is currently required by Ajax to transfer its total yearly output of 400,000 units of toldine to the Metals Division at total manufacturing cost plus 10 percent. Unlimited quantities of toldine can be purchased and sold on

the open market at $90 per unit. While the Mining Division could sell all the toldine it produces at $90 per unit on the open market, it would have to incur a variable selling of $5 per unit.

Brian Jones, manager of the Mining Division, is unhappy with having to transfer the entire output of toldine to the Metals Division at 110 percent of cost. In a meeting with the management of Ajax, he said, "Why should my division be required to sell toldine to the Metals Division at less than market price? For the year just ended in May, Metals' contribution margin was over $19 million on sales of 400,000 units while Mining's contribution was just over $5 million on the transfer of the same number of units. My division is subsidizing the profitability of the Metals Division. We should be allowed to charge the market price for toldine when transferring to the Metals Division."

Presented below is the detailed unit cost structure for both the Mining and Metals Divisions for the fiscal year ended May 31, 1993.

Cost Structure Per Unit		
	Mining Division	**Metals Division**
Transfer price from Mining Division	—	$ 66
Direct material	$12	6
Direct labor	16	20
Manufacturing overhead	32[1]	25[2]
Total cost per unit	$60	$117

[1]Manufacturing overhead cost in the Mining Division is 25 percent fixed and 75 percent variable.

[2]Manufacturing overhead cost in the Metals Division is 60 percent fixed and 40 percent variable.

Required   A. Explain why transfer prices based on cost are not appropriate as a divisional performance measure.

B. Using the market price as the transfer price, determine the contribution margin for both the Mining Division and the Metals Division for the year ended May 31, 1993.

C. If Ajax Consolidated were to institute the use of negotiated transfer prices and allow divisions to buy and sell on the open market, determine the price range for toldine that would be acceptable to both the Mining Division and the Metals Division. Explain your answer.

D. Identify which one of the three types of transfer prices—cost-based, market-based, or negotiated—is most likely to elicit desirable management behavior at Ajax Consolidated and thus benefit overall operations. Explain your answer.

33.   Estimated time 30 minutes (December 1992)

The management of JEM Associates Inc., a manufacturer of farm machinery, has begun the process of implementing a formal planning system incorporating strategic and operational planning. After three months of management discussions, JEM management has defined the following strategic goals for the next three years.

• Develop better integrated relations with Japan, Korea, and Mexico in order to minimize the cost of steel and parts used in manufacturing.

• Develop new marketing strategies in the agrarian economies of emerging nations.

• Procure additional funds from the public investment community to acquire and develop new products.

• Perform a human resource audit of JEM personnel to develop training programs in order to fill planned job vacancies with internal personnel.

• Procure and implement a computerized system to accommodate the global growth objectives.

After two months of submissions and revisions, JEM management has completed the operational and financial plans for the first year of operations under the newly established strategic goals. The managers are now concerned with being able to measure progress toward these goals and are considering various ways of controlling and evaluating performance. The managers are also concerned about how their employees will react to these performance measures.

Performance controls can be introduced at one or more of three general points—before, during, or after the goal attainment process. The chart below shows how controls can focus on the inputs, attainment, and outputs of the goal attainment process.

Required   A. Identify at least three reasons why JEM Associates Inc. needs an effective control system in order to realize their strategic goals for the next three years.

B. Define preliminary, screening, and post-action controls and give an example of each.

C. 1. Explain why employees frequently resist controls.

2. Identify those characteristics that make controls effective and acceptable.

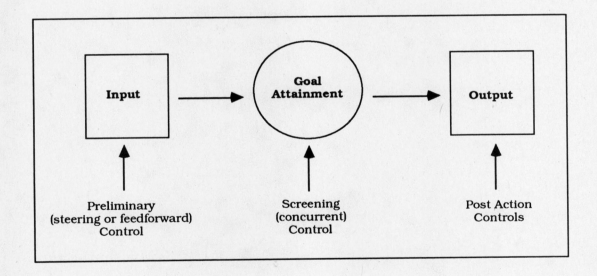

Solutions

1.

1. Classical management theory can be contrasted with modern organizational theory in the area of organizational goals as follows.

Issue	Classical	Modern
Principal objective	The principal objective of business activity is profit maximization.	In the modern complex business enterprise there are many diverse goals.
Goal structure and development	Goals are set by a few people because they are the only ones knowledgeable to do so.	Organizations are coalitions of individual participants. The organization itself cannot have goals, only individuals can have goals. Those goals are, in fact, the objectives of the dominant members of the coalition.
	Goals are additive—what is good for the parts of the business is also food for the whole.	There appears to be no valid basis for the assumption that goals are homogeneous and thus additive —what is good for the parts of the organization is not necessarily good for the whole.

2. Classical management theory can be contrasted with modern organizational theory in the area of employee behavior as follows:

Issue	Classical	Modern
Motivation	Organization participants are motivated primarily by economic forces.	Organization participants are motivated by a wide variety of psychological, social, and economic needs and drives.
Authority versus responsibility	There must be a balance between the authority a person has and the responsibility for performance.	Responsibility is assigned from above and authority is accepted from below.

3. Classical management theory can be contrasted with modern organizational theory in the area of management behavior as follows:

Issue	Classical	Modern
Role of business manager	The role of the business manager is to maximize the profits of the firm.	The management role is essentially a decision-making process subject to the limitations on human rationality and cognitive ability, and favorable for the organization.
	The manager uses employees as necessary components of the technical system.	The primary role of the business manager is to maintain a favorable balance between: (1) the contributions required from the participants and (2) the inducements (i.e., perceived need satisfactions) which must be offered to secure those contributions.
Management control	The essence of management control is authority. The ultimate authority of management stems from its ability to affect the economic reward structure.	The essence of management control is the willingness of other participants to accept the authority of management. This willingness appears to be a nonstable function of the inducement-contribution balance.

1. (Continued)

4. Classical management theory can be contrasted with modern organizational theory in the area of accounting as follows:

Issue	Classical	Modern
Primary function of accounting	The primary function of management accounting is to aid management in the process of profit maximization.	The management accounting process is an information system whose major purposes are: (1) to provide the various levels of management with data which will facilitate the decision-making functions of planning and control; and (2) to serve as a communications medium within the organization.
Accounting system	The accounting system is a goal-allocation (planning) device which permits management to select its operating objectives and to divide and distribute them throughout the firm. The accounting system is also a control device which permits management to identify and correct undesirable performance.	The effective use of budgets and other accounting planning and control techniques requires an understanding of the interaction between these techniques and the motivations and aspiration levels of the individuals to be controlled.
	There is sufficient certainty, rationality, and knowledge within the system to permit an accurate comparison of responsibility for performance and the ultimate benefits and costs of that performance.	The objectivity of the management accounting process is largely a myth. Accountants have wide areas of discretion in the selection, processing, and reporting of data.
	The accounting system is neutral in its evaluations—personal bias is eliminated by the objectivity of the system.	In performing their function within an organization, accountants can be expected to be influenced by their own personal and departmental goals in the same way that other participants are influenced.
Behavior	Employees have the capacity to behave in only a few ways and are adaptive to specific situations or self-initiative.	Human behavior within an organization is essentially an adaptive, problem-solving, decision-making process.
	Employees behave in ways only which satisfy individual primary needs.	The efficiency and effectiveness of human behavior is usually directed toward attempts to find satisfactory need gratification.
Productivity	Work is essentially an unpleasant task which people will avoid whenever possible. Therefore, productivity improvements must be realized through control of the technical elements of the job such as rate and quality of work and incentive pay.	Productivity improvements are realized by managing antecedents and consequences of effort such as total work setting, climate, socialization and non-monetary rewards.

2.

1. According to current organization theorists the classical economic entrepreneurship model does not fit modern organizations, whether profit-making or not-for-profit in nature. There is no longer typically a single entrepreneur whose personal goals, even if they were solely economic (which is also questioned), can dominate the objectives of the organization and all of its participants. In fact no single goal of any kind is seen as sufficient to explain the observed behavior of modern organizations. Rather there appear to be a series of goals, any one of which may dominate at a particular point in time. The accounting model as described in the paragraph would be inadequate to measure the results of an organization's activities

because some objectives are noneconomic and because the model focuses on only one economic goal. In fact, organization theorists would say that the organization itself can have no goals but rather what we view as organizational goals are merely the goals of the dominant members of the organization. Another contrast between classical and modern organization theory has to do with the nature of subunit goals. The classical view is that the subunit goals will fit into an overall and congruent goal structure, which will lead to the single goal of profit maximization, whereas the modern organization theorists' view is that it is highly likely that such subunit goals will be in conflict with each other and with higher unit goals.

2. Current organization theorists also take exception to the classical economic view of the profit goal being established by the entrepreneur at the top of the organization and the appropriate subunit goals developed from it and imposed upon the rest of the organization from the top. Rather, the establishment of the organization goals is viewed as a political process of bargaining or coalition formation. The goals that derive from this process will be those of the dominant members of the organization (or a dominant coalition of powerful members), subject to constraints imposed by the environment and by other nondominant but significant participants in the organization. It also follows from this that organization goals can shift over time in response to significant changes in any of these factors.

3.

A. 1. Denny Daniel's perception of John Scott the controller is as:

• an accountant who knows and cares little about the production aspects of organization.

• unsympathetic and not helpful in providing services to the production departments.

• an accountant who is unwilling to change or request top management to make changes in reporting requirements.

2. Denny Daniel's perception of corporate headquarters is as:

• unfair in that they are only using the cost report to judge performance thereby ignoring product quality, employee pride and motivation.

• insensitive to the needs and concerns of production people.

• resistant to change in reporting policies and budgetary processes.

3. Denny Daniel's perception of the cost report is as:

• a short-sighted report overemphasizing cost minimization as a single objective.

• inflexible and not subject to the changing conditions of a dynamic production process.

• a biased report highlighting shortcomings and failing to give proper recognition to improvements in performance or innovative processes.

4. Denny Daniel's perception of himself is as a:

• qualified production manager interested in a quality product at a reasonable price.

• frustrated manager unable to get satisfactory cooperation from the accounting department or top management.

• discouraged production manager recognizing that the current reporting situation is nearly hopeless, and that others before him have been equally unsuccessful.

Denny Daniel's perceptions adversely affect his behavior and performance as a production manager. Operating in a "no win" situation in which he believes performance reports do not fairly represent his accomplishments, plus the inability to communicate his desires or needs to appropriate people in top management, can inhibit motivational desires and curtail incentive.

B. Three changes, with supporting reasons, which could be made in the cost report to provide top management more meaningful information while at the same time be less threatening to the production managers, are as follows.

• Use a flexible budget rather than a static master budget for measuring performance so that changed conditions, volume changes and fixed versus variable costs are recognized in the reporting process.

• Separate controllable costs from noncontrollable costs and clearly identify those elements of the report for which the production manager is directly responsible. These actions will provide a more meaningful analysis of operations and managers will know responsibilities.

• A variance column which highlights both favorable and unfavorable circumstances would provide a less negative report. Significant variances could be highlighted to draw attention to them. Variance analysis may also be developed based upon standard cost.

4.

A. Operational benefits that accrue to an organization from a participative budgeting process include the following:

• The participant has the greatest knowledge, both general and detailed, about the activities covered by a specific budget.

• Goals are more appropriate to specific situations leading to goal congruence.

• Participative budgets may improve productivity.

Behavioral benefits for participants with a participative budgeting process include:

• a sense of belonging to the management team.

• a sense of satisfaction in helping to set performance levels and provide information.

• a better knowledge of what is expected so that improved motivation and morale result.

B. *Deficiencies*	*Recommendations*
1. Setting an upper spending constraint gives indirect approval to spending up to that level whether justified or not.	1. Weidner could institute zero-base budgeting, which would provide that all expenditures be substantiated.
2. Setting prior constraints such as maximum limits and inclusion of noncontrollable fixed expenditures prior to departmental input defeats the purpose of participative management.	2. Divisional constraints should be known to managers prior to budgeting, but individual limits should be determined with the input of managers.
3. Arbitrary allocation of the approved budget defeats the purpose of a participative budget process.	3. The department managers should be involved in the reallocation of the approved budget.
4. The Division Manager holds back a specified percentage of each department's appropriation for discretionary use.	4. Contingency funds should not be part of a departmental budget. These funds should be identified and provided for before the allocation process to departments.
5. Exception form reporting and evaluation based on performance to budget must be accompanied with rewards.	5. Recognition should be given to those attaining budget goals, not just exceptions.

5.

A. 1. The directive could have a significant effect on the care with which the budgets are prepared and the commitment that the division managers will make to achieve the budgeted results. The budget may have reduced significance as an operating plan, which will increase the uncertainty as to the validity of the approved budget. There also appears to be a decrease in the authority of the division managers, and there is likely to be less cooperation and coordination between division and corporate management.

2. The new directive would likely affect the preparation of future travel budgets as follows. The budget amount for travel expense may be inflated above actual needs to allow room for unforeseen trips, and there may be less care in preparation of the travel budget due to the division managers' decreased authority over travel.

B. The morale and motivation of the division manager and research staff are likely to be lowered by the directive because their autonomy, authority, and degree of participation in the budget process appear to be reduced.

6.

A. The budgetary control system of Ferguson & Son appears to have several very important shortcomings which reduce its effectiveness and may in fact cause it to interfere with good performance. Some of the shortcomings are itemized and explained below.

• *Lack of coordinated goals.* Emory had been led to believe high quality output is the goal; it now appears low cost is the goal. The employees do not know what the goals are and thus cannot make decisions which lead toward reaching the goals.

• *Influence of uncontrollable factors.* The actual performance relative to budget is greatly influenced by uncontrollable factors (that is, rush orders, lack of prompt maintenance). Thus, the variance reports serve little purpose for evaluation of performance or for locating controllable factors to improve performance. As a result, the system does not encourage coordination among departments.

• *The short-term perspectives.* The monthly evaluation and the budget tightening on a monthly basis results in a very short-run perspective by the supervisors. This will result in inappropriate decisions (that is, inspect the fork lift trucks rather than repair inoperative equipment, fail to report supplies usage).

• *System does not motivate.* The budgetary system appears to focus on evaluation of performance even though most of the essential factors for the purpose are missing. The focus on evaluation and the weaknesses take away an important benefit of the budgetary system—motivation of management employees.

B. The improvements in the budgetary control system must correct the deficiencies described above. The system must

• more clearly define the company's objectives.

• develop an accounting reporting system which better matches controllable factors with supervisor responsibility and authority.

• establish budget values for appropriate time periods which do not change monthly based on prior performances.

The entire company from top management down must be educated in sound budgeting procedures so that all parties will understand the total process and recognize the benefit to be gained.

7.

A. Division and plant personnel biases which may be included in the submission of budget estimates include:

• Budget sales estimates probably would tend to be lower than actually expected because of the high volatility in product demand and the current reward/penalty system for exceeding or missing the budget.

• Budget cost estimates will be higher than actually expected in order to protect the divisions against the effects of downside risk of business slumps and the possibility of increased higher costs. The reward/penalty system encourages this action.

• Plant and division management can incorporate "slack and padding" into the budget without the likelihood that it will be removed because corporate headquarters does not appear to get actively involved in the actual budget preparation.

B. Sources of information that top management can use to monitor divisional budget estimates include:

• industry and trade association sales projections and performance data.
• prior year performance by reporting units as measured by their financial, production and sales reports.
• performances of similar divisions and plants.
• regional and national leading economic indicators and trends in consumer preference and demand.

C. Services which could be offered by corporate management in the development of budget estimates are as follows:

• Provide national and regional industry sales forecasts for products as developed by corporate management or obtained by management from other sources.
• Sponsor training programs for plant and divisional personnel on budgeting techniques and procedures.
• Inform divisions of overall corporate goals in terms of sales, market share and net income.
• Provide economic forecasts with regard to expected inflationary trends and overall business cycles.

D. Top management should weigh the costs and benefits and the resulting behavioral effects of its actions before getting more involved in the budgeting process. The costs to be evaluated would include:

• increased costs at the corporate level because more time and perhaps additional staff will be required.
• lower profits due to an unfavorable change in division and plant management attitudes and motivation.

The benefits to be considered would include improved profits from:

• more accurate budget estimates which might reduce lost sales and/or reduce costs incurred.
• more effective management because of more realistic budgets.

• improved coordination and control of the budget process.

The behavioral variables to be considered would include:

• the effect of goal congruence.
• the effect on the communication channels between top management and divisional management.
• the effect of restricting authority over the budget process at the divisional level.
• the possible negative effect on motivation and morale due to loss of authority and autonomy.
• the effect on performance due to a potential reduction in bonuses.

8.

A. The performance measurement system does not properly capture the objective of better citizen service at a lower cost for a number of reasons. First, the system does not relate cost to service. The point budget is constructed on the basis of the number of hours worked rather than on the basis of estimated services to be performed. In addition, the system attempts to give credit for service performed as if the department and branch offices had responsibility for generating the activity in their offices, when in fact the services are provided because a citizen is required by law to use the services.

Second, although the department appears to be concerned with citizen service, the influence of citizen comments is so small as to make it a relatively unimportant facet of the evaluation process. Also, no organized program for obtaining citizens' comments was described.

Third, the only way a branch can improve its point total in a stable community (other than by citizens' comments) is to increase the number of failures on drivers' tests. This provides an incentive that is counterproductive to the department's objective of better citizen service.

B. The results for 1974 for the Barry County branch office are misleading. The branch office did not improve performance despite being closer to budget.

The budget performance points were reduced for 1974 to reflect a more realistic level of operations. This reduction was effected by reducing the number of budgeted clerical employees. While budgeted and actual performance points are closer, the branch office has not reduced costs because they have operated with the same number of clerical people in 1974 as in previous years.

There also appears to have been an undesirable practice in 1974 to increase actual performance points. The number of road test failures more than doubled in 1974—an extremely large increase from past experiences in 1972 and 1973. At the same time there was a decrease in the number of favorable citizen comments and a 200 percent increase in the number of unfavorable citizen comments. Both of these occurrences indicate a decrease in performance during 1974.

9.

A. The budget practices described in the problem are not likely to produce very effective budget control in the long run. Several weaknesses can be identified.

1. There appears to be no participation of plant personnel in the budget development.
2. Given that there have been five managers in four years, the managers have had no opportunity to assess whether the budget is realistic.
3. It appears that adjustments to the budget subsequent to its adoption are not permitted even in the light of new information.
4. The budget is being used to pressure the plant manager.

B. The immediate effect will be either a frustrated manager who will not make the budget because she/he is unwilling to sacrifice the future for the present and thus be replaced, or a frustrated manager who meets the budget by making decisions that sacrifice the future for the present. In either case, Drake Inc. is unfavorably affected.

The long-term effect will be to reduce the management effectiveness of Drake Inc. employees. The arbitrary method of budget development, lack of participation, and the use of the budget as a pressure device will result in loss of talented managers, development of nonproductive methods by managers to "beat" the budget, decisions taken to meet budget but that are detrimental to the company in the long-run, and probably low morale and motivation.

If the present methods of budget administration continue, David Green may adopt nonproductive methods and become an ineffective manager. However, if he is talented and continues to raise such issues as the poor condition of the plant and his short tenure, it is likely that he will resign or be fired.

10.

A. Features and characteristics of a standard cost system that make it an effective cost control tool include the following.

• Standards reflect an acceptable level of performance that should be recognized as legitimate or as readily attainable through normal efficient operations.

• Standards are generally set for routine activities which are easily identifiable and measurable. The standards can be associated with specific cost factors of uniform products such as material usage and direct labor time in production process.

• Standard setting can be a participative process. Those individuals most familiar with the variables associated with the standard setting can often provide the most accurate information for the standard. This sense of participation will help to establish the legitimacy of the standard and give the participants a greater feeling of being a part of the operation.

• Standards promote cost control through the use of performance reports. Variation analysis can be used to identify and isolate potential problem areas in the production process which may lead to cost control procedures applied to specific operations.

B. 1. The standard cost system appears to have had an unfavorable impact on cost control. The variances have been unfavorable since the introduction of the system and the amount of the variance has grown larger each month. The apparent cause of the ineffectiveness of the cost system is the reduction in employee motivation.

2. The standard cost system appears to have had an unfavorable impact on employee motivation. The significant increases in turnover and absenteeism are strong indicators of the decline in motivation.

C. The employee dissatisfaction would reduce the motivation and morale of the employees. Probable causes for the dissatisfaction are that the employees suffered a reduction in authority, the employees did not have an opportunity to participate in the standard-setting process, and the standards were set too tightly.

11.

A. To the extent that an accounting information system does not supply information to meet the needs of management, it will be ignored or resented as a waste of time and money. Because necessary information is not provided by the accounting information system, managers will seek other sources of information and develop an informal communication network. If the necessary information cannot be obtained from either a formal or an informal communications network, decision-making will be impeded, the planning function will suffer, control will be lacking, and no information will be available to evaluate centers, projects or individuals. This can lead to frustration and a decrease in motivation. The organization will experience a lack of goal congruence, suboptimization, waste and inefficiency as inaccurate, or possibly falsified, information is used.

B. 1. The perceptions of the B&B Company employees indicate that there is a problem with the accounting system because some employees believe the accounting system is:

• adequate when the information derived for performance reporting reflects favorably on that individual (i.e., George Vector).

• inadequate for cost control when last year's actual costs are utilized as a standard to measure present performance (i.e., Dora Hepple).

• is weak operationally when information is neither timely nor relevant and the same information regarding current operations must be requested each month (i.e., Vern Hopp).

2. The perceptions of the B&B Company employees indicate there is a problem within the firm because there is an atmosphere of distrust, i.e., employees perceive the firm as a separate entity of which they are not an integral part.

C. 1. Behavioral Factor	2. Management Action to Address Behavioral Factor
• Complacency or belief that the present system is satisfactory	Management should explain the ineffectiveness of the present system and emphasize the desired results of the new system.
• Distrust of the new system	Management should maintain an attitude of openness and honesty by reporting findings and recommendations throughout the design and implementation of the new system.

- Feeling threatened by the new system

Management should encourage participation in the design and implementation of the new system by those affected by it.

- Fear of change

Management should explain the need for change and disclose the relevant findings of the System Review Task Force. Management should conduct training programs for operational personnel and retraining programs for accountants.

12.

A. Segment information in the annual financial report is prepared to meet public reporting standards. The statements are prepared in conformity with generally accepted accounting principles using segment definitions set forth by the FASB. Thus, these statements may lack sufficient detail to evaluate segment managers properly and may identify segments that do not coincide with management desires.

The annual financial report does not segregate costs by behavior or by controllability. These statements incorporate full absorption accounting including the allocation of common costs incurred for the benefit of more than one segment. The allocation of these common costs is necessarily arbitrary. The evaluation of segment managers should be based on reports incorporating responsibility accounting and should not include the allocation of nontraceable common costs. In addition, the annual financial report does not include budgeted amounts.

B. No, the best interests of Parton Co. are not likely to be served because segment information in the annual financial report is not generated for the purpose of evaluating segment managers. Arnston's suggestion is expedient at best and reveals a lack of understanding at worst. Segment managers would become frustrated and dissatisfied because they would be held responsible for an earnings figure that includes the arbitrary allocation of common costs, costs traceable to but not controllable by them, and no comparison with budgeted amounts for a segment for which they may not even be entirely responsible.

C. Parton Co. should prepare reports incorporating responsibility accounting for its various segment responsibility centers. Management should define the segment responsibility centers rather than using the segment rules developed for public financial reporting.

The report should utilize the contribution approach that would separate costs by behavior and assign costs to segments only if they could be traced to the segment. The contribution margin statement could disclose contribution margin, contribution controllable by segment managers, and contribution by segment, all of which are useful in evaluating segment management performance. The report should include budgeted amounts, actual amounts, and variances.

13.

A. Four factors that generally determine the level of employee participation in an organization's control system include management style, organizational environment or culture, performance measures, and the employee's desire to participate.

Managerial style, participative or directive, is a primary determinant in the level of employee participation. Regardless of the organizational environment, directive managers utilize low to medium levels of employee involvement based on the subordinates' desire to participate and the accuracy level of the control. Participative managers need to assess the organizational culture as participative or non-participative. Non-participative organizational cultures force these managers to maintain low to medium levels of participation (similar to directive managers), while participative organizations allow for medium to high levels of employee participation based on each employee's desires to become involved.

An organizational environment that is subject to turbulent changes, may require rapid decision making at lower levels and, consequently, greater employee participation.

B. The current standard cost system at the western plant failed to achieve the desired employee perception of a participatory management style. Ways to improve the situation include

- improving communications with the employees. While employees were involved in developing data for standard setting their recommendations were not necessarily incorporated.

- conducting frequent reviews of the standards to ensure that they are continually revised to attainable levels.

- establishing training programs to prepare employees to achieve the standards. The employees' current job skills may not be sufficient to meet management's standards.

- having top management explain the company's goals and the desired employee involvement in achieving those goals.

C. In addition to the control over work, other benefits that were derived at the southern plant from the installation of stop buttons include

- safety features that can stop action to avoid serious accidents.

- cost reductions as errors can be corrected before long runs of defective equipment is turned out.

- improvement in employee morale, increased concern for quality, and reduced resistance to change.

D. The ways that the northern plant and its employees could benefit from the introduction of quality circles include

- establishment of a participatory environment with the employees who would be affected by procedural changes.

- increased employee self-esteem and interest due to working jointly with management in the review of problems and their solutions.

- more immediate implementation and acceptance of decisions.

14.

A. Advantages that EGA Inc. might have realized from using an imposed budgetary approach for Bradley Resources include

• ensuring coordination, communication, and uniformity of corporate objectives while providing the Bradley employees with immediate feedback on the corporate planning process. This helps the new managers understand EGA's requirements and assists them in decision making.

• facilitating effective, direct, and more objective control over Bradley's operations and the allocation of resources. Security of critical corporate forecast information (i.e., new product developments, technological inventions, or corporate entity changes) is ensured.

B. EGA Inc. could have used communication to better advantage in implementing the imposed budgetary system by having a meeting with Bradley Resource's management and explaining that, due to the imposed budgeting process this year, strict accountability for actual performance as compared to the budget would not be justified. Therefore, the individual manager's concerns about his/her operating unit performance would be minimized. EGA's management should have informed Bradley Resource's management that a vehicle would be provided to reflect budget changes during the year for material adjustments, that an open-door policy was in place to discuss the budget further, and/or that Bradley Resource's management would participate in the budgeting process next year.

C. The advantages of the participatory budget system that EGA Inc. is now proposing for Bradley Resources are that the participatory budget system

• motivates and stimulates creative thinking, while positively affecting employee productivity and morale.

• promotes a willingness to be held accountable for goal achievement.

• elicits more comprehensive input from operations management about the budget and budget contingencies. There would be better control by line management in daily operations with the implementation of budget objectives.

The disadvantages of the participatory budget system that EGA Inc. is now proposing for Bradley Resources are that the participatory budget system

• takes more time (increasing the risk of the loss of market position) and is more costly (i.e., use of increased manhours and training costs).

• promotes conservative projections for later budget comparisons, non-efficient costs from increasing the budget by a percentage over last year's spending, and the manipulation of financial information to meet budget goals, which can lead to mediocre performance.

15.

A. The probable behavioral effects on the product-line unit managers of Spiral Laboratories caused by each of the four cost allocation methods is described below.

• **Charge based on sales.**
This arbitrary method without regard to actual usage of the legal services may cause the unit manager to argue that the charge is unfair or unjust and, thereby, cause interdepartmen-

tal conflict. The manager may feel penalized for good sales performance which results in an increase in legal costs. There is no incentive for the manager to be cost effective as (s)he will use as much legal service as possible, without regard to limits of the resource.

• **Corporate headquarters absorbs all charges.**
There is no incentive for the manager to be cost effective as to legal costs as (s)he will use as much legal service as possible, without regard to limits of the resource. The manager will typically react favorably to this method.

• **Fixed hourly charge based on competitive rates.**
Since the manager is now charged on a usage basis, (s)he is in control and will tend to react responsibly and with confidence. The manager may choose an external, rather than internal, legal source based on qualitative or urgency reasons as (s)he is indifferent to the costs of either source.

• **Fixed hourly charge based on full cost recovery.**
Since the manager is now charged on a usage basis, (s)he is in control and will tend to react responsibly and with confidence. If the underapplied and overapplied absorption of legal costs is distributed to the product lines on an annual historic basis, this will be perceived as a fair method, and the manager will react positively.

B. The possible effects on the adequacy and quality of legal services to be provided and/or utilized under each of the cost allocation methods is described below.

• **Charge based on sales.**
This arbitrary method, without regard to actual usage of the legal services, may produce a more than adequate level of legal attention being given to each business unit providing that the internal Legal Department is not at full capacity and that annual requirements are properly budgeted. If less than adequate requirements are provided legal efforts may be fragmented, of lesser quality, and may leave the corporation open to risk.

• **Corporate headquarters absorbs all charges.**
This arbitrary method, without regard to actual usage of the legal services, may also produce a more than adequate level of legal attention being given to each business unit providing that the internal Legal Department is not at full capacity and that annual requirements are properly budgeted. The product-line unit manager may overconsume legal resources.

• **Fixed hourly charge based on competitive rates.**
This method should provide adequate and quality service, as the product-unit managers will be indifferent to choosing internal or external legal services. The Legal Department would be most efficient using this method because it is competing with external legal services.

• **Fixed hourly charge based on full cost recovery.**
This method should provide adequate and quality service; however, the Legal Department could be inefficient due to a lack of competition with external legal services.

C. The probable effects on the behavior of Spiral Laboratories' corporate attorney caused by the use of each of the four cost allocation methods is described below.

• **Charge based on sales.**
The corporate attorney will continue to build staff to meet the

demand for services from the product-line unit managers as there appears to be no limits on the costs in the department.

• **Corporate headquarters absorbs all charges.**
The emphasis will be on corporate projects first while product unit needs will be a low priorty.

• **Fixed hourly charge based on competitive rates.**
This method would cause the corporate attorney to perform most efficiently, give the highest quality service, and become diplomatic with product-line unit managers.

• **Fixed hourly charge based on full cost recovery.**
This method may cause the corporate attorney to build staff to meet the demand for services from the product-line unit managers as the total cost of the department will be absorbed. The setting of priorities of legal projects will be determined by the corporate attorney with emphasis on corporate projects first since his/her performance review is done by corporate.

16.

A. 1. The characteristics that should be present in a standard cost system in order to encourage positive employee motivation include

  • participation in setting standards from all levels of the organization including purchasing, engineering, manufacturing, and accounting.

  • the integration of organizational communication by translating the organizational goals and objectives into monetary terms for the employees.

  • support of the standard cost system by management.

  • incorporation of standards that are perceived as achievable and accurate and apply to controllable costs.

2. A standard cost system should be implemented to positively motivate employees by

  • communicating the corporate objectives of a standard cost system.

  • soliciting from employees standards for which they will be held accountable.

  • tying the individual's performance in the standard cost system to the individual's performance review and reward system.

B. 1. "Management by exception" is the situation where management's attention is focused only on those items that deviate significantly from the standard. The assumption is, that foregoing a thorough, detailed analysis of all items, the manager has more time to concentrate on other managerial activities.

2. The behavioral implications of "Management by exception" include both positive and negative implications.
   On the positive side, this technique increases management efficiency by concentrating only on material variances, allowing time for the manager to concentrate on other activities.
   On the negative side, managers tend only to focus on the negative variances rather than positive ones limiting their employee interactions to negative reinforcement or punish-

ment. This technique may not indicate detrimental trends at an early stage and fragmentation of efforts can occur from dealing only with the specific problems rather than global issues.

C. Employee behavior could be adversely affected when "actual to budget" comparisons are used as the basis for performance evaluation. Employees may subvert the system and submit budgets that are low so (s)he can meet or exceed the budget favorably, thereby averting negative reinforcement for varying unfavorably to budget. There can be a minimal level of motivation since exceptional performance is not rewarded. Employees may strive for mediocrity and not work up to his/her full potential.

17.

A. Criteria to be used when selecting the operational activities for which performance measures are to be established include the following:

• The activity should be repetitive in nature, with repetition occurring in relatively short cycles.

• The input and output (product or service) of the activity should be measurable and uniform.

• The input and output (product or service) of the activity should be measurable and uniform.

• The elements of cost, such as direct material, direct labor and overhead, must be defined clearly at the unit level of activity.

B. Behavioral issues that need to be considered when selecting the level of performance to be incorporated into the cost standards include the following:

• The standards must be established in such a way so as to be legitimate. The standards need not reflect the actual cost of a single item or cycle. However, they will ideally represent the cost that will be incurred in the production of a given product or the performance of a given operation.

• The standards must be established in such a way so as to be attainable. When the standards are set too high, the repeated failure to achieve them will tend to reduce the motivation for attainment. The converse is true. Standards which are too loose represent an invitation to relax.

• The participant should have a voice or influence in the establishment of standards and resulting performance measures. Involvement in the formulation of standards give the participant a greater sense of worth in the decision-making aspects of the company.

C. 1. The role of the Accounting Department in the establishment of standards is to determine the suitability of standards in terms of their ability to be quantified and to provide dollar values for specific unit standards.

2. The role of the department in which the performance is being

measured in the establishment of standards is to provide information for realistic standards and to allow for subsequent performance evaluation for the purpose of detecting problems and improving performance.

3. The role of the Industrial Engineering Department in the establishment of standards is to provide reliable measures of physical activities related to the standards of performance and to verify the consistency of the performance measures between departments.

18.

A. The benefits, other than better cost control, that are likely to accrue to Extra Strength Materials (ESM) from the implementation of departmental budgeting include

• improved communications and coordination among departments.

• earlier identification of problems and/or potential company weaknesses.

• better definition of accountability (responsibility accounting) and performance expectations.

B. The behavioral issues that the introduction of a departmental budgeting system is likely to raise with ESM's department managers may be both positive and negative.

Positive issues are likely to include

• increased motivation to achieve budgets if they are perceived as attainable.

• acceptance of the risks and rewards associated with budget accountability.

• acceptance of performance evaluations if budgeting was participative.

Negative issues may include

• fear of punishment if budgets are not achieved.

• fear of loss of control and authority.

• confusion over the options of achieving the budget vs. schedule vs. quality.

C. The behavioral issues that the introduction of a departmental budgeting system is likely to raise with ESM's production workers may be both positive and negative.

Positive issues are likely to include

• acceptance of performance evaluations based on attainable budget expectations.

• a sense of commitment and ownership if they participate in the budget-setting process.

Negative issues are likely to include

• fear of punishment for not achieving budgets.

• fear that greater control could lead to loss of jobs.

• sabotage of the budgeting system or giving up if it is perceived that budgets are not attainable.

D. The likely reactions of ESM's employees after several months experience with actual results vs. budget include the following.

• If objectives are not attained, employees could

  - see them as unrealistic and become negative or ignore budgets.

  - become stressed and adversely affect performance and performance evaluations.

• If employees feel objectives are/were attainable, they could

  - increase motivation by fostering a spirit to improve operations if they participated in the budgeting process.

  - foster a feeling of partnership with management in achieving results.

• View management as an enemy.

• Perceive a feeling of more ocntrol over their jobs since job direction and constraints are well defined; however, employees may also have fears of job loss due to the increased control.

19.

A. Based on the conversation between Terry Travers and Bob Christensen, it seems likely that their motivation would be stifled by the variance reporting system at Aurora Manufacturing Company. Their behavior may include any of the following.

• Suboptimization, a condition in which individual managers disregard major company goals and focus their attention solely on their own division's activities.

• Frustration from untimely reports and formats that are not useful in their daily activities.

B. 1. The benefits that can be derived by both the company and its employees from a properly implemented variance reporting system include the following.

• Variance analysis can provide standards and measures for incentive and performance evaluation programs.

• Variance reporting can emphasize teamwork and interdepartmental dependence.

• Timely reporting provides useful feedback, helps to identify problems, and aids in solving these problems. Responsibility can be assigned for the resolution of problems.

2. Aurora Manufacturing Company could improve its variance reporting system, so as to increase employee motivation, by implementing the following.

• Introduce a flexible budgeting system that relates actual expenditures to actual levels of production on a monthly basis. In addition, the budgeting process should be participative rather than imposed.

• Only those costs that are controllable by managers should be included in the variance analysis.

• Distribute reports on a more timely basis to allow quick resolution of problems.

• Reports should be stated in terms that are most understandable to the users, i.e., units of output, hours, etc.

20.

A. The performance evaluation process of Roland Industries has the following apparent weaknesses.

- Performance measures should be based upon the organization's objectives and on how each division can contribute toward the accomplishment of those objectives. Roland's top management apparently has not gone through this process in selecting performance measures for each division, but instead has accepted a single index to be used by all divisions.

- Although the performance measure was communicated to Futak when he became the Division Manager, he was not told the target ROA for his division. In addition, the feedback given to Futak during the year lacked specificity, and the communication between Poskey and Futak has been insufficient.

- The performance measure was not mutually agreed upon in advance by Poskey and Futak.

B. Motor Works' assets were increased by plant expansion that consisted of additions, both to the buildings and to the equipment, and replacement of obsolete and fully depreciated equipment. The equipment replacement would have increased the amount of assets employed because the book value of the old equipment was zero. The expansion and improvement of the facility should result in a correspondingly greater output, but a catchup period during which new markets are developed would normally be required.

C. The following criteria should be used in selecting performance measures to evaluate operating managers.

- The measures should be objective and verifiable and should relate only to that which is controllable by the operating managers. The measures should be congruent with the organization's goals and objectives and include a standard for comparison with actual results.

- The measures should address efficiency and effectiveness and should be mutually agreed upon by operating managers and their superiors.

D. The three criteria of dollar profit, receivables turnover, and inventory turnover are appropriate. They satisfy the criteria for performance measures discussed in Requirement C. The three criteria emphasize the need to balance profit making activities with the control of receivables and inventories. There is no conflict among the three performance measures which means that their use should not be counter-productive. Dollar profit is an appropriate measure because it avoids the problem of how to value the asset base that occurs with ROA; thus, the division manager can emphasize revenue generation and cost control to maximize dollar profit. Receivables turnover is an appropriate measure because the collection period should be kept as short as possible in order to minimize the investment in receivables. Inventory turnover is an appropriate measure because a company should move its inventory as quickly as possible in order to minimize the investment in inventory. Furthermore, because profits are a function of turnover, an increase in either receivables turnover or inventory turnover would increase the third criterion of dollar profit. The three criteria are consistent with

one another and allow an analysis and evaluation of the parts as well as the whole.

21.

1. The report has few desirable features in terms of its form and appearance in presenting the information requested. The desirable features include the following:

- The report includes an appropriate heading.
- Data is organized in columns for comparative purposes.
- Notes (1) and (2) are referenced to the body of the report.

Undesirable features in terms of its form and appearance in presenting the information requested include the following.

- Column headings lack specificity. The report should make clear that the first two columns are costs.

- The report should compare Alternative No. 1 to Alternative No. 2 instead of comparing each alternative to the irrelevant present operations.

- The report appears overly weighted to the notes, perhaps contrary to what the Committee expects from a Controller's presentation. In addition, notes (3) through (9) are not referenced to the body of the report.

2. The desirable features of the report in terms of its content are that the costs of each alternative are presented and the notes are included to help interpret the contents of the numerical schedule and to present additional qualitative information.

The undesirable features of the report in terms of its content include the following.

- The amount for the use of the existing building (1) is not relevant and should not be included because the amount is the historical cost of the existing building, i.e., a sunk cost.

- The report does not explicitly state that the straight-line method of depreciation will be used for tax purposes, although that is the implication of note (6). The straight-line method may not be the preferable method of depreciation for tax purposes.

- The tax effects of the alternatives should not be omitted. The fact that management is committed to following one or the other of the two courses of action does not change the fact that taxes, including the investment tax credit, would be different for the two alternatives.

- The salvage value of replaced facilities and new facilities should be included because their realization is different for the two alternatives.

- The description of the behavior of the production people and the assumption of the behavior's cause should not be included in the report.

- The logistics problem mentioned in note (5) lacks specificity and the backup schedules referred to in note (4) should be included with the report.

- The average savings of $1,200 per unit in note (3) lacks meaning because of the wide range of units, i.e., hitch-on trailers to motorized homes.

22.

A. The corporate practices and policies that must be present within Western Corporation for the strategic plan to be effective include:

- continued, visible management support for the plan.

- clear communication of the plan to all key personnel.

- structuring the organization to facilitate achievement of the plan's objectives.

- delegating the responsibility for implementing the plan.

- associating rewards with the achievement of the plan's objectives.

B. 1. The important characteristics that differentiate Western Corporation's three subsidiaries include growth potential, profitability, discretionary cash flow, regulatory involvement and level of risk.

2. The electric utility has limited growth because of regulatory constraints and complete market penetration. The division has predictable profits that will allow it to generate cash to support the other divisions. In order to maintain profitability, the division has been directed to concentrate on the efficiency of operations and effective relations with regulators.

The natural resources subsidiary has a high level of risk associated with both profit and growth potential. The plan to divest the low-potential assets will reduce the risk. The development of a profit and growth plan for the remaining assets coupled with an influx of cash from the electric utility would help this division contribute to the overall profitability of the corporation.

The electronics subsidiary exhibits a high potential for both growth and profitability with an acceptable level of risk. The corporation has placed a high priority on the development of this division by allocating discretionary resources to support its growth and diversification. The expansion of the subsidiary will make it a good training ground for the corporation's future officers.

C. The top management of the electric utility will be challenged by the strategic plan to operate the utility in the most efficient manner. However, their motivation will be limited by the lack of growth potential for this facility and by the diversion of discretionary funds to the electronics subsidiary. All of management, but especially middle management, will view the strategy of developing all future officers in the electronics subsidiary as career limiting. This may encourage the utility's managers to ask to be transferred to the electronics subsidiary or to seek employment elsewhere.

23.

A. The advantages associated with the use of incentive plans include:

- generating potentially higher income levels as managers try to meet their objectives by reducing operating costs or developing strategies providing quick returns.

- forcing management to plan and develop goals and to review its operations.

- promoting employee participation in goal formulation, making goal congruence and acceptance more likely.

- developing objective performance measures that provide communication and feedback to managers so that they know what is expected of them.

The disadvantages associated with the use of incentive plans include:

- too much emphasis on short-term rather than long-term objectives or the shifting of events between periods to enhance short-term performance.

- rejection or manipulation of plans because employees perceive the goals as unattainable or too complex.

- manipulation of earnings to take advantage of incentive plans.

- negative cost/benefit of the plan.

B. 1. Galaxy's incentive plan proposal evaluates and compensates the manager and key personnel in each division. These are the personnel in the operating unit that bear the brunt of all of the unit's decisions and, therefore, should share in the reward.

The plan's measurement standard, each division's annual operating plan, is the most basic method of evaluation because it is easily understood and a normal function of operations. This measure eliminates noncontrollable expenses from the base for the bonus. Furthermore, the division's operating plan was developed by the divisional manager and approved by corporate management during the annual budget process promoting participation, determination, and acceptance of objectives by management. Reliance on one central measurement, the operating plan, may not provide a tight enough standard but the possible inclusion of complementary standards such as plan improvement over last year's results would help put managers on the right track.

The minimum acceptable level for performance, i.e., 90 percent of the division's budgeted operating income before corporate and capital allocations, is easily understood and performance is objectively determined.

The graduated bonus should provide an incentive to achieve the maximum unless the dollar impact is too small. The setting of an upper limit can cause managers to not put forth their best effort or to shift events. The fact that achievement above the maximum percentage will be reviewed by the Compensation Committee of the Board of Directors for any additional bonus awards provides a means of flexibility in awarding exceptional performance.

The review by the Compensation Committee of the Board of Directors provides additional flexibility and rewards for non-financial results or the achievement of strategic goals as determined by upper management. However, it introduces an element of subjectivity into the plan and, therefore, opens the door for politics and bias.

2. The key management personnel of each of Galaxy's four divisions could be influenced by the plan's provisions as follows.

- The management of Star Manufacturing would likely find the plan acceptable because it is in a growth industry. Star should be able to reach its planned operating income and also readily achieve 110 percent of its goal, particularly if conservative goals are set. The company would then focus on qualifying for the additional bonus awarded by the Compensation Committee. The fact that Star's business is affected by uncontrollable factors such as the economy and strong competition could discourage the division's personnel.

• Because of its patents and the monopolistic nature of its market, Sun Appliances could determine an achievable operating plan that would motivate its key personnel. However, the division has little potential for growth, and Sun's executives could resent the key personnel of the growth divisions. In order to increase its market share, Sun would have to incur the expense of developing new products. This type of expenditure could qualify Sun for the 15 percent additional bonus.

• The management personnel of Venus Services are likely to be highly motivated by the plan as the division has strong growth and profit potential. The fact that the plan includes a cap of 110 percent of budgeted operating income could slow the growth of the division because there is no reward for exceeding the cap. The division could shift emphasis to the next year or the 15 percent additional bonus.

• The management of Comet Engineering should have little difficulty developing an achievable operating plan because of the nature of the Division's contracts. However, because of the fixed fee constraints of its contracts, Comet will be unable to achieve outstanding performance and the key personnel may not be motivated by the plan and could resent the executives of the growth divisions.

24.

A. A business has the characteristics required for decentralized profit centers when the segments of the business exercise responsibility for both producing (or purchasing) and marketing a product or group of products. Newworld Co. possesses these characteristics.

While Newworld is considering reorganizing its company according to product lines, many of the company's functions have already been organized in that manner. The production facilities for the two products (plastic and brass) are in separate plants because the technologies are different. The marketing effort is already segregated within the present sales function. With the reorganization by product line, each product center would be responsible for sales policy, manufacturing policy, and product development of existing lines. Consequently, the product centers of Newworld are profit centers because they are responsible for both producing and marketing the products under their control.

B. Mr. Knight is probably correct in his assessment that the proposed capital investment framework grants too much freedom to the divisions. Newworld's long-run performance is dependent upon its capital investments. While divisions must have some responsibility for capital investments for the proposed organization structure to be effective, corporate management must maintain adequate control to direct the future course of the firm. Under the proposed framework, division management controls a substantial portion of the capital budget and in some years few funds would be available for investment by corporate management. The present proposal would reduce corporate management's ability to diminish a

product line, and it also would impair management's ability to have adequate funds available for investment in new businesses.

Capital investment procedures should involve both division and corporate managements in such a way that corporation management should still be able to control the future direction of the firm. Such procedures might include classification of capital projects into groups, some of which could be approved by division management without corporate management study.

An alternative to the Newworld capital investment program might have the following features:
1. All proposed investment projects would be classified according to their nature—replacement, cost savings, expansion.
2. Replacement and cost savings projects could be adopted by division management alone without approval of corporate management, providing an individual project did not exceed a specified dollar limit and the total of such projects did not exceed another specified dollar limit. The dollar limits would reflect the nature and size of each division's operations.
3. All expansion projects or other projects that exceed the dollar limit would be submitted to corporate management for evaluation and approval.

25.

A. Clarkson Company appears to have a very well developed budgetary system. Budgets for each of the important areas requiring attention—sales, production, inventory levels, expenses, and capital investments—are included in the process. Insufficient details are provided to properly evaluate the construction and use of the budgets for sales, capital investment, and production and inventory levels. Thus, the analysis in this case must focus on the expense of the budgeting process.

Although there appears to be an elaborate budget process, analysis of the expense procedures reveals a number of shortcomings for planning and control purposes. The basic input to the expense budget for the coming year is the first six months of the current year's actual performance, the expense budget (modified to reflect uncontrollable events), and the corporate expense reduction percentage. The next expense budget is basically last year's actual costs reduced by the computed expense percentage.

This approach does not capture the full potential of the budget for planning purposes. A budget for planning purposes should be forward-looking. The Clarkson budget is based primarily on past results and does not recognize any planned changes in operating activities. The across-the-board corporate expense reduction target does not consider the differences among plants for opportunities for cost improvements. The review with division management may permit the "strong" managers to build slack into the budget. And, the facts do not make clear whether the proposed budget is based upon the current year sales volume or the planned volume for the budget year. If such adjustment is not made, then this is an additional weakness of the Clarkson procedure.

The process also falls short for control purposes. The major shortcoming is its failure to incorporate changes in operations that occur subsequent to August. Comparisons of performances that include these late changes with budgets that do not will not provide useful information for control. The inclusion of allocated corporation and division costs in plant budgets would make the expense budgets less effective for control purposes because they contain irrelevant data. The possibility that some division managers may be able to introduce slack into their budgets also reduces the effectiveness for cost control.

The budget process appears to omit the plant managers from active participation in budget preparation and revision. Participation by them likely would improve the cost control and planning benefits of the budget process. The use of across-the-board expense cuts and inclusion of allocated costs in the budgets used for performance measurement is further evidence that the company has failed to consider the effect of its system on management employees.

The company does have a budgetary system and does make an effort to provide for planning and control of its operations. Clarkson probably is better off for having developed its system to this point. However, further benefits could be gained by improving upon the weaknesses of its procedures.

B. Return on assets is not a good measure for evaluating the performance to the Dexter Plant. Too many factors used to compute the ROA are not within the control of plant management. The plant management appears to have effective control only over the plant level incurred costs. A significant portion of the "return"side of the measure is determined by the action of higher level management—sales and allocated costs. The same is true for the asset base. Corporate and division assets are allocated to the plant. In addition, it appears that specific assets may be charged to the plant even though the decision was made at a higher level.

C. The question states that the recommendations for promotions and salary increases for plant managers are influenced by the comparison of the budgeted return on assets to the actual return. It appears that this plant manager is reacting in direct response to this measurement system. Two events have occurred, both outside the manager's control (the sales decline and extra land charges), which will reduce the ROA measure. The manager has responded by affecting those components of the measure that he/she controls and which will improve this measure. The costs reduced—training, maintenance and repair, and certain labor—would not affect sales volume in the short-run. It is also likely that reduction of inventory levels will not influence the sales in the short-run. By these actions the manager has improved the ROA for 1973, but it may well be at the expense of 1974 or later.

26.

A. The proposed Achievement of Objective System (AOS) would be an improvement over the current measure of divisional performance for the following reasons:

• There appears to be greater participation in the establishment of objectives by divisional managers.
• The use of multiple criteria for performance measures should be a more equitable standard of evaluation. This performance measure tends to reduce over-emphasis on single measurement

criteria and may also balance extremes in performance in one area versus another.
• Realistic planning encourages accurate budget estimations and promotes intermediate and long-range planning objectives which enhance goal congruence.
• Static budgets established six months before the start of the year would be replaced by flexible budgets which would be subject to change as needed.
• The emphasis on performance is based upon factors controllable by and upon efforts actually directed by divisional managers.

B. Specific performance measures for the criteria "doing better than last year" could include total sales, contribution margin, controllable costs, net income, net income as a function of sales, return on investment, market share, and productivity. Measurement of these items should be compared in absolute terms or by percentages to the prior year.

Specific performance measures for the criteria "planning realistically" could include an analysis of variance between actual and budget and the use of a flexible budget to determine sales, net income as a function of sales, and return on investment.

Specific performance measures for the criteria "managing current assets" could include accounts receivable turnover, inventory turnover, return on current assets, and year to year comparisons of current assets in total and by account classification.

C. The motivational and behavioral aspects of the achievement of objectives system depend upon the level of acceptance of the system by top management and the divisional managers.

• Divisional managers could have a sense of participation in the role of goal setting and budget development which could encourage goal congruence.
• Multiple criteria enhance a sense of equity or fairness, and remove pressures to pursue measured goals, the achievement of which may conflict with corporate long-run objectives (i.e., promotes goal congruence).
• Divisional managers should have an increased sense of responsibility and control over activities within their divisions once they are not held responsible for uncontrollable factors.
• Top management support along with timely and regular reviews of performance will promote division manager's feeling of self-worth.

Programs which may be instituted to promote morale and give incentives to divisional managers in conjunction with the achievement of objectives system include the following.

• Intrinsic motivators can be provided by allowing the manager to assess his/her own achievement and his/her own worth.
• Extrinsic motivators can be developed through a manager's competition against him/herself or with other divisions with recognition given to the successful participants in the form of awards or monetary incentives.
• Increased morale can result from participation in budget setting and management level decisions as well as having positive feedback.

27.

A. Roach division management's attitude at the present time should be positive to each of these prices in decreasing order because Roach apparently has unused capacity. Roach division management performance is evaluated based on return on investment (ROI) and each of these prices exceed variable costs which will increase Roach's ROI.

At the time when all existing capacity is being used, Roach division management would want the inter-company transfer price to generate the same amount of profit as outside business in order to maximize division ROI.

B. Negotiation between the two divisions is the best method to settle on a transfer price. The MBR Company is organized on a highly decentralized basis and each of the four conditions necessary for negotiated transfer prices exist. These conditions are:

- An outside market exists that provides both parties with an alternative.
- Both parties have access to market price information.
- Both parties are free to buy and sell outside the corporation.
- Top management supports the continuation of the decentralized management concept.

C. No, the management of MBR should not become involved in this controversy. The company is organized on a highly decentralized basis which top management must believe will maximize long-term profits. Imposing corporate restrictions will adversely affect the current management evaluation system because division management would no longer have complete control of profits. In addition, the addition of corporate restrictions could have a negative impact on division management who are accustomed to an autonomous working environment.

28.

A. A cost-based human resource accounting (HRA) system basically views the costs of obtaining and improving the talent of the firm's employees as having long-term benefits to the firm instead of current outflows with no future returns. Therefore, in a cost-based HRA system, the costs incurred in recruiting, hiring, training, and developing personnel would be capitalized as an asset. These costs would not be expensed in the period in which they were incurred unless their usefulness expired. These capitalized costs would be amortized over the period of expected benefit.

B. The costs incurred to hire and develop the 20 skilled employees are sunk costs and are not relevant to the firing decision per se. The accumulated amortization as well as the process of charging HRA amortization to income are not relevant to this decision.

However, to the extent that these costs represent costs which will be incurred in the future when new skilled people must be hired, they are useful input to the decision process. An estimate of future HRA costs (based on historical HRA costs) will indicate the costs to be avoided if the existing skilled people are maintained instead of being fired. It is possible that the costs avoided by keeping the existing people, perhaps in unskilled positions, would significantly influence the decision.

C. A current replacement value HRA system might be more useful in estimating the future costs to be avoided by not firing some or all of the 20 skilled workers. If people are terminated with no intended replacement, the HRA costs avoided would be zero; this is apparently the case with 15 of the 20 skilled workers in the Consumers Products Division of Liberty Manufacturing Company. Some assessment of the behavioral costs seems important although they would be difficult to measure. Also future costs of spoilage, inefficiency, damaged goods, etc., which occur during the learning phase of newly hired replacements should be estimated and considered along with other avoided costs.

29.

A. A responsibility accounting system seeks to provide reports of actual costs incurred as a result of a department manager's (or other suitable subdivision head within the organization) decisions (i.e., only those costs controllable by a manager would be included) for comparison with planned or budgeted costs. The resulting differences are analyzed allowing management to react to variances from budget conditions. The purpose of the system is to provide managers with information on their performance and to allow an evaluation of managers based on costs the individual manager can control.

A responsibility accounting system could help resolve the concerns of Kelly's production managers in that they would be held responsible only for services they ordered and used, and not for any inefficiencies of the Maintenance Center.

B. The primary behavioral advantage generally attributed to responsibility accounting systems is increased managerial motivation because managerial behavior is influenced by how the manager's performance is measured. A responsibility accounting system promotes a clearer understanding of goals of the subunit. It also provides increased awareness and control of costs and activities which require managerial attention. Regular feedback to managers may have independent motivational effects and will improve morale.

C. The overall responsibility for maintenance and control is a joint responsibility of both operating and maintenance management. The report should emphasize a team concept and aid the users in understanding the goals, both of their center and of Kelly Petroleum Company as a whole. The reporting system should assign costs on a causal/responsibility basis. For instance, the Maintenance Center Manager has responsibility for preventive maintenance costs, for efficient operation of the central shop, and for the overhead of a maintenance department. The production center managers have supervision responsibility for the repair of the machines in the field whether as the result of a breakdown or discovery during preventive maintenance. Thus, the responsibility reports should reflect this division of management control.

The actual costs incurred for central shop repairs and for preventive maintenance, parts at actual costs, and labor at predetermined hourly rates, for each class of labor, would be charged to the Maintenance Center Manager. The overhead costs of the Maintenance Center would be charged to him, also.

The budget for the Maintenance Center would include amounts for the costs within Pepper's control.

The costs incurred for field repairs—actual part costs plus repair labor time at predetermined hourly rates for each class of labor—would be charged to the production departments. The production departments' budgets would include amounts for these costs.

30.

A. 1. The annual report is a one-way communication device. This requires an emphasis on clarity and conciseness because there is no immediate feedback from the readers as to what messages they are receiving.

The preparer must attempt to identify the users/audience of the report, and to determine their values, beliefs, and needs. Then the preparer can determine the language, i.e., words and phrases, that would be appropriate and familiar to the users/audience.

The preparer must also consider the organization of the material in the report. Logical ordering and attractive formatting facilitate the transmission of ideas.

2. The different users of annual reports have differing information needs, backgrounds, and abilities. For some users, the annual report may serve as an introduction to the company and/or the only significant information about the company. By using the report to communicate to all users, the problems the corporation faces include the following.

• In an attempt to reach several audiences, a company may include information for each audience. As a consequence, the annual report may grow in size and complexity to the point where it contains more information than many users want to receive or are able to comprehend, i.e., information overload. In some cases, technical concepts may be reduced to more common concepts; this reduces precision and conciseness thereby leading to more generalization.

• Care must be taken in the presentation of information. Words and phrases familiar to one user group may not be understood by those in other user groups. Graphic displays that are meaningful to some may be meaningless to others.

B. 1. Annual reports meet the statutory requirement that publicly held corporations are to report annually to stockholders and report on the stewardship of management to both current and potential stockholders. The reports include the financial and operating disclosures necessary to evaluate the risks of and potential returns on investment. However, the volume of data presented in annual reports can result in information overload that reduces the value of the report. Confusion can result from reducing technical concepts to common concepts or by the presentation of duplicate messages by different forms of media.

2. The set of audited comparative financial statements provides the basis for analysis done by financial analysts. Notes, which are an integral part of the statements, describe or explain various items in the statements, present additional detail, or summarize significant accounting policies.

Financial analysts are the most sophisticated class of users of annual reports and are able to ignore subjective interpretations included in the reports. However, some data may be too condensed, and they may need information in addition to annual reports to facilitate their analyses.

3. Annual reports provide employees with a year-end review of the results to which they have contributed during the year. In this sense, the annual report provides reinforcement and rewards. The annual report also informs or reminds employees of the organization's values and objectives and sensitizes them to the aspects of the organization with which they are not familiar. On the other hand, the employee already knows how the organization is performing so the annual report does not provide any substantive additional information.

C. Management may decide to omit information entirely from the annual report or to disguise it because competitors have access to annual reports. The objective of reporting should be to reveal as much as possible without giving away proprietary information or a competitive edge.

31.

A. 1. The positive and negative behavoral implications arising from employing a negotiated transfer price system for goods exchanged between divisions include the following.

Positive

• Both the buying and selling divisions have participated in the negotiations and are likely to believe they have agreed on the best deal posible.

• Negotiating and determining transfer prices will enhance the autonomy/independence of the divisions.

Negative

• The result of a negotiated transfer price between divisions may not be optimal for the firm as a whole and therefore will not be goal congruent.

• The negotiating process may cause harsh feelings and conflicts between divisions.

2. The behavioral problems which can arise from using actual full (absorption) manufacturing costs as a transfer price include the following.

• Full-cost transfer pricing is not suitable for a decentralized structure where the autonomous divisions are measured on profitability as the selling unit is unable to realize a profit.

• This method can lead to decisions that are not goal congruent if the buying unit decides to buy outside at a price less than the full-cost of the selling unit. If the selling unit is not operating at full capacity, it should reduce the transfer price to the market price if this would allow the recovery of variable costs plus a portion of the fixed costs. This price reduction would optimize overall company performance.

B. The behavorial problems that could arise, if Lynsar Corporation decides to change its transfer pricing policy to one that would apply uniformly to all divisions, include the following.

- A change in policy may be interpreted by the divisional managers as an attempt to decrease their freedom to make decisions and reduce their autonomy. This perception could lead to reduced motivation.

- If managers lose control of transfer prices and, thus, some control over profitability they will be unwilling to accept the change to uniform prices.

- Selling divisions will be motivated to sell outside if the transfer price is lower than market as this behavior is likely to increase profitability and bonuses.

C. The likely behavior of both "buying" and "selling" divisional managers, for each of the following transfer pricing methods being considered by Lynsar Corporation, include the following.

1. Standard full manufacturing costs plus a markup.

The selling divisions will be motivated to control costs because any costs over standard cannot be passed on to the buying division an will reduce the profit of the selling division.

The buying divisions may be pleased with this transfer price if the market price is higher. However, if the market price is lower and the buying divisions are forced to take the transfer price, the managers of the buying divisions will be unhappy.

2. Market selling price of the product being transferred.

Creates a fair and equal chance for the buying and selling divisions to make the most profit they can and should promote cost control, motivate divisional management, and optimize overall company performance. Since both parties are aware of the market price, there will be no distrust between the parties, and both should be willing to enter into the transaction.

3. Outlay (out-of-pocket) costs incurred to the point of transfer plus opportunity cost per unit.

This method is the same as market price when there is an established market price and the seller is at full capacity. At any level below full capacity, the transfer price is the outlay cost only (as there is no opportunity cost) which would approximate the variable costs of the good being transferred.

Both buyers and sellers should be willing to transfer under this method because the price is the best either party should be able to realize for the product under the circumstances. This method should promote overall goal congruence, motivate managers, and optimize overall company profits.

32.

A. Among the reasons transfer prices based on cost are not appropriate as a divisional performance measure are because they

- provide little incentive for the selling division to control manufacturing costs as all costs incurred will be recovered.

- often lead to suboptimal decisions for the company as a whole.

B. Using the market price as the transfer price the contribution margin for both the Mining Division and the Metals Division for the year ended May 31, 1993 is as calculated in Exhibit 1 below.

Exhibit 1		
Ajax Consolidated Calculation of Divisional Contribution Margin For the Year Ended May 31, 1993		
	Mining Division	Metals Division
Selling price	$90	$150
Less: Variable costs		
Direct material	12	6
Direct labor	16	20
Manufacturing overhead	24[1]	10[2]
Transfer price		90
Unit contribution margin	$38	$ 24
Volume	x 400,000	x 400,000
Total contribution margin	$15,200,000	$9,600,000

[1] Variable overhead = $32 x 75% = $24.
[2] Variable overhead = $25 x 40% = $10.

Note:
The $5 variable selling cost that the Mining Division would incur for sales on the open market should not be included as this is an internal transfer.

C. If the use of a negotiated transfer price was instituted by Ajax Consolidated, which also permitted the divisions to buy and sell on the open market, the price range for toldine that would be acceptable to both divisions would be determined as follows.

The Mining Division would like to sell to the Metals Division for the same price it can obtain on the outside market, $90 per unit. However, Mining would be willing to sell the toldine for $85 per unit as the $5 variable selling cost would be avoided.

The Metals Division would like to continue paying the bargain price of $66 per unit. However, if Mining does not sell to Metals, Metals would be forced to pay $90 on the open market. Therefore, Metals would be satisfied to receive a price concession from Mining equal to the costs that Mining would avoid by selling internally. Therefore, a negotiated transfer price for toldine between $85 and $90 would benefit both divisions and the company as a whole.

D. A negotiated transfer price is the most likely to elicit desirable management behavior as it will

- encourage the management of the Mining Division to be

more conscious of cost control.

• benefit the Metals Division by providing toldine at less cost than its competitors.

• provide a more realistic measure of divisional performance.

33.

A. At least three reasons why an effective control system is necessary for JEM Associates inc. to realize their strategic goals for the next three years include

• measurement of progress against established strategic control points ensuring goal congruence.

• allowance for timely corrective action of identified problems.

• adapting to changing conditions.

B. Preliminary controls are used to control input resources prior to the organizational transition process to prevent problems before they occur. Instead of waiting for results and comparing them with goals, control can be exerted by limiting activities in advance. These controls include policy manuals, budgets, rigid quality standards when purchasing from vendors, monitoring customer credit ratings before allowing purchases, and appropriate raining programs for internal personnel.

Screening controls are used to oversee the ongoing transformation process, guaranteeing that organizational objectives are being met. These controls are the heart of the control system. Included are quality controls while a product is being manufactured such as inspectors or calibration machines, and controls to ensure that a product is timely produced in the correct quantities. Also included are monitoring of labor productivity on a daily basis while the products are produced and online verification of customer accounts for the sales representatives.

Post-action controls are used to control the output of the process after the transformation is completed and to provide corrective action for problems encountered. These controls include variance analysis reports, analysis of scrapped material, performance evaluations, and feedback such as employee quality circles, customer surveys, and comments.

C. 1. Employees frequently resist controls because controls may imply that someone else is watching for that the employee is now accountable to someone else. Controls can restrict the individual's actions which can negatively affect status and other social needs. Employees who naturally resist change may also resist controls due to a change in expertise and power structures and a lack of understanding or knowledge of organizational objectives.

2. The characteristics that make controls effective and acceptable include

• employee participation in the establishment of valid performance standards in clear and concise terms (such as management by objectives) to increase employee acceptance.

• timely feedback information with clear measurement and variance analysis.

• checks and balances within the system to ensure objective evaluation of employee performance that includes positive reinforcement and rewards.

Index

Competence, 11
Competitive ability, of firms, 70
Completeness, of financial statements, 6
Compound interest method, of
  depreciation, 208
Confidentiality, 11
Conservatism, in financial statements,
  3, 4
Continuous budgets, 18, 19
Contribution margin, 83, 129, 132,
  134-143
Control accounts, 20, 22
Controllable variance, 167
Controlling, of business operations, 92,
  131
Conversion costs, 17, 18
Cost Accounting Standards Board, 23, 24
Cost allocation, 17-27
Cost centers, 205, 235
Cost classification, 17
Cost control, 129
Cost object, 24
Cost of Production Report, 27, 28
Cost system, standard, 138
Cost-volume-profit analysis, 83-89,
  129, 132, 138
Costing:
  absorption, 99, 129-141
  direct, 18, 19, 129-131
  job order, 18-27
  process, 18, 19, 24-38
Costs:
  allocation of, 20-34, 242, 243
  related to volume and profits, 129,
    132, 133
  relevant range of, 87
  of replacement, 207, 208
  of selling division, in transfer pricing,
    211-212
  types:
    administrative, 23
    budgeted, 168
    committed, 86-87
    common, 19, 132, 134
    controllable, 230
    conversion, 18
    differential, 24
    direct, 17, 103, 129-143
    direct labor, 17
    discretionary fixed, 134
    fixed, 18, 85, 86
    fixed manufacturing, 129
    full, 24, 183
    historical, 5, 6, 7
    incremental, 19, 22, 24, 132, 134, 212
    indirect labor, 18
    indirect materials, 18
    job cost, 183
    joint, 24-29, 132, 134, 136
    managed, 86

Costs: (continued)
  types:
    manufacturing, 17
    marginal, 132, 212
    mixed, 87
    nonmanufacturing, 18
    opportunity, 19, 212, 213
    overhead, 20-34
    prime, 18
    programmed, 86
    responsibility, 24, 230
    semivariable, 18, 87
    service departments, 23,
    standard, 18, 19, 138, 168, 170, 182
    sunk, 18, 19
    value added, 19
    variable, 18, 83, 86, 90, 129, 134
Cross-impact analysis, 72, 73
Crowing shield, Gerald R. 179
Current value statements, 208
Currently attainable standards, 167
Cycle time, 42, 43

Data, 1, 2
Decentralization, 205-206
Decisions, 241
Defective units, 17
Delphi method, of forecasting, 73, 74
Denominator variance (see Volume
  variance)
Depreciation, compound interest
  method, 209
Differential costs (see Incremental costs)
Direct costing, 19, 100, 129-143
  advantages of, 133
  compared to absorption costing,
    130-131
  disadvantages of 133
  external use of, 133-134
  internal use of, 131-133
  and profit, 129-130
Direct costs, 132
Direct labor:
  budget, 95, 98
  costs, 17
  standards, 170-171
Direct materials, 168-171
  costs, 17
  purchase budget, 95, 96
Discontinued operations, 132
Discretionary costs (see Managed costs)
Discretionary fixed costs, 134
Distributions, to owners, 8, 9
Divisional autonomy, 210, 211, 245
Divisional performance evaluation, 205,
  243, 245
Divisionalization, 206
Drucker, Peter, F., 69, 70
DuPont Company, 206
Dysfunctional behavior, 232-234

Earnings, retained, 17
Econometric models, 74
Economic activity, and accounting
  information, 3
Economic measurements, 7
Economic value, 207, 208
Efficiency, standards, 171, 172
Employees, motivation of, 168
Environmental forces, 69, 70, 236, 237
Equivalent units, 27
Ethical conduct, standards, of, 11-12
Expansion, of product line, 132
Expected annual level, of activity, 173
Expense budgets, 95, 99
Expenses, 7
External users, of accounting
  information, 2

Factory overhead, 18, 171-175
  budgeting, 98
Fair value, 5, 6
Falsification of data, 326
FASB (see Financial Accounting
  Standards Board)
Feedback, 75, 237, 240
FIFO (see First-in, first-out method)
Financial Accounting Standards Board
  (FASB), 4-6
  Statements of Financial Accounting
  Concepts:
    Recognition and Measurement in
    Financial Statements of Business
    Enterprises, 8
    Statement No, 1, 7
    Statement No., 97, 103
Financial policy, 71
Financial reporting, 6-8
  objective, 7
Financial statements, 5-8
  cash flow statement, 103
  criteria for, 5-6
  complete set of, 7-8
  interrelation of, 7
  qualitative objectives of, 5-6
Finished good inventory, 18
First-in, first-out (FIFO) method, for
  tracing inventories, 28, 29-31, 132,
  134-136
Fixed costs, 18, 86, 90, 134
  discretionary, 134
  manufacturing, 129
Fixed overhead, 172, 173
Flamholtz, Eric, 248
Flexible budgets, 19, 86-91, 129, 138, 174
Flexible flow lines, 43
Forecasting, 72-75
Foreign currency translation
  adjustments, 8
Full cost, 24
Funds statement, 7